Women Across Cultures
A Global Perspective

Third Edition

Shawn Meghan Burn

California Polytechnic State University

Mc
Graw
Hill

Connect
Learn
Succeed™

The McGraw·Hill Companies

Mc Graw Hill — Connect Learn Succeed™

WOMEN ACROSS CULTURES: A GLOBAL PERSPECTIVE, THIRD EDITION

This book is printed on acid-free paper

4 5 6 7 8 9 0 DOC/DOC 1 0 9 8 7 6 5 4

ISBN: 978-0-07-351233-4
MHID: 0-07-351233-8

Vice President & Editor-in-Chief: *Michael Ryan*
Vice President EDP/Central Publishing Services: *Kimberly Meriwether David*
Publisher: *William Glass*
Senior Sponsoring Editor: *Gina Boedeker*
Executive Marketing Manager: *Pamela S. Cooper*
Managing Editor: *Meghan Campbell*
Project Manager: *Erin Melloy*
Design Coordinator: *Margarite Reynolds*
Cover Designer: *Mary-Presley Adams*
Photo Research Coordinator: *Brian Pecko*
Cover Image: *Martin Child/Getty Images*
Buyer: *Susan K. Culbertson*
Media Project Manager: *Sridevi Palani*
Compositor: *S4Carlisle Publishing Services*
Typeface: *10/12 New Baskerville*
Printer: *R. R. Donnelley*

Library of Congress Cataloging-in-Publication Data

Burn, Shawn Meghan.
  Women across cultures: a global perspective/Shawn Meghan Burn.—3rd ed.
    p. cm.
  Includes bibliographical references and index.
  ISBN-13: 978-0-07-351233-4
  1. Women–Social conditions–Cross-cultural studies. 2. Women–Economic conditions–Cross-cultural studies. 3. Women's rights–Cross-cultural studies 4. Sex role– Cross-cultural studies. 5. Sex discrimination against women–Cross-cultural studies. I. Title

HQ1161.B87   2011
305.42'—dc22   2010023782

www.mhhe.com

Contents

Preface

In the last twenty-five years, women's studies scholars embraced diversity when they realized that women's experiences are shaped by contextual and intersectional variables. This diversity is true not only in our own countries, but globally, and it tremendously influences gender equality efforts. Stimulated by the United Nations' Fourth Women's World Conference in 1995, other conferences, and by the Internet, awareness of the global diversity in women's experiences and equality struggles continues to grow. *Women Across Cultures: A Global Perspective* demonstrates this diversity and integrates it with feminist theory and practice. This global women's studies book documents women's low status and power, violations of women's human rights due to their gender, and hope in the form of courageous women organizing for change. This work addresses the diversity and similarity of women's experience worldwide. The book's content reflects the perspective that women's human rights and respect for cultural diversity are not mutually exclusive, and in fact, must go hand-in-hand.

In this book, I try to convey the scope of gender injustice and the contextual and intersectional factors that contribute to it. Chapter 1 orients readers to a cross-national, multicultural approach to women's studies and summarizes some basic women's studies concepts, and outlines four themes of global women's studies (gender inequality as a sociocultural, socially constructed phenomenon; activism and empowerment; a multicultural, contextual, intersectional approach; and women's rights as human rights). Chapter 2 provides an overview of women's status worldwide. In Chapter 3, I move on to a discussion of reproductive health and rights and their relationship to women's status and power. Chapter 4 focuses on women's sexuality and sexual rights. Women's unpaid and underpaid labor are discussed at length in Chapter 5 as causes and effects of women's lower power and status. Women and development is the focus of Chapter 6, with the emphasis on feminist critiques of traditional development approaches and feminist efforts to bring women into the development process. Chapter 7 is on the ways that globalization has reshaped women's lives worldwide. Chapter 8 presents feminist critiques of religion as well as women's efforts to reform and reconstruct religions. Although all of the chapters to some extent focus on women's empowerment, the final three look more closely at women's political efforts. Chapter 9 examines women in national politics, Chapter 10 examines women's gender equality movements, and Chapter 11 examines the transnational women's human rights movement.

I hope that readers will be struck by the scope of gender injustice but equally struck by the scope of women's resistance and the possibilities for change. Global women's studies can read like a study of women's victimization but in fact it is increasingly a study of women's empowerment cross-culturally. Throughout the book are many examples of women's actions—from the small grassroots effort, to the use of international law for attaining gender justice. These diverse actions demonstrate that there are many meanings of feminism based on the needs, issues, cultures, and goals of diverse women. Boxed material profiling activist women and organizations, and end-of-chapter websites further illustrate the scope of women's actions for gender equality. Opportunities for readers to take action are also provided at the end of each chapter.

There is a lot of information in the book. As a long-time teacher, I am sympathetic to students' concerns about how to read and master textbook content. To this end, I have included a number of pedagogical elements. Headings alert readers to upcoming content. Important terms and concepts appear in boldface in the text and appear in a glossary at the end of the book. To liven up the often technical and factual textual material, are thought-provoking quotes in the margin and examples of women's history. Figures graphically depict text concepts to help students pull out key themes. Each chapter includes boxed examples of feminist thought and action from all over the world, including activist profiles of individuals and groups. Study questions are listed at the conclusion of each chapter. Students may use these to make sure they understand the major points of the chapter and to structure the study of text material. Discussion questions and activities follow the study questions. These are intended to stimulate critical and creative thinking and discussion. Instructors may use these as assignments or for class discussion. The book's chapters are organized by issues rather than by country or region, but an appendix provides an overall sense of women's status on a country-by-country basis using economic, educational, and health indicators. Students can use this information as the basis for country or regional reports on the status of women. This information may be enhanced by use of the end-of-chapter informational and activist organization websites.

Changes from the Second Edition

This third edition of *Women Across Cultures* is the result of a major overhaul of the second edition. The introduction has been expanded to provide more of an orientation to global women's studies including the addition of four global women's studies themes. These themes (gender as a social construction; intersectionality and contextualization; women's activism and empowerment; and women's rights as human rights) are woven throughout the text. Several chapters are significantly different from the second edition. The chapter on reproductive rights is now on women's reproductive health and reproductive rights. The chapter on lesbians is now on women's sexuality and sexual rights (although it still retains a focus on non-heterosexual women). The chapter on women's rights as human rights and the role of the UN in gender equality is now on women's transnational feminist movements and networks and the reciprocal relationship between the UN and transnational women's networks (although it retains a focus on women's human rights). All chapters were changed based on current trends and scholarship and all include more discussion questions and activities, and updated websites. All received statistical updates, which although tedious at times, provided the opportunity to see improvement on some key indicators such as literacy, political representation, and domestic violence legislation in the last five years. In the end, I hope the result is a readable text that inspires others to share my passion for global women's studies scholarship and feminist activism.

Acknowledgments

Writing a book is a time-consuming and somewhat insane endeavor. It is also something that few of us can do without support. The librarians at California Polytechnic State University once again deserve my thanks—especially those in interlibrary loan. I greatly appreciate the assistance of recently-graduated Megan Drabinski who gathered the material for a good part of the Appendix (bless her for her love of global women's studies and her attention to detail). I am grateful to the reviewers who provided thoughtful feedback for this third edition and I hope that they feel their suggestions were honored. These reviewers were: Ann Andaloro, Morehead State University; Beth Berila, St. Cloud State University; Geraldine R. Finn, University of Findlay; Barbara LeSavoy, The College at Brockport, State University of New York; Samantha A. Morgan-Curtis, Tennessee State University; Piya Pangsapa, State University of New York at Buffalo; Judith M. Roy, Century College; Craig Warkentin, State University of New York at Oswego; Michele Wilson, Portland Community College

My editors at McGraw-Hill, Janice Wiggins, Meghan Campbell, Erin Melloy, and Joyce Watters, were easy to work with and helped shepherd this new edition from beginning to end.

I must also thank all those who are working to bring about women's equality and all the great scholars who appear on the pages here—these are my heroes, and I feel I have been in the presence of greatness by reading their work and studying their efforts. Last, thanks to my husband, the always-supportive Gene Courter (T-Gene!); my son, the brilliant and talented Kane Lynch; my always-supportive friends Lois Petty and Karla Feye; and my amazing sisters Colin Royall and Kevyn Burn.

Women Across Cultures
A Global Perspective

1

Introduction to Global Women's Studies

We must be courageous in speaking out about the issues that concern us; we must not bend under the weight of spurious arguments invoking culture or traditional values. No value worth the name supports the oppression and enslavement of women.

—Dr. Nafis Sadik, Fourth World Women's Conference, 1995

The global study of women emphasizes how women's issues and activism vary based on culture, religion, sexual orientation, class, region, history, and economic and political systems. While at times shocking and sad, hope comes in the form of courageous activism and signs of progress. © arabianEye/PunchStock

This global women's studies book is about women's issues and gender equality cross-culturally. The study of global women documents women's status worldwide. A key area of focus is the understanding of **gender inequality**—the disadvantage of females relative to males. As you'll soon learn, the extent of gender inequality is still quite profound and has enormous implications for women everywhere. Global women's studies also examines how gender inequality arises from traditional cultural practices—practices that have become embedded in social, economic, political, and legal systems and require targeted activism to change. Global women's studies also examines intersections between gender and other variables such as race, class, and sexual orientation. Global women's studies is interdisciplinary and draws on research and theory from psychology, sociology, economics, religion, political science, medicine, public health, history, philosophy, and law.

The global study of women is rich and rewarding because it requires that we learn about different customs, religions, and forms of government and that we imagine what it would be like to be a woman in another culture. Studying women's lives in other cultures also inspires a profound appreciation for women. The great strength that women possess and the work they accomplish despite their customary lower status and power is truly amazing. That being said, the cross-cultural study of women is at times very difficult, shocking, and disturbing. You may be horrified, surprised, and angered at some of the gender-based abuses that continue today—in your own country as well as others. The saying, "The truth will set you free, but first it will make you mad" (and sometimes sad), applies to the subject matter of this book. Fortunately, this bad news is often tempered by courageous stories of activism and resistance and evidence of hopeful progress. To provide you with a finer sense of what global women's studies is about, here are four key themes that characterize the field.

Theme 1: Global Women's Studies Sees Gender Inequality as a Historical, Sociocultural Phenomenon

It is hard to understand why women are so disadvantaged economically, politically, legally, and socially relative to males. Why is it that despite women's respected role as childbearers and childrearers, they are still so often treated as second-class citizens? Global women's studies scholars typically answer this question with materialist and sociocultural explanations.

Materialist explanations for gender inequality view the oppression of women as a social, historical, and alterable phenomenon (Khan, 2006). Family and social institutions that arose out of material forces, such as the ownership of private property, led to male dominance and female subordination, and these materialist forces maintain gender inequality. For example, in Chapter 2 you'll learn that many societies are structured such that women are economically dependent on men and this makes it difficult for them to leave

"At certain points we may find that the idea of equality is unpalatable to ordinary people, beyond the pale of consensus. These are the raw nerves of the social construction of sex that, when tickled, arouse ridicule; the primal roots of gender roles that, when exposed, invoke a protest of incredulity and irritation."
Carmel Shalev

"Female subordination runs so deep that it is still viewed as inevitable or natural rather than as a politically constructed reality maintained by patriarchal interests, ideology, and institutions."
Charlotte Bunch

"The oppression of women in any society is in its turn a statement of an economic structure built on land ownership, systems of inheritance and parenthood and the patriarchal family as an inbuilt social unit."
Nawal El Saadawi

3

"To look for origins is, in the end, to think that we are something other than the product of our history and our present social world, and more particularly, that our gender systems are primordial, transhistorical, and essentially unchanging in their roots."
Michelle Rosaldo

"Men and women live on a stage, on which they act out their assigned roles, equal in importance. The play cannot go on without both performers. Neither of them 'contributes' more or less to the whole; neither is marginal or dispensable. But the stage set is conceived, painted, and defined by men. Men have written the play, have directed the show . . . assigned themselves the most interesting, heroic parts."
Gerda Lerner

"Man was not made a tyrant by nature, but had been made tyrannical by the power which had, by general consent, been conferred upon him; she merely wished that woman might be entitled to equal rights, and ac- knowledged as the equal of man, not his superior."
Lucretia Mott, speaking at the Women's Rights Convention at Seneca Falls, New York, 1848

situations of abuse. The idea that gender inequality is embedded in family, cultural, economic, political, and social structures is sometimes referred to as **patriarchy** and social systems that serve males' dominance over females are referred to as patriarchal. Materialist theorists trace the development of patriarchy to the Neolithic period when agriculture developed and the labor of children was needed to increase production and further surpluses. At that point women came to be viewed as commodities—resources to be acquired, traded, and controlled (Lerner, 1986).

Like materialist explanations, **social constructivist** and **sociocultural explanations** emphasize how gendered power relations are socially con- structed. These explanations also assume that gender is *dynamic*—active and changing rather than permanently fixed. Sociocultural perspectives on gender inequality also explain *how* gender relations became embedded in culture, and are passed on socially. The sociocultural approach also distin- guishes between **sex**, which refers to inborn biological differences between females and males relating to reproduction and sex organs, and **gender,** which refers to the socially constructed roles, behaviors, activities, and attri- butes a given society considers appropriate for males and females.

The sociocultural approach does not deny that males and females are biologically different and that these differences are important. Indeed, many see gender inequality as arising out of these differences. Think about it this way. At one time, all cultures had no means of birth control, no infant formula, and no convenient tampons or sanitary napkins. This, along with males' greater size and strength, made some types of work more "appropri- ate" depending on gender. Women's work became concentrated in the **private sphere** or domestic domain of the home, and men performed the labor in the **public sphere** outside the home because they were not con- strained by childcare (Sanday, 1974). In other words, a gendered division of labor arose and women ended up doing the work that was compatible with the unavoidable female life course of bearing and nursing children (Chafetz, 1990; Lerner, 1986). Once societies based on money evolved, men's labor ap- peared to have more value because it was more likely to be used in exchange for money or goods. Men's dominance in the public sphere led to them hav- ing greater property rights and economic and political power, which they then used to further consolidate their control. Political and economic systems were constructed based on these traditional gender-role arrangements.

The sociocultural approach explains the mechanisms by which we learn to "do gender." Once a gendered division of labor arose and women and men had different roles (**gender roles**), people then constructed **gender stereotypes** (beliefs about the qualities of each gender) and **gender norms** (social rules regarding what is appropriate for each gender to do) that sup- ported these divisions. These passed on culturally through **gender socialization** (the process by which societal beliefs and expectations about gender are instilled in us). Parents, peers, myths, literature, media, religion, etc. teach children what is expected of them based on their gender in order to prepare them for adulthood and help them get along in society. Conformity to gender norms and gender roles is maintained by granting social status and approval to conformers and by ostracizing violators.

There is also a reciprocal relationship between gender stereotypes and gender roles—in other words, gender stereotypes lead to gendered roles but gendered roles also lead to gender stereotypes. This idea comes from **social roles theory** (Eagly, 1987). People develop gender stereotypes about women and men from seeing them in different (gendered) roles because we assume that if men and women are doing different things, it must be because they are truly different. Once people develop gender stereotypes, these beliefs operate as expectations regarding appropriate roles for people from those groups—in this way, gender stereotypes lead to gender roles. These processes appear to operate in all cultures and explain how gender is socially constructed and maintained. Social roles theory maintains that because gender is socially constructed, it is dynamic and can be changed if gender stereotypes or gender roles change.

Cross-cultural and temporal (across time) variations in women's treatment testify to the large part culture plays in gender inequality. In many parts of the world, gender roles have changed rapidly and as Rosenthal and Rubin (1982, p. 711) once said, these changes have occurred "faster than the gene can travel." Also, anthropological evidence tells us that gender inequality hasn't always been so. For example, today's anthropologists generally agree that in the foraging societies of early history, which covered much more time than the 120,000 years or so from the Neolithic to the present, the sexes were probably complementary and of equal importance (Ehrenberg, 1989). Even today there are some cultures with egalitarian gender relations (Bonvillian, 2001). Gender-egalitarian cultures were also common to hunter-gatherer and horticultural societies prior to colonization (Sanday, 1981) and there is some evidence from ancient times of matriarchies—societies in which women had greater power than men (cf. Bachofen, 1967; Diner, 1975; Gimbutas, 1991; Gross, 1996).

As you will see throughout the book, there is good evidence that gender inequality is, in fact, socially constructed and embedded in our legal, economic, political, and cultural practices. Our hope for change lies in our transformation of these human-created systems, beliefs, and practices.

Theme 2: Global Women's Studies is About Activism and Empowerment

Although global women's studies seeks a scholarly understanding of gender inequality cross-culturally, this is not an end in itself; the hope is that this will serve change toward gender equality and contribute to women's **empowerment** (their ability to advocate for their rights and have decision-making power in their public and private lives). Our task is a positive one rather than a negative one. It is less about women as victims and more about women bringing about change for gender justice. It will quickly become apparent to you that wherever

"The women we honor today teach us three very important lessons: One, that as women, we must stand up for ourselves. The second, as women we must stand up for each other. And finally, as women we must stand up for justice for all." *Michelle Obama, First Lady of the United States at the International Women of Courage Awards, which honored women in Afghanistan, Guatemala, Iraq, Malaysia, Niger, Russia, Uzbekistan, and Yemen who have stood up for women and human rights.*

Sor Juana Inés de la Cruz (1651–1695) was a brilliant Mexican poet and intellectual. To avoid marriage and to continue her self-education, Juana entered a Catholic convent. When told by a bishop to give up her writing, she spiritedly defended the right of women to engage in intellectual pursuits, saying in a 1681 letter, "Who has forbidden women to engage in private and individual studies? Have they not as rational a mind as men do?" Ultimately, she lost her battle and was forced to give up her writing and her books.

BOX 1.1   *The "F" Word*

Are you hesitant to identify yourself as a feminist even though you believe women should be full and equal participants with men at all levels of social life? Research in the United States finds that although many women endorse feminist beliefs, they hesitate to describe themselves as feminists because of the stereotype that feminists are anti-male, along with other negative stereotypes of women who identify themselves as feminists (Anderson, Kanner, & Elsayegh, 2009). As Anderson et al. (2009, p. 216) said,

In some quarters, feminists and feminism have been directly and indirectly blamed for a variety of social problems, including the comparatively lower rate of college entrance of young men (Sommers, 2000), the claimed decline in "manliness" in American culture (Mansfield, 2006), and even the attacks of September 11, 2001 (Falwell, 2001) . . . Such representations of feminism affect the extent to which women are willing to identify as feminists.

Because feminism seeks social change it is considered subversive, therefore efforts are made to discredit it by labeling feminists "man-haters," "anti-family," or "lesbian." This is not just true in the United States, where feminists are sometimes referred to as "Femi-Nazis." Participants in an African women's leadership conference made a list of terms used to describe feminists in their societies that included, "Lesbians, Power hungry, Emotionally deprived, Sexually frustrated, Unmarriageable, Against God's plan," or "Castrators." Stereotypes of feminists aren't supported by the facts and it is a misunderstanding to believe that feminism requires or condones hatred of men. Indeed, in a recent U.S. study, feminists reported lower levels of hostility toward men than did nonfeminists (Anderson, Kanner, & Elsayegh, 2009). In my experience, once people learn more about gender inequality and feminism, these negative and inaccurate views of feminism fall away.

Christine de Pizan (approximately 1365–1430), a French woman, was the most successful female writer of the Middle Ages. Furthermore, in her 1405 book *The City of Ladies,* she became one of the first to argue in writing against women's inferiority.

The feminist movement challenges the very root of patriarchy, the idea that one person can be humanly superior to others and entitled to superiority over them.
Marilyn French, American feminist

women's rights are violated, there are women who resist and rally for change, even in the face of social rejection and physical danger.

Global women's studies is a feminist endeavor and conceives of **feminism** as a commitment to changing the structures that keep women lower in status and power (Sen & Grown, 1987). Gender inequality is viewed as part of multiple, interlocking forms of domination including racism, colonialism, economic injustice, and discrimination on the basis of sexual identity, nationality, or physical ability (Hunt & Jung, 2009). Box 1.1 talks more about feminism since it is often negatively stereotyped and misunderstood. In every chapter you will find examples of women coming together to achieve gender justice.

In addition to efforts made by governments, there are literally thousands of nongovernmental organizations (NGOs) working for gender equality. These range from small, local grassroots organizations to large international organizations. In addition to the efforts of Western women, with which you may be familiar, there is a long history of struggle for women's equality in the Middle East, Latin America, Asia, and Africa. You will read about these efforts worldwide to increase the status of women. Box 1.2 provides an example from Afghanistan. Starting with Chapter 2, at the end of every chapter you will also find a feature called "Action Opportunities," so that you can take action on issues that move you. Many of the websites listed at the end of each chapter also provide ways to help.

BOX 1.2   *Activist Profile: The Revolutionary Association of Women in Afghanistan (RAWA)*

The Revolutionary Association of the Women of Afghanistan (RAWA), is a good example of women's activism in the face of gendered oppression. RAWA began in Kabul, Afghanistan, in 1977 as an independent political/social organization of Afghan women fighting for human rights and for social justice. After the Soviet occupation of Afghanistan in December 1979, RAWA became directly involved in the war of resistance. RAWA also established schools with hostels for boys and girls, and a hospital for refugee Afghan women and children in Quetta, Pakistan with mobile teams. They also conducted nursing courses, literacy courses, and vocational training courses for women. One of RAWA's founders, Meena, was assassinated in 1987, possibly by the Soviets or by religious fundamentalists. Once the Taliban overthrew the Soviets in 1992, the focus of RAWA's political struggle became the Taliban's atrocities against the people of Afghanistan in general and women in particular. Under Taliban rule, RAWA worked to draw international attention to the oppression of women under the Taliban and continued to secretly educate girls and women despite laws outlawing it. RAWA continues to work on behalf of women in Afghanistan and runs an orphanage, schools and literacy programs, income-generating projects for women, and a rehabilitation program for prostitutes. For more information on RAWA, go to www.rawa.org.

Theme 3: Global Women's Studies Takes a Multicultural, Intersectional, Contextualized Approach

The cross-cultural study of women requires a multicultural approach. **Multiculturalism**, or interculturalism, emphasizes helping people to understand, accept, and value the cultural differences between groups, with the ultimate goal of reaping the benefits of diversity (Ferdman, 1995). The goal is to both celebrate differences and emphasize the dimensions of commonality or inclusion that supersede these differences (Devine, 1995). Although it sounds contradictory, women are both the same and different cross-culturally and intra-culturally (within the same culture, country, or region) and this matters for our global study of women.

The Importance of Similarity

In some ways women all over the world have a lot in common. Almost everywhere, women work extremely hard in both paid and unpaid labor, get married, structure their lives according to their children's needs, worry about unplanned pregnancies, experience gender discrimination, and are at some risk for gender violence such as rape, sexual assault, or domestic violence. Most women live in cultures where heterosexuality is expected and where bearing and caring for children are a source of status and identity. Almost everywhere, women are lower in status and power than men and live in societies with legal, political, and cultural structures that support this (see Chapter 2). The shared biology of women also gives rise to commonalities that affect women everywhere, such as menstruation, pregnancy, childbirth, and mothering. Women's commonalities are an important topic of this book and create connection between diverse women as well as forming the basis for **transnational feminisms**—feminisms that cut across cultures and unite women's struggles from many parts of the world. Global feminism emphasizes the interconnections between women. The idea is that the oppression of women in one part of the world is often linked to conditions in other countries due to globalization, and that no woman is free as long as others are oppressed (Bunch, 1993; Tong, 2009).

The Importance of Difference

Although women undoubtedly share certain experiences due to their gender, the form and specifics of these commonalities vary based on culture. For example, women everywhere menstruate, but this experience is shaped by cultural attitudes and conveniences. Women's experiences within a culture also vary widely depending upon race, class, ethnicity, nationality, disability, age, sexual orientation, region, and religion. The interplay of these different social categories is referred to as **intersectionality** (Cole, 2009). Gender is "intersectional" because the way it is enacted and experienced depends on the way it interacts with other social categories and identities. It is also important to **contextualize** women's issues and activism. This means that to fully understand them, you have to consider the contexts in which they are situated—cultural, social, political, historical, and economic. Acknowledging intersectionality and contextualizing no doubt complicates our task. But a failure to do so ultimately restricts our understanding of women and reduces the usefulness of our study to promoting gender equality.

> "We . . . find it difficult to separate race from class from sex oppression because in our lives they are most often experienced simultaneously."
> *Combahee River Collective, a group of Black American feminists*

A truly global feminism recognizes this diversity and acknowledges that there are diverse meanings of feminism, each responsive to the needs and issues of women in different regions, societies, and times. Throughout this book, you will see that there are many differences in the issues facing women across countries and within countries (often based on intersectionality and context). For example, Indian women's groups strive to stop bride burnings and dowries, Muslim feminists lobby for interpretations of the Koran that promote women's equality, Kenyan women's groups attempt to stop female genital cutting, Irish women's activists pursue greater access to contraceptives, Brazilian women's groups fight to reduce domestic violence, and Mexican feminists battle to reduce rape. In the United States, workplace discrimination and reproductive rights have been the primary focus of Euro American feminists but Native American and African American feminists frequently connect their struggle as women to the struggles of their communities against racism and economic exploitation.

> "The more diversity is affirmed, the more difficult inclusivity becomes, simply because human diversity is almost infinite."
> *Rita Gross*

Although global women's studies should describe and reflect all of this diversity, you should understand that this small book cannot begin to convey the diversity of women's lives worldwide or to speak for all women everywhere. Given the enormity of the task and the fact that data are lacking on women in many parts of the world, the best this book can do is give you a sense of the great diversity of women's issues and activism and the contextual and intersectional influences on them.

The Challenge of Multiculturalism

As some of the more dramatic instances of women's lower status and power are chronicled, you should not become complacent about gender inequalities in your own country or feel that your culture is superior. Those cultural aspects that do not result in the oppression of women or others deserve our respect. Admittedly, multiculturalism is not always easy. It goes against our natural human tendencies to reject people and cultures that are different from our own and to defend our own cultural traditions. Humans, it appears, have a general discomfort of diversity that is driven by a natural inclination to categorize people as one of "us," or one of "them," and to prefer those that are similar to us (social psychologists call this "ingroup-outgroup bias"). We like to believe that our culture's way of doing things is "right," and we like those things that are familiar to us. People are often **ethnocentric**—quick to think their culture's way is the right and only way, and quick to judge and reject the way other cultures do things. This means that we may have trouble acknowledging the ways in which our own culture permits discrimination and suffering among identifiable groups of people and that we may be quick to stereotype other cultures as all bad.

We have to override these tendencies because a multicultural approach to women's studies is not about judgment, cultural superiority, or the imposition of our ways on other cultures (what is sometimes called "cultural imperialism"). On the contrary, it is about understanding the influence of culture on women's issues and women's experiences, and "looking in our own backyard" and bringing about change in our own societies as we support women in other cultures. We have to find a way to be critical of practices that are harmful to women, but understand that the issues of greatest concern to women in our country may not be the major issues of concern to women in other countries. While talking about women's lives in different cultures, we also must take care to acknowledge the wide range of women's experiences within any given culture. We want to be culturally sensitive and avoid assuming that our way is the right way and that the path to gender equality is the same regardless of culture. We want to support international women's movements for equality while respecting the rights of women within particular countries to initiate their own movements in ways that work for them in their cultures.

Theme 4: Global Women's Studies Views Women's Rights as Human Rights

Some people suggest that cross-cultural women's studies cannot be done honestly because our own cultural biases inevitably lead to distortion. Others are uncomfortable with people from one culture making value judgments about the treatment of women in another culture when those judging cannot possibly understand the cultural context in which the treatment occurs. These concerns have some validity and caution is clearly required. But sometimes people mistakenly assume that respecting cultural diversity requires that we accept all cultural practices (the idea that right and wrong are culturally determined is called **cultural relativism**). And yes, while it is true that just because a culture is different from our own does not mean that it is wrong, global women's studies takes the position that culture should never be used to justify gender inequality.

Global women's studies scholars typically favor a human rights framework to help us determine when we should respect cultural practices and when we should work for their change. They take a **women's rights as human rights perspective**. The idea is that regardless of culture and gender, people are entitled to certain basic rights and that governments must do what they can to ensure these rights are protected. For example, the Universal Declaration of Human Rights adopted by United Nations (UN) member nations in 1948 stipulates that by virtue of being human, we are all entitled to full and equal rights (Articles 6 & 7); everyone has the right to life, liberty, and security of person (Article 3); no one should ever be tortured or held in slavery (Articles 4 & 5); everyone has the right to freedom of movement (Article 13); everyone has the right to own property and to participate politically (Articles 17 & 21); and everyone has the right to an education, to work for pay, and to be compensated fairly (Articles 22 & 23). Many of the situations described in this book may be viewed as violations of these and other basic human rights, and respect for cultural diversity should not be used to justify them. For instance, violence against women is not okay even if it is standard cultural practice. Domestic violence is a form of torture and rape violates women's freedom of movement and their right to security.

One of the most important human rights documents pertaining to women is the **UN Convention on the Elimination of Discrimination Against Women (CEDAW)**, basically an international bill of rights for women. The 1979 treaty (signed by almost all United Nations member states), requires ratifying nations to eliminate discrimination against women in employment, education, and politics and to provide proof of progress (sadly, the United States has not yet ratified CEDAW; see Chapter 11). The **Beijing Platform for Action**, the product of the Fourth World Conference on Women (FWCW) held in Beijing, China, in 1995 is also very important. The Platform, negotiated by 5,000 delegates from 189 countries, identifies "critical areas of concern" such as the feminization of poverty, inequalities in education, politics, and the economy, violence against women, and persistent discrimination against and violation of the rights of the girl child. It is called the Platform for Action because for each critical area of concern, it specifies strategic objectives and actions to be undertaken by governments. Throughout the book, you will read about these and other UN conventions and declarations that speak to women's rights.

Human rights are protected under international law and are monitored by the United Nations and human rights organizations but they are

"It is good to swim in the waters of tradition but to sink in them is suicide." *Mahatma Gandhi*

"All human beings are born free and equal in dignity and rights." *United Nations Universal Declaration of Human Rights*

The **United Nations (UN)** is an international organization with 192 participating countries. Its purposes are international peace and security, human rights, and the correction of international economic, social, environmental, and humanitarian problems. Many UN agencies figure prominently in this book because of their work on behalf of gender equality.

UN **conventions** are treaties, or legally binding agreements between countries; **declarations** are agreements that are not binding.

also an activist tool. Throughout the text you will see how feminists work to ensure that women's rights are included in human rights instruments and mechanisms and how they use these to challenge gender inequalities. This is deemed important because describing a particular discriminatory act as a human rights violation gives it more value than simply calling it unfair (Tomasevski, 1993). Once a government has signed on to an international human rights convention or declaration, activists can use that agreement to hold their government accountable for harms done and to pressure them to adopt, enforce, and implement consistent policies, programs, and laws. Both CEDAW and the Beijiing Platform for Action are used in this way. Educating women about their human rights also motivates and empowers grassroots challenges to gender inequalities.

At first glance it may appear that advocating for women's human rights internationally and valuing cultural diversity are mutually exclusive. How-ever, global women's studies and transnational feminism require that we do both. The way to accomplish this is to recognize the cross-cultural variation in the challenges women face and to let women be the architects of change in their own countries. The best way to respect cultural diversity and advo-cate for women's rights is to focus on those practices of concern to women in their own countries and to support their efforts to do something about it. Besides, going into another country and telling women what to be concerned with and what to do about it almost always backfires; either because we lack the cultural understanding necessary to effectively bring about change, or because our efforts are met with accusations of cultural imperialism which lead to a backlash (especially likely in countries with a history of colonization by western countries). We are most helpful when we share organizational strategies, help call international attention to abuses, lobby for international organizations to classify violations of women's rights as human rights viola-tions, contribute money to their campaigns, respond to their "action alerts," compare stories of struggle, and respect their right to be the architects of their own change.

Overview of the Book

The book begins with an overview of women's status in the world today. Chap-ter 2 makes the case that women are still disadvantaged in today's world. The chapter provides a summary of women's lower status and power, both politi-cally and economically, and provides data on key women's issues globally. A major theme in the chapter is violence against women, women's sexual objecti-fication, and how these relate to women's economic and political power.

The topic of Chapter 3 is reproductive health and reproductive rights. Reproductive health conditions are the leading cause of death and dis-ability in women of childbearing age worldwide. Reproductive rights refer to the right to reproductive health care and the right to reproductive self-determination. These rights include women's ability to control the number and spacing of their children and their access to a range of birth control methods from which they may freely and knowledgeably choose. The relationship between women's reproductive rights and their status, power, economic situation, and health are emphasized in Chapter 3.

Chapter 4 is on the topic of sexuality and sexual rights. Women's sexual rights are important to gender equality—how free can people be if they cannot determine their sexuality? Unfortunately, women's sexuality is often defined in terms of men's sexual pleasure, and as it relates to her family and community's honor. Sexual rights also include rights based on sexual orientation and gender identity. Sexual orientation affects a woman's experience in her society and is an important intersectional variable, especially because most societies discriminate against lesbian and bisexual women. Chapter 4 also includes the study of lesbians and bisexual women and their efforts to gain equality.

Chapter 5 investigates the topic of women's work, both paid and unpaid, and in the formal and informal economic sectors through a feminist economics lens. The ways that women often experience discrimination in the world of work are highlighted with an examination of the gender pay gap, the glass ceiling, and sexual harassment along with an examination of maternity protections and child care. The challenges that women face in balancing work and family are explored. Self-employed women are another focus. The undervaluing of women's unpaid labor and its relationship to women's status and power are key chapter themes as well.

Feminists generally believe that economic development should be an agent of women's empowerment. Chapter 6 takes a close look at women in economically developing countries. The chapter begins by describing traditional approaches to economic development and common feminist critiques of the traditional development process. The chapter also explores feminist efforts to bring gender into the development process, and the important role of women in sustainable development—development that meets the needs of the present without compromising the future. The role of women's nongovernmental organizations (NGOs) in bringing about change is also featured.

Chapter 7 describes how a world economy dominated by transnational corporations affects women. The chapter begins by explaining what globalization is and how structural adjustment programs and economic fluctuations impact women's labor and poverty. Globalization often leads women in search of work to migrate to other countries to alleviate poverty and provide for their families; this is a major chapter topic. Some women work in transnational corporate factories and others migrate to other countries where there is a demand for low-wage workers, sending most of their wages back home. Migrant women's work in domestic service, sex work, and nursing and home health work are discussed, along with the phenomenon of mail-order brides. The trafficking of women and girls into prostitution as part of the global sex industry is also presented as one of the effects of globalization.

Chapter 8 tackles the subject of women and religion. Many feminists view religion as part of the social systems that perpetuate gender inequality.

The chapter provides feminist critiques of religion and includes an overview of women in the world's major religions. Of course, religion is profoundly important to many women, including many feminist women. Feminist efforts to reform existing religions or to create new women-centered religions are a major topic in Chapter 8.

Feminists agree that women's political activity is one key to their equality, and Chapter 9 examines women in national politics. This chapter explores women's representation in political parliaments, congresses, and cabinets and the factors that lead to greater numbers of women in formal politics. The chapter provides an analysis of women as heads of government: How do they come to occupy these positions? How does their leadership differ from that of men? Are they more likely to promote domestic policies favorable to women and children? Do they typically pursue feminist agendas? The chapter concludes with a discussion of women's political activity in social protest movements. When we consider this form of political activity, it is evident that women are more political than they might appear at first glance.

Chapter 10 investigates local and national women's movements. The chapter begins by noting the many forces that operate against women's activism and how, despite these, women still frequently protest gender injustice. One of the main points of the chapter is that women's movements assume a variety of forms. In most countries you will find women's rights activist groups that focus on national policy, women's research groups that attempt to document the status of women and raise public awareness, and women's grassroots organizations that help women on a local level by providing shelter for battered women, providing credit for women-owned businesses, and so on. The chapter also describes the political and economic conditions, local and national, that affect women's movements, both positively and negatively, throughout the world. The chapter includes an examination of "state feminism"—government structures and policy machinery that promote women's rights and address women's issues. The chapter concludes with a discussion of the successes and failures of women's movements.

Transnational feminism relies on a women's rights and human rights framework for asserting women's rights. Chapter 11 focuses on transnational feminist movements. These movements span across multiple nations and involve the coming together of feminist NGOs to work across regional or international borders in coalitions and campaigns. The chapter explores the role of the United Nations in transnational women's movements and networks, including the four international UN women's conferences and important treaties and conventions such as the Convention on the Elimination of All Forms of Discrimination Against Women (CEDAW) and the influence of transnational feminist influences on the UN and human rights.

Throughout each chapter, you will find quotes from women scholars and activists, as well as examples of "sheroes" and women's history. Bolded terms appear in the glossary toward the end of the book. In addition to the "action opportunities" and websites mentioned earlier, the end of each chapter provides study questions, and discussion questions and activities.

The study questions are intended to help you structure your review of the information provided in the chapters. The discussion questions and activities are provided to stimulate your critical thinking on chapter topics. Finally, an appendix at the end of the book provides some key statistical indicators on women's status in 198 of the world's countries. These data remind us of the great diversity of women's status worldwide. However, information on the status of women is often hard to come by, as many governments do not compile accurate statistics, or, if they do, they may only release them periodically. This means that you should regard these statistics cautiously, and it means that throughout the text you will frequently find statistics that are several years old.

Study Questions

1. According to materialist approaches, what is the source of gender inequality?

2. What are the main features of sociocultural explanations for gender inequality?

3. What is the core idea behind feminism? How is global women's studies about action and empowerment?

4. What does it mean to say that women worldwide are "both the same and different"? What does this mean to the study of women cross-culturally?

5. What is intersectionality? Why is it so important to global women's studies?

6. What is multiculturalism? Why is it important to avoid ethnocentrism and to take a multicultural perspective when studying women cross-culturally? How does global or transnational feminism exemplify a multicultural approach?

7. What is the women's rights as human rights perspective and what does it say about cultural diversity and women's rights?

Discussion Questions

1. Do you call yourself a feminist? Why or why not? Do you agree with the chapter's claim that many people have a negative view of feminism but that most people agree with the aims of feminism? Does it matter whether we call ourselves feminists as long as we're doing our part to promote gender equality? Would we be more effective if we distanced ourselves from the feminist label?

2. The chapter emphasizes multiculturalism when studying women cross-culturally but at the same time says that regardless of culture, women have basic human rights. Make a list of any cultural practices in regard

to women in other countries that you are critical of (for example, many Americans are critical of Muslim women's head coverings). Should you override your ethnocentrism in regard to these practices, or are they violations of basic human rights?

3. According to the chapter, one of the risks of looking at some of the more dramatic instances of women's lower status and power is that it can foster feelings of cultural superiority. Why is this wrong, or is it?

4. The chapter makes the point that we should be careful in telling women in other cultures what to be concerned about and what they should do about it. What criticisms might an "outsider" make of your culture's treatment of women and how would you feel about them demanding change?

2 Women's Low Status and Power

Although we are divided by race, class, culture, and geography, our hope lies in our commonalities. All women's unremunerated household work is exploited, we all have conflicts in our multiple roles, our sexuality is exploited by men, media, and economy, we struggle for survival and dignity, and, rich or poor, we are vulnerable to violence. We share our "otherness," our exclusion from decision making at all levels.

—PEGGY ANTROBUS, Coordinator of Development with Women for a New Era (DAWN) and Director of Women and Development at the University of the West Indies

All over the world, women act to reduce the sexual and domestic violence faced disproportionately by women and to assist those who experience it. This violence is only one indicator of women's lower status and power relative to men.
© EMMANUEL DUNAND/AFP/Getty Images

If you wonder whether there is really a need to study women across cultures, this chapter should help you see the importance and urgency of women's issues globally. It provides an overview of the current status of women and introduces you to some of the gender inequalities that exist in the world as well as some of the explanations for women's lower status and power. As you will see, worldwide, females are generally lower in status and power relative to males (see Figure 2.1). In other words, there is gender inequality. In the sections that follow, pay attention to the material conditions that gave rise to and perpetuate gender inequalities and how societies are typically structured in ways that foster and condone gender inequality.

Men's Greater Economic Power

Many feminists view men's greater economic power to be at the heart of women's lower status and power. Men's control of economic resources increases women's dependence on men and gives men more power over them. For example, women's economic power is positively related to having a say in household decisions (UNICEF, 2006). Worldwide, men control economies

FIGURE 2.1 *Evidence of Gender Inequality*

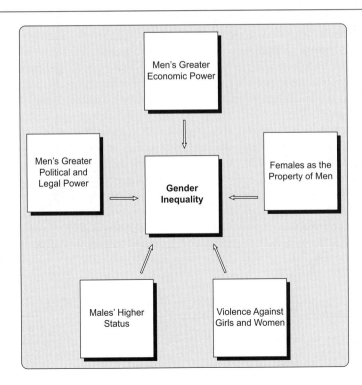

and resources, own more property, and occupy more positions of power in business and banking. This is true in virtually every country, including industrialized nations such as the United States. For example, in Pakistan, women own only 3 percent of the land, in Cameroon 10 percent, and in Mexico 22 percent (UNICEF, 2006). Men's economic power also provides them with greater control of legal, judicial, and political systems where gender inequality is often enshrined. Where women have little economic power, gender inequality is typically great.

Men's economic power is also related to women's status. Once societies based on money and trade developed, men's labor appeared to have more value because women's labor was largely for the family's use (**private use value**) whereas men's labor yielded money or the exchange of goods, and thereby had **public use (exchange) value** (Glenn, 1992). Additionally, women's unpaid labor is often not seen as real work because it is considered part of women's "natural" role as wife and mother. Of course, women often do work for pay (approximately 40 percent worldwide; UNICEF, 2006). But women's greater household and childcare responsibilities place them at a disadvantage for full-time employment and, on average, they earn 15 percent less than men, although there is great regional variation (ILO, 2007; ITUC, 2009). For example, in industrialized nations such as the United States, women earn 20 percent less, in the Middle East they earn 70 percent less, and in sub-Saharan Africa, they earn 50 percent less (UNICEF, 2006). As you will learn in Chapter 5, "Women and Work," only part of this **gender wage gap** can be explained by differences in educational attainment, job experience, and part-time work.

Women's lack of economic power is also related to their strong presence among the ranks of the poor. In addition to a smaller presence in the paid labor force and lower wages, in many parts of the world, gender biases in property and inheritance laws and education also leave women at greater risk for poverty, particularly when marriages end, or a husband dies (UNICEF, 2006; UNIFEM, 2009a). Poverty is said to have a "woman's face" because the majority of the 1 billion people living on one dollar a day or less are women (UNIFEM, 2009a). For example, in the country of South Africa, two-thirds of female-headed households are poor, compared to one-third of male-headed households and in Malawi, there are three poor women for every poor man (UNIFEM, 2009a). The gap between women and men caught in the cycle of poverty has widened in the past decade, a phenomenon commonly referred to as the **feminization of poverty.** Chapter 6, "Women and Development," and Chapter 7, "Women and Globalization," discuss the feminization of poverty in more detail.

Close to 60 percent of U.S. women are in the labor force and of the 63 percent of women with children under age six, 75 percent worked part-time.
United States Department of Labor

"More than 1 billion in the world today, the great majority of whom are women, live in unacceptable conditions of poverty, mostly in the developing countries."
United Nations, 2009

Men's Greater Political and Legal Power

Men's greater political and legal power also provides some evidence of their higher status and power. In 2010, women comprised only 9 percent of presidents and prime ministers and 19 percent of lawmakers in parliaments and congresses. Without women representatives and women's activism, most male lawmakers are not inclined to think about rape, domestic violence, women's health issues, and childcare. Men lawmakers are less likely to make laws that serve women and children's interests. But most of the world's lawmakers are men (Inter-Parliamentary Union, 2010). The United States, with 16 percent, ranked seventy-fifth among the 186 countries with representatives. Rwanda, Sweden, South Africa, and Cuba had the greatest percentages of women (51, 46, 43, and 43 percent respectively). The Nordic countries have the highest percentages of female representatives (42 percent) and the Arab states the lowest (10 percent; Inter-Parliamentary Union, 2010). When men control political systems, they sometimes use their power to create and maintain legal systems that support gender inequality and compel women to conform (Moncrieffe, 2005). As you will learn, in many places, women have fewer legal rights than men and even when laws are in place, male-dominated police and justice systems do not enforce them. Informal justice systems, which include forums of community representatives that decide on local disputes, usually consist of men who uphold customs and religious laws favoring men (UNIFEM, 2009).

Despite their somewhat poor representation in formal politics (parliaments, congresses, heads of state), women are often very political. In later chapters you will see that much of women's political influence comes from their activities in grassroots organizations that place pressure on formal political institutions. Increasing women's political participation and representation has long been a focus of women's activists. In the twentieth century, the focus was gaining women the right to vote (called **women's suffrage**). By 2005, all countries that allow males to vote had granted women that same right (U.S. women received voting rights in 1920). Kuwait was the last of these countries. Box 2.1 discusses the efforts of Kuwaiti women to gain the vote and increase the numbers of women in parliament. Chapter 9 focuses on women in politics and how women gain political power. Another focus for activists is the reform of legal and justice systems that allow the violation of women's human rights. This includes working for the passage and implementation of laws and constitutions that give women legal standing and guarantee women equal rights, increasing women's **legal literacy** (knowledge of their legal rights), improving women's access to legal advice and the courts, and reforming law enforcement institutions such that they are responsive to crimes against women such as sexual assault and domestic violence.

"The concept of democracy will only assume true and dynamic significance when political policies and national legislation are decided upon jointly by men and women with equitable regard for the interests and aptitudes of both halves of the population."
Interparliamentary Union, 1994

In Liberia, one of the first laws passed following the election of President Ellen Johnson Sirleaf was a law criminalizing rape and making it a nonparole offense.

Huda Shaarawi (1879–1947) was the founder of the modern Egyptian women's movement and encouraged Egyptian women to participate in politics. She organized meetings of Arab feminists from other countries and led delegations of Egyptian women to international conferences.

Males' Higher Status

Although progress has been made, in many ways and in many places, males are still more valued than females and enjoy a higher social standing. **Job prestige** is one example of women's lower status. Margaret Mead, the famous anthropologist and one of the first scholars to pay serious attention to the activities of women, noted, "Whatever the arrangements in regard to descent

BOX 2.1   *Kuwaiti Women Seeking Political Rights*

Kuwait, an oil-rich, predominantly Muslim country, is located in the Persian Gulf in the Middle East. By law, Kuwaiti women are assured equal rights but they were not granted the right to vote and run for political office until 2005. During the occupation by Iraq in 1990 and 1991, Kuwaiti women courageously smuggled food, weapons, and information to resistance fighters and were surprised that post-war, they were not rewarded with political rights. Those opposed argued that "the man speaks for the family" and that politics would take women away from their home and children. To win their rights, women demonstrated outside parliament chanting "Women's rights now!" and carried signs saying, "Our democracy will only be complete with women." The activists wore blue T-shirts with slogans like "Half a democracy is not a democracy." Wearing their blue shirts, they attended parliamentary sessions.

Less than a month after getting their voting rights, Prime Minister Emir Sheikh Sabah al-Ahmad al-Sabah named rights activist Massouma al-Mubarak as Kuwait's first woman Cabinet minister. However, Massouma al-Mubarak's swearing-in was marred by Islamist and tribal MPs (ministers of parliament) banging their desks and shouting insults. She was forced to resign in 2008 after intense pressure. In 2008, the Emir appointed Nouriya al-Subaih as Education Minister. She has been under fire since she defied Islamist calls for her to cover her hair when she was sworn in. Since 2006, approximately twenty-five women have run in each parliamentary election and in spring 2009, women finally won four seats in parliament despite resistance from Islamists (fundamentalist Muslims). Islamists then tried to oust those who did not wear traditional dress but were overruled.

or ownership of property, and even if these formal outward arrangements are reflected in the temperamental relations between the sexes, the prestige values always attach to the activities of men" (1935, p. 302). Likewise, anthropologist Michelle Zimbalist Rosaldo (1974) said it is striking that male activities, as opposed to female activities, are always recognized as predominantly important, and cultures bestow authority and value on the activities of men. According to the UN, although well-educated women have advanced and the share of women managers is increasing, most women remain in low-status, less-valued jobs and face greater barriers to higher-level positions (Millennium Development Goals Report, 2008).

Not only are male activities valued over female ones, but in many countries, families value male children over female children, in what is known as **son preference.** All over the world, people greet the birth of boys and girls differently (Mosse, 1993). For instance, among the Turkana people of northern Kenya, great feasting accompanies the birth of a boy, but there is no feasting if the baby is a girl.

In countries where there is a combination of son preference and small family size (by choice or by government coercion), some families use female infanticide and neglect and abandonment of girls to achieve the desired number of sons (Hesketh & Xing, 2006). In most countries, the mortality rate for children under age 5 is close to the same for boys and girls. However, in

"The most gifted and beautiful girl is not as desirable as a deformed boy."
Ancient Chinese proverb

"Daughters are not for slaughter."
Indian women's movement slogan

some countries with son preference, like Afghanistan, China, India, Nepal, and Pakistan, discrimination against girls leads to neglect of their health care and nutrition such that female children aged 1 to 4 are more likely to die than male children (Hesketh & Xing, 2006; UN Statistics Division, 2007a). Evidence of discrimination in the feeding and care of girl children also can be seen in countries like Afghanistan, Bangladesh, Burundi, Cambodia, Cameroon, China, India, and Viet Nam, where the percentage of underweight girl children is greater than the percentage of underweight boys (UN Statistics Division, 2007b).

The good news is that the influence of gender on childhood malnutrition and infant and child mortality has dramatically decreased in the last twenty years; the bad news is that in some places it has been replaced by a different type of disadvantage: **sex-selective abortion** (Hesketh & Xing, 2006). The United Nations Population Fund reports that the use of ultrasound equipment and amniocentesis has led to the selective abortion of so many female fetuses that, on average, 120 males were born for every 100 females in China and India (Tucker, 2008), though it should be noted that there is great regional variation in these countries. For example, in China, where the government allows families in urban areas only one child, families living in large cities are more likely to sex-select with the first pregnancy than are rural families allowed more than one child. It is estimated that in Asia, at least 60 million girls are "missing" as the result of sex-selective abortion, infanticide, abandonment, and neglect, most them in countries like China, South Korea, India, Nepal, and Viet Nam, where son preference is strongest (UNDP, 2007). In India alone, it is estimated that 700,000 girls a year (that's about 2,000 per day) go missing as a result of illegal sex determination and consequent elimination; this translates to as many as 10 million girls missing in the two and half decades between 1981 and 2005 (Kulkarni, 2007). In the next 20 years, there is expected to be 12 to 15 percent fewer women in China and India as a result of son preference (Hesketh & Xing, 2006). Son preference has contributed to imbalanced sex ratios in countries like Afghanistan, Bangladesh, China, India, Iran, South Korea, and Pakistan where there are between 78 and 94 women per 100 men (the natural ratio is around 105 to 100; UNFPA, 2007; UN Statistics Division, 2007c).

Governments and activists are concerned and taking action. Due to Indian women's activism, a national law was passed in 1994 banning the use of prenatal diagnostic techniques for sex selection and an amended law was passed in 2002 prohibiting the determination and disclosure of the sex of the fetus, outlawing advertisements related to preconception and prenatal determination of sex, and prescribing punishments for violators. The Chinese and South Korean governments have also adopted and carried out a series of policies, laws, and public awareness campaigns to address the issue. Rather than increasing their value and status, a scarcity of women for marriage is expected to put women at greater disadvantage for rape and violence and has already increased the trafficking of women (the recruitment, transportation, harboring, or receipt of people for the purposes of slavery, forced labor, and

"Female feticide has created a big demand for women and it's being met by trafficking . . . People have made their daughters vanish but they still desperately need women."
Ravi Kant, executive director of Shakti Vahini, an organization that has rescued thousands of minor girls being trucked into some regions of India

servitude) (UNFPA, 2007). Poor women from other regions or countries are "imported" (some women are willing to relocate for purposes of economic survival and some poverty-stricken parents are willing to sell their daughters; see Chapter 7). As commodities bought for sex, baby-making, and household labor and as outsiders unfamiliar with local customs and languages, these women have few rights and little status. In some parts of India where shortages of women are severe, **polyandry,** the practice of brothers sharing a wife, has arisen (Dhillon, 2007).

Despite government efforts, son preference continues because it is rooted in traditional practices and customs. According to the UN, the practice of son preference emerged with the shift from subsistence agriculture, which was primarily controlled by women, to settled agriculture which is primarily controlled by men (UN High Commissioner for Human Rights, 2009). In the patrilineal landowning communities prevalent in the Asian region, where sons carry on the family name and property inheritance is through the male line, the economic obligations of sons toward parents are greater. Sons are the source of family income and provide for parents in their old age. Sons bring prestige to the family. They interpret religious teachings and perform important rituals, especially following the death of their parents. They hold the political power positions and high-status jobs. They are the soldiers that protect the community. In contrast, daughters are expected to marry, leave the family, and have children. Consequently, they do not have the potential to enhance the family's economic or social position the way that sons do. Daughters in some cultures are viewed as wasted investments because any investment made in a girl is enjoyed only by her husband's family when she moves in with them upon marriage.

Historically, son preference has also meant that girls were less likely to receive an education than boys and, in many regions, women's literacy rates are still notably lower than men's (UNICEF, 2006). Globally, over the past thirty years, primary school enrollments for girls have risen from 52 percent to 90 percent but in the developing nations of sub-Saharan Africa and South Asia, girls still suffer disproportionately from educational disadvantage, especially in secondary and tertiary education (post-high school education such as college) (UNICEF, 2006). This is important because women's education levels are clearly linked to their children's survival and well-being and tertiary education is essential for leadership roles in politics, the economy, and administration (UNIFEM, 2009a).

Son preference and the perception that daughters are an economic liability are aggravated in cultures with large dowry requirements (UNFPA, 2005). A **dowry** consists of money or goods paid by the bride's family to the groom or his family, mostly in the countries of Southeast Asia. Hundreds of years ago, dowries were property of the bride and provided her economic protection within the marriage. Women could not inherit land from their parents, and dowry was viewed as their inheritance. Dowry inflation is a problem in many countries, particularly in India where some families with sons view dowries as a way to increase family wealth and acquire material things (Srinivasan & Bedi, 2007). This makes daughters expensive, especially for those who are poor. For example, in Bangladesh, paying a dowry to the future husband's family is illegal

BOX 2.2   *Walking Away from the Wedding Due to Dowry Demands*

In May 2003, Nisha Sharma, a 21-year-old computer student in New Delhi, became a role model to Indian women on the day of her wedding. As is common in upper middle-class Indian society, her parents found the bridegroom by placing a classified ad and interviewing prospective grooms. When the groom's family made a last-minute demand at the wedding for $25,000 in rupees, on top of the car and appliances they had already been promised, an outraged Nisha picked up her cell phone and called the police to report a violation of the Dowry Prohibition Act of 1961, and called off the wedding. Her courageous move earned her worldwide attention and praise. Interviewed on television and by newspapers, she posed wearing a sash reading "Anti-dowry," and encouraged other brides to walk away when in-laws request more dowry.

Others, like Pooja Pathak, soon followed Nisha's example. Barely two hours after the wedding ceremony, Pooja's husband and father-in-law said they would not accept the young woman into their home unless she also came with a new color television and video player. "I was very angry," Pooja recalled. "We had given so much, and yet their mouths were still open." Her family called the police, who arrested the groom and his father. Although dowry has been illegal in India since 1961, the fight to eradicate the practice has been uphill. Notwithstanding the publicity generated by Nisha Sharma's case and others like it, police are reluctant to bring dowry charges, and convictions are rare.

Source: Devraj, 2003; Vasudev, Menon, Vinayak, David, & Muralidharan, 2003; Lancaster, 2005.

but is still practiced by most rural families. Dowry payments are typically more than 200 times the daily wage and aggravate the poverty of families with daughters (University of Bath, 2008). One study in rural south India (Srinivasan, 2005) found that the expectation of a large dowry payment tops the list of causes for the undesirability of daughters. The expected dowry burden influences decisions regarding the number of daughters and is the primary justification for sex-selective abortion and female infanticide (Srinivasan & Bedi, 2007). Box 2.2 tells how Indian women are rebelling against demands for increased dowry. Many women, however, are in favor of dowry, believing that it is essential to marrying a "good" man, that it increases their value in their husband's family, and that it is their share of their family's wealth (Srinivasan & Bedi, 2007).

Females as Property

When people are thought of as commodities or property, they are diminished and dehumanized and do not have the power to make their own life choices. Sadly, there are a number of ways in which females are treated as the property of men and as commodities to be bought and sold.

The **trafficking of women and girls** for labor or sex is one instance of women as property and is a form of modern-day slavery. Typically, after

"I am a poor man, and this is how I can feed my large family. What else could I do? Many others are doing the same thing."
Afghan man who sold his 9- and 10-year-old daughters to wealthy opium poppy growers

winning the trust of women or the parents of girls, agents of local criminal networks acquire and sell the victims to criminal networks in destination countries. **Sex trafficking,** which pulls women and girls into prostitution against their will, is the most common identified form of human trafficking (79%); other forms of trafficking are probably underreported and include forced or bonded labor, domestic servitude, and forced marriage. Most identified trafficking victims are women (66 percent) and girls (13 percent; boys are 9 percent) and the estimated number of trafficked women runs as high as 10 million (UNODC, 2009). Trafficking in girls and women is discussed in more detail in Chapter 7.

In many cultures, an unmarried woman is considered the property of her father and he may choose when and to whom she will marry; this is called **forced marriage.** In forced marriage, one or both of the partners cannot give free or valid consent to the marriage. Forced marriages involve varying degrees of force, coercion, or deception, ranging from emotional pressure by family or community members to abduction and imprisonment. Forced and early marriage mainly affect young women and girls.

Victims are forced into marriage for many different reasons. To families living in poverty or financial difficulty, a daughter's early marriage may reduce financial strain. Forced marriages are also common where there is poverty in combination with **brideprice** (sometimes called bridewealth or *lobala*). Brideprice involves the groom giving money, goods, or livestock to the parents of the bride in return for her hand. Common in many African ethnic groups and parts of Papua New Guinea, India, and Afghanistan, the practice provides a financial incentive for parents to marry off their young daughters. For example, in Afghanistan, an estimated 57 percent of girls are forced to marry before the age of 16, often to men decades older (Ertürk, 2006). Forced marriages of girls can also be used to settle men's debt. In Afghanistan, Pakistan's North West Frontier Province, and the tribal territories, as well as in sub-Saharan Africa, girls are sometimes forced to marry in order to settle the debt of a father or brother. While forced and early marriages are less common than they once were, they persist in parts of the world. Forced marriage also includes **bride kidnapping,** an issue in the former Soviet Union countries of Kyrgyzstan and Uzbekistan, where it developed as a way for poor men to avoid paying brideprice. In Kyrgyzstan, up to a third of ethnic Kyrgyz women are estimated to be wedded in nonconsensual bride kidnappings and in Uzbekistan, as many as one in five women is abducted for marriage (Parrot & Cummings, 2008; UNIFEM, 2007).

Many women go from being the property of their father to the property of their husband. In sub-Saharan Africa, wives have little say over household decisions regarding health care, purchases, visits to relatives, and even what food to cook (UNIFEM, 2007). In the sub-Saharan African countries of Burkina Faso, Mali, Nigeria, Malawi, and Benin, over 70 percent of women say their husbands alone make decisions regarding their (the wife's) health (UNICEF, 2006). Laws sometimes sanction husbands' rights to control women and consider wives the property of husbands to do with as they wish.

82%, 75%, 63%, 57%, and 50%: The percentage of girls in Niger, Bangladesh, Nepal, India, and Uganda, respectively, who marry before the age of 18.
International Center for Research on Women (ICRW)

"If a man wants to marry a woman, the man gets a delegation of about ten men who go to the woman's home. When they reach there, they find another delegation of men from the woman's side. The speaker from the woman's side says the number of cows, goats, and money that are 'worth' their daughter and the speaker from the man's side says what they are willing to pay, the process of 'please reduce and you must increase' continues as though they are in a commercial or political negotiation."
Woman from Uganda, 2000

For example, wives in Saudi Arabia and Iran cannot travel without their husbands' permission, in Ethiopia marital rape is legal, and until 2004, Moroccan law dictated that women had to obey their husbands.

Violence Against Women (VAW)

Violence is often "gendered" in that some types of violence, such as rape and domestic violence, are experienced disproportionately by females, and because women and girls are victims because they are female. Gender-based violence is used to reinforce men's power over women, to keep women in their place, to remind them that men are "boss." The fact that it is common, accepted (or at least ignored), and that police and legal systems frequently fail to intervene, is an indication of women's lower status and power. For example, since 1993, in Ciudad Juárez and Chihuahua, Mexico almost 400 women and girls have been murdered (many were raped and mutilated) and more than 70 remain missing (Amnesty International, 2006; Herbert, 2006). It is widely accepted that the police and government systematically failed to prevent and punish perpetrators. VAW is a major public health problem and is a violation of human rights (World Health Organization, 2008). It is sustained by cultures of silence, denial of the serious health and social costs of abuse, and gender inequality and traditional gender norms (UNFPA, 2009a; WHO, 2008).

The United Nations *Declaration on the Elimination of Violence against Women* (1993) defines **violence against women** as "any act of gender-based violence that results in, or is likely to result in, physical, sexual, or mental harm or suffering to women, including threats of such acts, coercion or arbitrary deprivation of liberty, whether occurring in public or in private life." The United Nations Fund for Women (UNIFEM) suggests that violence against women includes: prenatal sex selection in favor of male babies, female infanticide, sexual abuse, female genital cutting, sexual harassment in schools and the workplace, trafficking, forced prostitution, dowry-related violence, domestic violence, battering, and rape and other forms of sexual assault. Violence against women and girls occurs in every segment of society but it is definitely influenced by intersectionality (Merry, 2009). Race, class, disability, sexual orientation, age, and religion all affect a woman's experience of gendered violence.

The study of violence against women also shows how women's social, political, and economic subordination are not only issues in and of themselves but are interrelated and influential in a variety of women's issues. You will see how the perception of women as men's property contributes to their abuse by husbands, to war rape, and to the selling of daughters into prostitution or marriage. Women's lack of political power means that legal and police protections against domestic and sexual violence are often absent or minimal. Women's lack of economic power means some are unable to leave abusive situations. Women's lower status leads to an acceptance of violence against them by families and authorities. Figure 2.2 shows the forms of violence against women discussed in this chapter.

"Women's struggles cannot be left solely to women. Men need to show solidarity, because they are living proof that there are men who repudiate this form of aggression and will do everything in their power to ensure that the number of people who practice violent acts— which unfortunately is very high across all classes and all parts of the world—continues to be reduced by democratic opposition on the part of both men and women."
Boaventura de Souza Santas, Brazil

"Through violence men seek both to deny and destroy the power of women. Through violence men seek and confirm the devaluation and dehumanization of women."
Rhonda Copelon, professor of law and Co-Director of the International Women's Human Rights Clinic

November 25th is International Day for the Elimination of Violence Against Women

FIGURE 2.2   *Forms of Violence Against Women*

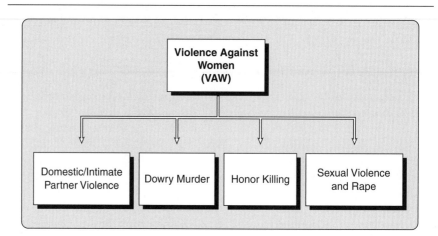

Domestic or Intimate Partner Violence

Domestic violence or **intimate partner violence (IPV)** includes bodily harm, usually accompanied by verbal threats and harassment, emotional abuse, or the destruction of property as means of coercion, control, revenge, or punishment on a person with whom the abuser is in an intimate relationship (Human Rights Watch, 1995). Domestic violence is a concern of feminists worldwide because it is exists in all regions, classes, and cultures, although rates vary widely based on culture. In the United States, each year women experience about 4.8 million intimate partner related physical assaults and rapes; 6 to 25 percent experience IPV (Bornstein, 2006; Center for Disease Control, 2006). Global studies find that between 10 and 69 percent of women report having experienced IPV and 12 to 25 percent have experienced attempted or completed forced sex in their intimate relationship (UNFPA, 2005). Box 2.3 shows the incidence of IPV in a sample of countries. As women's status and power increase and a country progresses toward gender equality, IPV usually decreases. This is largely because women in gender-unequal societies have few alternatives to staying in an abusive relationship and some men abuse the power this gives them.

A lack of laws and enforcement are one way in which some societies are structured such that women have few alternatives but to remain in abusive relationships. In many countries, neither government laws nor the police protect women from IPV, as it is viewed as a private family matter and a husband's right. Activists work hard to get domestic violence laws passed and they are making progress: 109 of 192 countries (56 percent) now have domestic violence laws, most enacted in the last ten years (UN Secretary General, 2009).

BOX 2.3   *Prevalence (in percentage) of Violence Against Women by An Intimate Partner*

Country	Ever Experienced Physical Violence	Ever Experienced Sexual Violence	Experienced Both
Peru (province)	61	47	69
Peru (city)	49	23	51
Ethiopia (province)	49	59	71
Tanzania (province)	47	31	56
Tanzania (city)	33	23	41
Bangladesh (province)	42	50	62
Bangladesh (city)	40	37	53
Samoa	41	20	46
Thailand (province)	34	29	47
Thailand (city)	23	30	41
Brazil (province)	34	14	37
Brazil (city)	27	10	29
Namibia (city)	31	16	36
Serbia & Montenegro (city)	23	6	24
Japan (city)	13	6	15

Source: World Health Organization Multi-Country Study on Women's Health and Domestic Violence against Women. Geneva: WHO, 2005.

For example, following years of activism, Japan enacted its first law against domestic violence in 2001 and by 2008 had forty-seven women's shelters (up from five in 1995). Zimbabwe passed its first domestic violence law in 2006, and Mexico, in 2007. Often, following the passage of legislation, women's groups have to work for the laws' implementation, refinement, and enforcement. Take the case of Romania. A law to counter domestic violence was passed by Romanian parliament in 2003 but it is largely ineffective because it provided no restraining orders, gave police no authority to enter homes in cases of suspected IPV, provides no resources for shelters, and requires victims to obtain an expensive medical-legal certificate to prove domestic abuse (Ciobanu, 2009). The National Coalition of Non-Governmental Organisations Involved in Programmes Against Domestic Violence is now lobbying to have it amended.

"Every woman thinking of leaving worries about finances. Women find themselves forced back into abusive marriages because they can't earn a living."
Ritsuko Nomoto, Japanese woman who opened a restaurant to give jobs to battered women

Help and services for domestic violence are available. The U.S. National Domestic Violence Hotline number is: 1-800-799-SAFE.

Research indicates that women's economic dependence on the men in their lives also increases their risk and tolerance of domestic violence (Bornstein, 2006). Some societies are structured such that an adult woman, especially one with children, will have extreme economic difficulty should she leave her relationship. Economic dependencies result from a multi-layered system of gender inequality (Carillo, 1992). First, much of women's labor is unpaid and therefore not valued. Second, even in paid jobs, women work for longer hours for lower pay with fewer benefits and less job security. Physical abuse can also increase women's economic dependence on men when it undermines women's ability to obtain and retain adequate employment due to increased absenteeism (from injury) and when abusers behave inappropriately at a partner's workplace (Bornstein, 2006).

Shelters play a critical role in women's ability to leave IPV situations because they provide alternatives to staying. Women frequently need psychological services as they recover from trauma, and financial and social services so they can become self-sufficient and do not have to return to their abuser. They also need a safe place to stay: Many have good reason to believe that their abuser will kill them or their children, or stalk them if they leave. This is not an unfounded fear. For example, in the United States, 60 percent of female homicide victims were wives or intimate acquaintances of their killers (Violence Policy Center, 2008) and half of the murdered women in the world are killed by their current or former husbands or partners (UNIFEM, 2009). Most countries have no such shelters or services, leaving activists to work to provide alternatives for women seeking to leave abusive situations. They lobby for government funding and often start and run their own women's shelters without government help. This is what happened in the 1970s and 1980s in the United States (Engle, 2009). Prior to that time there were no shelters for those experiencing domestic violence.

Women's social dependence on men also increases their risk for and tolerance of IPV (Carillo, 1992). In many cultures women are socially dependent on men because women's status is tied to marriage. Unmarried, divorced, and even widowed adult women have very low status. Leaving one's husband, regardless of circumstances, is shameful and divorce is stigmatized (this was true in the United States until the 1970s and remains true in some American subcultures). Where women cannot own or inherit property and are excluded from the economic and political power bases of their society, their class position is tied to their relationships with men (Lerner, 1986; WHO, 2008). This increases women's dependence upon marriage and increases their husband's power. Carillo (1992) also points out that women are trained to believe that their value is attached to the men in their lives—fathers, husbands, and sons. They are often ostracized if they disobey these men, and social norms frequently equate being a good woman with being an obedient woman. For example, in Ethiopia, where IPV rates are among the world's highest (71 percent), 79 percent of women interviewed felt wife-beating was justified if a woman disobeyed her husband (WHO, 2005).

According to the United Nations, IPV is also higher in countries with restrictive divorce laws (UNFPA, 2009a; WHO, 2008). Many societies are structured such that women cannot leave abusive relationships because laws make it difficult for them to divorce. For instance, Iranian women have the right to divorce if their husband signed a premarital contract granting that right or if the husband cannot provide for his family, or is a drug addict, insane, or impotent. However, a husband is not required to cite a reason for divorcing his wife and is given priority in child custody after a child reaches the age of 7 and if the wife remarries. In the United Arab Emirates, Muslim men can initiate divorce by simply saying, "I divorce you" three times but Muslim women can only initiate divorce if they can prove physical abuse (a woman must provide at least two male witnesses, or a male witness and two female witnesses to attest to the injury) or petition the Shari'ah court, and pay compensation or return their dowry to their husband (in the UAE dowry is the woman's property). If she remarries, she may have to forfeit her children. Israeli women must be granted a *get*, a Jewish divorce writ than can only be granted by husbands; many will demand that she forfeit property, alimony, and child support in exchange. In the Sudan, the man has the right to divorce but can deny his wife's request for a divorce. In Ireland—a country strongly influenced by the Roman Catholic Church, which is opposed to divorce—divorces were not granted until 1997 and in Chile, another Catholic country, divorce was illegal until 2003. Activists in these countries frequently work to change these and other family laws that are discriminatory to women.

Dowry Murder

Dowry murder (also known as *bride burnings* or *dowry deaths*) is a form of IPV and refers to the murder of wives by husbands or in-laws in the Southeast Asian countries of Bangladesh, India, and Pakistan for dowry purposes. These staged deaths occur when the bride's family is unable to provide the agreed upon dowry, when the husband's family wants to get rid of her so that they may get another dowry from a new bride to increase their family's wealth, or when a woman does not produce a son. In India, dowry deaths are sometimes called bride burnings because most victims are held over the cooking stove until their saris catch fire. In 2009, researchers found that 106,000 Indian women burn to death every year (an average of 12 women an hour, the average ratio of fire-related deaths of young women to young men was 3:1); many of these deaths are believed to the result of domestic violence and dowry disputes (Sanghari, Bhalla, & Das, 2009). In Pakistan and Bangladesh, there have been many incidents of acid attacks due to dowry disputes, often leading to blindness, disfigurement, and death (UNIFEM, 2009b). Since the 1970s, dowry deaths have been a leading concern of Indian feminists. In 1986 they won their battle to strengthen the Dowry Prohibition Act of 1961 (Bumiller, 1990). These Indian women continue to work to raise public awareness and fight for enforcement of laws.

Honor Killing

In 2007, in Kurdistan in northern Iraq, relatives and neighbors of 17-year-old Du'a Khalil Aswad beat and stoned her to death for falling in love with someone her community did not approve of (Amnesty International, 2007a). The killing was filmed on a cell phone and posted on YouTube. This is an example of another form of IPV, **honor killing,** a tradition whereby a man is obliged to kill a close female blood relative if she does something to dishonor the family such as having premarital sex (including being raped), marital infidelity (or suspected infidelity), seeking divorce, flirting, wearing makeup or nontraditional dress, and dating without parental approval. Honor killings occur in Bangladesh, Syria, Iraq, Egypt, Jordan, Morocco, Turkey, Palestine, and Uganda as well as in North American and European countries where immigrants have engaged in the practice. It is most common where there is a strong belief in family honor and a woman's disobedient behavior hurts the family's reputation and where a man's prestige is linked to the sexual behavior of the woman under his charge (Khan, 2006; Parrott & Cummings, 2006). The United Nations estimates that 5,000 women are killed each year in the name of honor but this is likely an underestimate (Chesler, 2009; WHO, 2008). It is believed that the actual number of honor killings is four times higher than reported figures; many girls simply go missing or deaths are reported as suicides (Khan, 2006).

Honor killings are viewed as a way to promote moral stability and perpetrators often go unpunished. For example, Syrian and Brazilian law allows for reduced sentences in the case of a murder committed in the name of honor. Turkey recently revamped its penal code and imposed life sentences for honor killings, prompting some families to force daughters to commit suicide or to kill them and disguise the deaths as suicides (Wilkinson, 2007). Honor killing differs from other forms of domestic violence in that it occurs in cultures where honor and morality are viewed as a collective family matter, and it usually involves multiple family and community members that conspire to kill a daughter/sister because she has dishonored the family through disobedience and "immoral" behavior (Chesler, 2009).

Before 1993, honor killings received little public attention or government action (Khan, 2006). Consequently, activists began working (and continue to work) to bring attention to the issue and for the passage and enforcement of laws criminalizing honor killing. They also work to aid potential victims. For example, the Organization for Women's Freedom in Iraq (OWFI) has created the Underground Railroad for Iraqi Women, which, inspired by the network of courageous individuals who operated the Underground Railroad during slavery in the United States, seeks to provide women threatened with honor killing with the means and resources to escape and begin to build a new life. They have also initiated a campaign calling on the Iraqi Kurdistan government to hold perpetrators accountable (International Campaign Against Honour Killings, 2009). This work is quite dangerous and activists and journalists working on honor killing-related violence are constantly threatened and in some cases killed (Khan, 2006).

Rana Husseini, reporter for the *Jordan Times,* received the 1998 Reebok Human Rights Award at age 26. Despite the risk of serious physical harm, she continues to investigate and write about the practice of honor killing in Jordan.

Sexual Violence and Exploitation

Women routinely experience sexual assault in ways that have no immediate parallels for men (Chowdhury et al., 1994). Women are disproportionately sexually victimized (as in the case of rape) and sexually exploited (sexually abused for others' sexual gratification or for financial gain, as in the case of prostitution and pornography). This is further evidence of women's lower power and status, for if women and men were equal, women would not be sexually subjugated, and, if they were, there would be severe consequences. Barry (1995) summed it up well when she said that **sexual exploitation** objectifies women by reducing them to sex; this **sexual objectification** incites violence against women and reduces them to commodities for market exchange: "In the fullness of human experience, when women are reduced to their bodies, and in the case of sexual exploitation to sexed bodies, they are treated as lesser, as other, and thereby subordinated" (Barry, 1995, p. 24).

Rape

The defining feature of **rape** is the lack of choice by the woman to engage in sexual intercourse (Koss, Heise, & Russo, 1994). **Non-normative rape** is rape that is both against a woman's will and in violation of social norms. Sadly, **normative rape,** rape promoted or allowed by a society, is common in many places (Koss et al., 1994).

Rape is a major concern of feminists all over the world. Globally, you will find women's activists working to pass and strengthen rape laws and their enforcement, educating men to see rape as wrong, training police in sensitive procedures for handling cases, and providing assistance to rape victims, largely through rape crisis centers. Rape is a concern of feminists for six main reasons:

1. *Rape is a very real threat to women everywhere.* For instance, in the United States, 17.7 million American women have been victims of attempted or completed sexual assault in their lifetime (one in six women; 16.6 percent) and in 2007 alone, there were 248,300 victims of sexual assault (RAINN, 2009). The rate is even higher for American Indian and Alaskan women (34 percent; RAINN, 2009), and for women U.S. military soldiers, the rate is approximately 30 percent (Benedict, 2009; Jamail, 2009). Estimates of the prevalence of sexual violence by nonpartners are difficult to establish, because in many societies, sexual violence remains an issue of deep shame for women and often for their families, and most rapes go unreported (UNIFEM, 2009b). The UN estimates that worldwide, one in five women will become a victim of rape or attempted rape in her lifetime. For more information, see the Appendix.

2. *Rape laws are weak and poorly enforced.* About 50 percent of countries have sexual violence laws (UN Secretary General, 2009). Haiti was

one of the most recent with passage of a law in 2008. Traditionally, rape was condemned not because of its harm to women but because it was seen as a violation of a man's honor and exclusive right to sexual possession of his woman/property (Copelon, 1995). For example, in Somalia, cases are usually dealt with by having the attacker pay compensation to the victim's father or husband, but never to her. Until 2006, in Pakistan, a woman who was raped could be prosecuted for having sex outside of marriage. In many societies, the legal system and community attitudes add to the trauma that rape survivors experience. Women are often held responsible for the violence against them, and in many places laws contain loopholes that allow the perpetrators to act with impunity and the police and judiciary often fail to investigate reports of rape and other sexual assaults (Onyejekwe, 2008; UNIFEM, 2009b). In Ecuador, a rapist can go free under the Penal Code if he marries his underage victim and in Burundi, girl victims can be forced by their families to marry their attacker. Ethiopia and the Bahamas have an exception for marital rape. In many countries, rape victims receive little support and have to prove that they were not responsible for the rape (Onyejekwe, 2008). They are shamed and humiliated, which results in secondary victimization from family, the police, and the legal system. These are examples of normative rape.

3. *The threat of rape limits women's freedom of movement and denies them control over their sexuality.* More than any other crime, fear of rape leads women to restrict their movements and their life choices or, alternatively, to prepare for battle (Niarchos, 1995).

4. *Many of the victims of rape are girl children and adolescents, often raped by an adult relative or acquaintance.* The World Health Organization's study of violence against women and girls (2005) found varying rates of sexual abuse before age 15 from a high rate of 21 percent reported by women in Namibia to a low of 1 percent of Bangladeshi women reporting abuse. Other high rates were reported by women in Peru (19%), Japan (14%), and Brazil (12%).

5. *The fact that men can and do rape women, whereas the reverse is not true, intimidates women and gives power to men.* Some feminists, such as Brownmiller (1986), view the threat of rape as the basis of men's power over women. Rape is an expression of dominance, power, and contempt, a rejection of women's right to self-determination (Niarchos, 1995). The threat of rape also makes women dependent on fathers, brothers, or husbands to protect them. This places women in a subordinate position to men. Brownmiller (1986) suggests that, historically, marriage and women's subjugation by men arose because women needed men to protect them from other men. Furthermore, says Brownmiller (1986), the price a woman paid for this protection was her male protector's exclusive ownership of her body.

6. *Sexual assault is traumatic and has serious psychological, physical, and social costs.* The World Health Organization (2008) reports that sexual violence is associated with sexually transmitted infections such as HIV/AIDS (forced sex results in greater abrasion, providing an avenue for the virus). Other physical effects include unintended pregnancies, gynecological problems, induced abortions, miscarriage, abdominal pain, and poor overall health status. Sexual violence is also associated with depression, emotional distress, and post-traumatic stress disorder (enduring physical and psychological symptoms after an extremely stressful event). Women may be unable to work or take care of themselves and their children. Rape is often associated with stigma and rejection of the victim, adding to its emotional costs. In some countries, women may be rejected by their husbands or become unmarriageable due to the loss of virginity. Sexual abuse as a child is associated with greater sexual risk-taking, substance abuse, and further victimization.

Sexual Violence in Conflict and Post-Conflict (War Rape)

War magnifies the gendered structure of violence (Nikolic-Ristanovic, 1996). During times of war, women often experience great hardship. War often displaces women and their dependent children from their homes and makes them refugees, leaves them without husbands and fathers, and makes meeting basic needs difficult. If this weren't bad enough, they also face the increased prospect of rape. Writings from as early as 420 c.e. document **war rape**—the rape of women during wartime. During World War II, Moroccan soldiers raped Italian women, Japanese soldiers raped Korean women, and Nazi soldiers raped Jewish women. In the 1970s, Pakistani soldiers raped Bengali women. In the 1980s, war rapes occurred in El Salvador and Guatemala. In the 1990s, Bosnian Serb soldiers raped between 20,000 and 50,000 Muslim women in the former Yugoslavia. An estimated 250,000 to 500,000 women and girls were raped during a civil war in less than 100 days in Rwanda in 1994. In the first decade of this century we have already seen hundreds of thousands of war rapes committed in Iraq, Burundi, Somalia, Sudan, the Central African Republic, the Democratic Republic of Congo, Côte d'Ivoire, Liberia, Sierra Leone, and Uganda (Stop Rape Now, 2009). Women and girls remain at risk for rape in the post-conflict period due to ineffective or unstable new governments and undeveloped police and justice systems. For example, in Burundi, high levels of rape and sexual violence have continued since the end of the civil conflict in 2003 (Amnesty International, 2007b). Most women suffering injuries or illnesses caused by war rape and post-conflict instability do not have access to medical care, and the stigma of rape often leads to their abandonment by their partners or families.

The UN identifies four kinds of war rape, summarized in Figure 2.3 (UN Integrated Regional Information Networks, 2003). One type, **genocidal rape,**

Help and services for sexual assault in the U.S. are available. Call the National Sexual Assault Hotline (U.S.) at 1-800-656-HOPE or go to http://apps.rainn.org/ohlbridge/ for the online hotline.

"Violence against women will end when legal, philanthropic, governmental and nongovernmental organizations and impassioned individuals unite and stand up to say it is a priority, to say that the time for ending violence is now."
Eve Ensler, founder of VDay, playwright and women's activist. Ensler's play "The Vagina Monologues," is staged every February in the U.S. and Europe. Millions of dollars in proceeds have been donated to women's shelters and rape crisis centers.

I was raped by them in front of my husband. They held him down while they did it. I was released afterwards because my husband and children pleaded with them, and cried saying "They will kill maman." I was raped by more than three men. I cannot remember the exact number because I lost consciousness. Afterwards a neighbor helped me, because I was bleeding. She boiled water and some herbs for me."
Human Rights Watch interview, Bukavu, October 16, 2003.

The persistence and painstaking research of Yoshiaki Yoshimi, a Japanese history professor, as well an international tribunal organized by transnational feminist networks, was instrumental in getting the Japanese government to admit that Japanese soldiers had used girls and women from Korea and China as "comfort women." The Japanese government had covered up the situation for more than forty years.

FIGURE 2.3   *Four Types of War Rape*

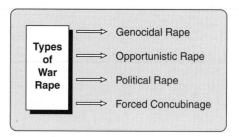

such as that seen in Rwanda and the Balkans, is intended to destroy an ethnic or political group perceived as the enemy. **Opportunistic rape** occurs when men take advantage of the breakdown of law and order that can occur during wartime to commit crimes against women, knowing it is unlikely they will face consequences. **Political rape** punishes individuals, families, or communities that hold different political views. When daughters or wives are raped to punish their male relatives, political rape is a variation on the woman-as-property theme. The desecration of the female is viewed as the torture of the male (Chesler, 1996). Women are the male enemy's property, and they are used as an instrument to defeat or punish the enemy (Brownmiller, 1986; Nikolic-Ristanovic, 1996). Many of the rapes occur in the presence of the victim's family, the local population, or other victims, and many involve sexual torture and sadism (Niarchos, 1995). **Forced concubinage** involves the kidnapping of girls and women to wash, cook, serve, and have sex with soldiers and militia. It takes the form of forced prostitution in "rape camps." For example, during World War II, the Japanese enslaved between 200,000 and 400,000 Korean, Filipino, Chinese, Indonesian, and Dutch women in "comfort stations" for sexual use by Japanese soldiers (Copelon, 1995). Ninety percent of these women died in captivity (Copelon, 1995).

Although war rape has occurred with every war, it was not until 1996 that UN postwar courts prosecuted sexual assault as a crime of war. This was an important first step in changing war rape from normative to non-normative. On June 27, 1996, a United Nations tribunal indicted eight Bosnian Serb military and police officers in connection with the rapes of Muslim women during the Bosnian war. In 2001, the International Criminal Tribunal for the former Yugoslavia indicted eighty men for war rape, and in February 2002, three Bosnian Serbs were the first to be jailed for war sex crimes in a case involving sex enslavement (Taylor, 2002). In 1998, the majority of the world's governments agreed to form a permanent independent international organization, called the International Criminal Court (ICC), to investigate and prosecute genocide, crimes against humanity, and war crimes. The ICC's draft treaty initially did not acknowledge rape as a war crime, leading women's activists and legal experts to work to have women's concerns incorporated into the treaty establishing the ICC (Frankson, 1998). It took until 2002 for the statute forming the court to be ratified by the required sixty countries and, by 2008, 108 states were party to the ICC and the court was ready to begin its work (ICC, 2009). The first cases to be prosecuted by the court all include indictments for war rape. In March, 2009 the ICC issued a warrant for the arrest of Omar Hassan Ahmad Al Bashir, the President of Sudan, for war crimes in Darfur including war rape (although many believe he will never be captured and stand trial). The ICC also began trials of military leaders who instigated widespread war rape in the Democratic Republic of Congo and the Central African Republic and issued arrest warrants for leaders in Uganda (International Criminal Court, 2009).

Prostitution

Prostitution is plainly about the sexual objectification of women, and it is clearly driven by economics. Although some women choose sex work as a profession and are not subservient or enslaved to their customers or to pimps (Chuang, 2005), the majority of women involved in prostitution are sexually exploited; this is a reflection of their lower worth in the world (Parrot & Cummings, 2008). Prostitution is most often about females as commodities to be bought and sold and about how poverty leads to prostitution. Activists say that cultural attitudes that consider prostitution a victimless crime, or that suggest women are sexual objects, must be changed.

Barry (1995) argues that prostitution is a form of sexual slavery because women and girls are held over time for sexual use and because getting out of prostitution requires escape. Although the prostitute herself typically earns barely enough to survive, an extended network of people profit from her body and her labor: The police and other government officials fine prostitutes or receive bribes to look the other way; pimps, bar, brothel, and hotel owners get a cut of her wages; airlines, travel agencies, and foreign customers also benefit. It is estimated that pimps control 80 to 95 percent of prostitution. These pimps find naive and needy young women, manipulate them into prostitution, and then take the majority of their money (Barry, 1995). Sex trafficking, where girls and women are tricked or coerced into leaving their home country and forced to become sexual slaves in another, is another case where devalued and marginalized women and girls are used for profit by men and for men (Parrot & Cummings, 2008). Other forms of sexual slavery include forced concubinage (sexual slavery in war camps) and forced marriage (since conjugal relations are required and often forced) (Parrot & Cummings, 2008).

The effect of prostitution on women is overlooked by governments such as Thailand, Korea, and the Philippines where **sexual tourism** is a major source of cash for economic development. Sexual tourism—when men travel to other countries to buy sex, often as part of tourism packages—is discussed at greater length in Chapter 7. The sexual exploitation of women is also overlooked by militaries, such as the U.S. Army, who see "sexual recreation" as vital to the well-being and morale of its troops and so permit

"Whether it's burkas or bikinis, the humiliation of women as property or sex objects is an affront to human dignity. It creates a market for women and girls who are traded like commodities."
Antonio Maria Costa, Executive Director of the UN Office on Drugs and Crime (UNODC)

"I have often heard men say that I had a choice, and I did, it was either work as a prostitute or starve to death."
Dawn, who became a prostitute at age 16 (Canada)

"The sexual control of women has been a cornerstone of patriarchal power."
Andrea Parrot and Nina Cummings

the **military sexploitation of women.** For example, U.S. military bases in the Philippines, Korea, and in Okinawa, Japan, coordinated with government authorities and entrepreneurs to provide U.S. servicemen with sex provided mostly by women trafficked from the Philippines and the former Soviet Union (Coronel & Rosca, 1993; Demick, 2002; Enloe, 1996). The Korean Special Tourism Association lobbied the government to allow the import of foreign women, saying that it was essential to prevent American GIs from harassing and raping Korean women.

Conclusion

"It's not governments or superheroes that will change the world—it's ordinary people who realize that governments and superheroes aren't doing anything."
Lauryn Oates, age 20, Canadian Human Rights Activist

This chapter documented women's lower power and status but is in no way intended to suggest that men are by nature evil beings intent on the oppression of women. Rather, as you will see throughout the book, men's individual, intentional acts of dominance over women are the reflections of cultures' overall systems of gender power relations. As Lips (1991) notes, the occurrence of many forms of routine oppression of women by men is mindless and unintentional, often unrecognized by either the perpetrator or the victim. Individuals, more or less unaware of the structure of power that surrounds them, participate in, maintain, and are limited by the power structures of their societies. For instance, many cultures define masculinity in ways that encourage the denigration of women and define femininity in terms of submissiveness and subordination to men. Both females and males are socialized into cultures that emphasize men's power over women and are taught by their parents and other agents of socialization (such as peers) to participate in traditional gender systems. It must also be acknowledged that many men actively support gender equality and many men do not personally perpetrate gender discrimination or violence against women. These male allies should be greatly appreciated.

It is also important to realize that it is not uniquely male to create groups in which some individuals have greater power and status than do others. Women often discourage their girl children from challenging traditional gender relations and they often participate in the social systems that oppress women. For instance, it is usually adult women that perform the physically traumatizing genital cutting of girls common in some countries. Similarly, the brokers that trick young women into sexual slavery are sometimes women, and women of the upper classes often exploit women of the lower classes (especially those of other ethnicities) for household labor. It generally takes a great deal of activism and vigilance to override the human inclination to exploit and dominate other humans and then justify it by seeing the victims as "lesser."

Finally, to suggest that women have limited power and status in comparison to men is not to overlook their great strength. Women are really quite remarkable—carrying on, often under conditions of great adversity, in order to keep their families going. Although their lives are frequently difficult, they find pleasure in their friends and family, and pride in their strength. Also, despite barriers to their political activity, they fight for their rights, and they have brought about significant change in the last fifty years through their efforts. For instance, there are many organizations working on the issues discussed in this chapter.

The following chapters pick up on some themes started here. Chapters 5, 6, and 7 return to the topic of women's labor and the feminization of poverty. Chapter 8 shows religion is sometimes an agent of patriarchy. Chapters 9, 10, and 11 all explore aspects of women's political activity and empowerment. The next chapter, Chapter 3, explores how women's power and status are affected by their role as "reproducer" and the importance of reproductive freedom for the achievement of gender equality and women's health.

Study Questions

1. What evidence does the chapter provide for the idea that women have less economic power than men? Why does this matter?
2. What evidence does the chapter provide for the idea that women have less political and legal power than men? Why does this matter?
3. How are job prestige and son preference an indication of females' lower status? Where son preference is profound, why does it occur and what are its effects?
4. What are some of the ways in which females are thought of as commodities or property?
5. How common is domestic violence? How is domestic violence linked to women's dependencies on men, and why is it difficult for women to leave abusive situations?
6. What are dowry murders and honor killings? Where and why do they occur?
7. Why are feminists so concerned about the rape of women?
8. How do the world's rape laws and war rape illustrate the concept of normative rape? What are the four types of war rape?
9. What is sexual exploitation? How is the sexual exploitation of women evidence of their lower power and status? What is the role of economics in the sexual exploitation of women?
10. How can prostitution, sex trafficking, forced marriage, and forced concubinage be seen as forms of sexual slavery?

Discussion Questions and Activities

1. In most cultures, it is expected that women will take their husband's name upon marriage, and most women do (in the United States about

75 to 90 percent do). Does this tendency reduce a female's value in her family of origin because she doesn't "carry on the family name"? Does this practice contribute to the perception that a woman is the property of her husband and is secondary to him? What do you think of the practice of women taking their husband's name upon marriage? How about how fathers "giving their daughters away" at the wedding and how the family of the bride is expected to pay for the wedding?

2. The chapter stated that women are socialized to believe that their value is attached to the men in their lives and that this is one of the factors that contribute to women's abuse by men. Some researchers have suggested that women feel like they must have a husband or boyfriend to have any social value; therefore, heterosexual women will put up with a lot rather than be without a man, and gay and bisexual women will sometimes choose heterosexual romantic relationships. Do you know women who fit this model? How is your answer influenced by your culture? How is it influenced by your generation? Would it be different if you were older or younger?

3. Some researchers have argued that paradigms used to explain lower female status may reflect a Western cultural bias with its denigration of domesticity and the devaluation of informal power. What do you think? Are women really lower in status and power, or is their status and power just different from men's? Explain your answer.

4. This chapter discussed women's status in generalities, when in fact there is great diversity not only across countries but within them based on geographic location, religion, ethnicity, and social class. Interview a woman from another culture using questions developed from the topics covered in this chapter. Make sure you ask her how long she lived in the other culture, whether where she lived was rural or urban, and from what social class she came. Share with her the information about women's status in her country of origin (see the Appendix) and ask for her thoughts.

5. Using UN and human rights websites, identify and classify current war rape situations.

6. Where can women go in your community if they need to escape IPV or have experienced rape? The chapter says that most of these organizations are nonprofits started by local women's groups. What is the history of your community's shelter and sexual assault prevention and treatment organization?

7. The chapter identifies many reasons for the importance of rape as a critical women's issue. One was that fear of rape inhibits women's freedom of movement. What do you think about this? How is your freedom of movement (i.e., travel, going out at night, etc.) affected by your efforts to reduce your risk of rape? Do you agree that women's need for protection increases their dependency on men? Is that a problem?

Action Opportunities

1. Become a volunteer at your local rape prevention and crisis center or domestic violence shelter. Even if you don't have time to go through the training to be a counselor, you can help out with office duties or fund-raising events.

2. Get involved with a "Take Back the Night" demonstration. Held annually around the country in April during Sexual Assault Awareness Month, and often organized by women's university centers, these events usually feature a nighttime walk followed by a rally with speakers. Contact your local women's center.

3. Contact your local domestic violence shelter and ask what types of donated goods they need. Common needs include toiletries and cleaning products. To collect the items, you could give people a list as they enter a store and request that they purchase one item to be dropped off to you when they leave.

4. Create wallet-sized cards that provide local statistics about violence against women and list local women's resources such as the local shelter and rape prevention and crisis center. Distribute in public places and get permission to leave small piles of them where they may be useful.

5. Be part of a letter-writing campaign by checking the Amnesty International and Human Rights Watch websites for campaigns (http://www .amnestyusa.org and http://www.hrw.org). Both organizations have campaigns on behalf of individual women and violence against women.

Activist Websites

Africa Feel Free Network http://www.feelfreenetwork.org

Equality Now http://www.equalitynow.org/english/index.html

UNIFEM'S Global Campaign to Eliminate Violence Against Women http://www.unifem.undp.org/campaign/violence

UN Action Against Rape in Conflict http://www.stoprapenow.org/

V-Day A Global Movement to End Violence Against Women and Girls http://www.VDAY.org

Informational Websites

WomenWatch http://www.un.org/womenwatch/

UN's Declaration on the Elimination of Violence against women http://www.umn.edu/humanrts/instree/e4devw.htm

Progress of the World's Women http://www.unifem.org/progress/2008/ publication.html

3

Reproductive Health and Reproductive Rights

". . . Good health is essential to leading a productive and fulfilling life, and the right of all women to control all aspects of their health, in particular their own fertility, is basic to their empowerment."

—United Nations Fourth World Conference for Women, Beijing Platform for Action, para. 92

This woman is from Mali, a country where women have little access to contraception and experience high rates of maternal death and disability. Women's reproductive health and rights are critical women's issues worldwide although they vary based on intersectional and contextual factors. © CONNIE COLEMAN/Getty Images

The focus of this chapter is women's reproductive health and reproductive rights. **Reproductive health** includes an array of topics and concerns including family planning, reproductive tract infections such as sexually transmitted diseases and HIV/AIDS, infertility, maternal mortality (pregnancy-related death) and morbidity (pregnancy-related illness and disability), unsafe abortion, reproductive tract cancers, and traditional harmful practices such as female genital cutting. Reproductive health conditions are the leading cause of death and illness in women of childbearing age worldwide (UNFPA, 2009b). Many of these deaths and illnesses are entirely preventable. **Reproductive rights** refer to the right to reproductive health care and the right to reproductive self-determination (Center for Reproductive Rights, 2006). These rights rest on the recognition of the basic right of all couples and individuals to decide freely and responsibly the number, spacing, and timing of their children and to have the information and means to do so, and the right to attain the highest standard of sexual and reproductive health. They also include the right of all to make decisions concerning reproduction free of discrimination, coercion, and violence (ICPD Programme of Action, 1994, para 7.3).

Reproductive rights mean having **reproductive control.** According to Jacobson (1992), a woman's reproductive control can be determined by her answers to the following questions: Can she control when and with whom she will engage in sexual relations? Can she do so without fear of infection or unwanted pregnancy? Can she choose when and how to regulate her fertility, free from unpleasant or dangerous side effects of contraception? Can she go through pregnancy and childbirth safely? Can she obtain a safe abortion on request? Can she easily obtain information on the prevention and treatment of reproductive illnesses? Where women are socially, politically, and economically disadvantaged, the answers to these questions are likely to be no, and high rates of reproductive illness and death are usually common.

Women's reproductive rights are a critical transnational feminist issue because of the intimate relationship between women's reproductive choice and their status, power, economic situation, and health. Women's ability to bear and nurse children profoundly affects their lives and the mother role is frequently a source of status. Yet women often lack the freedom to control the timing and number of their children and to make informed decisions regarding their reproductive health. Indeed, at least 200 million women want to plan their families or space their children, but lack access to safe and effective contraception (UNFPA, 2009b). Because of this, thousands of women die from unsafe abortions and experience pregnancy-related deaths and disability. Many have multiple children in close succession and spend most of their adult lives in poverty while pregnant, nursing, and caring for small children. These important private sphere responsibilities limit their participation in the paid labor force and in the formal political sphere, and consequently, reduce their power. Without the ability to control the number and spacing of their children, many women often do not have the power or the

"Reproductive health and rights are cornerstones of women's empowerment."
United Nations Population Fund

"When a woman is denied her reproductive rights—when she is denied obstetric care, birth control, the facts about reproductive health, or safe abortion . . . she is denied the means to direct her own life, protect her health, and exercise her human rights."
Center for Reproductive Rights

time to contest cultural practices that are discriminatory to women. Having more children than one can economically support pushes women and their families further into poverty. Figure 3.1 shows the many factors that constrain women's reproductive rights and health.

Although the focus here is on women's reproductive health and rights, there are many ways in which health risks, experiences, and outcomes are different for women and men, girls and boys (WHO, 2007). The name for this is **gender health disparities.** Gender discrimination leads to many health hazards for women including physical and sexual violence, malaria, and chronic obstructive pulmonary disease from cooking over open fires or traditional stoves (WHO, 2009). In many parts of the world, parents are more likely to seek medical attention for a sick boy child than for a sick girl child and girls suffer from higher malnutrition rates (UN Statistics Division, 2007b). In industrialized nations such as the United States, medical training and research have disproportionately focused on men, and medical insurance costs more for women than for men and often doesn't cover contraception; this has

FIGURE 3.1   *Common Factors Affecting Women's Reproductive Rights and Choice*

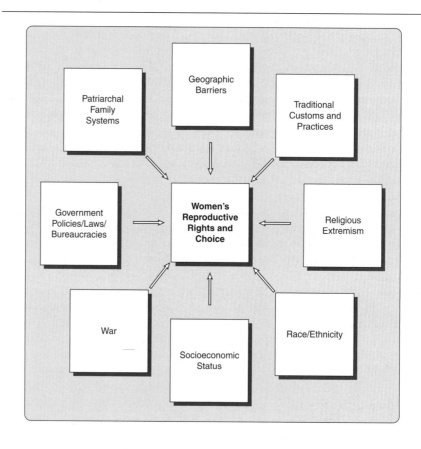

created gender health disparities in diagnosis and treatment (Center for Reproductive Rights, 2009a; Lorber, 2000). It is also important to recognize the role of intersectionality in gender health disparities—the health threats that women face and the degree of health-care availability are influenced by age, class, ethnicity, culture, region, and religion. For example, in the United States, non-White women fare worse than White women on every major health indicator from maternal mortality to the incidence of cervical cancer (CDC Office of Minority Health and Health Disparities, 2009; Center for Reproductive Rights, 2009a).

Maternal Mortality and Morbidity

Maternal Mortality

Every minute, a woman dies during pregnancy or in childbirth and every year 536,000 women die from pregnancy-related causes, leaving more than 1 million children motherless and vulnerable (UNFPA, 2009c). **Maternal mortality** refers to the death of a woman while pregnant or within forty-two days of termination of pregnancy from any cause related to or aggravated by the pregnancy or its management. According to the United Nations Population Fund (UNFPA, 2009d), more than 80 percent of maternal deaths arise from five direct causes: hemorrhage, sepsis (systemic infection), unsafe abortion, obstructed labor, or toxemia (hypertensive disease brought on by pregnancy). Another 25 percent of maternal deaths are due to diseases that are more likely to be fatal in combination with pregnancy such as malaria, anemia, and AIDS.

"No woman should die giving life."
United Nations Population Fund

Maternal mortality rates by region are shown in Box 3.1 and rates by country can be found in the Appendix. Maternal mortality ratios show that of all health indicators, the greatest gap is between rich and poor countries; 99 percent of maternal deaths occur in developing countries, primarily in Africa and South Asia (UNFPA, 2009e)[1]. Maternal mortality rates also differ within countries based on health-care availability. For example, in the United States, the rate is 8.1 per 100,000 live births for white women and 31.2 for African American women (Hoyert, 2007). These health disparities occur because quantity and quality of reproductive health care available to pregnant women—as well as women's knowledge of and ability to take advantage of the services that are available—are unequally distributed in favor of wealthier nations, urban locations, and social groups with higher incomes and education (Dixon-Mueller, 1993).

"It would cost the world less than two and a half days' worth of military spending to save the lives of 6 million mothers, newborns, and children every year."
Thoraya Obaid, Director of the UN Population Fund

Improving women's reproductive health is part of Goal 5 of the United Nations' Millennium Development Goals (MDG), which aim to cut in half the number of people living in absolute poverty by 2015. Specifically, Goal 5 calls for a 75 percent reduction in maternal mortality between 1990 and 2015 and universal access to reproductive health care by 2015. The United Nations Population Fund (2009b) says meeting this goal requires that all women have access to contraception to avoid unintended pregnancy, that all pregnant women have access to skilled care at the time of birth, and that those with

"Meeting unmet needs for **contraception** (birth control) would reduce as much as a third of maternal deaths globally."
United Nations Population Fund (UNFPA)

---

[1] Developing countries are countries with low standards of living and high poverty relative to countries with more developed economies. See Chapter 6 for a list.

BOX 3.1   *Maternal Death Rates*

A woman's lifetime risk of dying to maternal causes is:

- 1 in 22 in sub-Saharan Africa

- 1 in 210 in North Africa

- 1 in 61 in South Asia

- 1 in 1,200 in Eastern Asia

- 1 in 290 in Latin America and the Caribbean

- 1 in 7,300 in developed regions

Source: United Nations Populations Fund, State of the World Population, 2008.

---

pregnancy complications have timely access to quality emergency obstetric care (see Figure 3.2). Although maternal mortality ratios (the number of maternal deaths per 100,000 live births) are declining globally at a rate of 1 percent annually, a 5 percent decline is necessary to meet the goal; however, dramatic progress has been made in some countries including Jamaica, Malaysia, Sri Lanka, Thailand, and Tunisia (UNFPA, 2009e).

Maternal Morbidity (Disability)

"In 1948, the Universal Declaration of Human Rights of the United Nations said: 'Everyone has the right to . . . medical care. Motherhood and childhood are entitled to special care and assistance.' Therefore, we also see fistula as a basic violation of human rights, a call to action to cry out against this injustice."
Worldwide Fistula Fund

For each woman who dies as a result of pregnancy or childbirth, another twenty survive but suffer from pregnancy-related disability **(maternal morbidity)** caused by complications from pregnancy or childbirth (UNFPA, 2009e). There are a variety of such disabilities, including **uterine prolapse,** a condition wherein the supporting pelvic structure of muscles, tissue, and ligaments gives way, and the uterus drops into or even out of the vagina. The condition occurs due to difficult prolonged labor, frequent pregnancies, inadequate obstetric care, and carrying heavy loads. Often accompanied by chronic back pain and incontinence, the condition makes daily chores and sex difficult or impossible. In some countries, like Nepal, one in ten women suffers from uterine prolapse.

Depression, anemia, and obstetric fistula are also common pregnancy-related disabilities. **Obstetric fistula** is a current focus of activism and advocacy efforts. It arises from prolonged and obstructed labor, often in young women who are not physically mature or in those who have a small pelvis as a result of nutritional deficits during childhood. Fistula occurs when tissues between the

FIGURE 3.2   *Three Pillars of Maternal Health*

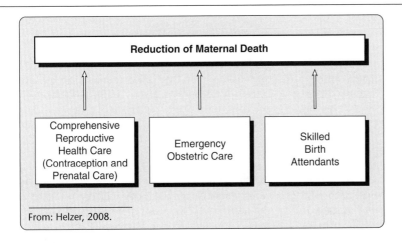

From: Helzer, 2008.

vaginal wall and the bladder or rectum are torn during childbirth, resulting in incontinence, infections, and ulcerations. Access to medical care has virtually eliminated fistula in industrialized countries but an estimated 2 million women live with fistula in developing countries, with an additional 50,000 to 100,000 new cases occurring annually (UNFPA Campaign to End Fistula, 2009). Their babies usually die from the obstructed labor and the women are often ostracized and abandoned because fistula makes personal hygiene difficult to maintain. Box 3.2 tells the story of Elena, a Tanzanian woman who experienced fistula. The UNFPA's (United Nations Population Fund) Campaign to End Fistula operates in 40 countries and emphasizes a variety of preventative measures, including increasing family planning services, improving access to maternal health care, reducing early marriage, and improving girls' nutrition. In addition to prevention, the UN and local and international nongovernmental organizations promote programs to repair physical damage through surgery (a simple surgery that costs about $300 can repair most fistulas) and treat emotional damage through counseling.

Female Genital Cutting

Another source of reproductive health problems for women is the practice of **female genital cutting** (FGC), also known as female genital mutilation (FGM) and female circumcision (FC), although there is controversy regarding terminology. We'll use the term FGC because it is more culturally sensitive than FGM (and sensitive to those who have undergone it) and yet it is not as benign a term as FC, which some feel minimizes the harmfulness of the practice. FGC refers to all procedures involving partial or total removal of the external female genitalia or other injury to the female genital organs for cultural or other nonmedical reasons (UNFPA, 2009f).

"Circumcision makes women clean, promotes virginity and chastity and guards young girls from sexual frustration by deadening their sexual appetite."
Female defender of FGM in Kenya

BOX 3.2   *Elena's Story*

Elena was about to complete her last year of primary school in Tanzania when her father arranged for her to marry one of his friends. When Elena tried to refuse the marriage proposal, her father treated her very harshly, so Elena ran away to a sympathetic aunt. Eventually, she fell in love with a young man named Nasibu. Her aunt knew Nasibu to be a good man, and Elena and Nasibu were married. Soon after, Elena conceived a child. She stayed with her aunt since it is customary in many cultures for a woman to stay with parents, close relatives, or in-laws during a first pregnancy. Her labor started in the afternoon when she was washing. The pain was strong, so she sent her cousin to bring her aunt from the fields. They returned after an hour, and told her to push whenever she felt pain. She pushed for the whole night.

Her husband came in the morning and found Elena very tired. He had no money to take her to the hospital,

so Elena had to continue the delivery at home. At 2:00 in the afternoon, they called a traditional birth attendant (TBA). The TBA came quickly and gave Elena an episiotomy using a razor. The TBA pulled the baby out, but it had already died. By now, Elena was unconscious and bleeding a great deal, so friends of her husband took her to the health center using a traditional bed tied between two bicycles. It usually takes six hours to get to the health center, but since it was night and raining, it took even longer. When the medical officer examined Elena, he saw that she was leaking urine. Due to her prolonged and obstructed labor and the lack of access to proper emergency obstetric care, Elena suffered a fistula.

Source: Women's Dignity (Utu Mwanamke)
http://www.womensdignity.org/home/index.php.

"FGM is one of the worst forms of violence against women."
Zipporah Kittony, Member of Kenya's Parliament

In some areas, FGC is carried out during infancy; in others, during childhood, at the time of marriage, during a woman's first pregnancy, or after the birth of her first child. The most typical age is between 7 and 10 years or just before puberty. Some 3 million women and girls are expected to undergo FGC every year, while some 100 to 140 million have already undergone the practice (UNFPA, 2009f). FGC is most common in the African countries of Benin, Burkina Faso, Cameroon, Central African Republic, Chad, Cote d'Ivoire, Democratic Republic of Congo, Djibouti, Egypt, Ethiopia, Eritrea, Gambia, Ghana, Guinea, Guinea-Bissau, Kenya, Liberia, Mali, Mauritania, Niger, Nigeria, Senegal, Sierra Leone, Somalia, Sudan, Tanzania, Togo, and Uganda. It is also practiced by some ethnic groups in the Asian countries of India, Indonesia, Malaysia, and Pakistan; by some groups in Oman, Saudi Arabia, United Arab Emirates, and Yemen; and by certain immigrant groups in Europe, Israel, Australia, Canada, and the United States. Incidence often varies by country and within a country based on region and ethnicity (Muteshi & Sass, 2005). Although religion is sometimes used to justify FGC, it is practiced by Muslims, Christians, Ethiopian Jews, and Copts, as well as by followers of certain traditional African religions (UNFPA, 2009f).

There are four types of FGC (Muteshi & Sass, 2005; World Health Organization, 2000):

- Type 1: Excision of the prepuce, with or without excision of part or the entire clitoris; the most common type (approximately 80% of cases).

BOX 3.3 *The Genital Cutting of Hannah from Sierra Leone*

"I was genitally mutilated at the age of 10. I was blind-folded and stripped naked. I was forced to lie flat on my back by four strong women, two holding tight to each leg. Another woman sat on my chest to prevent my upper body from moving. A piece of cloth was forced in my mouth to stop me screaming. I was then shaved. When the operation began, I put up a big fight. The pain was terrible and unbearable. I was genitally mutilated with a blunt penknife. The stuff they put on my wound stank and was painful. I was not given any anesthetic in the operation to reduce my pain, nor any antibiotics to fight against infection. Afterwards, I hemorrhaged and became anemic. This was attributed to witchcraft. I suffered for a long time from acute vaginal infections."

Source: Amnesty International (2003).

- Type 2: Excision of the clitoris with partial or total excision of the labia minora.
- Type 3: Excision of part or all of the external genitalia and stitching/narrowing of the vaginal opening (infibulation); one of the least common types (approximately 15% of cases).
- Type 4: Others; includes pricking, piercing or incising, stretching, burning of the clitoris, scraping of tissue surrounding the vaginal orifice, cutting of the vagina, and introduction of corrosive substances or herbs into the vagina to cause bleeding or to tighten the opening.

"I will circumcise my daughter because I don't want people to say that my girl is empty, I want her to be beautiful and her thing [to be] shiny like a mirror."
Somalian Mother

There are often intra-country differences in the type of FGC practiced depending on education, residence, economic status, and ethnicity (Muteshi & Sass, 2005). In most cases, a midwife or practiced village woman performs FGC using various tools (knives, razors, scissors, rocks, glass) that may or may not be sterilized. There is also variation in the use of anesthesia and antibiotics. In some countries, most notably Egypt, the procedure is often performed by medical personnel.

The health consequences of FGC are significant. Short-term medical consequences include pain, severe bleeding, infection, and death. The long-term consequences are serious, especially in the case of Type 3 (infibulation) and include difficulty urinating, menstruating, and having and enjoying sex; fistula; and complications in giving birth. Women who have undergone FGC are at significantly higher risk for adverse obstetric outcomes such as Caesarean sections, hemorrhaging, prolonged labor, resuscitation of the infant and low birth weight, and maternal mortality with the risks especially great for those with more extensive FGC forms (UNFPA, 2009f). Box 3.3 tells of the genital cutting of Hannah from Sierra Leone.

"If female circumcision is an everyday reality or province that women control, it is inconceivable that it could be eradicated without their input."
L. Amede Obiora

Efforts are underway to eradicate FGC. Human rights approaches emphasize that FGC violates major international human rights such as the right to be free from all forms of gender discrimination, the right to be free from torture, the right to health and to bodily integrity, and children's right to special protections. Legislative approaches focus on the passing of laws criminalizing the practice. Since the early 1990s, eighteen countries where FGC is practiced have enacted laws criminalizing FGC with penalties ranging from fines to life in prison. Twelve industrialized countries that receive immigrants from countries where FGC is practiced have also passed laws (Center for Reproductive Rights, 2008a). Health risk approaches have focused on educating about the harmful medical consequences of FGC. While government commitment, human rights, and medical perspectives are important, cultural practices often prevail. Cultural approaches use knowledge of local customs and mores and the involvement of affected women to derive solutions and also include information about health risks. Because FGC is embedded in cultural beliefs and practices, this approach is increasingly acknowledged as the most effective and culturally sensitive.

Women in the cultures where FGC is practiced are the best sources of cultural knowledge; thus, culturally based programs that involve them appear to be most effective. For example, in Kenya, Uganda, and Gambia, where the practice is an important rite of passage and initiation into womanhood, community-based women's groups have developed alternative "healthy initiation celebrations," "circumcision without cutting," and "circumcision with words" (Muteshi & Sass, 2005). In Senegal, where the practice is viewed as necessary for health, a movement to end FGM by educating women about the negative health consequences has almost ended FGM in 800 villages, saving an estimated 43,000 girls (Armstrong, 2003). In countries like Ghana, where the practice is a major source of income and respect for the women who perform it, a successful program trained practitioners to become traditional birth attendants (Muteshi & Sass, 2005).

In Chapter 1 it was said that it is important to avoid ethnocentricity and cultural superiority when studying global women. Cultural sensitivity is clearly important when it comes to FGC. African feminists often feel that Western feminists (feminists from Western Europe and the United States) are arrogant and demeaning in their study of and attitudes toward those who practice FGC. Although it is tempting to see cultures where FGC is practiced as barbaric and woman-hating, it is important to understand that FGC is not intended to harm girls and women. FGC occurs because parents love their daughters and want them to be socially accepted so that they can have a good future and because parents believe that it is good for their daughters (Muteshi & Sass, 2005).

Some African feminists criticize Western efforts to help as leaving out input from affected women on how to best change the practice (Hale, 2005; Obiora, 2005). They have also accused Western feminists of focusing on FGC in Africa to make them feel culturally superior while failing to wage an equally vigorous fight against the abuse of the female body in their own countries (Nnmaeka, 2005). These concerns further underscore the need for culturally sensitive approaches that empower women to change their own circumstances and remind us to look in our own backyard where there is business to take care of. After all, millions of Western women face mental and physical health difficulties due to social pressures that lead them to alter their bodies through surgery and restricted eating practices, many leading to eating disorders. Western women, especially American women, are preoccupied with weight and body image and have their bodies cut, shaped, stapled, and manipulated to conform to cultural beauty standards. Almost 400,000 American women get breast implants every year (Seager, 2009).

Contraception and Reproductive Choice, and Reproductive Health

Reliable and safe contraceptives (birth control) are essential to women's health and are an important reproductive right. The burden of having many children in close succession means that when women have the option, they seldom choose to have as many children as biologically possible. The average woman must use some form of effective contraception for at least twenty years if she wants to limit her family size to two children, and sixteen years if she wants four children (Guttmacher Institute, 2008). True reproductive choice and freedom require that women be able to make informed choices about a variety of birth control options (Hartmann, 1995). Unfortunately, reproductive choice is often limited, leading to maternal morbidity and mortality and increases in abortion rates.

Unintended pregnancies are an issue for women worldwide but contraceptive use is complex and affected by an array of personal and social variables including contraceptive knowledge and sex education, contraceptive availability, health-care system barriers (including lack of insurance coverage or money to pay, lack of facilities, or poor access due to geography), and a woman's partner situation (men often determine whether and what contraception is used). Box 3.4 provides an overview of the most common birth control methods, along with their advantages and disadvantages.

Intersectionality is important when considering contraceptive methods—the method that is best for one woman may not be the best for another, depending on her personal situation, age, and unique biology, and where she lives. The advantages and disadvantages of a method vary cross-culturally because culture influences the tolerability of side effects and because the danger of a reproductive technology depends on information and medical care availability. For example, the IUD (intrauterine device), a small plastic or copper device, is highly effective, and the most common side effect of heavy bleeding is experienced by some women but not by others. It is also a greater concern for women in developing nations who are more likely to be nutritionally deficient and have difficulty obtaining clean materials for menstruation (Hartmann, 1995). Prolonged bleeding is also a problem for women in some

In 2008, a grassroots British group put stickered messages such as "You are normal, this is not" on subway ads for plastic surgery and ads with emaciated models.

"It is very little to me to have the right to vote, to own property, et cetera, if I may not keep my body and its uses, in my absolute right."
Lucy Stone, American suffragist, 1855

Margaret Sanger (1883–1966) founded the birth control movement in the United States. Despite harassment and arrest, she successfully pushed the federal courts to change laws preventing physicians from providing birth control information and devices. In 1921 she founded the organization that would later become Planned Parenthood. Although Sanger was an important figure in the history of women's reproductive choice, she was a supporter of eugenics, a movement to limit the reproduction of "undesirable" groups.

"Women still face the dilemma that the safest contraceptives are not the most effective, while the most effective are not necessarily the safest."
Joni Seager

BOX 3.4   *Common Birth Control Methods*

Behavioral Methods

Abstinence—Continuous abstinence is not having sex play with a partner at all. It is 100 percent effective in preventing pregnancy and sexually transmitted infections (STIs). However, people may find it difficult to abstain for long periods of time, and women and men often end their abstinence without being prepared to protect against pregnancy or infection.

Outercourse—Sex play without vaginal intercourse, or oral or anal sex. It includes body rubbing and mutual masturbation. Nearly 100% effective against pregnancy if ejaculate or pre-ejaculate isn't spilled in the vagina. Most methods of outercourse also carry no risk of sexually transmitted infections/HIV transmission.

Fertility Awareness (Rhythm Method)—Uses calendars, cervical mucous, or temperature to chart the menstrual cycle. Abstinence or barrier methods are then used during the woman's fertile period. Can be effective with consistent and accurate monitoring but this is difficult for many women, especially those with irregular periods or those who are breast-feeding. Effectiveness is also reduced without men's commitment to abstain or use barrier methods during the fertile period. This method provides no protection against sexually transmitted diseases.

Withdrawal—An unreliable method requiring that the man withdraw his penis from the vagina before or when he feels he has reached the point when ejaculation is likely. It requires great control and experience on the part of the man. It does not protect against sexually transmitted disease and pregnancy may still occur due to the possibility of semen in pre-ejaculative secretions.

Barrier Methods

Diaphragm—Soft latex, shallow cup that holds spermicide and fits over the cervix to block and kill sperm. Proper fitting requires the help of a health-care practitioner. Does not protect against STIs but is 94 percent effective in pregnancy prevention if used correctly.

Cervical cap—Thimble-shaped, rubber cap that fits over the cervix. Like the diaphragm, it is used with a spermicide to block and kill sperm and must be fitted by a health-care practitioner. Does not protect against STIs but is 86 percent effective in pregnancy prevention when used correctly.

Vaginal sponge—Small, circular, polyurethane sponge that contains spermicide and prevents sperm from entering the uterus. It has a dimple on one side that fits over the cervix and a loop on the opposite side to aid in removal. Does not protect against STIs but is 84 to 87 percent effective in pregnancy prevention with proper use.

Male condom—Thin sheath, usually of latex, that covers the penis during sex. Condoms are highly effective (95 to 98 percent) if used correctly and offer protection against sexually transmitted infections (STIs) such as HIV/AIDS. However, some men's unwillingness to use them has increased women's STI rates and unplanned pregnancies.

Female condom—Sheath made of polyurethane with two flexible rings at either end that is inserted into the woman's vagina to prevent semen, vaginal fluid, and blood from being passed between sexual partners. It is the only female-controlled barrier method offering protection against STIs, including HIV/AIDS. Female condoms are 79 to 95 percent effective in pregnancy prevention; effectiveness is increased with use of a spermicide.

Hormonal Methods

These methods deliver the hormones progesterone, estrogen, or both to suppress ovulation or thicken the cervical mucus, blocking sperm penetration. They are 92 to 99 percent effective in pregnancy prevention but offer no protection against STIs and may produce a variety of undesirable side effects. Some of the more common side effects are bleeding, weight gain or loss, breast tenderness, nausea, headache, change in sexual desire, and depression. Less common are blood clots in legs, lungs, heart, or brain, high blood pressure, and liver tumors, gallstones, and jaundice. Antibiotics and other medications may reduce effectiveness.

continued

Oral Contraceptives (Birth Control Pills, the Pill)—Synthetic hormones taken daily that prevent pregnancy; a prescription drug in most countries.

Contraceptive Implant—Synthetic hormones released gradually from match-size capsules inserted in the arm by a trained professional. Prevents pregnancy for up to five years by inhibiting ovulation and thickening cervical mucus (this impedes sperm activity). Removal is tricky and requires a skilled health-care practitioner.

Contraceptive Injection (Depo-Provera)—Injectable contraceptive that prevents pregnancy for up to three months by inhibiting ovulation and thickening cervical mucus.

Contraceptive Patch—Thin, plastic patch placed on the skin of the buttocks, stomach, upper outer arm, or upper torso once a week for three out of four weeks.

Contraceptive Ring—A small, flexible ring inserted by a woman into the vagina once a month, left in place for three weeks, and taken out for the remaining week. A vaginal ring with multiple antiviral drugs that prevent HIV infection is currently under development.

Emergency Contraceptive Pills (EC or the "Morning After Pill")—Small dose of birth control pills taken within 72 hours of unprotected intercourse; useful for preventing pregnancy in the event of rape, barrier method failure (condom breaks or slips, etc), or any other unprotected vaginal intercourse. It is not an abortion pill because EC *prevents pregnancy* by delaying ovulation, preventing fertilization, or inhibiting implantation of a fertilized egg in the uterus.

Intrauterine Devices (IUDs)

The most widely used form of reversible birth control in the world, the IUD is highly effective against pregnancy but provides no STI protection and has an array of possible negative side effects such as bleeding and infection. IUDs are small devices that fit in the uterus with a small string that extends into the upper vagina. Some contain copper or hormones. They prevent pregnancy until removal and must be inserted and removed by a qualified health-care practitioner. IUDs can be used as emergency contraception if inserted within five days after unprotected intercourse.

Permanent Methods—Sterilization

This highly effective and permanent form of birth control is achieved through surgery. It is generally safe with few negative side effects if performed by a skilled professional in a sterile setting. In women, the fallopian tubes are blocked or cut in a procedure called a *tubal ligation* or, a "micro-insert" is placed in the fallopian tube to block it. In men, a procedure called a *vasectomy* cuts the vas deferens so that sperm cannot mix with the seminal fluid. Sterilization provides no STI protection.

Sources: Boston Women's Health Collective, 1992; International Planned Parenthood Federation, 2009; Planned Parenthood, 2003.

Muslim countries where a woman's everyday activities are curtailed during menstruation for religious reasons (Jacobson, 1992). Women with IUDs run a much greater risk of pelvic inflammatory disease (PID), an infection of the upper reproductive tract that may lead to sterility due to scarring of the fallopian tubes. The risk of infertility means that this method may not be appropriate for young women who have not yet had children and may be exposed to sexually transmitted infections (IUDs can worsen infections and infertility likelihood). PID risk is also heightened in developing nations where the IUD is more likely to be inserted or removed under less than sterile conditions by poorly trained personnel.

". . . Countries wishing for slower population growth will attain it by purely voluntary means. . . . Freedom of choice, backed by information and the means to make choices, will result in smaller families and slower population growth."
Dr. Nafis Sadik, Executive Director, UNFPA

> "When women are given a real choice, and the information and means to implement their choice, they will make the most rational decision for themselves, their community, and ultimately the world."
> *Dr. Mahmoud F. Fathalla, Egyptian gynecologist and former president of the International Federation of Planned Parenthood*

> "Reproductive health programs are . . . likely to be more efficacious when general health and development are served."
> *Gita Sen, of DAWN (Development Alternatives with Women for a New Era)*

Another example is the contraceptive pill. One of the most common reasons cited for discontinuing hormonal methods of contraception is disruption of the menstrual cycle (Jacobson, 1992). Many women view such bleeding as a sign of good health and fertility, and in some cultures it is viewed as a cleansing of bad blood or spirits. Reduced lactation caused by hormonal contraceptives containing estrogen is another side effect that affects women in some countries more than others. Hartmann (1995) suggests that it is one of the greatest dangers of the contraceptive pill in developing nations. For millions of infants, breast milk is the main source of nutrition for several years. Use of hormonal contraceptives during lactation can contribute to infant malnutrition and higher infant mortality rates. Hormonal methods are also more dangerous to a woman depending on where she lives. In most Western countries, a physician prescribes the pill, and a woman must have a Pap smear once a year to get her prescription renewed. This permits screening for cervical cancer and allows the dosage to be adjusted if there are side effects. The prescription requirement also provides the opportunity for screening out those women for whom the pill is contraindicated, such as those with heart disease or diabetes and those who smoke. However, in some countries (including Brazil, Mexico, Nigeria, and Bangladesh), hormonal methods are sometimes sold without a prescription. Long distances to healthcare facilities often preclude the monitoring that increases the safety and effectiveness of contraceptive methods.

Abortion

> "Abortion is a parody of choice, when there is no contraception."
> *Janet Hadley*

Many women's activists believe that the availability of safe and legal abortion is an important reproductive right that is critical to women's health. Approximately 50 percent of pregnancies are unintended, many due to poor availability and knowledge of contraception and of these, an estimated half (42 million) end in induced **abortion.** In developed regions, nearly all abortions (92%) are safe, whereas in developing countries, more than half (55%) are unsafe (Guttmacher Institute, 2008). An estimated 68,000 women die each year as a result of unsafe abortion, 5 million are hospitalized, millions suffer infections and other complications such as infertility, and approximately 220,000 children lose their mothers from abortion-related deaths (Guttmacher Institute, 2008; UNFPA, 2008).

> "As long as it remains possible for a woman to become pregnant without wanting to be, abortion will be a necessity and its denial a punishment of women—for having sex."
> *Rosalind Petchesky*

Abortion laws vary widely. Close to 40 percent of countries permit induced abortion without restriction as to reason; 21 percent allow it on economic grounds; almost 10 percent for mental health reasons; and about 26 percent prohibit it or allow it only to save the life of the mother (Center for Reproductive Rights, 2008). In Australia, the United States, and Mexico, there are within-country differences in legality and restrictions based on state law. Countries also vary in whether spousal or parental authorization is required, whether there are limits based on gestational age, and whether medical abortion (abortion resulting from ingestion of medically supervised drugs) is permitted.

The legal status of abortion also does not fully reflect availability and access. Class, race, age, and geographical location all make a difference (Seager, 2009). For example, in Nepal, an abortion in a government hospital can cost more than the average monthly salary, and 80 percent of rural women are not even aware that abortion is legal (Center for Reproductive Rights, 2009b). Some countries with seemingly liberal abortion laws restrict abortion in other ways. For instance, in the United States, some states have passed legislation requiring extensive counseling and waiting periods and have restricted public funding and insurance coverage for abortion.

Restricting legal abortion does not reduce abortion incidence and legalizing abortion does not increase it (Guttmacher Institute, 2008); rates are lowest in countries where it is legal and contraceptives and reproductive health information are widely available. For example, when Barbados, Canada, Tunisia, and Turkey liberalized their laws to increase access to legal abortion, abortion rates did not increase. The Netherlands, with a nonrestrictive abortion law, widely accessible contraceptives, comprehensive sex education, and free abortion services, has one of the lowest annual abortion rates in the world (Center for Reproductive Rights, 2005a). In the United States, where contraceptive access is strongly influenced by income level, low-income women are four times more likely than affluent women to have an unplanned pregnancy and three times as likely to have an abortion (Cohen, 2008; Gold, 2006). When women cannot attain legal abortions, they often get illegal ones or travel to neighboring countries where abortion is legal. In Indonesia, where abortion is prohibited except to save a woman's life, it is estimated that 1 to 2 million abortions are performed annually. In Ireland, 7,000 Irish women travel to England or Wales each year to have a legal procedure. In the United States, where abortion was generally illegal prior to 1973, data from the 1950s and 1960s shows that an estimated 700,000 to 800,000 illegal abortions took place each year (Center for Reproductive Rights, 2005b).

Although legality does not strongly influence the incidence of abortion, legality strongly influences abortion safety. Hartmann (1995) notes that in general, legalization of abortion leads to reductions in mortality rates. In the United States, an average of 292 women died per year from illegal abortions prior to legalization in 1973, after which the figure fell to 36. Romania legalized abortion in 1990 and its abortion-related mortality rate dropped by one-third in one year. Beginning in 1998, South African women were able to have legal abortions; prior to the law, illegal abortions caused approximately 425 deaths annually. When abortion was legalized in Guyana in 1995, hospital admissions from complications following illegal abortions declined 41 percent in six months.

Women on Waves is a Dutch organization that promotes legal, safe abortion by operating a mobile clinic on a ship that sails to countries where abortion is illegal. Their mission is to provide reproductive health services, provide sexual education, and support local initiatives to further women's reproductive rights.

"We should unite around a common goal of reducing the amount of abortions, not by making them illegal . . . but by preventing unintended pregnancies in the first place through education, contraception, accessible health care and services . . . We have a very high value placed on individual choice and individual responsibility. But we don't often empower people to be able to make those choices in a responsible way."
Hillary Clinton, US Senator and Secretary of State

The Agents That Control Women's Reproductive Choice and Health

Male partners, governments, corporations, and religious organizations are a major influence on women's reproductive lives. In the public sphere, corporations and governments sometimes make women's health concerns a low priority in the marketing and availability of contraception. Governments concerned with population control, and corporations concerned with profit, sometimes endanger women's health and, at the very least, restrict women's options. Powerful religious groups may also influence reproductive choice. Meanwhile, in the private sphere, male partners often restrict women's reproductive choices. Many women are socialized through religion, cultural taboos, and other social mechanisms to accept sexual subordination and even sexual oppression (UNIFEM, 2003). However, women are also agents of reproductive rights and health, and advocacy and activism for reproductive rights is quite common.

Government

Reproductive choice is frequently limited by governments. For example, because sex education is typically government funded, governments often determine reproductive knowledge. Governments also legalize some contraceptives and ban others. They affect options by regulating contraceptives as pharmaceuticals and through government family planning programs with limited services and options that create racial and class disparities in reproductive health. For example, in Japan, the government banned hormonal contraceptives in the 1960s, saying that they were unhealthy and promoted promiscuity. This changed in 1999, after thirty years of lobbying by women's activists. In Kenya, where contraceptives are supposed to be available for free or heavily subsidized at government clinics and hospitals, bureaucratic obstacles and insufficient funds have increased unplanned pregnancies, maternal deaths, and unsafe abortion (Mulama, 2009). In the United States, the Title X national family planning program passed by Congress in 1970 is intended to fund Medicaid family planning services so that poor women have greater access to contraception. However, funding varies depending on Congress and presidential administration; by the end of President George W. Bush's eight-year term, funding for low-cost, confidential family planning services was 61 percent lower in constant dollars than it was in 1980. President Obama's first budget in 2009 increased funding by $7.5 million (Jacobson, 2009).

Many governments have population policies aimed at shaping the composition, size, and growth of national populations (Center for Reproductive Rights, 2006). These policies can impact women's reproductive health and decision-making positively if they provide resources to expand women's reproductive empowerment and health, or impact them negatively if they control women's reproduction in the name of social needs or national interests. For example, countries with **pronatalist policies** seek to increase birth rates and do this by reducing or banning contraception and abortion and providing government benefits based on family size. Pronatalist policies are sometimes intended to replace wartime casualties. Following large casualties from war with Iran, in the 1980s Iraq banned contraceptives. Increasing the workforce is another common goal. The Romanian government outlawed

> "The personal is political."
> *American Feminist Slogan*

> "Reproductive freedom means the freedom to have as well as to not have children."
> *Rosalind Petchesky*

contraception in the 1970s and 1980s because it was feared that population growth was too low to keep up with projected labor needs (note: contraception and abortion became legal and available in Romania in 1990). Pronatalist policies may also be in response to falling birth rates.

More common than pronatalist programs are antinatalist programs. **Antinatalist policies** seek to reduce birth rates and strongly encourage or require that women limit their fertility. They tend to provide a limited range of contraceptive options, emphasizing those that are high in effectiveness but have greater health risks. Coercive antinatalism typically occurs when concerns about reducing population growth eclipse concerns about women's health and control over their bodies (Dixon-Mueller, 1993). Women are persuaded, tricked, and even coerced into sterilization or contraceptive methods with the lowest failure rates, irrespective of the health risks these methods pose. They are often not told enough to make informed choices. And because nonmedical personnel often administer population control programs and fail to screen and monitor women, the health risks of these methods are increased. These methods also do not protect women from sexually transmitted infections. Antinatalist programs that incorporate persuasion, incentives, and targets for family planning workers have been documented in China, Indonesia, Thailand, Sri Lanka, Bangladesh, the Republic of Korea, Colombia, Mexico, Tunisia, and India (Dixon-Mueller, 1993). China's one-child family policy, first instituted in the 1970s, provides one of the more dramatic examples of coercive antinatalism. In its early incarnation, parents were issued permits to have children, and those who had additional children could be fined; lose their jobs, land, or homes; or be demoted (Chow & Chen, 1994; Fang, 2003; Hartmann, 1987, 1995). There were also reports of forced abortion, and women could be fitted with an IUD after their first child and sterilized after their second (Pan, 2002).

Coercive antinatalism is sometimes selective within a country, targeting lower-income women or women from an ethnic group deemed undesirable by government officials. For instance, in 1976, it was revealed that the U.S. government had sterilized 3,000 Native American women in a four-year period without obtaining adequate consent (Hartmann, 1995). The involuntary sterilization of Mexican immigrant women, African American women, and Puerto Rican women also occurred through the 1970s in the United States (Davis, 1990; Guitterez, 2008). In the Czech Republic, Romany (Gypsy) women were sterilized without their consent as late as 2004 in order to limit the Roma population, a growing and unpopular minority (Amnesty International, 2008). In 2003, the Peruvian minister of health issued an apology for the forced sterilization of over 200,000 indigenous women from 1997 to 2000 (Kearns, 2009). Governments often view coercive antinatalism as necessary to reduce poverty and promote economic development but demographers, the United Nations Population Fund, and women's activists strongly believe that these goals can be achieved without sacrificing women's reproductive rights. When women have higher status, when conditions are such that child mortality is low, when women have access to information and a variety of

"Women are denied their right to free and accurate information about their bodies, and this greatly contributes to their inability to protect themselves from infection."
Lydia Cacho, a feminist and journalist in Mexico

"Reproductive politics in the United States inevitably involves racial politics."
Dorothy Roberts

ways to control their fertility, they have fewer children (Dixon-Mueller, 1993; Hartmann, 1995).

Politics and political administration changes also significantly affect the reproductive choices available to women. Policies affecting women's reproductive rights are often made at the executive level, without legislative approval, and this means that when governments change, policies often change as well. The U.S. approval of Mifepristone, a chemical alternative to aspiration abortion used in early pregnancy, is a good example. Because surgical facilities are not needed for medical abortion, it can help make abortion more available and lower in cost. The drug became available in France in 1988 but activists opposed to abortion threatened to boycott its manufacturer Roussel Uclaf should it be marketed in the United States. By 1991, President George H.W. Bush put the pill on a list of medications banned by the United States. In 1993, newly elected President Clinton called on the FDA to test the drug. Roussel Uclaf gave the rights to the drug to a nonprofit group, the Population Council. This group had to raise millions of dollars to conduct clinical trials of the drug, because none of the major pharmaceutical companies was interested due to the controversial nature of abortion in the United States. Seven years later, the drug was approved for use in the United States, largely due to the efforts of activists who felt strongly that Mifepristone should be available to American women (Bernstein, 2000).

Where family planning programs receive foreign aid to fund family planning programs, the policies of the government of one country may affect the reproductive choices of women in other countries. In his first act as President of the United States in 2001, George W. Bush reinstated the "Mexico City policy," or "Global Gag Rule." This policy restricted foreign nongovernmental organizations (NGOs) that receive USAID family planning funds from using their own, non-U.S. funds to provide legal abortion services, lobby their own governments for abortion law reform, or even provide accurate medical counseling or referrals regarding abortion. The administration also attached abstinence-only program requirements to U.S. funding for international family planning and AIDS relief despite evidence that these programs are ineffective (Elders, 2008). Ironically, the administration's action may have increased abortion rates since reduced family planning services mean more unplanned pregnancies, and poor women often resort to abortion when they cannot afford more children. The Bush administration also withheld hundreds of millions of dollars pledged to the United Nations Population Fund (UNFPA) for family planning programs in other countries, claiming that the UNFPA supported forced abortions in China (Jacobson, 2009).

Men

Cross-culturally, it is not uncommon for males to control sexual decision making, including the use of contraception. Women's bodies are sometimes viewed as the property of their husbands, and so it is husbands that decide the number and spacing of the children (Jacobsen, 1992). Many men fear that their partner's use of contraception will lead to her promiscuity, and they therefore oppose it. Many cultures believe that if women could enjoy sexual relations and could prevent pregnancy, then sexual morality and family security would be jeopardized (Cook, 1995). In some cultures, having many children is a sign of male virility and men in such cultures may oppose their partners' efforts to prevent this. The family planning literature documents that women's contraceptive use is inhibited by fear of male reprisal in the form of violence, desertion, or accusations of infidelity (Heise, 1995). Sanctions against abortion historically originated on behalf of the family, tribe, state, or husband. The idea was that a woman did not have the right to deprive these agents of their "property" (French, 1992; Petchesky, 1984; United Nations, 1993). In a dozen countries (Malawi, Syria, the United Arab Emirates, Republic of Korea, Equatorial Guinea, Kuwait, Maldives, Morocco, Saudi Arabia, Japan, Taiwan, Turkey), a married woman must have her husband's consent for an abortion (Center for Reproductive Rights, 2008b). In the next chapter, men's control of women's sexuality is linked to HIV/AIDS in women.

The Global Economy and Corporations

Corporations play a large role in the reproductive technologies available to women and they are motivated primarily by profit, not by concerns about women's reproductive rights or health. For instance, in the United States, the Today Sponge, (250 million of which were sold from 1983 to 1995) was taken off the market when pharmaceutical giant Wyeth didn't want to pay for plant upgrades. The popular product was unavailable to American women until a small company bought the rights to it in 2003. It reappeared in 2005 under new ownership, before being sold to another company that declared bankruptcy in late 2007, taking the Today Sponge out of production until a new company began selling it again in 2009 (Singer, 2009).

Activists are also concerned that in an effort to keep research and development costs down and maximize profit, pharmaceutical companies emphasize benefits and downplay side effects and risks. For example, Corea (1991) showed that Upjohn, the developer of Depo-Provera, presented incomplete information from Depo-Provera drug trials in order to receive U.S. Food and Drug Administration approval. In addition, the common side effects of depression and loss of sexual arousal were portrayed as "minor" (Corea, 1991). Pharmaceutical corporations from industrialized countries make contraceptives and aggressively market them to government-run population control programs in developing nations with the goal of monetary profit. These agencies play a major role in advertising, promoting, and distributing pharmaceutical contraceptives developed in industrialized capitalist countries such as the United States (Hartmann, 1995). Owners and presidents of U.S. pharmaceutical companies even sit on the boards of international population organizations, donate money to them, and lobby Congress for population appropriations (Hartmann, 1987). In short, the local availability of different birth control technologies may depend very much on international politics and economics of other countries. This is an example of globalization, the topic of Chapter 7.

Religious Organizations

"Each and every marital
act must of necessity
retain its intrinsic
relationship to the
procreation of human
life."
*Pope Paul VI in Humanae
Vitae (Of Human Life),
1968 which banned
contraception*

Religious extremism and fundamentalism challenge women's reproductive rights when government officials formulate policy and law based on absolutist religious interpretations that overlook scientific evidence and the realities of women's lives (Center for Reproductive Rights, 2006). Religious fundamentalists who favor traditional gender roles for women and see women primarily as mothers and reproducers are often associated with the curtailing of women's reproductive rights (Heyzer, 2002). For instance, under the fundamentalist Islamic Taliban, Afghan women had virtually no access to contraception or abortion. In the United States, fundamentalist Christians opposed to abortion act politically to reduce the availability of abortion, non-abstinence sexual education, and emergency contraception.

Worldwide, Catholicism has had a particularly strong influence on women's reproductive rights. The attitude of the Roman Catholic Church has been the most important obstacle to the wider use of contraception worldwide; indeed, no other religion has the same dogmatic opposition to contraception (Simelela, 2006). With the exception of the calendar or rhythm method, the Catholic Church is officially opposed to the use of contraception and is strongly opposed to abortion. Most of the countries that have the strictest laws on abortion are predominantly Catholic, and Catholic leaders exert pressure on governments to enact policies consistent with Vatican positions (for example, Poland, Ireland, the Philippines, Brazil, Chile, Nicaragua, and El Salvador). Influenced by the country's Catholic bishops and the Vatican, the Chilean Constitutional Court outlawed the distribution of emergency contraception in public health clinics (Malinowski, 2008). The Philippines, a largely Catholic country (81 percent), has one of the highest birth rates in Asia and as many as 500,000 women have illegal abortions each year, with some 80,000 going to the hospital due to complications (J. Adams, 2009). Despite this, politicians have been reluctant to fund family planning programs or legalize abortion due to resistance from the Catholic Church (Gonzales, 2008). Almost all Catholic hospitals in the United States will not perform sterilizations and abortions, or provide emergency contraception, even in cases of rape (about one in six Americans is treated in a Catholic health-care institution). Catholic hospitals are guided by the *Ethical and Religious Directives for Catholic Health Care Services* (the *Directives*), which were issued by the nation's Catholic bishops (Catholics for Choice, 2009).

Anti-abortion groups led by the Roman Catholic Church have also been influential in countries like the United States, Poland, Slovakia, Lithuania, Italy, Nicaragua, Brazil, and Hungary. In the strongly Catholic country of Italy, many doctors and hospitals refuse to perform abortions. Although a first-trimester abortion has been legal since 1978, the law permits any health-care worker or administrator to claim conscientious objector status and to refuse to participate. In the first year, 72 percent of Italian doctors became objectors (Boston Women's Health Collective, 1992). In 2009, public outcry ensued when a 9-year-old Brazilian victim of sexual abuse who was pregnant with twins, was given an abortion (in Brazil, the procedure is legal only in cases of rape or to save the mother's life). A Brazilian archbishop excommunicated the child's mother and doctors from the Catholic Church (G. Adams, 2009). Due to the influence of the Catholic Church, in 2006 Nicaragua banned all abortions, including those for medical reasons or in cases of rape or incest.

The Catholic Church explains that its opposition to contraception is based on the belief that it involves setting the will of individuals against God's will. However, some writers suggest that the Church's opposition is partly due to its desire to maintain authority over the traditional (patriarchal) family and to its declining numbers of religious adherents (Dixon-Mueller, 1993). Others argue that the Church's battle is about controlling women's sexuality since traditionalists believe that contraception leads to nonprocreative sex (Meacham & Shallat, 2002). It should be noted that the influence of the Roman Catholic Church is not always enough to override government concerns for reducing birth rates and Catholics' desires to limit the size of their families. For example, 60 to 70 percent of Brazilian and Mexican couples use modern contraceptive methods including oral contraceptives, injectable contraceptives, IUDs, or sterilization (Seager, 2009), and, in 2006, Guatemala passed legislation ensuring equal access to all family planning methods despite fierce opposition from the Catholic Church (Center for Reproductive Rights, 2006).

Women

Because pregnancy and reproductive health are concerns of almost all women at some point in their lives, it is perhaps unsurprising that women's activists often work to expand reproductive choice and advocate for safe contraception and reproductive health. All over the world, women's groups can be found working for legislation and population policy changes, running nonprofit organizations that provide reproductive health-care services, and working with governments and communities to increase reproductive choice. Large nongovernmental organizations like the Center for Reproductive Rights and the International Federation of Planned Parenthood, and thousands of small, grassroots nongovernmental organizations are devoted to providing women with control over their reproductive lives.

One area of activism centers on contraception. For instance, Naripokkho, a feminist activist group in Bangladesh, proved that Norplant, a hormonal contraceptive, is widely promoted to poor women without educating them as to side effects and without adequate follow-up. In the 1970s, American women of Puerto Rican, Black, Chicana, and Native American descent waged a campaign against sterilization abuse (Davis, 1983). U.S. women's groups also successfully worked to make emergency contraception available over-the-counter in 2006; they continue to work to increase access. Women in Manila

"We won, we won! Never underestimate the women of the world." June Zeitlin, Executive Director of the nonprofit Women's Environment and Development Program (WEDO), following successful protests to restore language promoting women's reproductive rights to the final document of the 2002 World Summit on Sustainable Development. Religious conservatives lobbied for the exclusion of the language.

(a major city in the Philippines) are currently battling for the repeal of an executive order issued in 2000 that bans city health centers and hospitals from providing contraception to women. In Chile, activists work to increase the availability of contraception and in 2008, 10,000 marched to protest a court decision to outlaw the distribution of emergency contraception in public clinics. Women's activists in China highlighted the conflicts between the government's family planning program and women's health care, the negative effects of certain contraceptive methods, abortion abuse, and the connections between the government's program and female infanticide (Zhang & Xu, 1995); some liberalization of policies has occurred due to their efforts.

Activism around the issue of safe, legal, and available abortion is also common. The number of countries legalizing abortion has grown dramatically in the last twenty years, largely due to women's activism. This is because where there are no safe and affordable abortions, almost all women have themselves experienced or know someone who has experienced the dangers of illegal abortion. In the 1970s, feminists in the United States and Western Europe worked for legalization by lobbying legislatures and staging demonstrations and speak-outs (Jenson, 1995; Wolfe & Tucker, 1995). In 1988, when Brazil was rewriting its constitution, Brazilian women's activists presented a petition to the government for an amendment to legalize abortion. The petition included 30,000 signatures. Although abortion was not legalized, activists felt that their efforts were successful in that the stricter penalties advocated by the Catholic Church were not adopted (Soares et al., 1995). In Poland, following the end of communist rule, the Catholic Church moved quickly to outlaw abortion and hundreds of women's organizations emerged to prevent Parliament from criminalizing abortion. The Polish Parliament decided that only the physician performing the abortion was to be punished, not the woman undergoing it (Matynia, 1995). The Family Planning Association of Nepal successfully worked for the passage in the Nepalese Parliament of a bill that would legalize abortion. Prior to its legalization in 2002, women were imprisoned for having abortions. Activists now seek the release of women imprisoned for life under the previous law banning abortion and work for increasing knowledge of the law and availability. Because of feminist activism, in 1998 South Africa passed one of the world's most liberal reproductive rights laws. After three decades of activism, in 2009, Portugal changed its abortion law to allow abortion up to the tenth week of pregnancy (abortion was illegal unless the mother's life is at risk, the fetus is deformed, or in cases of rape; otherwise, women who obtained abortions faced a prison sentence of up to three years). In 2006, over 150,000 Italian protestors took to the streets of Milan to protest the Vatican's efforts to undo Italy's law legalizing abortion in the first trimester. In Nicaragua, activists currently fight for the reinstatement of therapeutic abortions; they have sent fifty-four appeals to the Supreme Court to declare the law unconstitutional and have staged many street protests.

Conclusion

It is paradoxical that women's role as "reproducer" is a source of status yet plays a key role in their lower status. Without mothers, there would be no children to grow up to be workers, to continue family lineages, to fight wars. And although it is often believed that men are better suited for public sphere roles, it is commonly believed that women, relative to men, excel in the private sphere, particularly in regard to children. In many societies, adult women attain status through marriage and children, particularly by giving birth to male heirs. But women's importance as reproducers contributes to efforts to control them and their fertility and has at times reduced them to their bodies. Because women get pregnant, and because men sought certainty regarding paternity, many societies have sought to control women's sexuality. For example, a high premium is placed on women's virginity, and premarital virginity is sometimes ensured through various means such as female genital cutting, honor killing, and by rendering nonvirgins unmarriageable. Governments and religious leaders also recognize women's important role as reproducers. They have at times restricted women's reproductive rights to serve their own ends with little regard for the effects of their actions on women and their children.

> "In a sane world, it would seem, humankind would place a high value on life and those able to provide it."
> *Marilyn Waring*

This chapter illustrates the four global women's studies themes identified in Chapter 1. For example, reproductive and sexual health and being able to control the number and spacing of one's children are basic human rights agreed upon at major international UN conferences by UN member nations. As early as the 1968 UN International Human Rights Conference, it was acknowledged that family planning is a human right—that is, that couples should be able to freely decide how many children they want and the spacing of those children (Dixon-Mueller, 1993).

It is also evident that women's reproductive situations are not simply the result of biology but are strongly-influenced by sociocultural, political, and material factors. Women's reproductive choice is socially constructed because it is influenced by social conditions and government policies and practices (Petchesky, 1990). Because women's reproductive rights and health vary greatly depending on these factors and on how women are situated within their culture, change strategies have to be *contextualized* (developed for the specific situation) based on intersectionality. Women are often the most effective architects of change in their culture because they have an understanding of these factors in ways outsiders do not. And, as we saw in the case of FGC, ethnocentrism can hurt outsiders' efforts to bring about change in other cultures. Finally, the chapter underscored the theme of women's activism and empowerment. The diversity and range of women's reproductive rights activism is remarkable and has resulted in many advances in women's reproductive choices and health.

Study Questions

1. What are reproductive health, reproductive rights, and reproductive control?

2. What are gender health disparities? How are they affected by intersectionality?

3. What is maternal mortality? What are its causes? What factors affect its incidence? How is its reduction related to the UN's Millenium Development Goals and how can these be met?

4. What is maternal morbidity? What two types are discussed in the chapter? What is being done to prevent and treat obstetric fistula?

5. What is female genital cutting? Where is it practiced? What is its purpose? What health problems does it create? What is being done to stop it? Why are cultural approaches to FGC eradication probably the best approach?

6. Why is access to contraception an important human right? How is access related to women's reproductive health? How does intersectionality relate to women's access to contraception and their experience of side effects?

7. How common is abortion? How does legality affect the incidence and safety of abortion? How do abortion laws vary cross-culturally?

8. In what ways do governments and politics determine women's reproductive choice?

9. How do men sometimes control women's reproductive choice?

10. What role do corporations and the global economy play in women's reproductive choice?

11. What influence does religion have on women's reproductive choice?

12. How do women act to promote their reproductive rights?

13. How does the chapter illustrate the four global women's studies themes outlined in the book's introduction?

Discussion Questions and Activities

1. What do you think about African feminists' charge that Western women are quick to criticize African nations for FGC while failing to fight against the abuse of the female body in their own countries?

2. How is women's reproductive choice in your culture affected by the government, men, and religion? Would your answer be different if you were a different age, age, ethnicity, sexual orientation, or religion?

3. How do you feel about one country making financial aid to another country contingent upon adoption of population control programs or rejection of certain types of family planning programs (e.g., ones with comprehensive sexual education or referrals for safe abortion)? Do countries have a right to do this?

4. Interview several people from another generation. Ask them about the contraceptive methods available when they were of childbearing age and ask what happened when unplanned pregnancies occurred. Were they able to decide how many children they wanted and the spacing of those children? How was this determined by sociocultural and material factors?

5. In the United States, the rates of unintended teenage pregnancy (750,000 every year) and sexually transmitted infections (19 million new cases every year) are higher than those in virtually every other Western nation (Elders, 2008). This has major implications for the reproductive health of U.S. women. Using chapter concepts, how can you explain this and what should be done about it?

6. The chapter suggests that women's reproductive health depends on many things, including knowledge. What kind of sex education did you receive? Was it effective in promoting women's health and reproductive choice? Was it influenced by religion and the government?

Action Opportunities

1. Do a project to increase women's reproductive choice in your community. For instance, distribute wallet-sized cards on public transportation with the locations and numbers of family planning clinics in your area, or volunteer at a family planning clinic.

2. Why don't young women ask men to use condoms? How can this be changed? Develop a program to help young women develop the skills to request that male sexual partners use condoms. Present your workshop in the dorms, at sorority meetings, or to at-risk teen girls.

3. All over the world activists work to increase the availability of emergency contraception and women's knowledge about it because they believe that it will reduce unwanted pregnancies and abortion. Do an informational campaign to educate women in your community about emergency contraception and where it may be obtained.

4. Get involved in the effort to reduce gender disparities in health-care coverage in the United States. Compared to men, U.S. women spend approximately 68 percent more money out-of-pocket on health care, largely because employer health-care plans provide poor coverage for reproductive health care (only 49% of group insurance plans cover contraception and only 15% of large group plans cover the five most common reversible forms of contraception). Twenty-three states have contraceptive equity laws although seventeen have exemptions for religious organizations.

5. RAINBO, the Research Action and Information Network for the Bodily Integrity of Women, is an international nonprofit organization working to eradicate female genital cutting. They work with nongovernmental organizations in Africa to promote alternatives to FGC and provide information to immigrant women and doctors. To help, you can spread the word about their work and their website (http://www.rainbo.org), link your website to theirs, or make a financial contribution.

Activist Websites

UNFPA Campaign to End Fistula http://www.endfistula.org/index.htm

Worldwide Fistula Fund http://www.wfmic.org/

Feminist Majority Organization http://www.feminist.org/rrights/index.asp

Women on Waves http://www.womenonwaves.org/index_eng.html

Catholics for Free Choice http://www.cath4choice.org/

International Women's Health Coalition http://www.iwhc.org/
    index.php?option=com_content&task=view&id=3583&Itemid=1244

Engender Health http://www.engenderhealth.org/

Informational Websites

Guttmacher Institute http://www.guttmacher.org/index.html

Center for Reproductive Rights http://reproductiverights.org/

Association of Reproductive Health Professionals http://www.arhp.org/

International Planned Parenthood Federation (IPFF) http://www.ippf.org

United Nations Population Fund (UNFPA) http://www.unfpa.org

World Health Organization's Department of Reproductive Health and
    Research http://www.who.int/reproductive-health/index.htm

4

Women's Sexuality and Sexual Rights

No woman can determine the direction of her own life without the ability to determine her sexuality. Sexuality is an integral, deeply ingrained part of every human being's life and should not be subject to debate or coercion. Anyone who is truly committed to women's human rights must recognize that every woman has the right to determine her sexuality free of discrimination and oppression.

—PALESA BEVERLY DITSIE of South Africa, speaking at the 1995 Fourth World Conference on Women

Feminists believe that women have the right to make their own decisions about their sexuality and sexual activity. Some take action to promote the rights of non-heterosexual women. The photo above is of one such person, Kanako Otsuji, Japan's first openly gay member of parliament. © TORU YAMANKA/AFP/Getty Images

T his chapter focuses on women's **sexual rights.** Sexual rights are human rights related to sexuality—they are about the rights of people to make personal decisions about their sexuality and sexual activity. Like women's reproductive rights, family, religions and governments often regulate, limit, restrict, and define women's sexuality in the name of the national interest, the family, community, or culture. Those who challenge traditional gender and sexuality norms often face hostility, condemnation, and violence (Fried, 2003).

A Woman's Sexuality is Often Not Her Own

A woman's sexuality is often not her own. It belongs to her family and community and is proof of *their* morality and righteousness (Serhan, 2003). Honor killing, described in Chapter 2, is an extreme example of this. In many societies it is still the case that a woman's sexuality is confined to heterosexual marriage and a woman's virginity is to be guarded by her father and saved for her husband. For example, in Turkey and Morocco, many families require that the bride present proof of her virginity from a physician before the groom's family will approve the marriage (Sciolino, & Mekhennet, 2008). In the United States, at more than 1,400 purity balls, girls have pledged their virginity to their fathers for keeping until marriage (Valenti, 2009). The virgin/whore dichotomy is often used to regulate young women's sexuality (Cisneros, 1996). An unmarried woman's morality is reduced to her virginity; an unmarried, sexually active woman is a "bad" woman (Valenti, 2009). Note the many American slang words for a woman who is not sexually exclusive versus the number of terms for similarly behaving men. Language in Latin America also reflects and reinforces gendered messages about sexuality that suggest sexual power for men and sexual passivity for women (Chant, 2003).

Sexuality is a social construct, operating within the field of power (Giddens, 1992). In many places, a woman's sexuality is not at all about her sexual pleasure, but rather about her as an object of sexual satisfaction to her husband (or other males) (Bay-Cheng & Zucker, 2007). Women's sexuality is often reduced to heterosexual reproduction and family; sex is only endorsed when linked to marriage and family (Chant, 2003; Sharma, 2007). Mainstream Western culture, including media representations of women, often contributes to a female sexuality defined by women's sexual objectification and subordination to men (Dworkin, 1987; Kilbourne, 2003; Nelson & Paek, 2005; Stankiewicz & Roselli, 2008). Most religious frameworks emphasize women's sexual restraint, sexual duties to husbands, and sex for procreation and do not acknowledge or affirm women's capacity for sexual pleasure; the result is often guilt and shame about sexuality (Daniluk & Browne, 2008). Some conservative religions see women's sexuality as a dangerous and corrupting influence on men (see Chapter 8) and some require that women keep their sexuality under wraps through modest dress and behavior. For example, the Taliban of Afghanistan require that women be completely covered with only a small mesh screen through which to see. The control of women's sexuality and

"Likewise, ye wives, be in subjection to your own husbands; that, if any obey not the word, they also may without the word be won by the conversation of the wives; while they behold your chaste conversation coupled with fear. Whose adorning let it not be that outward adorning of plaiting the hair, or of wearing of gold, or of putting on of apparel; but let it be the hidden man of the heart, in that which is not corruptible, even the ornament of a meek and quiet spirit, which is in the sight of God of great price. For after this manner in the old time the holy women also, who trusted in God, adorned themselves, being in subjection unto their own husbands . . ."
Apostle Peter in the Bible (1 Pet. 3:1-5)

BOX 4.1   Women and HIV/AIDS

- Women comprise half of all people living with HIV worldwide, an estimated 15 million (UNAIDS, 2008). Nearly 60 percent of these women live in sub-Saharan Africa.

- In sub-Saharan Africa, 61 percent of adults (ages 15+) with HIV/AIDS are female.

- In the Caribbean, 43 percent of adults (ages 15+) with HIV are women, up from 30 percent in 1995; unprotected sex between sex workers and clients is a leading mode of transmission.

- In the United States, women represent 27 percent of AIDS diagnoses, up from 8 percent in 1985. Of new AIDS diagnoses among women (ages 13 and older), African Americans count for 66 percent, Caucasians 17 percent, and Latinas 16 percent.

- In China, women constituted 39 percent of reported HIV cases in 2004, up from 25 percent two years earlier.

- Women in some studies report not obtaining an HIV test, not disclosing test results, or not requesting that their partner be tested, use condoms, or remain faithful because of a fear of being beaten or abandoned by their partner.

- Increasing gender equality and reproductive health education, developing and distributing reproductive technologies that reduce transmission, and providing alternatives to sex work are important for prevention.

- Reducing stigma and improving medical access are important for women with HIV/AIDS; many delay diagnosis and lack access to life-extending medical care.

Sources: International Women's Health Coalition, 2009; UNIFEM: Women, Gender, and HIV/AIDS in East and Southeast Asia, 2003b.

"Women are not expected to discuss or make decisions about sexuality and they cannot request, let alone insist on using a condom or any form of protection."
World Health Organization

"Women's empowerment is one of the only AIDS vaccines available today."
UNIFEM (United Nations Development Fund for Women)

its definition by men has led some feminists to suggest that female sexuality has been corrupted by male power and the practices of masculinity (Weeks, 1999).

Sexuality for women is often defined in terms of monogamy, passivity, and receptivity to their male partners, while men's sexual urges are believed to be uncontrollable, such that they are not expected to be monogamous (Chant, 2003). This sexual double standard and male control of sexual decision-making is not only a violation of women's sexual rights, but it has serious health consequences for women. In particular, it is believed to significantly increase women's risk for **AIDS,** an autoimmune disease resulting from infection with the Human Immunodeficiency Virus (HIV). Women are two to eight times more likely than men to contract HIV during vaginal intercourse and more than four-fifths of new infections in women occur in those who are married or in long-term relationships with men. HIV/AIDS in women is related to cultural or social norms that restrict women's access to basic information about sexual and reproductive health. But it is also related to gender norms that prescribe an unequal and more passive role for women in sexual decision making that undermines women's autonomy, exposes many to sexual coercion, and prevents them from insisting on monogamy or condom use by their male partners (UNAIDS, 2008). Where it is common for married men to engage in extramarital sexual relations the spread of HIV/AIDS is fueled, especially when women are unable to negotiate the use of a condom or discuss fidelity with their partners without physical violence or the threat of violence (UNAIDS, 2008). Rape, sexual abuse, and sex work arising from economic hardship also put millions of girls and women at risk of HIV infection because women and girls in these situations do not usually have the power to negotiate the terms of sex. Young women and girls are at greater risk of rape, sexual coercion, and sex trafficking because they are perceived to be more likely to be free from infection, or because of the erroneous but widespread belief in some regions that sex with a virgin can cleanse a man of infection. Box 4.1 provides additional facts about HIV/AIDS and women.

Sexual Rights as Human Rights

Sexual rights are part of universal human rights, such as the right to privacy, the right to security of the person, and the right to be free from torture and from cruel, inhuman or degrading treatment or punishment (see Figure 4.1).

FIGURE 4.1 *Some Human Rights from the UNDHR Relevant to Sexual Rights*

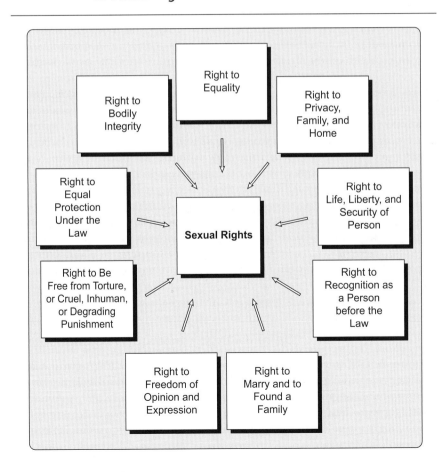

"That's right. You heard me. Women's sexual rights. We have sexual rights including a right to ask for sex when we want it ('Come on baby I'm in the mood'); a right to say no ('Put that thing away, I'm tired'); a right to enjoy it ('Oh yeah! A little to the left!'); and a right to safe sex ("No glove, no love"). And guess what? These rights are enshrined in the Namibian Constitution and a host of other legally binding instruments including the AU protocol on the rights of women."
Trainer from Sister Namibia, Namibian Women's Rights Group

That many women lack sexual rights is apparent when you think back to some previous chapter topics. What are rape, sexual coercion, and sex trafficking but the denial of a person's right to privacy, security, and right to be free from torture or degrading treatment? Female genital cutting is a sexual rights violation because it violates a right to bodily integrity and violates women's right to sexual pleasure.

Sexual Rights, Sexual Orientation, and Gender Identity

"Sexual rights are a fundamental element of human rights. Sexual rights include the right to liberty and autonomy in the responsible exercise of sexuality."
Health, Empowerment, Rights and Accountability (HERA), an international women's health advocacy group

Sexual rights also include rights based on sexual orientation, gender identity, and the rights of intersex people (often called LGBTI rights). At its most basic, **sexual orientation** is whether a person feels sexual desire for people of the other gender (heterosexual), the same gender (homosexual), or both genders (bisexual). Sexual orientation is different from **gender identity** (the psychological sense of being male or female). **Transgender** people are those whose gender identity or expression differs from conventional expectations of masculinity or femininity, including those whose gender identity does not match their assigned gender; they can be homosexual, heterosexual, or bisexual. While we tend to view sex as binary (i.e., male *or* female), the reality is that approximately 17 of every 1,000 people is **intersex**—they have chromosomal and anatomical features of both males and females (Fausto-Sterling, 2000). Often the term LGBT is used as an inclusive term (lesbian, gay, bisexual, transgender) but some favor LGBTI (adding "intersex") or LGBTQ (adding "queer" to include those to eschew sexual categorization). Although most societies currently view homosexuality and bisexuality as a sickness or deny their existence entirely, most psychologists and biologists believe that they are just instances of many human variations. Following significant lobbying activism from LGB political organizations, the American Psychiatric Association removed homosexuality from its list of mental disorders in 1974. The APA currently takes the position that it is no more abnormal to be homosexual than it is to be left-handed, which 15 percent of the population is. The World Health Organization removed homosexuality from its list of diseases in 1991.

"Women's sexuality or sexual autonomy carries enormous symbolic significance as well as material consequences— for fundamentalists and religious extremists as well as for feminists and women's rights advocates. Women's sexual autonomy and bodily integrity are core aspects of struggles for and against women's ability to exercise all of their human rights and to live lives of dignity."
Susana Fried, International Gay and Lesbian Human Rights Commission

Efforts to Define Sexual Rights as Human Rights

Because women's sexuality is so often seen as the domain of the family and community, women's sexual rights are a sensitive topic, especially when they are defined to include sexual orientation. Indeed, it was not until the 1990s that sexual rights were put on the human rights agenda and not without struggle. In 1995 at the UN's World Conference on Women in Beijing, sexual and reproductive rights were hotly debated. Of particular concern to many countries was language in draft documents referring to sexual orientation. Ultimately, this language had to be dropped and women's sexual and reproductive rights were defined in the final Platform for Action as including the rights of women to

BOX 4.2 *World Health Organization's Definition of Sexual Rights*

According to the World Health Organization, sexual rights include the right of all persons, free of coercion, discrimination and violence, to:

- The highest attainable standard of health in relation to sexuality, including access to sexual and reproductive health-care services

- Seek, receive, and impart information in relation to sexuality

- Sexuality education

- Respect for bodily integrity

- Choice of partner

- Decide to be sexually active or not

- Consensual sexual relations

- Consensual marriage

- Decide whether or not, and when to have children

- Pursue a satisfying, safe and pleasurable sexual life

Source: Rothschild (2005).

. . . have control over and decide freely and responsibly on matters related to their sexuality, including sexual and reproductive health, free of coercion, discrimination and violence. Equal relationships between women and men in matters of sexual relations and reproduction, including full respect for the integrity of the person, require mutual respect, consent and shared responsibility for sexual behaviour and its consequences. (paragraph 96)

In 2002, the World Health Organization adopted a working definition of sexual rights that did not specifically include sexual orientation, although it did say women had the right to "choice of sexual partner" (see Box 4.2). More recently, greater worldwide affirmation and delineation of sexual rights has occurred. In 2008, the International Planned Parenthood Federation released "The Declaration of Sexual Rights." According to the declaration, sexual rights encompass sexual activity, gender identities, and sexual orientation. Sexual rights require a commitment to "negative" rights such as protection from sexuality-related harm including violence and abuse of a physical, verbal, psychological, and sexual nature because of gender, gender identity, or sexual orientation. They also include more "positive" rights such as the right to pursue sexual pleasure and to choose one's own partner. At the General Assembly of the United Nations in 2008, sixty-six countries from five continents agreed to a statement confirming that international human rights protections include sexual orientation and gender identity.[1] In 2009,

"What intercourse is for women and what it does to women's identity, privacy, self-respect, self-determination, and integrity are forbidden questions; and yet how can a radical or any woman who wants freedom not ask precisely these questions?"
Andrea Dworkin, American feminist

---

[1] The annual General Assembly includes representatives from most of the world's countries and may draft conventions, resolutions, and treaties that when ratified are legally binding as part of international law. They may also draft and vote on declarations that are not legally binding but serve as international guidelines and general commitments.

"In most communities, the option available to women for sexual activity is confined to marriage with a man from the same community. Women who choose options which are disapproved of by the community, whether to have a sexual relationship with a man in a non-marital relationship, to have such a relationship outside of ethnic, religious or class communities, or to live out their sexuality in ways other than heterosexuality, are often subjected to violence and degrading treatment. . ."
Radhika Coomaraswamy, former UN Special Rapporteur on Violence Against Women

"Contrary to the views of many governments around the world, established human rights principles are fully inclusive of sexual minorities, including lesbian, gay, bisexual and transgender people."
Paula Ettelbrick, Executive Director of the International Gay and Lesbian Human Rights Commission (IGLHRA)

the Organization of American States (OAS) approved a resolution on human rights related to sexual orientation and gender identity in the countries of the Americas at its 39th General Assembly session in San Pedro Sula, Honduras. The resolution condemns acts of violence and related human rights violations committed against individuals because of their sexual orientation and gender identity.

The remainder of this chapter focuses on **sexual orientation** and sexual rights. Sexual orientation affects a woman's experience as a woman in her society and is thereby an important intersectional variable. Although we'll use the sexual orientation terminology of *heterosexual/homosexual/bisexual/lesbian*, terminology varies considerably cross-culturally and, in many places, there are no categories or concepts that include nonheterosexual sexuality, or only derogatory terms for people who don't fit traditional sexuality norms (Herdt, 1997; Laboy, Sandfort, & Yi, 2009). You should also be aware that **queer theory** opposes sexuality classifications as artificial, limiting, and inaccurate and instead focuses on challenging **heteronormativity,** the assumption that heterosexuality is the one and only way to be human (Butler, 1990; Cohen, 2005; Herdt, 1997).

The International Gay and Lesbian Human Rights Commission (IGLHRC) relates the rights of gays, lesbians, bisexuals, and transgender people to the Universal Declaration of Human Rights (UNHDR) and other international treaties. For example, the UNDHR specifies that everyone is entitled to equal protection under the law but the IGLHRC points out that those who challenge sexual and gender norms regularly experience discrimination related to housing, social security, and employment, such as when they are denied jobs because of their appearance or evicted from their homes because of their sexual orientation or gender identity. The UNDHR also specifies that everyone has a right to privacy and this is generally taken to include the right to a family life and to make decisions about one's body. The IGLHRC notes that those who challenge sexual and gender norms regularly experience violations of this right—ranging from being forced into heterosexual marriage to being prohibited from cohabiting with a same-sex partner.

The UNDHR also states that everyone has the right to security of the person and protection against violence or bodily harm, and also that everyone has the right to be free from torture and from cruel, inhuman, or degrading treatment or punishment. However, the IGLHRC observes that torture, violence, and abuse permeate the lives of those who challenge sexual or gender norms. The IGLHRC was part of an international team supported by the UN that developed the 2007 *Yogyakarta Principles on the Application of International Human Rights Law in Relation to Sexual Orientation and Gender Identity*. Named after an international seminar that took place in Yogyakarta, Indonesia at Gadjah Mada University in 2006, the principles clarify governments' human rights obligations in relation to sexual orientation and gender (Yogyakarta Principles, 2007). The hope is that these principles and accompanying recommendations will help governments progress toward sexual orientation equality.

Sexual Orientation and Global Women's Studies

It is important to include lesbians and bisexual women in our study of global women not only because it illustrates global women's studies' human rights theme, but because it fits with the goal of multiculturalism, including and valuing a wide range of women's experiences. Although allegedly committed to women's diversity, heterosexual feminists have regularly overlooked lesbian and bisexual women, despite the fact that many women are not heterosexual. Perhaps this is unsurprising given that **homophobia** (fear of homosexuals) and **heterosexism** (prejudice against homosexuals and bisexuals) are often used as weapons against feminism. **Lesbian-baiting/sexuality-baiting** are used to discredit women's rights activists and their work, especially those focusing on sexual or reproductive rights (Rothschild, 2005). Women often distance themselves from feminism for fear of being labeled "lesbian" and the losses that this label entails (such as in employment, approval of friends and family, community, children, and safety) (Pharr, 1988). Calling feminists lesbians, whores, or bad mothers is a way of ostracizing and disempowering feminism. It is a way to keep women conforming to traditional gender roles and gender stereotypes (Greene, 1994).

It is interesting to consider this equation of feminism with lesbianism given that mainstream feminism is often guilty of ignoring the issues of nonheterosexual women. Lesbian activists from Chile, Colombia, Costa Rica, Hong Kong, Latvia, Mexico, Romania, the Philippines, Malaysia, Thailand, India, Germany, the United States, the United Kingdom, and Italy have all reported barriers to advancing lesbian rights within their feminist movements (Chant, 2003; Dorf & Perez, 1995; Mak et al., 1995; Nur, 1995; Rondon, 1995; Rothschild, 2005; Sharma, 2007). The truth is that women's movements vary significantly in the extent to which they address issues of sexual orientation (Basu, 1995). Sometimes heterosexual feminists are oblivious to these issues. Other times they want to enhance their credibility with the larger public and therefore distance themselves from lesbians (Rothschild, 2005). Basu (1995) notes that the stronger women's movements are, and the less worried they are about survival, the more likely it is that they will be inclusive and advocate for lesbian rights.

Just as it is true that most feminists are not lesbians, it is also true that most lesbians are not feminists. Yes, it is true that lesbianism can be a feminist political statement and identity, a point discussed later in the chapter. But feminism is not the usual motivator of lesbianism. Indeed, for most lesbians, lesbianism is a quiet, personal matter that arises out of a natural sexual attraction to women or from falling in love with a woman. In most cases, lesbianism is not intended as a political statement. Lesbians, like heterosexual women, are diverse in their feminism and vary in their awareness of women's issues and in their activism for women's equality.

Lesbian and Bisexual Women

It is important to understand that women in every culture and throughout history have undertaken the task of independent, nonheterosexual, women-connected existence (Rich, 1980). Examinations of ancient literature, art,

"Around the world, state and non-state actors intentionally deploy what they see as pejorative ideas about women's sexuality to discredit individual women, the organisations they work for, and their political agendas. This phenomenon, described as 'sexuality-baiting' and 'lesbian-baiting,' is a particularly potent method through which women's activism, advocacy and leadership are threatened. No matter what our gender-related agendas, we are susceptible to attack. Our opposition calls us 'unnatural,' deviant, bad wives, bad mothers, and promiscuous."
Rauda Morcos, Aswat-Palestinian Gay Women, Palestinian Citizen of Israel

"The truth is that while the differences in sexual orientation and gender identity or expression are probably inborn—who would be so crazy to choose to be a lesbian in an extremely homophobic country?—the same cannot be said for homophobia, which is often the result of a certain time and context in history, a time and a context always marked by a strong inequality between men and women."
Renato Sabbadini, International Lesbian, Gay, Bisexual, Trans and Intersex Association (ILGA)

"What is important is not the gender of the two people in the relationship with each other but the content of that relationship. Does that relationship contain violence, control of one person by the other? Is the relationship a growthful place for those involved?"
Suzanne Pharr

"When any woman curtails her freedom or fails to take an action or say what she believes out of fear of being labeled a lesbian, then homophobia has denied her independence and sapped her strength."
Charlotte Bunch, Human Rights Lawyer & Activist

and anthropology reveal that lesbians have always existed and have not always been viewed as unacceptable and deviant. The designation *lesbian* comes from ancient Greece and the life of the lyric poet Sappho, who lived on the island of Lesbos (600 B.C.E.). Some of her poetry described her strong love for women. Cavin (1985) notes that it is ironic that lesbians are omitted from discussions of early society because, according to her, their existence is documented in the earliest recorded history, art, and literature of Western society: lesbians in Sparta and Crete (400 B.C.E.), and among the Celts described by Aristotle. Lesbianism was also reported in Athens (450 B.C.E.) and in Rome (100 C.E.). Several ancient Chinese sexual handbooks also describe lesbian activities, and lesbian relationships are celebrated in a number of Chinese plays and stories dating from the tenth to the eighteenth centuries (Ruan & Bullough, 1992).

Cavin (1985) examined anthropology's Human Relations Area Files and found evidence of lesbians in thirty different societies from all over the world. Lesbians did not appear to be more common to any one type of economy, family or household type, marriage form, stratification system, or marital residence. In other words, the lesbian sexual orientation reaches across a number of societies and social categories. Anthropological accounts indicate that being lesbian was acceptable in a number of cultures prior to Western colonization (Allen, 1992; Blackwood, 1984; Greene, 1994). As Kendall (1998) says of her studies of lesbianism in Lesotho, an African country, "Love between women is as native to southern Africa as the soil itself, but . . . homophobia . . . is a Western import" (p. 224). Native American Paula Gunn Allen (1992) claims that colonizers of Native American tribes tried to make Native American culture resemble the European patriarchy. The flexible and fluid sexuality found in many tribes did not fit this paradigm. Thus, colonization is linked to the growth of prejudice against lesbians (Allen, 1992). Anthropologists also believe that Native American women from the Mohave, Maricopa, Cocopa, Klamath, and Kaska tribes could marry other women and make love with other women without being stigmatized (Blackwood, 1984).

In many cultures, female–female romantic relationships occur prior to heterosexual marriage. Faderman (1981) found numerous examples of female–female romantic love relationships among European women from the seventeenth through the early twentieth centuries when she studied their letters to each other and the poetry and fiction written by women at that time. Likewise, in Lesotho, it is not uncommon for women to have romantic relationships with each other prior to and even during heterosexual marriage (Gay, 1986; Kendall, 1998). However, it appears that the acceptability of such relationships is due in part to their not being defined as "sexual" relationships (because no penis is involved!). For instance, Faderman's exploration suggests that it was not until after World War I, when the possibility of their sexual nature was acknowledged, that these intense romantic friendships were stigmatized. Similarly, Kendall (1998) concludes that although lesbian or lesbian-like behavior is common among Lesotho women, it is not viewed as sexual, nor as an alternative to heterosexual marriage. Both Kendall (1998) and Gay (1986) note the decline of lesbian-like relationships in Lesotho women exposed to Western ideas.

Although homosexuality has not always been viewed as aberrant and unacceptable, it is generally viewed as such by contemporary cultures. In Western cultures, by the nineteenth century and through much of the twentieth, lesbians were viewed as ill and in need of treatment. Confinements in mental asylums, clitoridectomy, and psychotherapy have all been used to "treat" lesbians. The presentation of lesbians in the medical literature further contributed to extreme and negative stereotypes of lesbians (Stevens & Hall, 1991). In some countries, such as Russia, lesbians are still subjected to "cures" such as involuntary psychiatric treatment and electroshock therapy. In China, lesbians can be jailed or forced to receive electroshock or aversion therapy (Dorf & Perez, 1995; Ruan & Bullough, 1992). Although many argue that females and males are "designed" to have sex with one another for procreative purposes and that homosexual sex is therefore unnatural, the fact that same-gender sexual relations persist across time and culture, despite societies' efforts to discourage them, indicates that it is natural for many people.

Compulsory Heterosexuality and Heteropatriarchy

Sexual rights include the right of lesbians and bisexual women to live nonheterosexual lives, but in many cultures, **compulsory heterosexuality** prevents this. In other words, most modern cultures present wife and motherhood as "natural" and "unquestionable" and essentially require that women live heterosexual lives (Rich, 1976). Compulsory heterosexuality is generally assured through **heteropatriarchy** (Penelope, 1990). Laws that outlaw homosexuality, religions that forbid it, police and justice systems that allow harassment and violence against lesbians, economic systems that make it difficult for women to live independently of men, and social norms that pressure women to marry men and define their lives in relation to them—are all features of a heteropatriarchal society. Being lesbian or bisexual is also viewed as a violation of the traditional female role, and as you'll see a little later, the social consequences of such deviation are often quite severe. Simply stated, women are expected to enter and stay in heterosexual unions and to enact a specific role as adult women. Those who don't may get in trouble.

Many feminists take the position that compulsory heterosexuality and its embedding in social structures is motivated by a desire to protect patriarchy. As Adrienne Rich noted in her classic book *Of Woman Born* (1976), patriarchy could not survive without motherhood and sexuality in their institutional forms. If it was acceptable to live as a lesbian and women believed they could live independently of men, then men would be less able to exploit women's sexuality and to use them as a source of unpaid labor. In short, men would have less control over women and would have sexual and emotional access to women only on women's terms. For example, Trujillo (1991) says that Chicana lesbians pose a threat to the Chicano community because they threaten the cultural beliefs that women should define themselves in terms

"One distressing thing is the way men react to women who assert their equality: their ultimate weapon is to call them unfeminine. They think she is anti-male; they even whisper that she's probably a lesbian."
Shirley Chisholm, first Black woman elected to the U.S. Congress and the first major-party black candidate for the President of the United States

"So what does one do in an effort to keep from being called a lesbian? She steps back into line, into the role that is demanded of her, tries to behave in such a way that doesn't threaten the status of men, and if she works for women's rights, she begins modifying that work."
Suzanne Pharr

"Being comfortable with homosexuality in societies that view your life as being not only abnormal but in fundamental opposition to patriarchal notions of the family, love, and heterosexual norms of desire is never an easy process, no matter where one lives."
Kaushalya Bannerji

of men and should be subservient to men. The existence of Chicana lesbians, she says, is a threat to the established order of male control and oppressive attitudes toward women. (Note: *Chicana* and *Chicano* are used by some Latin Americans instead of *Hispanic*, a term adopted by the U.S. government and rejected by some activists.)

Lesbian and Bisexual Invisibility

One means of keeping heterosexuality compulsory is to hide the existence of lesbians and bisexual women. In most contemporary societies, lesbians and bisexual women are rendered invisible by cultures that cannot deal with them and because they hide their sexual orientation to protect themselves and their families. This tendency for nonheterosexual women to live quiet, hidden lives and for societies to ignore or deny their existence is called **lesbian and bisexual invisibility.** Some people have suggested that bisexual invisibility may even be more pronounced than lesbian invisibility because societies tend to dichotomize sexual relations as either homosexual or heterosexual, which obscures bisexuality (Bennett, 1992), and because bisexuals may find it easier to "pass" as heterosexuals than those that are exclusively lesbian (Herek, 2009).

Lesbian and bisexual invisibility is part of heteronormative cultures that present heterosexual relationships as the only normal and natural relationships in society. There are a number of ways in which cultures contribute to this invisibility. For example, Rich (1976) suggested that lesbian existence has been written out of history and kept hidden as a means of keeping heterosexuality compulsory. Heterosexual marriage and romance are idealized in art, literature, media, and advertising as if this was the only form of sexuality (Rich, 1976). Heteronormativity as contributing to lesbian invisibility can be seen in the fact that there is no word for lesbian in most Asian languages (Greene, 1994). One of India's top scientists insisted that homosexuality is alien to India because "there are laws against it" (Dorf & Perez, 1995). Likewise, some country representatives at the UN's Fourth Women's World Conference balked at resolutions designed to protect lesbian rights, claiming there were no lesbians in their countries and that lesbianism was a Western cultural notion. However, if it seems that lesbianism is confined to Western White women, it is only because other lesbians face more obstacles to visibility (Bunch, 1995). Anthropology and the social sciences have also contributed to lesbian invisibility by failing to acknowledge it, document, and study it. (Blackwood, 1986; Blackwood & Wieringa, 1999; Cavin, 1985; Herdt, 1997).

The stigma and risk associated with acknowledging one's lesbian or bisexual identity also keeps lesbians and bisexual women invisible. Cross-culturally, lesbians keep their sexual orientation hidden in order to hold onto their jobs (Dorf & Perez, 1995). In Argentina, Mexico, and Peru, for example, lesbians have been fired for being lesbian and excluded from prominent public positions (Chant, 2003). Lesbians often expect negative consequences for disclosing their sexual orientation and do not disclose it

Enforced heterosexuality is tied to women's lack of economic power and the restriction of female activity to the domestic sphere. Further, the embeddedness of sexuality with gender roles in Western societies proscribes homosexual activity and defines women as male sex objects."
Evelyn Blackwood, anthropologist

"For the lesbian of color, the ultimate rebellion she can make against her native culture is through her sexual behavior. . . . We're afraid of being abandoned by the mother, the culture, la Raza, for being unacceptable, faulty, damaged. . . . To avoid rejection, some of us conform to the values of the culture, push the unacceptable parts into the shadows."
Gloria Anzaldua

In 2003, the United States Supreme Court struck down laws making gay and lesbian sex illegal. The ruling voided laws in thirteen states that prohibited sex between same-sex partners.

BOX 4.3   *Workplace Manifestations of Sexual Orientation Discrimination*

- Refusal of employment, dismissal, denial of promotion

- Harassment: unwanted jokes, innuendo, verbal abuse, malicious gossip, name calling, bullying and victimization, false accusations of child abuse, graffiti, abusive phone calls, anonymous mail, damage to property, blackmail, violence, death threats

- Employment benefits denied to the same-sex partner

Source: ILO, 2007.

"If lesbians were truly perceptible, then the idea that women can survive without men might work itself into social reality."
Sarah Lucia Hoagland

"Imagine if every gay military person said, 'If I can't be open, I'm out of here—send the straight people to war, and I'll stay home and go to gay pride parades . . . The impact would be phenomenal.'"
Margaret Cammermeyer, Retired U.S. Colonel, honorably discharged when she came out as lesbian. She fought the decision and was reinstated by a federal judge.

in fear that it will negatively affect relationships with coworkers, and interfere with their promotion and advancement (Griffith & Hall, 2002; Ragins, Singh, & Cornwell, 2007). In thirty states of the United States, it is still legal for employers to fire employees because they are gay or lesbian, and the military's "Don't Ask, Don't Tell" policy prevents openly gay and lesbian people from serving their country (Human Rights Campaign, 2009). Box 4.3 summarizes some common consequences of disclosing nonheterosexual sexual orientations at work.

The potential loss of family approval, acceptance, and love also contributes to lesbian and bisexual invisibility. Almost every lesbian and bisexual woman struggles with when and how (or if) to tell her family. In collectivist cultures where deviant behaviors bring shame on the family and people define themselves primarily in terms of family and community, this is an especially big issue. For many families, a daughter's heterosexual marriage is a duty. The pressure to marry and have children is explicit and intense and strict obedience to parents is expected (Greene, 1994). In many countries, lesbians are expelled from their homes, disowned, and subjected to physical and emotional abuse by their families. For these reasons, most lesbians and bisexual women worldwide marry men. For example, in South Korea, lesbians typically marry heterosexual men to fulfill familial and social obligations and sometimes even enter into "contract" marriages with male homosexuals to appear that they are living a heterosexual life (Cho, 2009).

Lesbians and bisexual women must often keep their sexual orientation secret for fear of losing their children. Most societies continue to believe that only heterosexuals can be good parents. For example, in Mexico, Uruguay, the United States, Germany, Serbia, and Nicaragua, lesbian mothers

"There have been many cases where women have been raped by their husbands, their brothers, even their fathers, in a bid to cure them. Some have been locked in a room for days and starved until they admitted it was all lies."
Betu Singh, co-ordinator of the Delhi India lesbian support group Sangini

"Lesbians in Iran face violence and harassment in existing lesbian organizations and no attention to lesbian issues from women's groups or other organizations, lesbians who experience such violence have few places to turn."
Vahme-Sabz

"In 1994 in Lima a very violent raid was carried out in the capital where about seventy-five lesbian women were beaten up and ill-treated by the police. Prostitutes get a very rough time in jail. But the treatment of lesbians was even worse. Lesbians were beaten up because, however degrading prostitution can be, it is still regarded as normal behavior, whereas lesbianism is seen as too threatening to the status quo."
Anonymous Peruvian witness

are often denied custody of their children on the grounds of their "immoral lifestyle" and the assumption that lesbian mothers will abuse their children or raise them to be homosexual (Duda & Wuch, 1995; Gonzalez, 1995; Martinez, 1995; Minter, 1995; Perez & Jimenez, 1995; Todosijevic, 1995). This is despite research studies in the United States, Britain, and the Netherlands finding no relationship between a mother's sexual orientation and her child's mental health, no evidence that homosexual parents are more likely to be sexually inappropriate with their children, and no evidence that their children are more likely to become homosexual (American Psychological Association, 2009a). Additionally, researchers have examined lesbians' parenting abilities and have consistently found them to match those of heterosexual mothers (Shapiro, Peterson, & Stewart, 2009). Despite this, lesbians are regularly denied their right to have children through artificial insemination and adoption and are refused custody of their biological children (Dorf & Perez, 1995; Herrera, 2009; Patterson & Redding, 1996). Lesbians also remain closeted to protect their children from the stigma of having a lesbian parent (Shapiro, et al., 2009; Skattebol & Ferfolja, 2007).

Lesbians and bisexuals typically keep their sexual orientation hidden to avoid physical and verbal attacks and, in some countries, to avoid criminal prosecution. In the United States, approximately half of sexual minority adults report having experienced verbal abuse due to their sexual orientation; 20 percent also report a crime against them or their property because they are gay, lesbian, or bisexual (Herek, 2009). Despite enacting the world's first constitution to explicitly protect against discrimination based on sexual orientation, South African lesbians still face abuse and violence and some are even raped and killed (Human Rights Watch, 2007a). Lesbians are also regularly denied their basic rights to freedom from torture, punitive psychiatry, and arbitrary arrest and incarceration (Dorf & Perez, 1995). In the east Asian nation of Kyrgyzstan, lesbians face beatings, forced marriages, and rape (Human Rights Watch, 2009a). There are eighty countries where being gay, lesbian, or transgender is a crime, seventy-two of which punish with prison time and seven (Iran, Mauritania, Saudi Arabia, Sudan, Yemen and parts of Nigeria and Somalia) where it is punishable by death (ILGA, 2009). In Uganda, for example, LGBTI people are regularly arrested and abused while in police custody (AWID, 2009). Figure 4.2 summarizes common reasons for lesbian and bisexual women's invisibility.

Consequences of Lesbian and Bisexual Invisibility

Heteronormativity and lesbian and bisexual invisibility have a number of consequences. The stress and strain experienced by lesbian and bisexual women due to their nonconformity to heteronormative expectations create what is known as **sexual minority stress** (Hequembourg & Brallier, 2009; Meyer, 2003). Invisibility not only makes it difficult for us to get an accurate picture of the lesbian and bisexual experience worldwide, it also makes lesbians

FIGURE 4.2 *Factors Contributing to Lesbian and Bisexual Invisibility*

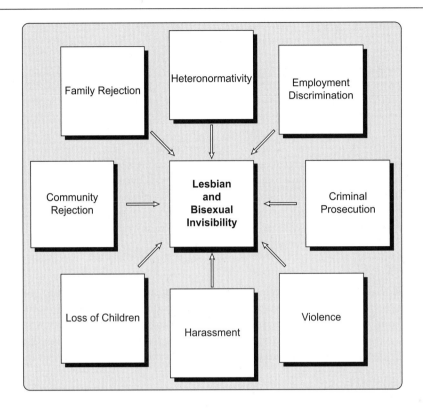

In Israel, ultra-Orthodox Jewish lawmakers have suggested establishing rehabilitation centers to cure homosexuality and have blamed GLBs for earthquakes and for "poisoning the Jewish state." Their comments are believed to have fueled a 2009 attack on the Tel Aviv Gay and Lesbian Center which killed two and seriously injured others (mostly teenagers seeking support).

"If we come out, we are more often than not exiled by the community. If we don't come out, we still feel that sense of exile because we are unable to share a very real part of ourselves with them."
Pratibha Parmar

Somebody that you know, probably somebody that you care about, is gay or is a lesbian. And are you willing, really, to say that that person should be treated differently because of their sexual orientation? I am not willing to do that."
Anita Faye Hill, American attorney known for her testimony against Supreme Court Justice nominee Clarence Thomas

and bisexual women invisible to each other. This makes it difficult for them to identify as nonheterosexual women and be part of an accepting community, which ameliorates minority stress (Meyer, 2003; Penelope, 1990). Sexual minority stress and the pressure to remain invisible also have negative mental health consequences such as depression and anxiety (American Psychological Association, 2009b; Hequembourg & Brallier, 2009).

In reading lesbians' accounts from around the world, one thing is evident: There is often a feeling of exile associated with being a lesbian. There are numerous sources of psychological stress for lesbians and bisexual women. First, they experience great psychological struggles because of a conflict between their sexual orientation and the perceived ideals of society. Raised in heterosexist, heteronormative societies, they have often internalized the societal message that nonheterosexuals are bad. Consequently, they experience lowered self-esteem and shame, as well as guilt about maintaining a false image as a heterosexual (Friedman & Downey, 1995). The greater the invisibility of lesbians and bisexuals in a culture, the greater the problem this presents. Young lesbians who have never met another lesbian and are told that lesbianism is a sickness are especially likely to suffer. This may result in

We want to live proudly and with dignity. But to want such things as Lesbians, is complicated and difficult because we live in cultures which have forbidden our existence, and scapegoated and murdered those of us they identified as Lesbians (or "unnatural," "sick," or "mad"). What might appear to be perfectly simple and reasonable desires are perceived by those who hate us as "unreasonable"; once they've defined us as subhuman, we can be denied the most basic of rights."
Julia Penelope and Susan Wolfe

"Woman-identification is a source of energy, a potential springhead of female power, violently curtailed and wasted under the institution of heterosexuality."
Adrienne Rich

"The one thing that most lesbians seem to have in common is the more or less conscious rejection of the social imperative that women must define ourselves in relation to men. In fact, it is the indifference to men that society finds so threatening."
Diane Griffin Crowder

self-directed homophobia and can lead to isolation, passive acceptance of persecution, exile, and even suicide (Dorf & Perez, 1995). For example, in India, where lesbians experience great social stigma and have difficulty living nonheterosexual lives, the suicide rate for lesbians is high. Newspapers regularly report suicide pacts between lesbians who would rather die than live apart (Harvey, 2008).

Even in more liberal countries, lesbians and bisexual women experience ongoing stress because of the effort required to conceal their sexual identity to avoid rejection, discrimination, and violence. Lesbians and bisexual women must continually decide who they can safely confide in—that is, who is safe to "come out" to. They often worry about the negative reactions that might occur should their sexual orientation become known. This actual and expected harassment creates an emotional stress that seriously impedes personal development (D'Augelli, 1992). As Pharr (1988) says, an overtly homophobic world that permits cruelty to LBGT persons makes it difficult for them to maintain a strong sense of well-being and esteem.

Lesbian Feminism

Earlier it was suggested that although uncommon, for some women, lesbianism is a political feminist statement. Lesbian feminism may be defined as a variety of beliefs and practices based on the core assumption that there is a connection between an erotic and/or emotional commitment to women and political resistance to patriarchal domination (Taylor & Rupp, 1993). For instance, Simone de Beauvoir, in *The Second Sex* (1953), presented lesbianism as a deliberate refusal to submit to the coercive force of heterosexual ideology, a refusal that acts as an underground feminist resistance to patriarchy. Similarly, Rich (1980) suggests that lesbian existence involves the rejection of a compulsory way of life and is a direct or indirect attack on male right of access to women. Ferguson (1981) said, "The possibility of a sexual relationship between women is an important challenge to patriarchy because it acts as an alternative to the patriarchal heterosexual couple, thus challenging the heterosexual ideology that women are dependent on men for romantic/sexual love and satisfaction" (p. 164). Audre Lorde (1984) suggested that sexuality between women looks away from male power for valuation and provides an alternate base for the creation and proliferation of power.

Lesbian feminism is a political movement that combines an interest in the liberation of women with an interest in the liberation of lesbians. The goals range from liberal lesbians' efforts to obtain lesbian civil rights within current patriarchal systems to the radical lesbian separatist goal of overthrowing world patriarchy in order to liberate all women (Cavin, 1985). Keeping homosexuals in the closet is viewed as the core of lesbian oppression. Therefore, "coming out"—that is, being open about one's lesbian identity with others—constitutes a political act. The strategy is that if everyone came out of the closet, lesbians and gays could not be oppressed because "they are everywhere" (Cavin, 1985). Many lesbian feminists resist the current movement in the United States and Australia to use the term "queer" as an inclusive, unifying term for nonheterosexuals. The concern is that this term masks the unique forms of oppression faced by lesbians because they are women (Blackwood & Wieringa, 2007).

According to Cavin (1985), lesbian feminism emerged twice as a political movement in the twentieth century, first in Germany and later in the United States. In Germany, lesbian feminists were politically active in both the early feminist and homosexual rights movements (1924–1935). Their activities continued until the Nazi regime sent them to the concentration camps, where they were forced to wear a pink triangle (now a symbol of lesbian and gay rights). Over 200,000 homosexuals died in Hitler's camps. The second emergence of lesbian feminism as a political movement began in the United States around 1970. It was stimulated in part by the neglect of lesbians by both the feminist and gay rights movements. Political lesbians learned that they had better speak for themselves or else they would not be heard at all (Cavin, 1985).

Most lesbian activism is not explicitly focused on the dismantling of patriarchy. Instead, the focus is on attaining the human rights and freedoms accorded to heterosexuals—rights like safety and privacy, and legal rights. Because they are not heterosexual, lesbians face particular challenges not experienced by heterosexual women. Heterosexual women may be oppressed, but at least society grants them a legitimate place as part of the cherished cultural unit of husband and wife. In addition to the safety, family, and employment losses lesbians face, they are denied the heterosexual privileges of social, cultural, and legal recognition. Lesbian activism is intended to remedy these problems.

A small minority of lesbian feminists identify themselves politically as lesbian separatists. **Lesbian separatism** began in the United States and Britain in the early 1970s. The idea is that lesbian liberation requires females' non-cooperation with the patriarchal system. This noncooperation ranges from a woman's choice not to be involved with men socially, emotionally, sexually, politically, or economically to physical separation from the institutions and jurisdiction of patriarchy (Cavin, 1985). Originally, lesbian "homelands"— free from sexism, racism, and ageism and embodying positive female values such as caring, compassion, and community—were seen as important in accomplishing these goals. In the 1970s and 1980s, some women lived in alternative separatist communities but by the 1990s, these were all but extinct. American lesbian separatist Jackie Anderson (1994) says that separatists begin with the assumption that injustices against women are expressions of hatred and violence and that the way to respond to this is to separate from men to the greatest extent possible.

Lesbian separatists and lesbian feminist movements do not characterize the lesbian experience in most of the world. Most lesbians live in countries where they must keep their sexual orientation secret and where they must live as heterosexuals to avoid persecution and for economic survival. In some countries, the lack of a lesbian community precludes a political lesbian existence. In many

"Separatists begin with the assumption that the social injustices we live with are best understood as expressions of hatred enforced with violence. . . choosing not to be violated is the objective of our action."
Jackie Anderson

places it is not possible for such communities and networks to develop. Lesbian publications are shut down, police harass women going into lesbian meeting places, and political activity on the part of lesbians is simply not allowed.

Wage earning, the ability to live separately from kin, and lesbian bars and gathering places all seem to be preconditions for the development of a more political lesbianism where lesbians see themselves as an oppressed minority with a right to exist. Indeed, lesbian feminist communities and organizations are more common in modern capitalistic societies, and in those, are more common among urban, educated lesbians. Blackwood (1986) suggests that in societies where women do not have control over their productive activities, and may not gain status independently of men, lesbian behavior is more "informal." Sometimes female same-sex practices are a normal part of some cultures, although they may not be labeled as lesbian (Blackwood & Wieringa, 1999).

Lesbian Responses to Heterosexism and Invisibility

Some lesbians feel that normalizing lesbianism and reducing negative stereotypes of lesbians requires that lesbians embrace the lesbian label and come out as lesbians. Staying invisible is thought to perpetuate the notion that lesbians are inferior. For instance, when the existence of lesbians is acknowledged by the larger heterosexual culture, it is often portrayed negatively and inaccurately (Cath, 1995; Ishino & Wakabayashi, 1995; Lindau, 1993; Mak et al., 1995; Ruan & Bullough, 1992). Poet Audre Lorde, a self-identified "black, feminist, lesbian," felt that lesbians in secure positions had the power to break the silence and encourage more women to empower themselves by speaking up (in Wekker, 1993). In the 1990s, a number of popular American entertainers came out in an effort to increase lesbian visibility and the accuracy of perceptions of lesbians (comedian Ellen DeGeneres, singer k.d. lang, and musician Melissa Etheridge are examples). Likewise, in Mexico, a number of artists have publicly come out as lesbians in support of lesbian rights. These include theatrical director Nancy Cardenas, musical performer Chavela Vargas, writer/director/comedian Jesusa Rodriguez, and writer and poet Rosamaria Roffiel. In 2005, Kanako Otsuji, a Japanese lawmaker in Osaka, came out as the first lesbian politician in Japan.

Not all lesbians agree on the need to come out and embrace the lesbian label. Some, such as Rupp (1997), even question whether the term should be used to describe women who would not use it to describe themselves. Some non-Western lesbians find the label restrictive and disrespectful of cultural traditions that support woman-woman relationships without calling attention to them (see Box 4.4). Also, in some non-Western cultures, *lesbian* is viewed as a Western word. Its use reduces the credibility of nonheterosexual relationships since detractors claim that lesbianism is a Western import or the result of Western colonization.

Lesbians sometimes adapt to their outsider status by developing their own lesbian communities and cultures within the larger culture. Lesbian

"...it is important to make a distinction between the secrets from which we draw strength and the secrecy which comes from anxiety and is meant to protect us. If we want to have the power for ourselves this silence must be broken. I want to encourage more and more women to identify themselves, to speak their name, where and when they can, and to survive."
Audre Lord, American poet and self-identified Black lesbian feminist

"For me this has been the most freeing experience because people can't hurt me anymore. I don't have to worry about somebody saying something about me, or a reporter trying to find out information. Literally, as soon as I made this decision, I lost weight. My skin has cleared up. I don't have anything to be scared of, which I think outweighs whatever else happens in my career."
Ellen DeGeneres, on coming out in 1997

BOX 4.4   *Two Perspectives on the Lesbian Label*

"I do not call myself 'lesbian' and I do not want to be called 'lesbian' either. Life is too complex for us to give names not derived from us, dirty, conditioned words, to the deepest feelings within me . . . Simply doing things, without giving them a name, and preserving rituals and secrets between women are important to me. Deeds are more obvious and more durable than all the women who say they are lesbian and contribute nothing to women's energy."

Astrid Roemer, Suriname poet

". . . it is important to make a distinction between the secrets from which we draw strength and the secrecy which comes from anxiety and is meant to protect us. If we want to have the power for ourselves this silence must be broken. I want to encourage more and more women to identify themselves, to speak their name, where and when they can, and to survive."

Audre Lord, American poet and self-identified black lesbian feminist

organizations exist in many parts of the world (see Box 4.5). These groups are important for the formation of a positive lesbian identity in the face of social stigma. They provide a social arena where lesbians do not have to hide. The Internet has also stimulated the development of lesbian community, providing electronic access to a wide range of lesbian organizations and chat groups. Some groups work to enhance lesbian visibility and serve a political function as well. Depending upon the country, lesbian activists may work for laws prohibiting discrimination based sexual orientation, the right to marry (especially important because so many governmental and employment benefits are shared with spouses), legal acknowledgment of partnerships, the right to adopt, the right to custody of their children, and the repeal of laws punishing homosexuality. The activities of these groups are acts of bravery, for in many countries, lesbian publications are shut down, members of lesbian organizations are harassed, and meeting places are raided and closed down. Lesbian political organizations also work to have lesbian rights acknowledged as international human rights. At the 1995 United Nations Fourth World Women's Conference in Beijing, lesbian advocacy groups worked toward including lesbian rights in the Platform for Action, the document that outlines women's human rights. This chapter's opening quote is from one of the activists.

Efforts are being made all over the world to reclaim homosexuals' place in history and to create archives and libraries to render the lesbian experience visible. The idea is that recovering lesbian history (herstory) will support current lesbian culture and inspire continued resistance to compulsory heterosexuality. Scholars such as Lillian Faderman (1991, 1997, 1999) and Leila Rupp (1996, 1997) document the lesbian relationships of Western women such as Jane Addams, Emily Dickinson, and Eleanor Roosevelt. Historian Vivien Ng (1996) looks for lesbians in Chinese history. Also, in the United States, there are the Lesbian Herstory Archives (LHA), the West Coast

BOX 4.5 *Women Around the Globe: A Sampling of Lesbian and Gay Organizations Working for Lesbian Rights*

Gays and Lesbian of Zimbabwe (GALZ) is a Zimbabwe group working for the attainment of full, equal rights and the removal of all forms of discrimination in all aspects of life for gay men, lesbians and bisexual people in Zimbabwe.

Al-Qaws is a Palestinian GLBT organization in Jerusalem.

Lesbians a la Vista is an Argentinean group demonstrating for lesbian rights as human rights.

Colectivo Ciguay is a group in the Dominican Republic working against discrimination and harassment in a country that considers homosexuality an "offense against morality."

Afro Lesbian and Gay Club in Ghana works against laws that ban homosexuality as "unnatural carnal knowledge" punishable by up to three years in jail.

Gay and Lesbian Organisation of Witwatersrand works to ensure that South Africa's new constitution provides civil rights protection to lesbians and gays.

The Asian Lesbian Network includes Asian lesbian groups from Bangladesh, India, Indonesia, Japan, Malaysia, Singapore, Thailand, the United States, the United Kingdom, the Netherlands, and Australia. These groups work together to document and combat discrimination.

RFSL is a Swedish group that has successfully assisted gay and lesbian refugees from the Middle East, Asia, and Latin America in their quest for political asylum in Sweden.

AKOE is a lesbian and gay group in Greece that provides support, protests antigay acts, and networks with other Mediterranean lesbians and gays.

Fiida is a group of Black lesbians in the Netherlands that works to combat discrimination based on race and sexual orientation.

Lambda became the first official gay and lesbian organization in Poland in 1992.

Society for the Protection of Personal Rights is an Israeli group working for legislation to protect lesbians and gay men.

Lesbian Collections, and the Women's Collection held at the Northwestern University library. Another example is the United Kingdom's South Asian gay and lesbian organization, Shakti Khabar. It is in the process of documenting the historical presence of homosexuality in South Asia. Recovering lesbian herstory is difficult because women who have loved women were often careful not to leave evidence of their relationships, or if they did, it was often suppressed or destroyed (Rupp, 1997). Also, because sexuality is greatly influenced by the social context, the lesbian experience in the past may look different than the lesbian experience of the present (Ng, 1996).

Conclusion

Women's sexual rights are an important part of gender equality. How free can a woman be if she does not have the power to determine her sexuality? Women are often unable to say no to sexual violence and to sex with their spouses or boyfriends. Their rights to sexual pleasure, bodily integrity, and sexual self-expression are sometimes disrespected by patriarchal cultures that define their sexuality in terms of men's pleasure and heterosexual roles of wife and mother. Laws, policies, and cultural practices often restrict women's sexuality. Women's lower status and power often make it difficult for them to challenge violations of their sexual rights.

Although a human rights approach to women's sexuality suggests that women everywhere have the same sexual rights, this is not to suggest that women's sexuality does not vary cross-culturally. Sexuality is socially constructed because how it is perceived and experienced are influenced by legal, political, and cultural factors. For example, depending on the culture, premarital virginity may be a strictly enforced social requirement, desired but not necessary, or entirely optional. Culture also strongly influences same-sex practices between women; there is no single way to be a lesbian. This is so much so that the word "lesbian" does not have a coherent, unifying meaning across cultures and great worldwide diversity in women's same-sex practices is found (Blackwood & Wieringa, 1999, 2007; Ferguson, 1990).

Sexuality is also intersectional—it varies based on a woman's age, religion, sexual orientation, location, disability, etc. and how these variables interact. Cultural and group identities such as class and ethnicity interact with nonheterosexual orientations to produce a variety of complex sexual identities. This means that even in the same country, experiences may differ. For example, in the United States, working-class lesbians typically eschew butch/femme roles but working-class lesbians are less inclined to do so. In San Francisco, there is an open, vibrant lesbian community but in most places in the United States, lesbians remain closeted, and lesbian cultures are harder to identify. Lesbians from discriminated-against racial or ethnic groups may be triply marginalized by race, gender, and sexuality. For instance, the experience of Latin American, African American, and Asian American lesbians may be very different from those of Euro American lesbians because the Latin, African, and Asian American groups face racism from outside their communities and heterosexism within them.

Like other chapters, this chapter also points to the material roots of women's disadvantage. Women's economic and social dependencies on men often put them in a position where they have to conform to others' definitions of their sexuality. The ability to lead a nonheterosexual life and to assert one's sexual rights is greater for women who can survive economically and attain social status without heterosexual marriage. The role of economic power in bringing about women's equality cannot be underestimated. This is the focus of chapter 5, "Women's Work."

"Sexuality is a natural and precious aspect of life, an essential and fundamental part of our humanity. For people to attain the highest standard of health, they must first be empowered to exercise choice in their sexual and reproductive lives; they must feel confident and safe in expressing their own sexual identity." *Jacqueline Sharpe, President of the International Planned Parenthood Federation*

Study Questions

1. What are sexual rights? In what ways are women's sexual rights often violated?

2. What is the relationship between HIV/AIDS and women's sexual rights?

3. How are sexual rights framed as human rights? How do they encompass both "negative" and "positive" rights?

4. What are sexual orientation and gender identity? What is heteronormativity? How have the rights of LGBT persons been framed as human rights?

5. Why is it important to include lesbians and bisexual women in global women's studies?

6. What is the relationship between mainstream feminism and lesbianism?

7. What evidence is provided for the commonality of lesbians?

8. What is compulsory heterosexuality? How is it assured by heteropatriarchy?

9. What is lesbian and bisexual invisibility? What are some of the ways in which cultures contribute to it? Why do some lesbian and bisexual women keep their sexual orientation hidden? What are the consequences of this invisibility?

10. What are some of the core beliefs and practices of lesbian feminism? How can lesbianism be viewed by some as a challenge to patriarchy? What is lesbian separatism and how characteristic is it of the lesbian experience?

11. How have lesbians attempted to overcome lesbian invisibility?

12. How is sexuality "socially constructed"? How is it "intersectional"?

Discussion Questions and Activities

1. The chapter suggests that women's sexuality is often not about their sexual pleasure or rights and is instead about women as objects of sexual satisfaction to men. It also suggests that women's virtue is equated with virginity and that there is a sexual double standard where men's sexual prowess is expected and encouraged and women's is negatively stereo-typed. In what ways are these things true of your culture?

2. Using Figure 4.1 and other chapter information on sexual rights as human rights, create your own "Declaration of Women's Sexual Rights." Make sure to include both "positive" and "negative" rights.

3. How heteronormative is your culture? Are you aware of occurrences of lesbian-baiting and sexuality-baiting? What happens if you tell people you are taking a women's studies or gender studies class? Do lesbian and bisexual women face prejudice and discrimination? How visible are lesbian and bisexual women in the media?

4. What would the world be like if homosexuality and bisexuality were not stigmatized? How would it affect children's play? How would it influence affection between those of the same sex? How would it affect what we wear? How would it affect what jobs we choose? How would it affect marriage?

5. Cavin says the predicament of the lesbian in heterosexist society is that of "unrecorded reality" and "recorded unreality." What did you know about nonheterosexual women prior to reading this chapter? Where did you get your information (TV, movies, family, church, personal experience)? Given lesbian and bisexual invisibility and negative stereotyping, how accurate do you think your impressions are?

6. Conduct an interview with a lesbian or bisexual woman using questions developed from the chapter section on factors contributing to lesbian and bisexual invisibility.

Action Opportunities

1. Find out if your school has a gay-straight alliance. If so, get involved, if not, start one. Ideas can be found at www.glsen.org.

2. Volunteer for Parents and Friends of Lesbians (PFLAG). You can call the national organization at (202) 467-8180, write to 1726 M Street NW, Suite 400, Washington, D.C. 20036, or go online to www.pflag.org for information and to locate your community's branch.

3. Volunteer for the Trevor Project, www.thetrevorproject.org, a suicide prevention hotline that provides information and support to lesbian, gay, bisexual, and transgendered youth.

4. Encourage your church or synagogue or school organization to reach out to lesbian and gay members. For instance, your organization can develop an anti-discrimination policy, or have a booth at the next local gay and lesbian pride event to show support.

5. Use strategies developed by the Gay, Lesbian and Straight Education Network to prevent heterosexism in the schools. Go to www.glsen.org for more information.

6. Join a letter-writing campaign sponsored by Amnesty International, http://www.amnestyusa.org/lgbt-human-rights/action/page .do?id=YIA0036022000E.

Activist Websites

International Gay and Lesbian Human Rights Commission http://iglhrc.org

International Lesbian and Gay Association http://ilga.org

Global Rights (Partners for Justice) www.globalrights.org/site/DocServer/
   Guide__sexuality_based_initiative.pdf?docID=10083

National Gay and Lesbian Rights Task Force (US) www.ngltf.org

Amnesty International OUTfront! Human Rights and Sexual Identity www
   .amnestyusa.org/outfront

Human Rights Campaign (USA) www.hrc.org

Informational Websites

National Sexuality Resource Center http://nsrc.sfsu.edu/

Kinsey Institute for Research in Sex, Gender, and Reproduction http://
   www.kinseyinstitute.org/about/index.html

World Association for Sexual Health http://www.worldsexology.org/about.asp

Lesbian Herstory Archives http://www.lesbianherstoryarchives.org/
   tourcoll2t.html

BiNet USA http://www.binetusa.org/

Safra Project (Muslim LGB women) http://www.safraproject.org/index.html

5 *Women's Work*

All women are working women whether they are engaged in market or nonmarket activities.

—MARY CHINERY-HESSE, Deputy Director-General of the International Labour Organization[1]

Women's paid and unpaid labor is extremely important to women's status, power, and family well-being but it is often undervalued. Like a quarter of women worldwide, this Mexican woman is self-employed and runs a small-scale enterprise where she is her only employee. © 1998 Copyright IMS Communications Ltd./ Capstone Design. All Rights Reserved.

---

[1] The International Labour Organization (ILO) is a United Nations agency that develops and monitors international labor laws and agreements and promotes gender equality in work.

Women have always worked, and work is a central part of women's lives all over the world. Most women work, and they work hard. The woman who enjoys a leisurely life paid for by her husband is a worldwide rarity. In fact, if women's unpaid labor contributions (i.e., housework, food preparation, child care, etc.) are included, women do more of the world's work than men do and on average work 60 to 90 hours a week (UNICEF, 2006). In only a few countries (Canada, Norway, Sweden, United Kingdom, and New Zealand) do men work almost as much as women when you consider both paid and unpaid labor (Seager, 2009). Women's paid labor is important because it reduces poverty. When women work for pay, they devote more of their income to family subsistence than do men, leading to better nutritional outcomes for children (Blumberg, 1995; UNICEF, 2006). Women's unpaid labor, such as obtaining or growing food, food preparation, cleaning, laundry, collecting fuel for family consumption and providing sanitation and health care to family members, is also essential to family functioning. Women's labor also matters because of its relationship to gender equality and women's quality of life.

How Women's Work, Status, and Power are Interrelated

Many Marxist feminists view women's economic dependence on men as the primary basis of patriarchy (Chafetz, 1991). This makes some sense when you think about it—as you have already learned, when women are economically dependent on men, they are less able to leave abusive situations, assert their reproductive and sexual rights, and challenge gender inequality.

Marxist feminists also point out that women's lower status and power are aggravated by the fact that their work tends to be unpaid or underpaid. Chafetz (1991) summarizes the thinking on this point. The argument goes like this: Societies designate household labor and care labor as women's work. This, combined with men's greater power in the home (**micro power**), means that men are able to avoid household and care labor, regardless of the other work women might do. In addition, the double workday experienced by wage-earning women reduces women's ability to compete for better-paying jobs, and this reinforces men's micro power advantages. Men's micro power can also be used to prevent women from entering the paid labor force or may restrict them to part-time jobs (for example, husbands may forbid their wives from working for pay at all or from working full-time). This further reinforces males' micro power advantage because they continue to be the major providers of money. Even when women do earn wages, their husbands' micro power is not totally eliminated because women can rarely match or exceed their husbands in the provision of economic resources. The fact that men generally enjoy greater **macro power** (public sphere power) plays into this as well. This power permits men—as employers, lawmakers, and so on—to segregate

Dolores Huerta (1930–) is the co-founder of the United Farm Workers Union in the United States. The mother of eleven has worked tirelessly for thirty years to gain a living wage and safe working conditions for farmworkers. Her recent focus is on the right of female farmworkers to work without sexual harassment and assault. She also works to get Latina women into leadership positions in unions and in politics.

In Ireland, until 1973, the government, banks, and most companies had a "marriage bar" that prohibited married women from employment.

Alexandra Kollontai (1872–1952; Russian) believed strongly in women's right to work for wages, their right to sexual freedom, and their right to control their fertility. She felt that women's equality with men required their economic independence from men. She organized women workers and played an important role in establishing the concept of women's rights in the newly developing USSR.

91

women into low-paying jobs, to restrict their opportunities to acquire skills and credentials needed for better jobs, or to even prevent them from paid employment altogether. Men's macro power is then reinforced as women tend to lack the resources to challenge it.

Feminist Economics

Feminist economics seeks to broaden the study of economics to include the importance of women's unpaid household and care labor to economies, women's labor in the informal sector, and the impact of economic policies on women. Much of women's labor is left out of governments' systems of economic accounting (Waring, 1988). Not only is much of women's labor unpaid household and care labor, but their wage earning often takes place in the **informal labor sector.** This informal sector work includes small enterprises, trading and selling at markets, work done on a contract basis in the home (such as garment sewing), and "under the table" and "off the books" employment (Beneria & Roldan, 1987; Tinker, 1995). The national accounting systems used by most governments define labor in terms of employment in the **formal labor sector** (where people get a paycheck and pay taxes). But over 60 percent of working women are in informal employment and, in the last decade, the number of women in the informal sector has grown in many regions: in sub-Saharan Africa, 84 percent of nonagricultural workers are women; in Asia, 65 percent; and in Latin America, 58 percent (UNIFEM, 2005).

Feminist economists like Marilyn Waring, Sakiko Fukuda-Parr, Devaki Jain, and Deniz Kandiyoti and activist organizations like the Women's Enviroment and Development Organization (WEDO) and the International Women Count Network, push governments to include women's unpaid labor and informal sector work as part of government accounting systems. They argue that women should be recognized for their contributions to economies and that such recognition would benefit women. For instance, assigning unpaid work a value would make it more likely that homemaker women would be treated fairly in divorce proceedings. It is additionally important because policy is often based on national accounting figures, and the undercounting of women's labor leads policymakers to make fewer policies and spend less money on programs and policies addressing women's needs. The idea is that what remains uncounted remains invisible and unvalued (Waring, 1988). Box 5.1 provides further insight on this point from feminist economist Lourdes Beneria.

Feminist economists also favor **gender-responsive budget analysis,** which examines how national budgets impact women and girls differently than men and boys. These analyses measure government commitment to women's specific needs and rights and include a focus on the unpaid care economy in which much of women's time is spent. For example, a UN gender budget analysis of domestic violence policies and laws in seven countries in Latin America revealed that appropriations for domestic violence programs and

"If women's work were accurately reflected in statistics, it would shatter the myth that men are the main breadwinners of the world."
Mahbub ul-Haq

"The international economic system constructs reality in a way that excludes the great bulk of women's work—reproduction (in all its forms), raising children, domestic work, and subsistence production."
Marilyn Waring, Feminist Economist

"A woman's work is never counted."
Peggy Kome, Canadian Activist

"What is not counted is usually not noticed"
J. K. Galbraith, Economist

BOX 5.1   *Feminist Economist Lourdes Beneria on Unpaid Labor*

Lourdes Beneria is a professor at Cornell University in the United States. She is the author of many books and articles and serves on the editorial board of the journal "Feminist Economics."

The challenge of accounting for women's unpaid work first surfaced for me in 1978 when I visited the picturesque town of Chechaouen in northern Morocco while I was working at the International Labor Office. . . . Statistics showed that the labor force participation rate for men and women in Morocco differed widely—more than 75 percent for men and less than 10 percent for women. But what I saw in the streets of Chechaouen told me a very different story. I saw many women moving about the busy streets, some carrying dough on their heads to bake bread in public ovens, others carrying wood on their backs or clothes to be washed in the brook bordering the town; still other women were carrying baskets or bags on their way to shopping, often with children at their side. The men were less busy—men were sitting outside the town's shops, idle and chatting, perhaps waiting for the tourist season to increase the demands for the beautiful crafts sold in the stores. I immediately thought something was wrong with the statistics I had seen. It was the first time I had thought about this type of discrepancy, but I soon found out how prevalent it was across countries and regions.

Source: Beneria, 1998.

---

interventions were nonexistent in some cases and there was evidence of gender discrimination in taxation policies (Elson, 2006). Feminist economists also recommend gender-disaggregated **time-use surveys** to study labor. These surveys provide information on how women and men, and girls and boys, spend their time in both market and nonmarket work. Such surveys reduce the invisibility of women's unpaid and informal sector labor.

Women's Unpaid Labor

Women's disproportionate responsibility for household labor and care labor affects their workforce participation, and as you'll learn later in the chapter, it also partly explains the gender pay gap and the glass ceiling.

Gender-Based Divisions of Household and Care Labor

Worldwide, who does the laundry, shopping, cooking, and child care, and looks after the family's medical needs and aging parents? In countries where water and fuel must be gathered and families must grow much of their own food, who takes care of these tasks?

The answer is, of course, women. In every society, women do most of the daily, routine household labor regardless of labor force participation (Seager, 2009; UN DESA, 2009). They are also the primary caregivers of children and sick or senior family members—what is known as unpaid

"Most of the household and care work is done by women in all parts of the world, regardless of their employment status. As a result of this dual workload, women work longer hours than men, and have less time for sleep, education, leisure and participation in public life."
UN Department of Economic and Social Affairs

BOX 5.2   *A Sampling of Weekly Hours of Household Labor in Industrialized Nations by Gender*

	Wives	Husbands
Latvia	18	11
Poland	21	12
Denmark	13	7
Russia	26	14
Great Britian	14	6.5
Israel	17	6
Brazil	35	10
Chile	37	10
Portugal	25	6
Japan	26	3

Data Source: Fuwa and Cohen, 2007.

care labor (UN DESA, 2009). This gender-divide of unpaid labor is true in both industrialized and developing countries, although it is more marked in developing nations. For example, in India, women spend approximately thirty-five hours a week on household tasks, child care, and sick and elder care; and men, only four hours a week (UNICEF, 2006). In the United States, women spend on average thirteen hours a week on housework compared to men's four hours (Seager, 2009). In Mexico, women in paid employment spend thirty-three hours a week on such tasks to men's six hours (UNICEF, 2006). Box 5.2 provides a sampling from industrialized nations of wives' and husbands' weekly hours of household labor.

Explanations for Gender-Based Divisions of Household and Unpaid Care Labor

There are three common explanations for gender differences in household labor and care labor, as shown in Figure 5.1. The **time availability perspective on gender-based divisions of household labor** suggests that because women spend less time in the paid workforce, they have more time to perform household tasks (Bianchi, Milkie, Sayer, & Robinson, 2000). This explanation is

"Before I leave home, I have to work. When I get home, I have to work." *Irene Ortega, Mexican woman who joined a one-day labor household labor strike. She normally puts in ten-hour days in the marketplace and does all the household labor.*

FIGURE 5.1 *Explanations for Gender-Based Division of Household Labor*

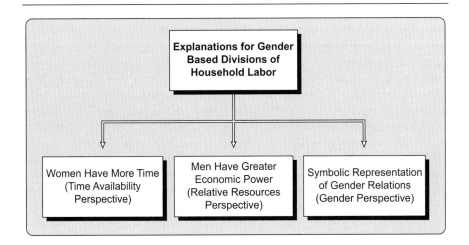

supported by studies finding that as wives' hours of employment rise, women's household and care labor decreases and husbands' household labor contributions often increase (Bianchi et al., 2000; Ishii-Kuntz, 1993). However, in some industrialized nations, such as the United States, the ratio of women's unpaid labor to men's has shrunk not because men are doing so much more but because women have reduced their in-home labor by lowering their standards and when they can afford it, by "outsourcing," such as buying prepared food and hiring home cleaning services (Bianchi et al., 2000). It is also true that research from a variety of countries indicates that employed women still do significantly more household labor than their male partners (Fuwa & Cohen, 2007; UNICEF, 2006). The fact that many employed women frequently work one shift in paid work and another unpaid second shift at home before or after paid work, is known as the **second shift** (Hochschild, 1989).

The **relative resources perspective** emphasizes that the division of household labor reflects the relative economic power of women and men; whoever has more resources is able to better avoid household labor (Bianchi et al., 2000). Because women are less likely to work for pay, are more likely to work part-time, and tend to be paid less than men, they do more household labor because they are expected to make up for their smaller monetary contribution to the household. According to this perspective, women with higher earnings should have more power to negotiate a more equitable division of labor (Fuwa, 2004). Some studies find that the smaller the income gap between an employed woman and her husband, the smaller the gender household labor gap (Batalova & Cohen, 2002; Blumstein & Schwartz, 1991). However, Sanchez (1993) found that wives' material conditions and relative resources had no consistent, significant effect on husbands' household labor in the five countries she studied (Indonesia, South Korea, Philippines, Taiwan, and the United States).

The **gender perspective on household labor** argues that household labor is a symbolic representation of gender relations, not merely a matter of who has time and who has the money (Bianchi et al., 2000). The idea is that husbands and wives display proper gender roles through the activities they perform in the home. Household labor, child care, and other care work are viewed as "women's work," and are stereotyped as female activities. An ideology of intensive motherhood valorizes intensive and exclusive maternal care, especially of young children, and defines male care-giving as insufficient (Hook & Chalasani, 2008). Socialization in childhood reinforces this perception. Women's employed work is seen as secondary to their primary role as wife and mother, and men's higher status is such that they have refusal power (Blumberg, 1991). Because gendered divisions of household labor and child care arise out of traditional gender ideologies, it follows that more egalitarian beliefs about the genders should lead to more egalitarian divisions of household labor. Indeed, one study of twenty-two countries found that gender empowerment (as measured by the number of women in government, administration, and professional careers) was related to more egalitarian divisions of household labor (Batalova & Cohen, 2002). The power of the gender ideology explanation for household labor distributions is shown by Fuma (2004). She found that both the relative resources and time availability perspectives explained gender differences in household labor in gender-egalitarian societies but not in nonegalitarian countries.

Women's Paid Labor

"The protection of pregnant workers and mothers is central to advance the rights, health, and employment of women."
International Labour Organization

Women's participation in the paid labor force has grown markedly. In the last decade, more than 200 million women have joined the global workforce (UNIFEM, 2009a). Women account for approximately 40 percent of employed people in the world (UNICEF, 2006) and the majority of women worldwide (60 percent) are employed (International Labour Organization, 2007). For example, nearly 53 percent of East Asian and Pacific women hold paying jobs, 61 percent in sub-Saharan Africa, and 60 percent of Central and Eastern European women. Box 5.3 lists the percentages of women in the paid workforce for a sample of countries. Cross-cultural differences are attributable to cultural factors such as traditional gender roles, economic factors, differences in fertility rates, and the availability of affordable childcare.

Effects of Paid Work on Women

Most feminists view women's economic empowerment as a key to women's equality, but there is some debate on the effects of paid work on women. On the one hand, earning money buys some freedom and

BOX 5.3 *Percentage of Women in the Paid Workforce 2006: A Global Sample by Age Group*

	15–24	25–34	35–54	55–64	Overall
Industrialized Countries					
France	26	79	81	38	62
Ireland	47	80	71	40	63
Japan	45	69	69	50	61
United States	60	76	77	58	60
Central and Eastern Europe/ Commonwealth of Independent States					
Albania	45	62	65	28	54
Romania	26	71	68	35	54
Kazakhstan	49	88	89	56	74
Latin America and the Caribbean					
Dominican Republic	37	60	55	42	45
Jamaica	34	73	73	48	60
Brazil	53	71	67	40	62
Chile	22	54	50	28	37
Mexico	33	49	50	32	43
East Asia and the Pacific					
Korea, Republic of	40	58	61	46	54
Philippines	42	63	69	56	34
Viet Nam	71	90	80	45	77
South Asia					
Afghanistan	38	42	43	45	40
Bangladesh	50	61	60	35	55
India	26	39	44	32	36
Pakistan	23	44	42	33	34
Africa					
Egypt	18	31	22	9	22
Ethiopia	72	80	74	55	73
Rwanda	69	93	92	80	85
Middle East					
Iran	36	53	46	21	42
Jordan	24	40	30	13	29
Syria	40	45	41	25	40

Source: United Nations Statistics Division, 2007.

some power in the home. On the other hand, this is often offset by the difficulties of balancing work and family, low wages, glass ceilings, and poor work conditions, including sexual harassment. The prevailing opinion is that employment is a necessary but not sufficient condition of high female status (Tinker, 1990). Indeed, Tinker notes that in some societies, women's social status is enhanced when they are economically dependent on husbands and don't have to work, and many poor, hard-working women would welcome such a situation. Furthermore, the extent to which women get to keep or control the income they generate varies greatly worldwide (Blumberg, 1991). Mere work in economic activities or even ownership of economic resources does not translate into benefits if the person has no control over them (Blumberg, 1991, 1995). The more a society's political, economic, legal, and ideological systems disadvantage women, the less a woman gets her "hypothetical dollar's worth of economic power for every dollar she brings to the household" (Blumberg, 1995, p. 213).

Maternity Protection and Child-Care

Maternity leave and child care are prerequisites for women's full participation in the labor force because it is common for women to get pregnant and have babies, and women have primary responsibility for children. Few countries provide adequate support for workers with family responsibilities. Government policies on child care and maternity leave can be seen as a reflection of a society's views about the "proper" role of women in society and whether women's participation in the labor force is desired (Sjöberg, 2004).

Maternity protection measures include policies and laws that ensure that pregnant employees will not face employment discrimination, that they will not be exposed to health hazards, that they will have time off to have children and return to the job without discrimination, and that they will be permitted breast-feeding breaks (ILO, 2008). **Maternity leave,** which provides time off for mothers following the birth of a child, is important both for women's health and for child development. The United Nations Convention on the Elimination of All Forms of Discrimination Against Women (CEDAW) affirms women's right to maternity protection.

71% of mothers in the U.S. are employed.

Most countries have laws guaranteeing women paid maternity leave and typically, women receive two-thirds to full wages during the covered period. A handful of countries (United States, Australia, Papua New Guinea, Lesotho, and Swaziland) do not require paid maternity leave (ILO, 2008b). Box 5.4 shows the best and worst countries as far as maternity leave. In approximately half of countries, wages are paid by social insurance or public funds, but in a quarter of countries, employers pay them, and in others the government pays some and employers make up the rest (ILO, 2008b). Most central Asian countries, countries in Central

BOX 5.4 *Maternity Leave Policies: The Best and the Worst*

	Weeks	Percent Pay	Source
The Best			
Sweden	68	480 days/100*	Social Security
Serbia & Montenegro	52	100	Social Security
Norway	42	100	Social Security
	52	80	
Albania	52	75	Social Security
Czech Republic	28	69	Social Security
The Worst			
United States	12**	Unpaid	
Lesotho	12	Unpaid	
Swaziland	12	Unpaid	
Solomon Islands	12	25	Employer
Libya	50 days	50	Employer

Source: International Labour Organization, 2008b.
*Swedish law requires parental leave of 480 days; each parent is required to take 14 weeks.
**Only guaranteed to women working in firms with more than 50 employees.

and Eastern Europe, and industrialized nations mandate a leave of fourteen to eighteen weeks (international standards recommend at least fourteen weeks). Most Latin American countries (except for Brazil, Costa Rica, Chile, Cuba, and Venezuela) provide less than fourteen weeks. About half of African countries have leaves of fourteen weeks and half have leaves of less than fourteen weeks. All Arab nations have leaves of less than fourteen weeks. However, maternity leave laws are unevenly enforced, often do not apply to women working in the informal sector, and may work against women when employers must pay all or part of the costs. In such cases, employers may choose to hire men or make women prove that they are not pregnant before hiring them (Morgan, 1996; Neft &

"When I had to go to work, I used to worry about my child. I would take him with me to the tobacco field. But my employer objected. Then I would leave him at home, but I still worried about him. But what could I do? I had to earn, and I had no option."
Agricultural labourer, India (UN State of the World's Women 2005)

BOX 5.5 *Recommended Gender-Equal Family-Friendly Work Measures*

- Offering paternity leave and making parental leave, after the initial maternity leave, available to both men and women and nontransferable

- Making "normal" work more family-compatible: Flexible arrangements with regard to working schedules

- Short leave for emergencies

- Flex-time and teleworking

- Reduction of daily hours of work and overtime

- Availability of affordable and good-quality child care

- More equal sharing of family responsibilities between men and women

Source: ILO, 2007.

Levine, 1998). Many working mothers do not take their full leave because they fear job losses or unfavorable reassignments (ILO, 2007a).

It is important to consider that how family leave policies are structured is, in some ways, a two-edged sword as far as gender equality (Fuwa & Cohen, 2007). For one, most countries do not provide for paternity leave; this reinforces the assumption that mothers are the primary parents. Family leave policies that provide leave for fathers may be more successful in promoting both gender equality and fathers' involvement with their children. Also, because maternity leave encourages women to withdraw from the labor force at least temporarily (hurting career progression and wages) and often offer low benefits, it may reinforce gender inequality in the market and in the family (Fuwa & Cohen, 2007). Extensive parental leaves, particularly in the absence of public or private supports for child care, may even encourage women to stay out of the labor force (Pettit & Hook, 2005). Long parental leave provisions for women may also reinforce perceptions that women are "costly" and unreliable (ILO, 2007a). Box 5.5 summarizes gender-equality-friendly recommendations from the International Labour Organization to promote work-family balance and offset some of these limitations.

Affordable child care also remains a significant problem for employed women and affects the type of work women take on and the number of hours they are able to work (UNICEF, 2006). In one study of nineteen industrialized nations, the provision of publicly sponsored child care was associated with higher employment rates for women (Pettit & Hook, 2005). Traditionally, nonworking female relatives, such as grandmothers, provided child care and elder care, but due to women's increased labor force participation and migration, this support is increasingly less available (ILO, 2004). When child care is unavailable or too expensive, women may leave their children alone, take older children (usually girls) out of school to care for younger ones, bring children to work with them (sometimes under unsafe conditions), and take on lower-paying or part-time work that makes poverty more likely (ILO, 2004).

Resources for child care may come from the family, government, nonprofit and religious organizations, and employers. In many countries, such as the United States and the United Kingdom, child care is viewed as the responsibility of parents, not the state. In such places, the greatest difficulties obtaining quality child care are experienced by low-income and single-parent households—ironically, those who need it the most (UNICEF, 2006). Sweden is one of the best countries for working parents. A Swedish law passed in 1985 guarantees a place in a day-care center for every child between the ages of 1 and 6, and a place in a "leisure time" center for every child between the ages of 7 and 12 (Neft & Levine, 1998).

The Gender Pay Gap: Explanations and Solutions

Women have entered the paid workforce in record numbers, but their economic power is diminished by the fact that they frequently receive less pay for their work than do men. This is known as the **gender pay gap** (the difference in average wages or earnings between men and women). Worldwide, women's wages are typically between 70 and 90 percent of men's (ILO, 2009). The pay gap ranges from 3 percent to 51 percent and, on average, women earn 22 percent less than what men earn (UNIFEM 2008; ITUC, 2009). Box 5.6 shows how much less women earn than men in a variety of countries. Rates vary based on gender job segregation, support of government for equal pay, differences in men's and women's education and training, union membership (the gap is lower for women in trade unions), traditional gender roles, and women's family responsibilities. In yet another example of intersectionality, the gender pay gap also varies within a country based on age and ethnicity. For example, in Brazil, Black women earn less than White men, Black men, and White women and in France, the gender pay gap is greater for older women (ILO, 2007a).

Why do employed women make less money than men? There are four main explanations: (1) Women are segregated and concentrated in lower-paying, female-dominated jobs, (2) family responsibilities lead to women working part-time, (3) women lack the experience and training for better-paying jobs, and (4) outright gender wage discrimination (see Figure 5.2).

"If money talks, women do not have a loud voice."
International Labour Organization

BOX 5.6   *Average Gender Pay Gap in a Sampling of Countries (2006–2009)*

Country	Percentage Less than Men
Georgia	51
Kazakhstan	38
Japan	33
China	32
Paraguay	31
Singapore	27
Botswana	23
USA, Germany, Slovakia, Colombia	22
Iran, Switzerland, El Salvador	19
European Union	16
Mexico, Sweden, Norway	16
Jordon, Lithuania, West Bank/Palestine	15
Australia, Bulgaria, New Zealand	14
Egypt, Poland	12
Thailand, Ireland, Italy, Portugal	9
Israel	7
Panama	4
Costa RIca	-2

Source: International Labour Organization, 2008a, UNIFEM, 2009a.

In most societies, employed women and men tend to work in different jobs and employment sectors and men hold the higher positions compared to women in the same job category. This is known as **gender job segregation** or **gender occupational segregation.** Gender occupational segregation is one reason why women earn less than men—"men's work" pays more than "women's work" and women are relegated to lower-paying positions. Some studies indicate that the majority of the gender

FIGURE 5.2 *Contributors to the Gender Pay Gap*

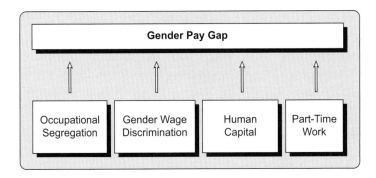

wage gap can be explained by occupational segregation (Charles & Grusky, 2004). There are two types of gender occupational segregation: horizontal and vertical.

Horizontal occupational segregation refers to the tendency for occupations mainly held by men to have substantially higher pay rates and status as compared to those mainly held by women. Men are more likely to be in core or salaried positions, whereas women are often in peripheral, insecure, less-valued positions (ILO, 2009; UNIFEM, 2009a). Women generally work in service sectors like secretarial work, sales, and domestic and care services and subsistence agriculture whereas men generally work in industry and transportation, management, administration, and policy (UNIFEM, 2009a).

Although horizontal segregation is less pronounced than it once was, it persists because many societies continue to believe that women and men are suited for different types of jobs and because gender socialization leads people to seek jobs consistent with their gender role (Charles & Grusky, 2004). Jobs are often labeled as "male" or "female" and this affects whether women are encouraged to pursue those jobs, whether they consider those jobs, and whether they get hired when they do. There are often barriers to women's entry into better-paying, traditionally male occupations, such as discrimination in selection and gender stereotyping (ILO, 2008c). Recruitment practices that favor men and barriers in the promotion or career development of women have the effect of excluding women or "segregating" them into certain jobs. Research indicates that women are less likely than equally qualified men to be hired for nontraditionally female jobs (Kawashima, 1995; Olson & Frieze, 1987).

On the face of it, the reduction of horizontal occupational segregation should reduce the gender pay gap. However, women still receive lower pay than men do even when working in the same job. This is partly due to gender wage discrimination (discussed a bit later) and vertical occupational segregation. **Vertical occupational segregation** refers to how, within occupations, there is a hierarchy of jobs and women tend to be more highly represented in lower-ranked, lower-paying positions than men are within the same

"A key employment challenge is tackling occupational segregation of traditionally accepted 'male' and 'female' jobs, and to break the gender barriers in opening up professions to both sexes. In many countries young women are still encouraged to train in relatively low-skilled and poorly paid 'feminine' occupations with little prospect of upward mobility, while young men are encouraged to go into modern technology-based training and employment, which often pay better."
Geir Tonstol of the ILO Bureau for Gender Equality

occupation. For example, in the United States, only 16 percent of partners in law firms (the highest rank) are women although women start careers in private law firms at the same rate as men (National Association of Women Lawyers, 2008).

The gender pay gap is partially due to women's part-time work and to family responsibilities that lead to gaps in employment and interfere with work experience and seniority. For example, many women leave the workforce during their children's early years. Part-time work is synonymous with low status, low pay, and limited training and career opportunities (ILO, 2007a). For example, in the United Kingdom, female part-time workers can expect to earn just 59 percent of the male full-time hourly rate (Tomlinson, 2008). Worldwide, women are more likely than men to be in the workforce part-time, and about three-quarters of part-time workers are women, although it should be noted that the majority of employed women work full-time (ILO, 2004; Seager, 2009). Family responsibilities can constrain opportunities for income generation, especially for those who cannot afford child care or to outsource household labor. Although part-time work is a desired choice for some women because it provides some income and time for family, for others it a choice forced by lack of affordable child care and unequal distributions of household labor.

Another explanation for gender differences in pay is provided by the **human capital approach** (Blau & Ferber, 1987; Jacobsen, 2003). *Human capital* refers to any attributes a person has that contribute to her productivity including education, skills, and focus. The idea is that women get paid less because they are less skilled, less educated, or less experienced workers than men typically are. These differences originate in gender discrimination in education and training, and also because many women enter and leave the workforce due to childbearing and rearing. Also, the thought is that the costs of employing women are higher because they get pregnant and take time off when their children are sick and that they are less focused on their work due to family concerns. According to research, the factors identified by the human capital approach explain from 4 to 50 percent of the male–female earnings differential, depending on the country (Jacobsen, 2003). For instance, women may have less work experience due to taking time out to have children or due to lack of training. In some countries, women's educational level is lower than men's.

Although occupational segregation, part-time work, and human capital may explain some of the pay gap, they do not explain it all. For example, one recent U.S. study found the gender pay gap remains even when education, experience, hours worked, and occupational segregation are held constant (Judge & Livingston, 2008). The ILO (2007a) says that after controlling for these factors, the unexplained portion of the gap in industrialized nations ranges between 5 and 15 percent and, in some countries such as South Korea and South Africa (20 percent) and China and Australia (80 percent), it is even greater. This leads to the conclusion that some of the gender wage gap is due to outright **gender wage discrimination**—paying women in the same jobs less just because they are women and because the skills associated with "women's jobs" are devalued.

Gender wage discrimination appears to have three main sources. One is the traditional devaluation of women's work. In general, women have been devalued and so has their work—if women do it, it is worth less than if it's done by men. Second, in some cultures, it is assumed that a woman can be paid less because her income is merely a supplement to her husband's and that her paid job is secondary to her unpaid job as wife and mother (Kawashima, 1995; Padavic & Reskin, 2002). Last, paying women less often has to do with employers' simply wanting to make more money. When employers can get away with paying women less, they often do—because saving on women's wages increases employers' profits.

The elimination of the pay gap is crucial to achieving gender equality and reducing the poverty of women and children. Elimination of the gap requires government commitment to enacting and enforcing pay equity legislation, commitment to international conventions regarding pay equity, reducing gender occupational segregation, and providing family supports such as child care. By the early 2000s, most countries had ratified the ILO's Equal Remuneration Convention, 1951 (No. 100) and the accompanying Recommendation (No. 90). The Convention requires that remuneration rates (pay) are to be established without discrimination based on the sex of the worker and that men and women workers obtain equal remuneration for work of equal value, not just for the same or similar work. The implementation of this principle requires an objective comparison among jobs to determine their relative value **(comparable worth).** Comparable worth uses detailed classification systems to compare jobs on skill, effort, responsibility, and working conditions so that compensation can be fair, instead of being based on whether the job is customarily held by women or men (United Nations, 1994). Ratifying states are also supposed to work with business to ensure equal pay, provide job trainings and counseling to reduce horizontal occupational segregation, and provide services to meet the needs of women workers with family responsibilities (ILO, 2003). Recent research suggests that ratification is associated with greater pay equity (ITUC, 2008).

Government commitment to equal pay for the genders is one important factor in cross-cultural variation in the gender pay gap (ILO, 2007a). The Equal Remuneration Convention suggests that countries enact national laws prohibiting gender pay discrimination, and many have. For example, Brazil, Britain, Canada, China, Cyprus, France, Ghana, India, Israel, Italy, Japan, Mexico, New Zealand, the Philippines, the United States, and Sweden all have such laws. In a study of the gender pay gap in eleven industrialized countries, Blau and Kahn (1996) found that countries with strong centralized unions and government participation in wage setting tended to have the smallest pay gaps. Unfortunately, equal pay legislation does not bring about gender pay equality when there are no penalties for violation of equal pay laws, or there is no monitoring or enforcement of such penalties.

Although some countries such as Ghana, the United States, and Hong Kong have specialized enforcement bodies to investigate and prosecute gender pay discrimination, they are limited in funding and staffing (ILO, 2003). In the United States, for example, complaints first go through federal, state, or local agencies, which are horrendously backlogged (Crampton, Hodge, & Mishra, 1997). The U.S. federal Equal Employment Opportunity Commission (EEOC) received 28,372 charges of sex-based discrimination complaints in the year 2008 alone (EEOC, 2009). Equal pay legislation also does not typically do much to address the sources of gender pay inequalities, such as gender occupational segregation. For instance, most of the countries that have equal pay laws make it illegal to pay women working the same job as men less money, but the truth of the matter is that occupational segregation means that in many countries, women are not found in the same jobs as men.

The Glass Ceiling: Explanations and Solutions

"I was kept in the lowest position no matter how many years I worked. And I was really working hard."
Noriko Narumi, Japanese woman who successfully sued her employer of thirty-eight years in a landmark case

Further evidence of gender discrimination in paid employment comes in the form of a **glass ceiling.** This term is used to refer to the various barriers that prevent qualified women from advancing upward in their organizations into management power positions. Worldwide, the percentage of women in senior management positions ranges from 3 to 12 percent (UNIFEM, 2009a). For example, in South Asia, one in eight full-time male workers is a senior manager but only one in fifty-five full-time women workers; in the Middle East and North Africa, one in nine men and one in thirty-eight women are senior managers; and in Latin America and the Caribbean, one in eight men and one in twenty-six women are senior managers. In the United States, fifteen Fortune 500[2] companies are run by women, and twenty-four Fortune 1000 companies have women in the top job (Fortune, 2009). Internationally, women make up a relatively small percentage of corporate boards; only 11.2 percent of all board seats in the Fortune Global 200 companies are held by women (Corporate Women Board of Directors International, 2009). Women fare somewhat better when lower and middle management are included. For instance, although only 11 percent of executive managers in top companies are women, 45 percent of managerial and professional positions are held by women (EOWA, 2008). In Austria, the Czech Republic, Denmark, France, Latvia, Poland, and Spain, women hold between 26 and 38 percent of administrative and managerial jobs (Seager, 2009). Intersectionality also applies to the glass ceiling. Consider also that in many countries, some women face the dual burden of racism and sexism in organizations, leading to a **concrete ceiling** (Nkomo & Cox, 1989). For instance, in the United States,

---

[2] Fortune 500 companies are the 500 largest publicly traded companies in the U.S. Fortune 1000 companies are the largest 1,000, and Fortune Global 200 are the largest international publicly traded companies.

where women make up 50 percent of managers and professionals combined, only 4 percent are Latina, 2 percent Asian American, and 5 percent African American (Catalyst, 2009).

Research on women and leadership does not support the idea that there are few women in higher-status positions because women have personality traits or behavior patterns that make them ill-suited for managerial positions (Eagly & Carli, 2007). Instead, the main culprits appear to be stereotypes that suggest that women are inappropriate for leadership positions, and organizational barriers such as a lack of mentoring and training of women for leadership positions. Three common explanations for the glass ceiling are represented in Figure 5.3 and are discussed next.

When you think of a leader, what types of qualities do you imagine? In your culture, are these qualities typically associated with males or females? Gender stereotypes are one contributor to the perception that women are inappropriate for leadership and managerial positions. If it is believed that a woman's place is in the home or that women are ineffective as leaders and decision makers, then women will be denied leadership positions (Stevens, 1984). The incompatibility between the female gender role and the leadership role is described by **role congruity theory** (Eagly & Karau, 2002). The idea is that we are less likely to assign people to roles that call for qualities associated with the other gender. The *agentic* qualities associated with

FIGURE 5.3 *Contributors to the Glass Ceiling*

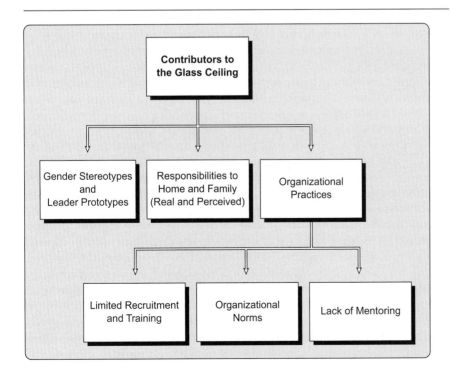

males (e.g., assertive, controlling, confident) are more consistent with the qualities expected of leaders compared to the *communal* qualities associated with females (e.g., helpful, nurturing, gentle). This leads to the conclusion that men are more suitable for leadership roles. Likewise, the **lack of fit model** proposes that there is a perceived lack of fit between the stereotypically based, nurturing and communal attributes and behaviors associated with women and the agentic, instrumental "male" attributes and behaviors believed necessary for success in powerful organizational positions; this incongruity leads to the perception that women are ill-equipped for these positions (Heilman & Okimoto, 2008). The concrete ceiling reflects greater negative stereotyping as a result of the combined effects of being female and from a negatively stereotyped ethnic or racial group. To the extent that both gender stereotypes and racial/ethnic stereotypes contradict "good leader" stereotypes, women from some groups may experience greater disadvantage (Sanchez-Hucles & Davis 2010).

In general, the characteristics associated with leadership roles (e.g., power, competition, authority) are ascribed more to men than to women (Garcia-Retamoro & López-Zafra, 2009). Studies in the United States, Australia, Germany, Japan, India, the United Kingdom, and Spain find that leadership continues to be associated with male rather than female stereotypes but there are cross-cultural variations; some studies find this to be more true of men than women, and others note a decline in the association in the United States (Duehr & Bono, 2006; Embry, Padgett, & Caldwell, 2008; Garcia-Retamoro & López-Zafra, 2009; Schein, Mueller, & Jacobson, 1989; Schein, Mueller, Lituchy, & Liu, 1996; Schein & Mueller, 1992; Sczesny et al. 2004). Research also indicates that gender-stereotypic images of occupations correspond to sex segregation in employment (Cejka & Eagly, 1999; Glick, 1991; Van Vianen & Willemsen, 1992). Gendered leader stereotypes, combined with the fact that there are relatively few women in positions of power, may make it hard for some people to imagine women as leaders and managers.

Gender stereotypes are but one cause of the glass ceiling. A second explanation is that common organizational practices sometimes dictate the hiring and promotion of males rather than females into management positions. This is often a self-perpetuating artifact of the organization's history. In other words, if the organization has historically hired and promoted men rather than women into leadership positions, this becomes the standard operating procedure as managers follow organizational precedent (Eagly & Carli, 2007). In some cases social norms suggest that women are not appropriate for high-level positions. Individuals within the organization may then comply with these norms regardless of their personal feelings regarding the appropriateness of women in leadership positions (Larwood, Szwajkowski, & Rose, 1988). Similarly, a qualified woman may not be promoted if upper management feels that employees' or clients' stereotypes might interfere with her effectiveness—for instance, that they won't be comfortable taking orders from a woman or won't find her a credible authority.

Another problem is that within the organization, women may be structurally disadvantaged due to gender occupational segregation. Basically this means that women are placed in jobs with less power and limited mobility, jobs that are less likely to lead to high-level positions in the organization (Baron et al., 1986; Bergmann, 1989). Women in prestigious male-typed organizations are usually segregated into female-typed specialties that offer fewer resources for power or are hired into departments with little power (Ragins & Sundstrom, 1989). They are also more likely to be hired into "staff" than "line" positions (managers in line jobs direct and control essential organizational activities, such as producing or selling products or services, whereas managers in staff jobs provide support and expertise to line managers) and managers in line positions typically have greater organizational power (Lyness & Heilman, 2006). For example, in Canada, in 2008 women held only 17 percent of all line positions—those important to advance to the highest levels (Apostolidis & Ferguson, 2009). One U.S. survey of executives and CEOs of Fortune 500 companies found that lack of line management experience was cited as the top barrier to advancement for women (Lyness & Heilman, 2006).

Yet another organizational barrier to women's progress is their relative lack of access to the political network and lack of mentoring. Mentoring occurs when a senior organizational member helps guide the career of a junior member by sharing knowledge about how to succeed in the organization. Mentoring is important because protégés receive more promotions, better compensation, and greater career mobility (Ragins, 1999). Women are less likely than men to receive personal support, job-related information, and career developmental support from their supervisors (Cianni & Romberger, 1995). Because of their gender and concerns about intimacy and sexual attraction, women are often excluded from the informal social relationships shared by their male counterparts where power transactions and mentoring often occur (Bhatnagar, 1988; Nelson et al., 1990; Noe, 1988; Powell & Mainiero, 1992). In many countries, such as parts of Afghanistan, Bangladesh, Cameroon, Pakistan, and Saudi Arabia, it is socially inappropriate for women to interact closely with men who are not husbands or family members.

Finally, the third explanation for the glass ceiling is that women's responsibilities to home and family, real and perceived, may prevent upward mobility in the organization. This can happen in two ways. First, when a woman is married and/or has children, employers often assume that her family responsibilities will interfere with her work commitment, and, consequently, they will not promote her into positions of responsibility. For example, in a U.S. study, mothers were expected to be less competent and were less likely to be kept in the running for advancement opportunities than were other female or male applicants who were applying for the same high-level managerial position (Heilman & Okimoto, 2008). Second, women remain disproportionately responsible for household labor and child care and these responsibilities are often incompatible with demands for the long hours, travel, and relocation required for advancement in the organization (Eagly & Carli, 2007). Because of the anticipated conflict between work and family, women in high-status careers frequently forgo or delay childbearing (Eagly & Carli, 2007). In a study of executives from North America, Latin America, and Asia, female executives were less likely than male executives to be married and more likely to delay or decide not to have children (Seager, 2009).

As mentioned earlier in regard to the gender pay gap, childbearing and women's primary responsibility for child rearing also affect women's pay and promotion in the workplace because many women take leaves of absence from their jobs in the formal sector while their children are small. For example, in Japan, advancement in the organization is highly dependent upon uninterrupted service to the organization and seniority. Japanese mothers generally do not participate in the paid sector because of difficulty reconciling the wife/mother role with the demands of paid employment (Harden, 2008). As Tanaka (1995) points out, marriage is more costly to a woman's career because only women are called upon to reconcile the competing demands of work and family responsibilities.

Because gender stereotyping appears to play a big role in the glass ceiling, it is important to reduce beliefs that women lack leadership skills and abilities. Progress is most evident in countries that have more gender-egalitarian beliefs. But changing gender-stereotyped leadership beliefs is not easy or swift—gender stereotypes often do not change until gender roles change, yet changing gender roles often requires changes in gender stereotypes. To jump-start this process, anti-discrimination legislation barring discrimination in hiring and promotion along with government policies and programs intended to reducing the structural disadvantage faced by women in organizations are sometimes needed. Programs that involve targeted recruitment efforts, training and mentoring programs to increase the number of qualified women in the leadership pipeline, considering gender as a "plus" factor in hiring, and even setting aside positions for women are ways to begin the process of gender role change and to reduce gender segregation in the workplace. Over time, as the presence of women in leadership positions becomes more common, gendered stereotypes of leadership should ease and pave the way for more women in leadership and such programs would become unnecessary. In Chapter 9, on women in politics, you'll learn that many of the countries with the highest numbers of women in politics used some of these methods. Changes in gendered divisions of household and care labor and family-supportive workplace and government policies would also clearly make a difference in eliminating the glass ceiling. In some countries, increasing educational parity between women and men is another key.

Sexual Harassment: Explanations and Solutions

Women have long been exposed to workplace harassment of a sexual nature but it wasn't until the 1970s that American women's activists gave it a name and demanded that it be recognized as sex discrimination under federal anti-discrimination legislation (Baker, 2005; MacKinnon, 1979; McCann, 2005). Since that time, it is increasingly recognized as a global problem that reflects and reinforces women's inequality in the workplace.

The ILO (2005) defines **sexual harassment** as "unwelcome sexual advances or verbal or physical conduct of a sexual nature which has the purpose or effect of unreasonably interfering with the individual's work performance or creating an intimidating, hostile, abusive or offensive working environment."[3] Fitzgerald's **tripartite model of sexual harassment** identifies three behavioral dimensions of sexual harassment, represented in Figure 5.4 (Fitzgerald, Swan, & Magley, 1997). **Gender harassment** refers to verbal and nonverbal behaviors that convey insulting, hostile, and degrading attitudes toward women. Displaying pornography, calling women "bitches" or "whores," and obscene gestures are in this category of sexual harassment. **Unwanted sexual attention** is just what it sounds like. It includes suggestive comments about a woman's body as well as unsolicited and unreciprocated sexual advances such as repeated requests for a kiss, a date, or sex. For example, in the 1990s, women at the U.S. Mitsubishi automobile plant in Normal, Illinois were subjected to repeated and unwelcome physical and verbal abuse. Among harassing behaviors were obscene graffiti demeaning to women, men exposing themselves to women and grabbing women's breasts, and men taunting women with crude names and pressuring them to have sex (Braun, 1998; Cray, 1997). Last, **sexual coercion** refers to requiring sex as a condition of employment or job rewards. Legally, it is often called *quid pro quo sexual harassment.*

"The señor wanted to take advantage of me, he followed me around . . . he grabbed my breasts twice from behind while I was washing clothes . . . I yelled, and the boy came out, and the señor left. I didn't tell the señora, because I was afraid. I just quit."
Maria Ajtún, domestic worker in Guatemala City

FIGURE 5.4   *Fitzgerald's Tripartite Model of Types of Sexual Harassment*

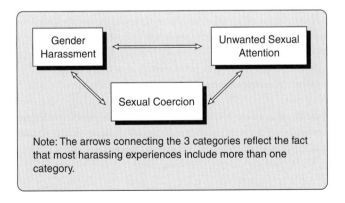

Note: The arrows connecting the 3 categories reflect the fact that most harassing experiences include more than one category.

---

[3] Although men sometimes experience sexual harassment (mostly young men, gay men, members of ethnic or racial minorities, and men working in female-dominated work groups), the vast majority of those who experience it are women (McCann, 2005).

"Frankly speaking, sexual harassment for many women in Korea is something that they have grown up with. Having been raised in this situation, women have tended to view sexual harassment as something they had to endure rather than something they had to protest. More women, especially in younger age groups, have started to raise the issue privately and publicly."
Korean woman

In Fiscal Year 2008, the U.S. EEOC received 13,867 charges of sexual harassment. 15.9 percent of those charges were filed by males.

Sexual harassment is perceived by victims as annoying, offensive, upsetting, embarrassing, stressful, and frightening (Fitzgerald et al., 1997). Sexual harassment often results in emotional and physical stress and stress-related illnesses (Chan et al., 2008; Gutek & Koss, 1993; Schneider, Swann, & Fitzgerald, 1997; Willness, Steel, & Lee, 2007). It is also potentially costly to organizations. Research in the United States indicates that harassment can lead to increased absenteeism, job turnover, requests for transfers, and decreases in work motivation and productivity (Chan et al., 2008; Willness, et al., 2007).

Statistics on the occurrence of sexual harassment worldwide are hard to obtain. The main source of information on sexual harassment in the workplace in most countries is the labor ministry or national office that processes complaints against employers, but in countries where there is no such office, there are almost no data (Report of the UN Secretary General, 2006). Like other forms of sexual violence, sexual harassment is underreported because women fear blame and retaliation. Available statistics suggest that sexual harassment is prevalent and that it cuts across social class and educational levels, although it is most commonly experienced by women who are young, single, separated, widowed, divorced, migrants, in traditionally male "blue-collar" jobs, supervised by men, and in the informal sector (McCabe & Hardman, 2005; McCann, 2005; Willness, et al., 2007).

In the United States, it is estimated that approximately one-half of employed women experience sexual harassment prior to retirement and that 65 to 79 percent of women in the U.S. military experience sexual harassment every year (Buchanan, Settles, & Woods, 2008).

According to the UN, European surveys find between 40 and 50 percent of women in the European Union reporting some form of sexual harassment or unwanted sexual behavior in the workplace; surveys in Asia-Pacific countries indicate that 30 to 40 percent of women workers report some form of harassment—verbal, physical, or sexual (Report of the UN Secretary General, 2006). Sexual harassment against girls and young women in educational institutions is also common. One study in the United States found that 83 percent of girls in grades 8 through 11 in public schools experienced some form of sexual harassment and 50 percent of schoolgirls in a Malawi study said they had been touched in a sexual manner without permission by either their teachers or male peers (Report of the UN Secretary General, 2006).

The intersection of gender, race, and class are also apparent in regards to sexual harassment. In what is termed **double jeopardy,** ethnic minority and migrant women are at increased risk for a combination of racial and sexual harassment (Berdahl & Moore, 2006; Buchanan & Fitzgerald, 2008). This is because minority group status denotes marginality and lack of power within the workplace (Murrell, 1996) and racism toward female ethnic minorities may be expressed as sexual aggression and harassment (Collins, 1990). It is interesting to note, for instance, that sexual harassment of women is reportedly widespread in factories owned by transnational corporations (this appears to be especially true when the supervisory staff is male and from a different country than the female subordinates). Minority women face an intersected type of harassment infused by racial stereotypes, particularly those based on their physical features (Buchanan & Fitzgerald, 2008). Ethnic minority women are also likely to see their harassment as arising from their minority status (Buchanan, Settles, & Woods, 2008; Collins, 1990; Murrell, 1996). This dual experience of racism and sexism, or sexual racism, exacerbates the negative experience of sexual harassment (Buchanan & Fitzgerald, 2008; Murrell, 1996).

Although the prevalence of sexual harassment varies cross-culturally and intra-culturally, research suggests that there is universality in the types of sexual harassment experienced. In a review of research, Gruber and colleagues (1996) found cross-cultural similarity in sexual harassment experiences. In studies with American, French, Spanish, Canadian, and Russian women, the most frequent form of harassment was verbal abuse and suggestive comments, followed by "sexual posturing" (including sexually suggestive looks or gestures, touching, following, and leering). Next were repeated requests for dates, sex, or a relationship; and last was outright sexual assault and coercion.

At its simplest, sexual harassment is a consequence of traditional power relationships between the genders in larger society and gender power differences within organizations. **Sex-role spillover** theory suggests that traditional expectations and relationships between the genders overflow into the workplace although they are irrelevant or inappropriate (Gutek & Morash, 1982). Men, used to perceiving women in sexual and traditional terms, carry this behavior into the workplace. Women, trained to interpret male attention as flattery and to avoid conflict, put up with it. Sexual remarks and behaviors toward women are normalized and therefore not perceived as problematic (Fitzgerald et al., 1997). From a feminist perspective, sexual harassment is also about power, because like other forms of gendered violence, it arises from and reinforces the subordinate position of women in society (Cleveland & McNamara, 1996; Menon & Kanekar, 1992). By intimidating and discouraging women from work, male dominance occupationally and economically is assured (Tangri, Burt, & Johnson, 1982). Also like other forms of violence against women, sexual harassment is considered to be a consequence of gender-role socialization processes that promote male dominance, the sexual objectification of women, and the cultural approval of violence against women (Cleveland & McNamara, 1996).

Sexual harassment is also about power because it frequently involves the abuse of organizational power. Men are often privileged in organizations and abuse their organizational power to sexually coerce or intimidate women (MacKinnon, 1979). For instance, most cases of sexual harassment occur between male superiors and female subordinates. Women's vulnerability to unemployment allows men with decision-making power to take sexual advantage of women (WIN, 1992). This is one reason why migrant women are at risk—they need their jobs and fear being turned over to immigration authorities if they lack required paperwork. At Mitsubishi, many of those who experienced sexual harassment did not complain because it was their supervisors who were doing the harassing (Braun, 1998; Cray, 1997). Ironically, according to the company's sexual harassment policy, sexual harassment complaints were supposed to be made through these very supervisors (Cray, 1997). Livingston (1982) points out that the relative social and economic power of harassers and victims influences the occurrence and severity of harassment as well as victims' responses.

Male peers also harass female peers, especially when the organization condones it or ignores it. More specifically, organizational tolerance—the degree to which an organization is perceived by employees to be insensitive or tolerant of sexual harassment—affects its frequency and severity (Hulin, Fitzgerald, & Drasgow, 1996; Kakuyama, Onglatco, Tsuzuki, & Matsui, 2003). In organizations that are tolerant of sexual harassment, complaints are not taken seriously, supervisors sexually harass, perpetrators are not meaningfully punished, and women who report sexual harassment face more harassment (Fitzgerald et al., 1997; Pryor et al., 1995). For example, in the Mitsubishi case referred to earlier, women who lodged complaints were subjected to hostile phone calls, the threat of rape, and stalking (Cray, 1997). Studies of *maquiladoras*, assembly plants in Mexico owned by multinational corporations, reveal that sexual harassment is common but few women report it because they fear reprisals and feel shamed and humiliated (Nauman & Hutchison, 1997). Hong Kong researchers Chang, Tan, and Chang (1999) link the reluctance to report incidents to collectivist cultures that emphasize harmonious relationships with others.

Sex-role spillover theory suggests that sexual harassment will decline as gender roles change and men get used to relating to women on the basis of their work roles rather than on the basis of traditional gender roles where men are the sexual pursuers and women are the sexually pursued. Also in a more gender-equal world, women will also be more likely to be assertive regarding the unacceptability of sexual harassment. They will not accept it as natural for males to harass and as part of their lot as females to put up with it. They will not try to minimize it by considering it a compliment, nor blame themselves for being too friendly or for wearing the wrong clothes. They will not hesitate to assert themselves out of a fear of not being nice or creating conflict. In the meantime, governments and organizations need to enact policies and programs that censure sexual harassment and require that it stop.

Sexual harassment is reduced when there are clear procedures to support victims and punish harassers and when there is a clear and consistent statement from management that sexual harassment will not be tolerated (Hulin et al., 1996). But the majority of organizations in the world have neither policies against sexual harassment nor procedures for handling it. Sexual harassment training, designed to prevent harassment from occurring, may also be effective if it is accompanied by strong managerial support. Unfortunately, sexual harassment training is often offered without procedures for ensuring that complaints will be taken seriously. At the Mitsubishi plant, the company's standard disciplinary measure was to require the harasser to watch a thirty-minute sexual harassment video (considered a joke by perpetrators) and to place a memo in the person's file (Cray, 1997).

National and international prohibitions against sexual harassment are also important. Over the last twenty years, international and national efforts to reduce sexual harassment have increased dramatically. Although there is no specific international agreement regarding sexual harassment, it is considered as a form of sex discrimination and a type of violence against women by the Convention to Eliminate Discrimination Against Women (CEDAW), the UN Declaration of Violence Against Women, and the ILO. The Bejiing Platform for Action calls for its elimination. Since the mid-1990s, the number of countries enacting sexual harassment laws has more than doubled (to 90); legislative provisions on sexual harassment have been enacted and existing provisions interpreted to combat harassment in countries in all regions (McCann, 2005). Some countries have national laws specifically prohibiting sexual harassment and others recognize it as a form of sex discrimination prohibited under equality or anti-discrimination laws.

Of course, once again, laws are of limited impact when they are vague or not enforced, and this is definitely the case when it comes to sexual harassment law. In the countries that have laws, violations rarely make it to court. This is partly because sexual harassment laws are often more progressive than the societies in which they are enacted, meaning that they are not taken seriously. Sexual harassment law is also new and confusing, and legal systems are not yet prepared to handle sexual harassment complaints. This means that few attorneys are familiar with it, and that it is often unclear what legal evidence is necessary to prove harassment. Women often have difficulty finding legal counsel willing to take their cases. Some countries require that complaints first be registered through under-funded and backlogged government agencies. Women frequently see little point in pursuing legal avenues of redress given the high personal and financial costs. However, some courageous women pursue their cases despite this, and eventually their efforts may have the effect of reducing organizational tolerance and increasing awareness. For example, you may be pleased to learn that in June 1998, U.S. courts ordered Mitsubishi to pay $34 million to 486 female workers at its Illinois plant.

Self-Employed Women

The Cuban woman who runs a beauty shop on the roof of her apartment building, the Peruvian woman who sells vegetables from her garden by the roadside, the South African woman who brews and sells her own beer, the Filipino woman who does others' laundry for pay, and the American woman who gets paid for watching her neighbor's children—are all self-employed women in the informal sector. Self-employed women in the informal sector rely on the skills and experience they already have, and so food processing and trading, sewing, and domestic and personal services are all common (Bullock, 1994).

"I eat and drink from my business. I built a house so that I no longer rent. I bought my plot from my earnings. I have been able to educate my children. That is very important—an even better achievement than building a house." *Betty Nakiganda, 48, Ugandan widow with eight children, sells mangos*

Sometimes the term **women's micro- and small-scale enterprises** (WMSEs), is used to describe this type of work (Dignard & Havet, 1995). The ILO uses the term **own-account workers** to refer to self-employed women without employees and notes that many of these women live in poverty. Over a quarter of the world's working women fall into this own-account category; almost 50 percent of women in sub-Saharan Africa, over 20 percent in Southeast Asia, South Asia, Latin America, the Caribbean, and the Middle East, but only 6 percent in more industrialized nations (ILO, 2007b). These women tend to return their profits to the family in the form of better food and living conditions, to what is called the "human economy" (Tinker, 1995).

One problem for own-account self-employed women is that they are not usually represented by unions; thus the power of collective organizing is unavailable to them and they are unprotected by labor laws. Another problem is that the invisibility of women's work in the informal sector, along with it not fitting standard definitions for economically successful business, means that women entrepreneurs have had difficulty getting credit (loans) from banks, governments, and development agencies. Berger (1995) summarizes some of the constraints on credit access for women micro-entrepreneurs. One of these is lack of collateral. Women often do not have clear title to land or property due to the widespread practice of registering property in the man's name and inheritance systems that favor men. Bank practices, such as those that require a male cosigner, also discourage women. In addition, many poor women lack the literacy to complete the complicated loan application forms. Consequently, for credit purposes, women micro-entrepreneurs frequently rely on moneylenders (who charge high interest rates), family, and friends (Berger, 1995).

Self-employed women have created their own solutions to these problems. For example, there are a number of self-employed women's unions such as the South African Domestic Workers' Union (SADWU) and the Union of Domestic Workers of Brazil. Perhaps the best-known self-employed women's union is SEWA of India, begun in 1972. One of SEWA's principal activities is the organization of cooperatives through which labor problems are addressed and loans are made. For example, SEWA helped the "push-cart vegetables cooperative" to fight for women's right to receive vending licenses (Bhatt, 1995). SEWA also offers retirement accounts and health insurance and the SEWA Bank provides capital for women's small-scale businesses (loans range from $100 to $1,000). As of 2009, SEWA had 84 different cooperatives providing capital to self-employed women, 181 rural producers groups, 6 organizations of health and child-care workers providing services to SEWA members, a training academy, 300,000 accounts in SEWA Bank, and a loan repayment rate of 98 percent (SEWA, 2009). A brief biography of Ela Bhatt, founder of SEWA, appears in Box 5.7.

The number of own-account workers is much smaller in industrialized nations, but the number of women employers—women who own their own businesses and have employees—is more common. Their businesses tend to be part of the formal sector and are directed toward growth. About 2 percent

"We may be poor, but we are so many. Why don't we start a bank of our own? Our own women's bank, where we are treated with the respect and service that we deserve."
Chandaben, old clothes seller, Founder - member, SEWA Bank

"How many times do we need to prove that poor women are bankable?"
Jayshree Vyas, M.D., SEWA Bank

Madam C. J. Walker (1867–1919), the first self-made woman millionaire in the United States, demonstrates the entrepreneurial spirit of African American women. She helped other women gain economic independence by hiring them to work at excellent wages for her hair-care products business.

BOX 5.7   *Activist Profile: Ela Bhatt of the Self-Employed Women's Association (India)*

Ela Bhatt, born in 1933 in India, is known as the founder of the Self-Employed Women's Association (SEWA). Bhatt's work as a lawyer for the textile industry brought her into contact with thousands of self-employed women workers such as street vendors and home-based piece rate workers. She realized that because the women were not organized, they were easily exploited, and because they worked in the informal labor sector, they could not appeal to the government for economic protections, and there were no unions to represent them. As Bhatt once said, "Personally, I don't think there can be any greater injustice to anybody in the world than to have one's work contribution negated. . . . Who is the backbone of any economy in the country? It's the poor! Yet they are not recorded as workers in the national census. They are described as non-workers!" Bhatt recognized that these women could be organized to demand better pay and work conditions, and that by pooling their resources they could provide loans to women's micro-enterprises that would otherwise be unable to obtain funding. With these goals, she founded SEWA in 1972. Today SEWA has hundreds of thousands of members and empowers women to have greater control of their economic lives. SEWA is the model for thousands of women's cooperatives worldwide.

of women worldwide fall into this category (in comparison to 4 percent of men) but there are regional variations, with the highest rates in industrialized nations (4 percent) and the lowest in South Asia (.4 percent) (ILO, 2007b). In contrast to the small-scale enterprises run by women in developing nations to provide for their families' basic needs (discussed further in Chapter 6), women in industrialized nations often choose self-employment to be their own bosses and to escape the glass ceiling.

Conclusion

This chapter illustrates the four global women's studies themes outlined in Chapter 1. For example, illustrating the theme that gender inequality is not inevitable and immutable is the fact that over the last twenty-five years, women have made huge advances in the world of employed work. Materialist and sociocultural factors are obvious influences on gender equality in the world of work—women's primary responsibility for household labor and care labor are factors in their workforce participation rates, the gender pay gap, and the glass ceiling and also impact occupational segregation. Cross-cultural and intra-cultural differences in women's work and the issues facing them once again demonstrate that multicultural and intersectional approaches are important if we are to be inclusive in our study of global women. For example, women in developing nations are more likely to work in the informal sector and this means that governments underestimate the value of their economic contributions and they frequently have fewer workplace protections.

Race, class, and gender intersect such that within a country, some groups of women are more likely to experience a glass ceiling or sexual harassment.

As is true of other chapters, this chapter highlighted efforts to cast working women's rights as human rights in international documents. We also saw the impact of women's activism in national legislation prohibiting gender discrimination and sexual harassment in the workplace and in the formation of self-employed women's unions and cooperatives when mainstream unions and governments were not responsive to their needs. Bullock (1994) suggests that the transformation of the situation of working women rests on three pillars: laws that establish equality principles, women's active participation in workers' organizations, and women's understanding of their rights. Workers' organizations, along with other NGOs (nongovernmental organizations), are important in pressing for the ratification of international labor standards and their implementation, as well as promoting women's legal literacy (Bullock, 1994). Chapters 9 and 10 focus more on these efforts. The next two chapters go into further depth on women in developing economies (Chapter 6) and how women are affected by globalization (Chapter 7).

Study Questions

1. Why is women's work important? What do Marxist feminists say about the relationship between women's work and women's micro- and macro-power?

2. What is feminist economics? Why do feminist economists recommend gender-responsive budgeting and time-use surveys? Why do they want governments to pay more attention to women's unpaid labor and their work in the informal sector labor?

3. What are gender-based household divisions of labor? What explanations for these divisions were provided in the chapter?

4. How common is women's participation in the paid labor force?

5. What does it mean to say that the effects of paid work on women are somewhat paradoxical? In what ways does working for pay benefit women?

6. What are maternal protection measures? Why are maternity leave and child care important? How common are government maternity leave polices and how are they paid for? Which countries have the best policies and which have the worst? How can maternity leave be a "two-edged sword" in regard to gender equality and what can be done about this?

7. What is the gender pay gap? How large is it? What explanations for it were given in the chapter? What is being done about it?

8. What is the glass ceiling? Worldwide, what is the percentage of women who hold senior management positions? What is the concrete ceiling?

9. How is the glass ceiling a function of gender stereotypes (role congruity theory and lack of fit theory)? What organizational practices contribute to it? What role do women's responsibilities to home and family play?

10. What is sexual harassment? What are the three main types according to the tripartite model of sexual harassment? What are the effects of sexual harassment? How common is it? What is double jeopardy? What are the three main explanations for sexual harassment? What needs to happen to reduce it?

11. What are WMSEs and "own account" workers? How common are these types of workers? How are self-employed women in industrialized nations somewhat different from those in less-industrialized ones? What are some of the difficulties facing self-employed women, and what have they done about them?

12. What are the "three pillars" on which the transformation of working women's situation rest?

Discussion Questions and Activities

1. The chapter suggested that government policies on child care and maternity leave may reflect a society's views about the "proper" role of women in society and whether women's participation in the labor force is desired. What do you think about this in regards to your country's maternity leave and child-care policies?

2. On International Women's Day (March 8) 2000, women in sixty countries took part in the first ever Global Women's Strike, demanding pay equity and wages for all "caring work." What would happen in your culture if women in heterosexual cohabitating or married relationships went on strike?

3. Discuss how the fact that women get pregnant, have children, and retain primary responsibility for children interferes with equal employment opportunities. This is a case in which women's differences from men mean that they need to be treated differently from men. Is this consistent with feminists' desire for women to be treated equally to men?

4. Discuss with others whether they have experienced sexual harassment in the workplace. Ask them to describe the type of harassment, how it affected their productivity, and its emotional and physical effects. How did they handle it and why? How did the answers of females and males differ? Summarize your findings.

5. Interview a woman in high-level management using questions formulated from the chapter discussion on the glass ceiling.

6. If you grew up in a two-heterosexual-parent home, who did the majority of the household labor—your mother or your father? Which of the three explanations for gender-based divisions of household labor seem to

best explain this? If your mother worked for pay, did she have a second shift? The gender perspective on household labor suggests that we unconsciously enact gender scripts for household and care labor. Do the unmarried heterosexual women and men you know seem to be doing this? What problems might this create as they become part of a dual-earner couple?

Action Opportunities

1. Hold a bake sale to draw attention to the gender pay gap. List your prices by gender (for example, in the U.S. charge men $1.00 for each item and women $.77). Explain to puzzled customers that your pricing scheme reflects the fact that women make that percent of what men make. When they argue that your pricing is not fair, remind them that the gender pay gap is not fair either. Donate your proceeds to a worthy women's cause such as UNIFEM, the United Nations Fund for Women.

2. Develop a project to increase the visibility of women's unpaid work. For instance, staff a table at a public event (activists call this "table-ing") where you have a display and pass out information. If you and your female friends tend to do all of the household labor for the males in your life, consider going on a strike for a day.

3. What is your university's policy on sexual harassment? What do students do to report sexual harassment? Educate your campus about what sexual harassment is and what to do about it. Write an article for your school newspaper, pass out information, design a web page and advertise the address, or post your information on bulletin boards on campus.

4. Check the Amnesty International and Human Rights Watch websites for campaigns related to working women's rights. Or, write letters to the U.S. Department of Labor and the ILO encouraging them to stay focused on women's labor issues.

5. Use your labor and ingenuity to create your own short-term microenterprise and donate all or part of your profits to The Global Fund for Women, an organization that uses monetary donations to fund women's micro-enterprises and empowerment all over the world. Learn more about the Global Fund for Women at http://www.globalfundforwomen .org Explain what the project taught you about self-employed women.

6. Go to http://www.now.org/issues/economic/and take action on an economic justice issue affecting women.

Activist Websites

National Association of Working Women (U.S.) http://www.9to5.org/

Alliance Against Sexual Harassment (Pakistan) http://www.aasha.org.pk/

The Wage Project (U.S.) http://www.wageproject.org/

Globewomen http://www.globewomen.org/

SEWA (Self Employed Women's Association India) http://www.sewa.org/

Mothers are Women (Meres et Femmes–Canadian) http://www
.mothersarewomen.com

Global Fund for Women http://www.globalfundforwomen.org

American Federation of Labor and Congress of Industrial Organizations
http://www.aflcio.org/issues/civilrights/

Informational Websites

Gender Responsive Budgeting http://www.gender-budgets.org/

International Labour Organization Gender Bureau http://www.ilo.org/
gender/lang-en/index.htm

Directory of UN Resources on Gender and Women's Issues: Women and
the Economy http://www.un.org/womenwatch/directory/women_and_
the_economy_3006.htm

Catalyst http://www.catalyst.org/

U.S. Equal Employment Opportunity Commission http://www.eeoc.gov/
index.html

Sexual Harassment Support http://www.sexualharassmentsupport.org/

Sexual Harassment at work: National and international responses (ILO)
http://www.ilo.org/public/english/protection/condtrav/pdf/2cws.pdf

6

Women, Development, and Environmental Sustainability

Development was to be a liberating project—a project for removal of poverty and leveling of socioeconomic inequalities, based on class, ethnicity, and gender. While the dominant image of "development" persists as a class- and gender-neutral model of progress for all, the experience of "development" has been the opposite, polarizing the dichotomizing society, creating new forms of affluence for the powerful, and new forms of deprivation and dispossession for the weak.

—Vandana Shiva

Like many women in developing nations, these Masai women in Tanzania Africa face increased workloads due to environmental degradation and have to travel farther and farther for water and fuel for family use. Efforts to help people in developing countries have been criticized by feminists for focusing on men and failing to acknowledge women's role in development. These critiques have resulted in improvements. © Brand X Pictures/PunchStock

The study of women and development is an important part of internationally oriented women's studies (Staudt, 1995). Women constitute 60 percent of the world's poorest people (United Nations Development Programme[UNDP], 2009a). Development projects are intended to promote economic development and reduce poverty. This chapter takes a close look at how women are affected by economic development efforts in their countries. As you will see, historically, gender equality has largely been ignored in development efforts. The result is that women's inequality was often untouched, and sometimes aggravated, by development projects, and development goals, such as the reduction of poverty, were unmet. The study of women and development is also another story of successful activism. After three decades of struggle by women's activists and scholars, gender is finally acknowledged as an important and central part of development.

> "The impact of economic development on gender equality is often neither automatic nor immediate. Nor is it sufficient."
> *World Bank*

The UNDP (United Nations Development Programme) works with countries to solve global and national development challenges, including poverty reduction. The program helps developing countries attract and use aid effectively and encourages human rights and women's empowerment. The UNDP provides important global data on human development.

Background

Development Terminology

An introduction to development terminology is necessary first. The term **developing nation** describes the less-industrialized or nonindustrialized nations of the world where poverty is the norm, health is poor, educational levels are low, and life expectancy is short. The United Nations identifies approximately 147 nations in Africa, Latin America, Asia, the Middle East, Central and Eastern Europe, and the Pacific as "developing." The fifty identified as "least-developed" (the poorest countries in the world with the lowest standards of living) are listed in Box 6.1. The majority of these least-developed nations are in the region known as sub-Saharan Africa. For example, in the sub-Saharan nations of Burundi, the Democratic Republic of Congo, and Zambia, over 50 percent of the population lives on less than $1.00 a day and life expectancy is less than age 50 (UNDP, 2008a).

The "developed" or **industrialized countries** are those that are industrialized and market based, such as Canada, France, Germany, Italy, Japan, the United Kingdom, and the United States. They have relatively high material standards of living and use advanced production techniques and equipment. In recent years, the terms **northern** and **southern countries** (also called **global north** and **global south**) have gained acceptance based on the relative geographic location of the industrialized nations in the northern hemisphere and developing nations in the southern hemisphere. These terms have largely replaced the terms "Third World" and "First World" countries.

In a nation, **development** is the process of growth that may include the following: emphasis on large-scale economic growth; focus on small-scale community development projects aimed at increasing individuals' self-reliance; creation or improvement of national infrastructures such as roads; provision of credit, training, or services that enable people to participate more fully in the economic, political, and social lives of their communities;

BOX 6.1   Countries Identified by The UN as "Least Developed"

Southern Asia

Afghanistan

Bangladesh

Bhutan

Maldives

Southeastern Asia

Cambodia

Laos

Myanmar (Burma)

Nepal

Middle East

Yemen

East Asia & the Pacific

Kiribati

Tuvulu

Vanuatu

Samoa

Solomon Islands

Timor-Leste

Caribbean

Haiti

Sub-Saharan Africa

Angola

Benin

Burkina Faso

Burundi

Cape Verde

Central African Republic

Chad

Comoros

Democratic Republic of Congo

Djibouti

Equatorial Guinea

Eritrea

Ethiopia

Gambia

Guinea

Guinea-Bissau

Lesotho

Liberia

Madagascar

Malawi

Mali

Mauritania

Mozambique

Niger

Rwanda

Sao Tome and Principe

Senegal

Sierra Leone

Somalia

Sudan

Tanzania

Togo

Uganda

Zambia

Source: UNICEF, 2006.

Note: Classified as least developed based on income (less than $750 annually per capita), level of economic diversification, and human resources such as life expectancy, nutrition, health, and literacy. Cape Verde, Maldives, and Samoa may soon be removed from the list.

improvement in access to health care; mechanisms for increasing agricultural yield; increased access to education for women and children; and expanded opportunities for political development (Mermel & Simons, 1991). The majority of development programs are funded through foreign aid, from the government of one country to the government of another country (called **bilateral aid**) such as that provided by USAID. **Multilateral aid** funded by the World Bank, the IMF (International Monetary Fund), and other UN agencies accounts for about 30 percent of funding (UNIFEM, 2008). Nongovernmental organizations (NGOs) such as OXFAM and the Global Fund for Women as well as foundations (like the Ford Foundation) also fund development projects.

Colonial History

Many of the countries in the global south spent years as colonies of northern countries, some well into the twentieth century. For example, the developing nation of Sri Lanka (formerly Ceylon) is an island country off the coast of India. Europeans dominated it for more than 400 years, first the Portuguese in the sixteenth century, then the Dutch, and later the British, who controlled it until 1948. Only two countries in Africa were never colonies (Liberia and Ethiopia). Belgium, Britain, France, Portugal, Holland, Germany, and Spain controlled the other African countries until a lengthy decolonization period following World War II. As colonies, these countries were exploited as sources of cheap labor and resources. Typically, profits were not shared with the natives.

Colonization permanently altered cultural features such as language and economies and, some would argue, negatively impacted women's status and power. Many feminist development scholars argue that colonization replaced egalitarian gender arrangements by removing women from the political decision-making spheres, limiting their access to and control over resources, and interfering with their legal rights and privileges (Boserup, 1970; Duley & Diduk, 1986; Sen & Grown, 1987). For example, Western patrilineal notions of land ownership contributed to a situation in which women own hardly any of the land in developing nations. Industrialization, which necessitated the movement of families into cities, increased women's dependence upon men for their livelihoods because offices and factories hire far fewer women than they do men, and urban work is often incompatible with traditional female roles.

Colonial experiences also affect how developing nations interpret Western attempts to help them. This fact is relevant to our study here. Colonizers often defended their behavior on the grounds that they were doing native cultures a favor by remaking them in the Western image and promoting economic development. The result, though, was the loss of many native traditions, increased poverty in many instances, and suspicion of Western intervention. Consequently, efforts to promote gender equality as part of development are often resisted with the charge of Western cultural imperialism.

Women in Developing Nations

"In sub-Saharan Africa, a woman's risk of dying from treatable or preventable complications of pregnancy and childbirth over the course of her lifetime is 1 in 22, compared to 1 in 7,300 in the developed regions."
UN Millennium Development Report 2008

Conditions for women in developing nations are especially challenging. For example, the majority of the world's 1 billion people living in poverty are women in developing nations (UNICEF, 2006). In the least-developed countries, nearly twice as many women over age 15 are illiterate compared to men (UN End Poverty Millennium Campaign, 2009). The majority of women with HIV/AIDS live in developing nations, and over 60 percent of adults with HIV/AIDS in sub-Saharan Africa are women (UNAIDS, 2008). Most maternal deaths (99 percent) and maternal disability (such as obstetric fistula) occur in developing nations due to poor access to skilled birth attendants and high birth rates resulting from the unavailability of contraception (UNFPA, 2008a, 2009e). The life expectancy of women in the least-developed nations is age 54 compared to 74 in more-developed regions (UNFPA, 2008a). Most of the countries that practice female genital cutting are developing nations in sub-Saharan Africa (UNFPA, 2009f). The majority of the hundreds of thousands of women subjected to war and post-conflict rape in the last fifteen years have lived in one of the least-developed nations in sub-Saharan Africa (Stop Rape Now, 2009). Two-thirds of the women in the developing world can be found working in the informal sector in low-paying, vulnerable jobs as own-account and unpaid family workers (UN, 2008).

Finally, women in the least-developed nations usually lack things we take for granted such as convenient stores, cooking stoves (many cook over fires), fuel (some have to gather wood or other fuel daily) and water (many have to travel long distances and carry it home). They often lack access to electricity, medical, and sanitation services. This means that the household and care labor typically performed by women is that much more difficult and time-consuming. For example, research indicates that women in sub-Saharan Africa spend around 40 billion hours a year fetching and carrying water (UNIFEM, 2009).

Feminist Concerns with the Development Process

"It is not possible to address society's needs at any level while ignoring the perspectives, priorities, and knowledge of more than half of the world's population."
Roshina Wilshire, UNDP

Historically, most development programs focused on economic growth and a conversion to capitalist market economies and modern technology. This focus is commonly associated with **modernization theory,** so-called because urban-based market economies were viewed as modern and desirable. Modernization proponents believed that modern capitalism and other forms of development go hand in hand. That is, if we transformed the economy of a developing country, then political and social development would follow. Traditional development programmers saw no need to consider gender since they believed that what benefited the economy would benefit both men and women. Unfortunately, economic growth does not necessarily increase women's status nor reduce their considerable workloads. Indeed, it can lead to increased income inequalities and can leave social and political inequalities untouched. The fact that some southern countries outperform richer industrialized countries in gender equality in politics, income, and professional positions (factors comprising the UN's gender empowerment index) demonstrates that economic development does not necessarily lead to increased gender equality. For instance, the developing nations of the Bahamas, Cuba, and Trinidad/Tobago are ahead of the industrialized nations of Japan, Switzerland, Hungary, Greece, Cyprus, and Israel on indicators of gender equality (UNDP, 2008a). This shows that economic development is no guarantee of women's equality.

In 1970, Ester Boserup expressed serious concerns about the effects of traditional development programs on women. Her now-classic book, *Women's Role in Economic Development* stimulated debate as the first major text in the women and development literature (Mosse, 1993). Boserup's research showed how contemporary development policies belittled women's economic contributions while relying on and exploiting their labor (Acosta-Belen & Bose, 1995). She also showed that economic development has a differential impact on men and women and that it often disrupted earlier, more egalitarian gender arrangements (Beneria & Roldan, 1987; Jaquette & Staudt, 2006). Boserup's book stimulated a number of feminist critiques of development programs, summarized into four categories below. Many of these criticisms are still valid today, although things have improved as a result of feminist development scholars and activists and "femicrats" (feminist bureaucrats) working for development organizations.

Traditional Development Programs Fail to Recognize Women's Economic Contributions

One common criticism is that development programs fail to acknowledge the importance of women's labor to the survival and ongoing reproduction of people in all societies and thus fail to meet important development goals such as poverty reduction and child mortality (Anand, 1993; Sen & Grown, 1987). Women devote more of their income and resources to their children than men do, so putting resources directly into their hands and strengthening their autonomy improves children's health and well-being (Amin & Li, 1997; Blumberg, 1995). Women produce between 60 and 80 percent of the food in most developing countries and are responsible for half of the world's food production (UN Food and Agriculture Organization [FAO], 2009a). Many water resource development and agricultural irrigation projects have failed due to the exclusion of women's important role in water management; women's participation is among the variables most strongly associated with project success (FAO, 2009b). Despite women's roles as the principal providers of basic needs (food, fuel, water, health care, sanitation, and so on) and the relationship between women's empowerment and important development goals, women have more difficulties than men in gaining access to development resources. This is attributed to the poor measurement of women's unpaid labor in government statistics (as noted in the previous chapter, what is uncounted often remains unnoticed).

BOX 6.2   *One Woman's Day in Sierra Leone*

4:00 A.M. to 5:30 A.M. Fish in local pond.

6:00 A.M. to 8:00 A.M. Light fire, heat washing water, cook breakfast, clean dishes, sweep compound.

8:00 A.M. to 11:00 A.M. Work in rice fields with four-year-old son and baby on back.

11:00 A.M. to 12:00 P.M. Collect berries, leaves, and bark, carry water.

12:00 P.M. to 2:00 P.M. Process and prepare food, cook lunch, wash dishes.

2:00 P.M. to 3:00 P.M. Wash clothes, carry water, clean and smoke fish.

3:00 P.M. to 5:00 P.M. Work in the gardens.

5:00 P.M. to 6:00 P.M. Fish in local pond.

6:00 P.M. to 8:00 P.M. Process and prepare food, cook dinner.

8:00 P.M. to 9:00 P.M. Wash dishes, then clean children.

9:00 P.M. to 11:00 P.M. Converse around the fire while shelling seeds and making fishnets.

11:00 P.M. to 4:00 A.M. Sleep.

Source: Food and Agriculture Organization, 2009f.

"In the vast and ever growing literature on economic development, reflections on the particular problems of women are few and far between."
Ester Boserup

"Neglecting women as agricultural producers and resource managers inhibits the attainment of food security goals."
UN Food and Agriculture Organization (FAO)

"If the average distance to the moon is 394,400 km, South African women together walk the equivalent of a trip to the moon and back 16 times a day to supply their households with water."
UNIFEM

Traditional Development Programs Have Not Reduced Women's Considerable Workloads

A second common criticism is that in most cases, development projects have not reduced women's considerable workloads. Women's work as the primary household food producers and preparers, and as water and fuel gatherers, has gone largely unappreciated and unaided even as this workload grows because of resource depletion and pollution (Bryceson, 1995). In many regions, women spend up to five hours a day collecting fuel wood and water and up to four hours a day preparing food (FAO, 2009a). Development programs often provide tools and technologies to aid in men's work but not women's work. For example, many women in developing nations could really use proper water and sanitation systems; energy-efficient, nonpolluting cookstoves; hoes and other hand-farming implements; and alternative fuel sources such as biogas and solar energy.

Box 6.2 gives you an idea of the average workday for a woman in the developing nation of Sierra Leone. You can probably readily think of development projects that could significantly reduce her work burden. Development projects focusing on irrigation systems for cash crops (crops grown for cash rather than local food production) are another good example of how development projects often negatively impact women. Such projects often divert water away from home gardens and other domestic uses, making it more difficult for women to provide for their families' food and water needs.

Traditional Development Programs Focus on Men's Income Generation

A third common criticism is that traditional development programs often assume a Western-style traditional gender-role arrangement in which men are breadwinners and women are homemakers. Consequently, they focus on fostering wage earning by male heads of household and on adult women in domestic homemaking roles. For instance, until the late 1970s, development efforts targeted at women viewed women primarily as mothers by focusing on mother–child health programs, feeding schemes, family planning, food aid, and so on (Moser, 1989). As Mosse (1993) points out, these programs do not do much to create independence and self-reliance among women, but they are politically safe in that they do not challenge women's traditional roles.

Assuming that what benefits husbands will benefit women and children, they also channel development resources through men (Youseff, 1995). This focus on males means that development programs have typically increased males' but not females' access to important sources of development such as land, credit, cattle, and technical know-how and thus create or maintain women's economic dependence on men. It also means that divorced, widowed, or abandoned women are particularly vulnerable to poverty because they often lack even indirect access to development resources (Bryceson, 1995). In the world's least-developed countries, 23 percent of rural households are headed by women (FAO, 2009a). The idea that progress involves the promotion of the male breadwinner/female homemaker roles also interferes with the extension of loan moneys to women entrepreneurs and women farmers. This is made worse by the fact that most development programs only lend to property owners. Yet there is widespread discrimination against women inheriting, owning or controlling property in most developing nations (Seager, 2009).

The male breadwinner focus of traditional development programs also means that extension programs, which provide education on new technologies, methods, and plant varieties to promote development, often exclude women. A recent FAO[1] survey showed that female farmers receive only 5 percent of all agricultural extension services worldwide (FAO, 2009e). Extension workers bypass women because women often do not own or control the land they farm and are therefore unable to obtain the credit to put extension education into action. Women are also bypassed because development often focuses on cash crops grown by men, and because cultural and religious customs sometimes make it socially unacceptable for women to interact closely with men who are not family members. Although efforts have been made to hire and train more female extension workers, only 15 percent of the world's extension agents are women (FAO, 2009e). The FAO has demonstrated significant benefits to including women in extension efforts.

"Experience shows that investing in women is one of the most cost effective ways of promoting development. As mothers, as producers or suppliers of food, fuel, and water, as traders and manufacturers, as political and community leaders, women are at the center of the process of change."
Gro Harlem Brundtland, former Prime Minister of Norway and former Head of the World Health Organization

---

[1] The FAO is the UN's Food and Agriculture Organization.

Following a national project targeting women in Kenya, corn yields increased by 28 percent, beans by 80 percent, and potatoes by 84 percent.

Traditional Development Programs Have Contributed to Erosions in Women's Status

Finally, a fourth criticism is that by encouraging or assuming a Western version of gender-role arrangements, development programs have contributed to erosions in women's status. The notion that a male breadwinner and a female housewife is a desired goal pervaded national and international agents of development until the 1980s, and that, combined with local patriarchal beliefs, contributed to women's continued lower status and power relative to men. Rogers (1980), in a highly influential book called *The Domestication of Women,* argued that because development efforts failed to provide incentives for women as producers, development projects eroded what had been a source of power and status for women. For instance, in many developing nations it is women who traditionally engage in improving and innovating plant and animal varieties (FAO, 2009d). This important source of status and control for women is lost when development projects give men, but not women, access to improved seed varieties and other farming technologies, as is typically the case. Likewise, many development projects resulted in women changing from being independent producers and providers to being housewives, economically dependent upon men as controllers of cash income. Furthermore, with cash, men gain access to banks and other modern institutions, leaving women further behind (Mosse, 1993).

> "Without specific attention to gender issues and initiatives, projects can reinforce inequalities between women and men and even increase imbalances."
> *UNDP*

> "Women are community managers, farmers, water collectors, entrepreneurs, caretakers of fragile ecologies, and as mothers they daily create and maintain life. Only when their expertise and value are realized will development initiatives have half a chance of succeeding."
> *Julia Mosse*

Women in Development Approach (WID)

Feminist criticisms of traditional development programs did have some impact. For example, in 1973, following considerable activism by American feminist development experts like Irene Tinker, the U.S. Congress enacted the Percy Amendment to the Foreign Assistance Act. It required that bilateral programs "give particular attention to those . . . activities that tend to integrate women into the national economies of foreign countries, thus improving their status and assisting the total development effort" (World Resources Institute, 1994–1995). In the 1980s, influenced by Boserup's critiques, the **women in development (WID)** approach emerged. This approach emphasized that directing development resources to women would improve food production and reduce poverty (Jaquette & Staudt, 2006). WID demanded increased attention to women's development needs and emphasized women's productive labor. WID projects can be classified into three general types: (1) income-generating projects, (2) projects that provide labor-saving technologies, and, (3) projects that improve women's local resource access (see Figure 6.1).

FIGURE 6.1   *Three Types of Women in Development Projects*

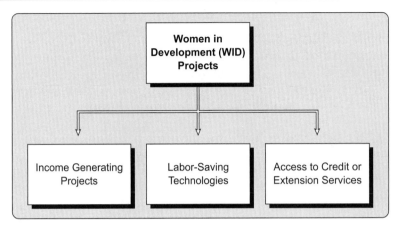

Income-Generating Projects

In the 1980s, development efforts began focusing on fostering women's economic participation in the public sphere. The thought is that women enhance family well-being and their own power within the household and society when they earn money, thereby increasing their status (Acevedo, 1995; Bryceson, 1995). Income-generating projects remain one of the most common types of women's projects under the WID approach but sometimes these projects are not very well thought out and often do not produce intended benefits.

The typical income-generating project for women focuses on traditional female skills such as sewing, embroidery, and handicrafts—all low in marketability and profit in comparison to the skills taught to men (Bryceson, 1995; Youseff, 1995). The projects are often unsuccessful because they are launched before it has been determined that there is a market for the goods produced and because they add to women's already considerable workloads (Afshar, 1991; Buvinic, 1995). Another problem is that this type of income-generating program frequently fails to include women in the project design process. Women are typically presented with the program instead of being asked to generate their own ideas. Involving women directly in the development process increases the likelihood that there will be a market for the item produced and that the item can be produced within the constraints of women's workload. It also gives women organizational skills and a sense of empowerment that lasts long after the donor has left the area. Under these conditions, income-generating projects can positively contribute to women's status and power (Mosse, 1993).

Although development programs sometimes still include small-scale income-generating development projects for women, particularly in rural areas, the trend since the mid-1980s is toward the employment of women by transnational corporations. As discussed in Chapter 7, these corporations have significantly increased profits by having much of their product assemblywork done by low-waged women factory workers and homeworkers

Song of an African Woman

I have only one request.

I do not ask for money

Although I have need of it,

I do not ask for meat . . .

I have only one request,

And all I ask is

That you remove

The road block

From my path.

From the Acholi poem, Song of Lawino by Okot p'Bitek

in developing nations. Indeed, women's work for transnationals constitutes a growing proportion of women's work in currently developing countries, especially in Asia, Latin America, and the Caribbean (Ward & Pyle, 1995). However, the women working for transnational corporations in factories frequently face harsh and unsafe working conditions, sexual harassment, and discrimination. This situation demonstrates that wage earning per se is no guarantee of a better life for women. "Homework," assemblywork done in the home, has also increased throughout the world and is often chosen by women who seek to combine wage earning with domestic responsibilities. Homeworkers are typically paid far less than factory workers are paid, and most of the time, neither group earns enough to get out of poverty. However, traditional measures of development success, such as increased gross national product (GNP) and per capita income, may lead to the perception that development based on providing low-cost labor to transnationals is an effective development strategy.

Labor-Saving Technologies

"In the Sudan, a project eased the duties of firewood collection among women through the provision of energy-saving gas cylinders and stoves."
IFAD

Because women's poor quality of life in developing countries is aggravated by the lack of technologies, including relatively simple tools, labor-saving technologies can be a useful development strategy. A number of development projects have reduced women's labor loads by providing such things as grinding mills, pumps, or cooking stoves. The main criticism of these projects is that they have disseminated only a narrow range of devices that merely begin to address the reality of women's multitask responsibilities (Bryceson, 1995). Also, because development agencies frequently fail to consult the women whom they wish to reach, the tools are often unsuccessful (Mosse, 1993). For example, in Ethiopia, where women are the primary water collectors, women were not consulted in the design of a water development program. Because of this, a pump that required two hands to operate was installed. Due to the traditional round-bottomed water jar used for collection, this meant that two people were required to collect the water.

Improving Women's Access to Development Resources

"The evidence indicates that . . . women microentrepreneurs . . . tend to do their utmost to succeed. They benefit (although they may increase their workday and self-exploitation), their children benefit, the credit project benefits, and the planet's equity account becomes a little less tilted toward power, privilege, and patriarchy."
Rae Lesser Blumberg, American Sociologist and Gender Stratification Expert

The UN's Convention on the Elimination of Discrimination Against Women (CEDAW) specifically addresses the rights of women in development. Article 14(9) of the convention promises women the right to "have access to agricultural credit and loans, marketing facilities, appropriate technology and equal treatment in land and agrarian reform as well as land resettlement schemes." As already noted, women's access to credit and loans is inhibited by the fact that they are unlikely to own land to use as collateral. This also affects women in the informal economic sector. For instance, women micro-entrepreneurs do such things as run beauty parlors out of their homes or make tortillas or clothing and sell them in the marketplace. In the 1980s and 1990s, aiding micro-entrepreneurs in the form of small loans became a popular form of development aid; however, male entrepreneurs are more likely to receive aid than females (Blumberg, 1995). Along with discriminatory loan practices (such as requiring male co-signers), assumptions that women are not serious entrepreneurs, that they will default on their loans, and that their businesses have no growth potential, have all made it difficult for women to obtain loans. Forrester (1995) points out that the reluctance to lend to women is ironic given that women have a repayment rate of 90 percent, even when interest rates are over 20 percent. Evidence from Bangladesh, the Dominican Republic, Guatemala, and Indonesia indicates that women micro-entrepreneurs have a payback record at least as good as or better than men's (Blumberg, 1995). Furthermore, Blumberg's (1995) research in the Dominican Republic, Ecuador, and Guatemala found that women's micro-enterprises often produce as many or more jobs than men's and often grow faster than men's do.

Fortunately, **microcredit,** the extension of small loans to women in poverty for small-scale economic enterprises, is gaining ground largely due to the efforts of nongovernmental organizations like SEWA (discussed in the previous chapter). Another well-known microlender is Bangladesh's Grameen Bank, which grants small loans to help women set up microenterprises. The bank now has 7.9 million members (90 percent women) in 84,487 villages, and a repayment rate of 97 percent (Grameen Bank, 2009). Thousands of nongovernmental organizations throughout Asia, Africa, and Latin America now use revolving credit funds and lend disproportionately to women (Fisher, 1996). For instance, ACCION, a private nonprofit organization, has a mission of giving people the financial tools they need to work their way out of poverty. They provide microloans (as small as $50), business training and other financial services, and operate in twenty-four countries in Latin America, the Caribbean, Asia, sub-Saharan Africa, and the United States (where they loan primarily to low-income minority Americans without access to traditional lending). Since 1998, ACCION-affiliated programs have made $23.4 billion in microloans to more than 7.7 million people (61 percent of them women), with a repayment rate of over 97 percent (ACCION, 2009). Women's credit programs benefit women in many ways. Studies indicate that women's credit programs positively impact their contraceptive use and nutritional status via the mechanisms of increased empowerment and autonomy (Amin & Li, 1997).

> The Grameen Bank, and its founder Dr. Muhammad Yunus, won the Nobel Peace Prize in 2006. Dr. Yunus, an economist committed to eradicating poverty, is considered the "Father of Microcredit."

Gender and Development Approach (GAD)

Critics of the WID approach pointed out that despite increased attention to women in development, development programs for the most part failed to increase women's status. In the 1980s, this led to a new approach to women and development. Called the **gender and development approach (GAD)** or **empowerment approach,** it focuses explicitly on improving women's status and power. The inclusion of the word "gender" in place of the word "women"

> "No man, planning economic development for the developing countries, intended to empower women."
> *Irene Tinker*

BOX 6.3 *Comparison of WID and GAD Approaches to Development*

Women in Development (WID)

Focus. Improve women's welfare.

How. By providing income-generating projects, labor-saving technologies, access to development resources like credit and extension services.

Top-down approach. Services determined and offered by development organizations. Women are passive recipients of aid.

Criticisms. Usefulness impeded by failure to consult women. Does not increase women's status or empowerment.

Gender and Development (GAD)

Focus. Transform society to promote gender equality.

How. By encouraging women's empowerment through women's organizations and activism, participation in politics, and decision making.

Bottom-up approach. Women are architects of their own development. Women are active participants of aid.

Criticisms. Difficult to translate into specific policies and programs. Resistance due to its "revolutionary" nature.

"Empowerment is the process of gaining control over the self, over ideology and the resources that determine power."
Srilata Balliwala

"There is a need to reconceptualize a development paradigm that can promote equity, social justice, sustainability, and self-determination."
Filomina Steady

reflects an emphasis on looking at the overall power relationships of women and men and their importance to development.

The GAD approach takes into account women's lives and labor, both inside and outside of the home. In addition, it emphasizes an approach in which women are not as much integrated into development, as they are the architects of their own development. Projects based on a GAD approach involve encouraging women to bring about positive change through women's organizations and activism. GAD differs from other approaches to women and development in that it sees the goals of development for women in terms of self-reliance, strength, and gender equality (Mosse, 1993). GAD emphasizes empowering women to work to change and transform the structures that contributed to their subordination (a bottom-up approach) (Moser, 1989).

Feminists from the south, in particular those in the organization DAWN (Development with Women for a New Era), embraced GAD (Braniotti, Charkiewicz, Hausler, & Wieringa, 1994; Sen & Grown, 1987). DAWN, a transnational feminist network launched as a global South initiative in 1984, includes representatives from Asia, Africa, Latin America, the Pacific, and the Caribbean. Many influential Southern Hemisphere feminists are members. DAWN's main purpose is to mobilize opinion and to create a global support network for equitable development (Dankelman & Davidson, 1988). DAWN emphasizes political mobilization, consciousness-raising, and popular education as crucial to women's empowerment. Box 6.3 summarizes the differences between the WID and GAD approaches.

In the 1990s, the leading development agencies began adding GAD-sounding rhetoric to their mission or goal statements. Since the early 2000s, bilateral and multilateral organizations have also increased funding to support gender equality, although only a fraction of development assistance is allocated to gender equality as a principal objective (UNIFEM, 2009). Most development agencies have also (to some extent) embraced **gender mainstreaming.** Gender mainstreaming requires a gender analysis to make sure that gender equality concerns are taken into account in all developmental activities rather than being marginalized into specialized women's institutions (Charlesworth, 2005). It also supposedly requires women's active participation in the development process.

All UN bodies and agencies have formally endorsed gender mainstreaming and most have corresponding statements, policies, programs, and activities. The UN's Millennium Summit and Declaration, which was adopted by 189 nations in 2000, set gender equality as a Millennium Development Goal (MDG-3) and as a condition for the achievement of the other goals, though it should be noted that concrete goals were lacking (see Box 6.4 for the MDG goals). In July 2005, ECOSOC (UN's Economic and Social Council) adopted a resolution calling upon all United Nations' funds and programs to intensify their efforts to address the challenges involving the integration of gender perspectives into policies and programs. Following a 2005 evaluation of gender mainstreaming, the UNDP concluded it had failed to create tangible and lasting results and initiated a series of remedies including senior management accountability, gender mainstreaming scorecards, and increased training and funding. The UNDP's 2008–2011 Gender Equality Strategy (UNDP, 2008b) also makes a specific commitment to address many of the gender problems associated with traditional development and provides a blueprint for doing so. The UNDP's gender mainstreaming tools advise programmers to incorporate gender specialists and representatives of women at all levels, to identify gender issues relevant to each project, to take all possible steps to ensure gender balance in project staff, and involve women's NGOs in project identification, formulation and appraisal.

In multilateral development organizations, gender mainstreaming is the primary tool for attacking gendered power relations but it has been criticized on a number of grounds. One concern is that despite positive rhetoric, there is a lack of accountability; proof of follow-through and effectiveness is lacking (UNIFEM, 2009). Another concern is that most cases, a women's empowerment focus has gotten lost in the process (Prugl & Lustgarten, 2006). Critics of gender mainstreaming charge that it has strayed from the original GAD vision of development as being about women's organizations and activism. This may be partly because GAD is viewed with suspicion by Southern Hemisphere governments who are uncomfortable with gender-role change and resist it with charges of cultural imperialism and cultural insensitivity. It has also been suggested that development organizations that are themselves based on gendered hierarchies (like UN agencies where leadership is predominantly male) cannot be expected to fully enact GAD (Charlesworth, 2005). It is apparent that gender mainstreaming is not an "end-all-and-be-all" and must be complemented by gender activists and scholars who hold development agencies accountable (Prugl & Lustgarten, 2006).

Joyce Banda was elected the first woman Vice-President in Malawi in March 2009. She left an abusive marriage with her three children and started her own successful business. As a Member of Parliament and Minister for Gender, Children's Affairs and Community Services, she fought for Malawi's recently enacted Domestic Violence Bill. She is the founder of Young Women Leaders, a girls' school, the Hunger Project in Malawi, and the National Association of Business Women, which has mobilized 30,000 women countrywide, disbursed $2 million in loans, and trained 12,000 women to run their own businesses.

"Women are indeed great, as I learn that they are better fighters against poverty than their men, have more calculative, stable, forward looking strategies to deal with their own environment. Everywhere in the country, we found that women were the most committed proponents of our future."
Ela Bhatt, Self-Employed Women's Association, India

BOX 6.4 *The Millenium Development Goals*

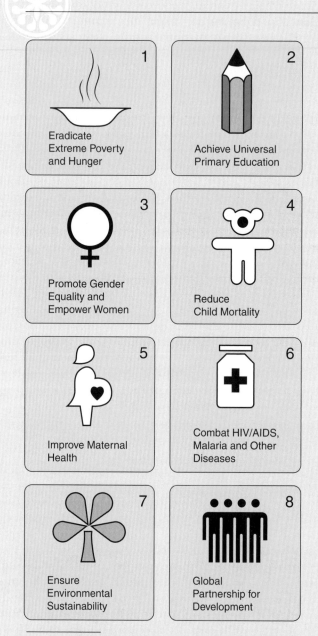

1 Eradicate Extreme Poverty and Hunger

2 Achieve Universal Primary Education

3 Promote Gender Equality and Empower Women

4 Reduce Child Mortality

5 Improve Maternal Health

6 Combat HIV/AIDS, Malaria and Other Diseases

7 Ensure Environmental Sustainability

8 Global Partnership for Development

Source: United Nations (2009). http://endpoverty2015.org/goals.

OXFAM, one of the world's leading nongovernmental development aid organizations, has also made changes consistent with a gender and development approach. In 1985, the gender and development unit was created to ensure that OXFAM's development and relief programs improve the quality of women's lives. OXFAM's gender policy states a commitment to the following: promoting the empowerment of women, confronting social and ideological barriers to the improvement of women's status, promoting women's independent access to development resources, helping women exercise their rights over their bodies and protect themselves from violence, and promoting initiatives with a gender focus. By the 1990s, OXFAM incorporated gender mainstreaming in a number of different ways, but following a self-review in 2001, OXFAM concluded that what it was doing was still too much of a WID approach and recommitted to fostering women's empowerment. By 2009, OXFAM had specific programs in place to promote women's political leadership to challenge gender inequality.

One way for development organizations to support GAD is to fund women's rights groups, but a 2007 study by AWID (Association for Women in Development) found the amount of aid reaching such groups is declining. The largest sources of funding for women's rights groups came from private foundations and nongovernmental organizations (such as OXFAM) although UNIFEM and UNFPA were among the top twenty donors (UNIFEM, 2009).

Women, the Environment, and Sustainable Development

In the mid-1980s, the United Nations, environmentalists, and policy makers concerned with the environment called attention to the environmental consequences of traditional development. Their main charge was that development, in both the north and the south, was not sustainable. Basically, **sustainable development** "meets the needs of the present without compromising the ability of future generations to meet their own needs" ("The Brundtland Report" World Commission on Environment and Development, 1987). This section explores women's role in promoting sustainable development, but first, some sustainability basics are in order.

Sustainability Basics

It is a fact that economic development has environmental consequences, many of which may significantly impact human health and survival. The environment is an eco*system* and, like other systems, change in one part affects the others. Take the case of deforestation, the conversion of forested land to nonforested land as a direct result of human activities, a problem faced on almost every continent but especially in developing nations (Greenfacts, 2009). The main causes are industrial logging, clearing of forests for conversion of

"We have learned that when women gain economic autonomy, the health, nutrition and education of other members of the household, especially children, improve at the same time."
Noleen Heyzer, Executive Director of UNIFEM

". . . governments and other actors should promote an active and visible policy of mainstreaming a gender perspective in all policies and programmes, so that, before decisions are taken, an analysis is made of the effects on women and men, respectively."
Beijing Platform for Action, Fourth World Conference on Women

"Think equality to end poverty."
Slogan from Women Environment and Development Organization (WEDO)

"The poor are not living in industrialized countries where the environment is distant— where you have to go out to appreciate it. Our lives depend upon it."
Wangari Maathai of Kenya, winner of the 2004 Nobel Peace Prize (for her contribution to sustainable development, democracy and peace)

land for agriculture or cattle ranching, fuelwood collection, and forest fires aggravated by climate change. Trees hold soil in place and, consequently, deforestation contributes to soil erosion. Agricultural yields are significantly decreased when valuable topsoil washes away. But the animal waste often used for fertilizer is sometimes burned for fuel when there are no trees left. This means that petrochemical fertilizers must be used to increase agricultural yields. However, over time these build up and increase the salinity of the soil. This results in desertification, which means that nothing will grow. Run-off of agricultural fertilizers pollutes waterways, thus reducing the amount of drinkable water and killing fish. Deforestation also contributes to global warming, as trees are major consumers of carbon dioxide, a greenhouse gas. These are only a few of the many effects of deforestation. The bottom line is that shortages of the basics of life, such as food, water, and clean air, may occur when development is not sustainable.

"The elimination of global poverty and the promotion of sustainable development are essential to a fair and equitable world. The current patterns of consumption and production are among the major causes of the degradation of the Earth's resources."
The Network of Women Ministers of the Environment

It might seem obvious that development should be conducted with regard to the future. However, the role of the north in southern development clouds the situation. Development in the global south is often guided and, in many cases, controlled by the global north countries that supply the capital for development. They often strike deals with developing nations that benefit corporations from their country. Corporations based in these northern countries open factories, develop large-scale agriculture or cattle operations, and resource harvesting operations (e.g., forests or petroleum) in developing nations. The corporations benefit from higher profits from lower labor and materials costs, and weaker environmental laws. The environmental costs are borne largely by the citizens of the southern countries, especially the poor, who are disproportionately women and children. Some people consider this **neocolonialism** because even though the former colonial powers granted independence to the colonies, the powers continue to use the former colonies for raw materials, minerals, and cash crops and control the area's resources indirectly through the business corporations and the financial lending institutions they dominate (Reuther, 2008).

You may not understand why the southern countries accept this type of development, but this too is complex. First, you must remember that some of the fault lies at the doorstep of the economic development strategies encouraged by traditional development programs. These programs encourage the replacement of small, localized economies with market-based economies that produce crops, minerals, goods, etc. for export to generate cash. International development programs arrange large loans (sometimes in the millions and billions of dollars) but in return often dictate what type of development is to occur (more on this in Chapter 7). Funding is based on projects' money-making potential, and environmentally sustainable development is often perceived as at odds with this goal. Remember also that economic progress is typically measured in terms of short-run economic goals, such as increases in per capita income and gross national product. Developing nations must demonstrate this type of progress in order to receive more aid. To make matters worse, what has often happened is that the cash generated goes to pay the interest on the loans. A high debt burden results and is aggravated when international markets fluctuate and prices fall. To come up with the money simply to pay the interest on their loans, governments are often forced to sell goods at rock-bottom prices and to exploit fragile natural resources.

Many people point out that the north's contribution to environmental degradation arises out of a consumer lifestyle and heavy fossil fuel use. Consider this evidence of consumption: The United States comprises only 4.6 percent of the world's population but accounts for 33 percent of the world's consumption of fossil fuels (World Resources Institute, 2009). The north's heavy diet of fossil fuels (it consumes as much as 70 percent; IFAD, 2009) and nonrenewable resources (once they're gone, they're gone) contributes to *global* environmental problems. Of particular concern is **global warming,** sometimes called **climate change.** Global warming is largely the result of human activities (in particular the burning of fossil fuels and deforestation) leading to a build-up of greenhouse gases that trap heat near the earth's surface. Global warming has already changed the earth's climate and is expected to lead to more severe weather events (like hurricanes), increased ecosystem stresses, shifting precipitation patterns, increased ranges of infectious diseases, coastal flooding, and other potentially devastating impacts (World Resources Institute, 2009). The people of the south, who are more reliant on rain-fed agriculture and natural resources and lack the technology and infrastructures to adapt, are more vulnerable to these effects of global warming (World Bank, 2009). While in the north global warming may mean adjusting thermostats, observing weather changes, and spending more on flood abatement, in the south it means more hunger from crop failure, more death from natural disaster, and increased workloads (UNDP, 2008c). There is great concern that global warming will worsen the poverty of southern nations.

In contrast, in the developing nations of the south, the damage is done in the quest to meet basic needs, not to sustain a consumer lifestyle. Local environmental problems, such as the degradation of a particular rangeland, soil erosion on farmland, water pollution from pesticides and fertilizers, and the loss of animal and plant habitats, directly affect the poor in the south because they decrease production, income, and food availability thereby increasing poverty (IFAD, 2009). Currently, about half of the world's poorest people earn their livelihoods in ecologically fragile areas. Such people often have little choice for survival other than to contribute to resource depletion and pollution.

Effects of Environmental Degradation on Women

Data is scarce on the impact of environmental degradation and climate change on women in developing countries. However, women are believed to be more vulnerable to their effects because they are the primary cultivators and gatherers of food, water, and fuel for family consumption, and environmental degradation significantly increases the amount of time that must be spent on these tasks (UNIFEM, 2009). Because poor women rely heavily on natural resources, they are among the first to notice and feel the effects of environmental stress (Steady, 1995).

Environmental degradation often increases women's already high workloads. Women must work harder and harder to coax crops from tired soils with limited rainfall. Drought and deforestation mean they must travel farther and farther to collect fuel, fodder, and water (Lambrou & Piana, 2006; World Bank, 2009). Close to 80 percent of rural women in Asia, 60 percent in Africa, and 40 percent in Latin America, are affected by fuelwood shortages (UNDP, 2009b). Contaminated water supplies (from fertilizers/pesticides, mining runoff, industrial pollution, or natural disasters resulting from climate change) also increase women's work because they have to travel farther for safe water and because it is usually women who care for those who are sick with diarrhea and other water-borne diseases. Increased workloads from environmental degradation interfere with the attainment of gender equality because they reduce women's time and opportunities for education, literacy, and income-generating activities (UNDP, 2003; World Bank, 2009). Environmental degradation may also result in the loss of income generation for women. For example, in Sri Lanka, forest destruction has reduced the availability of the nonwood forest products (such as wild fruits, flowers, seeds, and medicinal plants) that women harvested to sell in the market (FAO Sustainable Development Department, 2009).

Women's health is also affected by environmental degradation (Steady, 1995). For example, poor women must often cook with wood, crop residue, and animal dung, often in enclosed spaces, and suffer respiratory diseases, anemia, and cancer as a result (Chant, 2003; World Resources Institute, 1994–95; UNDP, 2009b). Carrying heavy loads of wood, often on their head, for long distances damages the spine and causes problems with childbearing (Dankelman & Davidson, 1988; UNDP, 2009b). As the primary water carriers and managers, they have the most contact with polluted water and are therefore most vulnerable to water-related diseases (UNDP, 2009c). Because it is women who care for the sick, they are more susceptible to contracting diseases from others (Chant, 2003). The longer hours that women work because of environmental degradation also increases their susceptibility to health problems. For example, a study of Sri Lankan women concluded that they suffered from persistent sleep deprivation because of their multiple roles (Lorentzen & Turpin, 1996).

The Role of Women in Sustainable Development

Women of the south play a critical role in sustainable development for two main reasons. First, in many cases they are the main managers of local natural resources. According to the Food and Agriculture Organization, women are often the principal caretakers and guardians of the forest. In developing nations, they are the ones who collect fuel, fodder, and food from trees and other plants. In the south, women are also largely responsible for collecting, supplying, and managing water. A World Bank review of 121 rural water projects found that women's participation was one of the variables most strongly associated with project effectiveness (FAO, 2009b). Also, in most of the developing world, women are the main producers of staple crops (FAO, 2009b).

Unfortunately, acknowledging the role that women play in resource use has sometimes led to blaming them for environmental degradation. However, it is important to realize that southern women often have no choice but to exploit natural resources in order to survive, even though they may have the knowledge to promote sustainability (Dankelman & Davidson, 1988; World Bank, 2009). Furthermore, evidence shows significantly more ecological damage results from development practices such as commercial logging and high-tech agricultural practices. For example, the main contributor to deforestation is commercial harvesting and the clearing of land for large-scale agriculture, not women collecting fuelwood (Brandiotti et al., 1994; Elliot, 1996). Indeed, as Shiva (1996) suggests, development projects have impaired the productivity and renewability of nature by removing land, water, and forests from women's management and control.

A second reason why women are important to sustainable development is that they often possess important knowledge about sustainability in their environments (FAO, 2009f). For instance, they often know which varieties of seed will yield drought- and pest-resistant plants and which seeds do not require petrochemical fertilizers. They often know which trees are easiest to grow and have the most practical value in their culture as sources of food, fuel, and medicine. Women's knowledge of water sources and water quantity and quality during wet and dry seasons makes them important sources of information when water resources are being developed. Some feminist environmentalists have suggested that one barrier to involving women in sustainable development is the dominant ideology that development should be propelled by the domination of nature (Steady, 1995). Current patterns of development and the use and management of natural resources are in line with male values that see the relationship with nature as one of control (Elliot, 1996). Box 6.5 profiles Vandana Shiva, an environmental feminist leader in India who voices similar concerns.

Progress in Acknowledging Women and Sustainable Development

Environmental degradation is now recognized as a critical development problem, and women are increasingly acknowledged as important contributors to sustainable development. This is reflected in a number of official reports and declarations that originated in the work of women's environmental conferences and activism. The 1991 World Women's Congress for a Healthy Planet, organized by the Women's Environment and Development Organization (WEDO), laid the foundation for a number of important documents. For instance, the 1992 UN Conference on Economic Development (UNCED), sometimes called the Rio Earth Summit, yielded a document known as "Agenda 21." It calls for specific agreements by governments to strengthen the role of women in creating and implementing sustainable development

"In the Third World, because women have remained in intimate contact with nature, they often give the early warning signals that something is wrong with the environment."
Vandana Shiva, Indian physicist and ecofeminist

"Women do not want to be mainstreamed into a polluted stream. We want to clean the stream and transform it into a fresh and flowing body. One that moves in a new direction—a world at peace, that respects human rights for all, renders economic justice and provides a sound and healthy environment."
Bella S. Abzug, U.S. Congresswoman and WEDO co-founder

BOX 6.5   *Activist Profile: Vandana Shiva and Ecofeminism*

Vandana Shiva, trained as a theoretical physicist and philosopher, is a well-known Indian environmental feminist and activist. She works closely with the Chipko movement as well as other rural environmental movements in India. She is currently active in the movement for biodiversity conservation. She advocates for indigenous people's rights in the face of globalization and biopiracy (when corporations patent forest products, seeds, medicines discovered by indigenous peoples to make money and then require them to pay to use them). Her 1989 book *Staying Alive: Women, Ecology and Development* is a classic in ecofeminism, a perspective suggesting that the domination of nature and the domination of women are linked. That book, along with later writings, argues that Western science and Western economic development have created both environmental destruction and the marginalization of women through the "death of the feminine principle." This feminine principle is "not exclusively embodied in women but is the principle of activity and creativity in nature, women, and men" (Shiva, 1989, p. 52). Shiva also suggests that women in the global south are uniquely suited to environmental activism: "Because of their location on the fringes, and their role in producing sustenance, women in Third World societies are often able to offer ecological insights that are deeper and richer than the technocratic recipes of international experts or the responses of men in their own societies" (Shiva, 1994, p. 1).

strategies (Steady, 1995). Women and sustainability are also mentioned in the Rio Declaration from the conference, which states "Women have a vital role in environmental management and development. Their full participation is essential to achieving sustainable development." Keep in mind that women's groups worked hard for these statements. The truth is that gender issues were given very little attention in the preparatory committees for UNCED and were only taken up after intense lobbying by women's NGOs and transnational feminist networks (Brandiotti et al., 1994; Elliot, 1996).

The United Nations Fourth World Conference for Women's Platform for Action, adopted unanimously by 189 delegations in Beijing in September 1995, also includes a section on women and the environment. This resulted from feminist environmental advocacy. Three strategic objectives are detailed: (1) involve women actively in environmental decision-making at all levels; (2) integrate gender concerns and perspectives in policies and programs for sustainable development; and (3) strengthen or establish mechanisms at the national, regional, and international levels to assess the impact of development and environmental policies on women. However, some feminist environmentalists were disappointed because the terms "environmental justice" and "environmental racism" were left out. These terms would have clearly reflected the fact that a disproportionate share of the burden of environmental degradation is experienced by the poor and by ethnic and indigenous groups that are low in power.

More recently, the 2008 UN Commission on the Status of Women (also known as Beijing +10) adopted a resolution urging governments to integrate: "a gender perspective in the design, implementation, monitoring and evaluation, and reporting of national environmental policies, strengthen mechanisms and provide adequate resources to ensure women's full and equal participation in decision making at all levels on environmental issues, in particular on strategies related to climate change and the lives of women and girls." Other recent international agreements acknowledging the importance of gender mainstreaming in efforts to address climate change include the UN Framework Convention on Climate Change, the Hyogo Framework for Action, and the UNEP Manifesto on Women and the Environment. Some countries (such as Norway, Paraguay, Slovakia, El Salvador, and Zambia) have also adopted sustainable development policy declarations with specific gender mainstreaming strategies and action plans (IUCN, 2002).

The incorporation of gender into climate change and sustainable development documents is notable but the criticisms levied earlier at gender mainstreaming apply here as well. In particular, we need much more research on the effects of environmental degradation and climate change on women and their role in sustainable development (sex disaggregated data). We also need greater movement from talk to action that truly engenders sustainable development. The formation of the Global Gender and Climate Alliance (GGCA) in 2007 may help in this regard. The alliance of twenty-five UN agencies and international organizations was formed to ensure climate change policies at the global, regional, and national levels are gender responsive. The involvement of WEDO, a well-established and respected advocate for women's empowerment, provides hope for follow-through. The GGCA's 2009 training manual is designed to increase gender mainstreaming capacity and help policy- and decision-makers advance gender empowerment in the context of climate change (GGCA, 2009).

Women and Environmental Activism

It is easy to view women as victims of ecological crisis. However, women often organize to prevent ecological destruction and, in many countries, women's environmental organizations and movements hold the key to sustainable development (Steady, 2005). It is women who are usually the first to become environmental activists in their communities because they are in direct contact with the natural environment and because environmental degradation affects their family's health (Dobash & Seager, 2001). As Vandana Shiva (1988) says, "I know for certain, no matter where you go, that if there is a scarcity of water, women have protested; if there has been an over-felling of trees, women have resisted it." Women's mobilization for the environment demonstrates the courage women have shown in the battle against the growing ecological degradation that surrounds them and against the traditional power structures that subordinate their needs (Sontheimer, 1991). As Elliot (1996) notes, women must not just be seen as victims of environmental degradation but as agents who must participate equally in the solution to these problems.

Women have had trouble gaining leadership positions in mainstream and radical environmental organizations and women's environmental issues have customarily been a low or nonexistent priority (Donash & Seager, 2001). Consequently, much of women's activism for the environment is the result

> "Women give life. We have the capacity to give life and light. We can take up our brooms and sweep the earth."
> *Isabelle Letelier*

of women's nongovernmental organizations (NGOs). Indeed, according to Fisher (1996), NGOs now serve as principal institutional resources for sustainable development in the south, both because of their own activities and because of their impact on governments. NGOs take two general forms: the **grassroots organizations (GROs),** locally based groups that work to develop and improve the community; and **grassroots support organizations (GRSOs),** nationally or regionally based development assistance organizations, usually staffed by professionals, that channel funds to grassroots organizations and help communities other than their own to develop (Fisher, 1996).

"Come arise, my brothers and sisters,

Save this mountain . . .

Come plant new trees, new forests,

Decorate the earth."

Song of the Chipko movement

The **Chipko movement** in the forests of Uttar Pradesh, India is a famous example of a GRO. In 1974, conflict escalated between logging companies supported by the state and the natives who depended upon the forest for food and fuel. The villagers were also aware that previous logging by commercial interests had resulted in erosion and flooding from which they had suffered dearly. The village men were away on the day the contractors arrived to cut 2,500 trees, but the village women took action. They wrapped themselves around the trees (*chipko* means "hug") and refused to move until the contractors left. The contractors did leave, and Indira Gandhi (the Prime Minister of India at the time) issued a fifteen-year ban on commercial logging in the forests of Uttar Pradesh (Dankelman & Davidson, 1988). The Chipko movement has spread throughout the Himalayas in India, Nepal, and Bhutan (Jain, 1991). The Chipko message is spread through sustainable development camps that meet twice a year (Fisher, 1996). This shows how GROs sometimes become GRSOs, which then support grassroots organizations elsewhere. In addition, Chipko-based resistance is now used throughout India to protest environmentally irresponsible road building, mining, and dam projects (Seager, 1993).

The **Greenbelt movement** in Kenya is a well-known example of the role of GRSOs in sustainable development involving women. The movement was begun in 1977 by Wangari Maathai, a Kenyan feminist, environmentalist, and national leader, in conjunction with the National Council of Women of Kenya (see Box 6.6 for an excerpt from Maathai's Nobel Peace Prize acceptance speech). By the 1970s, severe deforestation and soil erosion had created a shortage of fuelwood and food. The movement organized women to plant and manage trees for fuelwood and to guard against erosion. Maathai explains her focus on women by noting that it is women who use wood fuel for cooking and who also till the land (Katumba & Akute, 1993). More than 40 million trees have been planted and the movement now includes some 1,500 tree nurseries with more than 50,000 women participants. The women learn important leadership skills and gain economic power from the income generated by the sale of seedlings. The project also promotes organic farming and organizes workshops and seminars on sustainable development. The movement has been replicated in twelve other African countries including Tanzania, Uganda, Malawi, Lesotho, Ethiopia, and Zimbabwe (Greenbelt Movement, 2009).

Other GRSOs with a sustainability focus include the Secretariat for an Ecologically Sound Philippines, which addresses environmental problems affecting women, farmers, youth, and minorities, and KENGO, a Kenyan

BOX 6.6 *Activist Profile: Wangari Maathai*

A founder of the Greenbelt Movement in Kenya, Maathai was the first woman in East and Central Africa to earn a doctorate degree (her specialty is veterinary anatomy). She is also the first African woman to garner a Nobel Prize. She was a member of the Kenyan Parliament and Assistant Minister, Environment, Natural Resources & Wildlife, Republic of Kenya from 2003 to 2007. She is a leading global advocate for the cancellation of unpayable development loan debt for African nations. In 2005, she was honored by Time Magazine as one of the 100 most influential people in the world, and by Forbes Magazine as one of 100 most powerful women in the world. Here is an excerpt from her Nobel Peace Prize acceptance speech in 2004.

In 1977, when we started the Green Belt Movement, I was partly responding to needs identified by rural women, namely lack of firewood, clean drinking water, balanced diets, shelter and income.

The women we worked with recounted that unlike in the past, they were unable to meet their basic needs. This was due to the degradation of their immediate environment as well as the introduction of commercial farming, which replaced the growing of household food crops. But international trade controlled the price of the exports from these small-scale farmers and a reasonable and just income could not be guaranteed.

Through the Green Belt Movement, thousands of ordinary citizens were mobilized and empowered to take action and effect change. They learned to overcome fear and a sense of helplessness and moved to defend democratic rights.

It is 30 years since we started this work. Activities that devastate the environment and societies continue unabated. Today we are faced with a challenge that calls for a shift in our thinking, so that humanity stops threatening its life-support system. We are called to assist the Earth to heal her wounds and in the process heal our own—indeed, to embrace the whole creation in all its diversity, beauty and wonder. This will happen if we see the need to revive our sense of belonging to a larger family of life, with which we have shared our evolutionary process.

Sources: Greenbelt Movement, 2009; Nobelprize.org, 2004.

indigenous membership organization that promotes grassroots organizational involvement in renewable energy, environmental management and community development. International transnational feminist networks with a sustainability focus exist as well. Some examples include the Women's Environment and Development Organization and the International Women and Environment Network, which formed in 1989 in Managua, Philippines.

Conclusion

This chapter reinforces the importance of a multicultural approach to global women's studies. Western-style development efforts based on a breadwinner husband/homemaker wife model have not translated well to non-Western contexts. Some development efforts have been ineffective because developers failed to contextualize them; they did not consider the unique geographical, economic, sociocultural, environmental, and gendered situation when they intervened. It is also apparent in this chapter that the women's issues in one country may not be the same as the issues in another. For many women in developing nations,

"Women's empowerment is not a stand-alone goal. It is the driver of efforts to eradicate poverty and hunger, achieve universal primary education, reduce child and maternal mortality, and fight against major illnesses like HIV/AIDS and malaria. Women's empowerment is also a driver of sound environmental management and is, finally, essential for ensuring that development aid reaches the poorest through making women a part of national poverty reduction planning and resource allocation."
UNIFEM Progress of the World's Women 2008/2009: Who Answers to Women? (2009)

the issues center on the basic survival needs of themselves and their children. A multicultural view of women's activism was also evident in this chapter. The ways in which women act for gender justice reflects their unique cultures, as you saw with the Greenbelt and Chipko movements. Intersectionality was apparent in the discussion of sustainability because the effects of climate change and environmental degradation depend on gender and whether a person lives in a northern or southern country, and which country and region they live in.

This chapter further illustrates the global women's studies' theme of activism and empowerment. Feminists generally favor the gender and development approach to development because it integrates development, gender equality, and women's empowerment. It also specifically emphasizes that women themselves should set the agenda for women's development. Contrary to the belief that women in southern countries are content with their position, when given opportunity and support, women seek out ways of challenging and changing their situations (Mosse, 1993). Numerous cases show that local women are capable of being the agents of their own development (Moser, 1995).

While development agencies may be timid about promoting women's activism, this hasn't stopped women from organizing themselves. Local women have exerted pressure from the bottom up with some success (Moser, 1993). For instance, in many countries women are entitled to own land, but local customs prevent them from assuming ownership. This, as previously noted, prevents them from obtaining development loan moneys because they have no property for collateral, and it keeps them from receiving extension training. Women's NGOs in Thailand, China, Nicaragua, Malaysia, and Cuba have fought for women's land rights. According to Fisher (1996), over 200,000 grassroots organizations exist in Asia, Africa, and Latin America, over half of them organized by women. Additionally, her research indicates that there are 30,000 to 35,000 grassroots support organizations active in southern nations.

Women's activism is largely responsible for the changes in development programs we've seen so far. Women in local grassroots groups often demand inclusion in development projects. National and international women's organizations like DAWN and WEDO won't let development agencies ignore women. This activism will continue because, to borrow a phrase from Jahan (1995a), development agencies and organizations have only tinkered with the constraints on women's equality. They have yet to come forward with bold policies and adequate budgetary allocations. Networking and political pressure from a variety of women's organizations, which build on what happens at the local level, scale out the impact of women's NGOs at the grassroots level and scale up their impact on policy (Fisher, 1996).

Study Questions

1. What is a developing nation and an industrialized nation? Why are the terms "north" and "south" sometimes used instead? What is the process of development?

2. How does a past history of colonialism affect development efforts?

3. How is the experience of poverty affected by gender? That is, what are conditions like for many women in developing countries?

4. Does modernization necessarily lead to increases in women's status?

5. What are the four common feminist criticisms of traditional development programs?

6. What is the "Women in Development (WID)" approach to development? What are the three types of typical WID projects? What criticisms are made of these? Why is the WID approach criticized?

7. How does the "Gender and Development (GAD)" or empowerment approach differ from WID?

8. What is gender mainstreaming and why have development agencies adopted it? How has this been criticized as an incomplete version of GAD? What is one of the best ways for development agencies to support the empowerment piece of GAD?

9. What is sustainable development? How has it been compromised by neocolonialism and the high consumption rates of the north?

10. What is global warming and climate change? Why is it expected to worsen poverty in developing nations?

11. What are the effects of environmental degradation and climate change on women? Why are women important to sustainable development? What obstacles stand in the way of including women in sustainable development strategies? What progress has been made in including them? How have GROs and GRSOs like the Chipko movement and the Greenbelt movement acted for sustainability?

Discussion Questions and Activities

1. If southern women followed the footsteps of U.S. women, would they gain or lose? What cultural biases or values underlie your answers (adapted from Duley & Diduk, 1986)?

2. Do international development agencies have the right to intervene in the gender arrangements of a country? Is it morally wrong for them not to?

3. Consider this quote from DAWN's Peggy Antrobus: "We must never lose sight of the fact that the women's movement and the environmental movement are primarily *revolutionary* movements. If we give up that political challenge to the dominant paradigm, there is no hope for change." What do you think she means? Do you agree?

4. One theme is this chapter is the importance of including women in development. The UNDP has explicitly included gender in its "Millennium Goals" shown in Box 6.5. Look at the Millennium Development Goals and explain the importance of women to attaining each one.

5. Choose a development agency or NGO and find examples of development projects that reflect the GAD approach.

6. The chapter suggests that women's organizations play a key role in ensuring that women are included in development efforts. Do you think that eventually this may not be necessary? What would have to happen for their efforts to be no longer needed in this way?

7. Why should people in the north care whether their fossil fuel use, consumption patterns, and corporate practices impact people in southern nations? Why should they care about the significant challenges facing southern women? What changes should they make if they care? What are the barriers to their caring and changing?

Action Opportunities

1. Heifer International is a nonprofit organization that combats poverty and restores the environment by providing appropriate livestock, training, and related services to small-scale farmers worldwide. Heifer has a gender equity program called "WiLD" (Women in Livestock Development) that funds projects with women's groups. To help Heifer International help women, raise money so that Heifer can buy an animal for a project (the cost of different types of animals for projects are listed on the organization's website). You can also make an individual donation, or instead of holiday gifts to family and friends, make a donation in their names (Heifer will send a gift acknowledgment for each gift of $10 or more). Heifer International was featured on the Oprah television show in 2002. http://www.heifer.org

2. OXFAM is one of the world's leading nongovernmental, non-UN development organizations and has a GAD focus. Join an OXFAM letter-writing or fundraising campaign. http://www.oxfam.org/getinvolved.htm

3. One focus of this chapter was poverty. You can act locally or globally to reduce poverty. Locally, do a canned food drive for your local food bank, or volunteer at community organizations that serve low-income women. Globally, you can raise money for a NGO that recognizes the role of women's empowerment in alleviating poverty, such as The Hunger Project (http://www.thp.org/home). Or in October you can participate in the "Trick-or-Treat for UNICEF" program. UNICEF provides medicine, immunizations, nutrition, clean water and sanitation, education, and emergency relief to children in 158 countries. By asking people for their spare change for UNICEF, you can probably raise $100 in a few hours. See http://volunteers.unicefusa.org/activities/campus/ for information.

4. The chapter indicated that nations of the north are the biggest contributors to global warming. Do some research to determine how your household can reduce its "carbon footprint," create a "sustainable behavior" plan, and put it into action.

5. Go to the WEDO action site and choose a way to act on behalf of sustainable development and women's empowerment: http://www.wedo.org/category/act

Activist Websites

ACCION http://www.accion.org

Gender Action (promotes gender justice in the World Bank and IMF) http://www.genderaction.org/

AWID (Association for Women in Development)   http://www.awid.org/

The Greenbelt Movement   http://www.greenbeltmovement.org/w.php?id=3

Global Fund for Women   http://www.globalfundforwomen.org/cms/

Women's Voices for the Earth   http://www.womenandenvironment.org

Women's Environment and Development Organization   http://wedo.org

Development with Women for a New Era (DAWN) http://www.dawnnet.org

Informational Websites

United Nations Development Programme Gender Empowerment http://www.undp.org/women/

Dr. Muhammad Yunus's Nobel Peace Prize speech   http://nobelprize .org/nobel_prizes/peace/laureates/2006/yunus-lecture-en.html USAID Women and Development   http://www.usaid.gov/our_work/ cross-cutting_programs/wid/

OXFAM   http://www.oxfam.org.uk/resources/learning/gender/index.html

Who's Who of Women and the Environment   http://www.unep.org/ women_env/whoiswho.asp

The Greenbelt Movement   http://www.greenbeltmovement.org/w.php?id=3

UN Food and Agriculture Organization   http://www.fao.org/gender/ gender.htm

United Nations Fourth World Conference on Women Platform for Action: Women and the Environment   http://www.un.org/womenwatch/daw/ beijing/platform

7

Women and Globalization

Global economic and trade policies are not "gender neutral." The failure of governments and intergovernmental organizations to formulate and evaluate trade policies from a gender perspective has exacerbated women's economic inequity.

—Women's Environment and Development Organization (WEDO)

Globalization has had many effects on women, increasing women's migration for economic reasons as well as their employment in transnational factories. These textile workers in Managua's free trade zone produce goods for foreign-owned companies. Many transnational factories employ primarily women and are exempt from labor, health, and safety laws and provide low wages and poor working conditions.
© CHRISTOPHER PILLITZ/Reportage/Getty Images

This chapter discusses the ways that globalization has reshaped women's lives worldwide. In this chapter you will learn how the growing trend toward a world economy impacts women. By the year 2000, it was increasingly likely that the goods consumed by people in one country were grown, produced, or assembled in a multitude of other countries. Americans dine on fruit grown in Central America and wear clothes assembled in Vietnam or the Dominican Republic. Russians wear American-brand clothes manufactured in developing countries. South Africans smoke American cigarettes and drink Coca-Cola. Europe is dotted with Pizza Huts and Starbucks. An economic crisis in one country affects the economies of other countries. These are examples of globalization. **Economic globalization** refers to the integration and rapid interaction of economies through production, trade, and financial transactions by banks and multinational corporations, with an increased role for the World Bank and the International Monetary Fund, as well as the World Trade Organization (WTO) (Moghadam, 1999). **Cultural globalization** refers to the transnational migration of people, information, and consumer culture.

Critics of globalization are alarmed by the fact that the costs and benefits of globalization are not evenly distributed across nations. For example, more affluent northern governments provide subsidies to their farmers so that they can afford to sell their products for less in the global market. Farmers from southern countries where subsidies are unavailable are unable to compete and become poorer. Northern governments also frequently impose tariffs and import limits on goods from other countries. This keeps "cheaper" goods out of the home market and protects the profits of corporations in the home country. Liberalized trade agreements have eroded workers' rights and unionization. Environmental sustainability is compromised when poor countries, desperate for a piece of the global economic pie, let transnational corporations exploit or pollute their natural resources. Protests at world trade meetings are frequent, large, and often dramatic.

> "In the international women's movement, 'globalization' is a negative word because it has brought great harm to many women—by facilitating the systematic exploitation of women as a source of cheap domestic and migrant labor."
> *Jessica Neuwirth, founder of Equality Now, a human rights organization*

The Effects of Globalization on Women

The economic shifts that come with globalization create some jobs for women in their own countries, particularly low-paid jobs in the fresh export produce sector, the export clothing sector, and the outsourced service sector (UNIFEM, 2009). For example, Columbian women might package flowers for export to northern nations, Honduran women might sew clothing for export to northern nations, and Indian women might work in a service call center answering calls from people in northern nations.

Throughout the book you have read that employment has the potential to increase women's power and status, so you might expect that the creation of jobs for women is a positive benefit of globalization. There is some truth in this. For example, Lim (1990) found that women in developing countries often cite the benefits of employment, such as the ability to earn independent income and spend it on desired purchases; the ability to save for marriage or

FIGURE 7.1   *Effects of Globalization on Women's Labor*

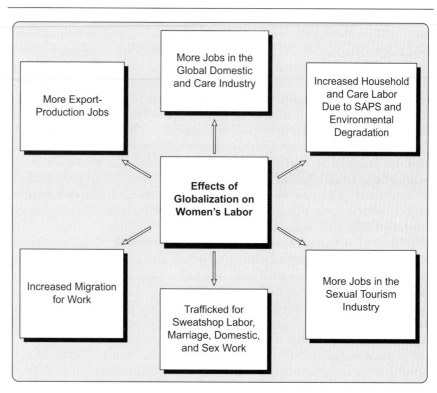

"Entering the labor
market for a woman does
not automatically mean
that she will have greater
control over income;
it may mean, instead,
increased work burdens,
greater drudgery, and
multiple responsibilities
as she is caught up
in a global assembly
line over which she has
little control."
Gita Sen

education, the ability to help support their families and "repay" their debt to
parents; the opportunity to delay marriage and childbearing and to exercise
personal choice of a marriage partner; and the opportunity to enjoy some
personal freedom, the companionship of other women, and to experience
more of what life has to offer, such as a "widening of horizons." Chant (1997),
in a study of Mexican women working in the tourist industry in Puerto
Vallarta, Mexico, also suggests that the ability to earn an independent income
reduces the pressure on women to marry. According to Blumberg (1995), data
from southern women indicates that a woman's absolute and relative income is
tied to increases in self-esteem and confidence, greater leverage in fertility decisions, and greater leverage in other household economic and domestic decisions.

However, whether paid employment benefits women depends on
whether she has control over the money she makes, whether her wages are
sufficient to escape poverty, whether she is still responsible for the majority of
household and care labor, and the work conditions. As will become apparent
later in the chapter, many of the jobs created by globalization for women are
poorly paid with little job security and offer difficult work conditions. Many
of the jobs are domestic and care labor jobs that replicate traditional gendered roles and may allow more affluent women to participate more equally
in labor force while confining migrant women to low-status gendered roles.

Globalization has affected women in other ways, besides creating jobs. One effect of special concern is how economic recessions and crises affect women. The integration of world economies results in a global economic *system* where the economy of one country or region is linked to others. This means that economic recessions and collapses in one country or region trigger economic problems in others. Research indicates that the effects of these economic downturns are disproportionately borne by women and, within a country, disproportionately affect women from certain ethnicities, classes, castes, and regions (Gunewardena & Kingsolver, 2007). For example, according to the World Bank, women in thirty-three developing countries, half of them in sub-Saharan Africa, are more vulnerable to effects from a world economic crisis (World Bank, 2009).

These negative effects of globalization on women first became apparent during the 1980s. During the decade's financial crisis, Southern Hemisphere commodity prices dropped, interest rates rose, and many developing nations could not make payments on their development loans. Debtor countries in Africa and Latin America were forced to ask for more money from the International Monetary Fund (IMF; the UN's international banking agency), and from wealthy northern countries. The new loans were made contingent upon a series of reforms (often called **structural adjustment programs,** or SAPs). The lenders said that without reforms, debt would continue to grow and economic development would be hindered. The reforms emphasized earning foreign exchange to service the debt by making it easier to attract international capital and transnational corporations. Production for domestic use was discouraged and production of cash crops and goods for exports was encouraged. To increase the amount they could pay on their loans, governments were pushed to cut budgets for social services, schools, hospitals, nutrition programs, public transportation, and utilities.[1] Ostensibly to deal with the economic crisis, there was also a shift from policies based on Keynesian economics to policies based on neoliberal capitalism (Mogadam, 2005). In a nutshell, neoliberalism emphasizes free market corporate capitalism, balanced government budgets, and the reduction of government services. This further fueled industrialized nations' emphasis on SAPs, reducing government spending and increasing austerity measures in developing nations.

Economic recessions and SAPs that lead to cuts in wages and social services, and rises in the costs of basic goods and services, have a greater impact on women because women are normally responsible for providing food, water, and health care for family members (Blumberg, 1995; Chang, 2000; Lorentzen & Turpin, 1996; Mosse, 1993). For example, women's unpaid labor increases as government services are cut and women must provide more care for children, elderly parents, and the sick (Chang, 2000; Desai, 2002). Women struggle to feed their families because the prices of household

---

[1] In northern countries like the U.S., recessions and neoliberal economic policies also lead to cuts in services and subsidies, cuts that disproportionately affect poor women and children.

About 1,700 people used to work here and all are unemployed now. Many women were pregnant, many are ill and are left with nothing. It's been three months since the factory closed and we haven't been paid anything, no severance, no social fund payments.
Ana Ruth Cerna, El Salvador

Moving to a new country exposes women to new ideas and social norms that can promote their rights and enable them to participate more fully in society.
UNFPA, State of the World Population: Women's Migration 2006

Human trafficking is a crime against humanity. It involves an act of recruiting, transporting, transferring, harbouring or receiving a person through a use of force, coercion or other means, for the purpose of exploiting them.
United Nations Office on Drugs and Crime (UNODC)

goods, especially food, rise as government subsidies are removed to save the government money. Food prices also rise from the globalization of the food industry. Food is less available because of reduced subsistence farming (for family consumption) as farmland is converted to commercial use. Women have less money due to high rates of unemployment and inflation.

Economic recessions also mean that in their desperation for cash, southern countries compromise environmental sustainability. To look attractive as sites for transnational factories (needed for jobs and cash), governments often relax environmental laws. As discussed in Chapter 6, this largely impacts women who must travel farther for water and have less access to arable land to grow food for their families. Women in poor, urban neighborhoods find their communities polluted by toxic chemical wastes and human wastes (Desai, 2002). In short, the costs of economic adjustment and change fall heavily on the shoulders of women already burdened by poverty.

Although globalization sometimes increases women's paid employment, which can benefit women, many of the jobs created for women by globalization are not secure jobs—their availability depends on consumption patterns in northern countries and whether their country provides the most favorable conditions for corporate profit. This means that if demand for consumer products falls in northern countries or corporations can relocate to another country where labor regulation is weaker, the jobs disappear. In times of economic downturns and transitions, women are often the first to lose their jobs. This is especially true in developing nations where women tend to work in the informal sector, or for transnational corporations in factories or services. In such places, economic crisis impacts female unemployment rates more than male unemployment rates. The effects of unemployment are greater because these employment sectors do not offer unemployment benefits and government safety nets are weak (Emmet, 2009; ILO, 2009). Women workers in export manufacturing, garments, electronics, and services (women constitute around 60 to 80 percent of this workforce in developing countries), are especially hard-hit as global demand falls (Emmett, 2009).

Globalization has also led to dramatic increases in women's migration to other countries for work, a topic covered at length later in this chapter. When women are unable to sustain their families, they may have no viable option but to leave their families and migrate for work (Chang, 2000). Migration can benefit women and their families by reducing their poverty. It can allow women to escape patriarchal societies and abusive marriages. It can also promote gender role change—women abroad sometimes play a role in promoting gender equality back home (UNFPA, 2006). However, in many cases migrant women end up in vulnerable types of employment marked by low pay and poor working conditions, and prejudice against migrants prevents their full and equal participation in the host country. Women seeking migration to better their lives are also subject to human traffickers who trick and coerce them into situations of forced labor and sexual exploitation in a form of modern-day slavery.

Women's Work in the Transnational Factory

In the global economy, knowledge-intensive aspects of the production process often remain in Western countries but labor-intensive activities are subcontracted to factories in developing countries where cheap female labor is abundant (Naples, 2002; Stearns, 1998). The United States was the first to relocate labor-intensive factory work such as garment-making and production of footwear and electronics to lower-wage sites in the Caribbean, East Asia, and Latin America (United Nations, 1999). **Free trade zones (FTZs), or export processing zones (EPZs),** were established in many cash-hungry southern nations to attract transnational factories. The ILO defines EPZs as "industrial zones with special incentives set up to attract foreign investors, in which imported materials undergo some degree of processing before being re-exported" but "imported material" also includes electronic data entry facilities and call centers (ILO, 2007c). In these zones, companies are generally exempt from labor, health and safety, and environmental laws and pay few, if any, taxes. According to the ILO, as of 2006, there were an estimated 3,500 EPZs in 130 countries, up from 93 countries and 843 EPZs in 1997 (Boyenge, 2007).

As neoliberalism gained hold, women in developing nations came to be viewed as sources of cheap labor that would lower the costs of production and consequently increase profits. Women dominate employment in most EPZs and are important part of **global supply chains** where different pieces of production are spread across geographic locations (UNIFEM, 2009). For example, many EPZ factories in Central America (which are often called *maquiladoras* or *maquilas*) assemble clothing; other parts of production are done elsewhere. Women constitute over 75 percent of the workers in EPZs in Cape Verde, El Salvador, Honduras, Nicaragua, Jamaica, Bangladesh, and Sri Lanka (Boyenge, 2007; UNIFEM, 2009). For instance, in Honduras, there are twenty-four EPZs employing over 350,000 people, 75 percent of them women. In Bangladesh, the export garment industry provides 75 percent of the country's foreign exchange and employs over 2 million workers, 85 percent of them impoverished women (Jaffer, 2009). In some cases, women migrate in order to work in EPZs in other countries. For example, Jordan employs tens of thousands of "guest" workers for apparel factories, mainly from Bangladesh and China (Greenhouse & Barbaro, 2006).

Women are the preferred labor supply because they can be hired for lower pay with no benefits, job guarantees, or social security (UNIFEM, 2009). In developing countries, they are treated by transnational corporations as a flexible, low-paid labor force that can be drawn in or dropped as needed (UNIFEM, 2009). Women's manual dexterity and docility (conditioned by culture), their desperation for work and lack of awareness about their rights, and their seemingly limitless supply have made them the choice factory workers of transnational corporations worldwide. Some theorists argue that women's low-wage labor for transnational corporations fuels global

"In today's global economy, the clothes we wear will have been sewed by workers across an ocean and passed from one business to another before being sold for a tidy profit by a retailer whose name we all know. Companies throughout the supply chain bear a responsibility and have the power to ensure that workers are treated fairly."
Clean Clothes Campaign

"I want my job and value it, because even though it tears me apart and exploits me, with my job I am able to feed my kids."
Nicaraguan Maquila Worker

BOX 7.1   *Conditions at the Meitai Plastics and Electronics Factory*

"We feel like we are serving prison sentences."

—Meitai factory worker making Micorsoft keyboards

The Taiwanese-owned Meitai Plastics & Electronics Factory in Dongguang City in Guangdong, China employs two thousand workers (75 percent women aged 18–25) and produces computer equipment for U.S. companies Dell, Lenovo, Microsoft, and IBM. Workers are prohibited from talking, listening to music, raising their heads, and putting their hands in their pockets. The young workers sit on hard wooden stools twelve hours a day, seven days a week as 500 computer keyboards an hour move down the assembly line (one every 7.2 seconds). Workers are allowed just 1.1 seconds to snap each key into place, repeating the same operation 3,250 times an hour, 35,750 times a day, 250,250 times a week and over one million times a month. Workers are fined for being one minute late, for not trimming their fingernails—which could impede the work, and for stepping on the grass. Workers are searched on the way in and out of the factory. Workers who hand out flyers or discuss factory conditions with outsiders are fired. Employees are required to live on-site in crowded dorms (10–12 workers share an 11 × 20 room) and have only a bucket with which to wash. On average they work 74 hours a week with only two days off a month. They are locked into the compound four days a week. Although they earn 76 cents an hour, this drops to 41 cents an hour after room and board are paid. These wages are below the Chinese minimum wage and are not a living wage.

Source: The National Labor Committee's (2009b) report "High Tech Misery in China."

production and is at the heart of corporate profits (Fuentes & Ehrenreich, 1983; Salzinger, 2003).

Women's Sweatshop Labor

"We work in the garment factory from 8 am to 10 pm. We do not get our salaries on time and we are not paid for overtime. We work in such crowded places that we cannot even breathe freely."
Takia, a garment worker in Bangladesh who works for a South Korean company

Unfortunately, many factories in EPZs are little more than **sweatshops**— businesses that do not provide a living wage, require excessively long work hours, and provide poor working conditions with many health and safety hazards. In sweatshops, mistreatment of women workers (such as verbal, physical, and sexual harassment) is common and those who speak out, organize, or attempt to unionize for better conditions are quickly shut down. In some sweatshops, such as those in the United States, Turkey, and Jordan, the workers are primarily impoverished migrant women (some illegal migrants) who tolerate abuses because their families are dependent on their meager income, because they fear immigration authorities, or because they are indentured to recruiters. The odds are good that the majority of your clothes, shoes, toys, and electronics were created with women's sweatshop labor in countries such as Bangladesh, Burma, China, the Dominican Republic, Haiti, Honduras, Indonesia, Guatemala, Malaysia, Mexico, Nicaragua, the Philippines, and Vietnam. See Box 7.1 for a report on a factory in a Chinese EPZ.

It is common for proponents of EPZs to say that these jobs benefit women by reducing their poverty and that the women are better off than they would be without the jobs. However, in most cases the wages are insufficient to escape poverty. Take for example, the Salvadoran women working for the Korean-owned Youngone maquila in Olocuilta, La Paz, El Salvador who sew jackets for the American company North Face. They are paid 94 cents for every $165 jacket and during the busy season work up to 91 hours a week. Due to soaring food costs they cannot afford milk and basic necessities for their children. It is estimated that if North Face required that the subcontractors pay the women $1.49 an hour (enough to make a difference in their standard of living), it would increase the direct labor costs to produce the jacket by only 68 cents, just four-tenths of 1 percent of the retail price of the jacket (National Labor Committee, 2008). Similarly, at the Korean-owned Nicotex maquila in Mixco, Guatamala, women sew garments for American apparel companies like Lane Bryant and JC Penney. The mostly indigenous women workers in their mid-twenties work a 64 to 69 hour work week. According to the U.S. State Department and National Labor Committee investigations, wages in Guatemalan EPZs are not enough to meet basic subsistence needs (National Labor Committee, 2008). In Nicaragua, the average worker in an EPZ makes 300 cordobas a month but needs 4,800 cordobas for groceries (ICFTU, 2006).

The fact that there are few better-paid jobs available for women is often used to rationalize their exploitation but this is a poor excuse for taking advantage of them—it is hardly a choice when these are the only wage-earning jobs available to them. Also, as mentioned earlier, EPZ jobs offer insecure employment. In some regions, such as the Caribbean, where export-production has been the major source of women's wage employment, women's unemployment has increased dramatically as corporations relocate to Asia where profit margins are greater (Werner & Blair, 2009).

Activism to Stop Sweatshop Labor

Although it is sometimes said that owners of transnational factories operating in EPZs prefer female workers because they are cheap and docile, they regularly attempt to organize themselves to advocate for a living wage, reasonable work hours, and safe working conditions. As Louie (2001) put it, they transform themselves from sweatshop workers to sweatshop warriors. Strikes and efforts to organize for better work conditions and pay are common, but are often swiftly and harshly punished, and collective bargaining agreements remain rare in EPZs (ICFTU, 2006). Organizers are fired, threatened with dismissal, intimidated in a variety of ways, and blacklisted such that they can't find work elsewhere. Strikes are shut down quickly, often with police help. When unions are formed, companies often close factories and move to friendlier locations. Governments often participate in the suppression of labor organizing because of competition with other economically struggling countries for foreign investment. They feel they need the jobs and foreign currency to pay off loans and know that transnational corporations will move their operations to other countries that do not enforce labor regulations.

Rubina Jameel, President of the Working Women's Organisation (WWO) in Pakistan, reported that women trade union activists face accusations of "bringing dishonour" on their families if they try to organize women workers.

Establishing a set of global norms and standards by which all corporations must abide by is one key to stopping corporate abuse of women's rights, livelihoods, and the environment (WEDO, 2009). Sweatshops are inconsistent with workers' human rights as defined by the ILO, and ILO conventions on labor human rights are routinely violated in many EPZs. For example, Conventions 87 and 98 support the right of employees to organize for better wages and work conditions yet many businesses operating in EPZs suppress and punish employee organizing and refuse to engage in collective bargaining. Conventions 29 and 105 require the elimination of all work that is forced or bonded or has elements of servitude or slavery. In EPZs, workers are routinely forced to work more excessively long hours without time off and are fired if they do not comply. They are sometimes denied wages due them. Forced confinement occurs in some sweatshops—workers are not allowed to leave the locked premises until supervisors release them. Migrant EPZ workers are sometimes trafficked, tricked, or coerced into migration and exploited through debt bondage. The majority of countries with EPZs that routinely violate these rights have ratified all or most of these conventions. International free trade agreements such as GATT (General Agreement on Tariffs and Trade), NAFTA (North American Free Trade Agreement), and CAFTA (Central American Free Trade Agreement) have aggravated poor labor conditions by making it easier for corporations to ask for and receive exemptions from laws that ostensibly interfere with free trade.

Ideally, international trade agreements would require compliance with International Labour Organization core labor rights conventions and the Universal Declaration of Human Rights. This would ensure a level playing field such that companies and countries honoring worker's rights will not be at a competitive disadvantage. Some have also suggested that the World Trade Organization play a role in enforcement of these international labor standards in EPZs (Moran, 2002; WEDO, 2009). Several bills have been introduced in the U.S. Congress to encourage compliance with ILO standards. "The Decent Working Conditions and Fair Competition Act" would have prohibited the import, export, and sale of goods made with sweatshop labor (it was supported by then-Senators Hillary Clinton and Barack Obama). The legislation would have required the Federal Trade Commission to investigate complaints and fine offenders and would have used the Homeland Security department for some aspects of enforcement. So far this bill and similar ones have died in committee and have not come up for a vote.

Nongovernmental organizations have played a key role in documenting abuses, organizing workers, mobilizing shareholders and consumers to exert pressure on corporations to clean up their act, and creating standards of conduct for corporations. For example, the Clean Clothes Campaign based in the Netherlands offers guidelines on what companies can do to better assess, implement, and verify compliance with labor standards in their supply chains, and eliminate abuses where and when they arise. The Maquila Solidarity Network (MSN) is a labor and women's rights organization that supports the efforts of workers in global supply chains to win improved wages and working conditions and a better quality of life. They work with women's and labor rights organizations in Mexico, Central America and Asia, through corporate campaigning and engagement, networking and coalition building, and policy advocacy. Some NGOs, like Green America, encourage northern consumers to avoid buying sweatshop-made items, and to push local businesses (including campus stores) and sports teams, to avoid sweatshop products. They also recommend that consumers write their favorite retailers and ask questions about labor practices in their supply chains. Those owning stocks are asked to vote in support of shareholder resolutions requiring the company to improve its labor policies.

Activist groups are sometimes successful in exacting change from corporations. Many corporations have adopted their own corporate social responsibility arrangements in response to activism but evidence is mixed on their success (UNIFEM, 2009). For example, in the 1990s, a number of NGO investigations revealed sweatshop conditions and labor rights violations in Nike's supply chain, where women comprise 80 to 90 percent of workers. Following activism, including consumer boycotts, Nike became the first in its industry to disclose its subcontracted factory locations. It also instituted a Code of Conduct to address minimum wages, freedom of association, and gender and maternity discrimination, and employed independent monitors to assess code compliance (WEDO, 2007). Although Nike has made progress, problems remain at many Nike subcontractors and in 2008, WEDO filed a complaint with the UN Global Compact Office (Nike had signed a trade compact monitored by this office that vows responsible business practices). Independent regulation and monitoring are favored by most activist organizations because monitors hired by the factories or corporations typically conduct limited investigations, often not even interviewing the workers.

Lawsuits are another avenue for change but many women lack the legal literacy, legal systems are not yet developed to support these types of complaints, and lawsuits require money and legal expertise often unavailable to affected women. However, in a victory for sweatshop activists, in 2004 the last of three lawsuits brought in 1999 by Sweatshop Watch, Global Exchange, Asian Law Caucus, Unite, and Saipan garment workers against dozens of U.S. big-name retailers and Saipan garment factories was settled (Bas, Benjamin, & Chang, 2004). The suits alleged violations of U.S. labor laws and international human rights standards in Saipan, an island in the U.S. Commonwealth of the Northern Mariana Islands. This island is home to a $1 billion garment industry, employing more than 10,000 workers, almost all young women from China, the Philippines, Thailand, Vietnam, and Bangladesh. Recruited with promises of high pay and quality work in the United States, the workers labored in sweatshop conditions to repay recruitment fees of up to $7,000. The retailers were also charged with misleading advertising by using the "Made in the U.S.A" label and promoting their goods as sweatshop-free. The companies agreed to improve work conditions, to pay $20 million in back wages (the largest award to date in an international human rights case), and to create a monitoring system to prevent labor abuses in Saipan factories

"Solidarity among workers should cross the border as easily as companies move production."
Mary Tong, Director for the Support Committee for Maquiladora Workers

"Jobs, Yes . . . but with Dignity!"
Campaign Slogan of the Network

The growth of ethical consumption, coupled with the campaigns of trade unions and NGOs for workers' rights, is obliging more companies to take account of the labour conditions throughout their supply chains.
UNIFEM, Progress of the World's Women 2008/2009

BOX 7.2   *Activist Profile: Chie Abad*

Upon graduation from high school in the Philippines, Carmencita "Chie" Abad, seeking a better life, responded to advertising that promised a good job in the United States in return for a recruitment fee. The job turned out to be working in a garment factory on the island of Saipan, in the U.S. Commonwealth of the Northern Mariana Islands. For six years Chie worked for the Sako factory, which produced clothing for U.S. retailers like the GAP. During that time, she endured sweatshop conditions, frequently working fourteen-hour shifts in dangerous conditions in order to meet unrealistic production quotas. Eventually, Chie attempted to organize Saipan's first garment worker union. Factory management intimidated employees and threatened to shut down the plant if they unionized; the union-certifying election was lost by five votes.

Because of her efforts, management refused to renew Chie's work contract. To prevent losing her job, she filed a complaint with the U.S. Equal Employment Opportunity Commission. In 1998 the EEOC prohibited Sako from firing Chie while they investigated, but in 1999, she decided to quit her job as an advocate for the workers in Saipan and other sweatshop seamstresses around the world. Chie was instrumental in the successful lawsuit brought against the Saipan factories and U.S. retailers. Chie now works with the Global Exchange, an NGO that advocates for a "people centered globalization that values the rights of workers and the health of the planet; that prioritizes international collaboration as central to ensuring peace; and that aims to create a local, green economy designed to embrace the diversity of our communities."

Source: Global Exchange, 2009.

(Bas et al., 2004; Collier & Strasburg, 2002). Increased public attention to sweatshops on Saipan has also led to greater enforcement of labor laws by the U.S. government (Bas et al., 2004). Box 7.2 profiles Chie Abad, a sweatshop warrior who worked in a Saipan factory for six years and assisted with the suit.

The Global Economy and Women's Migration

Women from Bangladesh, Indonesia, the Philippines, and Sri Lanka migrate to work in Bahrain, Oman, Kuwait, Saudi Arabia, Hong Kong, Malaysia, and Singapore. Women from Russia, Romania, Bulgaria, and Albania migrate to work in Scandinavian countries, Germany, France, Spain, Portugal, and England. South and Central American and Southeast Asian women migrate to the United States. African women migrate to Europe. France, for example, receives many female migrants from Morocco, Tunisia, and Algeria while Italy receives many from Ethiopia, Eritrea, and Cape Verde (Hochschild, 2002). Filipino women work in 160 different countries (Parrenas, 2008).

It is estimated that worldwide, there are over 47 million legal and illegal women migrants (UNFPA, 2006). Scholars now speak of the "feminization of migration" because in many countries, female immigrants outnumber male immigrants (UNFPA, 2006). This section focuses on how globalization makes economic survival difficult in some countries and how this leads poor women to migrate to more affluent countries where there is a strong demand for low-wage workers.[2] Many leave children behind in the care of family members. They typically send anywhere from half to nearly all of what they earn home to their families (**remittances**) and send a higher proportion of their earnings home than men do (Ehrenreich & Hochschild, 2002; UNDP, 2006). Governments in some countries, such as Sri Lanka, Vietnam, and the Philippines, encourage women to migrate because the money sent home contributes to the economy and reduces poverty (Chang, 2000; Ehrenreich & Hochschild, 2002; Parrenas, 2008). For example, the largest sources of foreign currency in the Philippines are remittances sent home from migrant women (Parrenas, 2008).

The work that women migrants do in the global economy is often a reflection of traditional gender roles and migrant women tend to work in traditionally "female" occupations marked by low wages and poor working conditions (UNFPA, 2006). They are the janitors, maids, and nannies, "hostesses" and "entertainers" (sex workers), nurses, and home health workers. Ironically, globalization and migration push women into wage labor that could conceivably result in economic independence and increased status, but at the same time, the type of work they tend to do reaffirms traditional gender roles (Parrenas, 2008). Women also sometimes migrate to become brides where there are shortages of women due to son preference or migration, or shortages of women that will accept traditional gender-role arrangements.

Women migrants are among the most vulnerable to human rights abuses (UNFPA, 2006). Migrant recruitment agencies often enable poor women to migrate to become domestic or care laborers, factory workers, or brides but leave them in a position of indenture (**debt bondage**) as they work to pay off the fees (Parrenas, 2008). Criminal networks not only traffic drugs and guns; they use deception, coercion and violence to traffic women for prostitution, domestic work, and sweatshop labor in what the United Nations calls the "dark underside" of globalization (UNFPA, 2006). During transit, women and girl migrants are often at risk for sexual harassment and abuse (UNFPA, 2006). Once they arrive, they often face multiple discriminations due to gender, race, class, and religion (UNFPA, 2006). Language, cultural barriers, and economic desperation interfere with migrant working women asserting their rights as women and workers and accessing services in cases of abuse. Undocumented workers without legal work papers and those who live where they work (like many nannies and domestics) are more likely to be exploited and to be physically or sexually abused since they face deportation or homelessness if they go to authorities.

> "We see migration as the result of structural adjustment programs—we give up our lands, our products, and finally people."
> *Eileen Fernandez of Malaysia, speaking at the Fourth World Women's Conference NGO Forum on Women*

> "While migration can be an empowering experience for millions of people worldwide, when it 'goes bad,' migrants can find themselves trapped in situations of extreme exploitation and abuse. Trafficked women and domestic workers are two groups that are particularly susceptible to major human rights violations and slave-like conditions."
> *UNFPA, State of the World Population: Women's Migration 2006*

---

[2] Women also migrate to escape war, violence, and persecution (there are approximately 6 million women refugees). See http://www.unhcr.org/pages/49c3646c1d9.html.

Migrating for Domestic and Care Work

The globalization of domestic and care work is exemplified by the migration of southern women to northern nations. Domestic service and care work is one of the largest fields of employment for female migrants; there are literally millions of migrant women domestic and care workers. Approximately 1.5 million women domestic workers, primarily from Indonesia, Sri Lanka, and the Philippines, work in Saudi Arabia alone (Human Rights Watch, 2008; UNFPA, 2006). Domestic and care work is neither socially nor intellectually fulfilling but is chosen for economic reasons (Parrenas, 2001).

The increased demand for these workers in affluent countries is partly due to the entry of educated women in northern countries into the workforce (UNFPA, 2006). As middle- and upper-class women enter the professional workforce and have less time to devote to household labor, they seek help with the traditional household duties typically done by women. For the most part, men have not provided this help. Indeed, research indicates that women's entry into the workforce has barely impacted the amount of child care and household labor performed by men (Ehrenreich & Hochschild, 2002; UNFPA, 2006). Not only have men not taken up much of the "slack," but in many industrialized nations like the United States, governments do not provide or subsidize child care, after-school care, or paid maternity and family leave, thus leaving employed women few choices but to turn to migrant domestics. Worldwide, migrant domestics are also common in the homes of the most affluent families with stay-at-home wives and mothers (Anderson, 2002). Many, if not most, migrant women domestics have children and migrate as a means to support them. They express guilt and remorse about leaving their own homes and children to care for the households and children of others (Hochschild, 2002). Box 7.3 describes the painful predicament experienced by many migrant mothers who work as nannies.

While many domestic workers enjoy decent work conditions, others endure a range of abuses including nonpayment of salaries, forced confinement, food deprivation, excessive workload, and instances of severe psychological, physical, and sexual abuse (Human Rights Watch, 2006, 2008). Abuses have been documented in many countries such as Lebanon, Singapore, Kuwait, Malaysia, Hong Kong, and Saudi Arabia (Human Rights Watch 2006; UNFPA, 2006). As migrants from other countries, they are often viewed as "lesser" by prejudiced employers who do not treat them as fully human. Because domestic work is done in the home, unfair work conditions are not visible and subject to regulation (UNFPA, 2006). Most abuses occur in countries like Kuwait, Saudi Arabia, and United Arab Emirates where domestic workers are not protected under law. Practices include taking women's passports upon arrival and law enforcement agencies' refusal to investigate or prosecute abuses, resulting in the return of domestic workers to their employers (UNFPA, 2006; Human Rights Watch, 2007a). Some women and girls are trafficked into domestic service (VOA News, 2009).

"It is hard to make a living back home. Working here and sending money home to my family is the only way I can take care of my family."
Dominique, New York City nanny from Trinidad

"The lifestyles of the First World are made possible by a global transfer of the services associated with a wife's traditional role—childcare, homemaking, and sex—from poor countries to rich ones."
Barbara Ehrenreich and Arlie Hochschild

BOX 7.3   *Rosemarie Samiego: Filipino Nanny Working in Italy*

"When the girl I take care of calls her mother 'Mama' my heart jumps all the time because my children also call me 'Mama.' I feel the gap caused by our physical separation especially in the morning when I pack lunch because that's what I used to do for my children. . . . I begin thinking that at this hour I should be taking care of my very own children and not someone else's, someone who is not related to me in any way, shape, or form. . . .

The work I do here is done for my family but the problem is that they are not close to me but far away in the Philippines. . . . If I had wings, I would fly home to my children. Just for a moment, to see my children and take care of their needs, help them, then fly back over here to continue my work."

Source: Parrenas, 2002.

In addition to human rights organizations like Human Rights Watch, a number of migrant workers' organizations work to expose abuses, fight for workers' rights, and assist victims of abuse. These include the British organization Kalayaan, RESPECT in Costa Rica, the Caribbean Female Household Workers Federation, and in the United States, the Break the Chain Campaign for Migrant Domestic Worker Rights. Activists and the UN would like to see more labor laws and codes protecting migrant domestics' rights, criminal laws and penalties for abuses, accessible complaint mechanisms, and better resources for identifying and assisting victims. They also call upon the "labor-sending" countries to use diplomacy to improve conditions and to improve services at embassies and consular offices that would enable workers to leave abusive situations (Human Rights Watch, 2006). The UN calls upon affected countries to ratify and enforce the ILO's International Convention on the Rights of All Migrant Workers and their Families.

Migrating to Marry

Another example of women migrating due to poverty is the phenomenon of **mail-order and Internet brides.** Women in poor economic circumstances are marketed as brides to American, European, and Asian men seeking traditional marriages and to Asian men who seek wives due to "bride deficits" caused by migration or son preference. For example, prenatal sex-selection and infanticide in some areas of India have led to a shortage of women. Villagers often turn to brokers to arrange for marriages between Indian men and Nepalese and Bangladeshi girls and women (UNFPA, 2006). Women are willing to migrate for marriage because they have few economic options. Sometimes they are under the impression that men in other countries will make better husbands and are less traditional than men in their country.

"The Russian woman has not been exposed to the world of rampant feminism that asserts its rights in America. She is the weaker gender and knows it."
Chance for Love Matchmaking Service Website

Some are forced; girls as young as age 13 (mainly from Asia and Eastern Europe) are trafficked as mail-order brides (UNICEF, 2009). In most cases these girls and women are powerless and isolated and at risk of violence.

There are thousands of commercial organizations that arrange introductions and broker marriages with foreign men. By the 1990s, international marriage agencies marketing women from the Philippines, India, Thailand, Eastern Europe, and Russia were established throughout Europe, the United States, Japan, and Australia. For a fee, potential customers can peruse hundreds of Internet mail-order bride sites and catalogues complete with photos and brief biographies. Some companies have package tours to countries like Russia and the Philippines to meet prospective brides. No firm statistics exist on the practice. However, in the United States alone, it is estimated that more than 500 international matchmaking services operate, annually arranging 9,500 to 14,000 marriages between American men and foreign women mostly from the Philippines and former Soviet Union (Lindee, 2007).

There is some evidence that mail-order and Internet wives are more susceptible to domestic violence but governments typically do not collect specific data on violence against this group of women (Lindee, 2007; Sassen, 2002). Imbalances in power, cultural differences, linguistic barriers, mail-order brides' lack of social and support networks, and the marketing of mail-order brides as submissive and deferential, likely increase risk (Lindee, 2007; UNFPA, 2006). In one famous U.S. case, Indle King, a 39-year-old man with a history of domestic violence murdered his wife of two years, Anastasia, a 20-year-old mail-order bride from Kyrgystan. It was later discovered that Indle, while planning Anastasia's murder, was already seeking another mail-order wife. Some also argue that international marriage brokers participate in human trafficking (Barry, 1995; Lindee, 2007). Not only do they generally treat women as commodities to be "sold" to men, but some international marriage brokers are little more than covers for sexual tourism operations and, in extreme cases, covers for prostitution rings that traffic recently immigrated mail-order brides (Lindee, 2007).

The Tahirih Justice Center (U.S.) protects immigrant girls and women from gender-based violence. The organization has assisted over 5,000 women and children. The organization is named for Tahirih, a poet and theologian who fought for women's rights in 19th-century Persia.

Nongovernmental women's organizations act to protect mail-order and Internet brides from abuse. For example, in the United States, the Tahirih Justice Center played a key role in getting the U.S. Congress to draft and pass the International Marriage Broker Regulation Act of 2005. Signed into law by President G.W. Bush in 2006, the act requires international marriage brokers to obtain criminal histories on their male clients, including any records from the National Sex Offender Public Registry, and provide a report to foreign women in their native language. It also requires that prospective brides receive an information packet with domestic violence resources. Gabriela, a Philippine-American women's organization, the Coalition Against Trafficking in Women, and the Global Alliance Against Trafficking in Women (GATW), also work on this issue. Domestic violence shelters in regions where mail-order and Internet brides are more common are also adapting their services to help those who experience domestic violence.

Women and Girls' Labor in the Global Sex Trade

Women have engaged in sex work for centuries but globalization has shaped the economics and practices of sex work in some remarkable ways.

Sexual Tourism

Easy global travel has changed the global sexual landscape, and travel for sexual purposes has grown with globalization. Sex work connected to tourism is known as **sexual tourism**. Sexual tourism is another effect of globalization and is made possible by a globalized system of communication and transportation (Cabezas, 2002). It arises out of a globalized economy that makes sex work one of the only ways for some women to earn a living wage and is fed by men from industrialized nations who draw on a racialized ideology where foreign females are thought be more submissive and available than women in their own countries (Enloe, 1989). Sexual tourism is based on inequalities of power based on race, gender, class, and nationality (Brennan, 2004). Governments that need the money brought by international tourism are willing to encourage, or at least ignore, sexual tourism; it is their way of getting their piece of the global economic pie. Sexual tourism is yet another example of how the effects of globalization are not gender-neutral.

"Far too many men, in Sweden and the rest of the world, see women as objects, as something that can be bought and sold. . . . A woman's body is not the same as a glass of brandy or an ice cream after a good dinner." *Swedish Deputy Prime Minister Margareta Winberg*

Sexual tourists are the hundreds of thousands of men who travel to other countries for sex holidays. Sex tourists come primarily from Australia, Canada, France, Germany, Japan, Kuwait, New Zealand, Norway, Qatar, Saudi Arabia, Sweden, the United Kingdom, and the United States (Seager, 1997). Their main destinations are Brazil, Cambodia, Costa Rica, Cuba, the Dominican Republic, India, Indonesia, Hungary, Kenya, Morocco, the Philippines, and Thailand. Thailand is one of the largest markets. Driven mostly by Australian, European, and American tourists, the number of prostitutes in Thailand ranges from 800,000 to 2 million, 20 percent of whom are 18 or younger (Guzder, 2009).

The nature of sex work in the global tourism industry varies based on region. For example, research in Sousa, Dominican Republic suggests that some women perceive sex work as a possible stepping-stone to marriage to a foreigner and migration to a better life in another country (Brennan, 2002, 2004; Cabezas, 2002). Some Dominican sex workers attempt to persuade European tourists to send them money or marry them. They keep in touch with clients through global communications such as telephones, faxes, wire transfers, and the Internet (Brennan, 2002, 2004; Cabezas, 2002). In contrast, in the so-called "sexual Disneyland" of Bangkok, Thailand, sexual tourists can find sexual services of almost any sort, including "freak shows" where women's bodies are reduced to grotesque objects exploited for tourists' entertainment, and opportunities for sex with children (Guzder, 2009). See Box 7.4 for the case of Tiew, a worker in the Thai sexual tourism industry. Children are also a part of some sexual tourism operations. For example, Mexico's social service agency reports that there are more than 16,000 children engaged in prostitution, with tourist destinations being among those areas with the highest number (UNICEF, 2009). Some sex workers in the sex tourism industry are trafficked from other countries.

The U.S.-based NGO Equality Now has successfully led several campaigns to shut down sexual tour companies operating in the United States.

BOX 7.4   *Tiew's Work in Thailand's Sex Tourism Industry*

Tiew was born in a city in Northeast Thailand. Tiew never learned to read or write because she had to help her family in the rice fields. In her early 20s, Tiew married and gave birth to a daughter. Shortly afterwards, her husband died. Looking for work, she migrated to Bangkok and eventually decided to try the life of a showgirl. "I thought it would be exciting and, if nothing else, at least help us survive," says Tiew. Tiew became part of a "Ping-Pong Show," where for foreign audiences, women perform tricks with their vaginas such as holding, ejecting, and blowing objects out of their vaginal cavities. Many of Tiew's co-workers come from Burma (Myanmar), Cambodia, and Laos. Tiew arrives at work at 6 P.M. and

leaves at daybreak. Each month, Tiew earns 6,000 Thai Baht (USD $181). The salary is more than Tiew has ever made in her life and, given her illiteracy, is probably more she can make anywhere else. "If I had any other options, I would obviously leave," says Tiew. Tiew says she only has sex with customers when she is desperate for cash. "It hurts too much and I hate it," says Tiew. "I try to get him to use a condom," she says, but admits that everything is negotiable for the right price when times are tough.

_____

Adapted from Guzder, 2009.

Sex Trafficking

Josephine Butler (1828–1906) of Great Britain was one of the first Western women to organize against prostitution and the trafficking of women. Despite threats of violence against her, she proved that the state-licensed brothels were participants in White slave traffic and the sale of children for prostitution throughout Europe.

The majority of sex workers are forced by economics and, often, by single motherhood, into prostitution, but it is economics, not others, that forced them. In stark contrast are the millions of sex workers coerced or tricked, and even sold into sexual slavery and taken away from their home countries. They are part of the multi-billion-dollar **sex trafficking** industry. Sexual trafficking is a form of **human trafficking,** the acquisition of people by improper means such as force, fraud, or deception, with the aim of exploiting them (UNODC, 2009). Trafficking can be intra-regional (within a country or region) or trans-regional (across regions). Trafficking criminals target and exploit desperate people who are simply seeking a better life and orphaned and poverty-stricken children. Women and girls comprise 80 percent of victims (UNODC, 2009). Earlier in the chapter, you learned that women and girls are sometimes trafficked into forced labor in sweatshops and into domestic work, but sex trafficking is the most common of human trafficking types (see Figure 7.2 for a summary of situations that girls and women are trafficked into). According to the United Nations Office of Drugs and Crimes (UNODC) 79 percent of all global trafficking is for sexual exploitation, and an estimated 1.2 million victims are children (Guzder, 2009).

Sex trafficking occurs all over the world, even in the United States, where an estimated 50,000 women are trafficked into the country each year (Seager, 2009). Here's just a sampling: Nepalese women and girls are trafficked to India; Bangladeshi women and girls are trafficked to Pakistan; Burmese women and girls are trafficked from Burma, Laos, and Cambodia to Thailand; women and children from East Asia, Southeast Asia, Eastern Europe, Russia, South America, and Latin America are trafficked to Japan; Nigerian and Balkan women (from Croatia,

FIGURE 7.2   *Situations Women and Girls Are Trafficked Into*

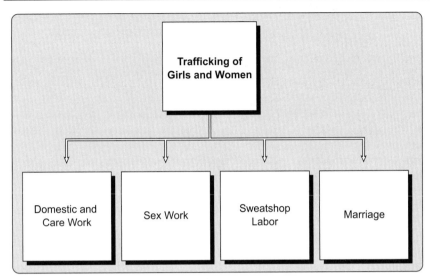

Bosnia-Herzegovina, Moldova, Yugoslavia, Kosovo, Macedonia, and Albania) are trafficked to Europe and Israel (Bales, 2002; Ebbe & Das, 2007; Seager, 2009; U.S. Department of State, 2009). Women and girls from Bangladesh, India, the Philippines, Pakistan, Afghanistan, Sri Lanka, Kenya, Ethiopia, and Sudan are trafficked into Arab countries such as Saudi Arabia, Qatar, United Arab Emirates, and Oman (Seager, 2009). Women and children from Malaysia, Thailand, the People's Republic of China (PRC), and the Philippines are trafficked to Papua New Guinea for forced prostitution there and from there to Australia and New Zealand; Vietnamese women and children are trafficked to China, Cambodia, Thailand, the Republic of Korea, Malaysia, Indonesia, Taiwan, and Macau for sexual exploitation (U.S. Department of State, 2009).

Trafficking agents, both women and men, are common. Agents use the offer of work to entice poor women to illegally immigrate to other countries. Women might be told they will work as maids, waitresses, or entertainers. Sometimes they are lured through false marriage offers. Upon arrival, however, their agent or "fiancé" sells them to a brothel or "club." Poverty-stricken parents may even sell their daughters to brothel brokers and agents, in most cases believing that the girls will work as maids, waitresses, or dishwashers, but sometimes understanding the work will be as a prostitute (Bales, 2002). According to Human Rights Watch, the recruiters often take advantage of families known to have financial difficulties. Debt bondage is not uncommon as women and girls are forced to continue in prostitution through the use of unlawful "debt" purportedly incurred through their transportation or recruitment (U.S. Department of State, 2009). They must first repay with interest the money given to their family or agent at the time of recruitment. This debt mounts as they are charged for food, shelter, and clothing. Should they try to leave the brothel without paying their debt, they are likely

"From 1970 I had been involved in initiating radical feminist action against rape, but until I learned of the traffic in women and explored pimping strategies in prostitution, I did not fully grasp how utterly without value female life is under male domination. Women as expendables. Women as throwaways. Prostitution—the cornerstone of all sexual exploitation."
Kathleen Barry

BOX 7.5   *Forced Prostitution: The Case of Lin Lin*

Lin Lin was thirteen years old when she was recruited by an agent for work in Thailand. Her financially destitute father took 12,000 baht (equal to $480) from the agent with the understanding that his daughter would pay the loan back out of her earnings. The agent took Lin Lin to Bangkok, and three days later she was taken to the Ran Dee Prom brothel. Lin Lin did not know what was going on until a man came into her room and started touching her breasts and body and then forced her to have sex. For the next two years, Lin Lin worked in various parts of Thailand in four different brothels.

The owners told her she would have to keep prostituting herself until she paid off her father's debt. Her clients paid the owner 100 baht ($4) each time. If she refused a client's requests, she was slapped and threatened by the owner. On January 18, 1993, the Crime Suppression Division of the Thai police raided the brothel, and she was taken to a shelter run by a local nongovernmental organization. She was fifteen years old and tested positive for HIV.

Source: Pyne, 1995.

to experience physical punishment by the brothel owner or the police. To keep them there, they are threatened with harm to their parents and with being arrested as illegal immigrants. Lack of familiarity with the local language or dialect puts them at a further disadvantage. Because trafficked women are often in the country illegally, law enforcement agencies respond to them as lawbreakers rather than as victims. To make things worse, they may be prosecuted for illegally leaving their own country should they attempt to return home.

Women forced into prostitution are exposed to significant health risks in the forms of violence and disease (Bales, 2002; Human Rights Watch, 1995; Pyne, 1995). Rapes and beatings are used to ensure compliance. Multiple daily clients, and the occasional sadistic client, inflict more pain. In brothels, women are exposed to sexually transmitted diseases, such as HIV/AIDS, because they are not allowed to negotiate the terms of sex and are forced to have sex with as many as twenty clients a day. Sex-trafficked women and girls face especially high risks of HIV infection. For example, HIV prevalence of 38 percent has been found among sex-trafficked females who have been repatriated to Nepal; up to a half of the women and girls trafficked to Mumbai, India have tested HIV-positive (UNAIDS, 2008). Although condoms may be available to clients, the client typically has the choice of whether or not to use them. The case of Lin Lin, a young woman from Burma (Myanmar), is described in Box 7.5 and illustrates these points.

Stopping human trafficking is difficult because demand is high and there is a steady supply of potential victims to feed it—a supply sustained by poverty, ignorance, organized crime, and government and police tolerance and corruption. Some suggest that the only way to reduce demand is through the apprehension and prosecution of perpetrators—this will require a big commitment from governments worldwide. Reduction of supply will only be accomplished through a lessening of poverty, educating potential victims, and the dismantling of criminal trafficking networks. Trafficking is also difficult to eradicate because it is based on prejudice against women, minorities, and lower socioeconomic groups (Ebbe & Das, 2007).

Due to globalization and sophisticated criminal networks, international cooperation is essential. The Protocol to Prevent, Suppress and Punish Trafficking in Persons, especially Women and Children, was adopted by the UN General Assembly in 2003 and by 2009 had been ratified by 132 member nations (UN Treaty Collection, 2009). It is the first global legally binding instrument with an agreed definition on trafficking in persons. Objectives of the Protocol are to prevent and combat the trafficking of women and children; to protect and assist the victims of trafficking; and to promote cooperation among governments to achieve these objectives. The UNODC (United Nations Office on Drugs and Crime) is coordinating international investigations and prosecutions. The UNODC also offers the "Toolkit to Combat Trafficking in Persons," which provides guidance, resources, and strategies to policymakers, law enforcement, judges, prosecutors, victim service providers, and NGOs.

There are many NGOs working on the issue. Human rights NGOs like Human Rights Watch and Amnesty International investigate the trafficking of women and girls and compile data that are useful in advocacy efforts. They pressure governments to bring their countries into compliance with international trafficking treaties. Donor countries are advised to use every opportunity to raise the issue of trafficking publicly and in official meetings. The Coalition Against Trafficking in Women-International (CATW), a GRSO that works with NGOs all over the world, was founded in 1988. CATW was the first international nongovernmental organization to focus on human trafficking, especially sex trafficking of women and girls. They have many programs, projects, and campaigns. The GRSO the Global Fund for Women has awarded over $3 million dollars to 300 groups in 71 countries, which work to prevent or stop trafficking and offer services and counseling to survivors. GROs like Shakti Samuha in Kathmandu, Nepal help survivors. Shakti Samuhu established the first shelter run by and for trafficking survivors in South Asia. NGOs such as Shared Hope International, with outreach efforts in the United States, India, Nepal, and Jamaica, and Safe House for Women in Yugoslavia, rescue women and provide them with medical treatment and counseling. Finally, sex worker NGOs, such as MODEMU in the Dominican Republic and Zi Teng in Hong Kong, work to advocate for the rights and welfare of sex workers (Cabezas, 2002; Lim, 2008). They seek to legitimize sex work as a profession where sex workers are not abused, persecuted, or exploited and have decent work conditions.

"It is a fundamental human right to be free of sexual exploitation in all its forms. Women and girls have the right to sexual integrity and autonomy."
Coalition Against Trafficking in Women (CATW)

Conclusion

In this chapter you learned that globalization has had mixed effects for women and girls. Although it has increased women's paid employment and consequently benefited some women, the costs of economic adjustment are also often disproportionately borne by women—especially women who are already poor. Such women are hit harder by economic downturns and are more likely to directly experience the effects of environmental degradation. Because they have few economic choices, they can be exploited in the global labor marketplace and by human traffickers. This is another example of how women's disadvantage arises out of material, economic forces. Globalization has also created a number of violations of women's human rights. We need to ask, as Hochschild (2002) suggested, what kind of a world globalization has created when working in a sweatshop, sex work, migration to work as a domestic, and becoming a mail-order bride are rational economic choices. These may appear to be individual choices but they are not really free—they are the result of economic globalization. This chapter also illustrates intersectionality because how globalization affects women depends on their race, region, and socioeconomic class. It further illustrates the connectedness of women everywhere.

"In my view, the singular achievement of globalization is the proliferation of women's movements at the local level, the emergence of transnational feminist networks working at the global level, and the adoption of international conventions such as the *Convention on the Elimination of All Forms of Discrimination Against Women* and the *Beijing Declaration and Platform for Action of the Fourth World Conference on Women.*"
Valentine Moghadam

Like other chapters, this one illustrates the global women's studies theme of activism and empowerment. Once again, we saw that where there are gendered wrongs, there are people working for women's rights. The "silver lining" of the globalization "cloud" is that in many cases globalization has inadvertently led to women's empowerment as women organize to combat its negative effects. Globalization can expose women to ideas and influences that inspire them to question and challenge gender inequality where they live. It opens up new spaces for resistance such as cross-border networks and transnational activism (Lim, 2008). Fueled by the dynamics of globalization itself, women all over the world fight the negative effects of globalization and use the transnational political stage to press for social, economic, environmental, and political justice (Cabezas, 2002; Desai, 2007). Transnational networks of activists play an increasing role in international and regional politics and may have progressive effects on policies regarding women, human rights, and the environment (Karides, 2002; Keck & Sikkink, 1999). They can expose injustices in an international arena. This is globalization from below, rather than from above. They use electronic communication and international and regional conferences to share information and expand political participation. Transnational feminism is discussed in more detail in Chapter 11.

Globalization is relevant to our next topic of women and religion. Under conditions of economic stress and cultural globalization, people often seek certainty and a return to a romanticized past. This makes them more open to conservative and fundamentalist religious ideas that are detrimental to women's status. Chapter 8, "Women and Religion," shows how religion is sometimes an instrument of gender inequality. It also shows how women seek to reclaim and reform their religions, and create their own spiritual traditions.

Study Questions

1. What is globalization?
2. What are some of the potentially positive effects of globalization on women?

3. How do global economic crises affect women? What are structural adjustment policies and how do they affect women's labor?

4. What are EPZs and FTZs? What percentage of workers in these zones are women? How is women's work in EPZs part of global supply chains?

5. What are sweatshops, and why do women work in them? Do jobs in EPZs help women get out of poverty? What is being done and what needs to be done to reduce women's sweatshop labor?

6. How does globalization influence women's migration? What does it mean to say "the work women migrants do is often a reflection of traditional female roles and stereotypes"? Why are migrant women vulnerable to human rights abuses?

7. How does globalization influence the supply of and demand for migrant women domestics? What types of abuses have been documented? What is being done and what should be done?

8. What are mail-order and Internet brides? What countries do they come from and why? What factors explain their increased susceptibility to domestic violence? What is being done, what should be done?

9. What is sexual tourism? How is it related to the differential effects of globalization based on gender, class, and race? Who are these "sexual tourists" and what are their destinations?

10. What is human trafficking? What different things are women trafficked to do?

11. What is sex trafficking? How does it work? How is debt bondage used to keep women and children enslaved? What are the effects on women? What is being done and needs to be done to stop it?

12. What was meant by saying that a "silver lining" of the "globalization cloud" is that globalization has stimulated activism and transnational feminist organizing?

Discussion Questions and Activities

1. How is your life affected by globalization?

2. How do migrant women contribute to your community? Which countries do they come from? What are the economic conditions in those countries that contribute to their migration? What types of work do they do—is it the domestic and care work traditionally done by women?

3. Interview a recent woman migrant using questions developed from the chapter.

4. Where were your clothes made? Choose an article of your clothing. Write a short story about the life of the woman who made it. To make it realistic, use the information in the text on women in the transnational

factory, information in the Appendix on the status of women in that country, and Internet research (for example, look for investigations by the National Labor Committee http://www.nlcnet.org/reports .php?id=560).

5. Cheap clothing and electronic products and large corporate profits (which mean good stockholder returns) are partly due to women's work in sweatshops. Is this free-market capitalism at its best or at its worst? How comfortable are you with northern people receiving more of the benefits due to this feature of economic globalization?

6. Locate websites that advertise mail-order brides (just type "mail-order brides" into a basic search engine and you'll find hundreds of sites). What countries do most potential "brides" come from? What are the economic conditions in those countries? Do the sites appear to cater to men seeking traditional gender-role relationships?

7. The chapter discusses how sex workers are victims of economics and a commercial sex industry that uses coercion and force to exploit them. However, some feminists argue that rather than eliminating sex work, we should work for sex workers' legal, political, and labor rights (Lim, 2008). They say this honors the choice of some women to choose sex work as an economic advancement strategy and will reduce the domination of sex work by criminal pimps and organized crime. What do you think? Can sex work be nonexploitative? Can sex work be revisioned as a form of legitimate work and regulated so that sex workers have decent work conditions and their human rights are respected? Would this stop sex trafficking?

Action Opportunities

1. Due to student activism, many colleges nationwide have signed on to help ensure that merchandise bearing their logos are made without sweatshop labor. Find out whether your college or university has a "no sweatshop policy" for their apparel. If they do, find out how it came about and how compliance is assured. If they don't, use some of the resources from Students United Against Sweatshops (http:// www.studentsagainstsweatshops.org/index.php?option=com_ weblinks&Itemid=22 to help bring such a policy about.

2. Go to Green America http://www.greenamericatoday.org/about/ and read the group's guide to ending sweatshop labor. Choose the strategies you think are realistic for you and your peers and use social networking tools to encourage others to adopt them.

3. Take action to educate others and inspire change on sex trafficking. Use resources from the UNODC's "Blue Heart Campaign" http:// www.unodc.org/blueheart/, Coalition Against Trafficking in Women

http://www.catwinternational.org/ and Stop the Traffik
http://www.stopthetraffik.org/resources/.

4. Help your local women's shelter develop a program to reach out to migrant women who experience abuse from male partners or employers.

5. Join one of Equality Now's campaigns to stop sex trafficking and sex tourism: http://www.equalitynow.org/english/campaigns/sextourism-trafficking/sextourism-trafficking_en.html

Activist Websites

Clean Clothes Campaign http://www.cleanclothes.org/

Maquila Solidarity Network http://en.maquilasolidarity.org/

Equality Now http://www.equalitynow.org/english/campaigns/sextourism-trafficking/sextourism-trafficking_en.html

Tahirh Justice Center http://www.tahirih.org/

Coalition Against Trafficking in Women http://www.catwinternational.org/about/index.php

Shared Hope International http://www.sharedhope.org

Informational Websites

Human Rights Watch http://hrw.org

Corp Watch http://www.corpwatch.org/

National Labor Committee http://www.nlcnet.org/reports.php?id=560

UNFPA's *State of the world population 2006: A Passage to Hope—Women and international migration.* http://www.unfpa.org/swp/2006/

UNIFEM Trafficking http://www.unifem.org/gender_issues/violence_against_women/facts_figures.php?page=5

UNODC Trafficking Resources http://www.unodc.org/unodc/en/human-trafficking/publications.html#Reports

Women and Religion

Now what about Islam? And what of the other great religions? When we think about religions in general, it seems to me that, more or less, they are the same. They all have a general human call for the equality of people—regardless of color, race, or sex. One finds this conception of equality in all of the religions, as well as in Marxism or existentialism. But when we come to the specifics, when we come to the daily lives of men and women, rich and poor, one race and another, this general sense of equality does not seem to be in evidence. Here we find oppression, including the oppression of women. So we must not have illusions about religion, because religion is used, and it is used often by those in power.

—Nawal El Saadawi

Religion is profoundly important to many women and religious feminists seek to reform and reclaim religion so that it promotes women's equality. This photo shows Jewish women from the "Women of the Wall" group, wearing Kipas and Tallits (veils) in the Old City of Jerusalem near the Wailing Wall. The Tallit and the Kipa are ritual articles usually worn only by men in Orthodox Judaism. The women in this group demand equal rights, including that of praying at the Wailing Wall.
© Menahem Kahana/AFP/Getty Images

This chapter focuses on women and religion and feminist theology. Religion is profoundly important to many women worldwide and can be a source of women's empowerment or their disempowerment. Inequalities based on gender, race, class, and sexuality can be seen as incompatible with a just, loving God and can motivate activism. Women's religious and spiritual leadership and participation in important rituals can strengthen them. Women can contest poor treatment by using scriptural references (Hoffman & Bartkowski, 2008). Religious affiliation may also empower women by giving them strength and hope in the face of patriarchal family structures and harsh economic conditions (Avishai, 2008). Unfortunately, though, religions are sometimes agents of gender inequality, presenting patriarchy as inevitable, inescapable, and correct (Daly, 1978; Sered, 1999). Religious feminists call attention to the ways in which their religions contribute to gender inequality and work for reform in their religions to promote women's empowerment. Some religions have been transformed by feminism and other religions (like goddess spirituality) have arisen out of feminism (Braude, 2006).

Diversity and the Study of Women and Religion

One of the challenges for global women's studies and the study of religion is that the great diversity of religious and spiritual traditions makes it hard to generalize about women and religion.

Religious and Spiritual Diversity

The relationship between religion and gender inequality is complex and depends on which religion you are talking about, the role it plays in a society or culture, and the role it plays in an individual's life. Even within a religion, there are variants, some of which are more supportive of gender equality than others. Likewise, the gendered practices of a religion can vary widely based on local norms. Although contextualizing religion and its effects on women is enormously important for this chapter, it is also exceedingly difficult given the immense variability of religions and religious contexts and limited scholarship on this variety.

Although the primary focus of this chapter is the world's major religions, it is important to keep in mind that smaller indigenous religions (religions in small-scale, kinship-based communities) often give women a greater role than do the world's major religions. In many indigenous traditions there are strong female mythological figures, female rituals, and no doctrine of male superiority and dominance (Gross, 1996; Sered, 1994, 1999). For example, in many traditional African religions, women play active roles as *diviners* (who foretell the future) and *healers* of physical and psychological illnesses (Mbon, 1987). In nonmainstream religions, women often have more power and autonomy (Gross, 1996; Sered, 1994; Weissinger, 1993). Sered (1994) examines twelve contemporary, woman-dominated religions in depth (Box 8.1 gives a sampling of her research). These religions are interesting in that they often

"Unquestionably 'religion' or 'spirituality' defined by and in the service of patriarchy is a force against freedom, vitality, and survival. But patriarchy's definition of religion is not the only one."
Sheila Ruth

BOX 8.1   *Some Contemporary Woman-Centered Religions*

Afro-Brazilian Religions (Brazil)

These combine elements of African tribal religions, Amerindian religions, Catholicism, and Kardecism (French Spiritism). The main features are curing and public rituals in which female mediums are possessed by spirits. They coexist with Catholicism.

Black Carib Religion (Central America)

This religion is centered around numerous rituals to honor and appease ancestral spirits and to protect the living against evil spirits and sorcery. Old women are the spiritual leaders. Most Black Caribs are also Roman Catholic.

Burmese Nat Religion (Upper Burma)

This religion centers around the appeasement of spirits called *nats*. These *nats* are also called upon to prevent and cure illness and to bring good luck. Most rituals are performed by women, and almost all shamans are women as well. The religion exists alongside Buddhist practices.

Christian Science (United States)

This religion was founded by Mary Baker Eddy in the nineteenth century. Christian Scientists believe that healing comes about through study and prayer.

Korean Household Religion

Korean women make offerings to gods for the well-being of their households and consult female shamans for guidance. This religion coexists with Buddhism.

Sande Secret Society (West Africa)

Adolescent girls are initiated into the societies at lengthy all-female retreats. At this time, they are taught about childbirth and other skills women are expected to know. Sande societies also control the supernatural and sacred realm. This religion coexists with male secret societies called *Poro*.

Za–r (parts of Africa and the Middle East)

Za–r are spirits that attack and possess women. Women then join za–r cults in which they participate in rituals to appease the possessing spirit and turn it into an ally. Women's za–r activities often serve as a counterpart to men's involvement in official Islamic practices.

Feminist Spirituality Movement

This is discussed at the end of the chapter.

Source: Sered, 1994.

exist alongside mainstream religions and frequently emphasize the appeasement of spirits for purposes of healing and bringing good tidings.

Religious Fundamentalism

As Ruether (2002) points out, it is a mistake to think that religiousness is authentically represented only by patriarchal, misogynist religious traditions; there are progressive, egalitarian principles within religious traditions. It is primarily the conservative and fundamentalist strains of the world's religions that most vociferously promote traditional roles for women and attempt to limit women's rights. This is true of fundamentalist strains of Islam, Judaism, Buddhism, Hinduism and Christianity (Armstrong, 2000; Helie-Lucas, 1999). **Religious fundamentalisms** are committed to the authority of ancient scriptures and believe them to be infallible; hold religion to provide a total worldview inseparable from politics; idealize a past when gender spheres were separate; require women to be modest and subordinate and regulate their sexuality; reject norms of universal human rights and multiculturalism; and have an "us versus them" mentality (Anwar, 1999; Furseth & Repstad, 2006; Hoffman & Bartkowski, 2008; Pollit, 2002). These religions see men and women as essentially different. They justify gender inequality as divinely mandated and use religious scriptures to support traditional views of gender roles (Daly, 1985; Glick, Lameiras, & Castro, 2002; Gross, 1996). They often condemn and resist feminism. Research confirms the idea that fundamentalism is a stronger predictor than religiosity in discriminatory attitudes toward women (Hunsberger, Owusu, & Duck, 1999; Kirkpatrick, 1993; Mangis, 1995).

Most fundamentalist and conservative religions do not hate women or see them as evil. Indeed, fundamentalist and conservative religions express great concern and respect for family, motherhood, and childrearing. And although they place men as the family head, restrict religious leadership to men, and expect women to submit to male authority, men are expected to be kind and compassionate in the use of their authority. This why adherents to these religions often react negatively to the suggestion that their religion is unkind to women—they feel women's role is honored and respected and women are well-cared for by their husbands and fathers. They may admit that the men's and women's roles are separate but they think this is what God intended and take exception to the suggestion that their religion promotes gender inequality.

This is consistent with what psychologists call "benevolent" sexism. **Benevolent sexism** has three domains: *Protective Paternalism* (i.e., men should protect and provide for women); *Complementary Gender Differentiation* (i.e., women are naturally suited for traditional female-specific gender roles); and *Heterosexual Intimacy* (i.e., heterosexual romantic relationships are essential) (Glick & Fiske, 2001). These domains are characteristic of conservative and fundamentalist religious ideologies and are found in key scriptures interpreted as the literal word of God. Psychologists point out that the net effect of benevolent sexism is still to support gender inequality. After all, it justifies traditional gender roles, restricts women's options, and privileges a gender hierarchy where men have greater power. Benevolent sexism also pacifies women's resistance to gender subordination by masking gender inequality with the cloak of chivalry, appearing to celebrate women's traditional role, and presenting traditional gender roles as religious imperative (Glick & Fiske, 2001; Glick et al., 2002). In some cases, this benevolent sexism may coexist with "hostile sexism," the perception of women as enemies or adversaries. For instance, there are elements in most fundamentalist religions that suggest women are temptresses that threaten men's religious study, relationships with the divine, and enlightenment, and consequently, women have to be controlled. The coexistence of these seemingly contradictory attitudes toward women is called *ambivalent sexism* (Glick & Fiske, 2001).

The heterosexual intimacy and complementary gender differentiation components of benevolent sexism also support heteropatriachy. Although many religions now welcome LGBT persons, some, especially fundamentalist and conservative religions, condemn homosexuality and compel followers to view it as a sickness to be overcome through spiritual practice. Scripture is read selectively to justify discrimination against LGBT persons. For example, many Christian denominations have excommunicated and oppressed LGBT persons, using the Sodom and Gomorrah narrative (Genesis 19: 1–29) to justify their actions (Monroe, 2009). In the United States, conservative Christian denominations have been instrumental in limiting the right of lesbians and gays to marry, claiming that it's wrong because the Bible clearly states that marriage is between a man and a woman. The Anglican Archbishop of Nigeria supported legislation that would have made homosexuality a crime, punishable by years in jail, for anyone to organize on behalf of gay rights, attend a gay marriage, or disseminate pro-gay media (Goldberg, 2008). Most fundamentalist and conservative religions will not ordain gays and lesbians or permit them to serve in religious leadership roles.

Critiquing and Deconstructing Religion

According to Peach (2002), almost all religions are patriarchal in origin, development, leadership, authority, and power. Feminist critiques of religion propose that the majority of the world's religions depict men's greater power and status relative to women as appropriate and acceptable. **Feminist theology** reconsiders the traditions, practices, scriptures, and theologies of religion from a feminist perspective with a commitment to transforming religion for gender equality (Watson, 2003). Feminist theology deconstructs religion by critiquing it through a feminist lens. Feminist theology suggests that gender inequality is legitimized and reinforced by the common presentation of God as male, by traditions of male leadership, by the exclusion of women from major religious rituals, and by religious texts that leave out the female experience and validate men's authority over women (see Figure 8.1). These concerns are described generally next and then later specifically in regards to each of the world's major religions.

FIGURE 8.1 *Negative Task of Feminist Theology: Critique of Religion*

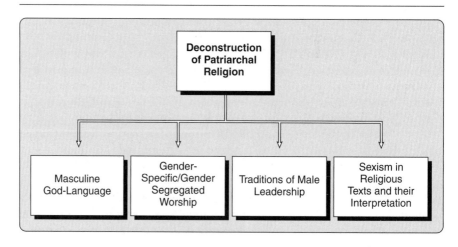

Masculine God-Language

Feminist critics of religion often cite the male imagery used by so many of the world's religions and regard it as both a source and a reflection of patriarchy. For instance, God or Allah is typically presented using **masculine God-language,** androcentric language arising from the patriarchal historical contexts in which the world's major religions emerged (Schüssler Fiorenza, 1992). The language used daily in worship and prayer, such as "Our Heavenly Father" and "He," gives the impression that God is thought of in exclusively masculine terms (Pagels, 1976). The concern is that this deifies male power because if God is male, then males are more God-like (Daly, 1973). Many feminists also object to conceptions of God as a stern, male father/ruler when God could as easily be conceptualized as having feminine, motherly qualities (Ramshaw, 1995; Ruth, 1995). Masculine God-language, along with the fact that the many religions portray God's main messengers on earth as male—Jesus (Christianity), Muhammad (Islam), and the Buddha (Buddhism) —also contributes to common cultural views that spiritual leadership and "family headship" are the domain of men and it is men that mediate our relationship with God. Some feminist theologians feel that the sexist and masculine focus of so many religions contributes to women's acceptance of male dominance by grounding it in the Divine (Daly, 1973; Ruth, 1995).

That it is frequently considered daring, degrading, or alienating to speak of God using female pronouns and imagery suggests that referring to God in gendered terms is, in fact, important in many religious traditions (Gross, 1979). For example, in 2009, Ruth Kolpack, a Catholic Pastoral Associate in Wisconsin, was fired by her Bishop for her Masters of Divinity thesis, which questioned the use of male imagery and language in the Catholic Church (Roberts, 2009). Some religious leaders argue that masculine God-language does not mean that God is gendered, nor does it imply the superiority of the male over the female. However, studies on gendered language (for example, using "he" or "man" to refer to all people), indicate that the generic masculine is not so generic after all and evokes male imagery (Hamilton, 1988, 1991; Hardin & Banaji, 1993). One study (McMinn et al., 1993) found that presenting God as male brought to mind the conception of God as "powerful" while presenting God as female brought to mind God as "merciful." Fundamentalist and conservative religions (such as evangelical Christianity), especially embrace the idea that masculine God-language and imagery reflect the true nature of God and they believe this supports male religious leadership and male headship of the family. To them, questioning masculine God-language is to question the truthfulness of the scriptures as the literal word of God.

Sexism in Religious Texts

Another focus of feminist criticism of religion is sexism in religious texts. Historically, in all major religions, it is men who have composed, transmitted, and interpreted the sacred writings. Over time these writings and their

> "If we do not mean that God is male when we use masculine pronouns and imagery, then why should there be any objections to using female imagery and pronouns as well?"
> *Rita Gross*

> "Consider the impact on your self-image of being 'in the likeness of God,' like Jesus, the Pope, and the 'Brothers of the Church' and contrast it with never finding yourself reflected in the sacred pronoun. Utter: God, He . . . ; God, Him. Now say: God, She. . . . Imagine the experience of seeing oneself reflected in the sacred images of power."
> *Sheila Ruth*

> "If Jews believe that all of us, male and female are created in the divine image, then why doesn't our liturgy reflect this basic theological conviction?"
> *Ellen Umansky*

interpretations increasingly reflected men's activities, achievements, and power as well as societal views of male superiority (Holm, 1994). Religious stories and texts often contain messages that perpetuate women's lower status and power: (1) Female sexuality is potentially dangerous; (2) female religious figures are subordinate to male religious figures (they are typically portrayed in relationship to males); (3) females should be subservient wives, mothers, and homemakers; (4) men and women have fundamentally different "natures" (essentialism); and (5) women's lower status is punishment for their sinful nature.

One key issue for feminists regarding the scriptures is the relative absence of females and female experience. As Ruether (1985) suggests, although women's experience may be found between the lines of religious texts, for the most part the norm presented for women is one of absence and silence. When women are portrayed, it is as objects praised for obedience or admonished for disobedience to men. A second issue is that men are the normative recipients of spiritual revelation in most religious texts (Smith, 2009). A third key issue for feminists with regard to the scriptures is that most of these texts sacralize patriarchy (present it as sacred) (Daly, 1985; Gross, 1996). Feminist theologian Mary Daly (1985) notes that the endorsement of traditional gender roles in religious texts makes women feel guilty or unnatural if they rebel against the role prescribed to them, and this condemns women to a restricted existence in the name of religion.

It is important to realize that it is not the scriptures themselves that lead to women's subordination; it is how people interpret them. **Hermeneutics** are the principles of interpretation for religious texts. For example, one hermeneutic is to interpret a text literally (as the word of God) and another is to interpret a text allegorically (as stories from which moral lessons are to be learned). A historical hermeneutic interprets a text as a reflection of the time in which it was written or translated. As noted earlier, fundamentalist strains are more likely to interpret texts as the literal word of God. Therefore, the traditional relationships between men and women found in the scriptures are seen as prescriptions for modern life as well.[1] In a study of American Christians, Burn and Busso (2005) found that benevolent sexism was positively related to scriptural literalism (the degree to which one interprets scriptures literally)—greater literalism was associated with the higher benevolent sexism scores. More liberal strains of the same religion will look at scriptures metaphorically and consider the historical context in which they were written. This hermeneutic provides more room for gender equality; passages that condone women's subordination can be seen as historical reflections rather than as role models for current gender relationships.

Feminist hermeneutics generally emphasize the importance of historical contextualization. Elisabeth Schüssler Fiorenza (1995) suggests a number of

---

[1] Note that even scriptural literalists do not take all scriptures literally. For example, the scriptures of Christianity, Judaism, and Islam all have passages supporting slavery (Gross, 1996).

feminist hermeneutics: *a hermeneutics of suspicion* (texts are not taken at face value; patriarchal interests are critically examined); *a hermeneutics of remembrance and historical reconstruction* (efforts are made to reconstruct women's history); *a hermeneutics of proclamation* (texts, passages, etc. are analyzed for their oppressive or liberating potential); and *a hermeneutics of creative actualization* (creative reading, interpreting, and envisioning of women in religious texts).

Gender-Segregated Religious Practices

A number of the world's religions have different rituals and forms of worship based on gender—that is, they have **gender-segregated religious practices.** In general, the religious practices of males are more public (for example, in the church, temple, or synagogue) and the practices of women are conducted in the home (for example, they prepare ritual and religious holiday meals).

Another instance of gender-segregated religious practices is that leadership roles in religions are usually reserved for males. Female ministers, bishops, priests, rabbis, gurus, mullahs and imams, and sadhus (holy people) remain rare or nonexistent in most religious traditions, even today (Eck & Jain, 1987). As Gross (1996) suggests, this is not the only important indicator of women's religious equality, but it is a way to quickly assess the status of women in a given religion.

Passages in religious texts are often used to justify why women should not hold religious leadership positions. Many religions also keep women theologically illiterate, thus ensuring that they are unqualified to hold high positions within the religion. For instance, women may not be permitted to study key religious texts, attend important religious ceremonies, or have access to theological education. Likewise, higher rates of illiteracy among females, and the lack of schooling in the languages of the texts, are in some cases obstacles. In most of the world's major religions (for instance, Christianity, Islam, and Buddhism), God's messengers on earth are male, and it is often said that only males may represent them. Some religions also maintain that women are spiritually inferior to men and that they are therefore unsuitable for religious leadership.

Many religious women maintain that just because women's role in religion is largely a private one, it is not a lesser one. Ahmed (2002) suggests that women's limited public role in Islam means that "women's Islam" is more spiritual and mystical than the "men's Islam" that focuses on religious texts and what some male religious leader says. It is also interesting that in virtually every culture, the heart of the religious tradition, at the local level and in the home, is performed, maintained, and transmitted by women (Eck & Jain, 1987). For instance, in most American Christian homes, it is the mother who gets the children ready for church and who prepares all religious holiday meals. Women's religious roles frequently provide the support necessary for the growth and maintenance of the tradition (Peach, 2002). Religious women often have a sense of importance in their religions from the knowledge that without them, those parts of religious traditions that take place in the home would not occur. Sered (1994) also maintains that even in many highly patriarchal cultures, women sacralize their domestic lives through holiday food preparation. In many cultures, food is one of the few resources controlled by women, and it plays a central role in women's religious lives (Sered, 1994).

Plaskow (1987) suggests that one benefit of the sex-segregated nature of religion is that it provides women with a common life, or **womanspaces**, where power and integrity come from their shared experiences and visions as women. For instance, in India, it is not uncommon for a married woman to live with her in-laws, and a household might consist of a number of sisters-in-law as well. Together these women run the household, and this domestic space is frequently a source of feminine support and friendship. Indeed, most of us can remember our mothers spending many hours working together with other women preparing for religious celebrations. Many of us have done this ourselves and can recall the special times spent with other women as we shared intimacies while we worked to prepare for elaborate meals and rituals (and then cleaned up afterward). However, as Plaskow (1987) cautions, perhaps these womanspaces are simply preserving an unjust system by rendering it bearable and providing shared self-validation.

Reforming and Reconstructing Religion

Feminist theologian Ursula King (1994) once said that feminist theology has two tasks. The negative task is the critique of and struggle against the oppression of women whereas the positive task is one of reform and reconstruction (King, 1994). In other words, feminist theology deconstructs and then reconstructs religion. Although there is great diversity in how feminists reform and reconstruct religion, reformists assume that although it is generally the case that religion has contributed to the oppression of women, this does not have to be so. Reformers argue that feminist reforms bring religion closer to its true heart and core of equality and freedom (Gross, 1996). Hartman (2007) argues that feminism and religion are not incompatible. We must be careful, she says, not to blur the distinction between the people in power who make decisions and speak in religion's name and the intangible, unbounded spiritual-human root of religion itself. There are four main reformist efforts (summarized in Figure 8.2). These are described generally next and later illustrated within discussions of each of the world's major religions.

One common reformist effort centers on the changing of God and prayer language to be more inclusive. For example, Jewish, Christian, and Muslim feminists have tried, with some success, to de-masculinize God-language. These efforts include avoiding the use of gendered pronouns altogether and not referring to God as the "Father" or alternating gendered pronouns and using God the "Mother" as well as the "Father." The idea is that without de-emphasizing the masculine face of God, women cannot be fully equal in the religious community.

Another reformist effort centers on the reexamination of religious texts and history in order to promote women's equality. A distinction is made between those aspects of the tradition that support women's empowerment and those that do not (Gross, 1996). As Carmody (1979) says in her book on

"If God had not intended that Women shou'd use their Reason, He wou'd not have given them any, for He does nothing in vain. If they are to use their Reason, certainly it ought to be employ'd about the noblest Objects, and in business of the greatest Consequences, therefore in Religion."
Mary Astell, 1705

"The first step in the elevation of woman to her true position, as an equal factor in human progress, is the cultivation of the religious sentiment in regard to her dignity and equality, the recognition by the rising generation of an ideal Heavenly Mother, to whom their prayers should be addressed, as well as to a Father."
Elizabeth Cady Stanton, The Women's Bible, 1895

FIGURE 8.2 *Reformist Efforts in Feminist Theology*

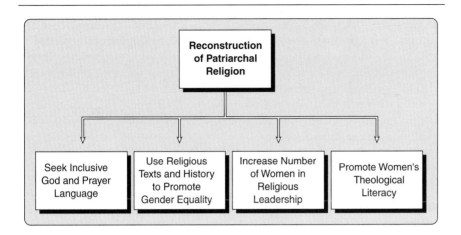

women and world religions, the task "is to winnow the wheat of authentic religion…from the religion's sexist chaff" (p. 14). Archeological, historical, and linguistic study are used to challenge inaccurate patriarchal interpretations and translations. Divine and prophetic texts are historically contextualized—analyzed in regard to the times in which they were written and translated (Smith, 2009). Historic analysis is also used to show that women's current low status in religion arose over time. For example, feminist scholars have shown that women had greater status in at least four religions (Islam, Christianity, Hinduism, and Buddhism) in the religions' formative years. In all of these religions it appears that once the original leaders died, new writings and interpretations emerged that justified the continuation of existing patriarchal traditions. Efforts are made to recover women's scriptural stories and to interpret texts in light of women's experiences (Smith, 2009).

Another, related reform effort is to increase women's theological literacy so that they are not dependent on male interpretations of scriptures that may be biased by patriarchal lenses. Feminist theologians promote women's access to scriptures and encourage women to read them for themselves. As noted earlier, higher rates of illiteracy among women and lack of access to key scriptures and religious books have meant women were dependent on male interpretations of religion.

Reformists also work to reduce sexism in religious practices. This includes working for women's ordination and leadership within their religious traditions as well as their rights to read sacred texts and perform sacred rituals. For many women, the realization that they are unequal in the eyes of their religions is experienced as a betrayal of deeply felt spiritual and ritual experience (Christ & Plaskow, 1979). Women who felt called to religious leadership and found themselves barred from these vocations have been instrumental in the fight for the right to become religious leaders (Christ & Plaskow, 1979).

"I heard the gospel long before I heard of the women's movement." *Nancy Hatch Wittig, one of the first women to be ordained as an Episcopal Priest in 1974 on "being called" to the priesthood.*

Women and the World's Major Religions

So far you have learned that religion can be an agent of gender inequality. Religious language, scriptures and texts (a religion's **canon**), gender-segregated religious practices, and masculine God-language contribute to traditional gender ideologies and are sometimes used to support the subordination of women. You have also learned that many women do not believe that God, or the founders of their religion, intended for their religions to be used to justify gender inequality. These women, along with supportive men, seek to reform their religions. This next section applies these ideas to each of the world's five main religions.

Islam

Islam is the fastest growing religion in the world. It originated in the Middle East and is now a major religion not only there, but also in Asia (in countries like Indonesia and Malaysia) and Africa (in countries like Algeria and Morocco). How Islam affects women's equality depends partly on how it blends with other cultural practices. There are different forms of Islam, including Sunni, Shiite, and Sufi. Islam began in the eighth century C.E., when Muhammad recorded the **Qur'an** (also spelled **Koran**). Muslims believe that the Qur'an is the unadulterated word of God as transmitted to Muhammad via the Angel of Gabriel (Hassan, 2003). The Qur'an is considered to be the primary source of Islam but there are other sources to which Muslims refer (Hassan, 2003). These include the *Sunnah* (the practices of Muhammad) and the Hadith(sayings attributed to Muhammad and what he approved; these developed over time and some are of questionable authenticity). Muhammad is seen as the final prophet of God, the last of a lineage beginning with Adam, and including Moses, Abraham, and Jesus (Peach, 2002). All Muslims are expected to observe the "Five Pillars of Islam": (1) to profess faith in God's oneness and to accept Muhammad as God's prophet, (2) to pray five times a day, (3) to fast during the holy month of Ramadan, (4) to give alms, and (5) to make a pilgrimage to Mecca at least one time.

"The Qur'an establishes that God is unique, hence beyond representation, and also beyond gender."
Asma Barlas

Although Islam opposes the used of gendered imagery for the Divine, Allah (God) is typically referred to as "He." Like many religions, there are scriptures that seem to support gender equality and others that do not. For example, in the Qur'an, Mohammed said, "Men and women are equal as two teeth on a comb" but another passage reads, "Men shall protect and maintain women because God has made some of them excel others, and because they support them from their means. Therefore the righteous women are obedient, guarding the intimacy which God would have them guard. As for those women whose rebellion you justly fear, admonish them first; then leave their beds; then beat them." Many of the sayings of hadith form the basis of religious law called **shari'ah.** Shari'ah often includes practices that restrict women and punish them for behavior characterized as immodest or immoral.

Religious practice is gendered in Islam and women and men are expected to show their devotion to God in distinctly different ways. Women play an important role in the practice of religious rituals in the home. Also, unlike men, many women show devotion through Islamic dress. Some wear the *hijab*, a headscarf that allows no hair to show (sometimes called a veil), or the *abaya*, a long dress or coat and a headscarf. (It should be noted that controversy about whether Islam truly calls for veiling has occurred for over 100 years. Although there are clearly cases where Islamic dress has been oppressively imposed on women, some women choose it as an expression of faith and appreciate that it frees them from sexual objectification.) For women, there are also ritual ways of washing after menstruation and after sex. Also, in contrast to men, menstruation restricts women's participation in some "public" religious practices; women are not allowed to enter mosques or touch the Qur'an until their period is over and they have taken a ritual bath. Mosques are also segregated by gender so that men and women are not distracted from prayer.

Women were important leaders in early Islam. Khadija, Muhammad's first wife, was the first person to accept his prophetic mission. After Khadija's death, Muhammad married A'isha and clearly said that she was to be accepted as an authority on the hadith ascribed to him (Hassan, 2003). She and her daughter Fatima carried the word of Muhammad long after his death. Women's authority as scholars and teachers of Islam was accepted and respected in early Islam (Shaaban, 1995). Rabi'a, a female saint, is also an important figure in early Islam. Despite women's importance as spiritual leaders in early Islam, there are now few opportunities for women's leadership outside of female groups that worship together. A hierarchy of *mullahs* (low-level religious officials) and *mojaheds* (high-ranking religious officials) serve as religious leaders and with only a few exceptions worldwide, these are men (Peach, 2001). In general, women are not allowed to lead prayer services.

Fundamentalist strains of Islam are the most oppressive to women and consider the Qur'an and hadith as divine and immutable. They seek religious states that rule according to shari'ah. Muslims with these ideas are sometimes called **Islamists** and the process by which states become governed by conservative forms of Islam is called **Islamization.**

Islamization   This is a trend in many Muslim countries including Pakistan, Afghanistan, Algeria, Sudan, Bangladesh, Nigeria, Yemen, and Iran. For instance, it was under shari'ah that twelve women in Sudan were arrested in 2009 for wearing pants (conduct or clothes in violation of public decency are a crime according to shari'ah in Sudan). The women were sentenced to forty lashes and made to pay a fine (McConnell, 2009). In Afghanistan, shari'ah is used to relegate women to domestic roles and to mandate that women wear the *burqua* in public (a cumbersome head-to-toe garment that covers the woman entirely). In 2009, a national law based on shari'ah was passed requiring Shiite women to obtain permission from their husbands to leave their houses, giving husbands the right to deny food to their wives if their sexual demands are not met, granting guardianship of children exclusively to their

In 2005 and 2008, Amina Waddud, an African-American Muslim feminist theologian, led prayer services. Although there is evidence that women led prayers in the time of Prophet Mohammed, nowhere in the world are women currently allowed to do so. Professor Waddud faced numerous threats to her life following these actions.

"If women's rights are a problem for some modern Muslim men, it is neither because of the Koran nor the Prophet, nor the Islamic tradition, but simply because those rights conflict with the interests of a male elite."
Fatima Mernissi

BOX 8.2   *Activist Profile: Shirin Ebadi of Iran*

"The discriminatory plight of women in Islamic states, whether in the sphere of civil law or in the realm of social, political and cultural justice, has its roots in the patriarchal and male-dominated culture prevailing in these societies, not in Islam."

Shirin Ebadi

Shirin Ebadi is the first Iranian and first Muslim woman to win the Nobel Peace Prize. The award was made for her years of legal work advocating on behalf of Iranian political activists, religious and ethnic minorities, women, and children. A lawyer, Ebadi became Iran's first female judge in 1970 and in 1980s began battling Islamists regarding the rights of women and children. Ebadi defended many of the democratic activists that

protested against the government in 1999 and served jail time for publicizing evidence that the government attacked pro-democracy forces. She has been instrumental in the successful drive to get women to elect candidates favorable to women's equality, including President Mohammad Khatami in 1997. Ebadi grounds her arguments for women's equality in the law and in the Koran. She insists that the true spirit of the Koran is consistent with women's rights. Ebadi continues to advocate for legal and human rights in Iran and is regularly harassed by government agents.

Source: Moaveni and Rotella, 2003; Mostaghim and Daragahi, 2009; nobelprize.org, 2003.

fathers and grandfathers, and allowing rapists to avoid prosecution by paying "blood money" to a girl who was injured when he raped her (Human Rights Watch, 2009b; Lozano, 2009). In March 2002, a shari'ah court in the state of Katsina in northern Nigeria sentenced 30-year-old Amina Lawal to death for having engaged in sex outside marriage (Human Rights Watch, 2002).The governments of more secular Muslim countries, like Syria and Turkey, do not base law on Islamic texts, and women in these countries have greater freedom (Moghadam, 2003).

There are many Muslim feminists and Muslim feminist theologians who challenge conservative Islamic interpretations that are oppressive to women. Because their efforts for gender equality are often greeted with charges that they are "Westernized" and untrue to Islam, they typically ground their arguments in Islam rather than the language of human rights or social justice values (Mogahadam, 2003). Those seeking an Islam more favorable to women emphasize the religious heritage of Islam and that Muhammad intended equality and dignity for women as well as men (Barlas, 2002; Hassan, 1991, 1999, 2003; Mernissi, 1987). They point to Khadija, Ai'sha, Fatima, and Rabi'a, early women leaders of Islam, and show how Muslims came to read inequality and patriarchy into the Qur'an to justify patriarchy. Muslim feminist theologians such as Riffa Hassan of Pakistan (1999, 2003) and Amina Wadud of the United States (1999, 2006) interpret the Qu'ran to show it is compatible with gender equality; they retranslate Arabic phrases and terms in the Qu'ran for precise meanings, and place Qu'ranic passages in historic context. Box 8.2 profiles Shirin Ebadi of Iran who, in 2003, won the Nobel Peace Prize for her women's rights and democracy work in Iran. She exemplifies those devout Muslim women who use the Qu'ran to show that Islam is compatible with women's rights.

Some activists work for women's literacy, feeling strongly that women's dependence on men for the interpretation of texts interferes with their ability to know their rights under Islam and they emphasize that early Islam stressed women's right to education and literacy. Egyptian feminist Leila Ahmed (2002, p. 120) put it this way: "Just because they were powerful, privileged in their societies and knew how to write, does this mean they have the right to forever to tell us what Islam is or what the rules should be?" As Nilofar Ahmad, the director of Daughters of Islam, a women's organization in Pakistan, said, "If I have any message for Muslim women it is that they must study their religion for themselves, learn what it really says, not accept someone else's idea. Only then will they be able to fight for their rights with the very weapon currently used against them—the Koran" (in Goodwin, 1994, p. 75).

Many Muslim women are concerned about fundamentalist movements and the reduction of women's rights in the name of Islam. They take action locally and transnationally. For instance, Women Living Under Muslim Laws is an international solidarity network formed in 1984. This transnational network monitors laws affecting Muslim women and publicizes gender-related acts of violence and oppression due to shari'ah, along with campaigns for justice. The Algerian feminist organization, Rassemblement Algerien des Femmes Democrates (RAFD), formed in 1993, is an example of local action against Islamist movements (Moghadam, 2003). In 1994, the group organized a protest involving tens of thousands Algerian women. They were responding to increased violence against women. Unveiled women, women living alone, and feminist activists were attacked and in some cases killed, apparently with the support of the government. Despite the risk, women also regularly protest the arrest and prosecution of women under shari'ah. In 2009, three of the Sudanese women arrested for wearing pants mentioned earlier in the chapter, decided to go to trial to challenge the law. One of them, Sudanese journalist Lubna Hussein, said the law is un-Islamic and oppressive and used her trial to rally support to change it. Sudanese police fired tear gas and beat women protesting outside the court, and some quietly protested by attending the trial wearing pants. Found guilty, Lubna Hussein chose to protest this misuse of Islam and serve her jail time rather than pay a large fine, but her fine was paid by someone seeking to quell the negative publicity and she is now free.

Judaism

Judaism is the world's oldest western religion. By 700 C.E., the Jewish tradition achieved most of the major features that it has today (Peach, 2002). Jews are found all over the world but the largest Jewish communities are found in Israel, Europe, and the United States. The two most important Jewish texts are the ***Torah*** (the first five chapters of the Old Testament), and the ***Talmud***

(a sixty-three volume of legal and theological teachings centering on the meaning of the Torah and the practice of Judaism).

Some consider Judaism among the world's most sexist religions (Gross, 1996; Heschel, 2003). This distinction stems from the masculine God-language, the paucity of female images in Judaism, the specific sexism of some religious texts, and because women are often excluded from the study of important texts, from leadership positions in the faith, and from participating in important rituals. However, this is truer of some forms of Judaism than others. Orthodox Judaism is the oldest and most traditional regarding women's roles, and one form, ultra-Orthodox Judaism (referred to as *haredi*), is a fundamentalist religion. Reconstructionist Judaism is the most progressive in regard to women's equality.

Masculine God-lanaguage and imagery is the norm in Jewish texts and liturgy[2] (Hartman, 2007). One of the best-known Jewish feminist theologians, Judith Plaskow, once said "Half of Jews have been women, but men have been defined as normative Jews, while women's voices and experiences are largely invisible in the record of Jewish belief and experience that has come down to us. Women have lived Jewish history and carried its burdens, but women's perceptions and questions have not given form to the scripture, shaped the direction of Jewish law, or found expression in liturgy" (1991, p. 1). The keeping of the Torah's commandments is the pride of Jewish life, yet very few of the 613 religious injunctions in the Torah apply to women (Carmody, 1994). The central concern of the *mitzvot,* the commandments of the Bible and the Talmud, is the religious life of Jewish men (Heschel, 2003). Parts of the Talmud can be interpreted to suggest that women's study of the Torah and their public religious worship should be restricted, and parts also portray women as sexual temptresses who distract men from prayer (Heschel, 2003). Indeed, the Talmud (the sixty-three volume explanation of the Torah) says: "Let the words of Torah rather be destroyed by fire than imparted to women."

Judaism is also based on various other texts, stories, and prayers not found in the Bible and these often contain negative images concerning women. For instance, a legend from *Genesis Rabbah* in the Midrash (a record of rabbis' biblical exegeses from 200–600 C.E.) explains that menstruation is one of women's punishments for Eve's sins (Schulman, 1974). One Orthodox Jewish prayer is the male's daily morning prayer: "Blessed art thou, O Lord our God, King of the Universe, who has not made me a woman." Heschel (2003) points out that although there are Jewish prayers for all sorts of bodily experiences, there is no prayer for giving birth. She provides this as an example of how the theological literature of Judaism was composed by men concerned primarily with the religious life of men, not women.

Gender-segregated religious practices are common in Judaism but this is less true of progressive variants and truer of Orthodox Judaism. Haredi Judaism excludes women from the majority of religious activities that take

In Israel, Orthodox Judaism is the official state religion.

---

[2] *Liturgy* refers to a religion's public forms of worship and ritual.

place outside of the home. The spiritual domain belongs to men; women participate by following the labor-intensive laws required to ensure the ritual purity of their homes. These included keeping the laws of family purity such as the ritual bath seven days after menstruation (the niddah), preparing kosher food, and doing the ritual work for home-centered religious holidays and the weekly Sabbath dinner. Married women in haredi communities cover their hair with hats or wigs, dress modestly, and on average have more children than do other Jewish women. Women's exclusion from the public religious realm is also apparent in Orthodox Judaism in the fact that women do not count as members of the *minyan*, the quorum of ten males required for public religious services. Women are also segregated from men in orthodox synagogues; typically women's sections are in the back, separated from the men by a wall or curtain. Services are conducted on the men's side. Orthodox Judaism also does not permit the ordination of women as rabbis and women cannot lead group prayers because they are not supposed to read from the Torah.

Over the last thirty-five years, Jewish feminists have brought about significant reform in their religion, especially in the non-Orthodox versions of Judaism. In many non-Orthodox synagogues, masculinist religious language has been changed. For "Blessed Are You, Lord Our God, King of the Universe" has become "Let us bless the source of life," and the names of the foremothers Sarah, Rebecca, Leah, and Rachel have been added to those of the forefathers Abraham, Isaac, and Jacob in Jewish prayer books (Cantor, 1995; Gross, 1996; Umansky, 1999). They have also created feminist liturgies and rituals (Heschel, 2003; Umansky, 1999) and re-envisioned parts of the Talmud. For example, Judith Plaskow (1979, 2005) reconceived the story of Lilith from one in which Lilith is a female demon and the first wife of Adam, spurned because she acted equal to him, to one in which she is a model for women's empowerment. Jewish feminists show how the Talmud supports gender equality, pointing out that it contains protections against the exploitation of women and advanced the status of women over what was common when it was written (Heschel, 2003).

Jewish feminists have also worked for permission to participate in the public sphere of religious life (Heschel, 2003). They use history to show that women held important roles as prophets, judges, and leaders during early Judaism (Heschel, 2003; Peach, 2002). They emphasized the strong female figures in the Old Testament such as Deborah, Jael (Yael), Esther, and Naomi (see Niditch, 1991 for a discussion). In the United States, where the greatest numbers of Jews live, women participate equally in most non-Orthodox synagogues. The reform, reconstructionist, and conservative Jewish traditions now permit women to be rabbis and cantors (directors of music and prayer in the synagogue), although it should be noted that they still face sexism in hiring and promotion.

Orthodox Jewish feminists like Blu Greeberg and Tova Hartman have also advocated for change but there is great controversy regarding their efforts and fierce resistance in some haredi communites. However, as a result of their work, there are some Orthodox communities that allow women to study and teach the Torah, study the Talmud, and who have synagogues where the

"The fact that, in traditional Judaism, women are not counted in a *minyan* (quorum required for public prayer) or called to the Torah amounts to our exclusion from the public religious realm."
Judith Plaskow, one of the first Jewish feminist theologians

"What is it after all that Jewish women seek? They do not ask to be excused or exempt. They do not wish to turn their backs on the tradition, to wash their hands of it and walk away. Rather, they desire to enter it more fully. They long to share a greater part of the tradition, to partake of its wealth of knowledge, to delight in the richness of ritual. For these reasons, their efforts should be welcomed, not scorned."
Blu Greenberg, one of the best-known Jewish Orthodox feminists and a founder of the Jewish Orthodox Feminist Alliance, a major source of information and activism

BOX 8.3   Activist Profile: Women of the Wall

The western Wailing Wall in Jerusalem, Israel is considered one of the holiest sites in Judaism. Custom has traditionally separated men and women and allowed only the men to read from the Torah, and pray as a group. In 1988, a group of seventy Jewish women from Israel, the United States, Europe, South America, and Australia from Orthodox, Conservative, Reform, and Reconstructionist forms of Jewry, went to the women's section of the Wall and prayed as a group and read from the Torah. They were immediately harassed and threatened but left unharmed. Committed to the quest for equal access to this holy site, the "Women of the Wall" (WOW), as they were now known, returned in early 1989 but this time Ultra-Orthodox (haredi) men threw heavy metal chairs at them over the high barrier that separated men from women and canisters of tear gas were thrown at them.

At the time, there was no law prohibiting what the women were doing but the violence escalated and they decided to go to the Israeli Supreme Court to ask for protection for their peaceful, religiously lawful prayer services. In 2002, following numerous appeals, the Court gave WOW permission to have its prayer groups in the women's section. Ultra-conservative politicians immediately introduced a bill to make it a criminal offense. Citing safety concerns, the Court reversed itself, although it did require the government to provide an alternate site, Robinson's Arch, which was opened in 2004. WOW still holds services once a month (on Rosh Chodesh, the monthly women's holiday) in the women's section of the Western Wall plaza.

_____

Sources: Chesler, 2008; Raday, 2005; Shalev, 1995.

women's section is on par with the men's section (Greenberg, 2000). There are even some haredi synagogues that hold women-only prayer groups and allow the Torah processional to pass through the women's section (Kress, 2009). Orthodox feminists also work for changes in religious laws that are detrimental to women, in particular, the one that allows only a man to initiate divorce (Jewish Orthodox Feminist Alliance, 2009; Umansky, 1999). Box 8.3 describes the activism of "Women of the Wall," a group seeking equal worship rights at a holy site in Jerusalem.

Hinduism

Hinduism, practiced primarily in India for 6,000 years, is the only major polytheistic religion in the world and is also the only one in which goddess worship is prominent and normal (Gross, 1996, 2009). Key concepts of Hinduism are *dharma*, a natural cosmic balance that exists in everything, and *karma*, the idea that one's present life is the result of actions taken in previous lives. Hinduism also has no single founder or single prophet—no male Son of God such as Jesus or male prophet such as Muhammad. Although the *Vedas* (written from 1750 to the sixth century B.C.E.) are the primary Hindu scriptures, there is no single authoritative scripture, no one sacred text (Carmody, 1991; Narayanan, 1999). One difficulty in defining Hinduism is the wide diversity of practices, beliefs, and cultural groups that emphasize different gods and goddesses, different scriptures, and have differing rituals (Erndl, 2006). Relative to many other religions, local customs, festivals, and rituals are far more important to the practice of Hinduism than the scriptures, which are written in Sanskrit, a language that most Indians cannot read (Narayanan, 1999, 2003). Drama, dance, and music are vehicles for religious expression and religious teaching (Narayanan, 2006).

Masculine God-language is not the issue in Hinduism that it is in the world's other major religions—there are both gods and goddesses. That said, how different goddesses are interpreted and whether they are centralized or marginalized in Hindu practice varies considerably based on local norms and the strain of Hinduism. In more progressive strains of the religion, goddesses are sources of power for women. Some of these goddesses suggest great female power. These goddesses include *Durga*, who rules strength and protection and is believed by some devotees to be the Supreme Being; *Sarasvati*, Goddess of Learning; *Lakshmi*, Goddess of Prosperity; and *Kali*, "the Dark One." Many Hindus celebrate and honor the goddesses Lakshmi, Saravati, and Durga during a ten-day fall festival called *Navaratri* (Narayanan, 2003, 2006).

Fundamentalist Hindus seek a Hindu state and, like other fundamentalist religions, interpret their religion in a way that promotes gender inequality. For example, goddesses are envisioned in ways that reinforce traditional gender ideologies (specifically, women's role as obedient wife) (Ross, 2008). They are seen as dangerously passionate, capable of giving and taking life, and needing the control of male gods so that they do not produce chaos (Carmody, 1989). In general, the unmarried goddesses are more likely to be presented as the dangerous ones. The married ones, such as Savitri, Sita, Parvati, and Lakshmi, are viewed as more virtuous and are more likely to be held up as models for women. For example, Savitri, a prominent female figure in Hindu mythology, is so devoted to her husband that she sacrifices her life for his. Similarly, another major female figure, Sati, wife of the god Siva, commits suicide by walking into a fire to avenge her husband's honor. Fire and the preservation of the husband's honor also figure in the story of Sita, who is kidnapped from her husband, Rama, by the demon Ravana. She is twice victimized—first, by the terror of abduction and captivity, and again, when she is rescued by Rama and must prove to him that she remained pure and faithful to him. She steps into a sacrificial fire but emerges unscathed because she was virtuous. Sita risked death to protect the honor of her husband (Robinson, 1985).

Like other religions, Hindu religious rituals differ depending on gender (Gold, 2008). The theme of *pativratya*, or husband devotion, is important to the practice of Hinduism for women in many Indian communities and fundamentalist Hindus see a woman's highest religious duty as being to her husband. Many believe that good karma comes to those women who are good and loyal wives. Men gain good karma, and therefore a higher level of rebirth, through the study of the Vedas and through meditation (Carmody, 1989). Traditionally, ideal Hindu wives ended their lives by throwing themselves on their husband's funeral pyre, a practice called *sati* or *suttee*. Although outlawed during the British colonial era, some Hindu fundamentalists have defended the practice and attempted to legalize it (Ross, 2008). Some Hindu fundamentalists still practice *purdah,* which requires that women stay indoors and segregated from all men other than their husbands and sons.[3]

Women are extremely important to the practice of many Hindu rituals. Women perform various life cycle and calendrical rituals at home, in public places, and in temples, on behalf of their families' well-being (Gold, 2008; Narayanan, 2006). Because Hinduism views women to be polluted when menstruating, more conservative and fundamentalist strains restrict their full participation in public sphere religious activities such as those in temples (Narayanan, 1999). Hinduism does not technically bar women priests but Hindu temple rituals and rites of passage are still primarily performed by male priests, and most Hindu teachers (gurus) remain male (Kaur, 2008; Young, 1987). The classical Hindu texts, especially the *Vedas* and early *Upanishads,* seem to suggest that women could receive religious education and perform religious ceremonies, but as time went on, these were closed to women (Carmody, 1991; Narayanan, 1999). In some areas of India, there are still restrictions on women's study of the *Vedas* and women are barred from entering temples (Kaur, 2008; Narayanan, 1999).

Hindu women who seek to reform their religion often look to the epic figure Draupadi, who does not allow men to dictate to her, and to the goddess Kali, who inspires terror and awe and is a model of female power (Gupta, 1991; Sugirtharajah, 1994). They seek to recast Hindu goddesses and religious figures as spiritual beings that show their devotion independent of husband devotion (Narayanan, 1999). They refer to the evidence that women contributed to the development of Hinduism, for example, composing hymns and performing rituals in the Vedic period (Peach, 2002). They study the ancient texts that support women's equality and point out how it was only over time that Hindu texts came to support the subordination of women. Box 8.4 provides a sampling of Hindu scriptures that celebrate the feminine divine. Many note how colonization by the British gave Hindu legal texts supportive of male power greater precedence than those that were more liberal in their attitudes toward women (Narayanan, 1999). They resist Hindu fundamentalism and its demands that women be restricted to their roles as wives and mothers, and its insistence that women not read the Vedas.

Hindu women seeking reform also work toward women's inclusion as spiritual leaders. Early Hinduism was more supportive of women's equality than later Hinduism. Women lost much of their freedom in seventh century B.C.E. when Hindu law, in particular the *Laws of Manu,* codified patriarchy (Gupta, 1991). Until recently, one barrier to women's leadership in Hinduism was that only males could study Sanskrit, the language of the religious texts. However, today the university study of Sanskrit is more likely to be undertaken by women because men generally pursue more lucrative professions. This is expected to elevate women's status in the religion since Sanskrit rituals and scriptures are important in the practice of Hinduism (Patton, 2007). In some

"Although Hindu traditions are portrayed, and quite correctly in some instances, as being patriarchal, the system has built-in mechanisms to allow for dynamic reinterpretation."
Vasudha Narayanan

[3] Some Muslims in tribal areas of Pakistan also practice purdah.

BOX 8.4   *Some Hindu Scriptures Venerating the Divine Feminine*

I am the Queen, source of thought,

knowledge itself!

You do not know Me, yet

you dwell in Me. I announce Myself in words both

gods and humans welcome.

From the summit of the world,

I give birth to the sky!

The tempest is My breath, all living creatures are My
    life!

Beyond the wide earth,

beyond the vast heaven,

My grandeur extends forever!

From the Devi Sukta

The Divine Mother revealed to me in the Kali temple
    that it was She who had become everything.

She showed me that everything was full of
Consciousness. The Image was Consciousness,
the altar was Consciousness, the water-vessels
were Consciousness, the door-sill was
Consciousness, the marble floor was
Consciousness—all was consciousness.

I found everything inside the room soaked, as it
    were in Bliss—the Bliss of Satchidananda. I saw
    a wicked man in front of the Kali temple; but in
    him also I saw the Power of the Divine Mother
    vibrating.

That was why I fed a cat with the food that was
    to be offered to the Divine Mother. I clearly
    perceived that the Divine Mother herself had
    become everything—even the cat.

From the Gospel of Ramakrishna

areas, women study the *Vedas*, recite the *Vedas*, and perform Vedic rituals, and, in more progressive areas, there are some women priests (Kaur, 2008; Narayanan, 1999; Young, 1994). Women gurus are less common but are growing in number, especially in Hindu communities in the United States and Canada (Narayanan, 2006).

Buddhism

Buddhism began in India in the fifth or sixth century B.C.E. after Siddhartha Gautama attained enlightenment and became the "Buddha" or the "awakened one" (Peach, 2002). Very generally, Buddha counseled that spiritual enlightenment requires devoting oneself to understanding and ending suffering, getting rid of ego and desire, seeking spiritual depth, and behaving morally (e.g., no killing, stealing, lying, gossiping, no intoxicants). Death and rebirth occur until enlightenment. Buddhism is practiced in Burma, China, Hong Kong, Japan, Sri Lanka, Nepal, Taiwan, Korea, Thailand, Cambodia, Laos, Burma, Tibet, Viet Nam, the United States, Canada, and Europe.

There are several forms of Buddhism and these differ in terms of gender equality. *Theravada* (Hinayana) Buddhism is more likely to view women as obstacles to spiritual progress and to suggest that women are inferior spiritual beings. Theravada denies the possibility of a female Buddha (a Buddha is a person who has achieved a state of perfect enlightenment and has been released from the cycle of birth and death). In contrast is *Mahayana* (Zen) Buddhism, which stresses that all human experience, male and female, is the source of enlightenment and that all things share one life because nothing can stand on its own. This is known as the Supreme Wisdom, *Prajnaparamita*, or the feminine principle (Bancroft, 1987). *Tantric* Buddhism, a less common form, is even more female-centered and includes the presence of strong, sexually active female sacred beings (Gross, 1996).

Although the Buddha is male, in Buddhism there are no gendered Absolute or Supreme Beings and no masculine God-language. However, like the world's other major religions, we find evidence of sexism in some Buddhist scriptures that describe women as filled with evil desires and as harmful obstacles to men's attainment of enlightenment (Uchino, 1985). Buddhist popular thought often regards women as impure, as having a more sinful karma than men (thus their poor situation), and as being unable to attain Buddhahood (the highest level of enlightenment) unless they are reborn as a man (Gross, 1999, 2003; Uchino, 1987). Women accomplish this by being good wives and mothers. There are also scriptures that suggest the genders are essentially different (Gross, 2004). However, like other major religions, there is also scriptural support for women's equality. Barnes (1987) argues that most of the main schools of Buddhism thriving today are egalitarian in doctrine and that the problems faced by women in Buddhist countries have more to do with social values that were not originated by Buddhist theorists.

Gender-segregated religious practices are common in Buddhism, especially in the Theravada tradition. The pursuits most honored in the Buddhist tradition—those of teachers, students, monastics, and meditators—have favored men (Derris, 2008; Gross, 2003). It has been expected that women show devotion through their domestic duties as wives and mothers, in lay devotional practices, and by feeding monks (monastic rules prohibit monks from farming or handling money).

Leadership in the Buddhist tradition has been predominantly male. In traditional Buddhism, the main religious leaders are the male monks, or *bhikkhu*. The female counterpart is the *bhikkhuni*, sometimes translated as "nun" although it is really the female form of the word *bhikkhu*. According to some historical accounts, women's right to enter the monastic order was granted by the Buddha following protest; 500 women with shaved heads and saffron robes walked 100 miles to plead with the Buddha, who relented after their third protest (Goonatilake, 1997). Despite this, in some countries—such as Burma, Cambodia, Laos, Tibet, Thailand, Nepal, Bhutan, and Burma—there are no orders of fully ordained *bhikkhuni*, even where there once were. Most of these countries practice Theravada, which does not ordain nuns, or does so under limited conditions (Bancroft, 1987; Barnes, 1994). In these countries, there are women who shave their heads as nuns and live as Buddhist devotees (Barnes, 1994). For instance, in Thailand, women may become *bhikkhuni* (nuns) or *mae chii* (female monks), but they are not fully ordained, receive no public or governmental support, and are marginalized within the religion (Falk, 2008; Kabilsingh, 1987).

Mahayana (Zen) Buddhism gives women greater equality in religious practice and leadership. In Taiwan, Buddhist nuns, or ascetics, have their own monasteries and enjoy social and financial support from the public. In Japan, nuns are ordained and may even perform some priestly duties in some sects. In general, though, Buddhist nuns have not fared as well as Buddhist monks in any period of history (Gross, 2003). There are fewer monasteries for them, fewer opportunities for economic support, and less family support since having a nun in the family does not bring the respect that having a monk does. The ordination process is more difficult for nuns, nuns' lives are more closely regulated than monks' lives, and male monks often have authority over nuns (Barnes, 1994).

Reform efforts in Buddhism include a review of the Buddha's history and conclude that it was not his intention to restrict women's participation in Buddhism (Falk, 2008; Kabilsingh, 1987). They also show that essential Buddhist teachings state that women and men have equal potential for enlightenment. Rita Gross's work (1993, 1996, 1999, 2003) is an excellent example of showing how Buddhism is fundamentally compatible with feminism. Buddhist feminists argue that Buddhist *dharma* (central truth or spiritual path) does not support patriarchy. As Gross (1999, p. 83) says, "the weightier texts, stories, and teachers argue that dharma is neither male nor female" and "there have always been important Buddhist thinkers that clearly said discrimination against women in Buddhism is inappropriate and un-dharmic."

Buddhist feminists work to discredit the orthodox Theravada view of women's inferiority by showing that the scriptures were not written down until 400 years after the Buddha's death and have changed over time (Bancroft, 1987; Derris, 2008). They recover and reimage scriptures that show that women are capable of enlightenment and draw attention to stories and texts supporting gender equality (Derris, 2008). They emphasize that the Buddha acknowledged the importance of women's religious leadership and that Buddhism's cannon includes the *Therigatha*, a volume of writings by female disciples of the Buddha (Boucher, 2006; see Box 8.5 for a sample). Reformist efforts have created new possibilities for women in Buddhism. Several recent Buddhist sects give women an equal place with men and have women in top administrative positions (Holm, 1994) and the number of Buddhist women teachers and leaders is steadily growing.

Buddhist women's activism for equal rights within their religion has a long history (Boucher, 2006; Falk, 2008; Goonatilake, 1997; Lavine, 2006). In one recent case of successful activism, Sakyadhita, the international association of Buddhist women, convinced Theravada male clergy in Sri Lanka to reestablish women's ordination (not since the eleventh century had they had this right) (Boucher, 2006; Falk, 2007).

Christianity

Christianity arose out of Judaism around the first century C.E. and is based on the life, death, and resurrection of Jesus of Nazareth. The main text of Christianity is the **Bible,** both the Old and New Testaments. The New Testament tells of Jesus

"When men know that spiritually we are the same as they are, they will have to judge us on our merits and our ability and not on what someone said thousands of years ago."
Reverend Master Jiyu Kennett Roshi ("Roshi"means Zenmaster), one of the few women who are heads of a Buddhist monastery in the United States

Sakyadhita, the International Association of Buddhist women, has created an international communication network for Buddhist women, educates women to be teachers of Buddhism, conducts research on women and Buddhism, and works for the ordination of women where it does not yet exist.

BOX 8.5   *Writings of Female Disciples of the Buddha*

Here are some Poems of Enlightenment that are attributed to female disciples of Buddha.

> While the breeze blows
> cool and sweet-smelling,
> I shall split ignorance asunder,
> as I sit on the mountaintop.
>
> *Therigatha 544*

> Awareness of impermanence
> practiced and developed,
> exhausts all desire,
> exhausts all ignorance
> and removes all conceit.
>
> *Therigatha 717*

> I am friend to all,
> companion to all,
> Sympathetic to all beings,
> and I develop a heart full of love,
> delighting in non-harming.
>
> *Therigatha 648*

---

and his followers and was composed between 50 c.e. and 90 c.e., long after Jesus' death (Gerhart, 2003). Most Christians believe that Jesus is the Son of God, and God personified on Earth.

Disagreements over biblical interpretation and practice led to three main forms of Christianity: Catholic, Protestant, and Orthodox. The Catholic Church and the Orthodox Church emphasize women's role as wife and mother and deny them most leadership roles. The official position of the Catholic Church is to prohibit abortion, contraception, and sterilization; to limit divorce and remarriage; and to deny the rights of gays and lesbians, although many Catholics do not agree with these positions (Kissling, 1999). In some versions of Christianity, most notably Latin American Roman Catholicism, Jesus' mother, Mary, is an important religious figure and model of womanhood. Mary is also presented as the perfect mother and a spotless virgin, ideals that some Catholic women have noted are difficult to live up to (Cisernos, 1996; Drury, 1994). Mary is also very important in Orthodox Christianity, which has a period of fasting dedicated to her as well as numerous feasts and festivals. There are also a number of female saints in Catholicism and Orthodox Christianity.

There are also dozens of different Protestant denominations. These different forms of Christianity vary considerably in their promotion of patriarchy; some are far more liberal about women's roles than are others. For instance, evangelical (fundamentalist) Christianity is explicitly antagonistic to feminism and promotes the traditional patriarchal family (Rose, 1999). Many conservative and fundamentalist Protestant Christian denominations rely heavily on scripture and use a literal hermeneutic. Other Christian denominations, such as the Episcopal Church, do not look at the canon this way and are decidedly more progressive regarding women's roles.

Because the Bible uses masculine God-language and the majority of biblical stories are the stories of men, many feminists view the Bible as a patriarchal document of a patriarchal society (although this does not necessarily mean that they recommend its complete abandonment). For instance, in Genesis (2:24), Eve is created as a companion ("help-meet") to Adam from his rib. This part of the story is often used to legitimate a husband's power over his wife in the most persuasive of ways—it is presented as divinely ordained. The story of Adam and Eve's fall from grace (Gen. 1:3) is frequently cited by feminist theologians as one of the most influential biblical stories affecting women's status because it has so often been used to justify women's subordination to men. Here, Eve is punished for eating from the tree of knowledge of good and evil. She is responsible for human's banishment from paradise, and because of her transgression, God tells her, "in sorrow thou shalt bring forth children; and thy desire shall be to thy husband" (Gen. 3:16).

Many passages in the Bible are consistent with benevolent sexism. For instance, this verse from the King James Version of the Bible is suggestive of *protective paternalism*, "But I would have you know, that the head of every man is Christ; and the head of the woman is the man; and the head of Christ is God" (Corinthians 11:3; see also Ephesians 5: 22–25 and Colossians 3:18–19). *Complementary gender differentiation* is suggested by this passage, "Wives, in the same way be submissive to your husbands so that, if any of them do not believe the word, they may be won over without words by the behavior of their wives, when they see the purity and reverence of your lives (1 Peter 3:1–7; see also Proverbs 31:10–15, 28 and Titus 2:5). *Heterosexual intimacy* is reflected in this passage, "And Adam said, this is now the bone of my bones, and the flesh of my flesh: she shall be called Woman, because she was taken out of Man. Therefore shall a man leave his father and his mother, and shall cleave unto his wife: and they shall be one flesh" (Genesis 2:24; see also Proverbs 5:18–20 and Ecclesiastes 9:9).

Gender-segregated religious practices are mostly seen in religious leadership. Christian and Catholic feminists sometimes refer to the barriers in the way of women's progression through the church hierarchy as the "stained-glass ceiling." In the late 1960s and early 1970s, feminists pointed out how males monopolized all visible roles in Christianity beyond singing in the choir, baking, and teaching young children (Gross, 1996). In some denominations, activism has led to the ordination of women and to the occupation

"God transcends all our human perceptions and language expressions . . . If Christianity preaches a God of love who liberates every person for new possibilities and discipleship, then we have to speak of this God in non-patriarchal, non-sexist terms."
Elisabeth Schussler Fiorenza

"The Christian tradition is by no means bereft of elements which foster genuine experiences and intimations of transcendence. The problem is that their liberating potential is choked off in the surrounding atmosphere of the images, ideas, values, and structures of patriarchy."
Mary Daly

by women of other church positions traditionally held by males, such as deacon. In the 1990s, women made up more than one-third of the student body at theological seminaries (Gross, 1996). But, change has been uneven. For instance, the Lutheran Church of America, the United Church of Christ, the United Methodist Church, the Presbyterian Church, and the Episcopal Church (most dioceses), all ordain women. However, despite the removal of official barriers to ordination in many Christian denominations and the surge of women graduating from seminaries, women still comprise less than 25 percent of the clergy leading mainline Protestant congregations. They are also more likely to be confined to lower-status positions such as assistant or associate pastor, and they are more likely to be paid less and to be offered part-time or temporary positions (Duin, 2001; Sentilles, 2008; Sullins, 2000).

There are Christian churches that still do not ordain women, including the Church of Jesus Christ of the Latter-day Saints (Mormons), some conservative branches of the Anglican Church, the Catholic Church, the Orthodox Church, and Southern Baptists. Those opposed to the ordination of women often point to 1 Timothy 2:12, which states that women should not teach or usurp the authority of men (Duin, 2001). The conservative Southern Baptist convention says that because of the sin of Eve, women cannot be deacons, chaplains, or ministers (Kissling, 2009). All women in the Catholic Church are laity, including nuns, because ordination to the clerical state is denied to women. Pope John Paul II defended this on the grounds that Jesus had no women among his twelve apostles and that because Jesus is male, only another male may represent him (the Orthodox Church makes the same argument). However, approximately 4 percent of Catholic churches are led by nuns or female lay ministers who are permitted to do everything but deliver the sacraments. There is a movement in the Catholic Church to ordain women. In defiance of the Vatican, the Roman Catholic Women Priests movement has ordained over forty women since 2002; the ordained women and the bishops who ordained them have been excommunicated from the Church (Roman Catholic Women Priests, 2009).

Ruether (1999) outlines Christian feminist reformist efforts in all regions of the world. In addition to trying to break the stained-glass ceiling and develop gender-inclusive liturgical language, Christian feminist theologians reexamine Christian texts and history to reveal those aspects that support women's equality. They refer to the Bible to show that Jesus is portrayed as freely talking to women, assigning them roles in his parables, and thinking of them as good friends and followers (Gross, 1996). They translate and interpret ancient documents that provide less-sexist versions of biblical stories (Arthur, 1987). They point out that Jesus' role as the Son of God was first revealed to a woman, as was his resurrection. They point to passages such as the one where the apostle Paul said, "There is neither Jew nor Greek, there is neither slave nor free, there is neither male nor female; for you are all one in Christ Jesus" (Gal. 3:28). They emphasize that women were major figures in the founding and spread of Christianity in its early years, and provide evidence that women were among Jesus' disciples (French, 1992; Gerhart, 2003; Schüssler Fiorenza, 1979; Stark, 1995).

Elizabeth Cady Stanton (1815–1902), one of the founders of the American women's movement, wrote and lectured on a variety of women's issues, including religion. Her *Women's Bible*, published in 1895, was the major nineteenth-century feminist interpretation of the Bible.

Christian feminist theologians also reinterpret biblical literature. For example, they show how the story of Adam and Eve can be reread in a way that is empowering to women (Trible, 1973). Asian Christian and Latin American Christian "Mariologists" reclaim and redefine Mary, the mother of Jesus Christ, as a model of liberation, suffering, and struggle (Gebara & Bingemer, 1994).

Intersectional Feminist Theologies

Most feminist theologies look at religion through the single lens of gender inequality but many newer and lesser-known feminist theologies look at it through intersectional lenses. For them, feminist theology is not just about deconstructing religion as an agent of patriarchy but as an agent of racism, classism, heterosexism, and colonialism. They reclaim their religions and revision them as agents of empowerment. For example, **liberation theologies** are activist theologies that focus on justice and equality for all people and use religious texts and specific stories and passages as a means to empower the poor and oppressed (King, 1994; Lev, 2009). Where women face multiple oppressions based on race, economics, and gender, feminist theologies are often liberation theologies. Some African and Asian feminist theologies are **post-colonial theologies** that seek to rediscover nonpatriarchal religious traditions and interpretations common before colonization. Anti-colonialism and anti-imperialism are important parts of these theologies as they examine associations between religion and Western colonization and re-appropriate theological symbols for empowerment and resistance (Pui-lan, 2007; Schüssler Fiorenza, 2007). These theologies sometimes mix parts of the religion brought by missionaries and colonizers with native traditions and rely on oral storytelling as the source of indigenous religion (Oduyoye, 2001; Pui-lan, 2007).

Theologies developed by marginalized women in industrialized nations also address the intersection of race, class, economics, and religion. For instance, **Womanist theology** is a newly developing Black women's feminist theology that began as a Protestant Christian African-American endeavor but increasingly includes the voices of other Black women; for example, those in the Caribbean (Townes, 2006). Womanist theology brings Black women's social, religious, and cultural experiences into the theological discourse (Townes, 2006; Williams, 1994). Womanist theology is a liberation theology in that it emphasizes justice for women and the oppressed and is envisioned as an instrument for theological and social change. Likewise, **Mujerista theology,** a Latin American feminist theology, has as its goal the liberation of Latinas (and all people) and the changing of church structures such that Latinas may participate fully in them (Isasi-Diaz, 1994, 2006). Mujerista theology also emphasizes the discovery and affirmation of God in Latinas' daily lives and communities. **Native American feminist theologies** challenge the patriarchal and colonial histories of Native Americans, histories in which women are

"Womanist is to feminist as purple is to lavender."
Alice Walker, African American writer and womanist

often absent and subordinate (Denetdale, 2007; Pesantobbee, 2005). They use oral tribal histories, rather than archival histories biased by colonization, to recover women's voices in Native American religion (Smith, 2009).

Feminist Spirituality

Some feminists question that equality for women can be found through revision of the world's major religions. They believe that the essential core of the world's major religions and religious organizations are so fundamentally sexist that reform efforts are all but hopeless (Hampson, 1987, 1990). Separating their feelings about God and the Spirit from traditional religion, they work to create new traditions and to embrace ancient ones that value women's experience, past and present. Recurrent themes are women and nature, the significance of community with other women, women-centered stories and rituals, and the use of female imagery and symbolism (Christ & Plaskow, 1979). These efforts often embrace *paganism*, an umbrella term for a wide variety of pre- and nonbiblical religions that include female images of the divine (Gross, 1996). These ancient religions are rich sources of positive female imagery and have the advantage of being rooted in tradition (Christ & Plaskow, 1979). Collectively, these groups are known as the **feminist spirituality movement** (Gross, 1996). However, others prefer the term **women's spirituality movement.** The feminist spirituality movement began in the 1970s and is mostly found in the United States, Australia, New Zealand, and Great Britain (Christ, 2006). These religions are among the few living religions created and led by women (Sered, 1994).

> "There is no way to find any feminist value in the Qur'an. If people say it is found, then either they lie, or they try to interpret the verses differently to make it suitable with the present day."
> *Feminist Bengali physician and writer Taslima Nasrin*

Many of these religions fall under the heading of **goddess spirituality** because the focus is on goddess worship, although there is a lot of variation in how these groups envision the goddess and the extent to which they include men (Griffin, 2003; King, 1987). Goddess spirituality is based in the belief that humans lived in peace and harmony with nature during a goddess-worshipping prehistory (Braude, 2006). Writers such as Starhawk (1979), Eisler (1987), and Gimbutas (1991) point to archeological artifacts and myths showing the important role of the goddess in early religion and civilization. For instance, feminine sacred beings (goddesses) were popular in the Greco-Roman traditions that co-existed with early Christianity and remain common in many indigenous African and Native American traditions as well as in Hinduism (Gross, 1996). Visual images of the Goddesses stand in stark contrast to typical male God imagery that suggests that legitimate spiritual power is male (Christ, 1995).

According to Christ (1995, 2006), it is common for those who worship the Goddess to have an altar in their home that includes a reproduction of a full-figured ancient goddess statue, objects from nature (e.g., feathers, rocks, flowers) that represent women's connection to the "web of life," and family photos. Goddess rituals have no set form but are often conducted in groups called "goddess circles." They are held on the days or nights of the new and full moons and on eight seasonal holidays such as the winter solstice and are also conducted for special occasions such as birth, menopause, and healing. Rituals may involve singing, dancing, chanting, and meditation and are often playful and inventive. They are intended to connect people to a divinity that is found in nature and in the natural cycles of birth, death, and regeneration (Christ, 1995).

Within the Goddess movement is the religion of **Wicca,** *or* **witchcraft,** a form of spirituality based on ancient wiccan (witchcraft) traditions that involve both Gods and Goddesses. Witchcraft is a magical earth religion whose main tenet is harmony with the earth and all life (Covenant of the Goddess, 2009). This type of witchcraft is *not* to be associated with Satanism or devil worship; in fact, most witches do not even believe in the devil. Although some witches do cast spells, the laws of wicca say that you can't cast a spell to "bend another person to your will," and you can't use a spell to harm another person.

There are numerous versions of Wicca. **Dianic witchcraft** is a feminist form that worships the feminine divine in mostly all-female covens. Dianic witches believe that before recorded history there were peaceful gender-egalitarian societies that worshipped the Goddess but that these were displaced by patriarchal forces through violence (Wise, 2008). Dianic witchcraft arose during the 1970s, stimulated by Merlin Stone's *When God Was a Woman* (1976) and Zsuzsanna Budapest's *The Feminist Book of Lights and Shadows* (1976), which eventually became *The Holy Book of Women's Mysteries* (1989). These books became the foundations of the Dianic tradition of Wicca. Starhawk is another well-known leader in Dianic witchcraft who practices a version known as Reclaiming. This type of witchcraft is an ecofeminist form emphasizing activism for peace and the environment.

Those who practice wicca often emphasize that common stereotypes of witches as dangerous and self-serving were perpetrated by those who sought to eliminate this source of power for women. Negative stereotypes originated in an eradication campaign by the Christian Church in the years 1560–1760. Historian Anne Barstow (1994) says that approximately 100,000 women were killed in European witch hunts during this time period and another 200,000 were accused of being witches. Old single women, seen as burdens, were especially likely to be accused, as were outspoken women and those who stepped out of the traditional female role. Barstow suggests that the European and American witch hunts had a number of effects on women's power. One is that fear of being accused of witchcraft kept women quiet and obedient. Another is that the campaign took away a source of power for women. Previously, witches had a lot of power as the village healers who delivered babies, performed abortions, set bones, and prescribed and administered herbal medicines. The attack on witchcraft had the effect of taking the practice of medicine away from women. The European and American witch hunts also essentially destroyed the religion of witchcraft, although it is now experiencing resurgence.

> "Through the Goddess, we can discover our strength, enlighten our minds, own our bodies, and celebrate our emotions. We can move beyond narrow, constricting roles, and become whole."
> *Starhawk*

Conclusion

Throughout the book we have used a human rights framework as a basis for gender equality advocacy and you may have noticed its absence in this chapter. That's because this framework presents special challenges when it

"Human rights is a universal standard. It is a component of every religion and every civilization."
Shirin Ebadi

comes to religion. Freedom of religion is affirmed as a human right in the UN Declaration on the Elimination of All Forms of Discrimination Based on Religion or Belief, but these religious rights may at times contradict the human rights of women. Indeed, conservative and fundamentalist religions often object to human rights instruments supporting women's rights and claim they are an infringement of religious freedoms. Some fundamentalists reject the concept of human rights altogether, viewing it as a Western strategy intended to eradicate their religious traditions or because they believe their scriptures are infallible and nothing can supersede them.

Many countries that ratified the Convention on the Elimination of Discrimination Against Women (CEDAW) did so with "reservations" based on religion (when governments enter a reservation to a treaty, it means that they will not be bound to those parts). In fact, fifty-six countries registered a total of 177 official reservations to CEDAW, most based on religious or cultural grounds. This is the highest number of reservations recorded for any international convention. For instance, Israel filed a reservation to Article 16, which states that parties undertake to eliminate discrimination against women in all matters relating to marriage and family relations (Shalev, 1995). Bangladesh, Egypt, Libya, and Tunisia all invoked Islam as the reason for their reservations to the Women's Convention (Mayer, 1995a). Some of the CEDAW provisions that are most in conflict with freedom of religion are equality in protection before the law; the abolition of all laws and practices that discriminate against women; equality in all areas of economic and social life; equality in all manner before the law; and equal rights in family life (Boden, 2007).

As Boden (2007) points out, there is no easy solution to this issue. We don't want to subordinate women's rights to religious rights or vice versa. We have to honor women's rights and dignity while honoring the role of faith and faith-based communities to women. The best way to do this might be changing patriarchal religious ideology (Boden, 2007). This is something that is best done by those within a given religious tradition. Otherwise, charges of violating freedom of religion and disrespect are likely. Besides, it is those within a religion who best understand it; they are the ones that are most qualified to deconstruct and reinterpret it. Indeed, religious feminists seeking equality in their religions often find it more effective to promote change based on scriptural study and the religion's history rather than appealing to human rights frameworks, though it should be noted that many religious people believe that their religion is fundamentally compatible with human rights (Mogahadam, 2003). As you saw in this chapter, the greatest changes have been brought by deeply religious feminist women.

This chapter, like those that preceded it, illustrates the multicultural, intersectional, contextual theme of global women's studies as well as the activism and empowerment theme. It reminds us of the courage displayed by those who work for change and who defy tradition. Once again there is evidence of positive results from women's activism. This activism theme is a major focus of the remaining chapters, which center on women's political activities.

Study Questions

1. How can religion empower women? How can it disempower them?

2. Why is it important to contexualize the study of women and religion?

3. What are the features of religious fundamentalism? How does benevolent sexism and hostile sexism apply to conservative and fundamentalist religions?

4. What is feminist theology? What are the common feminist critiques of religion?

5. What are hermeneutics and why do they matter in feminist theology? What are the feminist hermeneutics outlined in the chapter?

6. What basic assumptions underlie reformist efforts in feminist theology? What are some common reformist efforts?

7. For each major world religion examined in the chapter, briefly explain whether its canon is supportive of gender equality.

8. For each major world religion examined in the chapter, briefly review gender-segregated religious rituals and practices.

9. For each major world religion examined in the chapter, briefly outline gender equality progress resulting from the efforts of feminists from that tradition.

10. What are some of the basic features of the intersectional feminist theologies described in the chapter?

11. What is the feminist spirituality movement? Why have some abandoned reformist efforts in favor of new traditions? What are some common features of these traditions?

12. What is goddess spirituality? What is the religion of Wicca (witchcraft)? What is Dianic witchcraft? How was the eradication of witchcraft accomplished prior to the eighteenth century and how did it constitute an attack on women's power?

13. What challenges face the applications of a human rights framework to religion and women's human rights? Why do these challenges lead us to conclude that it is often most effective to promote change based on scriptural study and the religion's history?

Discussion Questions and Activities

1. Are traditional religions (Christianity, Islam, Hinduism, Judaism, and Buddhism) fundamentally sexist or have they merely been misinterpreted? Is it feasible that traditional religions can be reconceived or reinterpreted in a way that permits gender equality? Or will it be necessary for women to develop their own religions in order to achieve equality?

2. Does the use of the pronoun "He" to refer to God and the exclusion of women from most religious hierarchies condition women to view themselves as inferior to men?

3. Make a list of masculine adjectives that describe God and another list of feminine adjectives that describe God. What does this tell you about your conceptions of God? Is God male?

4. Interview a woman minister or rabbi, a practitioner of feminist spirituality (for instance, a witch), or a traditional religious woman, using questions developed from the chapter.

5. This chapter focused mostly on women in the world's major religions. Choose a lesser-known religion such as the Bahai, Sikh, or Jainism religions, a religion listed in Box 8.1, or a variant or denomination of a major religion like Sufism (Islam). Analyze the religion using feminist hermeneutics.

6. Find a story from a religious text that features women and interpret it in a way that empowers women.

7. Create your own goddess altar or invite a few friends over to do a ritual celebrating the feminine divine, the female body, a female rite of passage, or our connection with all things. See books by Starhawk or Zsuzsanna Budapest for ideas or create your own ritual.

Action Opportunities

1. If you worship regularly as part of an organized religion, lead a scripture study of passages suggestive of women's subordination to men. Be prepared to discuss their textual and historical context and whether they are otherwise consistent with the religion's conception of God.

2. If you are a member of an organized religion and you are dissatisfied with the treatment of women within your tradition, lead a change effort. For instance, you can lead a petition drive in favor of women being allowed to hold positions such as deacon, minister, or bishop or to change liturgical language to be more gender neutral. You can also meet with your religious leaders, and ask that they devote more time to presenting stories about women in the tradition and what they have to teach us.

3. Check the chapter websites for feminist activist efforts specific to your religion.

4. Go to http://www.Amnesty.org and http://www.HRW.org to participate in a letter-writing campaign for cases involving the persecution of women due to Shari'ah.

5. Do something to counteract religious conservatives' assault on women's rights in your country or community. Write letters to editors and your representatives in Congress about a particular policy area of concern to

you such as the restriction of women's reproductive rights or the prohibition of sex education. Enlist progressive clergy to speak out to counter people who use religion to promote gender inequality.

Activist Websites

Sisters in Islam http://www.sistersinislam.org.my/

Women of the Wall http://womenofthewall.blogspot.com/

Jewish Orthodox Feminist Alliance http://www.jofa.org/

Manushi (Hindu women's activism) http://www.manushi-india.org/

Sakyadhit (international association of Buddhist Women) http://www
.sakyadhita.org/pages/our_work.html

Roman Catholic Women Priests http://www.romancatholicwomenpriests.org/

Christians for Biblical Equality http://www.cbeinternational.org/

Informational Websites

Jewish Women's Encylopedia http://jwa.org/encyclopedia

Sufi Women's Organization http://www.sufiwomen.org/index.html

Theravada Buddhist Writings by Women http://www.enabling.org/ia/
vipassana/womenAuthors.html

Christian + Feminist http://www.users.csbsju.edu/~eknuth/xpxx/
index.html

Women and Theology http://www.earlham.edu/library/content/
outreach/acrlwss/wsstheo.html

Starhawk's Homepage http://www.starhawk.org/

Witches Voice http://www.witchvox.com/

Women in Politics

Political space belongs to all citizens, but men
monopolize it.

—United Nations Human Development Report, 1995

*Women's political empowerment is key to gender equality. This 2009 photo shows
Argentine President Cristina Fernandez de Kirchner (L) and Chilean President
Michelle Bachelet at the presidential palace in Santiago. Although women remain a
minority in formal politics, the last decade has seen major progress, much of it due
to women's activism.* © MARTIN BERNETTI/AFP/Getty Images

Women's political rights are enshrined in many international agreements. The Universal Declaration of Human Rights states that everyone has the right to take part in the government of his/her country (see Box 9.1). Increasing women's political power and representation is also consistent with Goal 3 of the UN's Millennium Development Goals (MDGs), "to promote gender quality and empower women" (UNIFEM, 2008). Unfortunately, women do not have the political status, access, or influence that men have in the overwhelming majority of countries in the world (Chowdhury et al., 1994). In other words, relative to men, women lack macro power. This is of concern because women's political empowerment is critical to gender equality. Women's underrepresentation in politics signifies their continued lower status and poses a barrier to women's issues advocacy. Like the domination of the economic sphere by men, male domination of the political sphere both reflects and perpetuates women's lower status and power. Indeed, a key focus of women's organizing worldwide has been political systems and processes so as to transform politics, shape public policy-making, and democratize power relations (UNIFEM, 2008).

"When we get involved in politics, we gain a better understanding of power and we discover that it is an indispensable goal if we want to have a voice in key decisions."
Otilia Lux, Member of Guatemala's Parliament

BOX 9.1 *Some International Agreements Enshrining Women's Political Rights*

Convention on the Political Rights of Women (1954)

Article I Women shall be entitled to vote in all elections on equal terms with men, without any discrimination.

Article II Women shall be eligible for election to all publicly elected bodies, established by national law, on equal terms with men, without any discrimination.

Article III Women shall be entitled to hold public office and to exercise all public functions, established by national law, on equal terms with men, without any discrimination.

Convention on the Elimination of All Forms of Discrimination Against Women (1979)

Article 7 States Parties shall take all appropriate measures to eliminate discrimination against women in the political and public life of the country and, in particular, shall ensure to women, on equal terms with men, the right:

  a. To vote in all elections and public referenda and to be eligible for election to all publicly elected bodies;

  b. To participate in the formulation of government policy and the implementation thereof and

to hold public office and perform all public functions at all levels of government;

  c. To participate in non-governmental organizations and associations concerned with the public and political life of the country.

Article 8 States Parties shall take all appropriate measures to ensure to women, on equal terms with men and without any discrimination, the opportunity to represent their Governments at the international level and to participate in the work of international organizations.

The Beijing Platform for Action (1995)
Women in Power and Decision Making (191-194)

Reaffirms the importance of women's equal participation in politics; acknowledges women's low levels of representation in formal politics, their leadership in "community and informal organizations," and their work in grassroots movements and non-govermental organizations; and identifies measures to "ensure women's equal access to and full participation in power structures and decision-making."

BOX 9.2   *A Snapshot of Women's Formal Political Power*

In 2010, worldwide,

- There were 17 women presidents and prime ministers (of these, nine were elected).

- Almost seventeen percent of countries (44) have achieved a critical mass of 30 percent or more women in their congress or parliaments.

- Women comprised about 18.99 percent of the membership of national parliaments and congresses; an all-time high.

- The following countries had the highest percentages of women in national legislatures: Rwanda (50 percent), Sweden (46 percent), South Africa (43 percent), Cuba (43 percent), Iceland (43 percent), Finland (40 percent), Noway (39 percent), Belgium (39 percent), Netherlands (39 percent), Denmark (38 percent), Angola (38 percent), Argentina (38 percent).

- Some countries have no women representatives including Qatar, Nauru, Micronesia, and Saudi Arabia.

- The region with the highest rate of women representatives in national legislatures is the Nordic region (42 percent), followed by the Americas (22.2 percent), Europe (excluding the Nordic countries; 19.9 percent), Sub-Saharan Africa (18.4 percent), Asia (18.7 percent), the Pacific (13.2 percent), and last, the Arab States (10.1 percent).

Source: Inter-Parliamentary Union, 2010.

When people think of politics, they often think of activities such as registering to vote, voting, running for and holding political office, and lobbying elected officials. The political sphere is also typically viewed as a masculine one and politicians as male. This is not surprising given that the majority of formal political positions continue to be held by men (see Box 9.2). Also, politics are a public activity, and the public sphere is associated with male activities. Add to this that media coverage of politics tends to be almost exclusively focused on male political actors. As well, until recently, political science has centered on male political activity and leaders (Lovenduski, 2008; Stevens, 2007).

Women, as you've almost certainly noticed in previous chapters, do act politically despite significant obstacles. That so many women overcome the barriers to their participation, at least to some extent, is a testimony to their commitment to the ideals of political citizenship (Lister, 2003). This commitment is especially evident in the sphere of **informal politics,** ("power from below") which includes local community-based action and national and international social movements (Lister, 2003). This chapter begins with a consideration of women's participation in **formal politics** ("political power from above") including voting, representation in parliaments and congresses, and women as heads of state. From there, it moves to a discussion of informal politics.

FIGURE 9.1   *Obstacles to Women's Presence in Representative Politics*

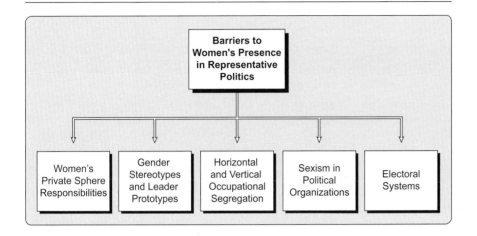

Women's Voting

Female voting, or **women's suffrage,** was a major aim of the early feminist movement from the mid-1880s through the first half of the twentieth century. Voting rights for women were hard-won, and women activists (suffragettes) were arrested and harassed while demonstrating for this right. For example, in the United States, it took seventy-two years of activism. In 1916, members of the National Women's Party (NWP), led by Alice Paul, picketed in front of the White House continuously. For this they were imprisoned and abused. To draw attention to their cause they staged a hunger strike. Media attention to the abuse of the activists led to increased popular support for their cause and led to the passage of the nineteenth amendment in 1920. Alice Paul (1885–1977) was an important women's rights leader. She began the fight for the Equal Rights Amendment, was a leader in the international women's movement, was instrumental in the UN including gender equality in its charter, and led a coalition that was successful in adding a sex discrimination clause to Title VII of the 1964 Civil Rights Act (Alice Paul Institute, 2009).

See Box 9.3, for a list of countries and the year women's suffrage was attained in each. Keep in mind, though, that there were often restrictions on *which* women could vote. For example, Native American women were not allowed to vote until 1924, four years after other American women; in Australia, White women won the vote in 1902 but Aboriginal women had to wait until 1967; and in South Africa, White women won the vote in 1931 but Indian and "colored" women waited until 1984 and Black women until 1994 (Seager, 2009). Saudi Arabia is now the only country where men may vote and run for office (municipal local elections) but women cannot. Unfortunately, most countries do not collect data on gender and voting so cross-cultural information on the voting rates of women relative to men is scarce. However,

"I never doubted that equal rights was the right direction. Most reforms, most problems are complicated. But to me there is nothing complicated about ordinary equality."
Alice Paul, leader in the women's suffrage movement whose hunger strike and organizing led to U.S. women gaining the right to vote in 1920

"It was we, the people; not we, the white male citizens; nor we, the male citizens; but we, the whole people, who formed the Union. . . . Men, their rights and nothing more; women, their rights and nothing less."
Susan B. Anthony, early leader in the fight for U.S. women's voting rights

BOX 9.3 *A Sampling of Women's Suffrage*

Years	Countries
1893–1919	Australia, Canada, Finland, Germany, Greenland, Iceland, New Zealand, Norway, Russia, Sweden, Turkey*
1920–1944	Brazil, Burma, Ecuador, France, Ireland, Lithuania, Philippines, Spain, Thailand, United Kingdom, United States
1945–1959	Argentina, Bolivia, Chad, Chile, China, Colombia, Costa Rica, El Salvador, Ethiopia, Guatemala, Honduras, India, Japan, Mali, Mexico, Morocco, Nicaragua, Niger, Pakistan, Portugal, Senegal, Venezuela, Vietnam
1960–1979	Algeria, Angola, Iran, Kenya, Libya, Nigeria, Paraguay, Peru, Sudan, Zaire, Marshall Islands
Since 1980	Hong Kong, Iraq, South Africa, Western Samoa, Vanuatu, Liechtenstein, Central African Republic, Namibia, Samoa, Kazakhstan, Moldova, Kuwait

Source: Inter-Parliamentary Union, 2009a.

*At that time the Ottoman Empire.

available information indicates that, in most cases, women vote at rates equal to or greater than the rates at which men vote (Paxton & Kunovich, 2007; Stevens, 2007). Unfortunately, even less is known about voting differences among women based on race, ethnicity, religion, and class.

Although there is little research on how women vote in comparison to men, most available evidence suggests that women, more than men, favor liberal or left-wing parties but this also appears to depend on gender roles in a society, women's religiosity, and age (older and more religious women often vote more conservatively). Research in the United States and Western Europe indicates that as traditional gender roles wane in a country, women's voting patterns shift from being more conservative than men's, to aligning with men's, to becoming more liberal than men's in a process called **gender realignment** (Giger, 2009; Inglehart & Norris, 2003; Iverson & Rosenbluth, 2006). It appears that as women become more educated and enter the labor force, they do not see conservative parties that support traditional gender roles as serving their interests. Gender differences in voting may also occur because women have more pro-environment, anti-military, and pro-social welfare political attitudes

(Stevens, 2007). Gender gaps in voting behavior are, however, a relatively new area of study with limited cross-cultural, comparative research.

Voting does not by itself guarantee equality of opportunity in politics (Abukhalil, 1994). In some countries, women's fathers, brothers, or husbands may interfere in their voting choices or discourage women from voting at all. Women's ability to exercise their voting rights freely is also impaired in those countries where there are discrepancies in the adult literacy rates of women and men. Finally, in some countries and for some women, voting is not a political act. For example, in parts of Egypt, it is not uncommon for women with low incomes to sell their votes for cash (Blaydes & El Tarouty, 2009).

Women Representatives in Parliaments, Congresses, and Cabinets

Women's voting is only one form of formal political involvement. Governments are complex organizational structures consisting not only of heads of state but of other formal political actors such as members of **parliaments** and **congresses** (often called national assemblies) and **government cabinets.**

As is evident in Box 9.2, women remain significantly underrepresented in parliaments and congresses. But there's good news: Although women occupy on average 18.8 percent of seats in national assemblies, this is an all-time high; an overall 50 percent increase in fifteen years, a .5 percent increase a year (Inter-Parliamentary Union, 2010). There is no question that women's activism is partly responsible for this increase. Rates vary internationally and, for reasons discussed later, industrialized Western nations do not necessarily exhibit greater gender parity in legislatures. For example, in 2010, the United States (16 percent), United Kingdom (19 percent), France (20 percent), Israel (19 percent), and Japan (18 percent) lagged behind Argentina (37 percent), Mozambique (39 percent), Rwanda (50 percent), and Uganda (31 percent). A glass ceiling is also in evidence: Only 14.55 percent of national assemblies are headed by women (IPU, 2010).

Women are even rarer as cabinet members, but like women in parliament, there's evidence of progress. Government cabinets consist of advisors to the head of state who frequently lead specific government agencies. Cabinets are often the originators of the policies considered by legislators and usually have control over spending and policies in their own department. In many countries, cabinet members are called *ministers* (as in Minister of Finance), but in some, such as the United States, they are called *secretaries* (as in Secretary of Labor). Depending on the region, on average, women hold from 7 to 28 percent of cabinet positions worldwide (UNIFEM, 2008). On average, women hold 16 percent of ministerial or cabinet posts (IPU, 2010). Only thirty of the world's countries have one-third or more women ministers and only four countries (Cape Verde, Finland, Norway, and Spain) have 50 percent or more (IPU, 2010). Women are typically appointed to cabinet positions in the areas of family, social affairs, health, women's affairs, and

"The achievement of democracy presupposes a genuine partnership between men and women in the conduct of the affairs of society in which they work in equality and complementarity, drawing mutual enrichment from their differences."
Universal Declaration on Democracy, 1997

"There is no democracy in our beautifully democratic countries. Why? Women have not the same part in decision making as men have."
Vigdis Finnbogadottir, President of Iceland

In 1986, Norway became the first country to have a cabinet with close to half of its members women.

In 1999 Sweden became the first country to have more female than male ministers in the cabinet.

In 1997, Madeleine Albright became the highest-ranking woman in the history of the U.S. government when she became U.S. secretary of state. Since that time there have been two others: Condoleeza Rice and Hillary Clinton.

"If you have only a few women, they are forced to concentrate their efforts in a few areas associated with women, usually education, health and social systems. If you have a large number of deputies and women in power, it is not possible to confine them to traditional women's issues."
Karin Junker, executive board of Germany's Social Democratic Party, member of the European Parliament

"The concept of democracy will only assume true and dynamic significance when political policies and national legislation are decided upon jointly by men and women with equitable regard for the interests and aptitudes of both halves of the population."
Inter-parliamentary Union

education and rarely to economic and defense positions. While this is likely an indicator of sexism and these ministries are often less powerful than others, it may be in these positions that they are best able to shape policies to reduce gender discrimination and benefit women and families (Atchison & Down, 2009). Indeed, there is some evidence that gender stereotypes may benefit women politicians promoting these policies as they are seen as credible authorities in regard to these issues (Paxton et al. 2007).

Importance of Women Representatives in Parliaments, Congresses, and Cabinets

Women's representation in these positions is of symbolic importance because it is consistent with the ideals of justice and equality at the heart of representative democracy. When we think about the true purpose of representative democracy, we should become alarmed that although women make up approximately half of the population, they constitute less than 20 percent of legislatures and rarely serve as party leaders. It is also of symbolic importance because women's presence in governance improves both men's and women's assessments of women's capabilities and has been found to provide positive political role models for girls and women, leading to their greater political engagement (Hughes, 2009; Wolbrecht & Campbell, 2007). Some research finds that women become more interested in politics when they see other women participating as candidates or representatives (Stevens, 2007).

Women political representatives are also of practical importance because they make a difference in law and policy. Researchers consistently find a positive relationship between the number of female legislators and the amount of legislation and social policy that is favorable to women and addresses social issues such as peace, child labor, and social justice (Atchison & Down, 2009; Hughes, 2009; Paxton, Kunovich, & Hughes, 2007; Saint-Germain & Metoyer, 2008; UNIFEM, 2008). The number of women cabinet members is also positively associated with social policies benefiting women (Atchison & Down, 2009). If women are underrepresented in politics, then issues such as gender violence, reproductive rights, and women's health may be neglected. For example, one study found that women legislators in Argentina, Colombia, and Costa Rica initiated 11 percent more women's issues bills (Scwindt-Bayer, 2006). A large-scale survey of members of parliaments found that over 90 percent agreed that women give priority to women's issues (UNIFEM, 2009).

The United Nations estimates that women need to constitute at least 30 percent of a legislative body in order to exert a meaningful influence on politics; this is sometimes called **critical political mass** (UNDP, 1995). The Beijing Platform for Action called for a 30 percent minimum for women in representative politics (UNIFEM, 2008). By 2010, this critical mass had been reached in forty-four (16.7 percent) of the world's countries (Inter-Parliamentary Union, 2010). As Lister (2003) suggests, increasing women's political representation is particularly important because women have special interests, some in conflict with men's interests, that need to be articulated directly by women in political debate and decision making. Of course, not all women representatives advance women's causes, but in sufficient numbers (at least 30 percent), they are more likely to make a difference.

This section emphasized the importance of women in politics both for symbolic reasons (the ideals of democracy) and for practical ones (to represent women's interests and benefit policy-making). But we should once again note that women's interests, even within a country, often vary based on intersectional categories of race, class, culture, region, and sexual orientation. Because women politicians frequently come from more educated, privileged backgrounds, they are not necessarily attuned to the issues concerning other women in their societies. Even if women are present, laws are likely to be designed and implemented in exclusive ways if minorities are not at the table (Paxton et al., 2007).

Explanations for Gender Differences in Political Representation

There are many explanations for gender inequality in political representation. Most may be categorized as one of two types: (1) Ideological or cultural, and (2) Structural or institutional.

Ideological or Cultural Explanations. These explanations suggest that traditional gender ideologies and culture are responsible for women's exclusion from politics. The dominant image of women in most cultures is that of the wife–mother who is competent in the private sphere of life, not the public one. Politics is stereotyped as a male domain, and as part of gender conformity, men are more likely to pursue formal politics than are women. One important factor for the election of women is to have a pool of women with the experience necessary to run and serve in the national legislature (Saint-Germain & Metoyer, 2008). Traditional gender ideologies reduce the supply of potential women politicians because they lead to traditional gender role socialization, which reduces women's political interest and ambition as well as the likelihood they will have needed resources, experience, and skills to run (Paxton & Kunovich, 2003; Paxton et al., 2007). For example, in many countries the pool of qualified women has been reduced by gender occupational and educational segregation. The jobs leading to formal political office are customarily male-dominated (law, military, big business) and women have been less likely to receive the higher education often associated with office-holding (Peterson & Runyan, 1999; Saint-Germain & Metoyer, 2008).

Another ideology-related issue is that in gender-role traditional cultures, women's responsibilities as wife and mother do not provide the time to run for and hold political office. Moreover, it is not only women's longer workday that interferes; it is their lack of control over when they will be available and whether (how) family obligations will interfere with political pursuits (Peterson & Runyan, 1999). Because of traditional gender ideologies and gender roles, combining family responsibilities and political office are much more of an issue for women; men are not forced to make these choices (Peterson &

"Young girls in Liberia now can speak about wanting to be a minister or a President or a leader. I hope that motivation will just spread."
President Ellen Johnson Sirleaf of Liberia, Africa's first women president, elected in 2006

"The gendered division of power makes possible not only the relative denial of formal power to women in the international system but also the exclusion of women's struggles and 'women's issues' from the world politics agenda."
V. Spike Peterson and Anne Sisson Runyan

"It is only when there is a critical mass of women in all their diversity in every country of the world in both appointed and elected decision-making positions and in all international bodies, that gender issues will be addressed in the policy agenda and the goals of equality, development, peace and human rights for all can be realized in the 21st century."
Women's Environment and Development Organization (WEDO)

"A woman's place is in the house, and in the Senate."
American feminist proverb

"The hand that rocks the cradle may be too tired to rule the world."
Carole Wade and Carol Tavris

"But what is true I think, is that women who want and need a life outside as well as inside the home have a much, much harder time than men because they carry such a heavy double burden . . . and the life of a working mother who lives without the constant presence and support of the father of her children is three times harder than that of any man I have ever met."
Golda Meir, 1975

Runyan, 1999). Too often women are disadvantaged by the fact that political systems are run on the assumption that those who participate have no family responsibilities (Norris & Lovenduski, 1995). Unlike men, many women who enter representative politics do not have children, or have waited until their children are grown.

Traditional gender ideologies also affect the demand for women politicians. Women do not match the prototype of political representative because historically we have only seen men in these positions. Traditional gender stereotypes suggest that men, not women, are more naturally suited for these roles. As Peterson and Runyan (1999) suggest, women are socialized into domestic roles that are antithetical to public political sphere activities, and the traits associated with political efficacy (ambition, aggression, competitiveness, authority) are seen as distinctly *un*feminine. The result is that some people have trouble accepting women as political agents (Peterson & Runyan, 1999). In some countries, such as Kenya, traditional gender ideologies have led to violence against women candidates, especially those with campaigns promoting gender equality (UNIFEM, 2008).

These ideologies also reduce political parties' support for women candidates. The culture and processes of formal political institutions (especially political parties) are major barriers to women's equal participation in institutional politics (Chowdhury et al., 1994). Women, in general, have not been welcome in the fraternity of formal politics. What Chowdhury (1994) says in regard to politics in Bangladesh is true in general: Women's participation in electoral politics is illustrative of male control of party organizations; men have a greater ability to build viable constituency and party support in favor of nominations; women lack access to the kind of money and patronage needed to win elections; and the aggressive electioneering tactics often employed discourage women's entrance into the fray. However, parties with more egalitarian ideologies (parties that lean farther left in their ideologies) are more likely to promote women candidates (Paxton et al., 2007). Historically, leftist parties have elected more women than have centrist or rightist parties (Saint-Germain & Metoyer, 2008).

Structural or Institutional Explanations. While it is generally true that the more gender-egalitarian the culture, the more women in national legislative politics, this is not necessarily true. This is because structural factors also play a big role in women's representation. Structural or institutional explanations for gender differences in political representation focus on how the structure of the political system, in particular, the electoral system, affects women's presence in representative politics. It is far easier for women to run and win elections under particular electoral arrangements. Indeed, the **electoral system** (the procedures by which representatives are elected) explains almost 30 percent of the varying proportions of women in democracies' national legislatures (Rule, 1994). Rule (1994) demonstrates this in an analysis of twenty-seven long-established democracies. The adoption of electoral systems that lead to more gender equality in political representation is also partly responsible for the high election rates of women in some newer democracies.

There are three types of electoral systems each with different effects on women's election to national legislative office: (1) In **party list/proportional representation systems** (PL/PR), three or more parties prepare lists of candidates for election from each district (party lists); seats are allocated roughly in proportion to the votes each party receives (e.g., if a party receives 30 percent of the votes, it gets 30 percent of the seats, and moves down its list until the party's seats are filled); and there are five or more representatives per district (multi-member districts). In contrast are the (2) **single member district systems** (SMD) or plurality/majority systems. These nonparty list/nonproportional representation systems are "winner-take-all" systems where there is usually only one seat per district, and the person who gets the most votes wins. Some countries have (3) **mixed systems,** with PR systems in some regions of the country and a plurality/majority system in others.

Female political representatives are far fewer in SMD systems. Unsurprisingly, under these systems, parties will usually choose and support only those candidates believed capable of winning the required number of votes. Historically, parties under these systems have believed that male candidates gave them the best chance of winning the district. Another problem is that male domination of political parties led to reluctance to support women candidates over male candidates (male leaders wanted the few available spots to go to men). SMD systems are one reason why nations like the United States, the United Kingdom, France, and Japan have relatively low numbers of women in their legislatures. The PL/PR system is used in the majority of the countries with the highest percentages of women legislators (Paxton & Hughes, 2007; Paxton & Kunovich, 2003). Under these systems, parties see an advantage in having some female candidates to attract more women voters and gain more seats, and the fact that women run for office does not prevent men from running (Paxton & Hughes, 2007). Within regions, there are often marked differences in women's representation based on electoral system. For example, in East Asia and the Pacific, a United Nations study showed that an average of 19 percent of seats were held by women in countries with PR systems compared to 6 percent in countries with non-PR systems (UNIFEM, 2008). In "mixed" systems, more women are elected from areas with PR systems.

As pointed out by Paxton and Hughes (2007), the effect of PL/PR systems on women's representation is complicated by the fact that PL/PR systems vary considerably. For example, the size of the multimember district (**district magnitude**) makes a big difference—the more seats per district, the better for women. **Party magnitude** (the number of seats a party expects to win in a district) also makes a difference for women. This is because parties move down their lists in order. Party leaders tend to be men and tend to put themselves at the top of the lists to ensure their election. When women are placed lower on the lists, their odds of election are lower, especially if the party tends to win only a small number of seats (Paxton & Hughes, 2007).

"We face many obstacles, but four of the more prevalent are stereotyping, the nature of the political beast, a rigid electoral system, and apathy."
Daisy Avance Fuentes, first woman deputy speaker in the Philippines House of Representatives

*Increasing the Number of Women Representatives
in Parliaments and Congresses*

Because women have a positive influence on policymaking regarding women's issues but their numbers remain relatively low, many feminist political scientists have studied how women gain greater power in representative democracies. Figure 9.2 summarizes the conditions leading to greater female representation in formal politics.

Electoral reforms, changes to the electoral system, are one way to increase the number of women representatives and may include the adoption of PL/PR systems and gender **quotas,** which involve such things as reserving a certain number of seats for women in parliament or congress, or requiring that a certain percentage of party candidates are women. Unfortunately, it is crisis that often opens the space for the adoption of systems favorable to increasing women's numbers in national legislatures. Many of the newly developing democracies that formed after intense strife chose PL/PR systems, with positive effects for women's representation. Women's movements were critical to the legislative and constitutional changes that carved out new roles for women in government (Tripp, Casimoro, Kwesiga, & Mungwa, 2009). International women's movements and the UN, especially following the Fourth World Conference for Women in Beijing in 1995, also encouraged new democracies to pass gender equity laws and policies, including legislated, national-level gender quotas (Franceschet & Piscopo, 2008).

The new democracy of Namibia adopted a PL/PR system in 1989. A total of fourteen women appeared on candidate lists, and women were elected to 6.9 percent of assembly seats. Although this may not seem significant, this was only the second election in which Namibian women were eligible to vote and run for office. By 2010, Namibian women representatives comprised 27 percent of the lower house and 27 percent of the upper house. Rwanda and South Africa

FIGURE 9.2 *Conditions Leading to More Women in Parliaments,
Congresses, and Cabinets*

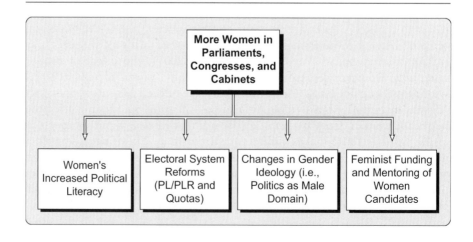

Despite their overall effectiveness, quotas are not without controversy. Critics charge that they are undemocratic, that they promote the election of unqualified women, that "quota women" are blindly loyal to male party bosses, and that quotas may become a ceiling on women's participation (countries may not be motivated to pursue further strategies to ensure equal participation) (Franceschet & Piscopo, 2008; Paxton & Hughes, 2007). Many agree that quotas are a point of departure rather than a point of arrival and point out that we must continue efforts to eliminate the factors that led to the problem in the first place (Bonder & Nari, 1995; Chowdury, 1994).

Feminist funding, advising, and training of women candidates are other avenues to increasing the number of women representatives. Indeed, strong women's groups and a national women's movement are associated with greater numbers of women in legislatures (Bystydzienski, 1994; Saint-Germain & Metoyer, 2008). In the 1970s in Norway, a coalition of women's groups mobilized women to run for office, worked through political parties, and taught voters how to use flexible voting rules (the system permits the writing in of names on ballots) (Bystydzienski, 1992b, 1995). Norwegian activists also convinced political parties to nominate women candidates and accept gender quotas, and female parliamentary representation has remained high. The result was the quadrupling of female political representation locally and nationally in a period of two decades.

In the SMD system of the United States, feminist groups have attempted to increase the number of female candidates by funding their campaigns. EMILY's List (the acronym stands for Early Money Is Like Yeast) is one example. At an average size of 550,000 residents, many U.S. congressional districts are larger than the entire populations of many nations, and U.S. congressional candidates need big money to reach them through mass media (Lauter, 1995). Unfortunately, women have had less access to the traditional business, professional, and political fund-raising networks (Lauter, 1995). Begun in 1985 by feminist Ellen R. Malcolm, EMILY's List helps female candidates by introducing them to a network of donors who provide funds. By 2010, EMILY's List had helped elect nine women governors, fifteen women to the U.S. Senate and eighty women to the U.S. House of Representatives, and 473 women to state and local political offices.

Another effective feminist effort to increase the numbers of women political representatives is a focus on increasing women's **political literacy.** Getting elected is a complex, expensive, and bureaucratic process and women have not always had the same access as men to information, money, and resources. Women's organizations sometimes step in to fill the gap. For example, Korean women's organizations such as the Women's Research Association, the Korean Research Institute for Women and Politics, and the Center for Korean Women in Politics work to educate and train potential female candidates (Darcy & Hyun, 1994). Emily's List in the United States also recruits and trains candidates and campaign professionals to effectively organize, fund-raise, and communicate their message. The UN also works to increase women's political literacy. UNIFEM partnered with Kenyan women's organizations to provide media

"Women's movements can expose women to the world of politics, offer opportunities for leadership, and create pathways to political office."
Michelle Saint-Germain and Cynthia Chavez Metoyer

BOX 9.4 *Activist Profile: Hazel Brown on Increasing Women's Political Literacy in Trinidad and Tobago*

Here Hazel Brown, Coordinator of the Network of NGOs of Trinidad and Tobago for the Advancement of Women, describes a campaign in the Caribbean for increasing women's political literacy and empowerment:

We decided to work together with women across the Caribbean, and exchange ideas on increasing women's participation locally. We developed eight strategies:

First, focus on cross-partisan activities. In the last local government elections in Trinidad and Tobago, of 100 who ran for office, 48 won. To increase the number of women running, we played each party against the others. When one party gave us a list with thirty-one women, we went to the other party and said, "Can I have your list please?" That list came up with forty-four women. We went back to the first party and said, "This party has forty-four—you can't go out there with thirty-one."

Second, women need consistent, supportive networks. For example, women often say campaigns can't be run without money. So how do we get the money? A cocktail party at the British High Commission included many men with money. I slid up to one and said, "We are running this campaign for women candidates, would you be willing to support it?" Some of them said, "I'm not giving my money to any party candidates," but we were able to promise to give their money to independent women candidates. We shared the pool of money raised equally among all the women who participated.

Our third strategy was to produce a manual on how to dress, how to read a speech, how to handle security, how to make eye contact with an audience, where to campaign, how to plan ahead, what to do about caring for your children, what you do about your husband. Everything was written down.

Fourth, we recommend using professional media. When we used professional media, we found ways to help ordinary people understand our messages. For example, a media professional translated our long message on how good it is to have women candidates into: "If the hand that rocks the cradle rules the world, then it is time for more of those hands to help." Everybody understood it, and it can run on the radio over and over again.

Fifth, build alliances—with church people, union people, business people—with anybody who supports your cause.

Sixth, target young voters. We found that it was young people who were willing to come out and work for our new paradigm. But most women in political parties don't appear to have a strategy for encouraging either youth or women voters.

The seventh strategy relates to sustainability after the elections. It is not enough only to get women elected, because nothing in the system supports them. After the election, we formed local government women's forums—combinations of women across each party, including those who won, lost, and worked on the campaigns. They now understand the dynamics of working together and the forum can be a valuable resource for women inside the political system.

The eighth strategy is to build links between women activists and politicians. Too often, politicians from the women's movement forget about us after they assume power; therefore we need to strengthen communications.

Source: Women's Environment and Development Organization, 2003 http://www.wedo.org/5050/trinadad.htm.

advocacy and training for women running for election; for the first time, six women were appointed to the cabinet and the number of women in parliament rose 3 percent (WIN, 2003). UNIFEM and UNDP have also provided training to help women run for office. Box 9.4 features a first-hand description of a political literacy campaign in Trinidad and Tobago.

Women Heads of State: Presidents and Prime Ministers

Although somewhat rare, powerful female leaders can be found throughout history. Women like Cleopatra (Egypt), Catherine the Great (Russia), Yaa Asantewaa (Ghana), and Tz'u-Hsi (China) acquired their positions through hereditary monarchies in countries where women were deemed largely incapable of exercising political power (Fraser, 1988). Currently three Western countries have reigning queens: Queen Elizabeth II, queen of the United Kingdom of Great Britain and Northern Ireland (since 1952); Margrethe II, Queen of Denmark (since 1972); and Queen Beatrix of the Netherlands (since 1980). In the twenty-first century, however, these queens wield little power and coexist with democratically elected governments. The true heads of state are considered to be the democratically elected or appointed presidents or prime ministers of their respective countries.

In 2010 there were just seventeen women presidents or prime ministers, about 6 percent of the world total (see Box 9.5). While numbers remain low, this is a 25 percent increase in just five years and almost 70 percent of these were "firsts"—the first woman in her country to hold the position. In some ways, major progress has been made in the last forty years, and although the glass ceiling is far from shattered, it has cracked. The first three women heads of state served in the 1960s, in the 1970s there were six, in the 1980s there were seven, in the 1990s there were twenty-six, and in the first decade of the twenty-first century, we matched the 1990s number.

It is true, however, that the power of the president or prime minister varies and in many countries, women presidents or prime ministers have few executive powers. Women in these positions are also more common in power-sharing

Prime Minister Johanna Siguroadottir is not only the first woman to hold this position in Iceland, she is the first openly gay head of state in the world.

In 1993, Agathe Uwilingiyimana became the first female prime minister of Rwanda but was assassinated in 1994.

In 2003, Finland became the first European country to have women as both president and prime minister.

BOX 9.5 *Women Presidents and Prime Ministers in 2010*

President Tarja Halonen* (Finland)

President Mary McAleese (Ireland)

President Gloria Macapagal-Arroyo (Philippines)

President Michelle Bachelet* (Chile)

Prime Minister Luisa Diogo* (Mozambique)

President Cristina E. Fernandez de Kirchner* (Argentina)

Prime Minister Helen Clark (New Zealand)

President Dalia Grybauskaité (Lithuania)

Prime Minister Emily Songh-Elhage (Netherlands-Antilles)

President Laura Chinchilla (Costa Rica)

Prime Minister Sheikh Hasina (Bangladesh)

President Ellen Johnson-Sirleaf* (Liberia)

President Borjana Kristo* (Bosnia)

Chancellor Angela Merkel* (Germany)

President Pratibha Patil* (India)

Prime Minister Johanna Siguroadottir* (Iceland)

President Yulia Tymoshenko* (Ukraine)

* First woman to hold this position in this country.

arrangements (e.g., systems with dual executives; both a president and prime minister, where one is male). Prime Minister Yulia Tymoshenko of Ukraine and Prime Minister Luisa Dias Diogo of Mozambique are two recent examples. In fact, an analysis of women leaders in 132 countries from 1996 to 2006 found that women are more likely to be executives when their powers are relatively few and generally constrained (Jalalzai, 2008). For instance, the presidency in Iceland, which has been held by two women, is a nonpolitical office in which the president has little power over domestic issues. Likewise, the Irish Constitution prevents the Irish president from participating in politics (there have been two women presidents of Ireland). That said, many women leaders in this situation, like Mary Robinson of Ireland, have used the symbolic power of their offices to promote social reform benefiting women. And, it should also be noted that three recent "firsts," President Michele Bachelet of Chile (2006), Chancellor Angela Merkel of Germany (2005), and President Ellen Johnson Sirleaf of Liberia (2006), occupy some of the most powerful executive positions in their regions. For example, in 2010, Angela Merkel was the only woman leading a Group of 8 (G8) country (a forum of the world's most powerful industrialized democracies), the only woman head of state in NATO (North American Trade Organization), and the only woman head of state in the European Union (Wiliarty, 2008). Feminists hope that these are not exceptions to the rule but the beginning of a new rule.

It is interesting to consider how women come to occupy these customarily male power positions and to ask how their leadership might differ from that of men. Unfortunately, the study of women heads of state has received less attention than the study of women in legislative politics and so the answers to these questions are preliminary. Quantification is difficult, partly due to the small sample of women executive leaders (Jalalzai, 2008). The differing and complex political, economic, and cultural contexts specific to a given woman's trajectory and experience also make generalization difficult and study challenging.

Paths to Power

Let's begin with the first question: How do women get to be president or prime minister of their country? Box 9.6, summarizes the many factors found to precipitate women's rise to executive office.

Historically, one of the most common paths to executive government office has been kinship. Many women heads of state have used kinship ties, as daughters or wives of political figures, to attain office (D'Amico, 1995; Jalalzai, 2008). Indeed, most women heads of state have become president or prime minister in countries where women's status lags behind men's; this is commonly attributed to the fact that many have benefited from kinship ties to past political leaders (Jalalzi, 2008). In many cases (especially in Latin America), women leaders have followed the "widow's walk" to power and are **political surrogates** (stand-ins) for husbands killed by natural or political causes and were expected to act as their husbands would. Likewise, some women leaders are the daughters of the country's founding fathers. This has

BOX 9.6 *Recipe for Woman Head of State*

One of more of these personal factors:

• Deceased husband or father who was a pro-nationalist or pro-democracy leader

• Served in national assembly, climbed party ladder

• Record of government service plus activism in a pro-democracy or anti-government corruption movement

• Educated, and from upper-class

+

One or more institutional/structural factors:

• Parliamentary system where prime minister or president isn't determined by the popular vote

• Dual executive system (both a president and a prime minister)

• Party structure with institutionalized leadership-selection processes

+

One or more sociohistorical factors:

• Government transition to democracy

• Society recovering from civil war, dictatorship, or political instability

• Recent history of government corruption

• Political party instability due to scandal, infighting, or death

• Active women's groups or movements

=

Woman Head of State

been more common in Asia than elsewhere. In contrast to the widows, the daughters of political martyrs typically have extensive political party experience. Their political pedigree helped them to get their foot in the political party door, where they eventually became political "insiders." It also gave them a credibility that aided in their election. However, once elected they often stray significantly from their father's leadership style and policies.

The world's first woman prime minister, Sirimavo Bandaranaike of Sri Lanka (1960–1965, 1970–1977, 1994–2000), took the widow's walk to power. Like most women heads of state, she came from an aristocratic, well-off family. Her husband, Solomon Dias Bandaranaike, was a leader in the movement to gain independence from Britain. He became prime minister in 1956, only to be assassinated in September 1959. New elections were set for March 1960, and Sirimavo Bandaranaike was asked to campaign on behalf of her husband's political party, the Sri Lankan Freedom Party (SLFP). In May 1960, she reluctantly accepted headship of the SLFP, and the party won the majority of seats in the House of Representatives. As head of the party, she became prime minister. At the beginning she acted as a surrogate for her dead husband, carrying out his political plans. However, over time she became a politician in her own right. In 1994 she was again appointed prime minister—this time by her daughter, President Chandrika Kumaratunga. Bandaranaike retired in 2000 at age 84 and died a few months later, only hours after voting in a public election.

In the case of most surrogates, the husband or father was assassinated and subsequently martyred by the citizenry as a persecuted leader of democratic change or national independence. When it appeared that the government was going in the direction of pre-struggle politics and there were no electable alternative candidates, political strategists sought the next best thing to the successful but now deceased challenger—his relatives. The wife or daughter was chosen when there were no male offspring to assume this role or when party leaders assumed that women would be more malleable and obedient than their male relatives (Jalalzai, 2008). During the campaign, references to the achievements and martyrdom of the husband/father were made repeatedly, and it was implied that the female candidate would serve as a stand-in for the cherished leader. With all but a few exceptions, these women were well educated and came from wealthy, political families. Most had little political experience when drafted by a political party.

In countries where attitudes toward women are especially traditional, the kinship path has historically been the most likely route to female national leadership. Violeta de Chamorro, president of Nicaragua (1990–1996) is a good example of this. According to Saint-Germain (1993), Nicaraguan women are expected to derive their identities from their male relatives and are respected to the extent that they sacrifice and submit to the demands of men. The line between public (political) and private (home) spheres is clearly demarcated, and women are expected to stay within the home sphere. Given this dual gender system, it is difficult for women to be political. To do so, they must typically present their political activity as an extension of their role in the home by emphasizing their wife and mother role during and after elections. For instance, during Chamorro's campaign, she said she was not a feminist but rather a woman dedicated to her home, as "taught" by her husband, Pedro Chamorro. She stated she was not a politician but was running "for Pedro and for her country." At one point she said that she was "marked with the Chamorro branding iron." Violeta Chamorro's advisors modeled her image after the Virgin Mary, the ultimate long-suffering maternal mother in Nicaraguan culture. The idea of a national mother who could bring together war-torn Nicaraguans appealed to voters. This, in combination with U.S. promises to provide aid and stop encouraging the Contras should she be elected, resulted in her election to president in 1990. (The Contras were a rebel military force that launched numerous attacks across the country to topple the democratically elected Sandanista government.)

Benazir Bhutto, prime minister of Pakistan (1988–1990, 1993–1996) and the first woman elected to lead a Muslim state, is another example of how, in gender-traditional countries, women's political activism may be acceptable when it appears as though they are acting on behalf of male relatives. It is likely that Bhutto would not have been elected in the gender-conservative country of Pakistan were it not for the popularity of her martyred father, Zulfikar Ali Bhutto. Following her father's political imprisonment and her brothers' political exile abroad, Bhutto dutifully carried on her father's struggle against the authoritarian regime of General Mohammad Zia. Her father was eventually put to death by Zia, and Benazir was imprisoned. This treatment only cemented the Pakistanis' adoration of the Bhuttos. In time, international and domestic pressure led Zia to release Benazir, and, in 1988, Zia allowed elections. Benazir used her father's image skillfully, referring repeatedly to him in speeches and being photographed with his image in the background (Anderson, 1993). Zia was killed in a plane crash right before the election and Benazir's party, the Pakistan People's Party (PPP), won the majority of seats in the National Assembly, and Benazir became prime minister. In 1990, President Izhaq Khan dismissed Bhutto on charges of nepotism and corruption. She ran for office and won again in 1993, but three years into her five-year term, she was dismissed by President Farooq Leghari, again under charges of corruption. Bhutto went into self-imposed exile until 2007 when she returned to lead the PPP and run for parliament. She was assassinated by a suicide bomber during a campaign rally in December 2007. The terrorist group Al-Qaeda claimed responsibility and it is widely speculated that then-President Musharraf deliberately provided inadequate security.

Political party officials frequently assume that once elected or appointed, the female head of state will act as a figurehead and will leave the governing to party officials. For instance, it appears that few party officials had any intention of actually having Chamorro lead. As one of her brothers-in-law said, "We are not looking for someone to run the country. We are looking for someone who represents the ideal [of democracy]." One of her political advisors said, "Violeta wasn't chosen for her abilities as a president. Violeta was chosen to win" (Saint-Germain, 1993, p. 84). However, most surrogates become political leaders in their own right. For example, the Pakistani Political Party chose Benazir Bhutto to head the party because she was a Bhutto and had suffered political persecution by Zia. Although the party elders assumed that she would serve primarily as a symbol and had a difficult time accepting her leadership, she asserted herself and became a powerful leader (Anderson, 1993).

My father always would say, "My daughter will go into politics. My daughter will become prime minister," but it's not what I wanted to do. I would say, 'No, Papa, I will never go into politics.' As I've said before, this is not the life I chose; it chose me . . . But I accepted the responsibility and I've never wavered in my commitment."
Benazir Bhutto

A second common path to power for female leaders is that of **political insider** or climber (D'Amico, 1995). Women prime ministers and presidents typically have lots of political experience and many have served in political party leadership positions (Jalalzai, 2004). These women earn their prime minister or president position through dedicated service to their party and by climbing the party's promotion ladder. As is the case with parliamentary representation, institutional factors make a difference, and it is easier for women to attain executive political office under some political systems than others. This path to power is especially likely in parliamentary systems where prime ministers are elected by parliament or granted the position based on the application of party rules. Under these systems, women can work their way up in a party, become party head, and bypass a potentially biased public (Jalalzai & Krook, 2008). This is also why women executives are more common in parliamentary systems than in presidential systems where women must be elected by popular vote (Jalalzai, 2008). Although D'Amico (1995) hypothesized that this is an infrequent path to power for women because women are statistically underrepresented in the professions that serve as political stepping-stones (that is, the law, military service, and business), this appears to be changing as more women enter "feeder" professions and positions and as the pool of qualified women increases due to growth in women's presence in national legislative assemblies. Global, regional, and national women's movements have played an important role in this development, pushing for higher levels of women's political representation, making the idea of women politicians more acceptable, and registering women voters (Adams, 2008; Wiliarty, 2008).

Indira Gandhi of India is one example of a leader who took the insider path but her trajectory also has kinship/surrogate elements. She became a member of the Congress Party in 1948, was elected to its Working Committee in 1955, to its presidency in 1959, to the upper house of Parliament in 1964, and served an appointed position as Minister of Information and Broadcasting before assuming the presidency of India in 1966 (Carras, 1995). Although she certainly presented herself as a political surrogate early on (her father was leader in the movement to gain independence from Britain and the first prime minister following independence), her party granted her power in part because she had earned her status within the party hierarchy. Similarly, Margaret Thatcher of Great Britain began working for the Conservative Party in the 1950s, was elected to the House of Commons in 1959, became Parliamentary Secretary to the Ministry of Pensions and National Security in 1961, became Secretary of State for Education in 1970, leader of the Conservative Party in 1975, and finally, prime minister in 1979.

Golda Meir, the first and only woman prime minister of Israel, was clearly a political insider. Her government service to Israel began in the state's formative years. As a teenager in the United States, she became a Zionist, organizing and raising funds for an independent Jewish state in Palestine. In 1921, she moved to Palestine. For a time, she lived on a kibbutz, a communal experience dedicated to Zionism. In 1928 she took a position as secretary of the Women's Labor Council. Meir raised hundreds of millions of dollars for the fledging Israeli state. She spent a good part of the 1930s and 1940s

"My father was a statesman, I am a political woman. My father was a saint. I am not."
Indira Gandhi

traveling the world raising funds for the Jewish settlers in Palestine. She was active in the formation of the Mapai political party and served in many positions. She was responsible for settling the thousands of immigrants arriving from Europe in the late 1940s and orchestrated the building of thousands of homes. She served as the first Israeli ambassador to the Soviet Union, secretary of labor, foreign minister, head of the Mapai Party, and, finally, in 1970 as prime minister.

The first women who took the insider path to power appeared to function as "honorary males." They dismissed the relevance of gender to their leadership and saw themselves as one of the political "boys." Indira Gandhi once said, "As Prime Minister, I am not a woman. I am a human being" (quoted in Everett, 1993). Golda Meir (1975) said, "The fact is that I have lived and worked with men all my life, but being a woman has never hindered me in any way at all. It has never caused me unease or given me an inferiority complex or made me think that men are better off than women—or that it is a disaster to give birth to children. Not at all." Perhaps without these attitudes these women would not have been able to rise through the party ranks.

Many women executives come to power under unique sociohistorical circumstances, entering office during transitions to national independence or democratic governance, party instability, or the opening of political opportunity due to the sudden removal, resignation, or death of an executive (Jalalzai, 2008). Many are compromise candidates in the case of a divided political party (D'Amico, 1995). For example, it is generally agreed that Indira Gandhi may not have come to power at all were it not for the unexpected death of Prime Minister Lal Bahadur Shastri, a divided political party, and a desire to prevent a particular individual (Morarji Desia) from becoming prime minister (Carras, 1995; Everett, 1993). Likewise, Margaret Thatcher became head of the Conservative political party because the person expected to run for the post refused to run, and there was a shortage of qualified competitors. As Genovese (1993) suggests, Thatcher's first election to prime minister had more to do with the failure of the Labour Party to solve severe domestic and trade union problems than it did with her policy proposals or charisma. Like Thatcher, Golda Meir probably would not have become prime minister of Israel in 1970 were it not for some unusual circumstances. Israel's Prime Minister Levi Eskol died suddenly from a heart attack when Israel was on the verge of war with Egypt, and disagreements within Eskol's coalition cabinet prevented the selection of a leader from the cabinet. It made sense to appoint the steady Meir as an interim prime minister rather than engage in political infighting when Israel was on the verge of war.

Some recent examples of the tendency for women to come to power in cases of divided parliaments or parties include Han Myung-Sook and Angela Merkel. South Korea's first woman prime minister, Han Myung-Sook, elected by parliament in 2006, was a bi-partisan compromise selected to mediate a bitter relationship between government and opposition parties. Merkel, the first female Chancellor of Germany (the head of Germany) was trained as a physicist and chemist. An East German, she got involved in German politics in 1989 after the fall of the Berlin Wall during the period of reunification of East and West Germany. She held a variety of elected and appointed positions in government and worked her way up her party's hierarchy. In 2005 she was elected by the majority of delegates in the Bundestag (Germany's parliament) where she was a compromise candidate following a major scandal in her political party that caused party leaders to step down.

Some women executives have come to power as their countries recover from brutal dictatorships, corrupt governments, or transition to democracy. These women seem to benefit from a combination of government service experience and a past history of activism in pro-democratic or anti-corruption movements; this seems to increase people's trust that they will serve democratic ends rather than use their power for personal gain and political repression. This too may be a case where women benefit from gender stereotypes that women are more ethical, less corrupt, less selfish, and less violent than men. Whether these stereotypes are true or not, they may provide an important advantage to women candidates in postconflict environments (Adams, 2008).

President Michele Bachelet, the first woman president of Chile, is an example. Elected in 2006, this pediatrician and epidemiologist with advanced training in military defense, never served in Parliament. Her party chose her to run because of her popularity with the electorate; her visible and successful performance in both the Minister of Health and Defense Minister roles, her personal history as a political prisoner under the dictator Pinochet, and her expertise in the effects of trauma due to political oppression (helpful in a country still recovering from a brutal dictatorship). In Chile, where differences between women and men are taken for granted, the qualities attributed to women include generosity, a commitment to service, an interest in the common good, little ambition for power or wealth, incorruptibility, and closeness to citizens' concerns; these qualities appealed to the Chilean people who sought an incorruptible leader who was interested more in the nation than in petty party concerns (Rios Tobar, 2008).

Like Bachelet, Ellen Johnson Sirleaf, elected by popular vote in 2005 as Liberia's first women president and Africa's first woman elected head of state, also benefited from a combination of leadership experience and participation in the pro-democracy movement. She came to power after Liberia experienced 23 years of political repression, corruption, and civil conflict. Because of this, she is also an example of the fact that many women executives come to power following political instability and corruption. Johnson Sirleaf had served as Liberia's Finance Minister, worked for the UNDP, the World Bank, and for Citibank in senior positions. As Finance Minister, she became known for challenging the government's economic policies and corruption, and did prison time for speaking out. During the election, she capitalized on perceptions that women in Liberia were peacemakers rather than those responsible for sparking and prolonging the conflict, and she took a strong stance against corruption, building on the widespread view that women are less corrupt than men (Adams, 2008).

"I am here as a woman, representing the defeat of the exclusion which we have objected to for so long."
Michelle Bachelet, Chile's first woman president, elected in 2006

In addition to Ellen Johnson Sirleaf, Africa has had six women prime ministers and seven vice presidents and deputy presidents and from 1997–2007, 27 African women ran for president of their country.

Gender Differences in Leadership

Accepting the characterization of aggressiveness and authoritarianism as male traits, many feminists have assumed that women world leaders would govern in a more peaceful and democratic way than do male leaders. Some have also assumed that women political leaders will be more ethical than men political leaders. However, evidence indicates that none of this is necessarily true. Indeed, there is great variability in women leaders, just as there is in men. Simply put, it is difficult to generalize about women leaders. Their policy agendas and styles of leadership are diverse and often challenge gender-based notions of feminine values and behavior (D'Amico, 1995). As Gonzalez and Kampwirth (2002) concluded in regard to Latin American women in politics, the evidence does not clearly support the position that men are inherently more violent and women inherently more peaceful. Also, contrary to our images of women as nurturers and peacemakers, women leaders are not necessarily less likely to use their militaries to resolve conflicts. Many of the women profiled in this chapter did not hesitate to use the military against domestic protesters or go to war to defend territorial interests. Indeed, Fraser (1988) suggests that many women leaders "have found in the crucible of war—if successfully survived—the fiery process which has guaranteed them passage into the realms of honorary men" (p. 10). There are also, unfortunately, examples of women political leaders who did not use their power for the democratic good.

> "We can't be certain that women would make different decisions than men, but they might if there were enough of them to affect the decision process and its environment."
> *Jeanne Kirkpatrick, first female U.S. ambassador to the UN, 1981–1985*

The world's first female prime minister, Sirimavo Bandaranaike of Sri Lanka, increased defense spending, bought armaments from all over the world, and used them to control rebellion against her government. The military was used to squash ultra-leftists, who felt Bandaranaike was not moving quickly enough, and to combat the Tamils, a minority group that revolted when she decreed Buddhism the national religion and Sinhalese the national language. Indira Gandhi oversaw the most ambitious program of military buildup in India's history, presided over India's first underground nuclear explosion, built up the navy to become the principal naval power in the region, and went to war with Pakistan over East Pakistan's desire to become an independent state (Bangladesh).

> "Women are not inherently passive or peaceful. We're not inherently anything but human."
> *Robin Morgan*

Margaret Thatcher sent British forces to the Falkland Islands in 1982 to reclaim them from the Argentinean government. She did not hesitate to use the police in strike situations and showed little sympathy for the citizens injured (Genovese, 1993). Eugenia Charles, prime minister of Dominica, appealed to U.S. president Ronald Reagan for assistance in invading Grenada in 1983 following a political coup there. Golda Meir was quite willing to use force in conflicts with Israel's neighbors, seeing it as necessary to the establishment and preservation of a Jewish state in Palestine. As foreign minister she was ready to use force against Egypt in 1956, and she supported the Six-Day War of 1967 with Egypt.

Tansu Ciller, the first female prime minister of Turkey (1993–1996) is yet another example of the fact that female leaders are often no more gentle, peaceful, and ethical than male leaders. While Ciller was prime minister, tensions between Greece and Turkey over the island of Cyprus escalated following the killing of a Greek protester who had tried to tear down a Turkish flag on the island. Ciller reportedly warned that anyone who tried to tear down the Turkish flag would have their hands broken. During her administration, human rights activists repeatedly called attention to the imprisonment and torture of political opponents and the evacuation and destruction of over 1,000 Kurdish villages. Ciller also introduced a law allowing the seizure and government sale of land that did not have a title issued since the last coup. Ciller personally benefited from such land seizures. Kurdish rebellion, economic instability, and charges of corruption led her to step down in 1996. She has remained active in politics, first as foreign minister, then as a member of parliament, and later as leader of the True Path Party.

Also contrary to the notion of women leaders as ethical is Benazir Bhutto, who lost her office amid charges of autocratic rule and corruption. Bhutto routinely bypassed parliament and awarded high positions in her administration to corrupt politicians, including her husband. In addition, many believe she was behind the death of her brother and political rival, who was ambushed and killed by police. In a country where the average person earns $1.18 a day, she proposed $1.1 billion in new taxes while she was in the process of purchasing a $4 million mansion in Britain (Dahlburg & Bearak, 1996). As UNIFEM (2000a) concluded, electing or appointing women to leadership positions will not on its own clean up government. Effective checks and balances on power are needed (democratic and transparent politics), whatever the gender of politicians.

That said, some women world leaders do fit the feminist image of peacemaker and ethical leader. For example, Corazon Aquino, president of the Philippines from 1986 to 1992 and a political surrogate for her martyred husband, Benigno Aquino, emphasized economic development and the peaceful resolution of long-standing internal conflicts (Boudreau, 1995; Col, 1993). She granted amnesty to guerrillas, declared cease-fires with rebels, and released political prisoners (Col, 1993). Nicaragua's President Chamorro, much to the chagrin of the UNO party that ran her as a candidate, cooperated with the defeated yet powerful FSLN party. She did this by appointing General Humberto Ortega, a director of the FSLN, to be her senior military officer. By cooperating with the FSLN and the Contras, she undoubtedly quelled some civil strife. In a country torn for many years by civil war, she consistently advocated consensus and reconciliation over confrontation and vengeance (Williams, 1995). Mary Robinson is another example. She consistently worked for a peaceful solution to the conflict in Northern Ireland.

A recent peacemaker head of state who has also done much to reduce government corruption is Ellen Johnson Sirleaf of Liberia. In a country scarred by fourteen years of civil conflict (during which an estimated 200,000 people died) and a corrupt government, she created a national action plan for promoting lasting peace that focuses on the role of women as peacemakers and peacekeepers (The Carter Center, 2009; Sussman, 2009). She also

"I have no experience in lying, stealing, or cheating like our male presidents have had. But then perhaps this better qualifies me to lead the nation well."
Corazon Aquino, the Philippines' first woman president, elected in 1986

"I think when women have equal qualifications, experience, capacities, they bring to the task a certain dimension that may be missing in men—a sensitivity to humankind. Maybe it comes from being a mother."
Ellen Johnson Sirleaf, President of Liberia and Africa's first elected woman president (2006)

emphasized the process of demilitarization, demobilization, and training and reintegration of ex-combatants. She was a founding member of the International Institute for Women in Political Leadership. Prior to her election to president, Johnson Sirleaf led the country's anti-corruption reform as Chairperson of the Governance Reform Commission.

As the evidence currently stands, female leaders are also not more likely than male leaders to exhibit a democratic leadership style. Some are, but it appears that many, like Turkey's Tansu Ciller, are described as combative, insensitive, arrogant, and power mad. It is not hard to find autocratic female leaders. These leaders have strong convictions regarding the directions that their countries should take, and they believe that only they are qualified to lead their countries there. For instance, in 2003, President Chandrika Kumaratunga of Sri Lanka suspended parliament and deployed troops around the capital while her prime minister and arch-rival Ranil Wickremesinghe was out of the country. She did this in part to signal her displeasure with his willingness to negotiate with Tamil rebels to end a twenty-year civil conflict that had left 65,000 dead. Margaret Thatcher and Indira Gandhi, who shared the moniker of "Iron Lady," are some of the best-known examples of women leaders who did not exhibit a democratic leadership style. Their external gentle appearance was at odds with their shrewd and ruthless leadership style. Indira Gandhi, for instance, tolerated little dissent from political advisors and cabinet members. When threatened with public opposition, she imposed martial law and used the military against Indian citizens to repress dissent. For this she was ultimately killed. Gandhi authorized a military operation (resulting in at least 576 deaths) against a Sikh temple from which alleged terrorist activities were conducted. Several months later, she was assassinated by two of her Sikh security guards.

As the privileged and doted-upon daughter of a national hero, Benazir Bhutto was reputedly an arrogant and imperious leader who surrounded herself with family members who had proven their loyalty (Anderson, 1993). Margaret Thatcher was also known for an aggressive leadership style and chose cabinet members based on their loyalty to her. As Genovese (1993) says, Thatcher's style was highly personalized and imperious. She did not believe in listening to divergent viewpoints within her cabinet, nor did she believe in seeking consensus. She believed in getting her way and did it by arguing, bullying, intimidating, and threatening, and was unapologetic about it. Like Indira Gandhi, she chose her cabinet based on loyalty and obedience and regularly shuffled her ministers in order to maintain control. Although less extreme than Gandhi or Thatcher, Golda Meir was known for toughness, especially in international relations. As an ardent international champion of Israeli interests, she became known for her confrontational style and her uncompromising opposition to concessions in the Arab-Israeli conflict.

Corazon Aquino is one national leader who was clearly consensus oriented and democratic in her leadership style. She came to power during a time when Filipinos were tired of the dictatorship of Ferdinand Marcos and longed for democracy. After nineteen years of rule by Marcos, wealth and

"Many women do not want to be mirror images of men in similar positions, but at the same time they must show authority or they will simply be swept aside."
Margaret Anstee, 1993, first woman to head a UN peacekeeping mission

"I accept that women are gentler at the moment, but if they had the same amount of power as men, they wouldn't be more virtuous."
Lynne Segal, 1987

"And I know, in the depth of my being and in all my knowledge of history and humanity, I know women will struggle for a social order of peace, equality, and joy."
Joan Kelly, 1982

Women will not simply be mainstreamed into the polluted stream. Women are changing the stream, making it clean and green and safe for all—every gender, race, creed, sexual orientation, age, and ability.
Bella Abzug, American congresswoman and women's rights advocate

"There is a special place in hell for women who do not help other women."
Madeleine K. Albright, first woman secretary of state in the U.S.

power were concentrated in the hands of a powerful few, and the people were angry. Cory Aquino represented human rights, civil liberties, ethics, and democracy. As leader of the Philippines, she sought to develop a political culture ruled by law, tolerance, and participation. In her commitment to democratic participation, she made decisions only after elaborate and lengthy consultations with as many people and groups as possible (Col, 1993). Although criticized as incompetent and indecisive, she remained committed to a democratic style of leadership.

Many feminists believe that there are no clear-cut gender executive leadership differences because female leaders are so aware of their precarious hold on power that they feel compelled to lead as men would. Carras (1995) points out that in time, this may change as the number of women leaders increases and as they feel less bound by the male rules of the current power game. Perhaps then the prediction that women leaders are more cooperative and community oriented in their approaches will be borne out. On the other hand, the fact that the behavior of female world leaders is not strikingly different from male behavior could be because leadership, male or female, is more influenced by situational factors and personality than it is by gender. Similarly, the customary ways of gaining, wielding, and holding onto power may erroneously be believed to be male ways of power because most power is held by males. If this is the case, the absence of a gender difference in world leader behavior is likely to persist regardless of women's increased presence in world politics. It may be that, regardless of gender, getting and maintaining political power often requires a certain ruthlessness and defensiveness.

Advocacy of Women's Issues

Many feminists believe that adding women to existing power structures will put women's issues on policymaking agendas (Peterson & Runyan, 2010), and there is some evidence for this position. However, this gender difference is not so clear at the head-of-state level, probably because most female heads of state are aware that being seen as a "women's leader" would quickly result in the loss of their already tenuous hold on power. Recall that most of these women gained power under very unusual circumstances. Women typically come into power during economic and political transitional periods. Therefore, it is not surprising that women's issues are frequently subordinated to other seemingly more pressing concerns, particularly economic ones affecting all citizens. Keep in mind as well that many female heads of state came into office without "feminist consciousness."

Of course advocacy of women's rights is often dangerous to a woman's political career. Although Benazir Bhutto made women's rights a major theme of her campaign and in writings favored a feminist interpretation of Islam, she was nonetheless criticized by feminists as being more concerned with political power than with women's rights (Anderson, 1993). Her arranged marriage, as well as the fact that she never appeared without the traditional Islamic head covering for women (the dupatta), further dismayed

Islamic feminists. However, Islamic fundamentalism was on the rise at the time, and many were antagonistic to the idea of a woman leader—especially a Western-educated one. Furthermore, Bhutto's party did not have a majority in the congress, and there were laws limiting the prime minister's power. Given these constraints, she may have had little choice other than to soft-pedal her women's rights agenda. Even so, Bhutto made some improvements for women. For instance, Bhutto prevented passage of an amendment that would have reexamined all laws in terms of their conformity to Islam. (Movements in this direction under Zia's Islamization programs resulted in the severe repression of women.)

Historically, many political insiders and "honorary men"—such as Indira Gandhi, Margaret Thatcher, Edith Cresson, and Golda Meir—were disinclined to pursue a feminist agenda. They advanced precisely because they minded their manners and proved to the party that they would advance a party line, not a feminist agenda. Margaret Thatcher once said, "The battle for women's rights has largely been won," and "The days when they were demanded and discussed in strident tones should be gone forever" (quoted in Harris, 1995). Her policies, which drastically decreased funding for education and social programs, disproportionately affected poor women and children, earning her the nickname "Maggie Thatcher the Milk Snatcher." As "honorary male" politicians, insiders seem no more likely than male politicians to encourage the appointment and election of females to political posts. For instance, Indira Gandhi appointed no women to her cabinet, and the number of women in the British cabinet decreased under Thatcher.

That said, it is increasingly common for women heads of state to come into office with a record of prior commitment to women's issues and organizations and many have appointed record numbers of women to their cabinets. For instance, Michele Bachelet kept a campaign promise to make her cabinet 50 percent women, a first for Chile. South Korea's first woman prime minister Han Myung-Sook, who served from 2006–2007 (she left to run for president but was not elected), was a feminist activist and pro-democracy leader before entering politics and is known as the founder of the Korean women's movement. Gro Harlem Brundtland, prime minister of Norway, appointed seven women of seventeen posts in her first cabinet and eight of eighteen in her second (D'Amico, 1995). She also extended maternity leave to twenty-four weeks, supported changing Norway's Constitution to include female inheritance of the throne, and was instrumental in the Labor Party's requirement that at least 40 percent of the party's candidates in any given election be female. Vignis Finnbogadottir, president of Iceland from 1980 to 1996, promoted feminist causes and had a long history with Iceland's feminist movements as a member of parliament and as a member of the Women's Alliance Party (Peterson & Runyan, 1999). Mary Robinson, Ireland's former president, was a vocal supporter of rights for women, greater reproductive freedom for women, and reform in family laws that limited women. As a member of the Irish Parliament, she introduced legislation to legalize contraception in Ireland (1969) and divorce (1976)—daring moves in a country dominated by the Roman Catholic Church.

"Women power is a formidable force."
Gro Harlem Brundtland, former Prime Minister of Norway

Women in Informal Politics: Social and Protest Movements

Ordinary women act politically when they organize and put pressure on established power systems from the bottom up, and the results of these efforts are significant. As D'Amico and Beckman (1995) note, a feminist perspective on women in world politics sees women as engaged in politics when they are working to prevent rape, to stop female genital cutting and dowry deaths, and to influence how development aid is allocated.

Although relatively few women are official "state actors" and politics continues to be stereotyped as a male domain, women all over the world are political, active, challenge gender dichotomies, and change world politics by their political agency (Peterson & Runyan, 1999). As stated early in the chapter, the invisibility of women's political activity is in part due to defining politics narrowly as participation in formal politics. Women's political activity is especially high when we take into account local, community-based actions in which women are a driving force (Lister, 2003); that is, their participation in so-called informal politics. West and Blumberg (1990) suggest that there are four general types of issues that draw women into social protest: (1) issues linked to the economic survival of themselves and their children; (2) issues related to nationalist and racial/ethnic struggles; (3) issues addressing broad humanistic/nurturing problems (e.g., peace, environment); and (4) issues identified as women's rights issues. They also note that these might overlap—a protest of economic conditions may lead to a larger, nationalist struggle, as was the case when women's demands for food helped to spark both the French and Russian revolutions. Other examples can be found in the fact that peace and environmental causes are often part of the agendas of feminist movements, and women's movements, particularly in the Global South, may connect their struggles as women to their struggles against racism.

In 2002, approximately 20,000 Colombian women marched in Bogota to demand an end to the civil war, many shouting "We won't give birth to more sons to send to war" (Seager, 2009). This is an example of the fact that much of women's informal political activity can be viewed as an extension of their traditional feminine roles, especially their mother role. Women who might be otherwise uncomfortable in the political sphere can use **maternalism** as a way to rationalize the expansion of their nurturing roles into the public sphere (West & Blumberg, 1990). As Lister (2003) says, it is primarily (but not solely) as mothers that women transgress, and feel justified in transgressing, the public-private divide in their struggle to protect their families and communities. Women who do not generally see themselves as political may take political action when their families and communities are threatened. It is interesting to think of this in private sphere–public sphere terms. In short, when public policies and conditions make it difficult for women to meet their private sphere responsibilities, they may act publicly on behalf of private sphere concerns such as the food, shelter, and safety needs of their families.

> . . . a political struggle that does not have women at the heart of it, above it, below it, and within it is no struggle at all.
>
> *Arundhati Roy, Indian women's activist*

This has been called **accidental activism** (Hyatt, 1992), wherein women are often the active citizens of deprived communities.

Although maternal concerns often motivate women's political activity, this shouldn't be overstated. Motherhood is not the only motivation for women's political participation and it is a mistake to reduce women's political participation to maternalism. To do so is to possibly contribute to women's marginalization within politics, a situation wherein they will be seen as credible political actors only within the context of isses that affect women and children (Pateman, 1992). It is also exclusionary in the sense that it may leave no room for political women who are not mothers or are not motivated by maternal concerns (Lister, 2003). Emphasizing maternalism also runs the risk of reinforcing women's traditional roles (Dietz, 1985; Segal, 1987; Strange, 1990).

Social protest actions taken by women as extensions of their nurturing wife–mother roles may be viewed as less of a gender violation than women's participation in the formal political sphere, but they are still often dangerous. Women's political activism is frequently punished. This is perhaps not surprising when you consider that to be political activists, women violate their gender role and challenge male-dominated institutions of power. Violence as a consequence of women's social protest is well documented, and this punishment is frequently gendered in the sense that it may involve verbal sexual slurs, rape, sexual torture, and violence against their children (Amnesty International, 1990). Women also face criticism from their husbands and families, who may see them as stepping out of their proper role at the expense of their husbands and children. Historians have often failed to record the important roles women have played in social protest and women's informal political activity is understudied by political scientists (West & Blumberg, 1990).

The first three types of social protest described by West and Blumberg (1990) are examined next. The fourth type, political action for women's rights, is the focus of the final two chapters of the book.

> "Everyone knows what a woman must suffer who undertakes to act against bad men. My reputation has been assailed, and it is done so cunningly, that I cannot prove it to be unjust."
> *Sarah Winnemucca, 1855, American Indian rights activist*

Women's Action Around Economic Issues

On April 30, 2008, more than 1,000 women gathered outside of Peru's Congress in Lima, banging pots and pans and demanding that their government do something about food shortages; similar protests occurred in thirty-four other countries (UNIFEM, 2009a). Women's protests in regard to economic conditions are one of the most durable and pervasive examples of women as political actors (Peterson & Runyan, 1999). Women have led and taken part in food riots, welfare protests, labor struggles, tenants' rights, and other similar actions (West & Blumberg, 1990). In the chapter on women and work, women's labor organizing around the world was noted. In the chapter on women and economic development, you learned about women-organized grassroots organizations dedicated to promoting women's economic development.

> "Every moment is an organizing opportunity, every person a potential activist, every minute a chance to change the world."
> *Dolores Huerta, Mexican-American labor rights organizer*

Many of women's actions in this category fit with what was said earlier about political activity often being an extension of women's maternal, private sphere role. For instance, Nigerian women have staged a series of protests against multinational oil companies in Nigeria. Since 2002, they have taken over numerous oil facilities, refusing to leave until their demands are met. In one case in 2002, over 150 Nigerian women took over a Chevron facility for eight days, resulting in a loss to the company of 500,000 barrels of oil a day (BBC, 2002). They did not leave until Chevron promised to hire locals and to build schools, water, and power facilities. In 2003, a group of eighty Nigerian village women, ranging from 25 to 60 years old, took over a Shell Oil pipeline station (Mbachu, 2003). Their action was precipitated by the company's moves to build a chainlink fence around the station—preventing the women from drying the vital local staple, manioc, in the heat of gas flares, an unwanted byproduct of oil. They called for employment opportunities, infrastructural development, and microcredit lending programs from the multinational corporation and accused the company of exploiting the environment and neglecting the country's poverty. The women occupied the pumping station after driving employees out and replacing the locks. Shell was forced to shut down facility operations, resulting in a daily loss of 40,000 barrels of crude oil.

"They are very brave. They go and they get beat up every day and they come back and they say 'I hurt, I hurt there' and then the next day they go back and they get pepper-sprayed, beaten up. It's amazing."
Kelly Nikinejad, editor of Tehranbureau.com, on women protestors in Iran in 2009

"We are not myths of the past, ruins in the jungle, or zoos. We are people and we want to be respected, not to be victims of intolerance and racism."
Rigoberta Menchu Tum, Guatemalan indigenous rights activist and Nobel Peace Prize winner

Women's Action Around Nationalist and Racial/Ethnic Issues

Throughout history, women have initiated and joined protests and movements demanding liberation and equality (West & Blumberg, 1990). In the United States, Black women were important organizers of civil rights actions, and Rosa Parks, famous for refusing to give up her bus seat for a White man, was a long-term activist in the NAACP, a major civil rights organization (West & Blumberg, 1990). Millions of women have participated in countless uprisings, guerrilla movements, and revolutions—ranging from the French, American, Russian, and Chinese revolutions to the more recent revolutionary struggles throughout Latin America, the Caribbean, Africa, and the Middle East (Peterson & Runyan, 1999). Women have mobilized to challenge authoritarian regimes in Argentina, Brazil, Chile, Nepal, Peru, and the Philippines, among others (UNIFEM, 2009a). For example, Iranian women have been on the front lines of anti-government, pro-democracy protests in 2009. The face of an Iranian woman, Neda Agha Soltan, 27, who was captured on video dying of a gunshot wound from government forces, has become the symbol of the opposition (Bazar, 2009). In 2008, thousands of Nigerian women in the Ekti State, all dressed in white and barefoot, protested the delay of local government elections (Africa News, 2008). Following elections in 2009, thousands of women once again took to the streets, this time half-naked (breaking a taboo), to protest electoral fraud, saying that their votes must count (Africa News, 2009). Additional examples of women's roles in independence movements are found in the next chapter on women's movements, as many women's movements originate in nationalist liberation struggles.

Women's Action Around Humanistic/Nurturing Issues

Women have been leaders and mass participants in movements that address such issues as peace, environmentalism, public education, prison reform, mental health care, and hospices (West & Blumberg, 1990). Their actions in these arenas are sometimes extensions of their wife–mother roles. In the chapter on women and development, the role of women in the environmental sustainability movement was illustrated using the Chipko movement and the Greenbelt movement. In the United States, women have taken leadership roles in the movement against hazardous wastes. For example, American Lois Gibbs uncovered the contamination of her home community (Love Canal in New York State), organized collective action to protect those living there, and now runs an organization that helps other women fight pollution in their communities.

"What women want, God wants. Congolese women want peace." Chant of Congolese women marching for peace in 2002

Another example is the Argentinean group, Mothers of the Plaza de Mayo. A military junta took over the government in 1976 and began a terrorist regime in which an estimated 30,000 citizens (thought to be a political threat to the government) were kidnapped and killed (Feijoo, 1998; Navarro, 2001). People were taken without warning, and families were unable to obtain any information about the whereabouts of their loved ones, who came to be known as the "disappeared," or *desaparecidos*. The mothers (and grandmothers) marched defiantly and silently with photographs of their disappeared loved ones; they talked and made tapestries to share the truth about their loved ones; they used drama, speech, and other art forms to publicize their political message (West & Blumberg, 1990).

Women have been the backbone of peace movements worldwide (Cockburn, 2007; West & Blumberg, 1990), and their protests against war are often maternally inspired (Strange, 1990). One example of women's organized resistance to war occurred in 1915, when 1,500 women from twelve countries met at the International Congress of Women in The Hague to discuss women's role in ending World War I. They linked women's suffrage with peace, arguing that if women were allowed greater political participation, war would be less likely. After the meeting, envoys from the conference visited leaders in fourteen countries and called for peace and mediation by neutral countries. There is evidence that these women had a positive effect on the peace process (Stienstra, 1994).

We choose pink, the color of roses, the beauty that like bread is food for life, the color of the dawn of a new era when cooperation and negotiation prevail over force. Code Pink, U.S. Women's Peace Organization

In the 1980s, women's activist antinuclear groups emerged in Australia, Canada, Holland, Italy, the United States, the United Kingdom, and West Germany (Cockburn, 2007; Peterson & Runyan, 1999). Their activism here also appears to be strongly connected to their maternal roles; you can't, they declare, "hug children with nuclear arms" (Strange, 1990). In the last two decades, women's groups have built pressure for peace talks and agreements in Sierra Leone, Liberia, Uganda, Sudan, Burundi, Somalia, Timor-Leste, the Democratic Republic of Congo, and the Balkans, although in many cases they had to demand inclusion in the peace process (Fleshman, 2003; Tripp et al., 2009; UNIFEM, 2009a). African women and women's groups have also engaged in grassroots peace activism, using a variety of tactics including rallies and boycotts and negotiating with rebels to release abducted child soldiers (Tripp et al., 2009). In 2002 and 2003, American women took a leading role in protesting the U.S. war in Iraq. Women in Black chapters held candlelight vigils all over the country to draw attention to the human costs of war. At protests, the women dressed in black to signify mourning for the war dead. Code Pink, a women's peace organization that uses the color pink in their demonstrations, staged creative demonstrations in many major U.S. cities and handed out "pink slips" to legislators who supported the war in Iraq.

Women more than men can strip war of its glamour and its out-of-date heroisms and patriotisms, and see it as a demon of destruction and hideous wrong.
Lillian Wald, reformer and peace activist, 1914

Women organize for peace in their communities and at the national and regional levels, but they are rarely a part of the official peace process from the start (WomenWarPeace.org, 2009). The UN notes that the marginalization of women from equal participation in peace negotiations denies half the population equal access to the political process and denies all people the benefits of having a female perspective in political decision-making. When women gain access, they often make a difference. For example, Mairead Corrigan and Betty Williams of Ireland won the Nobel Peace Prize in 1976 for their decade-long effort to stop the bloodshed between Protestants and Catholics; their work laid the foundation for a peace agreement (see Box 9.7 for other women winners of the prize). The United Nations Security Council Resolution 1325 on women, peace, and security (adopted in 2000) is the first effort toward gender mainstreaming in the peace and security process. The resolution specifically addresses the impact of war on women, and women's contributions to conflict resolution and sustainable peace. The International League for Peace and Freedom (the world's oldest women's peace organization) coordinates the "PeaceWomen Project," which monitors and works toward the full implementation of Resolution 1325 and coordinates NGO efforts for including women in peace efforts. The group's web page includes contact information for hundreds of local grassroots women's peace organizations, national women's peace organizations, and international women's peace organizations.

Although the motivation of much of women's activism against war and the military has been their association with and responsibility for mothering, it should be noted that many mothers support the war effort. Not all women are maternalist pacifists opposed to war (Strange, 1990). Maternalism and patriotism are often linked, and women frequently see their role as calling for their support of military operations (Strange, 1990). Women, like men, are not innately peaceful and have always served militaries and supported wars (Peterson & Runyan, 1999). Also, women do take up arms and support national liberation struggles, evidence that women are not naturally peaceful (Peterson & Runyan, 1999). For example, in the first decade of the twenty-first century, female suicide bombers killed themselves (and hundreds of others) for the political causes in Russia, Israel, and Iraq.

BOX 9.7   *Women Winners of the Nobel Peace Prize*

1905 – Bertha von Suttner (Austria) for her leadership in the European peace movement and her writings about the perils of nationalism and militarism

1931 – Jane Adams (United States) for her work in the international peace movement and on behalf of the poor in the United States

1946 – Emily Greene Balch (United States), founder of the Women's International League for Peace and Freedom

1976 – Betty Williams (Ireland), founder of the Northern Ireland Peace Movement

1976 – Mairead Corrigan (Ireland), founder of the Northern Ireland Peace Movement

1979 – Mother Teresa (India) for her work in bringing help to suffering humanity

1982 – Alva Myrdal (Sweden) for playing a central role in the United Nations' disarmament negotiations

1991 – Aung San Suu Kyi (Burma) for her nonviolent struggle for democracy and human rights

1992 – Rigoberta Menchu Tum (Guatemala) for her work on behalf of social justice and ethno-cultural reconciliation based on respect for the rights of indigenous peoples

1997 – Jody Williams (United States) for her work with the International Campaign to Ban Landmines

2003 – Shirin Ebadi (Iran) for her efforts for democracy and human rights, especially the rights of women and children

2004 – Wangari Maathai (Kenya) for her contribution to sustainable development, democracy, and peace

---

Source: http://nobelprize.org/nobel_prizes/lists/women.html.

Conclusion

Women's political rights have long been acknowledged in international human rights agreements and although progress has been made, it remains true that in most places, men monopolize political space. Like other chapters, this chapter shows that the oppression of women is a sociohistorical and alterable

"Women's equal participation in decision-making is not only a demand for simple justice or democracy but can also be seen as a necessary condition for women's interests to be taken into account. Without the active participation of women and the incorporation of women's perspectives at all levels of decision-making, the goals of equality, development and peace cannot be achieved."
Beijing Platform for Action, 1995

phenomenon. Ideological explanations for women's low levels in representative politics and executive leadership further illustrate how essentialism (beliefs that women and men are essentially different), contribute to gender inequality. The role of social structures in perpetuating gender inequality was also evident in the fact that women's representation and executive leadership are strongly affected by institutional factors such as the structure of political systems. The global women's studies empowerment theme was also strongly evident. Women have demanded their political rights and exercised them through social protest even when their numbers were low in representative politics. The ideas that the journey to gender justice is highly variable and a multicultural approach is needed were also in evidence. A country's history, culture, and political system greatly affect women's political participation and how they strengthen their political voices. Unfortunately, intersectionality remains a neglected topic in the study of women and politics. As noted by Paxton et al. (2007), research tends to compare women and men while ignoring distinctions among women. It is evident for example, that in most countries, women from some economic and ethnic groups have more political rights than others.

The story of women in politics is a story of a glass "half-full" of remarkable progress, and "half-empty" with staggering disappointment. It is exciting that each year gives us a new first for women in politics—a country's first woman prime minister, first woman defense minister, the world's first national parliament over 50 percent female, etc. In the last decade, most governments have pledged to reach a goal of 30 percent female representation. However, most governments and political parties have fallen far short in making changes that would fully include women. Male political control often poses significant barriers to women's rights advocacy. Also, too many women remain politically illiterate, unable to participate fully in politics and advocate for their rights. So, although there is room for cautious optimism, continued progress requires the transformation of the social structures and gender ideologies that interfere with women's full political participation. The next two chapters, one on women's movements and the other on women's rights as human rights, focus on the mechanisms for such transformations.

Study Questions

1. What are the main international agreements enshrining women's rights?

2. What are formal politics? What are informal politics?

3. What is women's suffrage? What was the first country to grant women voting rights? Which country most recently granted voting rights to women? How does women's voting differ from men's? What is gender realignment?

4. What is the global average of women's representation in national assemblies? What is the global average of women in government cabinets? What types of cabinet appointments are most common for women?

5. Why are women political representatives of symbolic importance? Why are they of practical importance? What is critical political mass?

6. How do ideological or cultural explanations explain gender differences in political representation?

7. How do cultural factors and traditional gender ideologies influence the supply of and demand for women political leaders?

8. How do structural or institutional explanations explain gender differences in political representation? How do the three types of electoral systems affect women's election? Why are more women elected under PL/PR systems? How does district magnitude and party magnitude affect women's election?

9. What are electoral reforms? Under what conditions are electoral systems changed to PL/PR systems? What role do gender quotas play in increasing women's representation? How common are quotas? When do they arise? Under what conditions are they most effective? What criticisms are made of quotas?

10. What role do feminist and women's organizing play in increasing women's representation?

11. How common are women heads of state? What kind of progress has been made in women's executive leadership? How much power do they have?

12. What are the paths to women's executive power? What personal factors are associated with women's executive leadership? What socio-historical circumstances are associated with women's executive leadership? What institutional factors?

13. Are women leaders more peaceful, ethical, and more democratic in their leadership style than men leaders?

14. What four issues draw women into social protest? How is their activity often a result of maternalism? What is accidental activism?

Discussion Questions and Activities

1. Conduct research to explain the low levels of women's political representation in the United States, Japan, or Britain using ideological and structural explanations.

2. Quotas are one of the main means of getting women into political office worldwide. What is your position regarding the use of quotas to increase the number of women holding political office? Why do you think they haven't been used in the United States to increase women's presence in national representative politics?

3. Do a biographical essay on a current woman president or prime minister. Analyze how she came to power using chapter concepts and explain whether she was an advocate for peace, ethics, and women's issues.

4. Do you agree that were it not for the fact that women leaders must act like men to get and stay in office, gender differences in leadership would be more apparent? Why or why not?

5. Interview a woman politician or activist in your community. Develop questions based on the chapter. For example, ask her how being a woman influences the issues of concern to her, her leadership style, and others' response to her political activity.

6. This chapter focused on women's presence in national assemblies and as national executives. Do some research on women representatives in your local and state government. How do the numbers compare to women in national office? How do you explain differences?

Action Opportunities

1. Take one of the political actions suggested by the *Women, Power, and Politics* global online exhibition (WPP). WPP showcases women from all walks of life claiming and exercising their power. http://www.imow.org/wpp/stories/viewTopic?topicid=320 and http://www.imow.org/community/act/index.

2. Do something to increase women's political literacy. For example, teach students how to use absentee ballots, or help women run for campus elected offices by explaining the process. Educate your local or campus women's group on political tactics such as "tabling," petitions, and running for student offices. Remember that your mission will be to teach others the specifics of participation in a political system.

3. Do some campaigning or fund-raising for a woman political candidate.

4. Women in social protest movements frequently face government persecution, such as imprisonment without due process. Participate in an Amnesty International letter-writing campaign on behalf of one or more female political prisoners (http://www.amnesty.org).

5. Become a political leader for an economic, racial, peace, or environmental issue.

6. Help change the image of politics as a masculine domain by creating an educational display of women political leaders that is posted in a public place at your university or public library.

Activist Websites

International Institute for Democracy and Electoral Assistance (International IDEA) http://www.idea.int/gender/

International Knowledge Network of Women in Politics (iKNOW Politics) http://iknowpolitics.org/

Emily's List http://www.emilyslist.org/home.htm

Peace Women Across the Globe http://www.1000peacewomen.org/eng/ueberuns.php

Women, Power, and Politics (online exhibition) http://www.imow.org/wpp/index?gclid=CN2e2fL5j50CFSNQagodc0YzAA

UNIFEM's portal on women, peace, and security http://www.womenwarpeace.org/

Informational Websites

Center for Women in American Politics (CAWP) http://www.cawp.rutgers.edu/fast_facts/index.php

Inter-parlimentary Union (IPU) http://www.ipu.org

Worldwide Guide to Women and Leadership http://www.guide2womenleaders.com/index.html

Council of Women World Leaders http://www.cwwl.org/

Beijing Platform of Action (Women in Power and Decision Making) http://www.un.org/womenwatch/daw/beijing/platform/decision.htm

Center for Women's Global Leadership http://www.feminist.com/cfwgl.htm

Politics and Gender (Research Journal) http://journals.cambridge.org/action/displayJournal?jid=pag

10 National and Local Women's Movements

While gender subordination has universal elements, feminism cannot be based on a rigid concept of universality that negates the wide variation in women's experience. . . . There is, and must be, a diversity of feminisms, responsive to the different needs and concerns of different women, and *defined by them for themselves.*

—GITA SEN and CAREN GROWN of DAWN

In every society, in every generation, women have fought for gender equality although there is great diversity in women's movements. This 2005 photo shows Kuwaiti women demonstrating in front of the parliament building in Kuwait City for the right to vote. © YASSER AL-ZAYYAT/AFP/ Getty Images

Throughout the book you have read about the remarkable efforts of women's activism to bring about gender equality and empower women. Without these efforts, it is almost certain that little progress toward gender equality would have been made. This chapter takes a closer look at women's movements and how these vary cross-culturally and intra-culturally based on contextual factors such as history, politics, identity, and culture. For our purposes, a **women's movement** is defined as the sum of campaigns by groups and associations using a variety of tactics, disruptive or conventional, to change women's position in society (Kumar, 1995; McBride & Mazur, 2005). Women's movements often include the "women's movement thinkers" who inspire awareness of gender inequality and the "women's movement actors" who work for change (McBride & Mazur, 2005). Women's movements may be independently organized or affiliated with political parties, they may be of short or long duration, they may rest on a narrow social base or on multi-class coalitions, they may focus on one issue or multiple issues, and they may be local, national, or international (Basu, 1995). As you'll see, the women's movement is not a distinct organizational entity worldwide, and even within a single country, the movement has broad ideological variety and a range of organizational expressions (Katzenstein, 1987). Indeed, it is far more accurate to speak of women's movements than *a* women's movement. Box 10.1 provides a sense of this variety.

Forces Operating Against Women's Activism

People are sometimes puzzled that women put up with gendered abuses and inequalities. Many people simply proclaim that it could all be stopped if women would just join together and stand up for themselves. There is a small truth in this—the system of patriarchy can function only with the cooperation of women. However, as Lerner (1986) points out, this cooperation is secured by a variety of means: gender indoctrination, educational deprivation, denying women their history of struggle and achievement, dividing women from one another, restraints and outright coercion, discrimination in access to economic resources and political power, and awarding class privileges to conforming women. In other words, standing up for women's rights is not such a simple matter after all.

It is important to understand the perils of women's activism and to acknowledge the courage of those women who challenge gender inequality. One danger in speaking out is the possible loss of social belongingness and social approval. Questioning tradition and seeking social change is one of the surest ways to trigger the wrath and rejection of others. Socially speaking, it is a risky business to speak out on behalf of gender justice. Many people are inhibited by a desire to fit in and be accepted by others. This social rejection may be experienced especially severely in collectivist cultures that emphasize

"Power is not something people give away. It has to be negotiated, and sometimes wrested from the powerful."
Devaki Jain, Indian writer and activist

"Believe not those who say the upward path is smooth,

Lest thou should stumble on the way

And faint before the truth."
Anne Brontë (1820–1849), British writer

"It has been difficult for me as an indigenous woman to find the confidence to speak publicly, particularly since we were raised to believe that the only role for women is to maintain a household and to bear children. If you broke with this role, you were seen as abandoning tradition and you would lose the respect of the people."
Rigoberta Menchu, Guatemalan winner of the Nobel Peace Prize

"Women have been taught for centuries that they are the slaves of men. I started writing because I wanted to wake them up."
Taslima Nasrin, Physician, poet, and activist

BOX 10.1   *Diversity in Women's Activism*

- In 1978 in Spain, as part of a national campaign in support of women on trial for having abortions, 1,000 women publicly proclaimed in a written document that they too had had abortions and should be tried. In a second document, both men and women stated that they had participated in abortions and insisted that they too be judged.

- In 1984, women in Iceland protested gender wage discrimination by jamming grocery stores and markets and insisting that they should only have to pay $.66 on the dollar for purchases. Their reasoning was that if they were only paid $.66 for every dollar men earned, they should only have to pay 66 percent of the price of consumer goods.

- The Centre de Promotion des Femmes Ouvrières (CPFO) was founded in Port-au-Prince, Haiti, in 1985. CPFO's work focuses on the rights of women workers, women's literacy, women's reproductive health, and legal counseling and assistance. The organization serves a population of about 30,000 women workers.

- In 1990, forty-seven veiled Saudi Arabian women drivers protested the law prohibiting women from driving cars by driving on the King Abdul Aziz Highway in Riyadh.

- The National Women's Lobby Group (NWLG), formed in Zambia in 1991, aims to promote the end of laws and customs that discriminate against women, to increase women's education and political participation, and to put women in political decision-making positions. The NWLG intensely campaigns to get women's issues on the government agenda, forms alliances with other NGOs, and does outreach to educate women as to the law and their rights.

- The Zena Zenama (Woman to Woman) Association was founded in Mostar, Bosnia-Herzegovina, in 1997, by a Serb woman and two Muslim women. Working out of a crowded apartment, they engage in a number of activities such as helping elderly women try to recover their homes, assisting battered wives, running support groups for survivors of ethnic massacres and war rape, and providing voter education.

- The Sri Lanka Federation of University Women (SLFUW) was formed almost fifty years ago by a handful of graduate women. Today the organization's focus is on helping women graduates and undergraduates and on training programs to enhance women's employment opportunities. The organization networks with a number of other organizations both nationally and internationally.

- In 2003, hundreds of Iranian women rallied for equal social and political rights in Tehran on International Women's Day. This was the first women's public protest since the 1979 Islamic Revolution.

- In 2008, young women's activists in the United Kingdom created a Facebook group called "Somewhat Strident But Who Cares?" that turned into an activist project where women put sticker messages on public ads for plastic surgery and on ads showing emaciated models. The stickers said such things as "You are normal, this is not!"

the subordination of individual goals for the sake of the community. In collectivist cultures, people's identity is strongly rooted in family and community. Speaking out for gender equality is that much harder in these cultures because individuals do not want to bring shame upon their family or community. However, even in Western, individualistic countries such as the United States, fears of social rejection inhibit people from identifying themselves as feminist or calling attention to sexism.

Another reason why women often do not resist is that their low power leads them to believe that there is not much point in defiance. Women often lack **self-efficacy** (the belief that their efforts will be effective) in regard to challenging the traditional gender order. Self-efficacy matters because if you are skeptical about your chances of success, then you are unlikely to try, or to persist if your efforts are not immediately fruitful (Bandura, 1986). Self-efficacy is fostered by personal success experiences with the task, by seeing people like you succeed at the task (role models), and by receiving social support and encouragement (Bandura, 1986). Looked at this way, it is not surprising that women sometimes put up with gender inequality. Females learn early that efforts to rebel are unlikely to be successful, particularly in cultures with rigid gender roles that tolerate little deviation, It is also the case that in such societies, females are unlikely to have ever seen females like themselves successfully step outside of their gender place. Instead, they have seen such individuals ostracized and otherwise punished. As Lerner (1986) points out, when there is no precedent, one cannot imagine alternatives to existing conditions. We must also consider that in these societies, others are unlikely to socially support deviation. This is because conformity is equated with survival. Given that there are few options for women outside of conformity to traditional roles, and knowing that punishment is the likely result of deviation, the loved ones of potential "deviates" encourage conformity. By communicating to women that they are empowered or disempowered as women, societal and family norms also affect women's perceived self-efficacy.

It must also be understood that responses to women's activism can be brutal and severe. In some countries, freedom of speech (including a free press) and freedom of political assembly (e.g., political meetings, organizations, and rallies) are limited or disallowed by the government. Women's rights activists are regularly harassed, attacked, beaten, imprisoned, and killed. In the Philippines from 2001 to 2006, over fifty women's activists were murdered (Feminist Majority, 2006). In 2009, women's rights activists in Nepal were victims of beatings, sexual attacks, and murder; in Fiji, the Women's Rights Movement Office was vandalized; in Iran, women's rights activists were arrested; in the Democratic Republic of Congo, women's activists were assaulted; in Guatemala, women's activists experienced sexual harassment and violence; in Guinea, thirty-three women and girls protesting sexual violence were raped by the military. Box 10.2 tells the story of a Bangladeshi physician turned novelist who faces death due to her feminist beliefs.

The amazing thing, then, is not that women don't always protest gender injustice, but that *they often do.* Indeed, in every society, in every generation, there have been efforts by women to fight their lower status. For instance, in nineteenth-century Persia (now Iran), Fatimah Umm Salamih fought for the equality of women. Murdered in 1852, thrown in a well, and covered with rocks, her last words were recorded as "You can kill me as soon as you like, but you cannot stop the emancipation of women" (Tomasevski, 1993).

"Our hands are empty, our homes are made of glass; there is a knot in our throats and no time to cry; our sisters are in jail; our days are filled with danger, and yet forever, until these laws change, we will leave traces of even more signatures on the campaign's petition."
Nafiseh Azad, Campaign for Equality activist (the petition demands equal rights for women in Iran)

BOX 10.2 *Activist Profile: Taslima Nasrin of Bangladesh*

Taslima Nasrin was born in August 1962 to a Muslim family in Bangladesh. She began writing when she was 15 years old, publishing poetry in the literary magazines. She continued to write even while in medical school. After receiving her medical degree in 1984, she worked in public hospitals for eight years.

Starting in 1986, she has published over twenty-four highly acclaimed books of poetry and literature. Taslima's critical writings about religion and women's oppression make her a controversial figure in Bangladesh, where most of her books and writings are banned. By 1990, Islamic fundamentalists began an intimidation campaign against her that included demonstrations and physical assaults, making it impossible for her to appear in public. In 1993, a fundamentalist organization set a price on her head because of her criticism of Islam, and she was confined to her house. The public unrest stirred by her writing led the government to ban her books and force her to leave the country. In 1998, without the permission of the government, she risked death to return to her country to be with her ailing mother. Again, fundamentalists demanded she be killed and again she was forced to leave Bangladesh. Since that time, she has lived in exile in Europe and the United States. Here is an excerpt from her response to the banning of her books (on her website http://taslimanasrin.com/).

What is the bottom line, and why the objections to my books?

Patriarchal minds object.

I am not supposed to write about equality and justice for women.

Patriarchal minds object.

I must not talk about the enjoyment of sex, if what I write includes showing the enjoyment of sex by women.

Patriarchal minds object.

I must not dare to challenge patriarchy.

For if it were to tumble down women would no longer be able to be treated as slaves, as sexual commodities, and men would have to make a shift in their viewpoints and actions.

I am a proud nonconformist. I accept the good from the past and reject the bad. But I do not accept the view that it is bad to express oneself freely.

Women are being oppressed everywhere, are they not? Well, this oppression simply has to stop!

Sources: Filkins, 1998, and Taslima Nasrin's official website http://taslimanasrin.com/.

Early (Mistaken) Assumptions About Women's Movements

Until recently, Western feminist academics dominated the study of women's movements.[1] Typically, they focused on movements in the United States and Europe and rarely on movements in postcolonial countries (Basu, 1995). These analyses often overemphasized the role of middle-class women, the role of economic development, and particular types of activities such as a focus on reproductive rights. This narrow definition left out movements that didn't fit this Western mold. Some Western scholars portrayed women

---

[1] The "West" or "Western nations" is sometimes used to refer to the industrialized nations of Western Europe and North America (the U.S. and Canada).

in developing nations as passive and without agency (Mohanty, 1991; Xu, 2009). However, there is a long history of struggle for women's equality in the Middle East, Latin America, Asia, Africa, and Central, Eastern, and South Eastern Europe; economic development is no guarantee of a strong women's movement; and women's movements comprise a range of struggles by women against gender inequality (Basu, 1995; Bystydzienski, 1992a; deHann, Daskalova, & Loutfi, 2006; Keddie, 2007; Tripp et al., 2009).

Assuming That All Women's Movements Use the Feminist Label

It also took a while for Western scholars to recognize that women's movements include individuals and groups that do not explicitly identify as feminist. Some women's movements embrace the feminist label, such as the Association of Women for Action and Research (Singapore), Action India, the Feminist Majority (United States), and Bat Shalom (Israel). However, many women's organizations that do the work of the women's movement avoid the feminist label or consider it irrelevant to the work they do.

One reason for avoidance of the feminist label is that feminism has a negative connotation in many cultures. In countries with a history of colonization (many African countries), or other antagonistic relationships with the West (many Muslim countries), the effectiveness of openly feminist organizations may be compromised by the public perception that feminism is a Western, imported notion. In countries like Iran and Egypt, Islamists will suggest that a group has ties to the West to discredit women's rights efforts (Keddie, 2007). In China, many in the women's movement prefer the term "womanism" to the term "feminism" not only to distinguish it from Western feminism but because it is seen as representing a less antagonistic view of gender relations (Xu, 2009). In other countries, antifeminist groups have successfully given feminism a negative image such that many with feminist leanings do not call themselves "feminists." For example, in the United States, many women's activists and organizations are "covertly" feminist because of the perception that support for women's policies and programs is reduced by association with the feminist label.

In a number of Latin American countries where socialist struggles have resulted in democratization, feminism is associated with the bourgeoisie (the middle and upper class) and imperialism. In Chile, for instance, feminists are considered bourgeois and elitist and insufficiently committed to the interests of the working class (Frohmann & Valdes, 1995). In Bolivia, feminism is viewed as alien to the working class and as divisive to the labor movement (Salinas, 1994). Similarly, feminist activists in Nicaragua often avoid the feminist label because feminism is often portrayed in the media as anti-family and anti-male, and the traditional Latin American political left believes feminism to be bourgeois and inappropriate for women in a poor country like Nicaragua (Chinchilla, 1994).

Many women's movements also avoid the feminist label because the term *feminism* is frequently associated with a narrow, Western view of women's issues and strategies. Women in some countries, including Poland, Russia,

"This demonization of feminism as Western totally ignores the fact that for more than two decades women of Asia, Africa, Latin American, and the Middle East have been creating their own contextualized forms of feminism and speaking about their rights and demands in their own voices."
Rosemary Ruether

"Every country has women's rights groups."
Mahnaz Afkhami

"The women's movement in Iran is very misunderstood by the West. If you could break the image that we are all one black mass under the hijab, you would understand women in Iran. What we care about is not what we wear on our heads, but much more important issues, more profound issues of law that affect our lives."
Mehranguiz Kar

"In its various guises and disguises, feminism continues to be the most avid manufacturer of gender consciousness and gender categories, inevitably at the expense of local categories such as ethnicity, seniority, race, and generation, that may be more locally salient."
Oyeronke Oyewumi

and Honduras, distance themselves from Western feminism because it is not seen as relevant to their own social and economic conditions (Sekhon & Bystydzienski, 1999). Many non-Western women feel that their struggle as women is connected to the struggles of their communities against racism, economic exploitation, and imperialism and believe that Western feminism does not address this. In other words, Western feminism has often ignored intersectionality, and to many non-Western women, it is seen as too singularly focused on the struggle against gender discrimination when their oppression cannot be limited to gender alone (Ghodsee, 2004; Johnson-Odim, 1991). As Mohanty (1991) says, "To define feminism purely in gendered terms assumes our consciousness (or identity) of being 'women' has nothing to do with race, class, nation, or sexuality, just gender. But no one becomes a woman purely because she is female. Ideologies of womanhood have as much to do with class and race as they have to do with sex" (p. 12). For instance, Black South African feminism is based on Black women's experience of multiple oppressions and includes issues, such as access to clean water and housing, that have not traditionally been defined as feminist (Kemp, Madlala, Moodley, & Salo, 1995).

Non-Western women often distance themselves from Western feminism for other reasons as well. They are often aware, for example, that Western women participated in the oppression of Southern women (Johnson-Odim, 1991; Kemp et al., 1995). It is sometimes difficult for them to think of these feminists as their sisters when these women received privileges on the backs of non-White women (Oyewumi, 2003). They are also cognizant of the fact that racism was present in the early women's movement in the Northern Hemisphere and that, up until recently, these White Western feminists dominated international women's conferences (Johnson-Odim, 1991).

Assuming Western Feminist Concerns Are the Concerns of All Women

Some of the concerns that have driven Western feminist movements, such as women's reproductive and sexual rights, do not characterize other non-Western feminisms and women's movements. Margolis (1993) gives the example of family planning. In the West, family planning and abortion have served as major mobilizing forces for the women's movement, but such programs often arouse suspicion and opposition from women in some developing nations, who may see these as attempts to limit the populations of their ethnic groups. This approach also does not make sense to women in countries where women's status is enhanced by having lots of children or where women need lots of children to help with the labor. Indeed, in contrast to Western feminisms that often focus on women in the public sphere of work and politics and women's reproductive and sexual rights, the focus of many Latin American, South American, and African feminisms and women's movements is motherhood (Oyewumi, 2003). Islamic feminists often argue that Western feminism, with its emphasis on equality in the labor force and White middle-class women, is irrelevant to the majority of the world's women, who seek an honored place as wives and as mothers (Afshar, 1996).

African feminisms are also often shaped by African women's resistance to Western hegemony (domination) and by African culture. Like African feminists, women working toward equality in Muslim countries frequently distinguish themselves from Western feminists to avoid charges that they have been influenced by "foreign" or Western ideologies (Keddie, 2007; Moghadam, 1991). Their efforts are often centered on recovering their own women's history and showing that women's equality is consistent with Islam (Keddie, 2007; Moghadam, 1991, 2003). Some non-Western feminisms are even rooted in a precolonial past in which women played strong roles and were high in status. For example, the creation of the first woman, according to the indigenous people of the Philippines, was simultaneous with the creation of the first man. Filipina feminists refer to this to show that as a person born whole and separate from man, the Filipina owns her body and self and can chart her own history and destiny (Santiago, 1995).

Because feminist struggles occur in unique cultural contexts unable to be fully understood by outsiders, women in their own cultures create the most effective women's movements. It is these women who know how to frame women's rights in cultural context. Also, associations with "outsiders" often compromise the legitimacy and, correspondingly, the effectiveness of movements. Feminist outsiders mean well when they try to change practices in other cultures, but at times they may unwittingly interfere with gender progress and other women's right to self-determination. Indeed, as you've read earlier in the book, those who are best suited to engineer and bring about lasting reform are typically women in their own cultures (Obiora, 2003). Box 10.3 summarizes the reasons why Western feminisms are not easily exportable to non-Western cultures. As this chapter proceeds, it will become increasingly evident that women's movements should be contextualized and have taken many forms.

Different Strands of Women's Movements

Even within a country, women's movements take many forms and employ many strategies. Consider this example from Alvarez (1994) describing the Brazilian women's movement of the 1970s and 1980s:

Women spearheaded protests against the regime's human rights violations; poor and working-class women crafted creative solutions to meet community needs in response to gross government neglect of basic urban and social services; women workers swelled the ranks of Brazil's new trade union movement; rural women struggled for their rights to land that were increasingly being usurped by export-agribusiness; Afro-Brazilian women joined the United Black Movement and helped forge other organized expressions of a growing antiracist, Black-consciousness movement; Brazilian lesbians joined gay males to launch a struggle against homophobia; young women and university students enlisted in militant student movements; some took up arms against the military regime, and still others worked in legally sanctioned parties of the opposition. By the

"The minute you hear about feminism one immediately puts it in the connotation of the European and North American women's struggles. These are women from societies which have long been independent—people who . . . support the governments that . . . support our oppression. I could never feel solidarity with that. . . . I think there will be a different feminism coming out of Africa."
Chase, Black Namibian activist

"In Islam and the Arab world, and in all our cultures, we must claim those things that are positive and discard without hesitation those things that are negative. In Egypt we have a long tradition of women in power. For thousands of years, for example, we have had the Goddess Isis, and her tradition. Thank God, thank Goddess, we still have her spirit with us."
Nawal el Saadawi

"Can an outsider be so arrogant as to assume that she is omniscient or omnipotent enough to unilaterally appropriate a lead role and articulate a viable reform agenda?"
L. Amede Obiora

BOX 10.3 *Differences Between Western and Other Feminisms*

- Western feminism may not apply to cultures with different economic and social conditions.

- Non-Western feminisms are often tied to other struggles (e.g., racism, poverty, imperialism) that are seen as equally important.

- Non-Western women do not always trust Western feminists because Western feminists have historically excluded women from developing nations from international conferences and non-Western women often come from countries with a history of imperialism.

- Motherhood is often central to non-Western feminisms.

- Non-Western feminisms are often rooted in precolonial past.

- Arab feminisms are often rooted in Islam.

- Western feminism is viewed suspiciously as a possible effort to impose Western culture.

- Association with Western feminism often hurts Southern hemisphere and Arab feminist efforts.

"Feminism in Mexico, as elsewhere, is not expressed in a single voice."
Victoria Rodriquez

"Because of cultural and historical differences, it would be naïve to assume that Indian women fight for change in the same ways American and European women did."
Mangala Subramaniam

1980s, thousands of women involved in these and other struggles had come to identify themselves as feminists (p. 13).

Three major "strands" of women's movements (see Figure 10.1) are found in many countries: (1) women's rights activist groups that raise women's issues at the national policy level; (2) women's research and advocacy organizations that raise public awareness; and (3) nongovernmental organizations that work to raise women's awareness and mobilize women at the grassroots level (Jahan, 1995b). Furthermore, these different types of groups often build coalitions in order to create change. Jahan (1995b) describes these three major strands in Bangladesh in her discussion of campaigns to eliminate violence against women in Bangladesh (from the late 1970s to early 1980s). Researchers documented violence against women, grassroots groups started intervention programs, and women's organizations pressured the government to enact laws against that violence.

Large, national organizations focused on legislative change are perhaps the most visible of the three "strands." For example, from the early to mid-twentieth century, women's organizations on every continent won women the right to vote. Another example of change sought by a large, national women's organization is Bangladesh's largest women's organization, Mahila Parishad. This organization collected 17,000 signatures and lobbied parliament for an antidowry law, which was passed in 1980. Likewise, the Concertación Nacional de Mujeres por la Democracia (National Coalition of Women for Democracy, or CNMD), a coalition of women's organizations in Chile, successfully lobbied to include women's issues on the agenda of the new democratic government formed in 1990. As you learned in Chapter 9, women's organizations have also played a major role in getting women's rights and parliamentary gender quotas enshrined in new Constitutions.

FIGURE 10.1 *Three Strands of Women's Movements*

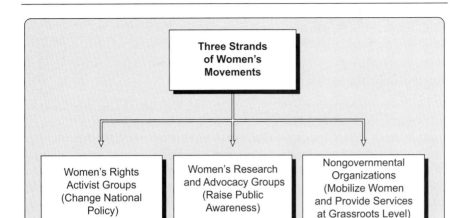

Despite the visibility of large national women's organizations, the vitality of women's movements lies primarily in small, local-level activist groups (Basu, 1995; Katzenstein, 1987). As discussed in Chapter 6, these grassroots organizations (GROs) include small, local-level groups that provide services such as shelter to battered women or credit to female micro-entrepreneurs, or engage in local protests or awareness campaigns. Grassroots support organizations (GRSOs) are another type of nongovernmental organization characteristic of women's movements worldwide. Recall that GRSOs are nationally or regionally based assistance organizations that channel funds and information to grassroots organizations; GRSOs are usually staffed by professionals. In every chapter you have encountered many examples of GROs and GRSOs that respond to women's issues.

Bystydzienski (1992a) suggests that in countries with a women's movement, there are generally two branches: an established older branch made up of organizations that have become institutionalized and that are more or less accepted as the mouthpiece for women's rights; and a younger, noninstitutionalized branch made up of small, loose groups outside of the mainstream. The older branch, she maintains, tends to be more ideologically liberal or moderate and essentially struggles for changes in laws and policies within the existing society. This branch also tends toward a hierarchical structure with some role specialization and formal rules. In contrast, the younger branch is more ideologically radical and seeks transformation of existing societies according to feminist principles. It consists of small, local groups, often linked by informal networks, and avoids formal rules and hierarchies. The activities of the younger branch focus on building alternatives outside of the system, such as cooperatives run by women, economic enterprises, women's shelters, health clinics, and daycare centers.

Contextual Factors Affecting Women's Movements

Every women's movement arises in a unique way based on a variety of contextual factors. Contextual factors also affect the success of women's movements.

Practical and Strategic Gender Interests

Women's movements arise in response to different issues and may focus on immediate needs or on gaining long-term rights. Molyneaux (1985) suggests that women's movements may arise out of either "practical gender interests" or "strategic gender interests." **Practical gender interests** usually develop in response to an immediate perceived need and do not generally have as their goal women's emancipation or equality. In contrast, **strategic gender interests** arise out of an awareness of a generalized patriarchy and a desire to challenge and change it. Both types of movements are important and necessary for easing and eventually eliminating gender inequality.

Peterson and Runyan (2010) propose that movements arising out of practical gender interests tend to be attempts at reforms of an existing system whereas movements arising out of strategic gender interests are oriented toward larger transformations. They also suggest that most women's activism arises out of local and immediate conditions that are perceived as obstacles to the realization of practical interests, but that as activists become aware of the relationship between local struggles and the overall system of gender subordination, they often move toward system-transforming politics. In this way, they say, participation in local resistance actions can lead to participation in (or at least support for) larger and sometimes global movements. This point is driven home in the next chapter on global feminism. It appears, however, that strategically motivated movements may also become more practically oriented. This seems to happen as activists discover just how deeply embedded gender inequality is in established social systems; they then focus on bringing about progress in recalcitrant social systems through incremental change. For example, Tanaka (1995) writes that the Japanese feminist movement that emerged in the 1970s changed from one that sought to "transform the whole set of cultural values" to one in the 1990s focused on "concrete social changes" and "women's assimilation into the male-dominated system" (p. 351).

Local Political and Economic Conditions

Local political and economic conditions also affect women's movements, both positively and negatively, and as these conditions change, women's movements change also.

On the positive side, women's movements frequently arise out of other political struggles. These include working-class struggles, movements opposing state repression, fights against colonialism or neocolonialism, and civil rights struggles. For instance, Nigeria's first women's activist association, the National

"This is a common story in many women. We began with the social struggle, and little by little we moved toward the struggle of women."
Gilda Rivera, one of the founders of the Honduran Women's Organization Centre de los Derechos de la Mujer

Ichikawa Fusae (1893–1981) led the women's suffrage movement in Japan. In 1919 she founded one of the first feminist organizations (the New Woman's Association), and was elected to the House of Councillors in 1952, where she continued her work on women's issues and served until her death.

Women's Union, was begun in 1947 by Funmilayo Ransome-Kuti and represented over 100,000 women who protested the colonial power's taxation policies and those prohibiting assembly (Abdullah, 1995; Tripp et al., 2009). Basu (1995) suggests that what initially motivates many women to organize is not necessarily a belief in the distinctive nature of their problems but rather a sense of shared oppression with other groups that have been denied their rights. West and Blumberg (1990) suggest that women's consciousness is also raised when they begin to see the contradictions in ignoring their own oppression while fighting other injustices. They add that in the course of participating in these other struggles, women also gain valuable leadership training, skills, and confidence.

On the negative side, gender equality is often subordinated to other political and economic issues. Reforms intended to promote gender equality are often given a low priority while other pressing social and economic matters are attended to. Women's rights can seem like a luxury when the majority of people are struggling for basic survival (Margolis, 1993; Matynia, 1995). For example, Chowdhury (1994) states that women's issues are not perceived as major issues in Bangladesh, hidden as they are behind the country's poverty and underdevelopment. In Eastern Europe, the transition to market economies created inflation and unemployment for both genders and many women's issues are subordinated to these economic concerns (Aulette, 1999; Ghodsee, 2004; Gottlick, 1999). War also typically causes struggles for women's rights to be put on hold. To illustrate, from the early 1900s until 1937, the women's movement was strong in Japan. Women such as Kishida Toshiko, Fukuda Hideko, Ishimoto Shizue, and Ichikawa Fusae spoke against the oppression of women, advocated women's rights, organized women's groups, and joined political parties (Ling & Matsumo, 1992). However, when Japan invaded China, the Japanese women's movement was prohibited, feminist leaders were forced to cooperate with the war effort, and those who persisted in feminist organizing were arrested and some killed (Fujieda, 1995; Ling & Matsumo, 1992). Likewise, Black South African women began protests against "pass laws" in 1912, but the campaign was suspended at the outbreak of World War I (Kemp et al., 1995). In the 1990s, war in Bosnia-Herzegovina reduced attention on women's rights (Wilkinson, 1998).

Likewise, during times of political turmoil and repression, women's resistance of male oppression is often relegated to the margins, separated from other class and national struggles and subordinated to the wider and presumed higher cause of national liberation (Acosta-Belen & Bose, 1995). In Iran, in the late 1970s through the 1980s, women's demands for equal rights coincided with anti-colonial and nationalist discourses; any criticism of the patriarchal aspects of Muslim culture were seen as betrayals (Mir-Hosseini, 2001). In cases in which the state is highly repressive, the vast majority of men also experience oppression, and it is therefore difficult for women to present a case that they are particularly oppressed (Bystydzienski, 1992b). As a case in point, under Soviet communism, Polish, Hungarian, Czech, and Slovak women *and* men felt equally repressed by the state, and the energies of every social movement were directed toward activities with the potential for large-scale change

"Hum Bharat ki nari hain, phool nahin, chingari hain." ("We, the women of India, are not flowers, but fiery sparks.")
Indian feminist slogan

(Matynia, 1995). In some cases, feminists believe that gender progress will not occur until authoritarian governments are overthrown, and so they work for other social changes under the assumption that women's liberation will follow. This was the case in the Philippines from 1950s until the 1970s. Many feminists joined the nationalist movement against dictator Ferdinand Marcos, believing that national liberation would bring about women's equality (Santiago, 1995).

Another example comes from India. The newly developing Indian women's movement of the 1970s was interrupted by the declaration of a state of emergency by Prime Minister Indira Gandhi in 1975. Most political organizations were driven underground, and those that remained focused on civil rights such as freedom of speech and association and the right to protest (Kumar, 1995). Kemp and colleagues (1995) describe a similar phenomenon in regard to Black South African feminism in the twentieth century. In the 1950s, women's activism was banned along with other opposition to the White, separatist government. In the 1970s, a resistance movement reemerged, but the immediacy of the state's attack on Black people and the constant bannings and detentions of Black activists meant that the debate over issues of gender and women's oppression had to wait until the battle for national liberation was won.

Women's Movements Arising From Class Struggles

India in the 1970s provides numerous examples of women's organizations arising out of political movements that fought class differences. These include the Self-Employed Women's Association (SEWA), founded in 1970 in Gujarat by trade unionist Ela Bhatt; the Progressive Organization of Women (POW) of Hyderabad and the Stree Mukti Sangathana (Women's Liberation Organization) of Bombay (both of which arose out of the Maoist communist movement), and Mahila Samta Sainik Dal (League of Women Soldiers for Equality) of Maharashtra, which was associated with the anticaste *dalit* movement (Kumar, 1995).[2] In many Latin American countries, the origins of women's movements are easily traced to efforts by the working class to organize, unionize, and struggle for better wages and working conditions. In Chile, for example, women workers began organizing around both class and gender issues in the early 1900s (Frohmann & Valdes, 1995).

Women's Movements Arising From Nationalist Struggles

Women's movements sometimes arise in tandem with nationalist struggles. Historically, women have played important roles in movements for national liberation, and women's activists frequently promote women's rights in

---

[2] Those born into the *dalit* or untouchable social class have the lowest status in India's caste system.

tandem with other nationalist struggles for freedom. One early example is Huda Sha'rawi, an important Egyptian feminist of the twentieth century who actively involved women in the nationalist debate against the British in 1919. Women's public participation in a nationalist march empowered women to take a more public stand on women's rights, including the formation of feminist organizations and political activities on behalf of women (Sherif, 2001). Sha'rawi founded the Egyptian Feminist Union, one of many Egyptian women's rights organizations working in the first half of the twentieth century whose activism led to significant progress for women (Keddie, 2007).[3] Likewise, the rise of women's activism in India is traced to their involvement in the nationalist campaign against British colonialism (Desai, 2001). In Egypt and India, women learned the language of political rights in the nationalist movement and insisted that the full economic and political equality of women be guaranteed by the new constitution (Desai, 2001; Sherif, 2001).

The involvement of women in nationalist struggles stimulates women's activism in yet another way. When women work hard in the battle for liberation only to discover the patriarchy within the very liberation movement in which they are working, their feminist consciousness is often raised. For example, Elaine Salo, of the South African United Women's Congress (UWC), recalls how the UWC was called upon to provide the tea and snacks at a national conference on the media instead of being a full participant (in Kemp et al., 1995). Likewise, many of the present leaders of the Bangladeshi women's movement became aware of gender discrimination as a result of the war for independence from Pakistan. Despite their role in the national independence movement, the new government marginalized women. They responded by organizing the first autonomous women's research organization in Bangladesh (Women for Women). Their reports on the status of women provided the basis for much of women's activism from the mid-1970s onward (Jahan, 1995).

Women's Movements and Democratization

The transition to democracy (democratization) often opens up new spaces for political participation, including women's rights and issues activism. Women often mobilize to ensure that new government laws, policies, and structures promote gender equality and address specific women's needs. But this is not always the case and, unsurprisingly, it depends on particular contextual factors.

> "If particular care and attention is not paid to the ladies, we are determined to foment a rebellion and will not hold ourselves bound by any laws in which we have no voice or representation."
> *Abigail Adams, wife of U.S. President John Adams, and one of America's first feminists*

---

[3] Egypt's vibrant women's movement was suppressed following the assassination of Anwar Sadat in the early 1980s. Many of the gains resulting from the movement have since been reversed due to Islamization.

Women's Movements in New Democracies

Spain is an example of a country where democratization went hand-in-hand with a strong women's movement. The modern Spanish women's movement coincided with the end of a long struggle for democratic rule in 1975. Most of the movement leaders at this time were members or ex-members of leftist political groups who had struggled against the authoritarian rule of General Franco. Following the death of the dictator in 1975, Spanish feminists had to persuade the newly developing government that women's liberation was part of the task of building democracy and socialism (Threlfall, 1996). According to Threlfall (1996), the emerging movement was protected and encouraged by the fact that 1975 was the United Nations' International Women's Year. Feminists essentially got in on the ground floor of the newly developing Spanish government. From there, they encouraged the eradication of discriminatory legislation and the passing of legislation favorable to women. In 1983, the government set up the Instituto de la Mujer (Institute of Women). It is currently one of the largest women's public administrations in Europe, although it appears more effective in representing women's movement goals when a left-wing party is in office (Valiente, 2005).

South Africa is yet another example of how feminism may emerge in the space created by national liberation. The British and the Dutch colonized South Africa. By 1948, the Dutch-descended Afrikaners controlled the government and the country. The Afrikaans government restricted the rights and movements of all non-White citizens under a system called *apartheid.* All Black opposition parties were banned, and individuals who violated this ban were arrested. The majority of Blacks were forced to live in desolate "homelands" called *bantustans,* were not allowed to own property, and when in White areas, were required to carry passes proving they had permission to be there. It wasn't until 1992, following years of national and international protest, that apartheid was outlawed and a new constitution granted equal rights to all South Africans. As was the case in Spain, from the beginning, women's organizations in South Africa played an important role in the struggle for national liberation. They organized protests and other grassroots challenges to the state. National Women's Day, a public holiday on August 9, commemorates one particularly famous example. On August 9, 1956, despite the discouragement of male comrades, 20,000 South African women marched on the Union Building in Pretoria to protest the extension of "pass laws" to Black women and their children (Kemp et al., 1995).

As South African women's level of political awareness and experience grew, they demanded that women's issues be addressed in the national agenda. Having taken on co-responsibility for waging the political struggle, for sustaining and conserving it when it was really embattled, women expected to be included as equals in the new democracy (Kemp et al., 1995). Following the fall of apartheid, new women's organizations formed and old ones emerged from hiding. In 1992, the Women's National Coalition (WNC), representing eighty-one diverse women's organizations, was formed to ensure that women's rights were represented in the new constitution. Because the WNC represented a broad range of women's perspectives and was strongly activist, it was able to add women's issues to the national agenda of the post-apartheid government. In 1996, the new South African Constitution, which provides equality between women and men as well as protection for lesbian and gay rights, was ratified.

The Philippines also fit this model of the newly liberated country sympathetic to women's issues. Like Chile, Spain, and South Africa, Filipino women played important roles in the labor and liberation movements from the beginning. Santiago (1995) shows that feminist organizing and consciousness have a long history in the Philippines.

Beginning in the early 1900s, *feminista* organizations campaigned to achieve political equality. Philippine suffragists campaigned in the Philippine Assembly, in the media, in schools, and at gatherings, and in 1937 they became the first women in Asia to win the right to vote. During the liberation movement of the 1970s and 1980s, *feministas* became an integral part of the struggle and insisted that a feminist perspective be part of the national agenda. In 1984, they founded a feminist political party and the feminist coalition GABRIELA. In 1985, when dictator Ferdinand Marcos declared victory in the national elections, feminist organizations were central in challenging the election results. This challenge toppled the Marcos dictatorship and affirmed Corazon Aquino as president. The Filipino women's movement today is strong and consists of a large variety of women's organizations working on a wide variety of issues, including reproductive rights, eliminating violence against women, employment, and the dismantling of U.S. military bases (Santiago, 1995). However, as is so often the case, traditional gender attitudes (and in this case the Catholic Church) make the struggle ongoing and poor economic conditions often take precedence over social reforms for gender justice.

Factors Affecting the Influence of Nationalism and Democratization on Women's Movements

Although the fall of oppressive governments may lead to the adoption of reforms favorable to women and to climates supportive of feminist activism, this is not always true. The countries of the former Soviet Union demonstrate this. The new "masculine democracies" that arose in countries of the former Soviet Union gave little space to women's needs, interests, civil rights, and organization in the policy process (Molyneaux, 1996). For example, maternity policies were curtailed, women's legislative quotas dismantled, and abortion rights threatened (Vitema & Fallon, 2008).

Initially it is puzzling that the falls of oppressive governments in Spain, the Philippines, and South Africa have led to positive developments for feminism but not in the former Soviet republics. However, there are important differences. First, women's post-transition movements benefit from women's pretransition activism because there is a base of experienced activists and

> "Twenty years are but the wink of an eye in the vast historical terrain of womankind's struggle for emancipation and liberation. The next 20 years will be another wink of an eye. But if we find the southward-flowing river, we can likely make the way easier and achieve the dreamt-of society sooner, with no backward sliding."
> *Ninotchka Rosca, GABRIELA activist*

networks, and this prior activism legitimates present-day feminist demands (Vitema & Fallon, 2008). This was true in Spain, the Philippines, and South Africa where politically active feminists played key roles in the nationalist struggle. There was already a fairly strong feminist consciousness and familiarity with political advocacy that was used to advocate for women's rights during the transition to democracy. This was not the case in the majority of the Eastern bloc countries. Soviet communism collapsed unexpectedly in 1989, the collapse was not the result of a democratic movement of the people, and, the Communist Party stifled women's pretransition mobilizations (Ghodsee, 2004; Vitema & Fallon, 2008). Indeed, the countries with the most active women's movements during the democratic transition (such as Poland) had a longer history of organized rebellion against the Soviet Union (Waters & Posadskaya, 1995).

Second, democratic transitions introduce new ideologies and to the extent that these are compatible with women's rights, women's movements will have greater influence in the "design" of the new state (Vitema & Fallon, 2008). For example, unlike the Spanish democracy that arose during the International Decade for Women and the South African transition that arose out of a movement emphasizing equality for all, the new democracies of the 1980s and 1990s arose in a climate emphasizing free markets (neoliberalism) and minimal government protections (Molyneaux, 1996). This was true in Eastern Europe, where new governments were not designed around an ideology of equality but rather around an ideology of the free market shaped by Western Europe and the United States (Ghodsee, 2004). Add to this that some transitions to democracy are guided by other countries (typically Western industrialized nations) with masculinist political systems, and the importation of these systems may not leave space for women's inclusion (Fallon, 2008). Such was the case in the countries of the former Soviet Union and some new democracies in sub-Saharan Africa. Furthermore, in the former Soviet republics, much of the language of feminist ideology—emancipation, equality, oppression—resembled the propaganda of the Communist regime (Cravens, 2006). Consequently, the very fact that the Soviet regime espoused the idea of women's equality was enough to bring it under suspicion (Molyneaux, 1996; Waters & Posadskaya, 1995). Many women even favored a return to traditional roles because "Soviet-style" gender equality forced women into the workplace without providing any relief at home, and because the pre-Soviet past is romanticized (Matynia, 1995; Cravens, 2006).

Successful nationalist struggles may also interfere with women's equality when the ideology of the "winning" regime is a conservative religious one, incompatible with gender equality. This type of nationalism often seeks inspiration from an imaginary past and usually advocates redomesticating women and controlling their sexuality (Basu, 1995). Religious states and traditional women's roles are presented as necessary to preserve centuries-old cultures in the face of globalization and the importation of Western values and culture. The battle between those who desire a secular modernist state and those favoring a traditional religious state continues to be waged in many countries including Algeria, Morocco, Iran, Iraq, Saudi Arabia, and Afghanistan. Who wins will greatly affect women's lives.

The traditional religious state won for a time in Afghanistan, where a nationalist religious movement succeeded in ending ten years of Soviet occupation. Prior to that, chaos reigned for almost nine years as the freedom fighters turned against one another. It was the nationalist Taliban group that brought peace. However, as you may recall, the ruling Taliban government enforced an extreme version of Islam that prohibited women from working outside the home, prevented girls from going to school, and required that women in public be completely by a *burqa*. The Taliban was overthrown following U.S. intervention in 2001, but by the end of the decade, it had regrouped and resurged. In 2003, the Loya Jirga's (Grand Council) draft constitution did not recognize women's rights as equal to men's, nor did it grant women the right to vote. Due to the activism of women's rights advocates in Afghanistan and internationally, the final version passed in January 2004 explicitly states that men and women have equal rights under the law, pledges to promote education for women, and guarantees women a place in government. However, the Constitution also states, "no law can be contrary to the beliefs and provisions of the sacred religion of Islam." Women's rights activists are concerned that this leaves women's rights vulnerable. Inadequate funding for reconstruction, political instability and violence, and traditional Islamic views also interfere with the enforcement of Afghan women's rights (Maloney, 2004; Moghadam, 2003). It remains dangerous for girls to go to school and for women to work—there are attacks on women who do not conform to traditional dress norms and on girls on their way to school, and the destruction of girls' schools continues (Filkins, 2009; Keddie, 2007).

Iran is yet another case in which women's rights were significantly curtailed following a nationalist religious revolution. In Iran, a 1979 revolution led to an Islamist state. The new government restricted women's activities and rights, and Iranian women fought to regain the ground they lost (Afshar, 1996; Mir-Hosseini, 2001). They did this by anchoring their arguments in favor of women's rights in the teachings of Islam. As Afshar (1996) says, "Given the Islamic nature of the national political discourse, which posits the government as the defender of the faith, women were able to take the Republic to task for failing to deliver on its Islamic duty" (p. 203). They referred to parts of the Koran that favor respect for women and support for females' education and training. Muslim women also referred to educated and powerful female role models such as Muhammad's wives Khadija (politician and businesswoman) and A'isha (politician and religious expert). Consequently, in the 1990s, Iranian women successfully argued for the removal of many of the barriers placed upon educating women, women practicing medicine and law, and women owning and running businesses. They also successfully sought representation in parliament and hoped to change laws such as those that require women to have their husbands' permission to work and that say a woman's word in the courts counts for half of a man's. But in the first decade of the twenty-first century, Iranian women's rights defenders have been beaten

Meena (1957–1987) of Kabul, Afghanistan, dangerously campaigned against the occupying Soviet forces, began a feminist women's magazine, founded the Afghan feminist organization RAWA, advocated against Islamic fundamentalist views of women, and established schools for Afghanistan refugee children in Pakistan and micro-enterprises for their parents. She was assassinated in 1987 by the Soviet secret service (KGB) and their fundamentalist accomplices.

"Whenever women protest and ask for their rights, they are silenced with the argument that the laws are justified under Islam. It is an unfounded argument. It is not Islam at fault, but rather the patriarchal culture that uses its own interpretations to justify whatever it wants."
Shirin Ebadi

by police at public rallies, arrested and tortured, and sentenced to prison (Amnesty International, 2008). For example, in 2009, Shadi Sadr, an Iranian women's activist, was arrested, beaten, and jailed along with other women's activists. Sadr, an attorney, was director of *Raahi,* a legal advice center for women, until it was closed down by the government. She also launched the first website about women's rights activism in Iran and is a leader in Women's Field, a women's rights organization that has launched several campaigns including the "Stop Stoning Forever" campaign (Amnesty International, 2009). She was questioned about women's rights NGOs, charged with illegal assembly, collusion against national security, disruption of public order and refusal to obey the orders of the police; fortunately, she was released on bail after several weeks (AWID, 2009). In November 2009, Sadr was awarded the Tulip Award, the Dutch Human Rights Defenders Award.

Following the overthrow of Saddam Hussein by U.S. forces in 2003, Iraq struggled to design a government that would satisfy those preferring a progressive democratic government enshrining the rights of women and those desiring a government based on the precepts of Islam. Initially, the U.S.-backed Governing Council passed a resolution that put family law under shari'ah (recall that shari'ah is Islamic religious law and is often interpreted in ways that promote gender inequality). U.S. and Iraqi women's activists lobbied the Bush administration not to approve the interim constitution with this provision. Eventually, the Governing Council agreed to tone down the language to say that Islam would be *a* source of legislation, rather than *the* source. However, this compromise still leaves the door open for future leaders to apply shari'ah to family law, and it is unclear whether a new government will rewrite the constitution once the U.S. leaves. New women's organizations like the Iraqi Women's League and the Organization of Women's Freedom are working hard to guarantee women's rights (Keddie, 2007), but given the political organization of Islamists, their resistance to women's empowerment, and the dangers facing women's activists, it is still to be determined how much women will benefit in the post-Saddam Hussein era. Fundamentalism is on the rise in Iraq and there are many who view women's rights as an affront to Islam. Some are willing to use violence to discourage challenges to traditional gender roles and efforts to empower women. Fern Holland, a women's activist who worked for the U.S.-led Coalition setting up women's centers across south-central Iraq and who helped draft the women's rights section of the interim constitution, was assassinated in March 2004, two weeks after the constitution was signed.

Box 10.4 summarizes the conditions under which women's movements have the most impact in new democracies.

Women's Movements and State Feminism

The term **state feminism** refers to activities of government structures that are formally charged with furthering women's status and rights (Stetson & Mazur, 1995). These government structures are sometimes called "women's

---

BOX 10.4 *Factors Affecting the Impact of Women's Movements in New Democracies*

Women's movements have the most impact in new democracies when:

- The ideology of the new democracy emphasizes equality.

- Women were active in the struggle for democracy.

- There is feminist consciousness, experience with feminist organizing, and feminist networks.

- Other countries or international organizations aiding the democratic transition emphasize the need to incorporate gender equality in new government policies and structures.

---

policy machinery." The feminist bureaucrats who sometimes work as part of these government structures are referred to as "**femocrats**" (Stetson & Mazur, 1995). State feminism assumes a variety of forms at many levels of government, ranging from temporary advisory commissions to permanent ministries (Mazur, 2001). Box 10.5 provides a synopsis of the modern Chinese women's movement and the movement's primary women's policy machinery, the All-China Women's Federation (ACWF). Ideally, women's policy agencies (WPAs) are government allies of women's movement actors and ensure that women's movement goals are translated into government policy and action (Haussman & Sauer, 2007). For example, Norway serves an example of an effective state feminism with centralized government offices that have integrated gender equity principles into policy and fostered the empowerment of women's groups (Stetson & Mazur, 1995). Although the Equal Status Council (ESC) remains the main agency responsible for gender equality, gender has been mainstreamed into most state agencies. The state actively promotes women's equality through childcare subsidies, generous parental leave policies, quotas, and publicly appointed boards, committees, councils. The cases of Norway and China show the importance of contextualizing women's movements, including state feminism.

In the last twenty-five years, there has been a proliferation of state (government) agencies to promote women's status and rights (Lovenduski, 2008). Many governments have added offices, commissions, agencies, ministries, committees, and advisors to deal with women's issues and gender equality. This development has been stimulated in part by the 1995 Beijing Platform for Action of UN Fourth World Conference on Women. The Platform called upon governments to eliminate gender-based discrimination and incorporate gender equality at all stages of policymaking; in other words, to practice

"Women hold up half the sky."
Chinese saying

BOX 10.5   *The Chinese Women's Movement*

The modern Chinese women's movement shows how women's movements may develop in tandem with nationalist movements and how new governments with ideologies of equality can lead to state feminism. The nationalist movement at the turn of the twentieth century rejected Confucianism, which justified dynastic rule and the rule of women by men, and replaced it with an egalitarian ideology that included gender equality. Women like Qiu Jin (1875–1907) played important roles in anti-dynastic uprisings while also emphasizing women's emancipation (Qiu Jin was ultimately beheaded for leading a thwarted rebellion and became a hero). Feminism, nationalism, and class struggle became linked. After the overthrow of the Qing dynasty, women's groups worked to ensure women's rights in the new republic.

The Chinese Communist Party (CCP), which has ruled the country since 1949, created the All-China Women's Federation (ACWF) to mobilize and represent the interests of Chinese women. Although its influence has varied, it can be said that the ACWF has advanced

women's interests. Since the early 1980s, other women's organizations and NGOs have arisen, although they must have a formal link with a state agency to supervise their activities. Dramatic growth in the number of women's NGOs occurred following the UN Beijing Fourth World Women's Conference and many use global feminist frameworks such as gender and development, empowerment, and gender mainstreaming, although these are often "indigenized" (adapted into uniquely Chinese practices). Women's studies as an academic discipline, along with women's publications and literature, have grown. Although women's status has improved, workplace discrimination due to maternity, reproductive rights, son preference, the "second shift," and domestic violence remain of concern, and it is said that more attention needs to be paid to the difficulties faced by rural Chinese women.

Sources: Yuan, 2005; Xu, 2009; Zhang & Xu, 1995.

---

gender mainstreaming (Tripp et al., 2009). Women's activism is also a critical mechanism by which states can become more gender equitable; states generally do not adopt feminist changes without pressure from organized women's groups (Vitema & Fallon, 2008). These groups articulate women's concerns to government through "platforms," and push these platforms using media, lobbying, and protests.

Norway's successful state feminism is an example of the role of women's organizations as a mechanism for making states more gender equitable. Although Norway's state feminism is due in part to Norway's commitment to the values of equality and justice and the belief that it is the state's role to promote equality, Norway's active women's movement played a large role in creating a state responsive to women's needs (Bystydzienski, 1992b, 1995). Norwegian women have always been strong and political; this is reflected in Norwegian literature dating back to the tenth century. The modern movement has its roots in the 1800s (As, 1996; Morgan, 1996). During the 1960s and 1970s, women representing traditional women's organizations and the so-called new feminists formed a successful coalition that raised public

"We do not want a piece of the pie; we want to change the basic recipe of the pie."
Birgit Brock-Utne

consciousness regarding women's disadvantaged status and called on the government to respond. In the 1970s, they united on the issue of abortion, and the Storting (the Norwegian Parliament) gave women the right to abortion within the first twelve weeks of pregnancy. One particular goal of the feminist coalition that significantly impacted state feminism was to increase the number of women in public office (as discussed in Chapter 9). The growing responsiveness of the Norwegian government to feminist activists clearly coincides with the increased number of women in public offices, for many of these women received their political training in the women's movement and were sympathetic to feminist demands. As more women entered government, the state became more responsive to women's demands from below, and women began to participate in forming state policy. For example, in 2002, the government ordered companies to ensure that at least 40 percent of their board members are women (Seager, 2009). Because of the influence of feminist organizations, the major political parties have all adopted sex quotas for political campaigns (at least 40 percent female and 40 percent male in any given election).

Debate About the Role of the State

In theory, women's policy agencies (WPAs), or "women's national policy machinery," represent women's interests in state decision-making (Lovenduski, 2008). But whether these agencies and bureaucracies promote a feminist agenda is highly variable. Some critics concede that states should play a role in solving women's problems but contend that many governments undermine change by co-opting women's organizations and weakening them such that they become part of the system rather than a challenge to it. For example, in Mexico during the 1930s, the United Front for Women's Rights was founded and had more than 50,000 women members from different social classes and ideological viewpoints. The movement was incorporated into the official party, Partido Revolucionario Mexicana (predecessor of today's ruling Partido Revolucionario Institutional). Its activities were then restricted, ostensibly to prevent "political instability" (Pablos, 1992).

Some countries are not allowed much of an independent women's movement, and almost all women's issues advocacy is done by government commissions and government-sponsored women's organizations. In Egypt, for example, all nongovernmental organizations have to be registered and supervised by the state, which has the right to dissolve NGOs and put government representatives on their boards (Keddie, 2007; Sekhon & Bystydzienski, 1999). Egyptian women's NGOs must also accept the authority of the government's National Council for Women (Keddie, 2007). Basu (1995) also points to cases in which governments created women's organizations so that they could control women's activism. These governments required that women's interests be pursued through these organizations and not independently. The problem is that under these conditions, governments decide what women's problems are and how to solve them. The result is the appearance of

"A true feminist agenda challenges the state."
Hussaina Abdullah

progress despite the fact that key women's issues are ignored, and traditional gender relations and gender power differentials remain largely intact. A number of examples come from Latin America. In Chile, SERNAM, the main governmental organization devoted to women's issues, is perceived by many feminists to be too cautious and conservative, as an instrument through which the women's movement has been co-opted, and to have failed to establish good links with grassroots women's organizations (Frohmann & Valdes, 1995; Waylen, 2008), although others argue that over time this has become less true (Franceschet, 2003). Grassroots feminists in Brazil make similar charges regarding state women's organizations (Alvarez, 1994).

It is important that state feminist inclusion of societal actors empower those interests without co-opting or dominating them (Mazur & Stetson, 1995). As Stetson and Mazur (1995) caution, "If interests become overly dependent on the state, not only is their autonomy threatened, but their own fortunes become intertwined with those of the policy offices, and these are often linked to the fate of a governing party coalition" (p. 276). The United States is a typical example. In general, feminist organizations have worked to cement alliances with the Democratic Party, and when this party is in power, more feminist policies are adopted. However, these are often reversed when the Republicans control the government. For instance, it was very difficult to get equal rights legislation passed under Republican presidents Ronald Reagan, George H. W. Bush, and George W. Bush. By the early 1990s, many of the gains made in the 1970s were significantly weakened by these three administrations.

Nicaragua provides yet another example of how feminist-government alliances are somewhat risky because governments change and state feminist machineries may be dismantled. As was the case in many Latin American countries, a nationalist struggle for independence from a dictatorship stimulated the growth of the women's movement. Nicaraguan women played an important role in the overthrow of the Somoza dictatorship and, in the process, honed their political skills and confidence and earned the right to inclusion in the new Sandinista government. AMNLAE (Asociación de Mujeres Louisa Amanda Espinosa) became the Sandinista-affiliated women's organization and by 1985, played an aggressive role in educating Nicaraguan society about women's issues. The Sandinista government also funded a number of significant feminist research projects and created a Women's Legal Office, located in the president's office, in order to participate in strategic planning (Chinchilla, 1994).

In 1990, however, the Sandinistas lost the election to the conservative UNO party, and, the women's movement lost traction due to its association with the FSLN, the Sandinista party. Violeta de Chamorro became president and her government advocated traditional gender roles and the rhythm method as the only acceptable form of birth control, and cut services that benefited women (Chinchilla, 1994). These events stimulated intense discussion within the Central American women's movement about the meaning and importance of autonomy for feminist organizations (Chinchilla, 1994).

Antifeminist movements in Nicaragua have since gained ground (Kampwirth, 2006). To regain and retain power, the FSLN aligned itself more closely with the Catholic Church. Once again in power, they outlawed all abortion (in 2006), prevented demonstrations by women's organizations, and raided the offices of the Nicaraguan Autonomous Women's Movement, a vocal critic of the government's policies (Booth, 2008; Lacey, 2008). Although state feminism is now weak, this and the antifeminist movement have stimulated the growth of an independent women's movement.

Factors Affecting the Success of State Feminism

The potential dangers of state feminism, including the possibility of the state co-opting women's movements, inconsistencies due to changes in political administrations, and failing to bring about real change, seem greater when there is no independent women's movement. For example, in Australia, women's policy machinery and feminist-inspired programs have waned as an autonomous, active, and oppositional women's movement has gradually disappeared (Andrews, 2008). A robust, independent women's movement has the advantage of being able to exert continued pressure on government so that it cannot fail to keep gender-equality promises. A diverse movement of women's groups focused on a variety of women's issues and the needs of women that vary based on race, sexual orientation, and class, also prevents governments from responding to only a narrow range of women and issues. If state feminism is weak, an independent women's movement often provides needed services through GROs and can exert pressure on government to respond to women's issues and needs.

Tripp and colleagues (2009), in a discussion of state feminism in Africa, note a variety of factors influencing the effectiveness of state machineries in promoting women's interests. These include: (1) how much authority they have to make and enforce policy; (2) whether they have a clear mandate and are given adequate resources to meet it; (3) whether the leaders of the agency or ministry are true femocrats or simply government bureaucrats or political appointees without gender consciousness; (4) whether they are part of strategic government units or marginalized; and (5) whether they coordinate and collaborate with women's NGOs or actively weaken them. Others have noted that state feminism does the most for women when the state is defined as the site of social justice, has the structural capacity to institutionalize demands for equality, and supports feminist organizations and reform politics in unions and political parties. In sum, state feminism seems to work best when the agency or bureau is a separate ministry (rather than subsumed under another); when they have a clear mandate; when they have adequate (and technically trained) staff and money; when they are run by true femocrats rather than bureaucrats; and when they have a strong, positive relationship with women's movement GROs and GRSOs, letting them help set the agenda and providing them with funding (Hausman & Sauer, 2007; Waylen, 2008).

"The women's
movement, not only
here in the U.S., but
worldwide, is bigger and
stronger than ever before
and in places where it
has never been. It has
arms. It has legs. And
most importantly, it has
heads."
*Bella Abzug, U.S.
Congresswoman
and cofounder of
Women's Environment &
Development
Organization (WEDO)*

Evaluating the Success of Women's Movements

Women's struggles for equality are by no means new, but this fact, combined with women's continued lower status and power, suggests that these struggles have been less than effective. Indeed, the record of success is mixed. On the one hand, significant gains have been made (see Figure 10.2 for some women's movement successes). On the other hand, women's movements have not achieved many of their goals. Constant vigilance seems necessary to keep steps forward from being followed by steps backward. It is also obvious that the countries of the world still have a considerable distance to go before gender equality is achieved. Jahan's (1995) statement regarding the success of the women's movement in Bangladesh has broad applicability: While public pronouncements on the importance of including women are common, and women's participation at all levels has increased, the social structures and institutions perpetuating women's inequality remain largely intact.

Many explanations have been offered for the uneven success of women's movements. One thought is that many middle-class women's movements have failed because they did not mobilize poor women and assumed that class interests could be subordinated to gender interests (Basu, 1995). For example, Australian Aboriginal women frequently feel that talking about women's rights is irrelevant when they are oppressed by racism and poverty and when the destruction of Aboriginal society deprives men, more than women, of status and self-respect (Sawer, 1994). Likewise, women's national, cultural, or ethnic identities may be of equal or greater concern to women, and many women may not support movements that fail to take this into account. LaFromboise, Heyle, and Ozer (1990) note that Native American women are at least as concerned with the preservation of their race and culture as they are with women's equality. They also suggest that Native American gender equality movements will differ from non-Native movements as Native women seek a feminism that works within the context of Native American families, their nations, and their cultures.

Countermovements against feminism often challenge the success of women's movements. In 1980s India, for example, Indian feminists were accused of being Westernists, colonialists, and cultural imperialists. Feminists worked against dowries, sati (a widow's immolation on her husband's funeral pyre), and arranged marriage. Irate families, the police, and the courts (which ruled against feminist positions) attacked them. Traditional Hindu nationalist women agitated in favor of women's right to *sati* (Kumar, 1995).[4] In the United States, feminists are accused of being manlike and man-haters and antifeminists actively work to limit women's reproductive rights. Antifeminist movements often draw attention to their female members and then charge that feminists do not represent the true interests of women and are forcing women into change that they do not want. In Australia, repudiations of the excesses of feminism have recently been used to support the reversal of policies

---

[4] *Sati* is a funeral practice in which a woman throws herself on her husband's funeral pyre (a combustible heap on which the dead are burned).

FIGURE 10.2 *Successes of Women's Movements*

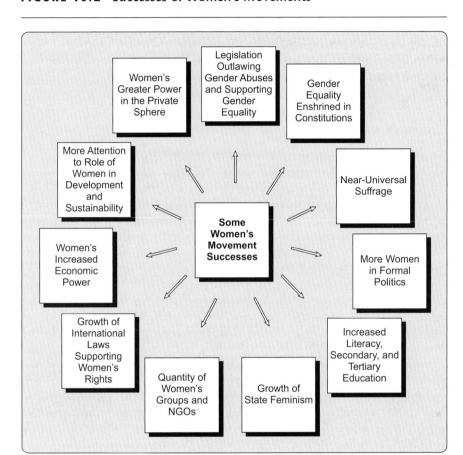

supporting working women, particularly working mothers (Andrews, 2008). As Basu (1995) points out, the opposition to women's equal rights is often better funded and better organized and often has the weight of the state, and tradition, behind it. Changing deeply entrenched gender ideology is a long-term process, particularly in the face of resistance and hostility from conservative and extremist groups using religion to legitimize a bid for social and political control (Jahan, 1995b).

Women's movements also sometimes face significant challenges from within, as feminist groups differ about what they see as critical issues and about how to go about solving them. Consider the case of Brazil. There, the women's movement was torn apart in the 1980s because of profound differences among feminist groups on which party to support during the election and controversy regarding whether the movement should remain autonomous from the state

(Alvarez, 1994; Soares et al., 1995). In Muslim countries, for example, some feminists try to promote a liberation theology as a way toward gender equality whereas others fight for secularism (a separation of religion and state) as a way to gain equality (Moghadam, 1991). Simply put, there are a variety of feminisms, often within one country, and these differences sometimes threaten the solidarity that it takes to challenge entrenched systems.

Conclusion

"Never doubt that a small group of thoughtful, committed citizens can change the world—indeed, it's the only thing that ever has."
Margaret Mead

This chapter illustrates the variety of ways in which women collectively work to change gender ideologies and state policies and structures and how they act to create groups and organizations to serve women's needs and promote their interests. The array of contextual factors that influence how women's movements arise and whether they succeed illustrates that the path to gender equality in one place is likely to be different than the path in another place. The importance of intersectionality was once again apparent; some movements have failed because they have been too narrowly focused on women's interests without considering how these interact with nationalism, class, or other important identities. As we suggested in Chapter 1, a truly global feminism recognizes diversity in women's movements and acknowledges that there are diverse meanings of feminism, each responsive to the needs and issues of women in different regions, societies, and times. A multicultural approach to global women's studies requires that we respect the rights of women to initiate their own movements in ways that work for them in their countries. Ethnocentrism is regard to women's movements is foolhardy—not only do the strategies of women in one country often fail to translate to another, but believing that the path taken by women in one's country is the only path leads to an incomplete understanding of women's movements.

While this chapter focuses on challenges to the traditional gender roles of a particular community by women in that community (that is, national and local movements), the next chapter focuses on transnational women's movements and international legal instruments as a means for change. These two approaches to gender equality are not mutually exclusive—on the contrary, they are mutually supportive. Positive changes in international law frequently result from the coordinated efforts of grassroots women's movements. Furthermore, without the influence of grassroots movements, international law may not have relevance in the day-to-day lives of women and may coerce cultural variety into a false unity (Toro, 1995). International laws regarding the equality of women also serve grassroots movements by legitimizing their struggles and providing mechanisms for change where women's movements are suppressed. By building regional and international linkages, women's ability to develop effective political and legal strategies for their local struggles is enhanced (Human Rights Watch, 1995; Tripp et al., 2009). International laws also strengthen feminism worldwide by placing pressure on governments to respond to women's movements (Basu, 1995).

Study Questions

1. What is a women's movement? Why is it more accurate to speak of women's movements rather than *a* women's movement?

2. What forces operate against women's activism? What are women up against when they ask for equal rights?

3. What early (mistaken) assumptions were made about women's movements by Western feminist scholars?

4. Why do some women's movements distance themselves from the feminist label? What are some differences between Western and other feminisms?

5. What are the three major strands of women's movements found in most countries?

6. What are practical and strategic gender interests?

7. How can local political and economic conditions affect the development of women's movements, both positively and negatively?

8. What are some specific examples of how women's movements can arise out of nationalist struggles for liberation? Why does women's involvement in nationalist struggles often stimulate women's movement activism?

9. What are some examples of women's movements arising in new democracies? What are some examples where democratization didn't benefit women's movements? What factors seem to explain these differences?

10. What is state feminism? What is a femocrat? What are some of the concerns about state feminism? What are some examples of state feminism not doing much to help women's equality and some examples of it helping? What accounts for the difference?

11. What gains have been made by women's equality movements?

12. What are some of the explanations given for the uneven success of women's movements?

13. Why is an intersectional, multicultural approach to women's movements recommended?

Discussion Questions and Activities

1. Considering the broad definition of women's movements given at the beginning of the chapter, identify the various women's GROs and GRSOs in your community and explain what they do.

2. Would you recommend that women's organizations in your culture use the feminist label? Why or why not?

3. What state feminism structures exist in your national government and your state government? To what extent do these women's policy machineries serve women's interests? To what extent do they reflect a feminist view?

4. One of the themes of the chapter is that women's movements vary cross-culturally and that gender social change is something that women in a culture do for themselves. If this is true, how can feminists in one culture assist feminists in another culture, or can they?

5. The chapter discussed the cases of Iran, Iraq, and Afghanistan. In 2010, in all three countries, women's rights were uncertain as those favoring an Islamist government and traditional gender roles conflicted with those favoring a more progressive government and society. What has happened since? What is the current status of women's rights in those countries?

6. Research the women's movement in a newly democratic country not covered in this chapter. Use the factors discussed in the chapter to explain why democracy has (or has not) benefited the women's movement.

Action Opportunities

1. Volunteer your time to help a women's organization in your community. If you don't want to make a long-term commitment, many can use occasional office help or assistance with fund-raising efforts.

2. There are many specific types of feminist groups, including feminist groups for different religions, ethnicities, etc. Identify and explore a feminist organization that reflects you from an intersectional perspective.

3. Identity a women's movement organization in your country that advocates for women at a national level and participate in one of their campaigns.

4. Create your own campaign on a women's issue of your choice. Organize women (and men) to take action on a women's issue in your local or university community (for example, is women's safety an issue on your campus? Is emergency contraception available at your university's health center?), or on a national or international women's issue. Remember women's activists use a range of tactics—you can do a "teach-in," a rally, a petition drive, a letter-writing campaign, fund-raising drives, or organize a picket, etc. You can also use art, music, and other creative means to increase awareness.

5. Go to Amnesty International's website and take action to support a currently jailed or imprisoned women's rights activist, http://www .amnesty.org.

Activist Websites

Feminist Majority (US) http://www.feminist.org

National Organization for Women (US) http://www.now.org

All India Democratic Women's Association http://www.aidwa.org

Defending Women: Defending Women's Rights http://www
.defendingwomen-defendingrights.org/press_release_putan
_observatory.php

Women's Field http://www.meydaan.com/

Global List of Women's Organizations http://www.distel.ca/womlist/
womlist.html

Informational Websites

National Council of Women's Organizations (US) http://www
.womensorganizations.org

SAWNET South Asian Women's Organizations http://www.umiacs.umd
.edu/users/sawweb/sawnet/orgn.html

International Council for Research on Women http://www.icrw.org

Women's Equality Day (celebrating the day in 1920 when U.S. women won
the right to vote) www.nwhp.org/resourcecenter/equalityday.php

International Feminist Journal of Politics http://www.tandf.co.uk/journals/
titles/14616742.asp

11

Transnational Women's Movements and Networks

Challenging prevailing concepts of, and reinterpreting the movement for, human rights from a feminist perspective is not merely a matter of semantics. It is about the lives and deaths of individual women, everywhere, everyday. . . . Yet even as the international human rights community has begun to recognize gender-based violations as pervasive and insidious forms of human rights abuse, we must work further to see that concerted actions against such practices are taken. . . . Only through community responsibility and state accountability, day by day, place by place, will we counter the massive violation of women's human rights in the world.

—CHARLOTTE BUNCH,
Center for Women's Global Leadership

The transnational feminist movement involves women working across national borders to insure that women's interests are addressed by intergovernmental treaties and policies. Transnational feminist organizing was stimulated by four United Nations international conferences on women. This photo shows women at the Fourth World Women's Conference in Beijing, China in 1995. © AP/Wide World Photos

The last chapter focused on women's movements in different countries. Here the focus is on international women's movements, or as they are sometimes called, **global** or **transnational feminist movements.** Transnational feminist movements span across multiple nations and have at their core the belief that women are entitled to the same rights as men, regardless of where the women live, and their ethnicity, sexual orientation, religion, and social class. These movements involve the coming together of feminist NGOs to work across regional or international borders in coalitions and campaigns (Porter, 2007). However, transnational feminisms recognize diversity and acknowledge that there are diverse meanings of feminism, each responsive to the needs and issues of women in different regions, societies, and times. Diversity and difference remain central values in transnational feminisms, values to be acknowledged and respected, not erased in the building of alliances (Mohanty, 2003).

Transnational feminisms are not new. The first transnational feminist organization, *Association Internationale des Femmes,* was founded in 1868 in Geneva, Switzerland (Tripp, 2006a). In 1887, American suffragists Elizabeth Cady Stanton and Lucretia Mott called a meeting of the International Council of Women to be held the following year in Washington, D.C. Their call recognized the "universal sisterhood" of women and noted, "The position of women anywhere affects the position of women everywhere." They expressed the hope that the international council would "devise new and more effective methods for securing the equality and justice of women" and would help them realize their power in combining together to these ends (Fraser, 1987). This 1888 meeting resulted in the first formal international women's organization, the International Congress of Women (ICW) (Stienstra, 1994). Many early international women's organizations emphasized women's suffrage. For example, in 1904, U.S. feminists Elizabeth Cady Stanton, Susan B. Anthony, and Carrie Chapman Catt formed the International Women's Suffrage Alliance (IWSA) with the goal of securing women's right to vote. Following World War I, international women's groups worked to ensure that the newly forming League of Nations (later the United Nations) included women's representatives and addressed issues affecting women and children. Other early international feminist organizations include the Women's International League for Peace and Freedom (1905) and the International Alliance of Women (1926). Women's international nongovernmental organizations were also instrumental in the establishment of the United Nations in 1945 (West, 1999).

International and regional conferences where information is shared and strategies are developed remain a key part of transnational women's movements but the modern transnational women's movement has been stimulated by globalization and aided by advances in information and communication technologies (Desai, 2007). As noted in Chapter 7, "globalization from above" has had many negative effects on women, but one positive effect is "globalization from below" is seen in the growth of **transnational feminist networks (TFNs),** the

"Women are taking the lead and making a huge contribution to defining the international agenda in term of human rights, macroeconomics, conflict/peace, and sustainable development. We have a valuable and unique perspective on these issues as women and as human beings. We recognize that feminism in one country is not sustainable—we need feminism on a global scale."
WIDE (Women in Development Europe)

March 8 is International Women's Day (IWD). Celebrated since 1901, it was originally intended to highlight the struggles of working-class women and to promote women's suffrage. The idea is that on this day, every year, women would speak together with one voice. In many countries, IWD is a day for rallies and marches to call attention to women's economic, political, and reproductive rights.

FIGURE 11.1   *Activities of Transnational Feminist Networks*

Form Coalitions to Influence Policy and Intergovernmental Organizations

Share Strategies, Information, and Research

Research, Advocate, and Lobby to Influence Policy and Awareness

Partner with Labor, Environmental, Human Rights, and Humanitarian Organizations

Activities of Transnational Feminist Networks

Protest Negative Effects of Globalization on Women, the Poor, and the Environment

Create and Use Global Networks to Support Specific Gender Equality Struggles

Ensure Women's Issues and Rights are Mainstreamed in UN Agencies and Human Rights Instruments

Use Human Rights Instruments like CEDAW to Promote Women's Rights

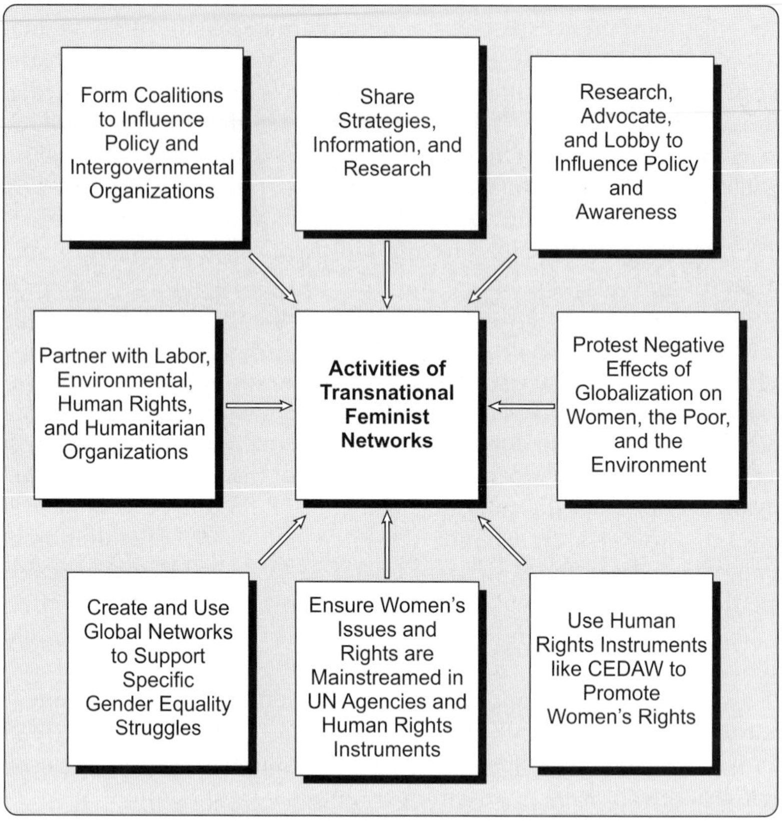

organizational expression of the transnational feminist movement (Moghadam, 2005). These networks operate across national borders to resist inequalities created by globalization, to influence policymaking, and to insert a feminist perspective in transnational advocacy and activism (Moghadam, 2005). For example, some TFNs ensure that United Nations' treaties and organizations address women's rights and issues and practice gender mainstreaming; some work to stop the trafficking of women; some focus on environmental sustainability; some focus on peace and the effects of conflict on women; some resist patriarchal nationalism and fundamentalisms; and others monitor, document, and protest the gendered effects of world trade agreements. Figure 11.1 summarizes the many activities of TFNs.

Although this chapter focuses primarily on the transnational feminist movements and networks, the United Nations, and human rights, it is important to note that the activities of TFNs are broader than this. For example, regional TFNs in Africa and Latin America have influenced peace initiatives

BOX 11.1   *Women Living Under Muslim Laws*

Women Living Under Muslim Laws (WLUML) is a TFN that operates across seventy countries. WLUML focuses on the often diverse practices and laws classified as "Muslim" (resulting from different interpretations of religious texts and/or the political use of religion) and the effects these practices have on women. WLUML was formed by nine women from Algeria, Morocco, Sudan, Iran, Mauritius, Tanzania, Bangladesh, and Pakistan in 1984 in response to three cases where women were being denied rights by laws said to be Muslim. See WLUML's website for interviews with some WLUML's founders: http://www.wluml.org/section/media/latest.

WLUML engages in a variety of activities in concert with NGOs transnationally. These include coordinating international action alerts. A current campaign is the Global Campaign to Stop Killing and Stoning of Women (http://www.stop-killing.org/home). WLUML uses a human rights framework and international agreements on the rights of women to make their case. WLUML also provides support to individuals in the form of advising on legal rights, providing assistance with asylum applications, and providing information on support resources such as shelters or counseling. WLUML promotes networking among women and organizations and responds to requests for information from academics, activists, the media, international agencies, and government institutions. WLUML also collects, analyzes, and circulates information regarding women's diverse experiences and strategies in Muslim contexts and holds training sessions, workshops, and conferences. WLUML has offices in Senegal, Pakistan, and the United Kingdom.

_____

Sources: Moghadam, 2005; WLUML, 2009.

in civil conflicts (Tripp, 2006a). Box 11.1 profiles Women Living Under Muslim Laws, a TFN that operates across seventy countries and focuses on the human rights of women in Muslim countries.

The Transnational Women's Movement and the United Nations

The resurgence of the transnational women's movement in the latter part of the twentieth century is often attributed to the UN Decade for Women (1975–1985). NGO forums at four UN international conferences on women and the numerous preparatory conferences that preceded them were central to the formation and growth of the modern transnational women's movement (Desai, 2007; Porter, 2007). Growth in the modern movement was especially noticeable from the mid-1980s to mid-1990s when the third and fourth UN conferences and pre-conferences increased networking and organizing opportunities for TFNs and helped them raise funds for projects. This, combined with feminist resistance to the negative effects of economic globalization and conservative religious and political forces, fostered the development of a new global feminist identity and solidarity (Moghadam, 2005).

The UN's World Women's Conferences

"The obstacles to the equality of women created by stereotypes, perceptions of and attitudes towards women should be totally removed. Elimination of these obstacles will require, in addition to legislation, education of the population at large through formal and informal channels, including the media, non-governmental organizations, political party platforms and executive action."
Nairobi Forward-Looking Strategies for the Advancement of Women 1985

The United Nations designated 1975 as International Women's Year and the ten years from 1975 to 1985 as the **United Nations Decade for Women.** During the Decade for Women, the UN promoted transnational feminism through the creation of national and international forums for action, gathered data about women, and held three world women's conferences. These international conferences on the status of women (1975– Mexico City; 1980– Copenhagen, Denmark; 1985–Nairobi, Kenya) catapulted the international connections among women to a qualitatively different level as women from very different backgrounds worked together on committees, caucuses, and networking (Chowdhury et al., 1994). A fourth world conference was held in Beijing, China, in 1995. Since the Beijing conference, follow-up sessions have been held by the Committee on the Status of Women in five-year intervals (known as Beijing +5 and Beijing +10; Beijing +15 was held in 2010). These sessions are intended as an opportunity to review progress and promote transnational feminist networking.

Because UN world conferences are media events, these conferences and the declaration of United Nations Decade for Women (1975–1985) publicized the low status and power of women in the world. In some cases this publicity led to increased grassroots activism. The international women's conferences and UN Decade for Women also encouraged national commitments to increase the status of women through the development of women's bureaus and commissions and through legal and constitutional changes. Preparations for the first international women's conference held in 1975 in Mexico City revealed that the UN had very little information on the status of women worldwide. As a result, the UN pushed for the collection of statistical data and now publishes regular reports on the status of women.

"Unless the human rights of women, as defined by international human rights instruments, are fully recognized and effectively protected, applied, implemented and enforced in national law as well as in national practice in family, civil, penal, labour and commercial codes and administrative rules and regulations, they will exist in name only."
Beijing Platform for Action, 1995

Member nations sent delegates to the women's conferences to discuss proposals regarding women's rights. For example, at the first women's conference in Mexico City in 1975, 133 delegates reached agreement on the "World Plan of Action," agreeing to work to end discrimination against women. In 1985, at the Third World Conference on Women in Nairobi, Kenya, 1,899 delegates reached agreement on the "Nairobi Forward-Looking Strategies for the Advancement of Women." This document set goals that were to be reached by the year 2000. The **Beijing Platform for Action (BPFA)** was the product of the Fourth World Conference on Women (FWCW) held in Beijing, China, in 1995 and is considered to be the most comprehensive agenda ever negotiated for women's empowerment. The BPFA, negotiated by 5,000 delegates from 189 countries, identifies twelve "critical areas of concern" (see Box 11.2). It is called the *Platform for Action* because for each critical area of concern, it specifies strategic objectives and specific actions to be undertaken by governments. For example, violence against women is one critical area of concern and includes three strategic objectives: (1) take integrated measures to prevent and eliminate violence against women (thirty recommended actions); (2) study causes and consequences of violence against women and

BOX 11.2 *The Beijing Platform for Action*

The Platform for Action is an agenda for women's empowerment. It aims at accelerating the implementation of the Nairobi Forward-Looking Strategies for the Advancement of Women and at removing all the obstacles to women's active participation in all spheres of public and private life through a full and equal share in economic, social, cultural, and political decision-making. Governments are called upon to take strategic, specified actions in regard to twelve critical areas of concern:

1. The persistent and increasing burden of poverty on women

2. Inequalities and inadequacies in and unequal access to education and training

3. Inequalities and inadequacies in and unequal access to health care and related services

4. Violence against women

5. The effects of armed or other kinds of conflict on women, including those living under foreign occupation

6. Inequality in economic structures and policies, in all forms of productive activities and in access to resources

7. Inequality between men and women in the sharing of power and decision-making at all levels

8. Insufficient mechanisms at all levels to promote the advancement of women

9. Lack of respect for and inadequate promotion and protection of the human rights of women

10. Stereotyping of women and inequality in women's access to and participation in all communication systems, especially in the media

11. Gender inequalities in the management of natural resources and in the safeguarding of the environment

12. Persistent discrimination against and violation of the rights of the girl child

Source: DAW, 2005.

the effectiveness of prevention measures (four recommended actions); and (3) eliminate trafficking in women and assist victims of violence due to prostitution and trafficking (five recommended actions). Activists from all over the world have used the Platform to lobby governments and call for women's empowerment (Moghadam, 2007).

At Beijing +5, Beijing +10, and Beijing +15 the implementation and outcomes of the Beijing Declaration and Platform for Action were reviewed and national, regional, and global reports were presented. In 2000, at the Beijing +5 conference, delegates from 180 countries approved the Political Declaration. This declaration included a statement agreeing to eradicate "harmful customary or traditional practices" and one that stated "women have the right to decide freely and responsibly on matters related to their sexuality . . . without coercion, discrimination, and violence." The Political Declaration also affirmed governments' responsibility to implement the Beijing Platform for Action. Women's NGOs played important roles at all UN women's conferences, influencing the content of conference documents and engaging in transnational feminist organizing. The **Commission on the Status of Women (CSW)**

"We the Governments, at the beginning of the new millennium, reaffirm our commitment to overcoming obstacles encountered in the implementation of the Beijing Platform for Action and the Nairobi Forward-Looking Strategies for the Advancement of Women and to strengthening and safeguarding a national and international enabling environment, and to this end pledge to undertake further action to ensure their full and accelerated implementation, inter alia, through the promotion and protection of all human rights and fundamental freedoms, mainstreaming a gender perspective into all policies and programmes and promoting full participation and empowerment of women and enhanced international cooperation for the full implementation of the Beijing Platform for Action."

Beijing +5 Political Declaration

is the UN body responsible for monitoring the implementation of conference agreements such as the Nairobi Forward Looking Strategies (from the third women's conference in 1985) and the BPFA.

The UN women's conferences illustrate the complexities of international politics and cooperation regarding women's rights. All four of the conferences became bogged down at some point by international politics that had little to do with the status of women. The 1980 conference in Copenhagen was perhaps the worst in this regard; the official conference agenda was superceded by resolutions dealing with nationalist concerns (Jaquette, 1995; West, 1999). Language issues and the fact that the UN uses a consensus model of decision making also made for difficulty. The final conference documents are usually somewhat unwieldy because the language must be translated into all of the languages of the UN system and because each government wants to make sure its viewpoint is included (Fraser, 1987). For instance, at the Fourth World Conference, voting on the 149-page "Platform for Action" was delayed by wording difficulties. There were translation problems with the word *gender*, which does not exist in some languages, as well as terms such as *gender-neutral* and *feminization*. Some countries had problems with the phrase "universal human rights," arguing that human rights are relative to the culture. Ultimately this issue was resolved by dropping the word *universal*. Likewise, it took sixteen hours of debate before a subcommittee could accommodate the contrary views of countries who believe that sex education encourages risky youth sexual behavior and those who insist such education reduces youth risk. Beijing +5 was also marked by strong disagreement. Wider protection of women's reproductive rights and protections for lesbians and gays were blocked by some Catholic and Islamic delegations. Affirmation of the Beijing Platform for Action at Beijing +10 was held up by demands from the United States (under then-president George W. Bush) that the UN renounce abortion rights.

The evolving character of the four women's conferences and Beijing +5 also symbolize the development of women's issues within the UN. For instance, at the 1980 Copenhagen convention, male dominance was evident. Indeed, it became a joke that male delegates always replaced women delegates in the lead delegate chair during important votes and debates. By the end of the Nairobi conference in 1985, however, women delegates dominated (Fraser, 1987). Similarly, male delegates took over the early women's conferences to complain about issues they had with other countries (Bernard, 1987).

International attention and commitment to women's rights and status were important outcomes of the UN women's conferences. However, an equally important outcome is the contribution of the conferences to the transnational feminist movement. At conference "nongovernmental forums," thousands of NGO representatives from around the world shared information and networked. In contrast to the formal political spaces of the official conferences, the NGO forums were "counter-political spaces," mixing serious political discussion, networking, and coalition building with women's

BOX 11.3   *Two Women's Impressions of the Beijing Conference's NGO Forum*

"The vast majority of Chinese women attending the NGO forum in Huairou saw or heard the slogan, "women's rights are human rights," there for the first time. . . . On arriving at the site of the 1995 NGO forum, Huairou, a banner with the slogan, "Look at the world through women's eyes," flew high above the road. This was a reminder, a resounding call. . . . We were used to seeing the world through the class struggle, now we are getting used to seeing it from the perspective of a commodity economy; women have almost never thought about how to use their eyes to see the world."

Journalist Chuan Renyan of China

"On a hill above the Beijing suburb of Huairou, the Older Women's Tent of sweeping yellow canvas welcomed over 2,000 women from every continent. This Tent was one of seven "diversity tents" designated for special issues, such as disabled, indigenous, refuge, youth, and lesbian women. . . . Over the subsequent days, older women succeeded in putting aging concerns on the international NGO agenda. They built a strong Older Women's Caucus that met daily at both the Tent and the Government Conference in Beijing. Each day, women crowded under the Tent to hear speakers and hold debates on a wide range of issues. . . . On the last day of the Forum at the Tent, women decided to build a global older women's network. Despite differences of culture and economy, many core issues are the same across regions: elder rights, economic security, and a desire to participate fully in the life of society."

Susanne Paul, Coordinator of the Older Women's Tent at Beijing

cultural events and shopping (West, 1999). Box 11.3 shares the experiences of two women that attended the conference.

The growth of the NGO forums from the first women's conference to the fourth in Beijing reflects the growth of transnational feminism. For example, approximately 6,000 people attended the NGO forum in 1975 at Mexico City, approximately 8,000 attended in 1980 at Copenhagen, and approximately 14,000 attended in 1985 at Nairobi (Fraser, 1987). In 1995 at Beijing, this number grew to 30,000 (West, 1999). Fraser (1987) suggests that this growth is more than merely numerical. By the time of the Nairobi conference, women had moved from the consciousness-raising and outrage of the early conferences to collective activism. The growth of the forums also sent a message to the world that there is determination and solidarity among diverse women (Fraser, 1987). For instance, at the Fourth World Conference on Women in Beijing, tens of thousands of people, mostly women, participated in the Non-Governmental Organizations Forum on Women despite its location in the hard-to-reach suburb of Huairou, 35 miles from the conference site. Originally, the NGO forum was supposed to be in Beijing but Chinese officials, hoping to prevent human rights protests, moved it in an effort to discourage attendance and reduce its visibility.

"The Holy See cannot accept ambiguous terminology concerning unqualified control over sexuality and fertility particularly as it could be interpreted as a societal endorsement of abortion and homosexuality."
One of the Holy See's Reservations on the Beijing Platform for Action (the Holy See is the home of the Pope and the central administration of the Roman Catholic Church)

There is agreement among transnational feminist scholars that the UN women's conferences enabled the growth of the transnational feminist movement but there is also agreement that the movement cannot rely on the UN to provide this type of forum. Although specialized NGOs working on the implementation of CEDAW are part of the annual meetings of the Commission on the Status of Women (CSW) and the follow-ups to Beijing, the women's "megaconferences" have probably come to end. Many question whether additional UN women's conferences will create real change given the influential voices of the Vatican, fundamentalist Christians, and Islamists on UN women's platforms and declarations (Porter, 2007). For example Beijing +5 and +10 reaffirmed the Platform and added to it in areas, such as HIV/AIDS, but they are less bold in spirit and reflect the impact that conservative forces have had on governments' attitudes toward women's issues, especially in areas like sexual and reproductive rights (Bunch, 2007). Alternative forums such as AWID (Association for Women in Development), the International Interdisciplinary Congress on Women, and the International Feminist Dialogues (held prior to the World Social Forums) have to some extent taken the place of the UN women's conference NGO forums (Porter, 2007). The Internet has also created new spaces for transnational feminist networking, organizing, advocacy, and information-sharing; TFNs use websites, ListServs, and email alerts to communicate and network across borders (Moghadam, 2005).

Transnational Feminist Influences on the UN

"Transnational women's groups have demystified the idea that women's issues are narrow; they have shown how gender matters in macroeconomic issues, in trade and finance. It is an accomplishment that the World's Bank president announced that gender justice is a worthy goal."
Zenebeworke Tadesse, founder of AAWORD (a TFN based in Ethiopia)

The relationship between the UN and the transnational women's movement is also reciprocal; over time, the influence of transnational feminist networks on the UN and the human rights agenda has grown. Because the numbers of women in governmental delegations have been small, women's organizations and movements have long played an important role in bringing the views of women into the UN (Bunch, 2007). Transnational feminists use lobbying and other forms of activism to ensure that women are not left out of the UN mission. Due to this activism, the UN and many of its specialized agencies, funds, and programs, now prioritize women and gender in their publications, policies, and programs (Moghadam, 2005). Throughout the book you have seen many examples of successful transnational feminist organizing that have impacted the UN and international agreements. These successful actions include the addition of war rape as a crime to be prosecuted by the International Criminal Court; gender mainstreaming in UN organizations and development programs; a UN focus on women's literacy and reproductive health as key to poverty reduction; the inclusion of gender equality in the constitutions of new democracies; acknowledgment of the importance of women's unpaid labor and their labor in the informal economy to economies; the provision of microcredit to women's enterprises; the inclusion of sexual and reproductive rights in human rights protections; gender responsive budget analysis; attention to the role of women in environmental sustainability;

actions to stop sweatshop labor and sex trafficking; and actions to increase women's representation in formal politics.

Equality Now (based in the United States and Kenya) is an example of a transnational feminist network that uses international law and UN mechanisms to advance gender equality while continuing to pressure the United Nations to advocate for women's rights. Recent campaigns include the organization of transnational feminist organizations to support the UN appointment of a Special Rappoteur on National Laws and Practices that Discriminate Against Women (currently under UN consideration) and a call for the consideration of women candidates in the election of the next United Nations Secretary-General. They worked with activists at the national level to prepare submissions for the UN Human Rights Committee on the status of women's rights in various countries being reviewed by the Committee for their compliance with the International Covenant on Civil and Political Rights. They participated in the Beijing Conferences and pre-conferences. Additionally, they called for the implementation of United Nations Security Council Resolution 1325 on Women and Peace and Security in Afghanistan and the Middle East.

TFNs often cooperate with one another to maximize their impact on specific campaigns and strategies. Throughout the 1990s, TFNs joined together to make sure that UN meetings and documents did not neglect economic and gender justice (Moghadam, 2005). For example, in 1993, women's rights advocates from all over the world organized and cooperated to get the United Nations World Conference on Human Rights to include discussions of women's human rights. The conference organizers did not intend to include a specific discussion of women's human rights on the agenda but TFNs circulated petitions throughout their networks; approximately 500,000 people from 123 countries signed a petition demanding that the conference address women's human rights. This effort was orchestrated by two women's human rights TFNs: the Center for Women's Global Leadership, and the International Women's Tribune Center. Box 11.4 profiles activist Charlotte Bunch, who as leader of the Center for Women's Global Leadership, was one of the leaders of this effort.

One major goal of activists for the Vienna conference was that the UN affirm the rights of women as universal human rights and, in particular, recognize that all forms of violence against women are a violation of human rights (Bunch, 2007). Success came in the form of the **Vienna Declaration and Programme of Action,** which documents women's rights abuses in five areas: (1) abuse within the family, (2) war crimes against women, (3) violations of women's bodily integrity, (4) socioeconomic abuses, and (5) political participation and persecution abuses. The document also includes recommendations for the reduction of such abuses although it does not adequately address the problem of compliance with these (Friedman, 1995). At the conference, TFNs also advocated for the UN appointment of a Special Rapporteur on Violence Against Women. Rapporteur Radhika Coomaraswamy of Sri Lanka was appointed from 1994 and served until 2003. Since then there

"Violence against women violates human dignity as well as numerous rights, including the right to equality, physical integrity, freedom and non-discrimination." *South African human rights lawyer Rashida Manjoo, UN Special Rapporteur on Violence Against Women*

BOX 11.4   *Activist Profile: Charlotte Bunch of the Center for Women's Global Leadership*

Charlotte Bunch of the United States has been advocating for women's rights for over thirty-five years. As a young feminist in the 1960s, she was one of the first American feminists to work for lesbian rights. In 1989 she founded the Center for Women's Global Leadership (CWGL), an organization dedicated to including gender and sexual orientation on the international human rights agenda. Under her leadership, CWGL organized TFNs and individuals to successfully demand the inclusion of women's rights at the 1993 Vienna Human Rights Conference. CWGL remains one the world's leading women's human rights organizations and is a presence at most UN conferences. CWGL promotes networking internationally for women's rights, provides training, and organizes international campaigns such as CWGL's

16 Days of Activism Against Gender Violence (during this annual campaign, women all over the world take action to protest gender violence). In 2000, Bunch was a lead organizer of the Women's International War Crimes Tribunal on Japan's Military and Sexual Slavery, which presented evidence of the sexual slavery of over 200,000 women by the Japanese military. Results from the tribunal were used to influence the International Criminal Court to include the prosecution of war rape as part of war crimes. Recently, CWGL worked for adoption of the new UN women's agency. Bunch is the author of many books and reports and the recipient of many awards. She is currently Executive Director of CWGL and a professor in the Women and Gender Studies Department at Rutgers University.

have been two others: Dr. Yakin Erturk (Turkey; 2003–2009), and Rashida Manjoo (South Africa; since 2009). The annual Rapporteur reports detail human rights standards on VAW and outline governments' responsibilities to abide by those standards in concrete policy terms (Bunch, 2007). The 1993 Vienna conference represented a major success in bringing the women's human rights agenda into the human rights agenda and is viewed by transnational feminist activists as a turning point in the effort to link women's rights to human rights (Moghadam, 2005). It also led to the definition of practices such as sati, dowry deaths, domestic violence, and FGC as "violence against women." Previously these practices were considered "cultural customs and traditions" and were not considered to be human rights violations (Jain, 2005; Tripp, 2006a).

In February 2008, the TFN WEDO launched the GEAR (Gender Equality Architecture Reform) Campaign. Partnering with other TFNs and hundreds of activists, they called on United Nations member states to create a strong, fully resourced women's entity at the UN so that governments can better deliver for women on the ground.

In the last decade, transnational feminist organizations have continued to work together to influence the UN. Women from the North and the South worked together to get the UN Security Council to pass Resolution 1325 in 2000, which requires that women be included in peace negotiations and peacekeeping missions (Tripp, 2006a). From 2000 to 2005, transnational feminist activists worked for a gender perspective to be included in the UN's Millennium Development Goals (MDGs) (Bunch, 2007). Although one of the MDG goals was gender equality, it initially included only one concrete target: equal access to primary school education. Activists worked with MDG task forces to expand this goal and to bring a gender perspective into the other MDG goals. New targets were added, such as ensuring universal access to sexual and reproductive health services through the primary health-care system; eliminating gender inequality in access to assets and employment; achieving a 30 percent share of seats for women in national parliaments; and reducing by half the lifetime prevalence of violence against women.

A recent victory of transnational feminist organizing occurred in September 2009 when the UN General Assembly approved the creation of a new UN body to focus on gender equality and women's empowerment. This was the result of a three-year effort by a coalition of over 300 organizations in 80 countries led by WEDO and the Center for Women's Global Leadership. They called their campaign GEAR (Gender Equality Architecture Reform). The new high-level agency is intended to replace four small, poorly funded UN women's agencies (UNIFEM, DAW, INSTRAW, and the Office of Special Advisor on Gender Issues). GEAR argued that these agencies had overlapping missions and competed for resources, impeding their ability to effectively address women's needs worldwide and that a stronger and single, fully-resourced women's entity at the UN was needed. They acknowledged that other UN agencies sometimes do important work on gender equality, but said that it is a small part of their mandate, and often receives low priority. The combined budget of the four agencies to be replaced by the new entity was $221 million and the new agency is expected to receive a budget of at least $1 billion (Ward, 2009). Activism continues to ensure that the establishment of the agency occurs quickly, including filling the new agency's Under-Secretary-General position, as well as approving the budget and guaranteeing ambitious, committed funding (WEDO, 2009).

Transnational Feminism and Women's Rights as Human Rights

Contemporary transnational feminism relies on a human rights framework as the basis for asserting women's rights (Desai, 2007). The idea behind the women's human rights approach is to wed women's rights to human rights, which are protected under international law and are monitored and enforced by the United Nations. This lends legitimacy to political demands because the protection of human rights is already accepted by most governments and brings with it established protocols for dealing with abuses (Friedman, 1995). Whether used in political lobbying, in legal cases, in grassroots mobilization, or in broad-based educational efforts, the idea of women's human rights has been a rallying point for women across many boundaries and has facilitated the creation of collaborative strategies for promoting and protecting the rights of women (Bunch & Frost, 2000). Coalitions of NGOs and local activists lobby governments, corporations, international financing institutions (like the World Bank), and regional and international intergovernmental bodies, to create the necessary political, economic, and human rights conditions for equality, sustainable human development, and social justice (Tripp, 2006a).

Former U.S. congresswoman Bella Abzug (1920–1998) was a pioneer of the twentieth-century U.S. women's movement and of global women's organizing. Abzug also fought to make governments accountable for their promises to promote women's equality. Toward this end, Abzug issued annual report cards to 187 nations, grading them on their progress toward women's equality. Abzug was also the founder of WEDO (Women's Environment and Development Organization). A few days before she died, she said, "This is the time to declare, as we approach the great millennium, that women must be made free."

Our starting point is that there can be no human rights without women's rights. . . .
UN Office of High Commissioner for Human Rights

"Women's rights are human rights."
Slogan of women's human rights movement popularized at the 1993 UN conference on human rights

"Discrimination against any group of human beings is wrong, not because it hurts that particular group but because, in the final analysis, the fact of its existence hurts all groups of society."
Minerva Bernardino, one of four women signatories of the charter establishing the UN

"The human rights of women and the girl-child are an inalienable, integral and indivisible part of universal human rights. Gender-based violence and all forms of sexual harassment and exploitation, including those resulting from cultural prejudice and international trafficking, are incompatible with the dignity and worth of the human person, and must be eliminated."
Vienna Declaration and Programme of Action, 1993

"The recognition of such issues as human rights abuses raises the level of expectation about what can and should be done about them."
Charlotte Bunch and Samantha Frost

As you learned in Chapter 1, according to the concept of **universal human rights,** everyone has certain inalienable rights simply by virtue of being human. This means that all humans are born free and equal in dignity and rights, which no one, including governments, can deny them. In theory then, women have the same economic, political, civil, and social rights as men. Although the principle of women's equality and nondiscrimination on the basis of sex was inscribed in the United Nations from the beginning through the UN Charter in 1945, and the Universal Declaration of Human Rights (UDHR) in 1948, it is important to note that this was the result of transnational feminist activism. Four women delegates attending the UN Charter Conference worked together with forty-two NGOs to ensure inclusion of sex in the antidiscrimination clause as well as to change "equal rights among men" to "equal rights among men and women." A similar effort was necessary in the drafting of the UDHR (Bunch, 2007; Jain, 2005).[1]

Framing discrimination against women as a violation of their human rights has not been easy. Human rights law has traditionally focused on violations in the public spheres of life, in particular violations committed by government agents (such as the imprisonment or torture of political dissenters). As Bunch (1995) notes, this is not surprising given that the Western-educated, propertied men who first advanced the cause of human rights most feared the violation of their civil and political rights in the public sphere. They did not fear violations in the private sphere because they were the masters of that territory. In contrast, the most common violations of women's rights often occur in the private sphere of the family and are condoned by religious and cultural practices. As a result, these violations were viewed as outside the scope of human rights law (Bunch & Frost, 2000; Mertus, 1995; Sullivan, 1995).

As advocates for women's rights point out, though, the public/private distinction breaks down upon examination because "private" behaviors such as wife murder, battery, and rape result from a public toleration of the subordination of women (Charlesworth, 1995). Governments condone abuses when they inadequately prosecute wife abuse, rape, and sexual harassment. Therefore, they are accountable for these abuses (Friedman, 1995). Furthermore, using the public/private distinction to justify states' lack of involvement with women's human rights abuses is hypocritical considering that marriage and family law is monitored by the state (Kerr, 1993).

CEDAW: The International Women's Bill of Rights

The **Convention on the Elimination of Discrimination Against Women,** sometimes called the Women's Convention and sometimes called **CEDAW** (although the monitoring committee also goes by this acronym), is viewed as one of the most far-reaching and important women's rights documents.

---

[1] The four women were: Minerva Bernardino (Dominican Republic), Bertha Lutz (Brazil), Wu Yi-Fang (China), and Virginia Gildersleeve (United States).

It is essentially an international bill of rights for women. The 1979 treaty,[2] developed during the UN's Women's Decade, defines discrimination against women as "any distinction, exclusion, or restriction made on the basis of sex which has the effect or purpose of impairing or nullifying the recognition, enjoyment or exercise by women, irrespective of their marital status, on a basis of equality of men and women, of human rights and fundamental freedoms in the political, economic, social, cultural, civil, or any other field." CEDAW consists of a preamble and thirty articles defining what constitutes discrimination against women and setting up an agenda for national action to end such discrimination. It is the only human rights treaty that affirms the reproductive rights of women and targets culture and tradition as influential forces shaping gender roles and family relations (DAW, 2009). Nations that ratify the Women's Convention commit to undertake a series of measures to end discrimination against women in all forms, including:

- incorporating the principle of equality of men and women in their legal system;
- abolishing all discriminatory laws and adopting appropriate ones prohibiting discrimination against women;
- establishing tribunals and other public institutions to ensure the effective protection of women against discrimination; and
- ensuring elimination of all acts of discrimination against women by persons, organizations, or enterprises.

Every four years, nations that have ratified the treaty are supposed to submit reports on their progress to the **CEDAW Committee,** a group comprised of twenty-three women's rights experts who monitor compliance with CEDAW and issue recommendations. NGOs are also encouraged to submit reports on their country's compliance with CEDAW and many develop "shadow reports" documenting the gap between official government statements and the actual status of women (Hawkesworth, 2006). Because there have been so many overdue reports, the UN offers technical report assistance to those countries that seem to have trouble meeting this treaty requirement. The Optional Protocol to CEDAW, adopted by the General Assembly in 1999, offers two mechanisms to hold governments accountable for their obligations under CEDAW: (1) a communications procedure that provides individuals and groups the right to lodge complaints with the Committee on the Elimination of Discrimination Against Women (CEDAW Committee), and (2) an inquiry procedure that enables the CEDAW Committee to conduct inquiries into serious and systematic abuses of women's rights. These procedures apply only to countries that have ratified the Optional Protocol.

> "If we consider women's rights to be human rights, then we must work to make the reality of our lives match the ideals laid out by the rights standards that international law extends to all human beings."
> *Ilka Tanya Payan, 1995*

> ". . . the full and complete development of a country, the welfare of the world and the cause of peace require the maximum participation of women on equal terms with men in all fields."
> *From the Convention on the Elimination of All Forms of Discrimination Against Women (CEDAW)*

---

[2] Recall that a treaty (also referred to as convention or covenant) is an international legal instrument that legally binds, in international law, those States that choose to accept the obligations contained within it.

BOX 11.5   *The United States and CEDAW*

The United States is one of the only UN members that has not ratified CEDAW and is the only democracy in the world not to do so. President Carter signed it in 1980, but the U.S. Senate has not yet ratified it due to resistance from political conservatives. Neither the Reagan nor Bush (George H. W. and George W.) administrations even sought Senate ratification. In 1993, sixty-eight senators signed a letter asking President Clinton to support ratification of CEDAW but a group of conservative senators blocked a Senate floor vote on CEDAW. Conservatives favoring a unilateral approach to international relations object to CEDAW, claiming that it will give the UN too much power over U.S. laws. Also, they say that ratifying CEDAW would be giving in to "special interests" (read: feminists). Some claim that it would force the United States to keep abortion legal.

In June 2002, the Senate Foreign Relations Committee voted twelve to seven in favor of sending CEDAW to the full Senate for ratification but then Senate Majority Leader (Republican Bill Frist) did not allow it to come up for a vote. The election of President Barak Obama and a democratic majority in Congress has given new hope for ratification. President Barack Obama, Vice-President Joe Biden, and Secretary of State Hillary Clinton all support ratification and Sen. Barbara Boxer (D-Calif.), chair of the new Senate Foreign Relations Subcommittee on International Operations and Organizations, Human Rights, Democracy and Global Women's Issues, intends to begin hearings. Unfortunately, it is likely that the United States will register a number of reservations to the Convention to relieve the U.S. government from any obligation to adopt paid maternity leave and alleviate the gender wage gap, and provide health-care services to poor women.

> In our country—where we have worked so hard against domestic violence, where we have worked so hard to empower women—it is to say the least, an embarrassment that the U.S. has not ratified CEDAW.
> *U.S. President Bill Clinton, 1996*

As of 2010, 186 countries have signed and ratified CEDAW (over 95 percent). Only a small number of countries have not ratified CEDAW, including the United States, Iran, Somalia, and Sudan. Box 11.5 discusses why the United States has not yet ratified CEDAW. It is important to note that many of the countries that ratified CEDAW did so only with "reservations" (when governments enter a reservation to a treaty, it means that they will not be bound to particular parts of that treaty). Charlesworth and colleagues (1991) suggest that the CEDAW process shows that the international community is ready to acknowledge the considerable problem of women's inequality only if they are not required to alter the patriarchal practices that subordinate women. The fact that the international community tolerates these reservations, many of which are incompatible with the purpose of the CEDAW, further underlines the inadequacy of current international law regarding women's human rights (Charlesworth et al., 1991).

The Optional Protocol to CEDAW has been ratified by ninety-nine nations as of October 2010. This is far less than the number that have ratified CEDAW. This may be partly due to the time it takes for government bodies to ratify UN documents through their domestic legal and legislative systems. However, it may also be due to the Protocol's emphasis on accountability. It is one thing for governments to support women's rights in theory; it is yet another thing for them to agree to take responsibility for women's rights violations in an international venue.

BOX 11.6   *Conventions Adopted by the UN General Assembly Specific to the Rights of Women*

- *Convention on the Political Rights of Women* (1952). Requires that women be granted full political rights: the right to vote and to be eligible for election to all publicly elected bodies, and to be entitled to hold public office and to exercise all public functions on equal terms with men, without any discrimination.

- *Convention on the Nationality of Married Women* (1957). This convention provides for the general principle that men and women have equal rights to acquire, change, or retain their nationality.

- *Convention on Consent to Marriage, Minimum Age for Marriage and Registration of Marriages* (1962). This convention requires national legislation establishing equal rights for both spouses in connection with marriage, including that marriages be entered into with the free and full consent of both spouses and a minimum age for marriage.

- *Convention on the Elimination of All Forms of Discrimination Against Women* (1979). This convention is described in detail in the chapter.

Other conventions and covenants adopted by the General Assembly concerning the status of women include:

- Convention for the Suppression of the Traffic in Persons and of the Exploitation of the Prostitution of Others

- Supplementary Convention on the Abolition of Slavery, the Slave Trade, and Institutions and Practices Similar to Slavery

- International Covenant on Economic, Social, and Cultural Rights

- International Covenant on Civil and Political Rights

- Optional Protocol to the International Covenant on Civil and Political Rights

Source: United Nations, http://www.un.org/womenwatch/un/iinstrum.htm.

Women's rights activists use CEDAW as a tool to press their governments to adopt gender equality legislation and constitutional amendments and to petition courts for change. They use their country's CEDAW reviews to press for change. For example, in Brazil (1988) and Colombia (1991), feminists used CEDAW to shape new national constitutions recognizing women's rights, and in India (1992), a group of women's NGOs successfully petitioned the Supreme Court to draft a sexual harassment law by arguing that the lack of one was in violation of CEDAW (Hawkesworth, 2006). CEDAW is the most far-reaching convention specific to the rights of women, but there are other conventions that address women's rights. Box 11.6 lists some other conventions that address the rights of women adopted by the UN General Assembly.

Challenges to a Women's Human Rights Agenda

The global movement for women's human rights has made impressive progress but it faces many challenges. These are summarized in Figure 11.2. One challenge is that *we must move from visibility of abuse to actual accountability of abuse*

FIGURE 11.2 *Challenges to a Women's Human Rights Agenda*

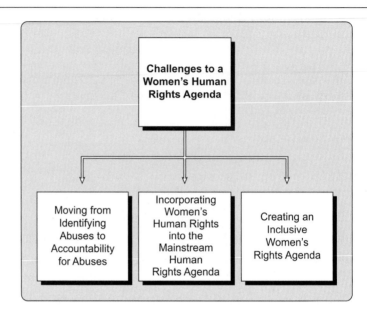

Rhonda Copelon was a U.S. law professor and international human rights activist. She pioneered the use of international law to prevent and prosecute crimes against women such as war rape.

"My responsibility as UN High Commissioner is to adopt and to foster a rights-based approach across the whole spectrum of 'civil, cultural, economic, political, and social rights, to promote and protect the realization of the right to development and specifically to include women's rights as human rights.'"
Mary Robinson

(Thomas in Friedman, 1995; emphasis added). It is remarkable that virtually all of the abuses documented in this book can be seen as violations of human rights according to *existing* UN conventions and treaties. Yet there is no question that these abuses continue. This is due in part to a lack of proper implementation machinery (Coomaraswamy, 1994). Treaty bodies merely declare the rights of women and outline the states' responsibilities but they do not enforce compliance—they only monitor and encourage compliance (Johnstone, 2006). For example, the CEDAW Committee that monitors compliance with the Convention on Elimination Against Discrimination does this largely through the examination of reports submitted by member states and by dialogues with government representatives. However, this committee has not yet declared a government in violation of women's human rights conventions despite evidence to the contrary. This problem is worsened by the fact that women's rights are frequently enshrined in agreements that are not legally binding (like declarations) rather than in "treaties" that technically are (although they are often not enforced because this piece of international law remains underdeveloped). This choice is often an indicator of resistance to women's rights; it is harder to ratify treaties, which in the case of women's rights, often have to be relatively weak before member states agree to ratify them.

Several other obstacles hinder implementation. Many countries have an ideological resistance to human rights for women. Although the UN documents relevant to women's rights clearly imply that gender equality is a desirable value, this universal value is not so universal after all. Indeed, local customs and national and religious laws often contradict the treatment of women required by UN conventions and declarations. Furthermore, because of beliefs in state and cultural sovereignty, those local customs and national laws are usually given precedence. The governments of some countries reject the multilateral approach critical to the international human rights approach. For example, under President George W. Bush, the United States assumed a unilateral approach to international relations and refused to endorse multilateral women's agreements such as BPFA (Tripp, 2006a).[3]

Implementation of international laws and conventions is also hampered by the fact that in some cultures, talk about rights is not considered meaningful. Particularly in cultures with a history of colonialism, the human rights movement is disrespected, virtually ignored, and viewed as another tool of the West to eradicate indigenous cultures (Coomaraswamy, 1994). This may mean that unless movements *within* a society cause human rights values to take root, women's human rights will not be enforced (Coomaraswamy, 1994). If a country's own people demand change, these attempts to change things cannot be as easily resisted with accusations of cultural insensitivity. On the other hand, it is helpful to local women's groups to be able to appeal to international treaties. For instance, Plata (1994) explains how the Colombian government began to take women's groups seriously once it emphasized that the groups' requests were consistent with Brazil's signing of the Convention on the Elimination of Discrimination Against Women. As Coomaraswamy (1994) says, civil society is necessary for creating the conditions for law to be relevant, but without law, any human rights activist will only be tilting at windmills.

A second challenge to an international approach to women's human rights is that *women's issues must become part of the mainstream of the human rights agenda such that they will be considered at every level of human rights discussions rather than marginalized* (Thomas in Friedman, 1995; emphasis added). The long-term male domination of all-powerful political bodies nationally and internationally means that issues of concern to men are seen as general human concerns whereas women's concerns are relegated to a specialized and marginalized sphere (Charlesworth, 1995). Although there is an international convention on the rights of women (CEDAW), some transnational feminists and women's human rights proponents have suggested that CEDAW is evidence of the marginalization of women's human rights because women's human rights remained unaddressed by other UN human rights treaty bodies (Johnstone, 2006).

Stamatopoulou (1995) suggests that the creation of specialized bodies for addressing women's issues within the United Nations has contributed to their marginalization. Because there are specific UN groups designated to deal with women's issues, the more powerful, mainstream organs of the UN, such as the Commission on Human Rights, have paid little attention to

> "Isn't it revealing that women's human rights need to be discussed?"
> *Isabel Allende*

> "I don't know how we have survived so many years by thinking of women as a separate chapter. We are not a separate chapter, we are half the book."
> *Rosario Green, 1996, Assistant Secretary for UN Political Affairs (highest-ranking woman in the UN Secretariat)*

---

[3] A unilateral approach to foreign affairs involves acting individualistically, without consulting or involving other nations. A multilateral approach emphasizes transnational cooperation and agreements.

The fundamental challenge for the movement for women's human rights is that it not become a reformist project: Its recipe should not read 'Add women and stir,' but 'Add women and alter.'
Dorothy Q. Thomas, 1995, Human Rights Watch

women's human rights violations such as rape, forced marriage, transboundary trafficking of women, honor killings, and genital mutilation. These special women's agencies have resulted in the treatment of women's rights as "lesser rights" (Stamatopoulou, 1995) and have created a "women's ghetto" within the UN (Reanda, 1992). On the other hand, prior to creating separate institutional mechanisms for dealing with women's issues, women's human rights violations were still ignored. It is not that specialized agencies devoted to women's issues are necessarily bad. The problem is that they are chronically underfunded, given little authority, and often excluded from power bodies within the UN. This was one of the motivators for the GEAR campaign discussed earlier. Bunch (2007) maintains that history shows that women's equality should be pursued through separate UN entities *and* through the mainstreaming of gender into all other UN bodies.

A third and especially "tricky" challenge is that *we must continue to work and organize for an inclusive women's human rights agenda so that the interests of diverse women worldwide are represented* (Thomas in Friedman, 1995; emphasis added). At the heart of the women's rights as human rights endeavor is universalism—the idea that all humans share the same inalienable rights. Both the Universal Declaration of Human Rights and CEDAW specify the international human rights standard of legal and social equality between women and men, but the truth is that the needs and interests of women often vary based on their local and national contexts. In the early history of the modern transnational feminist movement (1975–1985), Western feminist conceptions of feminism and feminist concerns dominated and northern and southern feminists clashed. Transnational feminist organizations like DAWN, Women Living Under Muslim Laws, and Women in Law and Development in Africa, successfully engaged in their own activism within the transnational feminist movement so they could have a leadership role and create a more inclusive agenda. Today, TFNs in Africa, Latin America, and Asia lead in the use of human rights frameworks and transnational coalitions and networks to ensure issues of concern to women in their regions (such as trafficking, land reform, education, peace building, reproductive rights, violence against women, electoral quotas) are addressed (Tripp, 2006a).

Human rights notions of universality are also frequently undermined by beliefs that respect for cultural and religious diversity provides exceptions to human rights law. Claims for universality are sometimes rejected as imperialistic and as a way to uphold Western economic interests (Chinkin, 1999). The claim that international human rights are incompatible with respect for cultural diversity must be carefully considered. Cultural diversity and human rights must be balanced. Cultural diversity should not be used to excuse human rights violations; nor should a claim for universal values be used to justify the eradication of unique cultural practices that do not violate human rights. This issue is particularly acute in international law, which is concerned with transnational standards (Charlesworth, 1994).

Recall that cultural relativism is the notion that right and wrong are determined culturally. Cultural relativists and human rights activists often disagree on women's rights and every international conference discussing women's rights has seen conflict between feminists and cultural relativists (Coomarswamy, 1999). The most radical cultural relativists argue that there are no legitimate cross-cultural human rights standards and that the human rights endeavor, arising as it did out of the European Enlightenment, is, by its very nature, inapplicable to non-Western cultures (Coomaraswamy, 1999). In regard to women's rights, these cultural relativists suggest that Western condemnations of gender discrimination in other regions are insensitive and ethnocentric and are a version of cultural imperialism (Mayer, 1995a). For instance, El-Bakri and Kameir (1983) object to holding the role of women in the Middle East and Third World countries to the standards of Western democracies.

Other cultural relativists are more selective, taking issue with only some of the rights specified in human rights documents or their interpretation (Coomaraswamy, 1999). For instance, cultural relativists often emphasize that the treatment of women is often prescribed by a culture's religious practices; therefore calls for change are instances of religious intolerance (Jaising, 1995). As noted earlier, many of the countries that have ratified CEDAW did so only after registering "reservations" to those elements that they felt were contrary to important cultural or religious practices (indeed, CEDAW breaks the record for the most reservations recorded for an international human rights instrument). This problem for CEDAW symbolizes a problem that plagues the women's rights as human rights endeavor.

Human rights and feminist values may conflict with traditional customs, and it is a legitimate question to ask which should be privileged when this occurs (Katzenstein, 1989). We certainly do not want to be so presumptuous as to impose our worldview on others. Just because a culture is different from our own does not mean that it is wrong. Furthermore, there is no question that historically, Western imperialists and colonialists destroyed native cultures and defended their actions based on the superiority of Western cultural practices. On the other hand, we can go too far in the worship of cultural difference. Nussbaum (1992) cites a number of examples of scholars who defend disturbing cultural practices out of reverence for the culture at hand. As philosopher Rachels (1993) points out, it does not stand to reason that just because cultures differ, that right and wrong are matters of opinion. If we were to take cultural relativism too seriously, we would have to agree that all sorts of questionable behaviors were not immoral because those countries in which they occur do not define them as immoral. Domestic violence is, for example, an accepted practice in many cultures.

It is true that we shouldn't reject cultural practices just because they are not our own and that we should not presume to understand the experiences of those in another culture. And it is true that many cultural practices are nothing more than what Rachels (1993) calls "social conventions," which, objectively speaking, are neither right nor wrong and about which we should keep an open mind. But should we accept cultural practices that obviously result in serious harm to large segments of a society out of

"[s]tates should condemn violence against women and should not invoke any custom, tradition, or religious consideration to avoid their obligations with respect to its elimination."
Declaration on the Elimination of Violence Against Women

"Women from every single culture and every part of the world are standing up and saying we won't accept cultural justification for abuses against us anymore. We are human, we have a right to have our human rights protected, and the world community must respond to that call and throw out any attempts to justify abuse on the grounds of culture."
Dorothy Q. Thomas, director of the Women's Rights Project of Human Rights Watch

respect for the existing culture or tradition? If this had been the case in the United States, slavery would not have been abolished, women would not have been allowed to vote, and civil rights legislation would not have been passed. As Rachels says, moral progress cannot occur if we take cultural relativism too far.

Maryam Rajavi is president-elect of the National Council of Resistance of Iran. Rajavi uses UN women's human rights documents to critique what she calls the "gender apartheid" of Iran. Now living in exile, Rajavi continues to give speeches refuting the fundamentalists' use of the Koran to support their oppression of women. Rajavi emphasizes that democracy and world peace depend on the advancement of women.

Another problem with the cultural relativist's position is that it implies that there is a homogeneous culture upon which there is agreement. However, "culture is not a static, unchanging, identifiable body of information," but rather is a "series of constantly contested and negotiated cultural practices" (Rao, 1995). For instance, Mayer (1995b) points out that contrary to the view of a monolithic Islamic position on human rights, Muslims actually espouse a wide range of opinions regarding international human rights. These range from the assertion that international human rights are fully compatible with Islam to the claim that international human rights are products of alien, Western culture and represent values contrary to Islam. Libya, Tunisia, and Algeria are all examples of Islamic countries that have found it prudent to make concessions to citizen demands for the observance of international human rights (Mayer, 1995b). Women Under Muslim Laws (see Box 11.1) is a TFN that argues Islam is compatible with a women's human rights perspective, and in previous chapters you saw many other examples of Muslim feminists who felt likewise.

When pressured about international human rights, repressive governments often hide behind insincere claims of cultural imperialism as a way to remove the pressure. Their insincerity is evident when they show little respect for cultural diversity within their own nations and when internal demands for the recognition of international human rights show there is no cultural agreement. As Peters and Wolper (1995) say, when considering local, national, or international rulings, one must ask questions about context: What is the status of the speaker? In whose name is the argument from culture advanced? To what extent have the social groups primarily affected participated in the formation of the cultural practices being protected?

Some people doubt that it is possible to universalize feminism given the wide variety of women's experiences, and they question the usefulness of the international legal approach to women's rights. However, supporters of the international human rights approach point out that regardless of differences, women worldwide share the experience of patriarchy and the devaluing of women and all that experience encompasses (such as violence against women). They say we can respect cultural diversity *and* promote human rights as long as we recognize that cultural and class differences affect women's experience and how male domination can be contested. As Walter (2001) explains, culture determines the specifics of international human rights violations. For instance, she says that dowry deaths are an Indian manifestation of the international problem of domestic violence. To address the problem of dowry deaths, both the specific cultural context and the fact that they are a violation of women's human rights must be addressed. As noted throughout the book, this consideration of the cultural context is something that is best done by people in their own cultures. We can agree on human rights standards, but to be empowered and effective, people must be the architects of change within their own cultures.

Conclusion

This chapter further demonstrated the global women's studies theme of action and empowerment. Transnational women's organizing has resulted in impressive gains, particularly in regard to the inclusion of women's human rights in international human rights agendas and agreements—agendas and agreements that local and national activists then use as a basis upon which to further gender equality.

You have seen in this chapter the intersection of a multicultural approach to women's rights and a human rights perspective to women's rights. The challenge of balancing respect for diversity while embracing commonalities was identified in the book's introduction and reemerged here. It bears repeating that the success of the women's human rights movement requires embracing both universal human rights and cultural difference. It is important to emphasize the separate identities and histories of groups of women based on religion, ethnicity, nationality, sexual orientation, and economic position while at the same time avoiding a dangerous fatalism of unbridgeable differences among women (Chowdhury et al., 1994). We must agree that regardless of culture, it is unacceptable to deny women their equal rights, yet we must acknowledge the diversity of women's experiences to make our efforts relevant. We must respect those cultural features that do not lead to the oppression of women (and others) so as to preserve and respect cultural diversity. We must understand the nuances of a culture because they will affect the ease with which human rights mechanisms are applied. We must create approaches that avoid cultural relativist excuses for oppression, as well as ethnocentric forms of universalism (Walter, 2001). International actors must also remember that taking action that affects another society requires consulting local organizations regarding the advisability of a strategy, its timing, how it is framed, and to make sure that it is guided by accurate information; otherwise, efforts may be disrespectful, ineffective, or even hurtful (Tripp, 2006b).

Finally, yet importantly, to paraphrase Charlesworth and colleagues (1991), we must remember that the formal acknowledgment of women's rights as human rights by governments does not in and of itself resolve problems of inequality. That will require economic and cultural change that is unlikely to occur without women's activism. As Bunch and Fried (1996) point out, the UN documents that affirm women's equal rights (such as CEDAW and the Beijing Platform for Action) are only tools. The potential of these tools can only be realized through vigorous leadership, difficult political dialogue among different groups of women, and women's political activity at all levels—from the global to the local.

"Diversity and difference are central values here—to be acknowledged and respected, not erased in the building of alliances." *Chandra Talpade Mohanty*

"Feminism today, with all its local variation, is best understood to be a truly global phenomenon: a product of transnational dialogues and disagreements, coalitions and networks." *Myra Marx Ferree and Aili Mari Tripp*

Study Questions

1. What characterizes global or transnational feminist movements?

2. Are transnational feminisms new? When were the first international women's movements founded, and what was their focus?

3. How do current movements differ from the early movements? What activities do modern transnational feminist networks (TFNs) engage in?

4. What are the four international UN women's world conferences? How did they contribute to transnational feminist movements? How do they illustrate the complexities of international politics and cooperation regarding women's rights? How did they evolve over time? What is the role of NGOs in the conferences?

5. What is the Beijing Platform for Action (BPFA)? Why is it important? What is the purpose of the Beijing follow-up conferences?

6. How have transnational feminist networks and activists influenced the UN? What is the Vienna Declaration and Platform for Action? Why is it seen as a major breakthrough for transnational feminism and women's rights?

7. What are universal human rights?

8. What is the "women's rights as human rights" approach? How do human rights activists cast discrimination against women as a violation of their human rights? Why has this been difficult to do given the traditional focus of human rights laws? How can human rights instruments and mechanisms be used to challenge the abuse of women?

9. What is CEDAW? Why is it important? How do the problems in ratifying CEDAW represent a problem that plagues the women's rights as human rights endeavor?

10. What three challenges face the women's human rights movement?

11. What is the nature of the cultural relativist criticism that international human rights are incompatible with a respect for cultural diversity? How do "universalists" respond to cultural relativists' criticisms of the human rights approach?

12. How does the success of the women's movement require that we embrace both universal human rights and cultural difference?

Discussion Questions and Activities

1. What should be done when local customs and national and religious laws contradict the treatment of women as required by UN conventions and declarations?

2. Are you optimistic or pessimistic about a human rights approach to women's equality?

3. Charlesworth and colleagues (1991) suggest that it is significant that the major institutions of international law are dominated by men. Do you agree or disagree with their assertion that until there are more women in UN leadership roles, women's human rights will not receive the attention needed? Can and will men advocate for women's human rights?

4. Women's human rights lawyers often work on behalf of women experiencing gender-based abuses and try to help them obtain asylum in another country. Research the topic of gender-based asylum. Do you think that a fear of persecution based on gender should be a category for asylum under international refugee law? Does your country consider gender-based asylum claims?

5. Do some research to find out what happened at Beijing +15 and whether it further strengthened women's rights or whether conservative forces managed to weaken agreements. What role did women's NGOs and TFNs play in Beijing +15? (This website http://www.beijing15.org may be helpful). Has GEAR been implemented? Was additional TFN activism required? If a new agency has been created, is it well funded and staffed and structured in a way that will truly benefit gender equality? (The website http://www.un-gear.eu may be helpful).

6. Some transnational actions of Western feminist organizations like the Feminist Majority Foundation (FMF) have been criticized for culturally insensitive campaigns conducted on behalf of women in other countries. Evaluate the FMF's current international campaigns. Do these types of organizations contribute to a passive-victim image of women in other countries (one criticism)? Do they focus on concerns that are not key issues to women in other countries (another criticism)? Do they suggest American superiority over other cultures (yet another criticism)?

Action Opportunities

1. Join or start a campaign to ratify CEDAW by the United States. Go to http://www.womenstreaty.org/take.htm , http://www .hrw.org/campaigns/cedaw , or http://salsa.democracyinaction. org/o/1920/t/1019/campaign.jsp?campaign_KEY=6902.

2. The 16 Days of Activism Against Gender Violence is an international campaign originating from the first Women's Global Leadership Institute sponsored by the Center for Women's Global Leadership in 1991. Participants chose the dates, November 25, International Day Against Violence Against Women and December 10, International Human Rights Day, to symbolically link violence against women and human rights and to emphasize that such violence is a violation of human rights. This sixteen-day period also highlights other significant dates including December 1, which is World AIDS Day, and December 6, which marks the Anniversary of the Montreal Massacre. Go to http://www.cwgl.rutgers.edu/16days/ about.html for specific information on how to participate.

3. Do something to celebrate or inform on International Women's Day, March 8. Every year on this day, women around the world hold rallies and marches to call attention to women's economic and political rights. Hold a press conference, write a newspaper article or a letter to the editor, or have a table at a public venue. Celebrate the many people and organizations working on behalf of women's rights locally, nationally, or internationally.

4. Join a transnational campaign coordinated by one of the TFNs listed under the activist websites below.

Activist Websites

DAWN (Development Alternatives for a New Era) http://www.dawnnet.org/

WIDE (Women in Development Europe) http://www.wide-network.org

WEDO (Women's Environment and Development Organization) http://www.wedo.org/

WLUML (Women Living Under Muslim Laws) http://www.wluml.org/ english/index.shtml

SIGI (Sisterhood is Global Institute) http://www.sigi.org/

Equality Now http://equalitynow.org

CWGL (Center for Women's Global Leadership) http://www.cwgl .rutgers.edu/

Informational Websites

UN Conventions and Declarations relevant to women's rights
http://www.un.org/womenwatch/un/iinstrum.htm
Convention on the Elimination of Discrimination Against Women
http://www.un.org/womenwatch/daw/cedaw/cedaw.htm
Beijing Platform for Action http://www.un.org/womenwatch/daw/beijing/
pdf/Beijing%20full%20report%20E.pdf
United Nations Human Rights http://www.un.org/en/rights/
International Women's Day http://www.internationalwomensday.com/

Appendix: Statistical Indicators
of Women's Status Worldwide

This appendix provides data by country for the following:

1. Country's relative geographic location
2. Adult literacy (% of 15- to 24-year-old women who can read)
3. Life expectancy
4. Average age at marriage
5. The percentage of contraceptive use among married women (contraceptive prevalence rate)
6. Maternal deaths per 100,000 live births (includes women who die from unsafe abortion, pregnancy-related illness, and women who die in childbirth)
7. Abortion rate (number per 1,000 women)
8. Abortion law as of November 2009 (whether and under what conditions it is allowed)
9. Women's employment to population ratio (age 15+)
10. Women's share of legislators and managers

Notes

1. Most data is from government reports to the United Nations from 2005 to 2009. Data collection methods and years may vary across countries. Many countries lack the human and economic resources to reliably collect and analyze data on women's issues and status, so statistics must be interpreted cautiously. Countries for which there was no or little data were not included.

2. Geographic descriptions are from the CIA Factbook http://www.cia.gov/cia/publications/factbook. Other information comes from the United Nations Statistics Division (http://data.un.org/Browse.aspx?d=GenderStat); UNIFEM (2009.). *Progress of the world's women 2008/2009. Who answers to women? Gender and accountability.* http://www.unifem.org/progress/2008; UNICEF (United Nations Children's Fund). 2006. *The state of the world's children 2007: Women and children;* UNFPA (2008). *State of the world population 2008.* These sources update their information regularly; check for updates.

3. See the http://www.ipu.org/parline-e/parlinesearch.asp for current information on women in national assemblies (parliaments and congresses).

Country	Afghanistan	Albania	Algeria	Angola	Argentina
Location	Southern Asia, north and west of Pakistan, east of Iran	Southeastern Europe, bordering the Adriatic Sea and Ionian Sea, between Greece and Serbia and Montenegro	Northern Africa, bordering the Mediterranean Sea, between Morocco and Tunisia	Southern Africa, bordering the South Atlantic Ocean, between Namibia and Democratic Republic of the Congo	Southern South America, bordering the South Atlantic Ocean, between Chile and Uruguay
Adult Literacy (% of 15–24 yr old women)	18.4	99.5	86.1	63.2	99.1
Life Expectancy	42	79	72	43	78
Average Age at Marriage	17.8	22.9	25.9	17	23.3
Fertility Rate (births per woman)	7.5	2.2	2.5	6.8	2.4
Contraceptive Prevalence Rate (%)	10.3	75.1	57	8.1	74
Maternal deaths per 100,000 live births	1900	55	140	1700	82
Abortion Rate (number per 1,000 women)	No data	9.6	No data	No data	No data
Abortion Law (Whether and under what conditions it is allowed)	To save the woman's life	On request	To save the woman's life	To save the woman's life	To save the woman's life; rape
Women's Employment to Population Ratio (age 15+)	33.8	41.6	30.7	67.5	49
Women's Share of Legislators & Managers	No data	No data	5	No data	23

Country	Armenia	Australia	Austria	Azerbaijan	Bahamas
Location	Southwestern Asia, east of Turkey	Oceania, continent between the Indian Ocean and the South Pacific Ocean	Central Europe, north of Italy and Slovenia	Southwestern Asia, bordering the Caspian Sea, between Iran and Russia, with a small European portion north of the Caucasus range	Caribbean, chain of islands in the North Atlantic Ocean, southeast of Florida, northeast of Cuba
Adult Literacy (% of 15–24 yr old women)	99.9	99	99	99.9	No data
Life Expectancy	75	83	82	70	74
Average Age at Marriage	23	28.7	26.1	23.9	27.2
Fertility Rate (births per woman)	1.3	1.8	1.4	1.7	2.1
Contraceptive Prevalence Rate (%)	53.1	76	50.8	55.4	No data
Maternal deaths per 100,000 live births	55	8	4	94	60
Abortion Rate (number per 1,000 women)	13.9	19.7	1.3	9	No data
Abortion Law (Whether and under what conditions it is allowed)	On request	On request	On request	On request	To save the woman's life; to preserve mental or physical health
Women's Employment to Population Ratio (age 15+)	43.5	47.9	53.6	56	57.6
Women's Share of Legislators & Managers	24	37	27	5	43

Country	Bahrain	Bangladesh	Barbados	Belarus	Belgium
Location	Middle East, archipelago in the Persian Gulf, east of Saudi Arabia	Southern Asia, bordering the Bay of Bengal, between Burma and India	Caribbean, island in the North Atlantic Ocean, northeast of Venezuela	Eastern Europe, east of Poland	Western Europe, bordering the North Sea, between France and the Netherlands
Adult Literacy (% of 15–24 yr old women)	97.3	60.3	No data	99.8	99
Life Expectancy	77	63	79	75	81
Average Age at Marriage	25.6	18.7	31.8	22.8	27.9
Fertility Rate (births per woman)	2.5	3.2	1.5	1.2	1.6
Contraceptive Prevalence Rate (%)	61.8	58.1	55	50.4	78.4
Maternal deaths per 100,000 live births	28	380	95	35	10
Abortion Rate (number per 1,000 women)	11	No data	No data	31.7	7.5
Abortion Law (Whether and under what conditions it is allowed)	On request	To save the woman's life	To save the woman's life; rape or incest; economic or social reasons, fetal impairment, mental or physical health	On request	On request
Women's Employment to Population Ratio (age 15+)	27.4	50	57.2	47.7	39.9
Women's Share of Legislators & Managers	12	10	43	No data	32

Country	Belize	Benin	Bhutan	Bolivia	Bosnia-Herzegovina
Location	Central America, bordering the Caribbean Sea, between Guatemala and Mexico	Western Africa, bordering the Bight of Benin, between Nigeria and Togo	Southern Asia, between China and India	Central South America, southwest of Brazil	Southeastern Europe, bordering the Adriatic Sea and Croatia
Adult Literacy (% of 15–24 yr old women)	76.7	33.2	35	96.1	99.8
Life Expectancy	79	56	65	66	77
Average Age at Marriage	26.2	19.9	20.5	22.8	23
Fertility Rate (births per woman)	3.4	5.9	2.9	4	1.3
Contraceptive Prevalence Rate (%)	56.1	18.6	30.7	58.4	47.5
Maternal deaths per 100,000 live births	140	850	420	420	31
Abortion Rate (number per 1,000 women)	No data	No data	No data	No data	No data
Abortion Law (Whether and under what conditions it is allowed)	To save the woman's life; economic or social reasons; fetal impairment; to preserve mental or physical health	To save the woman's life; rape or incest; fetal impairment, to preserve mental or physical health	To save the woman's life; fetal impairment	To save the woman's life of rape or incest; to preserve mental or physical health	On request
Women's Employment to Population Ratio (age 15+)	36.3	49	43	58.9	51.6
Women's Share of Legislators & Managers	41	No data	No data	36	No data

Country	Botswana	Brazil	Brunei	Bulgaria	Burkina Faso
Location	Southern Africa, north of South Africa	Eastern South America, bordering the Atlantic Ocean	Southeastern Asia, bordering the South China Sea and Malaysia	Southeastern Europe, bordering the Black Sea, between Romania and Turkey	Western Africa, north of Ghana
Adult Literacy (% of 15–24 yr old women)	95.6	97.9	98.9	98.1	26.5
Life Expectancy	47	75	79	76	52
Average Age at Marriage	26.9	23.4	25.1	21.1	18.9
Fertility Rate (births per woman)	3.2	2.3	2.5	1.3	6.4
Contraceptive Prevalence Rate (%)	40.4	76.7	No data	42	13.8
Maternal deaths per 100,000 live births	100	260	37	32	1000
Abortion Rate (number per 1,000 women)	No data	No data	No data	21.3	No data
Abortion Law (Whether and under what conditions it is allowed)	To save the woman's life; fetal impairment; rape or incest; to preserve mental or physical health	To save the woman's life; rape or incest	To save the woman's life	On request	To save the woman's life; fetal impairment, rape or incest; to preserve mental or physical health
Women's Employment to Population Ratio (age 15+)	33.5	49.8	41.6	36.3	75.5
Women's Share of Legislators & Managers	33	35	35	31	No data

Country	Burundi	Cambodia	Cameroon	Canada	Cape Verde
Location	Central Africa, east of Democratic Republic of the Congo	Southeastern Asia, bordering the Gulf of Thailand, between Thailand, Vietnam, and Laos	Western Africa, bordering the Bight of Biafra, between Equatorial Guinea and Nigeria	Northern North America, bordering the North Atlantic Ocean on the east, North Pacific Ocean on the west, and the Arctic Ocean on the north, north of the conterminous US	Western Africa, group of islands in the North Atlantic Ocean, west of Senegal
Adult Literacy (% of 15–24 yr old women)	70.4	78.9	69	99	96.7
Life Expectancy	49	60	50	82	73
Average Age at Marriage	22.5	22.5	20.2	26.8	25.7
Fertility Rate (births per woman)	6.8	3.6	4.9	1.5	3.8
Contraceptive Prevalence Rate (%)	15.7	23.8	26	74.7	52.9
Maternal deaths per 100,000 live births	1000	450	730	6	150
Abortion Rate (number per 1,000 women)	No data	No data	No data	15.2	No data
Abortion Law (Whether and under what conditions it is allowed)	To save the woman's life; to preserve mental or physical health	On request	To save the woman's life; to preserve mental or physical health	On request	On request
Women's Employment to Population Ratio (age 15+)	83.5	73.2	47.6	57.2	31
Women's Share of Legislators & Managers	No data	14	No data	37	No data

Country	Central African Republic	Chad	Chile	China	Colombia
Location	Central Africa, north of Democratic Republic of the Congo	Central Africa, south of Libya	Southern South America, bordering the South Pacific Ocean, between Argentina and Peru	Eastern Asia, bordering the East China Sea, Korea Bay, Yellow Sea, and South China Sea, between North Korea and Vietnam	Northern South America, bordering the Caribbean Sea, between Panama and Venezuela, and bordering the North Pacific Ocean, between Ecuador and Panama
Adult Literacy (% of 15–24 yr old women)	46.9	23.2	99.2	98.5	98.4
Life Expectancy	45	52	81	70	75
Average Age at Marriage	19.7	18.1	23.4	23.1	23.1
Fertility Rate (births per woman)	5	6.5	2	1.7	2.5
Contraceptive Prevalence Rate (%)	27.9	2.8	56	90.2	78.2
Maternal deaths per 100,000 live births	1100	1100	31	56	130
Abortion Rate (number per 1,000 women)	No data		No data	24.2	No data
Abortion Law (Whether and under what conditions it is allowed)	To save the woman's life	To save the woman's life; fetal impairment; to preserve physical health	Prohibited	On request	To save the woman's life; fetal impairment; rape or incest; to preserve mental or physical health
Women's Employment to Population Ratio (age 15+)	64.4	60	33.6	66.8	52.9
Women's Share of Legislators & Managers	No data	No data	23	17	38

Country	Comoros	Congo	Congo, Democratic Republic of	Costa Rica	Cote d'Ivoire
Location	Southern Africa, group of islands at the northern mouth of the Mozambique Channel, about two-thirds of the way between northern Madagascar and northern Mozambique	Western Africa, bordering the South Atlantic Ocean, between Angola and Gabon	Central Africa, northeast of Angola	Central America, bordering both the Caribbean Sea and the North Pacific Ocean, between Nicaragua and Panama	Western Africa, bordering the North Atlantic Ocean, between Ghana and Liberia
Adult Literacy (% of 15–24 yr old women)	No data	96.5	63.1	98	52.1
Life Expectancy	60	54	46	81	48
Average Age at Marriage	23.6	22	No data	20.9	22
Fertility Rate (births per woman)	4.9	4.8	6.7	2.5	5.1
Contraceptive Prevalence Rate (%)	25.7	44.3	31.4	80	15
Maternal deaths per 100,000 live births	480	510	990	43	690
Abortion Rate (number per 1,000 women)	No data	No data	No data	No data	No data
Abortion Law (Whether and under what conditions it is allowed)	To save the woman's life; to preserve mental or physical health	To save the woman's life	To save the woman's life	To save the woman's life; to preserve mental or physical health	To save the woman's life
Women's Employment to Population Ratio (age 15+)	52.6	52.2	55.7	41.9	35.2
Women's Share of Legislators & Managers	No data	No data	No data	27	No data

Country	Croatia	Cuba	Cyprus	Czech Republic	Denmark
Location	Southeastern Europe, bordering the Adriatic Sea, between Bosnia and Herzegovina and Slovenia	Caribbean, island between the Caribbean Sea and the North Atlantic Ocean, 150 km south of Key West, Florida	Middle East, island in the Mediterranean Sea, south of Turkey	Central Europe, between Germany, Poland, Slovakia, and Austria	Northern Europe, bordering the Baltic Sea and the North Sea, on a peninsula north of Germany (Jutland)
Adult Literacy (% of 15–24 yr old women)	99.7	100	99.8	99	99
Life Expectancy	78	79	81	79	80
Average Age at Marriage	26.2	20	23.1	25.3	30.7
Fertility Rate (births per woman)	1.3	1.6	1.6	1.2	1.8
Contraceptive Prevalence Rate (%)	No data	79.3	No data	72	9
Maternal deaths per 100,000 live births	8	33	47	9	5
Abortion Rate (number per 1,000 women)	5.7	24.8	No data	12.2	14.3
Abortion Law (Whether and under what conditions it is allowed)	On request	On request	To save the woman's life fetal impairment; rape or incest; to preserve mental or physical health	On request	On request
Women's Employment to Population Ratio (age 15+)	38.3	42.8	50.8	47.4	55.5
Women's Share of Legislators & Managers	21	No data	31	15	28

Country	Djibouti	Dominica	Dominican Republic	Ecuador	Egypt
Location	Eastern Africa, bordering the Gulf of Aden and the Red Sea, between Eritrea and Somalia	Caribbean, island between the Caribbean Sea and the North Atlantic Ocean, about half way between Puerto Rico and Trinidad and Tobago	Caribbean, eastern two-thirds of the island of Hispaniola, between the Caribbean Sea and the North Atlantic Ocean, east of Haiti	Western South America, bordering the Pacific Ocean at the Equator, between Colombia and Peru	Northern Africa, bordering the Mediterranean Sea, between Libya and the Gaza Strip, and the Red Sea north of Sudan, and includes the Asian Sinai Peninsula
Adult Literacy (% of 15–24 yr old women)	13	No data	95.4	96.5	78.9
Life Expectancy	55	No data	74	77	72
Average Age at Marriage	19	No data	21.3	21.5	22.3
Fertility Rate (births per woman)	4.5	No data	3	2.8	3.2
Contraceptive Prevalence Rate (%)	9	50	69.8	72.7	59.2
Maternal deaths per 100,000 live births	730	No data	150	130	84
Abortion Rate (number per 1,000 women)	No data	No data	16	No data	No data
Abortion Law (Whether and under what conditions it is allowed)	To save the woman's life	To save the woman's life	To save the woman's life	To save the woman's life rape or incest; to preserve mental or physical health	To save the woman's life
Women's Employment to Population Ratio (age 15+)	No data	No data	32.7	53.6	15.1
Women's Share of Legislators & Managers	No data	48	31	28	11

Country	El Salvador	Equatorial Guinea	Eritea	Estonia	Ethiopia
Location	Central America, bordering the North Pacific Ocean, between Guatemala and Honduras	Western Africa, bordering the Bight of Biafra, between Cameroon and Gabon	Eastern Africa, bordering the Red Sea, between Djibouti and Sudan	Eastern Europe, bordering the Baltic Sea and Gulf of Finland, between Latvia and Russia	Eastern Africa, west of Somalia
Adult Literacy (% of 15–24 yr old women)	90.3	94.9	40	99.8	33.8
Life Expectancy	74	51	58	77	52
Average Age at Marriage	22.3	No data	19.6	22.1	20.5
Fertility Rate (births per woman)	2.9	5.6	5.5	1.4	5.8
Contraceptive Prevalence Rate (%)	67.3	No data	8	70.3	14.7
Maternal deaths per 100,000 live births	150	880	630	63	850
Abortion Rate (number per 1,000 women)	No data	No data	No data	33	No data
Abortion Law (Whether and under what conditions it is allowed)	Prohibited	To save the woman's life; to preserve mental or physical health	To save the woman's life; to preserve mental or physical health	On request	To save the woman's life; fetal impairment; rape or incest; to preserve mental or physical health
Women's Employment to Population Ratio (age 15+)	46.3	46.5	52.7	48.6	64.8
Women's Share of Legislators & Managers	29	No data	No data	34	16

Country	Fiji	Finland	France	Gabon	Gambia
Location	Oceania, island group in the South Pacific Ocean, about two-thirds of the way from Hawaii to New Zealand	Northern Europe, bordering the Baltic Sea, Gulf of Bothnia, and Gulf of Finland, between Sweden and Russia	Western Europe, bordering the Bay of Biscay and English Channel, between Belgium and Spain, southeast of the UK; bordering the Mediterranean Sea, between Italy and Spain	Western Africa, bordering the Atlantic Ocean at the Equator, between Democratic Republic of the Congo and Equatorial Guinea	Western Africa, bordering the North Atlantic Ocean and Senegal
Adult Literacy (% of 15–24 yr old women)	91	99	99	95.1	30
Life Expectancy	70	82	83	58	59
Average Age at Marriage	22.9	30.2	30.2	22.1	19.6
Fertility Rate (births per woman)	3	1.8	1.9	3.4	5.2
Contraceptive Prevalence Rate (%)	44	77	74.6	32.7	9.6
Maternal deaths per 100,000 live births	75	6	17	420	540
Abortion Rate (number per 1,000 women)	No data	11.1	16.9	No data	No data
Abortion Law (Whether and under what conditions it is allowed)	To save the woman's life; to preserve mental or physical health; economic or social reasons	To save the woman's life; fetal impairment; rape or incest; to preserve mental or physical health; social or economic reasons	On request	To save the woman's life	To save the woman's life; to preserve mental or physical health
Women's Employment to Population Ratio (age 15+)	48.8	52.3	43.2	49.8	54.3
Women's Share of Legislators & Managers	No data	29	38	No data	No data

Country	Georgia	Germany	Ghana	Greece	Grenada
Location	Southwestern Asia, bordering the Black Sea, between Turkey and Russia	Central Europe, bordering the Baltic Sea and the North Sea, between the Netherlands and Poland, south of Denmark	Western Africa, bordering the Gulf of Guinea, between Cote d'Ivoire and Togo	Southern Europe, bordering the Aegean Sea, Ionian Sea, and the Mediterranean Sea, between Albania and Turkey	Caribbean, island between the Caribbean Sea and Atlantic Ocean, north of Trinidad and Tobago
Adult Literacy (% of 15–24 yr old women)	98	99	65.5	99	No data
Life Expectancy	74	81	59	80	69
Average Age at Marriage	24.3	28	21.2	24.5	No data
Fertility Rate (births per woman)	1.5	1.3	4.4	1.3	2.4
Contraceptive Prevalence Rate (%)	47.2	74.7	25.2	No data	54.3
Maternal deaths per 100,000 live births	32	8	540	9	No data
Abortion Rate (number per 1,000 women)	19.1	7.8	No data	5	No data
Abortion Law (Whether and under what conditions it is allowed)	On request	On request	To save the woman's life; fetal impairment; rape or incest; to preserve mental or physical health	On request	To save the woman's life; to preserve mental or physical health
Women's Employment to Population Ratio (age 15+)	43	45.7	62.8	38.3	No data
Women's Share of Legislators & Managers	34	38	No data	28	No data

Country	Guam	Guatemala	Guinea	Guinea-Bissau	Guyana
Location	Oceania, island in the North Pacific Ocean, about three-quarters of the way from Hawaii to the Philippines	Central America, bordering the North Pacific Ocean, between El Salvador and Mexico, and bordering the Gulf of Honduras (Caribbean Sea) between Honduras and Belize	Western Africa, bordering the North Atlantic Ocean, between Guinea-Bissau and Sierra Leone	Western Africa, bordering the North Atlantic Ocean, between Guinea and Senegal	Northern South America, bordering the North Atlantic Ocean, between Suriname and Venezuela
Adult Literacy (% of 15–24 yr old women)	99	78.4	33.7	No data	98
Life Expectancy	77	73	55	47	66
Average Age at Marriage	24.4	20.5	18.7	No data	27.8
Fertility Rate (births per woman)	2.7	4.6	5.8	7.1	2.4
Contraceptive Prevalence Rate (%)	No data	43.3	9.1	7.6	34.6
Maternal deaths per 100,000 live births	No data	240	740	1100	170
Abortion Rate (number per 1,000 women)	No data	No data	No data	No data	No data
Abortion Law (Whether and under what conditions it is allowed)	No Data	To save the woman's life	To save the woman's life; to preserve mental or physical health	To save the woman's life	On request
Women's Employment to Population Ratio (age 15+)	No data	32.5	76.8	55.3	37.9
Women's Share of Legislators & Managers	No data	No data	No data	No data	25

Country	Haiti	Honduras	Hong Kong	Hungary	Iceland
Location	Caribbean, western one-third of the island of Hispaniola, between the Caribbean Sea and the North Atlantic Ocean, west of the Dominican Republic	Central America, bordering the Caribbean Sea, between Guatemala and Nicaragua and bordering the Gulf of Fonseca (North Pacific Ocean), between El Salvador and Nicaragua	Eastern Asia, bordering the South China Sea and China	Central Europe, northwest of Romania	Northern Europe, island between the Greenland Sea and the North Atlantic Ocean, northwest of the United Kingdom
Adult Literacy (% of 15–24 yr old women)	46	90.9	No data	99	99
Life Expectancy	60	73	84	77	83
Average Age at Marriage	22.3	20.4	28.6	26.3	30.5
Fertility Rate (births per woman)	4	3.7	0.9	1.3	2
Contraceptive Prevalence Rate (%)	28.1	61.8	86.2	77.4	No data
Maternal deaths per 100,000 live births	680	110	No data	16	0
Abortion Rate (number per 1,000 women)	No data	No data	No data	23.4	14.1
Abortion Law (Whether and under what conditions it is allowed)	To save the woman's life	To save the woman's life	No Data	On request	To save the woman's life; fetal impairment; rape or incest; to preserve mental or physical health; economic or social reasons
Women's Employment to Population Ratio (age 15+)	51.2	52	51.4	39.3	68.8
Women's Share of Legislators & Managers	No data	41	No data	35	30

Country	India	Indonesia	Iran	Iraq	Ireland
Location	Southern Asia, bordering the Arabian Sea and the Bay of Bengal, between Burma and Pakistan	Southeastern Asia, archipelago between the Indian Ocean and the Pacific Ocean	Middle East, bordering the Gulf of Oman, the Persian Gulf, and the Caspian Sea, between Iraq and Pakistan	Middle East, bordering the Gulf of Oman, the Persian Gulf, and the Caspian Sea, between Iraq and Pakistan	Western Europe, occupying five-sixths of the island of Ireland in the North Atlantic Ocean, west of Great Britain
Adult Literacy (% of 15–24 yr old women)	67.7	98.5	96.7	80.5	99
Life Expectancy	64	70	71	59	80
Average Age at Marriage	19.9	22.5	22.1	22.3	30.9
Fertility Rate (births per woman)	3.1	2.4	2.1	4.9	2
Contraceptive Prevalence Rate (%)	56.3	60.3	72.9	44	No data
Maternal deaths per 100,000 live births	540	230	76	250	5
Abortion Rate (number per 1,000 women)	3.1	13.9	No data	No data	No data
Abortion Law (Whether and under what conditions it is allowed)	To save the woman's life; fetal impairment; rape or incest; to preserve mental or physical health; economic or social reasons	To save the woman's life	To save the woman's life	To save the woman's life	To save the woman's life
Women's Employment to Population Ratio (age 15+)	32.2	44.3	33.7	13.4	51.9
Women's Share of Legislators & Managers	No data	14	13	No data	31

Country	Israel	Italy	Jamaica	Japan	Jordan
Location	Middle East, bordering the Mediterranean Sea, between Egypt and Lebanon	Southern Europe, a peninsula extending into the central Mediterranean Sea, northeast of Tunisia	Caribbean, island in the Caribbean Sea, south of Cuba	Eastern Asia, island chain between the North Pacific Ocean and the Sea of Japan, east of the Korean Peninsula	Middle East, northwest of Saudi Arabia
Adult Literacy (% of 15–24 yr old women)	99.6	99.8	91	99	99
Life Expectancy	82	83	75	85	73
Average Age at Marriage	25	28.4	33.2	28.6	25.3
Fertility Rate (births per woman)	2.9	1.3	2.6	1.3	3.5
Contraceptive Prevalence Rate (%)	No data	60.2	65.9	55.9	55.8
Maternal deaths per 100,000 live births	17	5	87	10	41
Abortion Rate (number per 1,000 women)	No data	10.6	No data	12.3	No data
Abortion Law (Whether and under what conditions it is allowed)	To save the woman's life; fetal impairment; rape or incest; to preserve mental or physical health	On request	To save the woman's life; to preserve mental or physical health	To save the woman's life; rape or incest; to preserve physical health; economic or social reasons	To save the woman's life; fetal impairment; to preserve mental or physical health
Women's Employment to Population Ratio (age 15+)	45.7	34.5	45.4	46.2	23.9
Women's Share of Legislators & Managers	30	34	No data	9	No data

Country	Kazakhstan	Kenya	Kiribati	Korea, North	Korea, South
Location	Central Asia, northwest of China; a small portion west of the Ural (Zhayyq) River in eastern-most Europe	Eastern Africa, bordering the Indian Ocean, between Somalia and Tanzania	Oceania, group of 33 coral atolls in the Pacific Ocean, straddling the Equator; the capital Tarawa is about half way between Hawaii and Australia	Eastern Asia, northern half of the Korean Peninsula bordering the Korea Bay and the Sea of Japan, between China and South Korea	Eastern Asia, southern half of the Korean Peninsula bordering the Sea of Japan and the Yellow Sea
Adult Literacy (% of 15–24 yr old women)	99.9	80.7	No data	99	96
Life Expectancy	71	52	No data	69	81
Average Age at Marriage	23.4	21.7	22	No data	26.1
Fertility Rate (births per woman)	2	5	No data	1.9	1.2
Contraceptive Prevalence Rate (%)	66.1	39.3	21	68.6	80.5
Maternal deaths per 100,000 live births	210	1000	56	67	20
Abortion Rate (number per 1,000 women)	35	No data	No data	No data	No data
Abortion Law (Whether and under what conditions it is allowed)	On request	To save the woman's life; to preserve mental or physical health	To save the woman's life	On request	To save the woman's life; fetal impairment; rape or incest; to preserve mental or physical health
Women's Employment to Population Ratio (age 15+)	59.9	58.2	No data	46.2	48.8
Women's Share of Legislators & Managers	38	No data	27	No data	No data

Country	Kuwait	Kyrgyzstan	Laos	Latvia	Lebanon
Location	Middle East, bordering the Persian Gulf, between Iraq and Saudi Arabia	Central Asia, west of China	Southeastern Asia, northeast of Thailand, west of Vietnam	Eastern Europe, bordering the Baltic Sea, between Estonia and Lithuania	Middle East, bordering the Mediterranean Sea, between Israel and Syria
Adult Literacy (% of 15–24 yr old women)	99.8	99.7	74.7	99.8	80
Life Expectancy	79	69	63	77	69
Average Age at Marriage	25.2	21.9	20.8	26.9	32
Fertility Rate (births per woman)	2.3	2.5	3.6	1.2	2.3
Contraceptive Prevalence Rate (%)	50.2	59.5	32.2	48	58
Maternal deaths per 100,000 live births	5	110	650	42	150
Abortion Rate (number per 1,000 women)	No data	15.8	No data	27.3	No data
Abortion Law (Whether and under what conditions it is allowed)	To save the woman's life; fetal impairment; to preserve mental or physical health	On request	To save the woman's life; to preserve physical health	On request	To save the woman's life
Women's Employment to Population Ratio (age 15+)	48.9	50	53.5	45.2	30.3
Women's Share of Legislators & Managers	No data	35	No data	41	No data

Country	Lesotho	Liberia	Libya	Liechtenstein	Lithuania
Location	Southern Africa, an enclave of South Africa	Western Africa, bordering the North Atlantic Ocean, between Cote d'Ivoire and Sierra Leone	Northern Africa, bordering the Mediterranean Sea, between Egypt and Tunisia	Central Europe, between Austria and Switzerland	Eastern Europe, bordering the Baltic Sea, between Latvia and Russia
Adult Literacy (% of 15–24 yr old women)	94	69.5	96.5	No data	99.6
Life Expectancy	46	45	76	No data	78
Average Age at Marriage	21.3	20.2	29.2	26	24.8
Fertility Rate (births per woman)	3.8	6.8	3	No data	1.3
Contraceptive Prevalence Rate (%)	37.3	10	45.1	No data	47
Maternal deaths per 100,000 live births	550	760	97	No data	13
Abortion Rate (number per 1,000 women)	No data	No data	No data	No data	13.9
Abortion Law (Whether and under what conditions it is allowed)	To save the woman's life	To save the woman's life; fetal impairment; rape or incest; to preserve mental or physical health	To save the woman's life	To save the woman's life; to preserve mental or physical health	On request
Women's Employment to Population Ratio (age 15+)	24.8	46.9	31	No data	47.6
Women's Share of Legislators & Managers	No data	No data	No data	No data	38

Country	Luxembourg	Macau SAR	Macedonia	Madagascar	Malawi
Location	Western Europe, between France and Germany	Eastern Asia, bordering the South China Sea and China	Southeastern Europe, north of Greece	Southern Africa, island in the Indian Ocean, east of Mozambique	Southern Africa, east of Zambia
Adult Literacy (% of 15–24 yr old women)	99	99.8	98.5	68.2	70.7
Life Expectancy	81	82	76	59	46
Average Age at Marriage	26	27.1	22.9	20.6	18.9
Fertility Rate (births per woman)	1.7	0.8	1.6	5.3	6
Contraceptive Prevalence Rate (%)	No data	No data	No data	27.1	32.5
Maternal deaths per 100,000 live births	28	No data	23	550	1800
Abortion Rate (number per 1,000 women)	No data	No data	18.4	No data	No data
Abortion Law (Whether and under what conditions it is allowed)	To save the woman's life; fetal impairment; rape or incest; to preserve mental or physical health; social or economic reasons	No Data	On request	To save the woman's life	To save the woman's life
Women's Employment to Population Ratio (age 15+)	42	59.5	25.3	73.9	78.1
Women's Share of Legislators & Managers	No data	No data	29	22	No data

Country	Malaysia	Maldives	Mali	Malta	Mauritania
Location	Southeastern Asia, peninsula bordering Thailand and northern one-third of the island of Borneo, bordering Indonesia, Brunei, and the South China Sea, south of Vietnam	Southern Asia, group of atolls in the Indian Ocean, south-southwest of India	Western Africa, southwest of Algeria	Southern Europe, islands in the Mediterranean Sea, south of Sicily (Italy)	Northern Africa, bordering the North Atlantic Ocean, between Senegal and Western Sahara
Adult Literacy (% of 15–24 yr old women)	97.3	98.3	16.9	97.8	55.5
Life Expectancy	75	66	54	81	64
Average Age at Marriage	25.1	21.8	18.4	22.2	22.1
Fertility Rate (births per woman)	2.9	2.8	6.7	1.5	4.8
Contraceptive Prevalence Rate (%)	54.5	39	8.1	No data	8
Maternal deaths per 100,000 live births	41	110	1200	21	1000
Abortion Rate (number per 1,000 women)	No data	No data	No data	No data	No data
Abortion Law (Whether and under what conditions it is allowed)	To save the woman's life; to preserve mental or physical health	To save the woman's life; to preserve physical health	To save the woman's life; rape or incest	Prohibited	To save the woman's life
Women's Employment to Population Ratio (age 15+)	45.1	48.6	64.8	32.2	50.2
Women's Share of Legislators & Managers	23	14	No data	19	No data

Country	Mauritius	Mexico	Micronesia	Moldova	Mongolia
Location	Southern Africa, island in the Indian Ocean, east of Madagascar	Middle America, bordering the Caribbean Sea and the Gulf of Mexico, between Belize and the United States and bordering the North Pacific Ocean, between Guatemala and the United States	Oceania, island group in the North Pacific Ocean, about three-quarters of the way from Hawaii to Indonesia	Eastern Europe, northeast of Romania	Northern Asia, between China and Russia
Adult Literacy (% of 15–24 yr old women)	93.7	97.6	71	99.7	98.4
Life Expectancy	75	77	68	71	68
Average Age at Marriage	23.8	22.7	No data	21.1	23.7
Fertility Rate (births per woman)	1.9	2.4	4.2	1.4	2.1
Contraceptive Prevalence Rate (%)	78.5	68.4	No data	67.8	67.4
Maternal deaths per 100,000 live births	24	83	No data	7	110
Abortion Rate (number per 1,000 women)	No data	0.1	No data	17.6	21.7
Abortion Law (Whether and under what conditions it is allowed)	To save the woman's life	To save the woman's life; rape or incest	To save the woman's life	On request	On request
Women's Employment to Population Ratio (age 15+)	36.4	38.7	No data	49.9	46.9
Women's Share of Legislators & Managers	20	31	No data	No data	48

Country	Montenegro	Morocco	Mozambique	Myanmar (Burma)	Namibia
Location	Southeastern Europe, between the Adriatic Sea and Serbia	Northern Africa, bordering the North Atlantic Ocean and the Mediterranean Sea, between Algeria and Western Sahara	Southeastern Africa, bordering the Mozambique Channel, between South Africa and Tanzania	Southeastern Asia, bordering the Andaman Sea and the Bay of Bengal, between Bangladesh and Thailand	Southern Africa, bordering the South Atlantic Ocean, between Angola and South Africa
Adult Literacy (% of 15–24 yr old women)	No data	60.5	36.6	93.4	93.5
Life Expectancy	77	72	45	63	53
Average Age at Marriage	No data	25.3	18	24.5	26.4
Fertility Rate (births per woman)	1.8	2.5	5.5	2.1	3.6
Contraceptive Prevalence Rate (%)	No data	63	16.5	37	43.7
Maternal deaths per 100,000 live births	No data	220	1000	360	300
Abortion Rate (number per 1,000 women)	No data	No data	No data	No data	No data
Abortion Law (Whether and under what conditions it is allowed)	On request	To save the woman's life; to preserve mental or physical health	To save the woman's life; to preserve mental or physical health	To save the woman's life	To save the woman's life; fetal impairment; rape or incest; to preserve mental or physical health
Women's Employment to Population Ratio (age 15+)	No data	23.7	77.8	66	29.6
Women's Share of Legislators & Managers	20	12	No data	No data	36

Country	Nepal	Netherlands	Netherlands Antilles	New Caldonia	New Zealand
Location	Southern Asia, between China and India	Western Europe, bordering the North Sea, between Belgium and Germany	Caribbean, two island groups in the Caribbean Sea-composed of five islands, Curacao and Bonaire located off the coast of Venezuela, and Sint Maarten, Saba, and Sint Eustatius lie east of the US Virgin Islands	Oceania, islands in the South Pacific Ocean, east of Australia	Oceania, islands in the South Pacific Ocean, southeast of Australia
Adult Literacy (% of 15–24 yr old women)	60.1	99	98.1	99.1	94
Life Expectancy	62	81	79	79	81
Average Age at Marriage	19	29.9	30.2	30.4	25.4
Fertility Rate (births per woman)	3.7	1.7	2.1	2.1	2
Contraceptive Prevalence Rate (%)	38.3	78.5	79	25	74.9
Maternal deaths per 100,000 live births	740	16	No data	No data	7
Abortion Rate (number per 1,000 women)	No data	10.4	No data	No data	19.7
Abortion Law (Whether and under what conditions it is allowed)	On request	On request	No data	No data	To save the woman's life; fetal impairment; rape or incest; to preserve mental or physical health
Women's Employment to Population Ratio (age 15+)	43.7	53	42.4	No data	58.7
Women's Share of Legislators & Managers	14	28	34	No data	40

Country	Nicaragua	Niger	Nigeria	Norway	Oman
Location	Central America, bordering both the Caribbean Sea and the North Pacific Ocean, between Costa Rica and Honduras	Western Africa, southeast of Algeria	Western Africa, bordering the Gulf of Guinea, between Benin and Cameroon	Northern Europe, bordering the North Sea and the North Atlantic Ocean, west of Sweden	Middle East, bordering the Arabian Sea, Gulf of Oman, and Persian Gulf, between Yemen and UAE
Adult Literacy (% of 15–24 yr old women)	88.8	23.2	81.3	99	96.7
Life Expectancy	74	54	47	82	76
Average Age at Marriage	20.6	17.6	21.4	31.4	21.7
Fertility Rate (births per woman)	3	7.4	5.8	1.8	3.7
Contraceptive Prevalence Rate (%)	68.6	14	12.6	74	23.7
Maternal deaths per 100,000 live births	230	1600	800	16	87
Abortion Rate (number per 1,000 women)	No data	No data	No data	15.2	No data
Abortion Law (Whether and under what conditions it is allowed)	Prohibited	To save the woman's life	To save the woman's life; to preserve mental or physical health	On request	To save the woman's life
Women's Employment to Population Ratio (age 15+)	33.1	66.6	41.9	61.7	21
Women's Share of Legislators & Managers	41	No data	No data	31	9

Country	Pakistan	Palestine	Panama	Papua New Guinea	Paraguay
Location	Southern Asia, bordering the Arabian Sea, between India on the east and Iran and Afghanistan on the west and China in the north	Middle East, west of Jordan, north of Egypt, contested areas of Israel including the West Bank and Gazastrip	Central America, bordering both the Caribbean Sea and the North Pacific Ocean, between Colombia and Costa Rica	Oceania, group of islands including the eastern half of the island of New Guinea between the Coral Sea and the South Pacific Ocean, east of Indonesia	Central South America, northeast of Argentina
Adult Literacy (% of 15–24 yr old women)	53.1	98.8	95.6	64.1	96.1
Life Expectancy	64	74	77	60	73
Average Age at Marriage	21.3	21.7	21.9	20.8	21.5
Fertility Rate (births per woman)	4	5.6	2.7	4.3	3.5
Contraceptive Prevalence Rate (%)	27.6	50.6	No data	25.9	72.8
Maternal deaths per 100,000 live births	500	100	160	300	170
Abortion Rate (number per 1,000 women)	No data	No data	No data	No data	No data
Abortion Law (Whether and under what conditions it is allowed)	To save the woman's life; to preserve mental or physical health	No data	To save the woman's life; rape or incest; to preserve mental or physical health	To save the woman's life; to preserve mental or physical health	To save the woman's life
Women's Employment to Population Ratio (age 15+)	30.2	8.3	44.7	69.8	58.4
Women's Share of Legislators & Managers	3	10	44	No data	35

Country	Peru	Phillipines	Poland	Portugal	Puerto Rico
Location	Western South America, bordering the South Pacific Ocean, between Chile and Ecuador	Southeastern Asia, archipelago between the Philippine Sea and the South China Sea, east of Vietnam	Central Europe, east of Germany	Southwestern Europe, bordering the North Atlantic Ocean, west of Spain	Caribbean, island between the Caribbean Sea and the North Atlantic Ocean, east of the Dominican Republic
Adult Literacy (% of 15–24 yr old women)	96.3	96.6	99	99.6	86.3
Life Expectancy	72	72	79	80	82
Average Age at Marriage	23.1	24.1	25.2	23.9	22.6
Fertility Rate (births per woman)	2.7	3.5	1.3	1.5	1.8
Contraceptive Prevalence Rate (%)	70.5	48.9	49.4	No data	77.7
Maternal deaths per 100,000 live births	410	200	13	5	25
Abortion Rate (number per 1,000 women)	No data	No data	No data	0.2	No data
Abortion Law (Whether and under what conditions it is allowed)	To save the woman's life; to preserve mental or physical health	To save the woman's life	To save the woman's life; fetal impairment; rape or incest; to preserve mental or physical health	To save the woman's life; fetal impairment; rape or incest; to preserve mental or physical health	On request
Women's Employment to Population Ratio (age 15+)	53	51.6	39.9	51.3	34
Women's Share of Legislators & Managers	30	57	36	32	41

Country	Qatar	Romania	Russia	Rwanda	Saint Lucia
Location	Middle East, peninsula bordering the Persian Gulf and Saudi Arabia	Southeastern Europe, bordering the Black Sea, between Bulgaria and Ukraine	Northern Asia (the area west of the Urals is considered part of Europe), bordering the Arctic Ocean, between Europe and the North Pacific Ocean	Central Africa, east of Democratic Republic of the Congo	Caribbean, island between the Caribbean Sea and North Atlantic Ocean, north of Trinidad and Tobago
Adult Literacy (% of 15–24 yr old women)	97.5	97.8	99.8	76.9	No data
Life Expectancy	75	75	72	45	74
Average Age at Marriage	26.3	24.1	21.8	22.7	33.7
Fertility Rate (births per woman)	2.9	1.3	1.3	6	2.2
Contraceptive Prevalence Rate (%)	43.2	63.8	65.3	17.4	47
Maternal deaths per 100,000 live births	7	49	67	1400	No data
Abortion Rate (number per 1,000 women)	1.2	27.8	53.7	No data	No data
Abortion Law (Whether and under what conditions it is allowed)	To save the woman's life; rape or incest; to preserve mental or physical health	On request	On request	To save the woman's life; to preserve mental or physical health	On request
Women's Employment to Population Ratio (age 15+)	34.8	46.4	50.8	72	No data
Women's Share of Legislators & Managers	7	28	39	No data	52

Country	St. Vincent & the Grenadines	Samoa	Sao Tome & Principe	Saudi Arabia	Senegal
Location	Caribbean, islands between the Caribbean Sea and North Atlantic Ocean, north of Trinidad and Tobago	Oceania, group of islands in the South Pacific Ocean, about half way between Hawaii and New Zealand	Southern Europe, an enclave in central Italy	Middle East, bordering the Persian Gulf and the Red Sea, north of Yemen	Western Africa, bordering the North Atlantic Ocean, between Guinea-Bissau and Mauritania
Adult Literacy (% of 15–24 yr old women)	No data	99.4	94.9	94.7	41
Life Expectancy	73	74	66	74	64
Average Age at Marriage	30.9	23.9	17.8	21.7	21.5
Fertility Rate (births per woman)	2.3	4.4	4.3	3.8	5.2
Contraceptive Prevalence Rate (%)	58	30	29.3	31.8	11.8
Maternal deaths per 100,000 live births	No data	No data	No data	23	690
Abortion Rate (number per 1,000 women)	No data	No data	No data	No data	No data
Abortion Law (Whether and under what conditions it is allowed)	To save the woman's life; fetal impairment; rape or incest; to preserve mental or physical health	To save the woman's life; to preserve mental or physical health	To save the woman's life	To save the woman's life; to preserve mental or physical health	To save the woman's life
Women's Employment to Population Ratio (age 15+)	No data	No data	No data	17	50.7
Women's Share of Legislators & Managers	No data	No data	No data	10	No data

Country	Serbia-Montenegro	Seychelles	Sierra Leone	Singapore	Slovakia
Location	Southeastern Europe, between Macedonia and Hungary	Archipelago in the Indian Ocean, northeast of Madagascar	Western Africa, bordering the North Atlantic Ocean, between Guinea and Liberia	Southeastern Asia, islands between Malaysia and Indonesia	Central Europe, south of Poland
Adult Literacy (% of 15–24 yr old women)	99.3	99.4	37.4	99.6	99
Life Expectancy	76	No data	43	81	78
Average Age at Marriage	23.1	24	19.8	26.5	25.4
Fertility Rate (births per woman)	1.7	No data	6.5	1.4	1.2
Contraceptive Prevalence Rate (%)	58.3	58	4.3	62	74
Maternal deaths per 100,000 live births	11	No data	2000	30	3
Abortion Rate (number per 1,000 women)	No data	21.6	No data	12.6	11.7
Abortion Law (Whether and under what conditions it is allowed)	On request	To save the woman's life; fetal impairment; rape or incest; to preserve mental or physical health	To save the woman's life; to preserve mental or physical health	On request	On request
Women's Employment to Population Ratio (age 15+)	42.6	No data	51.1	48	44.6
Women's Share of Legislators & Managers	35	No data	No data	31	31

Country	Slovenia	Soloman Islands	Somalia	South Africa	Spain
Location	Central Europe, eastern Alps bordering the Adriatic Sea, between Austria and Croatia	Oceania, group of islands in the South Pacific Ocean, east of Papua New Guinea	Eastern Africa, bordering the Gulf of Aden and the Indian Ocean, east of Ethiopia	Southern Africa, at the southern tip of the continent of Africa	Southwestern Europe, bordering the Bay of Biscay, Mediterranean Sea, North Atlantic Ocean, and Pyrenees Mountains, southwest of France
Adult Literacy (% of 15–24 yr old women)	99.9	No data	No data	94.3	99.6
Life Expectancy	80	63	47	56	83
Average Age at Marriage	29.8	21	20	27.9	26
Fertility Rate (births per woman)	1.2	4.4	6.2	2.8	1.3
Contraceptive Prevalence Rate (%)	73.8	11	1	56.3	80.9
Maternal deaths per 100,000 live births	17	130	1100	230	4
Abortion Rate (number per 1,000 women)	15.2	No data	No data	4.5	8.3
Abortion Law (Whether and under what conditions it is allowed)	On request	To save the woman's life	To save the woman's life	On request	To save the woman's life; fetal impairment; rape or incest; to preserve mental or physical health
Women's Employment to Population Ratio (age 15+)	50.4	51.9	53.6	31.4	39.7
Women's Share of Legislators & Managers	34	No data	No data	34	32

Country	Sri Lanka	Sudan	Suriname	Swaziland	Sweden
Location	Southern Asia, island in the Indian Ocean, south of India	Northern Africa, bordering the Red Sea, between Egypt and Eritrea	Northern South America, bordering the North Atlantic Ocean, between French Guiana and Guyana	Southern Africa, between Mozambique and South Africa	Northern Europe, bordering the Baltic Sea, Gulf of Bothnia, Kattegat, and Skagerrak, between Finland and Norway
Adult Literacy (% of 15–24 yr old women)	96.1	71.4	94.1	89.8	99
Life Expectancy	75	58	72	45	82
Average Age at Marriage	25.3	22.7	No data	26	32.3
Fertility Rate (births per woman)	2	4.8	2.6	3.5	1.7
Contraceptive Prevalence Rate (%)	70	9.9	42.1	0	No data
Maternal deaths per 100,000 live births	92	590	110	370	2
Abortion Rate (number per 1,000 women)	No data	No data	No data	No data	20.2
Abortion Law (Whether and under what conditions it is allowed)	To save the woman's life	To save the woman's life; rape or incest	To save the woman's life	To save the woman's life; fetal impairment; to preserve mental or physical health	On request
Women's Employment to Population Ratio (age 15+)	31.6	20.9	27	22.5	55.7
Women's Share of Legislators & Managers	24	No data	No data	No data	32

Country	Switzerland	Syria	Tajikistan	Tanzania	Thailand
Location	Central Europe, east of France, north of Italy	Middle East, bordering the Mediterranean Sea, between Lebanon and Turkey	Central Asia, west of China	Eastern Africa, bordering the Indian Ocean, between Kenya and Mozambique	Southeastern Asia, bordering the Andaman Sea and the Gulf of Thailand, south-east of Burma
Adult Literacy (% of 15–24 yr old women)	99	90.2	99.8	76.2	97.8
Life Expectancy	83	75	69	51	74
Average Age at Marriage	29.1	22	21.2	20.5	23.5
Fertility Rate (births per woman)	1.4	3.5	3.8	5.7	1.8
Contraceptive Prevalence Rate (%)	82	46.6	33.9	26.4	72.2
Maternal deaths per 100,000 live births	7	160	100	1500	44
Abortion Rate (number per 1,000 women)	7.3	No data	12.6	No data	No data
Abortion Law (Whether and under what conditions it is allowed)	On request	To save the woman's life	On request	To save the woman's life; to preserve mental or physical health	To save the woman's life; rape or incest; to preserve mental or physical health
Women's Employment to Population Ratio (age 15+)	58.1	31	41	82.7	65.2
Women's Share of Legislators & Managers	30	No data	No data	49	30

Country	Timor-Leste	Togo	Tonga	Trinidad & Tobago	Tunisia
Location	Southeastern Asia, northwest of Australia in the Lesser Sunda Islands at the eastern end of the Indonesian archipelago	Western Africa, bordering the Bight of Benin, between Benin and Ghana	Oceania, archipelago in the South Pacific Ocean, about two-thirds of the way from Hawaii to New Zealand	Caribbean, islands between the Caribbean Sea and the North Atlantic Ocean, northeast of Venezuela	Northern Africa, bordering the Mediterranean Sea, between Algeria and Libya
Adult Literacy (% of 15–24 yr old women)	No data	63.6	99.4	99.5	92.2
Life Expectancy	59	60	73	71	75
Average Age at Marriage	No data	21.3	25.5	26.8	26.6
Fertility Rate (births per woman)	7	5.4	3.7	1.6	1.9
Contraceptive Prevalence Rate (%)	10	25.7	33	38.2	62.6
Maternal deaths per 100,000 live births	660	570	No data	160	120
Abortion Rate (number per 1,000 women)	No data	No data	No data	No data	8.6
Abortion Law (Whether and under what conditions it is allowed)	No Data	To save the woman's life; fetal impairment; rape or incest	To save the woman's life	To save the woman's life; to preserve mental or physical health	On request
Women's Employment to Population Ratio (age 15+)	53.2	45.7	No data	43	24
Women's Share of Legislators & Managers	No data	No data	27	43	No data

Country	Turkey	Turkmenistan	Uganda	Ukraine	United Arab Emirates
Location	Southeastern Europe and Southwestern Asia bordering the Black Sea, between Bulgaria and Georgia, and bordering the Aegean Sea and the Mediterranean Sea, between Greece and Syria	Central Asia, bordering the Caspian Sea, between Iran and Kazakhstan	Eastern Africa, west of Kenya	Eastern Europe, bordering the Black Sea, between Poland, Romania, and Moldova in the west and Russia in the east	Middle East, bordering the Gulf of Oman and the Persian Gulf, between Oman and Saudi Arabia
Adult Literacy (% of 15–24 yr old women)	93.3	99.8	71.2	99	95.5
Life Expectancy	73	67	48	73	80
Average Age at Marriage	22	23.4	19.6	21.7	23.1
Fertility Rate (births per woman)	2.8	2.8	6.7	1.2	2.5
Contraceptive Prevalence Rate (%)	71	61.8	19.7	67.5	27.5
Maternal deaths per 100,000 live births	70	31	880	35	54
Abortion Rate (number per 1,000 women)	No data	No data	No data	27.5	No data
Abortion Law (Whether and under what conditions it is allowed)	On request	On request	To save the woman's life; to preserve mental or physical health	On request	To save the woman's life
Women's Employment to Population Ratio (age 15+)	25	54.3	78.1	46.4	39.3
Women's Share of Legislators & Managers	8	No data	33	39	10

Country	United Kingdom	United States	Uruguay	Uzbekistan	Vanatu
Location	Western Europe, islands including the northern one-sixth of the island of Ireland between the North Atlantic Ocean and the North Sea, northwest of France	North America, bordering both the North Atlantic Ocean and the North Pacific Ocean, between Canada and Mexico	Southern South America, bordering the South Atlantic Ocean, between Argentina and Brazil	Central Asia, north of Afghanistan	Oceania, group of islands in the South Pacific Ocean, about three-quarters of the way from Hawaii to Australia
Adult Literacy (% of 15–24 yr old women)	99	99	99	84	No data
Life Expectancy	81	80	79	70	70
Average Age at Marriage	26.4	26.3	23.3	20.6	22.6
Fertility Rate (births per woman)	1.7	2	2.2	2.7	4.2
Contraceptive Prevalence Rate (%)	84	72.9	84	67.7	28
Maternal deaths per 100,000 live births	13	17	27	24	No data
Abortion Rate (number per 1,000 women)	17	20.8	No data	7.8	No data
Abortion Law (Whether and under what conditions it is allowed)	To save the woman's life; fetal impairment; to preserve mental or physical health; economic or social reasons	On request	To save the woman's life; rape or incest; to preserve mental or physical health	On request	To save the woman's life; to preserve mental or physical health
Women's Employment to Population Ratio (age 15+)	53	57	51.4	51	No data
Women's Share of Legislators & Managers	34	43	40	No data	No data

Country	Venezuela	Vietnam	Yemen	Zambia	Zimbabwe
Location	Northern South America, bordering the Caribbean Sea and the North Atlantic Ocean, between Colombia and Guyana	Southeastern Asia, bordering the Gulf of Thailand, Gulf of Tonkin, and South China Sea, alongside China, Laos, and Cambodia	Middle East, bordering the Arabian Sea, Gulf of Aden, and Red Sea, between Oman and Saudi Arabia	Southern Africa, east of Angola	Southern Africa, between South Africa and Zambia
Adult Literacy (% of 15–24 yr old women)	98.1	93.6	58.9	66.2	97.9
Life Expectancy	76	75	62	39	40
Average Age at Marriage	22.1	22.1	20.7	21.1	21.1
Fertility Rate (births per woman)	2.7	2.3	6	5.6	3.6
Contraceptive Prevalence Rate (%)	70.3	78.5	23.1	34.2	53.5
Maternal deaths per 100,000 live births	96	130	570	750	1100
Abortion Rate (number per 1,000 women)	No data	35.2	No data	No data	No data
Abortion Law (Whether and under what conditions it is allowed)	To save the woman's life	On request	To save the woman's life	To save the woman's life; fetal impairment; to preserve mental or physical health; economic or social reasons	To save the woman's life; fetal impairment; rape or incest; to preserve physical health
Women's Employment to Population Ratio (age 15+)	48	70	26	60	61
Women's Share of Legislators & Managers	27	22	No data	19	No data

Glossary

Abortion   Surgical or chemical means of terminating a pregnancy.

Accidental activism   When women are drawn into politics because the safety and health of their families or communities is threatened.

AIDS   Acquired Autoimmune Deficiency Syndrome, a disease caused by the Human Immunodeficiency Virus (HIV) leading to a breakdown of the body's natural defenses and opportunistic infections.

Antinatalist policies   Government policies that seek to control population size by strongly encouraging or requiring that women limit their fertility; may involve persuasion, trickery, or force.

Beijing Platform for Action (BPFA)   An agreement from the UN Fourth World Conference on Women that identifies 12 critical areas of concern and specifies strategic objectives and specific actions for each area.

Benevolent sexism   A type of sexism that includes protective paternalism, complementary gender differentiation, and heterosexual intimacy and is more subtle than overt, hostile sexism.

Bible   The primary text of the Christian religion containing both Old and New Testaments.

Bilateral aid   Country-to-country development aid.

Biosocial (evolutionary) explanations   Explanations suggesting that male dominance and female submissiveness are genetically encoded because both contributed to the survival of the species.

Bride kidnapping   The practice of kidnapping a woman for purposes of forced marriage.

Brideprice (bridewealth or lobala)   A practice wherein the groom gives money, goods, or livestock to the parents of the bride in return for her hand in marriage.

Buddhism   A nontheistic religion based on the teachings of the Prophet Buddha in the fifth or sixth century; found throughout the world, especially in Asia.

Canon   A religion's scriptures and texts.

Care labor   Paid or unpaid labor focused on caring for children, the sick, or seniors.

CEDAW (1979 Convention on the Elimination of Discrimination Against Women)   An international bill of rights for women signed by the majority of UN member nations that defines gender discrimination and sets up an agenda for national action to end it.

CEDAW Committee   Monitors progress for women made in those countries that are the parties to the 1979 Convention on the Elimination of All Forms of Discrimination Against Women.

Chipko movement   A sustainable development GRO movement that began in India and uses passive resistance methods to stop environmentally destructive logging and mining.

Christianity   The Christian faith based on the life, death, and resurrection of Jesus Christ and on the Bible.

Commission on the Status of Women (CSW)   A UN body (part of the UN Economic and Social Council) dedicated to gender equality and the advancement of women that is responsible for monitoring the implementation of agreements from the Women's Conferences.

Comparable worth   The use of detailed classification systems to compare different jobs on skill, effort, responsibility, and working conditions so that compensation can be given accordingly.

Compulsory heterosexuality   The idea that societies "require" heterosexuality by giving women few economic options outside of marriage, and by hiding nonheterosexuality.

Concrete ceiling   The dual burden of racism and sexism in organizations; leads to low numbers of minority women in managerial positions.

Contextualize   When analyzing something, to consider how it is situated within multiple contexts (cultural, social, political, historical, economic).

Contraception Prevention of conception or impregnation through the use of various devices, agents, drugs, sexual practices, or surgical procedures.

Critical political mass The estimated 30 percent minimum for women in a legislative body necessary to exert a meaningful influence on politics.

Cultural globalization The transnational migration of people, information, and consumer culture.

Cultural relativism The notion that right and wrong are matters of culture and that there is no universal right or wrong.

Debt bondage The use of unlawful debt purportedly incurred through the transportation or recruitment of trafficked women and girls to force them to continue in prostitution.

Developing nation A less or nonindustrialized nation where poverty is the norm, health is poor, educational levels are low, and life expectancy is short. Also called *southern nations.*

Development The process of economic, political, or social growth in a nation.

Dianic witchcraft A feminist form of wicca that worships the female divine, mostly in all-female covens.

District magnitude The size of the multimember district; the number of seats in the district.

Domestic violence or **intimate partner violence (IPV)** Violence that includes bodily harm, usually accompanied by verbal threats and harassment, emotional abuse or the destruction of property as means of coercion, control, revenge, or punishment on a person with whom the abuser is in an intimate relationship.

Double jeopardy Refers to how minority women are at an increased risk for multiple forms of harassment because of their multiple minority status.

Dowry Money or goods given to the groom or his family by the bride's family.

Dowry murders The staged death of wives by husbands or in-laws so that the husband can remarry, also called *bride burnings* and *dowry deaths.*

Economic globalization The integration and rapid interaction of economies through production, trade, and financial transactions by banks and multinational corporations, with an increased role for the World Bank, International Monetary Fund (IMF), and World Trade Organization (WTO).

Electoral system The procedures by which representatives are elected (PR, SMD, or mixed).

Electoral system reform Changes in the procedures by which representatives are elected such as quotas or the adoption of PL/PR systems.

Empowerment The process by which women are able to advocate for their rights and have decision-making power in their public and private lives.

Female genital cutting (FGC) Procedures involving partial or total removal of the external female genitalia or other injury to the female genital organs for cultural or other nonmedical reasons; sometimes called *female genital mutilation* and *female circumcision.*

Feminism A variety of theories and approaches all committed to understanding and changing the structures that keep women lower in status and power.

Feminist economics Branch of economics that seeks to broaden the study of economics to include women's unpaid labor, women's labor in the informal sector, and the impact of economic policies on women.

Feminist hermeneutics Interpreting religions through a feminist lens with an emphasis on hermeneutics of suspicion, rememberance and historical reconstruction, proclamation, and creative actualization.

Feminist spirituality movement Variety of nonbiblical religions that include female images of the divine; also known as *women's spirituality movement.*

Feminist theology A study of religion that reconsiders the traditions, practices, scriptures, and theologies of religion from a feminist perspective with a commitment to transforming religion for gender equality.

Feminization of poverty Refers to the larger number of women in poverty, relative to the number of men.

Femocrats Feminist bureaucrats who work as part of government structures.

Forced concubinage The kidnapping of girls and women to wash, cook, serve, and have sex with soldiers and militia.

Forced marriage When girls or young women are forced by their parents to marry against their will or when they are kidnapped and raped so that they will have to marry.

Formal labor sector Official labor sector where people get a paycheck and pay taxes.

Formal politics Institutionalized politics such as voting, parliaments and congresses, and heads of state.

Free trade zones (FTZs) or **export processing zones (EPZs)**   Industrial zones with incentives (usually a relaxing of labor and environmental laws and tax breaks) to attract foreign investors.

Gender   The socially constructed roles, behavior, activities, and attributes a given society considers appropriate for males and females.

Gender and development approach (GAD)   Development approach that focuses explicitly on improving women's status, also called the *empowerment approach*.

Gender-based divisions of household labor   The tendency for women to do more of the core household tasks and child care.

Gender harassment   Type of sexual harassment characterized by verbal and nonverbal behavior that conveys insulting, hostile, and degrading attitudes toward women.

Gender health disparities   The ways in which health risks, experiences, and outcomes are different for females relative to males.

Gender identity   The psychological sense of being male or female.

Gender inequality   Women and girls' disadvantage relative to men and boys.

Gender mainstreaming   The inclusion of a gender perspective in all development activities; requires women's active participation in the development process.

Gender norms   Societal rules about how to behave as a function of gender.

Gender occupational segregation   Refers to the fact that employed women and men tend to work in different jobs and employment sectors and men hold the higher positions compared to women in the same job category.

Gender pay gap   The common gap between male and female earnings, with women generally receiving less pay.

Gender perspective on household labor   Explanation for gendered divisions of household labor because household labor is a symbolic representation of gender relations; household labor and child care are viewed as "women's work."

Gender-responsive budget analysis   Policy analyses examining how national budgets impact women and girls differently than men and boys.

Gender roles   Gender-based divisions of labor and social roles.

Gender-segregated religious practices   The notion that in most religions, women and men are expected to show their devotion to God differently; public religious roles and rituals are often designated as male.

Gender socialization   The processes by which gendered societal beliefs and expectations are instilled in us.

Gender stereotypes   Societal beliefs about how females and males are different.

Gender wage discrimination   The practice of paying women in the same jobs as men less just because they are women, because the skills associated with "women's jobs" are devalued, because it is assumed that a woman's income is supplemental to her husband's, or to maximize profits.

Gender wage gap   The common gap between male and female earnings; women generally receive less pay.

Genocidal rape   The practice of using rape to destroy an ethnic or political group perceived as the enemy.

Glass ceiling   The various barriers that prevent qualified women from advancing upward in their organizations into management power positions.

Global feminist movements   See *Transnational feminist movements.*

Global supply chains   A feature of economic globalization wherein different pieces of production are spread across geographic locations.

Global warming   Climate change resulting from the build-up of greenhouse gases as a result of human activities like deforestation and fossil fuel use.

Goddess spirituality   Pagan religions focused on goddess worship and based in the belief that humans lived in peace and harmony during a goddess-worshipping pre-history.

Government cabinets   The group of advisors to the head of state who frequently lead specific government agencies and wield considerable policy-making power.

Grassroots organizations (GROs)   Locally based groups that work to develop and improve the community.

Grassroots support organizations (GRSOs)   Nationally or regionally based development assistance organizations that channel funds to grassroots organizations and foster their development.

Greenbelt movement   A GRSO based in Kenya; organizes women to plant and manage trees for sustainable forestry use.

Hermeneutics   The principles of interpretation for religious texts.

Heteronormativity   The assumption that only heterosexuality is acceptable and normal.

Heteropatriarchy   Social structures, including laws, religion, and justice systems, that reinforce heterosexuality and traditional gender roles and make living as a nonheterosexual difficult.

Heterosexism   Bias in favor of heterosexuals and against nonheterosexuals.

Hinduism   A 6,000-year-old religion of India with numerous male and female deities.

Homophobia   Fear of nonheterosexuals.

Horizontal occupational segregation   The tendency for occupations with higher pay and status to be occupied by men.

Human capital approach   Idea that women get paid less because they are less skilled, less educated, or less experienced workers than men are.

Human trafficking   The acquisition of people by improper means such as force, fraud, or deception, with the aim of exploiting them.

Ideological or **cultural explanations for gender differences in political representation**   Ideas that explain gender differences in representative politics as arising from traditional gender ideologies and culture; affect the supply of and demand for women politicians.

Industrialized countries   Countries that have relatively high standards of material living, market economies, and advanced technologies; also called *developed countries* and *northern nations.*

Informal labor sector   "Under the table" and "off the books" employment such as small enterprises and trading and selling at markets.

Informal politics   Political actions including grassroots protests and political action organized by nongovernmental organizations.

Intersectional feminist theologies   Feminist theologies that deconstruct religion through the additional lenses of race, class, heterosexism, and colonialism and reconstruct religion for empowerment.

Intersex   A person who has chromosomal and anatomical features of both males and females.

Islam   Religion founded in the eighth century C.E., and based on the Prophet Muhammad's teachings.

Islamists   Muslim fundamentalists who use strict scriptural interpretations that restrict women and favor a state governed by religious law.

Islamization   The process by which states become governed by conservative forms of Islam.

Job prestige   The valuing of some types of work over others.

Judaism   The Jewish faith, which is based on study of the Torah and ritual practice as described in the Talmud.

Lack of fit model   Idea that a perceived lack of fit between female attributes and behaviors and the "male" attributes and behaviors believed necessary for success in powerful organizational positions, leads to the perception that women are ill-equipped for these positions.

Legal literacy   Knowledge of one's legal rights in the legal system.

Leisure gap   The common gap between the amount of leisure time women have relative to men; men have more leisure time.

Lesbian-baiting   The practice of accusing nonconforming women and women's activists of being lesbian to disempower them. See also *Sexuality-baiting.*

Lesbian and bisexual invisibility   The tendency for cultures to deny or hide the existence of lesbian and bisexual women and for such women to lead hidden lives.

Lesbian feminism   A variety of beliefs and practices connecting lesbianism and political resistance to patriarchy.

Lesbian separatism   A rare type of lesbian feminism emphasizing a complete rejection of patriarchy; may involve all-women communities and the avoidance of any relationship with men.

Liberation theology   Theology focused on freedom from oppression and the reduction of racism, classism, and sexism.

Macro power   Power in the economic and political or public sphere of life.

Mail-order and internet brides   Women who migrate to marry and use commercial organizations to arrange introductions and broker marriages with foreign men.

Masculine God-language   Religious language in scriptures, prayers, and liturgy that suggests God is male.

Maternity leave   Time off for mothers following the birth of a child.

Maternity protection measures   Policies and laws that ensure that pregnant employees will not face employment discrimination and will not be exposed to health hazards, that provide time off to have children and return to the job without discrimination, and that provide for breastfeeding breaks.

Maternal morbidity   Serious disease, disability, or physical damage such as fistula and uterine prolapse, caused by pregnancy-related complications.

Maternal mortality   The death of a woman while pregnant or within forty-two days of termination of pregnancy from any cause related to or aggravated by the pregnancy or its management.

Maternalism   Political activity that is an extension of women's role as wife and mother.

Microcredit   The extension of small loans to women in poverty for small-scale economic enterprises.

Micro power   Power in the home or private sphere of life.

Military sexploitation of women   Military support for its troops by sexually exploiting women.

Mixed system   An electoral system with PR systems in some regions of the country and a plurality/majority system in others.

Modernization theory   A traditional development approach focused on economic growth and a conversion to capitalist market economies.

Mujerista theology   A Latin American feminist liberation theology with the goal of liberating Latinas.

Multiculturalism   A perspective that emphasizes helping people to understand, accept, and value the cultural differences among groups, with the ultimate goal of reaping the benefits of diversity.

Multilateral aid   Development aid funded by international agencies such as the UNIFEM, the IMF, and the World Bank.

Native American Feminist Theology   Theology that challenges the patriarchal, colonial history of Native Americans and uses oral tribal history to recover women's voices in Native American religion.

Neocolonialism   When northern countries treat southern countries as pseudo-colonies, using them for raw materials and cash crops and controlling them through business corporations and lending.

Non-normative rape   Rape that is in violation of social norms for expected behavior.

Normative rape   Rape supported by social norms, often not investigated or punished; may include marital rape, punitive rape, war rape.

Northern countries   Industrialized nations in the Northern Hemisphere.

Obstetric fistula   A maternal disability arising from prolonged and obstructed labor; tears between the vaginal wall and bladder or rectum result in incontinence, infections, and ulcerations.

Opportunistic rape   Rape of women during wartime because men know it is unlikely they will face consequences.

Own-account workers   Self-employed women without employees.

Parliaments and congresses   National-level political bodies comprised of citizen representatives that create laws and policies; also called *national assemblies.*

Party list/proportional representation system (PL/PR)   Electoral system wherein parties receive seats in proportion to the votes they receive and party lists and multimember districts are common.

Party magnitude   The number of seats a party expects to win in a district.

Patriarchy   The idea that gender inequality is embedded in economic, political, cultural, and legal structures; a society in which men have greater power and status.

Political literacy   Knowledge of the processes required for political participation.

Political rape   Rape used to punish individuals, families, or communities that hold different political views.

Political surrogates   Women politicians who "stand-in" for a father or husband who was a national leader.

Polyandry   The practice of brothers sharing a wife.

Post-colonial theologies   Theologies that examine associations between religion and colonization, rediscover indigenous religions common before colonization, and reappropriate religion for empowerment and resistance.

Practical gender interests   A motivation for women's movements that arises out of concerns about an immediate issue facing women.

Private sphere   The domestic domain of the home.

Private use value   Unpaid labor for the use of the family.

Pronatalist policies   Government policies that seek to increase birth rates through the banning of contraception or abortion and providing government benefits based on family size.

Prostitution The selling of sexual services.

Psychoanalytic explanations Explanations suggesting that men's domination of women is rooted in unconscious motivations such as the envy or fear of women's bodies.

Public sphere The public domain outside of the home.

Public use value (exchange value) Labor exchanged for goods or money.

Queer theory A perspective favoring the abandonment of gender and sexual orientation categories and focusing on challenging heteronormativity.

Quotas When an electoral system or party requires that a certain number of seats be reserved for women in a parliament or congress, or a certain percentage of party candidates are required to be women.

Qu'ran The primary text of the religion of Islam (also spelled **Koran**).

Rape Sexual intercourse without the victim's choice or consent.

Relative resources perspective on household labor Idea that women do more household labor to make up for their smaller monetary contribution to the household.

Religious fundamentalisms Religions that are committed to the infallibility of scriptures, that see traditional gender roles as divinely mandated, and are antagonistic toward feminism.

Remittances Money sent home by migrant workers.

Reproductive choice The extent to which women can freely choose from a variety of birth control methods.

Reproductive health Health topics including family planning, reproductive tract infections and cancers, infertility, maternal mortality, morbidity, abortion, and female genital cutting.

Reproductive rights The right to reproductive health care and the right to reproductive self-determination.

Role congruity theory The idea that we are less likely to assign people to roles that call for qualities associated with the other gender.

Second shift Term describing how employed women frequently work one shift in paid work and another shift doing household labor before or after paid work.

Sex A person's biological maleness or femaleness as determined by chromosomes and sex organs.

Sex-role spillover theory Idea that sexual harassment occurs because traditional gender expectations and relationships overflow into the workplace although they are irrelevant or inappropriate.

Sex-selective abortion Aborting a female fetus because a son is desired.

Sex trafficking A form of human trafficking that pulls women and girls into prostitution against their will.

Sexual coercion *or* **quid pro quo sexual harassment** Type of sexual harassment in which sex is required as a condition of employment or job rewards.

Sexual exploitation or sexual objectification The use of women as sexual objects for financial gain or pleasure without regard to them as people; the reduction of women to their bodies.

Sexual harassment Unwelcome sexual advances or verbal or physical conduct of a sexual nature that has the purpose or effect of unreasonably interfering with the individual's work performance or creating an intimidating, hostile, abusive or offensive working environment.

Sexual orientation A person's sexual desire for people of the other gender, the same gender, or both.

Sexual rights Human rights related to sexuality; the rights of people to make personal decisions about their sexuality and sexual activity.

Sexual tourism Tourism based on the travel of men from northern countries to southern countries to have cheap sex with women and children.

Sexuality-baiting Questioning an activist's or nonconforming person's sexuality to disempower them; includes calling women "whores," "bad mothers," or "lesbians."

Shari'ah (or sharia) Islamic law based on sayings attributed to Muhammad; often conservative and supportive of traditional gender roles.

Single-member district system Electoral system in which the winning candidate is the one with the most votes and there is only one seat per district.

Social roles theory A theory that postulates a reciprocal relationship between gender stereotypes and gender roles and that suggests gender is "dynamic."

Sociocultural explanations Explanations emphasizing that gendered power relations are socially constructed and maintained.

Son preference Valuing male children over female children.

Southern countries Developing nations in the Southern Hemisphere.

State feminism Government structures such as bureaus and agencies that are charged with addressing women's issues and equality.

Strategic gender interests A motivation for women's movements that arises out of a desire to bring about large-scale gender social change.

Structural adjustment programs (SAPs) Government "belt-tightening" measures typically entailing cuts for social services, schools, hospitals, public transportation, and utilities; often required as a condition of lending.

Structural or institutional explanations for gender differences in political representation Explanations that focus on how the structure of the political system, in particular, the electoral system, affect women's presence in representative politics.

Sweatshops Businesses that do not provide a living wage, require excessively long work hours, and provide poor working conditions with many health and safety hazards; common in EPZs.

Sustainable development Meets the needs of the present without compromising the ability of future generations to meet their own needs.

Talmud Sixty-three volumes of legal and theological teachings centering on the meaning of the Torah and the practice of Judaism; in addition to the Torah, one of the most important Jewish texts.

Time availability perspective on household labor Explains gendered divisions of household labor by suggesting that women have more time to perform household tasks due to less time in the paid workforce.

Time-use surveys Labor surveys providing gender-disaggregated information on how people spend their time in both market and nonmarket work.

Torah The first five chapters of the Old Testament that make up one of the two most important Jewish texts.

Transgender Term that describes persons whose gender identity or expression differs from conventional expectation or does not match their assigned gender.

Trafficking of women and girls The recruitment, transportation, harboring, or receipt of women and girls for purposes of slavery, forced labor, and servitude.

Transnational feminisms Feminisms that cut across cultures and unite women's struggles from many parts of the world.

Transnational feminist movements Women's movements spanning across multiple nations to resist gender inequalities, influence policymaking, and insert a feminist perspective in transnational advocacy and activism.

Transnational feminist networks (TFNs) The organizational expression of the transnational feminist movement.

Tripartite model of sexual harassment Postulates three behavioral dimensions of sexual harassment: gender harassment, unwanted sexual attention, and sexual coercion.

United Nations Decade for Women A period (1975–1985) when the UN gathered data about the status of women and held three world women's conferences (1975–Mexico City; 1980–Copenhagen, Denmark; 1985–Nairobi, Kenya) that promoted transnational feminist activism.

Universal human rights Inalienable rights possessed by virtue of being human such as rights to life, liberty, and security of person.

Unwanted sexual attention Type of sexual harassment characterized by suggestive comments about a woman's body; unsolicited and unreciprocated sexual advances such as repeated requests for a kiss, a date, or sex.

Uterine prolapse A condition in which the supporting pelvic structure of muscles, tissue, and ligaments gives way, and the uterus drops into or even out of the vagina.

Vedas The primary Hindu scriptures.

Vertical occupational segregation Explains the pay gap by noting that even when men and women have the same occupation, women tend to be represented in lower ranks than men within the same occupation.

Vienna Declaration and Programme of Action A 1993 UN declaration resulting from transnational feminist activism that linked women's rights to human rights, documented women's rights abuses in five areas, and provided recommendations for their reduction.

Wicca Form of earth-based, magical, feminist spirituality based on wiccan (witchcraft) traditions.

Womanist theology An African American Christian feminist liberation theology reflecting Black women's social, religious, and cultural experiences.

Womanspaces   The "female-only" spaces provided by traditional religions; potentially a source of power, sharing, and integrity for women.

Women and Development (WAD)   Development approach focusing on women's empowerment and their involvement in the development process.

Women in development (WID)   Development approach that includes women through income-generating projects, labor-saving technologies, and improving women's local resource access.

Women's micro- and small-scale enterprises (WMSEs)   Small-scale business run by women in the informal labor sector.

Women's movement   The sum of campaigns by groups and associations using a variety of tactics, disruptive or conventional, to change women's position in society.

Women's rights as human rights perspective   A perspective emphasizing that regardless of culture, women and men are equally deserving of rights and freedoms; views abuses against women as human rights violations.

Women's suffrage   A name for women's voting rights.

Zipper quotas   The alternating of equal numbers of women and men on party electoral lists.

References

Abdullah, H. 1995. Wifeism and activism: The Nigerian women's movements. In *The challenge of local feminisms: Women's movements in global perspective,* edited by A. Basu. Boulder, CO: Westview Press.

Abukhalil, A. 1994. Women and electoral politics in Arab states. In *Electoral systems in comparative perspective: Their impact on women and minorities,* edited by W. Rule and J. F. Zimmerman. Westport, CT: Greenwood Press.

ACCION. 2009. ACCION http://www.accion.org Retrieved on August 4, 2009.

Acevedo, L. 1995. Feminist inroads in the study of women's work and development. In *Women in the Latin American development process,* edited by C. E. Bose and E. Acosta-Belen. Philadelphia: Temple University Press.

Acosta-Belen, E., and C. E. Bose 1995. Colonialism, structural subordination, and empowerment: Women in the development process in Latin America and the Caribbean. In *Women in the Latin American development process,* edited by C. E. Bose and E. Acosta-Belen. Philadelphia: Temple University Press.

Adams, G. 2009. Brazil rocked by abortion for 9-year-old rape victim; Church excommunicates mother and doctors—but not accused rapist. *The Independent (London),* 9 March, p. 20.

Adams, J. 2009. More Filipinos question birth-control taboo: A bill to provide contraception is the first to reach House debate in this largely Roman Catholic country. *Christian Science Monitor,* 10 March. http://www.csmonitor.com/2009/0310/p07s02-woap.html

Adams, M. 2008. Liberia's election of Ellen Johnson-Sirleaf and women's executive leadership in Africa. *Politics and Gender, 4,* 475–484.

Africa News. 2008. Nigeria; Women protest delay in conduct of LG poll. October 7.

———. 2009. Nigeria; Women protest half-nude over election results. April 30.

Afshar, H. 1991. *Women, development, and survival in the Third World.* New York: Longman.

———. 1996. Islam and feminism: An analysis of political strategies. In *Feminism and Islam: Legal and literary perspectives,* edited by M. Yamani. New York: New York University Press.

Ahmed, L. 2002. Gender and literacy in Islam. In *Nothing sacred: Women respond to religious fundamentalism and terror,* edited by B. Reed. New York: Thunder's Mouth Press/Nation Books.

Alice Paul Institute. 2009. *Alice Paul: Feminist, suffragist and political strategist.* http://www.alicepaul.org/alicepaul.htm Retrieved on September 29, 2009.

Allen, P. G. 1992. *The sacred hoop: Recovering the feminine in American Indian traditions.* Boston: Beacon Press.

Alvarez, S. E. 1994. The (trans)formation of feminism(s) and gender politics in Brazil. In *The women's movement in Latin America: Participation and democracy,* 2d ed., edited by J. S. Jaquette. Boulder, CO: Westview Press.

American Psychological Association. (2009a). *Lesbian & gay parenting.* Washington, DC: Author.

American Psychological Association. (2009b). *Answers to your questions for a better understanding of sexual orientation and homosexuality.* http://www.apa.org/topics/sorientation.pdf Retrieved on July 14, 2009.

Amin R., and Y. Li. 1997. NGO-promoted women's credit program, immunization coverage, and child mortality in rural Bangladesh. *Women and Health, 25.*

Amnesty International. 1990. *Women in the front line: Human rights violations against women.* New York: Author.

———. 2006. Mexico: Killings and abductions of women in Ciudad Juarez and the City of Chihuahua—the struggle for justice goes on. http://www.amnestyusa.org/document.php?id=engamr410122006&lang=e Retrieved on April 4, 2009.

———. 2007a. *Iraq: Amnesty International appalled by stoning to death of Yezidi girl and subsequent killings.* http://www.amnesty.org/en/library/info/MDE14/027/2007. Retrieved on April 4, 2009.

———. 2007b. *Burundi: No protection from rape in war and peace.* http://www.amnesty.org/en/library/info/AFR16/002/2007/en Retrieved on April 4, 2009.

———. 2008a. *Amnesty International International Report 2008.* http://archive.amnesty.org/air2008/eng/regions/europe-and-central-asia/czech-republic.html Retrieved on March 31, 2009.

———. 2008b. Iran: Women's rights defenders defy oppression. http://www.amnesty.org/en/library/asset/MDE13/018/2008/en/63dd8933-e16d-11dc-9135-058f98b1fb80/mde130182008eng.pdf Retrieved on September 30, 2009.

———. 2009. Iran: Women's rights activist and lawyer violently arrested - NEWS FLASH. http://www.amnesty.org/en/for-media/press-releases/iran-women039s-rights-activist-and-lawyer-violently-arrested-news-flash- Retrieved on September 30, 2009.

Anand, A. 1993. *The power to change: Women in the Third World redefine their environment.* London: Zed.

Anderson, B. 2002. Just another job? The commodification of domestic labor. In *Global woman: Nannies, maids, and sex workers in the new economy,* edited by B. Ehrenreich and A. R. Hochschild. New York: Metropolitan Books.

Anderson, J. 1994. Separatism, feminism, and the betrayal of reform. *Signs,* Winter, 437–448.

Anderson, K. J., M. Kanner, & N. Elsayegh. 2009. Are feminists man haters? Feminists' and nonfeminists' attitudes toward men, *Psychology of Women Quarterly, 33,* 216–224.

Anderson, N. F. 1993. Benazir Bhutto and dynastic politics: Her father's daughter, her people's sister. In *Women as national leaders,* edited by M. A. Genovese. Newbury Park, CA: Sage.

Andrews, M. 2008. Questioning women's movement strategies: Australian activism on work and care. *Social Politics: International Studies in Gender, State, and Society, 15,* 369–395.

Anwar, G. 1999. Reclaiming the religious center from a Muslim perspective: Theological alternatives to religious fundamentalism. In *Religious fundamentalisms and the human rights of women,* edited by C. W. Howland. New York: St. Martin's Press.

Apostolidis, S., and R. Ferguson. 2009. *Catalyst's report to women in capital markets: Benchmarking 2008.* http://www.catalyst.org/publication/88/catalysts-report-to-women-in-capital-markets-benchmarking-2008 Retrieved on July 23, 2009.

Armstrong, K. 2002. Fundamentalism. In *Nothing sacred: Women respond to religious fundamentalism and terror,* edited by B. Reed. New York: Thunder's Mouth Press/Nation Books.

Armstrong, S. 2003. Not my daughter: Villages in Senegal say no to female cutting. *Ms.,* Summer, 22–23.

Arthur, R. H. 1987. The wisdom goddess and the masculinization of western religion. In *Women in the world's religions, past and present,* edited by U. King. New York: Paragon House.

As, B. 1996. Norway: More power to women. In *Sisterhood is global,* edited by R. Morgan. New York: Feminist Press.

Atchison, A., and I. Down. 2009. Women cabinet ministers and female friendly social policy. *Poverty and Public Policy, 1,* 1–23.

Aulette, J. R. 1999. New roads to resistance: Polish feminists in the transition to democracy. In *Democratization and women's grassroots movements,* edited by J. M. Bystydzienski and J. Sekhon. Bloomington: Indiana University Press.

Avishai, O. 2008. Doing religion in a secular world: Women in conservative religions. *Gender and Society, 22,* 409–433.

AWID. 2009. Ugandan LGBTI activists challenge hostile climate. http://www.awid.org/eng/Issues-and-Analysis/Library/Ugandan-LGBTI-activists-challenge-hostile-climate/(language)/eng-GB Retrieved on August 5, 2009.

AWID (Association for Women's Rights in Development). 2009. Iran: Women's rights activist Shadi Sadr violently abducted. http://www.awid.org/eng/Issues-and-Analysis/Library/Iran-Women-s-rights-activist-Shadi-Sadr-violently-abducted Retrieved on September 30, 2009.

Bachofen, J. J. 1967. *Myth, religion, and mother right.* Princeton, NJ: Princeton University Press.

Baker, C. N. 2005. *The women's movement against sexual harassment.* Cambridge: Cambridge University Press.

Bales, K. 2002. Because she looks like a child. In *Global woman: Nannies, maids, and sex workers in the new economy,* edited by B. Ehrenreich and A. R. Hochschild. New York: Metropolitan Books.

Bancroft, A. 1987. Women in Buddhism. In *Women in the world's religions, past and present,* edited by U. King. New York: Paragon House.

Bandura, A. 1986. *Social foundations of thought and action.* Englewood Cliffs, NJ: Prentice-Hall.

Barlas, A. 2002. *Believing women in Islam: Unreading patriarchal interpretions of the Qu'ran.* Austin: University of Texas Press.

Barnes, N. S. 1987. Buddhism. In *Women in world religions,* edited by A. Sharma. Albany: State University of New York Press.

———. 1994. Women in Buddhism. In *Today's woman in world religions*, edited by A. Sharma. Albany: State University of New York Press.

Baron, J. N., A. Davis-Blake, and W. T. Bielby. 1986. The structure of opportunity: How promotion ladders vary within and among organizations. *Administrative Science Quarterly, 31,* 248–273.

Barry, K. 1995. *The prostitution of sexuality.* New York: New York University Press.

Barstow, A. L. 1994. *Witchcraze: A new history of the European witch hunts.* New York: HarperCollins.

Bas, N. F., Benjamin, M., and Chang, J. C. 2004. Saipan sweatshop lawsuit ends with important gains for workers and lessons for activists. http://www.cleanclothes.org/about-us/617-saipan-sweatshop-lawsuit-ends-with-important-ga Retrieved on August 17, 2009.

Basu, A., ed. 1995. *The challenge of local feminisms: Women's movements in global perspective.* Boulder, CO: Westview.

Batalova, J. A., and P. N. Cohen. 2002. Premarital cohabitation and housework: Couples in cross-national perspective. *Journal of Marriage and the Family, 64,* 743–756.

Bay-Cheng, L. Y., and A. N. Zucker. 2007. Feminism between the sheets: Sexual attitudes among feminists, non-feminists, and egalitarians. *Psychology of Women Quarterly, 31,* 157–163.

Bazar, E. 2007. Iranian women take key role in protest; calls for equality during election energized many. *USA Today,* June 25, 4A.

BBC News. 2002. Nigerian women's oil protest ends. 25 July. http://news.bbc.co.uk/1/hi/world/africa/2152264.stm Retrieved on June 29, 2003.

Bem, S. L. 1993. *The lenses of gender: Transforming the debate on sexual inequality.* New Haven, CT: Yale University Press.

Benedict, R. 2009. *The lonely soldier: The private war of women serving in Iraq.* Boston: Beacon Press.

Beneria, L. 1998. On paid and unpaid work. *Radcliffe Quarterly.* Fall.

Beneria, L., and M. Roldan. 1987. *The crossroads of class and gender: Industrial homework, subcontracting, and household dynamics in Mexico City.* Chicago: University of Chicago Press.

Bennett, K. 1992. Feminist bisexuality: A both/and option for an either/or world. In *Closer to home: Bisexuality and feminism,* edited by E. R. Weise. Seattle, WA: Seal Press.

Berdahl, J. L., and C. Moore. 2006. Workplace harassment: Double-jeopardy for minority women. *Journal of Applied Psychology, 91,* 426–436.

Berger, M. 1995. Key issues on women's access to and use of credit in the micro- and small-scale enterprise sector. In *Women in micro- and small-scale enterprise development,* edited by L. Divard and J. Havet. Boulder, CO: Westview Press.

Bergmann, B. R. 1989. Does the market for women's labor need fixing? *Journal of Economic Perspectives, 3,* 43–60.

Bernard, J. 1987. *The female world from a global perspective.* Bloomington: Indiana University Press.

Bernstein, S. 2000. Persistence brought abortion pill to U.S. *Los Angeles Times,* 5 November, A1, A24.

Bhatnagar, D. 1988. Professional women in organizations: New paradigms for research and action. *Sex Roles, 18,* 343–355.

Bhatt, E. 1995. Women and development alternatives: Micro- and-small-scale enterprises in India. In *Women in micro- and-small-scale enterprise development,* edited by L. Divard and J. Havet. Boulder, CO: Westview Press.

Bianchi, S., M. A. Milkie., L. C. Sayer, and J. P. Robinson. 2000. Is anyone doing the housework? Trends in the gender division of household labor. *Social Forces, 79,* 191–229.

Blackwood, E. 1984. Sexuality and gender in certain Native American tribes: The case of cross-gender females. *Signs, 10,* 27–42.

Blackwood, E. 1986. Breaking the mirror: The construction of lesbianism and the anthropological discourse on homosexuality. In *The many faces of homosexuality: Anthropological approaches to homosexual behavior,* edited by E. Blackwood. New York: Harrington Park.

Blackwood, E., and Wieringa, S. 1999. *Female desires: Same-sex relations and transgender practices across cultures.* New York: Columbia University Press.

———. 2007. Globalization, sexuality, and silences: Women's sexualities and masculinities in an Asian context. In *Women's sexualities and masculinities in a globalizing Asia,* edited by S. E. Wieringa, E. Blackwood, and A. Bhaiya. New York: Palgrave Macmillan.

Blau, F. D., and M. A. Ferber. 1987. Occupations and earnings of women work. In *Working women: Past, present, future,* edited by K. S. Koziara, M. H. Moskow, and L. D. Tanner. Washington, DC: BNA Books.

Blau, F. D., and L. M. Kahn 1996. Wage structure and gender earnings differentials: An international comparison. *Economica, 63,* 529–562.

Blaydes, L., and S. El Tarouty. 2009. Women electoral participation in Egypt: The implications of gender for voter recruitment and mobilization. *Middle East Journal, 63,* 364–380.

Blumberg, R. L. 1991. Income under female versus male control: Hypotheses from a theory of gender stratification and data from the Third World. In *Gender, family, and economy: The triple overlap*, edited by R. L. Blumberg. Newbury Park, CA: Sage.

———. 1995. Gender, microenterprise, performance, and power: Case studies from the Dominican Republic, Ecuador, Guatemala, and Swaziland. In *Women in the Latin American development process*, edited by C. E. Bose and E. Acosta-Belen. Philadelphia: Temple University Press.

Blumstein P., and P. Schwartz. 1991. In *Gender, family, and economy: The triple overlap*, edited by R. L. Blumberg. Newbury Park, CA: Sage.

Boden, A. L. 2007. *Women's rights and religious practice: Claims in conflict*. New York: Palgrave Macmillan.

Bonder, G., and M. Nari. 1995. The 30 percent quota law: A turning point for women's political participation in Argentina. In *A rising public voice: Women in politics worldwide*, edited by A. Brill. New York: Feminist Press.

Bonvillian, N. 2001. Women and men: Cultural constructs of gender, 3d ed. Upper Saddle River, NJ: Prentice Hall.

Booth, W. 2008. Democracy in Nicaragua in peril. *Washington Post.* November 20. A2.

Bornstein, R. F. 2006. The complex relationship between dependency and domestic violence. *American Psychologist, 61,* 595–606.

Boserup, E. 1970. *Women's role in economic development*. New York: St. Martin's Press.

Boston Women's Health Collective. 1992. *The new our bodies, ourselves*. New York: Simon and Schuster.

Boucher, S. 2006. The way of the elders: Theravada Buddhism, including the Vipassana movement. In *Encyclopedia of women and religion in North America (Vol. 2),* edited by R. S. Keller, R. R. Ruether, and M. Canton. Bloomington: Indiana University Press.

Boudreau, V. G. 1995. Corazon Aquino: Gender, class, and the people power president. In *Women in world politics: An introduction,* edited by F. D'Amico and P. R. Beckman. Westport, CT: Bergin and Garvey.

Boyenge, J. S. 2007. *ILO database on export processing zones (Revised)*. Geneva: International Labour Organization.

Brandiotti, R., E. Charkiewicz, S. Hausler, and S. Wieringa. 1994. *Women, the environment, and sustainable development*. Santo Domingo, Dominican Republic: INSTRAW.

Braude, A. 2006. Religions and modern feminism. In *Encyclopedia of women and religion in North America (Vol. 1),* edited by R. S. Keller, R. R. Ruether, and M. Canton. Bloomington: Indiana University Press.

Braun, S. 1998. Mitsubishi to pay $34 million in sex harassment case. *Los Angeles Times,* 12 June, A1, A18, A19.

Brennan, D. 2002. Selling sex for visas: Sex tourism as a stepping stone to international migration. In *Global woman: Nannies, maids, and sex workers in the new economy,* edited by B. Ehrenreich and A. R. Hochschild. New York: Metropolitan Books.

———. 2004. *Transnational desires and sex tourism in the Dominican Republic: What's love got to do with it?* Durham, NC: Duke University Press.

Bryant, E. 2003. Glass ceiling thrives in French politics. *United Press International,* 14 October.

Bryceson, D. F. 1995. Wishful thinking: Theory and practice of western donor efforts to raise women's status in rural Africa. In *Women wielding the hoe: Lessons for feminist theory and development practice,* edited by D. F. Bryceson. Oxford: Berg Publishers.

Brownmiller, S. 1986. *Against our will*. New York: Simon and Schuster.

Buchanan, N. T., and L. F. Fitzgerald. 2008. Effects of racial and sexual harassment at work and the psychological well-being of African American women. *Journal of Occupational Health Psychology, 13,* 137–151.

Buchanan, N. T., Settles, I. H., and K. C. Woods. 2008. Comparing sexual harassment subtypes among Black and White women by military rank. *Psychology of Women Quarterly, 32,* 347–361.

Budapest, Z. 1976. *Feminist book of lights and shadows*. Venice, CA: Feminist Wicca.

———. 1989. *Holy book of women's mysteries: Feminist witchcraft, goddess rituals, spellcasting, and other womanly arts*. Berkeley, CA: Wingbow Press Book People.

Bullock, S. 1994. *Women and work*. London: Zed.

Bumiller, E. 1990. *May you be the mother of a hundred sons: A journey among the women of India*. New York: Random House.

Bunch, C. 1993. Prospects for global feminism. In *Feminist frameworks*, 3rd ed., edited by A. M. Jaggar and P. S. Rothenberg. New York: McGraw-Hill.

———. 1995. Transforming human rights from a feminist perspective. In *Women's rights, human rights: International feminist perspectives,* edited by J. Peters and A. Wolper. New York: Routledge.

———. 2007. Women and gender: The evolution of women specific institutions and gender integration at the United Nations. http://www.cwgl.rutgers.edu/globalcenter/charlotte/UNHandbook.pdf Retrieved on October 28, 2009.

Bunch, C., and S. Frost. 2000. Women's human rights: An introduction. http://www.cwgl.rutgers.edu/globalcenter/whr.html Retrieved on March 10, 2003.

Burn, S. M., and J. Busso. 2005. Ambivalent sexism, scriptural literalism, and religiosity. *Psychology of Women Quarterly, 29,* 412–418.

Buss, D. M., and M. Barnes. 1986. Preferences in human mate selection. *Journal of Personality and Social Psychology, 50,* 559–570.

Butler, J. 1990. *Gender trouble: Feminism and the subversion of identity.* New York: Routledge.

Buvinic, M. 1995. Women's income generation activities in Latin America and the Caribbean: A commentary. In *Seeds 2,* edited by A. Leonard. New York: Feminist Press.

Bystydzienski, J. M. 1992a. Introduction. In *Women transforming politics: Worldwide strategies for empowerment,* edited by J. Bystydzienski. Bloomington: Indiana University Press.

———. 1992b. Influence of women's culture on public policies in Norway. In *Women transforming politics: Worldwide strategies for empowerment,* edited by J. Bystydzienski. Bloomington: Indiana University Press.

———. 1994. Norway: Achieving world-record women's representation in government. In *Electoral systems in comparative perspective: Their impact on women and minorities,* edited by W. Rule and J. F. Zimmerman. Westport, CT: Greenwood Press.

———. 1995. *Women in electoral politics: Lessons from Norway.* Westport, CT: Praeger.

Cabezas, A. L. 2002. Tourism, sex work, and women's rights in the Dominican Republic. In *Globalization and human rights,* edited by A. Brysk. Berkeley: University of California Press.

Cantor, A. 1995. *Jewish women, Jewish men: The legacy of patriarchy in Jewish life.* New York: Harper and Row.

Carillo, R. 1992. *Battered dreams: Violence against women as an obstacle to Development.* New York: UNIFEM.

Carmody, D. L. 1974. *Women and world religions.* Nashville: Parthenon Press.

———. 1979. *Women and world religions.* Nashville: Abingdon.

Carras, M. C. 1995. Indira Gandhi: Gender and foreign policy. In *Women in world politics: An introduction,* edited by F. D'Amico and P. R. Beckman. Westport, CT: Bergin and Garvey.

Catalyst. 2009. *Women of color/visible minorities.* http://www.catalyst.org/app Retrieved on July 21, 2009.

Cath. 1995. Country report on lesbians in India. In *Unspoken rules: Sexual orientation and women's human rights,* edited by R. Rosenbloom. San Francisco: International Gay and Lesbian Human Rights Commission.

Catholics for Choice. 2009. *Religious freedom and Catholic health care.* http://www.catholicsforchoice.org/topics/healthcare/religiousfreedomcatholichealthcare.asp Retrieved on May 9, 2009.

Cavin, S. 1985. *Lesbian origins.* San Francisco: Ism Press.

CDC (Center for Disease Control) Office of Minority Health and Health Disparities. 2009. *About minority health.* http://www.cdc.gov/omhd/AMH/AMH.htm Retrieved on May 16, 2009.

CDC. 2006. Understanding intimate partner violence. http://www.cdc.gov/ViolencePrevention/pdf/IPV-FactSheet.pdf Retrieved on April 12, 2009.

Cejka, M.A., and A. H. Eagly. 1999. Gender-stereotypic images of occupations correspond to the sex segregation of employment. *Personality and Social Psychology Bulletin, 25,* 413–423.

Center for American Women in Politcs. 2008. *The gender gap: Voting choices in presidential elections.* http://www.cawp.rutgers.edu/fast_facts/voters/documents/GGPresVote.pdf Retrieved on September 13, 2009.

Center for Reproductive Rights. 2005a. *Safe abortion: A public health imperative.* http://reproductiverights.org/sites/crr.civicactions.net/files/documents/pub_bp_tk_safe_abortion.pdf Retrieved on April 24, 2009.

———. 2005b. *Setting the record straight: The facts on some popular myths about abortion.* New York: Center for Reproductive Rights. http://reproductiverights.org/en/document/setting-the-record-straight-the-facts-on-some-popular-myths-about-abortion Retrieved on April 26, 2009.

———. 2006. *Gaining ground: A tool for reproductive rights law reform.* New York: Center for Reproductive Rights. http://reproductiverights.org/sites/crr.civicactions.net/files/documents/pub_bp_tk_myths.pdf Retrieved on April 27, 2009.

———. 2008a. *Female Genital Mutilation (FGM): Legal Prohibitions Worldwide.* http://reproductiverights.org/en/document/female-genital-mutilation-fgm-legal-prohibitions-worldwide Retrieved on March 26, 2009.

———. 2008b. *World abortion laws 2008 fact sheet.* http://reproductiverights.org/en/document/world-abortion-laws-2008-fact-sheet Retrieved on April 25, 2009.

———. 2009a. *Addressing disparities in reproductive and sexual health care in the U.S.* http://reproductiverights.org/en/node/861 Retrieved on April 26, 2009.

———. 2009b. *Court orders Nepal to improve women's access to abortion.* http://reproductiverights.org/en/press-room/court-orders-nepal-to-improve-women%E2%80%99s-access-to-abortion Retrieved on April 26, 2009.

———. 2009c. *Bringing rights to bear: Abortion and human rights.* http://reproductiverights.org/en/document/bringing-rights-to-bear-abortion-and-human-rights Retrieved on April 26, 2009.

Chafetz, J. S. 1990. *Gender equity: An integrated theory of stability and change.* Newbury Park, CA: Sage.

———. 1991. The gender division of labor and the reproduction of female disadvantage: Toward an integrated theory. In *Gender, family, and economy: The triple overlap,* edited by R. L. Blumberg. Newbury Park, CA: Sage.

Chan, D. K-S., Lam, C. B., Chow, S. Y., and S. F. Cheung. 2008. Examining the job-related, psychological, and physical outcomes of workplace sexual harassment: A meta-analytic review. *Psychology of Women Quarterly, 32,* 362–376.

Chan, K-S., C. S-K. Tang, and W. Chan. 1999. Sexual harassment: A preliminary analysis of its effects on Hong Kong Chinese women in the workplace and academia. *Psychology of Women Quarterly, 23,* 661–672.

Chang, G. 2000. *Disposable domestics.* Cambridge, MA: South End Press.

Chant, S. 1997. Female employment in Puerto Vallarta: A case study. In *Gender, work, and tourism,* edited by M. T. Sinclair. London: Routledge.

Chant, S. 2003. *Gender in Latin America.* New Brunswick, NJ: Rutgers University Press.

Charles, M., and D. B. Grusky. 2004. *Occupational ghettos: The worldwide segregation of women and men.* Stanford, CA: Stanford University Press.

Charlesworth, H. 1994. What are "women's international human rights"? In *Human rights of women,* edited by R. Cook. Philadelphia: University of Pennsylvania Press.

———. 1995. Human rights as men's rights. In *Women's rights, human rights: International feminist perspectives,* edited by J. Peters and A. Wolper. New York: Routledge.

———. 2005. Not waving but drowning: Gender mainstreaming and human rights in the United Nations. *Harvard Human Rights Journal, 18,* 1–18.

Charlesworth, H., Chinkin C., and Wright, S. 1991. Feminist approaches to international law. *The American Journal of International Law,* 85, 613–645.

Chesler, P. 1996. What is justice for a rape victim? *On the Issues,* Winter, 12–16, 56–57.

———. 2008. The Women of the Wall: Twenty years on. *Jewcy,* November 30. http://www.jewcy.com/post/women_wall_twenty_years Retrieved on August 29, 2009.

———. 2009. Are honor killings simply domestic violence? *Middle East Quarterly, Spring,* 61–69.

Chinchilla, N. S. 1994. Feminism, revolution, and democratic transitions in Nicaragua. In *The women's movement in Latin America: Participation and democracy,* edited by J. S. Jaquette. 2d ed. Boulder, CO: Westview Press.

Chinkin C. M. 1993. Peace and force in international law. In *Reconceiving reality: Women and international law,* edited by D. G. Dallmeyer. New York: Asil.

———. 1999. Cultural relativism and international law. In *Religious fundamentalisms and the human rights of women,* edited by C. W. Howland. New York: St. Martin's Press.

Cho, J. S. P. 2009. The wedding banquet revisited: "Contract marriages" between Korean gays and lesbians. *Anthropological Quarterly, 82,* 401–421.

Chodorow, N. 1978. *The reproduction of mothering: Psychanalysis and the sociology of gender.* Berkeley: University of California Press.

Chow, E. N., and K. Chen. 1994. The impact of the one child policy on women and the patriarchal family in the People's Republic of China. In *Women, the family, and policy,* edited by E. N. Chow and C. W. Berheide. Albany: State University of New York Press.

Chowdhury, N. 1994. Bangladesh: Gender issues and politics in a patriarchy. In *Women and politics worldwide,* edited by B. J. Nelson and N. Chowdhury. New Haven, CT: Yale University Press.

———, B. J. Nelson, K. A. Carver, N. J. Johnson, and P. L. O'Loughlin. 1994. Redefining politics: Patterns of women's political engagement from a global perspective. In *Women and politics worldwide,* edited by B. J. Nelson and N. Chowdhury. New Haven, CT: Yale University Press.

Christ, C.P. 1995. *Rebirth of the Goddess: Finding meaning in feminist spirituality.* London: Routledge.

Christ, C. P., and J. Plaskow. 1979. Introduction: Womanspirit rising. In *Womanspirit rising: A feminist reader in religion,* edited by C. P. Christ and J. Plaskow. San Francisco: Harper and Row.

Crist, C. P., B. J. Nelson, K. A. Carver, N. J. Johnson, and P. L. O'Loughlin. 1994. Redefining politics: Patterns of women's political engagement from a global perspective. In *Women and politics worldwide,* edited by B. J. Nelson and N. Chowdhury. New Haven, CT: Yale University Press.

Chuang, J. 2005. The United States as global sheriff: Using unilateral sanctions to combat human trafficking. *Michigan Journal of International Law, 27,* 437.

Cianni, M., and B. Romberger. 1995. Perceived racial, ethnic, and gender differences in access to developmental experiences. *Group and Organization Management, 20,* 440–459.

Ciobanu, C. 2009. Romania: Media spotlight on domestic violence. *Inter Press News Service,* 15 April.

Cisneros, S. 1996. Guadalupe the sex goddess. In *Goddess of the Americas, La Diosa del las Americas,* Ed. A. Castillo. New York: Riverhead Books.

Cleveland, J. N., and K. McNamara. 1996. Understanding sexual harassment: Contributions from research on domestic violence and organizational change. In *Sexual harassment in the workplace: Perspectives, frontiers, and response strategies,* edited by M. S. Stockdale. Thousand Oaks, CA: Sage.

Cockburn, C. 2007. *From where we stand: War, women's activism, and feminist analysis.* London: Zed.

Cohen, J. 2005. Punks, bulldaggers, and welfare queen: The radical potential of queer politics. In *Black Queer Studies,* edited by. E. P. Johnson and M. G. Henderson. Durham, NC: Duke University Press.

Cohen, S. A. 2008. Abortion and women of color: The bigger picture. *Guttmacher Policy Review, 11,* 1–12.

Col, J. 1993. Managing softly in turbulent times: Corazon C. Aquino, President of the Philippines. In *Women as national leaders,* edited by M. Genovese. Newbury Park, CA: Sage.

Cole, E. R. 2009. Intersectionality and research in psychology. *American Psychologist, 64,* 170–180.

Collier, R., and J. Strasburg. 2002. Clothiers fold on sweatshop lawsuit. *San Francisco Chronicle,* September 7, A1.

Collins, P. H. 1990. *Black feminist thought: Knowledge, consciousness, and the politics of empowerment.* Boston: Irwin Hyman.

Coomaraswamy, R. 1994. To bellow like a cow: Women, ethnicity, and the discourse of rights. In *Human rights of women,* edited by R. Cook. Philadelphia: University of Pennsylvania Press.

Coomaraswamy, R. 1999. Different but free: Cultural relativism and women's rights as human rights. In *Religious fundamentalisms and the human rights of women,* edited by C. W. Howland. New York: St. Martin's Press.

Cook, R. J. 1995. International human rights and women's reproductive health. In *Women's rights, human rights: International feminist perspectives,* edited by J. Peters and A. Wolper. New York: Routledge.

Copelon, R. 1994. Intimate terror: Understanding domestic violence as torture. In *Human rights of women,* edited by R. Cook. Philadelphia: University of Pennsylvania Press.

———. 1995. War crimes: Reconceptualizing rape in time of war. In *Women's rights, human rights: International feminist perspectives,* edited by J. Peters and A. Wolper. New York: Routledge.

Corea, G. 1991. Depo-Provera and the politics of knowledge. In *Reconstructing Babylon,* edited by H. P. Hynes. Bloomington: Indiana University Press.

Coronel, S., and N. Rosca. 1993. For the boys: Filipinas expose years of sexual slavery by the U.S. and Japan. *Ms., 5,* 10–15.

Corporate Women Directors International. 2009. http://www.globewomen.org/CWDI/Female%20Directors%20-%20Global.html Retrieved on July 28, 2009.

Covenant of the Goddess. *About witchcraft.* http://www.cog.org/wicca/about.html Retrieved on September 4, 2009.

Crampton, S. M., J. W. Hodge, and J. M. Mishra. 1997. The Equal Pay Act: The first 30 years. *Public Personnel Management, 26,* 335–344.

Cravens, C. S. 2006. *The culture and customs of the Czech Republic and Slovakia.* Westport, CT: Greenwood Press.

Cray, C. 1997. Conducive to sexual harassment: The EEOC's case against Mitsubishi. *Multinational Monitor,* October, 24–26.

Dahlburg, J. T., and B. Bearak. 1996. Pakistani president sacks Bhutto and government. *Los Angeles Times,* November 6, A1, A26.

Daly, M. 1971. After the death of God the Father. *Commonweal,* 12 March, 7–11.

———. 1973. *Beyond God the Father.* Boston: Beacon Press.

———. 1974. Theology after the demise of God the Father: A call for the castration of sexist religion. In A. L. Hageman (Ed.), *Sexist religion and women in the church: No more silence* (pp. 125–142). New York: Association Press.

———. 1985. *The church and the second sex.* 2d ed. Boston: Beacon Press.

D'Amico, F. 1995. Women as national leaders. In *Women in world politics: An introduction,* edited by F. D'Amico and P. R. Beckman. Westport, CT: Bergin and Garvey.

D'Amico, F., and P. R. Beckman. 1995. *Women in world politics: An introduction.* Westport, CT: Bergin and Garvey.

Daniluk, J. C. and N. Browne. 2008. Traditional religious doctrine and women's sexuality: Reconciling the contradictions. *Women and Therapy, 31,* 129–142.

Dankelman, I., and J. Davidson. 1988. *Women and environment in the Third World: Alliance for the future.* London: Earthscan.

Darcy, R., and C. M. Hyun. 1994. Women in the South Korean electoral system. In *Electoral systems in comparative perspective: Their impact on women and minorities,* edited by W. Rule and J. F. Zimmerman. Westport, CT: Greenwood Press.

D'Augelli, A. R. 1992. Lesbian and gay male undergraduates' experiences of harassment and fear on campus. *Journal of Interpersonal Violence, 7,* 383–395.

Davis, A. 1983. *Women, race, and class.* New York: Vintage Books.

———. 1990. Racism, birth control, and reproductive rights. In *From abortion to reproductive freedom: Transforming a movement,* edited by M. Gerber Fried. Cambridge, MA: South End Press.

DAW (Division for the Advancement of Women). 2005. *Beijing Platform for Action.* http://www.un.org/womenwatch/daw/beijing/pdf/Beijing%20full%20report%20E.pdf Retrieved on October 26, 2009.

———. 2009. *Convention on the Elimination of Discrimination Against Women.* http://www.un.org/womenwatch/daw/cedaw/cedaw.htm Retrieved on October 24, 2009.

de Beauvoir, S. 1953. *The second sex.* New York: Alfred Knopf.

deHaan, F., K. Daskalova, and A. Loutfi. 2006. *A biographical dictionary of women's movements and feminisms: Central, Eastern, and South Eastern Europe, nineteenth and twentieth centuries.* Budapest, Hungary: Central European University Press.

Demick, B. 2002. Off-base behavior in Korea. *Los Angeles Times,* 26 September, A1, A15.

Denetdate, J. 2007. *Reclaiming Dine history.* Tucson: University of Arizona Press.

Derris, K. 2008. When Buddha was a woman: Reimaging tradition in the Theravada. *Journal of Feminist Studies in Religion, 24,* 29–35.

Desai, M. 2001. India: Women's movements from nationalism to sustainable development. In *Women's rights: A global view,* edited by L. Walter. Westport, CN: Greenwood Press.

———. 2002. Transnational solidarity: Women's agency, structural adjustment, and globalization. In *Women's activism and globalization: Linking local struggles transnational politics,* edited by N. A. Naples and M. Desai. New York: Routledge.

———. 2007a. The messy relationship between feminisms and globalizations. *Gender and Society, 21,* 797–804.

———. 2007b. The perils and possibilities of transnational feminism. *Women's Studies Quarterly, 35,* 333–337.

Devine, P. G. 1995. Prejudice and out-group perception. In *Advanced social psychology,* edited by A. Tesser. New York: McGraw-Hill.

Devraj, R. 2003. Fiancée's rejection of a dowry reopens old debate. Inter Press Service, 28 May.

Dhillon, A. 2007. Land without brides. *South China Morning Post,* 3 January, 12.

Dietz, M. 1985. Citizenship with a feminist face: The problem with maternal thinking. *Political theory, 13,* 19–37.

Dignard, L., and J. Havet. 1995. Introduction. In *Women in micro- and small-scale enterprise development,* edited by L. Divard and J. Havet. Boulder, CO: Westview Press.

Diner, H. 1975. *Mothers and Amazons.* New York: Julian Press.

Dinnerstein, D. 1976. *The rocking of the cradle and the ruling of the world.* London: Souvenir.

Dixon-Mueller, R. 1993. *Population policy and women's rights: Transforming reproductive choice.* Westport, CT: Praeger.

Dobash, M., and J. Seager. 2001. *Putting women in place: Feminist geographers make sense of the world.* New York: Guilford Press.

Dorf, J., and G. C. Perez. 1995. Discrimination and tolerance of difference: International lesbian human rights. In Women's rights, human rights: International feminist perspectives, edited by J. Peters and A. Wolper. New York: Routledge.

Drury, C. 1994. *Christianity*. In *Women in religion*, edited by J. Holm. New York: St. Martin's Press.

Duda, A., and M. Wuch. 1995. Country report on lesbians in Germany. In *Unspoken rules: Sexual orientation and women's human rights*, edited by R. Rosenbloom. San Francisco: International Gay and Lesbian Human Rights Commission.

Duehr, E., & J. E. Bono. (2006). Men, women, and managers: Are stereotypes finally changing? *Personnel Psychology, 59*, 815.

Duin, J. 2001. Women break through the stained-glass ceiling. *Insight on the News, 17*, 26–30.

Duley, M. I., and S. Diduk. 1986. Women, colonialism, and development. In *The cross-cultural study of women: A comprehensive guide,* edited by M. I. Duley and M. I. Edwards. New York: Feminist Press.

Dworkin, A. 1987. *Intercourse*. London: Arrow.

Eagly, A. H. 1987. *Sex differences in social behavior: A social role interpretation*. Hillsdale, NJ: Erlbaum.

Eagly, A. H., and L. L. Carli. 2007. *Through the labyrinth*. Boston, MA: Harvard Business School Press.

Eagly, A. H., and S. J. Karau. 2002. Role congruity theory of prejudice toward female leaders, *Psychological Review, 109*, 573–598.

Ebbe, O. N. I. and D. K. Das. 2007. *Global trafficking in women and children*. Boca Raton, FL: Taylor & Francis.

Eck, D. L., and D. Jain. 1987. Introduction. *Speaking of faith: Global perspectives on women, religion, and social change*. Philadelphia: New Society Publishers.

EEOC. 2009. Sex-based discrimination. http://www.eeoc .gov/types/sex.html Retrieved on July 19, 2009.

Ehrenberg, M. 1989. *Women in prehistory*. Norman: University of Oklahoma Press.

Ehrenreich, B. 2002. Maid to order. In *Global woman: Nannies, maids, and sex workers in the new economy*, edited by B. Ehrenreich and A. R. Hochschild. New York: Metropolitan Books.

Eisler, R. 1987. *The chalice and the blade*. San Francisco: Harper and Row.

El-Bakri, Z. B., and E. M. Kameir. 1983. Aspects of women's political participation in Sudan. *International Social Science Journal, 35*, 605–623.

Elders, J. 2008. Sexual healing. *Ms.* (Summer), 79.

Elliot, L. 1996. Women, gender, feminism, and the environment. In *The gendered new world order*, edited by J. Turpin and L. A. Lorentzen. New York: Routledge.

Elson, D. 2006. *Budgeting for women's rights: Monitoring government budgets for compliance with CEDAW*. http://www.unifem.org/attachments/products/ MonitoringGovernmentBudgetsCompliance CEDAW_eng.pdf Retrieved on June 20, 2009.

Embry, A., M. Y. Padgett, and C. B. Caldwell. 2008. Can leaders step outside of the gender box? An examination of leadership and gender role stereotypes. *Journal of Leadership & Organizational Studies, 15*, 30–46.

Emmett, B. 2009. *Paying the price for the economic crisis*. http://www.oxfam.org.uk/resources/policy/ economic_crisis/downloads/impact_economic_ crisis_women.pdf Retrieved on August 14, 2009.

Enloe, C. 1989. *Bananas, beaches, and bases: Making feminist sense of international relations*. Berkeley: University of California Press.

———. 1996. Spoils of war. *Ms., 6*, 15.

EOWA. 2008. *EOWA Australian census of women in leadership*. http://www.catalyst.org/file/243/ eowa_census_2008_publication.pdf Retrieved on July 21, 2009.

Erndl, K. M. 2006. New Hindu movements. In *Encyclopedia of women and religion in North America (Vol. 2)*, edited by R. S. Keller, R. R. Ruether, and M. Canton. Bloomington: Indiana University Press.

Ertürk, Y. 2006. *Integration of the human rights of women and the gender perspective: Violence against women. Report of the Special Rapporteur on violence against women, its causes and consequences. Addendum. Mission to Afghanistan (9 to 19 July 2005)*. United Nations Commission on Human Rights.

Everett, J. 1993. Indira Gandhi and the exercise of power. In M. A. Genovese, *Women as national leaders*. Newbury Park, CA: Sage.

Faderman, L. 1981. Surpassing the love of men: Romantic friendship and love between women from the Renaissance to the present. New York: William Morrow.

———. 1991. *Odd girls and twilight lovers: A history of lesbian life in twentieth century America*. New York: Columbia University Press.

———. 1997. Who hid lesbian history? *Journal of Lesbian Studies, 1*, 149–154.

Falk, M. L. 2008. Gender and religious legitimacy in Thailand. In *Gender politics in Asia: Women maneuvering within dominant gender orders*, edited by W. Burghoorn, K. Iwanga, C. Milwertz, and Q. Wang. Copenhagen, Denmark: NIAS Press.

Falwell, J. (2001, September 13). 700 Club [Pat Robertson's television program]. www.pfaw.org/

pfaw/general/default.aspx?oid=1817 Retrieved July 16, 2006.

Fang, D. 2003. The one-child policy is here to stay. *South China Morning Post,* 12 July, 7.

FAO (Food and Agriculture Organization). 2009a. *Gender and food security: Division of labor.* http://www.fao.org/gender/en/labb2-e.htm Retrieved on August 2, 2009.

———. 2009b. *Women and food security.* http://www.fao.org/focus/e/Women/Sustin-e.htm Retrieved on August 2, 2009.

———. 2009c. *Women and water resources.* http://www.fao.org/focus/e/Women/Water-e.htm Retrieved on August 2, 2009.

———. 2009d. *Women: Users, preservers and managers of agro-biodiversity.* http://www.fao.org/focus/e/Women/Biodiv-e.htm Retrieved on August 2, 2009.

———. 2009e. *Gender and food security: Education, extension and communication.* http://www.fao.org/gender/en/educ-e.htm Retrieved on August 3, 2009.

———. 2009f. *Gender and food security fact files: One woman's day in Sierra Leone.* http://www.fao.org/gender/en/Facte/FL9719-e.htm Retrieved on August 6, 2009.

———. 2009g. *Gender and food security: Environment.* http://www.fao.org/gender/en/envb1-e.htm

FAO Sustainable Development Department. 2009. www.fao.org/sd/

Fausto-Sterling, A. 2000. The five sexes revisited. *Sciences, 40,* 18–24.

Feijoo, M. D. C. 1998. Democratic participation and women in Argentina. In *Women and democracy: Latin America and Central and Eastern Europe,* edited by J. S. Jaquette and S. L. Wolchik. Baltimore, MD: Johns Hopkins University Press.

Feminist Majority. 2006. *Feminist activist murdered in the Philippines.* http://www.feminist.org/news/newsbyte/uswirestory.asp? Retrieved on May 23, 2006.

Ferdman, B. 1995. Cultural identity and diversity in organizations: Bridging the gap between group differences and individual uniqueness. In *Diversity in organizations,* edited by M. M. Chemers, S. Oskamp, and M. A. Constanzo. Thousand Oaks, CA: Sage.

Ferguson, A. 1981. Patriarchy, sexual identity, and the sexual revolution. *Signs, 7,* 157–172.

Filkins, D. 2009. A school bus for Shamisa. *New York Times.* August 17. http://www.nytimes.com/2009/08/23/magazine/23school-t.html?pagewanted=all Retrieved on October 3, 2009.

Fisher, J. 1996. Sustainable development and women: The role of NGOs. In *The gendered new world order: Militarism, development, and the environment,* edited by J. Turpin and L. A. Lorentzen. New York: Routledge.

Fitzgerald, L. F. 1993. Sexual harassment: Violence against women in the workplace. *American Psychologist, 48,* 1070–1076.

Fitzgerald, L. F., S. Swann, and V. J. Magley. 1997. But was it really sexual harassment?: Legal, behavioral, and psychological definitions of the workplace victimization of women. In *Sexual harassment: Theory, research, and treatment,* edited by W. O'Donohue. Boston: Allyn and Bacon.

Fleshman, M. 2003. African women struggle for a seat at the peace table. *Africa Renewal, 16,* 1.

Forrester, A. 1995. From stabilization to growth with equity: A case for financing women in development programs. In *Women and the United Nations,* edited by F. C. Steady and R. Toure. Rochester, VT: Schenkman Books.

Fortune. 2009. Women CEOs. http://money.cnn.com/magazines/fortune/fortune500/2009/womenceos/ Retrieved on July 21, 2009.

Franceschet, S. 2003. "State feminism" and women's movements: The impact of Chile's Servicio Nacional de la Mujer on women's activism. *Latin American Research Review, 38,* 11–40.

Francheschet, S., and J. M. Piscopo. 2008. Gender quotas and women's substantive representation: Lessons from Argentina. *Politics & Gender, 4,* 393–425.

Frankson, J. R. 1998. Getting our day in court. *Ms.,* 7, May/June, 19.

Fraser, A. 1988. *The warrior queens: The legends and life of the women who have led their nations in war.* New York: Random House.

Fraser, A. S. 1987. *The U.N. Decade for Women: Documents and dialogue.* Boulder, CO: Westview Press.

French, M. 1992. *The war against women.* New York: Simon and Schuster.

Fried, S. 2003. An Interview with Susana Fried, the Director of Programs of the International Gay and Lesbian Human Rights Commission. *WHRnet,* http://www.awid.org/eng/Issues-and-Analysis/Library/The-LGBT-Community-and-Sexual-Rights Retrieved on June 25, 2009.

Friedman, E. 1995. Women's human rights: The emergence of a movement. In *Women's rights, human rights: International feminist perspectives,* edited by J. Peters and A. Wolper. New York: Routledge.

Friedman, R. C., and J. Downey. 1995. Internalized homophobia and the negative therapeutic reaction. *Journal of the American Academy of Psychoanalysis, 23,* 99–113.

Frohmann, A., and T. Valdes. 1995. Democracy in the country and in the home: The women's movement in Chile. In *The challenge of local feminisms: Women's movements in global perspective,* edited by A. Basu. Boulder, CO: Westview Press.

Fuentes, A., and B. Ehrenreich. 1983. *Women in the global factory.* Boston, MA: South End Press.

Fujieda, M. 1995. Japan's first phase of feminism. In *Japanese women: New feminist perspectives on the past, present, and future,* edited by K. Fujimura-Fanselow and A. Kameda. New York: Feminist Press.

Furseth, I., and P. Repstad. 2006. *An introduction to the sociology of religion: Classic and contemporary.* Hampshire, England: Ashgate.

Fuwa, M. 2004. Macro-level gender inequality and the division of household labor in 22 countries. *American Sociological Review, 69,* 69–92.

Fuwa, M., and P. N. Cohen. 2007. Housework and social policy. *Social Science Research, 36,* 512–530.

Garcia-Retamero, R., and E. López-Zafra. 2009. Causal attributions about feminine and leadership roles: A cross-cultural comparison. Journal *of Cross-Cultural Psychology, 40,* 492–509.

Gay, J. 1986. "Mummies and babies" and friends of lovers in Lesotho. In *The many faces of homosexuality: Anthropological approaches to homosexual behavior,* edited by E. Blackwood. New York: Harrington Park.

Gebara, I., and M. C. Bingemer. 1994. Mary—Mother of God, mother of the poor. In *Feminist theology from the Third World,* edited by U. King. New York: Orbis.

Genovese, M. A. 1993. Margaret Thatcher and the politics of conviction leadership. In *Women as national leaders,* edited by M. A. Genovese. Newbury Park, CA: Sage.

Gerhart, M. 2003. Christianity. In *Her voice, her faith,* edited by A. Sharma and K. K. Young. Boulder, CO: Westview Press.

Ghodsee, K. 2004. Feminism-by-design: Emerging capitalisms, cultural feminisms, and women's non-governmental organizations. *Signs: A Journal of Culture and Society, 29,* 728–752.

Giddens, A. 1992. *The transformation of intimacy: Sexuality, law, and eroticism in modern societies.* Cambridge, MA: Polity.

Giger, N. 2009. Towards a modern gender gap in Europe: A comparative analysis of voting behavior in twelve countries. *The Social Science Journal, 46,* 474–492.

Gimbutas, M. 1991. *The civilization of the goddess: The world of Old Europe.* San Francisco: Harper and Row.

Glenn, E. N. 1992. From servitude to service work: Historical continuities in the racial division of paid reproductive labor. Signs, 1–43.

Glick, P. 1991. Trait-based and sex-based discrimination in occupational prestige, occupational salary, and hiring. *Sex Roles, 25,* 351–378.

Glick, P., and Fiske, S.T. 2001. An ambivalent alliance: Hostile and benevolent sexism as complementary justifications for gender inequality. *American Psychologist, 56,* 109–18.

Glick, P., M. Lameiras, and C. Castro. 2002. Education and Catholic religiosity as predictors of hostile and benevolent sexism toward women and men. *Sex Roles, 47,* 433–441.

Global Exchange. 2009. *Carmencita Chie Abad.* http://www.globalexchange.org/getInvolved/speakers/5.html Retrieved on August 17, 2009.

Global Gender and Climate Alliance (GGCA). 2009. *Training manual on gender and climate change.* http://www.generoyambiente.org/archivos-de-usuario/File/ecosistemas_especificos.pdf Retrieved on August 6, 2009.

Gold, A. G. 2008. Gender. In *Studying Hinduism: Key concepts and methods,* edited by S. Mittal and G. Thursby. New York: Routledge.

Gold, R. B. 2006. Rekindling efforts to prevent unplanned pregnancy: A matter of 'equity and common sense.' *Guttmacher Policy Review, 9,* 1–7.

Gonzales, S. 2008. Population Philippines: Catholic Church damns the Pill. *IPS News,* http://ipsnews.net/news.asp?idnews=43280.

Gonzalez, M. B. 1995. Country report on lesbians in Nicaragua. In *Unspoken rules: Sexual orientation and women's human rights,* edited by R. Rosenbloom. San Francisco: International Gay and Lesbian Human Rights Commission.

Gonzalez, V., and K. Kampwirth. 2002. *Radical women in Latin America: Left and right.* University Park, PA: Pennsylvania State University.

Goodwin J. 1994. *Price of honor: Muslim women lift the veil of violence on the Islamic world.* Boston: Little, Brown.

Goonatilake, H. 1997. Buddhist nuns' protests, struggle, and the reinterpretation of orthodoxy in Sri Lanka.

In *Mixed blessings: Gender and religious fundamentalism cross-culturally.* New York: Routledge.

Gottlick, J. F. B. 1999. From the ground up: Women's organizations and democratization in Russia. In *Democratization and women's grassroots movements,* edited by J. M. Bystydzienski and J. Sekhon. Bloomington: Indiana University Press.

Grameen Bank. 2009. http://www.grameen-info.org/index.php?option=com_frontpage&Itemid=68 Retrieved on August 3, 2009.

Greenbelt Movement. 2009. http://www.greenbeltmovement.org/w.php?id=3 Retrieved on August 1, 2009.

Greenberg, B. 2000. Orthodox feminism in the next century. *Sh'ma: A Journal of Jewish Responsibility.* http://www.jofa.org/pdf/uploaded/962-QQQH9815.pdf Retrieved on August 30, 2009.

Greene, B. 1994. Lesbian women of color: Triple jeopardy. *Journal of Lesbian Studies, 1,* 109–147.

Greenfacts. *Scientific facts on forests.* http://greenfacts.org Retrieved on August 9, 2009.

Greenhouse, S., and M. Barbaro. 2006. An ugly side of free trade: Sweatshops in Jordan. *New York Times,* May 3.

Griffin W. 2003. Goddess spirituality and wicca. In *Her voice, her faith,* edited by A. Sharma and K. K. Young. Boulder, CO: Westview Press.

Griffith, K. H., and M. R. Hebl. 2002. The disclosure dilemma for gay men and lesbians: 'Coming out' at work. *Journal of Applied Psychology, 87,* 1191–1199.

Gross, R. M. 1979. Female God language in a Jewish context. In *Womanspirit rising: A feminist reader in religion,* edited by C. P. Christ and J. Plaskow. San Francisco: Harper and Row.

———. 1993. *Buddhism after patriarchy: A feminist history, analysis, and reconstruction of Buddhism.* Albany: State University of New York Press.

———. 1996. *Feminism and religion: An introduction.* Boston: Beacon Press.

———. 1999. Strategies for a feminist revalorization of Buddhism. In *Feminism and world religions,* edited by A. Sharma and K. K. Young. Albany: State University Press of New York, pp. 78–109.

———. 2003. Buddhism. In *Her voice, her faith,* edited by A. Sharma and K. K. Young. Boulder, CO: Westview Press.

———. 2009. *A garland of feminist reflections: Forty years of religious exploration.* Berkeley, CA: University of California Press.

Gruber, J. E. 1997. An epidemiology of sexual harassment: Evidence from North America and Europe. In *Sexual harassment: Theory, research, and treatment,* edited by W. O'Donohue. Boston: Allyn and Bacon.

Gruber, J. E., M. Smith, and K. Kauppinen-Toropainen. 1996. Sexual harassment types and severity: Linking research and policy. In *Sexual harassment in the workplace: Perspectives, frontiers, and response strategies,* edited by M. S. Stockdale. Thousand Oaks, CA: Sage.

Gunewardena, N., and A. Kingsolver. 2007. Introduction. In *The gender of globalization: Women navigating cultural and economic marginalities,* edited by N. Gunewardena and A. Kingsolver. Santa Fe, NM: School for Advanced Research Press.

Gupta, L. 1991. Kali the savior. In *After patriarchy: Feminist transformations of the world religions,* edited by P. Cooey, W. Eakin, and J. McDaniel. Maryknoll, NY: Orbis.

Gutek, B. A., A. G. Cohen, and A. M. Konrad. 1990. Predicting social-sexual behavior at work: A contact hypothesis. *Academy of Management Journal, 33,* 560–577.

Gutek, B. A., and M. P. Koss. 1993. Changed women and changed organizations: Consequences of and coping with sexual harassment. *Journal of Vocational Behavior, 42,* 28–48.

Gutek, B. A., and B. Morash. 1982. Sex-ratios, sex-role spillover, and sexual harassment of women at work. *Journal of Social Issues, 38,* 55–74.

Gutierrez, M., and O. Boselli. 2009. Politics-Italy: Where Are the Women? *IPS.* September 22.

Guttierrez, E. R. 2008. *Fertile matters; The politics of Mexican-origin women's reproduction.* Austin, TX: University of Texas Press.

Guttmacher Institute. 2008. *Facts on induced abortion worldwide.* http://www.guttmacher.org/pubs/fb_IAW.html

Guzder, D. 2009. Thailand: The world's sex capital. *Untold stories: Dispatches from the Pulitzer Center on Crisis Reporting.* August 14. http://pulitzercenter.typepad.com/untold_stories/2009/08/thailand-flesh-market.html#more Retrieved on August 20, 2009.

Hale, S. 2005. Colonial discourse and ethnographic residuals: The "female circumcision" debate and the politics of knowledge. In *Circumcision and the politics of knowledge,* edited by O. Nnaemeka. Westport, CT: Praeger.

Hamilton, M. C. (1988). Using masculine generics: Does generic *he* increase male bias in the user's imagery? *Sex Roles, 19,* 785–798.

———. 1991. Masculine bias in the attribution of personhood. *Psychology of Women Quarterly, 15*, 393–402.

Hampson, D. 1987. Women, ordination and the Christian Church. In *Speaking of faith: Global perspectives on women, religion, and social change*, edited by D. L. Eck and D. Jain. Philadelphia: New Society Publishers.

Harden, B. 2008. Japanese women shy from dual mommy role. *The Washington Post* August 28, A08.

Hardin, C., and M. R. Banaji. 1993. The influence of language on thought. *Social Cognition, 11*, 277–308.

Harris, K. 1995. Prime Minister Margaret Thatcher: The influence of her gender on her foreign policy. In *Women in politics: An introduction*, edited by F. D'Amico and P. R. Beckman. Westport, CT: Bergin and Garvey.

Hartman, T. 2007. *Feminism encounters traditional Judaism*. Walthan, MA: Brandeis University Press.

Hartmann, B. 1987. *Reproductive rights and reproductive wrongs*. New York: Harper and Row.

———. 1995. *Reproductive rights and wrongs: The global politics of population control*. Boston: South End Press.

Harvey, N. 2008. The fire inside: Lesbianism in India has traditionally been the great unmentionable—and the treatment meted out to women who love women still leads many couples to opt for suicide pacts, often burning themselves to death. *New Internationalist*, October, 23–28.

Hassan, R. 1991. Muslim women and post-patriarchal Islam. In *After patriarchy: Feminist transformations of the world religions*, edited by P. Cooey, W. Eakin, and J. McDaniel. Maryknoll, NY: Orbis.

———. 1999. Feminism in Islam. In *Feminism and world religions*, edited by A. Sharma and K. K. Young. Albany: State University Press of New York.

———. 2003. Islam. In *Her voice, her faith*, edited by A. Sharma and K. K. Young. Boulder, CO: Westview Press.

Hausman, M., and B. Sauer. 2007. Introduction: Women's movements and state restructuring in the 1990s. In *Gendering the state in the age of globalization: Women's movements and state feminism in postindustrial democracies*. New York: Rowman & Littlefield.

Hawkesworth, M. E. 2006. *Globalization and feminist activism*. New York: Rowman & Littlefield.

Heilman, M. E., and T. Okimoto. 2008. Motherhood: A potential source of bias in employment decisions. *Journal of Applied Psychology, 93*, 189–198.

Heise, L. L. 1995. Freedom close to home: The impact of violence against women on reproductive rights. In *Women's rights, human rights: International feminist perspectives*, edited by J. Peters and A. Wolper. New York: Routledge.

Helie-Lucas, M. A. 1993. Women living under Muslim laws. In *Ours by right: Women's rights as human rights*, edited by J. Kerr. Ottawa, Canada: North-South Institute.

Helzner, J. F. 2008. Three pillars of maternal health: Low-tech, low-cost ways to save women's lives. *Ms.* (Summer), 24–25.

Hequembourg, A. L., and S. A. Brallier. 2009. An exploration of sexual minority stress across the lines of gender and sexual identity. *Journal of Homosexuality, 56*, 273–298.

Herbert, B. 2006. Punished for being female. *New York Times*, 2 November, A27.

Herdt, G. 1997. *Same sex: Different cultures*. Boulder, CO: Westview Press.

Herek, G. M. 2009. Hate crimes and stigma-related experiences among sexual minority adults in the United States: Prevalence estimates from a national probability sample. *Journal of Interpersonal Violence, 24*, 54–74.

Herrera, F. 2009. Tradition and transgression: Lesbian motherhood in Chile. *Sexuality Research and Social Policy, 6*, 35–51.

Heschel, S. 2003. Judaism. In *Her voice, her faith*, edited by A. Sharma and K. K. Young. Boulder, CO: Westview Press.

Hesketh, T., and Z. W. Xing. 2006. Abnormal sex ratios in human populations: Causes and consequences. *Proceedings of the National Academy of Sciences (PNAS), 103*, 13271–13275.

Heyzer, N. 2002. Women are key to development. In *An agenda for the people: The UNFPA through three decades*, edited by N. Sadik. New York: New York University Press.

Hochschild, A. R. 2002. Love and gold. In *Global woman: Nannies, maids, and sex workers in the new economy*, edited by B. Ehrenreich and A. R. Hochschild. New York: Metropolitan Books.

Hochschild, A. R., and J. P. Bartkowski. 2008. Gender, religious tradition, and biblical literalism. *Social Forces, 86*, 1245–1270.

Hoffman, J.P., and J.P. Bartkowski. 2008. Gender, religious tradition, and biblical literalism. *Social Forces, 86*, 1245-1270.

Holm, J. 1994. Introduction. *Women in religion*. New York: St. Martin's Press.

Hook, J. L., and S. Chalasami. 2008. Gender expectations? Reconsidering single fathers' childcare time. *Journal of Marriage and Family, 70*, 978–990.

Horney, K. 1967. *Feminine psychology*. New York: Norton.

Hoyert, D. L. 2007. *Maternal mortality and related concepts*. National Center for Health Statistics. Vital Health Stat 3(33), 1–20.

Hughes, M. M. 2009. Armed conflict, international linkages, and women's parliamentary representation in developing nations. *Social Problems, 56*, 174–204.

Hulin C. L., L. F. Fitzgerald, and F. Drasgow. 1996. Organizational influences on sexual harassment. In *Sexual harassment in the workplace: Perspectives, frontiers, and response strategies*, edited by M. S. Stockdale. Thousand Oaks, CA: Sage.

Human Rights Campaign. 2009. *Laws. http://www.hrc.org/issues/workplace/workplace_laws.asp* Retrieved on June 25, 2009.

Human Rights Watch. 1995. *The Human Rights Watch global report on women's human rights*. New York: Human Rights Watch.

———. 2002. Sharia stoning for Nigerian woman. http://www.hrw.org/en/news/2002/08/20/sharia-stoning-sentence-nigerian-woman Retrieved on August 28, 2009.

———.2006. Swept under the rug: Abuses against domestic workers around the world. http://www.hrw.org/en/reports/2006/07/27/swept-under-rug-0 Retrieved on August 19, 2009.

———. 2007a. South Africa: Lesbians targeted for murder. http://www.hrw.org/en/news/2007/08/07/south-africa-lesbians-targeted-murder Retrieved on June 28, 2009.

———. 2007b. Exported and exposed: Abuse against Sri Lankan domestic workers in Saudi Arabia, Kuwait, Lebanon, and the United Arab Emirates. http://www.hrw.org/en/reports/2007/11/13/exported-and-exposed-1 Retrieved on August 19, 2009.

———. 2008. *"As if I am not human": Abuses against Asia domestic workers in Saudi Arabia*. http://www.hrw.org/en/reports/2008/07/07/if-i-am-not-human-0 Retrieved on August 19, 2009.

———. 2009a. Kyrgyzstan: Protect lesbians and transgender men from abuse. http://www.hrw.org/en/news/2008/10/06/kyrgyzstan-protect-lesbians-and-transgender-men-abuse Retrieved on June 25, 2009.

———. 2009b. *Afghanistan: Law curbing women's rights takes effect*. http://www.hrw.org/en/news/2009/08/13/afghanistan-law-curbing-women-s-rights-takes-effect Retrieved on August 28, 2009.

Hunsberger, B., V. Owusu, and R. Duck. 1999. Religious prejudice in Ghana and Canada: Religious fundamentalism, right-winged authoritarianism, and attitudes toward homosexuals and women. *The International Journal for the Psychology of Religion, 9*, 181–194.

Hunt, M. E., & P. B. Jung. 2009. "Good sex" and religion: A feminist overview. *Journal of Sex Research, 46*, 156–167.

Hyatt, S. 1992. *Putting bread on the table: The women's work of community activism*. West Yorkshire, UK: University of Bradford, Work and Gender Research Unit.

ICFTU (International Confederation of Trade Unions). 2006. *Annual survey of violations of trade union rights 2006*. Brussels, Belgium: Author.

ICPD Programme of Action (United Nations International Conference on Population and Development. 1994. http://www.iisd.ca/Cairo.html

IFAD (International Fund for Agricultural Development). 2009. *Combating environmental degradation*. http://www.ifad.org/events/past/hunger/envir.html Retrieved on August 6, 2009.

ILGA. 2009. *2009 report on State-sponsored homophobia*. http://www.ilga.org/news_results.asp?LanguageID=1&FileID=1251&FileCategory=9&ZoneID=7 Retrieved on June 28, 2009.

Inglehart, R., and P. Norris. 2003. *Rising tide: Gender equality and cultural change*. Oxford: Cambridge University Press.

International Campaign Against Honour Killing. 2009. *News: Honour killing in Iraq*. http://www.stophonourkillings.com/News/article/sid=1667.html Retrieved on April 27, 2009.

International Criminal Court (ICC). 2009. *Situations and cases*. http://www.icc-cpi.int/Menus/ICC/Situations+and+Cases/ Retrieved on May 27, 2009.

International Institute for Democracy and Electoral Assistance. 2006. *Global database of quotas for women*. http://www.quotaproject.org/ Retrieved on September 18, 2009.

International Labour Organization. 2003. *Time for equality at work. Global report under the follow-up to the ILO Declaration on Fundamental Principles and*

Rights at Work. Report of the Director-General, 2003. http://www.ilo.org/wcmsp5/groups/public/---dgreports/---dcomm/---publ/documents/publication/wcms_publ_9221128717_en.pdf Retrieved on July 27, 2009.

———. 2004. *Informational fact sheet: WF-1 Work and family responsibilities.* http://www.ilo.org/public/english/protection/condtrav/pdf/infosheets/wf-1.pdf Retrieved on July 15, 2009.

———. 2005. *ILO thesaurus 2005.* http://www.ilo.org/public/libdoc/ILO-Thesaurus/english/tr1259.htm Retrieved on July 24, 2009.

———. 2007a. *Equality at work: Tackling the challenges. Global report under the follow-up to the ILO Declaration on fundamental principles and rights at work. Report of the Director-General, 2007.* http://www.ilo.org/global/What_we_do/Publications/ILOBookstore/Orderonline/Books/lang--en/docName--WCMS_082607/index.htm Retrieved on July 14, 2009.

———. 2007b. *KILM 3 status in employment.* http://www.ilo.org/public/english/employment/strat/kilm/download/kilm03.pdf Retrieved on July 28, 2009.

———. 2007c. *What are EPZs?* http://www.ilo.org/public/english/dialogue/sector/themes/epz/epzs.htm Retrieved on August 15, 2009.

———. 2008a. *Remove the obstacles: On the right road to equality!* http://www.uneca.org/adfvi/documents/ILO-BrochSeptGB.pdf Retrieved on July 17, 2009.

———. 2008b. *Working conditions: Laws 2006–2007.* http://www.ilo.org/public/english/protection/condtrav/pdf/work_laws.pdf Retrieved on July 15, 2009.

———. 2008c. *Youth employment: Breaking gender barriers for young women and men.* http://www.ilo.org/gender/Events/Campaign2008-2009/lang--en/WCMS_097842/index.htm Retrieved on July 18, 2009.

———. 2009. Global employment trends for women report, 2009. http://www.ilo.org/global/What_we_do/Publications/lang--en/docName--WCMS_103456/index.htm Retrieved on July 18, 2009.

International Planned Parenthood Federation. 2009. *Contraception.* http://www.ippf.org/en/Resources/Contraception/Contraception.htm

International Women's Health Coalition. 2006. *Women and risk of HIV infection.* http://www.iwhc.org/storage/iwhc/docUploads/Women%20and%20HIV%206.4.08%20final%20update.pdf Retrieved on April 27, 2009.

Inter-Parliamentary Union. 2008. *Women in parliament in 2008: The year in perspective.* http://www.ipu.org/pdf/publications/wmn08-e.pdf Retrieved on September 13, 2009.

———. 2009a. *Women's suffrage.* http://www.ipu.org/wmn-e/suffrage.htm Retrieved on September 12, 2009.

———. 2010. *Women in national parliaments.* http://www.ipu.org/wmn-e/classif.htm Retrieved on April 13, 2010.

IPU/DAW. 2008. *Women in politics 2008 (Map).* http://www.un.org/womenwatch/daw/public/womeninpolitics2008/FemmeEnPolitique_UK_BD.pdf Retrieved on September, 23, 2009.

Isasi-Diaz, A. M. 2006. Mujerista theology. In *Encyclopedia of women and religion in North America (Vol. 3)*, edited by R. S. Keller, R. R. Ruether, and M. Canton. Bloomington: Indiana University Press.

Ishii-Kuntz, M. 1993. Japanese fathers: Work demands and family roles. In *Men, work, and family*, edited by J. C. Hood. Newbury Park, CA: Sage.

Ishino, S., and N. Wakabayashi. 1995. Country report on lesbians in Japan. In *Unspoken rules: Sexual orientation and women's human rights*, edited by R. Rosenbloom. San Francisco: International Gay and Lesbian Human Rights Commission.

ITUC (International Trade Union Confederation). 2008. *The global gender pay gap.* Brussels, Belgium: ITUC.

———. 2009. *Gender (in)equality in the labour market.* International Trade Union Confederation. http://www.ituc-csi.org/IMG/pdf/GAP-09_EN.pdf Retrieved on July 10, 2009.

IUCN. 2002. *The unavoidable current: Gender policies for the environmental sector in Mesoamerica.* San Jose, Costa Rica. http://www.genderandenvironment.org/admin/admin_biblioteca/documentos/GENDER%20POLICIES.pdf Retrieved on August 7, 2009.

Iverson, T., and F. Rosenbluth. 2006. The political economy of gender: Explaining cross-cultural variation in the gender division of labor and the gender voting gap. *American Journal of Political Science, 50*, 1–19.

Jacobsen, J. P. 2003. The human capital explanation for the gender gap in earnings. In *Women, family, and work*, edited by K. S. Moe. Oxford, UK: Blackwell.

Jacobson, J. 2009. Yes we can: Ending eight years of frustration, the Obama administration has revived reproductive justice in just a few months. *Ms.,* Spring, 12–13.

Jacobson, J. L. 1992. Women's reproductive health: The silent emergency. *New Frontiers in Education, 22,* 1–54.

Jaffer, M. 2009. Global: Kalpona: Sweatshop buster. *Women's Feature Service,* May 11.

Jahan, R. 1995a. The elusive agenda: Mainstreaming women in development. In *Seeds 2,* edited by A. Leonard. New York: Feminist Press.

———. 1995b. Men in seclusion, women in public: Rokeya's dream and women's struggles in Bangladesh. In *The challenge of local feminisms: Women's movements in global perspective,* edited by A. Basu. Boulder, CO: Westview Press.

Jain, D. 2005. *Women, development, and the UN: A sixty-year quest for equality and justice.* Bloomington: Indiana University Press.

Jain, S. 1991. Standing up for trees: Women's role in the Chipko movement. In *Women and the environment: A reader on crisis and development in the Third World,* edited by S. Sontheimer. New York: Monthly Review Press.

Jaising, I. 1995. Violence against women: The Indian perspective. In *Women's rights, human rights: International feminist perspectives,* edited by J. Peters and A. Wolper. New York: Routledge.

Jalalzai, F. 2004. Women political leaders. *Women and Politics, 26,* 85–108.

———. 2008. Women rule: Shattering the executive glass ceiling. *Politics and Gender, 4,* 205–231.

Jalalzai, F., and M. L. Krook. 2008. Beyond Hillary and Benazir: Women's political leadership worldwide. Paper presented at the Annual Meeting of the Northeastern Political Science Association, Boston, MA, November 13–15.

Jamail, D. 2009. US: Culture of unpunished sexual assault in military. *IPS,* April 30. http://www .ipsnews.net/news.asp?idnews=46674 Retrieved May 1, 2009.

Jaquette, J. S. 1995. Losing the battle/winning the war: International politics, women's issues, and the 1980 mid-decade conference. In *Women, politics, and the United Nations,* edited by A. Winslow. Westport, CT: Greenwood Press.

Jaquette, J. S., and K. Staudt. 2006. Women, gender, and development. In *Women and gender equity in development theory and practice: Institutions, resources,*

and mobilization, edited by J. S. Jaquette and G. Summerfield. Durham, NC: Duke University Press.

Jenson, J. 1995. Extending the boundaries of citizenship: Women's movements of Western Europe. In *The challenge of local feminisms, Women's movements in global perspective,* edited by A. Basu. Boulder, CO: Westview Press.

Jewish Orthodox Feminist Alliance. 2009. *JOFA advocacy for agunot.* http://www.jofa.org/about .php/advocacy Retrieved on August 30, 2009.

Johnson-Odim, C. 1991. Common themes, different contexts: Third World women and feminism. In *Third world women and the politics of feminism,* edited by C. T. Mohanty, A. Russo, and L. Torres. Bloomington: Indiana University Press.

Johnstone, R. L. 2006. Feminist influences on United Nations human rights treaty bodies. *Human Rights Quarterly, 28,* 148–185.

Jones, M. P. 2009. Gender quotas, electoral laws, and the election of women: Evidence from the Latin American vanguard. *Journal of Comparative Politics, 42,* 56–81.

Judge, T. A., and B. A. Livingston. 2008. Is the gap more than gender? A longitudinal analysis of gender, gender orientation, and earning. *Journal of Applied Psychology, 93,* 994–1012.

Kabilsingh, C. 1987. The future of the Bhikkhuni Samgha in Thailand. In *Speaking of faith: Global perspectives on women, religion, and social change,* edited by D. L. Eck and D. Jain. Philadelphia: New Society Publishers.

Kakuyama, T., M. L. Onglatco, Y. Tsuzuki, and T. Matsui. 2003. Organizational tolerance as a correlate of sexual harassment of Japanese working women. *Psychological Reports, 92,* 1268–1271.

Kampwirth, K. 2006. Antifeminist politics in post-Sandinista Nicraragua. *NWSA Journal, 18,* 73–100.

Karides, M. 2002. Linking local efforts with global struggle: Trinidad's national union of domestic employees. In *Women's activism and globalization: Linking local struggles transnational politics,* edited by N. A. Naples and M. Desai. New York: Routledge.

Katumba, R., and W. Akute. 1993. Greening takes root. *The Power to Change.* London: Zed.

Katzenstein, M. F. 1987. Comparing the feminist movements of the United States and Western Europe: An overview. In *The women's movements of the United States and Central Europe: Consciousness, political opportunity, and public policy,* edited by M. F. Katzenstein and C. M. Mueller. Philadelphia: Temple University Press.

———. 1989. Organizing against violence: Strategies of the Indian women's movement. *Pacific Affairs, 62,* 53–71.

Kaur, G. 2008. Indian city opens doorway to female Hindu priests. *Women's e-news.* http://www .womensenews.org/article.cfm/dyn/aid/3506/ Retrieved on September 1, 2009.

Kawashima, Y. 1995. Female workers: An overview of past and current trends. In *Japanese women: New feminist perspectives on the past, present and future,* edited by K. Fujimura-Fanselow and A. Kameda. New York: Feminist Press.

Kearns, R. 2009. Forced sterilization of indigenous case re-opened in Peru. *Indian Country Today.* February 20. http://www.indiancountrytoday .com/global/39910172.html Retrieved April 2009.

Keck, M. E., and K. Sikkink. 1998. *Activists beyond borders: Transnational advocacy networks in international politics.* Ithaca, NY: Cornell University Press.

Keddie, N. R. 2007. *Women in the Middle East: Past and present.* Princeton, NJ: Princeton University Press.

Kemp, A., N. Madlala, A. Moodley, and E. Salo. 1995. The dawn of a new day: Redefining South African feminism. In *The challenge of local feminisms: Women's movements in global perspective,* edited by A. Basu. Boulder, CO: Westview Press.

Kendall. 1998. "When a woman loves a woman" in Lesotho: Love, sex, and the (Western) construction of homophobia. In *Boy-wives and female husbands: Studies of African homosexualities,* edited by S. O. Murray and W. Roscoe. New York: St. Martin's Press.

Kerr, J. 1993. *Ours by right: Women's rights as human rights.* London: Zed.

Khan, T. S. 2006. *Beyond honour: A historical materialist explanation of honour related violence.* Oxford: Oxford University Press.

Kilbourne, J. 2003. Advertising and disconnection. In T. Reichert & J. Lambiase (Eds.), *Sex in advertising: Perspectives on the erotic appeal.* Mahwah, NJ: Erlbaum.

King, U. 1987. Goddesses, witches, androgyny and beyond? Feminism and the transformation of religious consciousness. In *Women in the world's religions, past and present,* edited by U. King. New York: Paragon House.

———. 1994. Introduction. In *Feminist theology from the Third World,* edited by U. King. Maryknoll, NY: Orbis.

Kirkpatrick, L. 1993. Fundamentalism, Christian orthodoxy, and intrinsic religious orientation as predictors of discriminatory attitudes. *Journal for the Scientific Study of Religion, 32,* 256–268.

Kissling, F. 1999. Roman Catholic fundamentalism: What's sex (and power) got to do with it? In *Religious fundamentalisms and the human rights of women,* edited by C. W. Howland. New York: St. Martin's Press.

Koss, M. P., L. Heise, and N. F. Russo. 1994. The global health burden of rape. *Psychology of Women Quarterly, 18,* 509–537.

Kress, M. 2009. The state of Orthodox Judaism today. *Jewish Virtual Library.* http://www.jewishvirtuallibrary .org/jsource/Judaism/orthostate.html Retrieved on August 30, 2009.

Kulkarni, P. M. 2007. *Estimation of missing girls at birth and juvenile ages in India.* United Nations Population Fund. http://www.unfpa.org/gender/ docs/missingirlsatbirth_india.pdf Retrieved March 28, 2009.

Kumar, R. 1995. From Chipko to Sati: The contemporary Indian women's movement. In *The challenge of local feminisms: Women's movements in global perspective,* edited by A. Basu. Boulder, CO: Westview Press.

Laboy, M. M., T. Sandfort, and Yi Huso. 2009. Introduction to Special Issue: Global perspectives on same-sex sexualities: Desires, practices, and identities: Part 1: Negotiating global sexual identities in local contexts. *Sexuality Research and Social Policy, 6,* 1–3.

Lacey, M. 2008. Sandinista fervor turns sour for former comrades of Nicaragua's president. *New York Times.* November 24. A6.

LaFromboise, T. D., A. M. Heyle, and E. J. Ozer. 1990. Changing and diverse roles of women in American Indian cultures. *Sex Roles, 22,* 455–486.

Lambrou, Y., and G. Piana. 2006. Gender: The missing component of climate change. http://www.fao .org/sd/dim_pe1/docs/pe1_051001d1_en.pdf Retrieved on August 7, 2009.

Lancaster, J. 2005. For bride, dowry is deal breaker. *Washington Post Foreign Service,* 27 March, A19.

Larwood, L., E. Szwajkowski, and S. Rose. 1988. Sex and race discrimination resulting from manager-client relationships: Applying the rational bias theory of managerial discrimination. *Sex Roles, 18,* 9–29.

Lauter, D. 1995. EMILY's List: Overcoming barriers to political participation. In *A rising public voice: Women in politics worldwide,* edited by A. Brill. New York: Feminist Press.

Lavine, A. 2006. Tibetan Buddhism. In *Encyclopedia of women and religion in North America (Vol. 2),* edited by R. S. Keller, R. R. Ruether, and M. Canton. Bloomington: Indiana University Press.

Lerner, G. 1986. *The creation of patriarchy,* Vol. 1. New York: Oxford.

Lev, S. L. 2009. Liberation through the textual looking glass. *Journal of Feminist Studies in Religion, 25,* 170–180.

Lim, A. 2007. Transnational feminist practices in Hong Kong: Mobilization and collective action for sex workers' rights. *The Asian Pacific Journal of Anthropology, 9,* 319–331.

Lim, L. Y. C. 1990. Women's work in export factories: The politics of a cause. In *Persistent inequalities,* edited by I. Tinker. Oxford: Oxford University Press.

Lindau, R. 1993. A sexualized image of lesbians in Sweden. *Off Our Backs,* June, 10, 20.

Lindee, K. M. 2007. Love, honor, or control: Domestic violence, trafficking, and the question of how to regulate the mail-order bride industry. *Columbia Journal of Gender & Law, 16,* 551–602.

Ling, Y., and A. Matsumo. 1992. Women's struggle for empowerment in Japan. In *Women transforming politics: Worldwide strategies for empowerment,* edited by J. Bystydzienski. Bloomington: Indiana University Press.

Lips, H. M. 1991. *Women, men, and power.* Mountain View, CA: Mayfield.

Lister, R. 2003. *Citizenship: Feminist perspectives,* 2d ed. New York: New York University Press.

Livingston, J. A. 1982. Responses to sexual harassment on the job: Legal, organizational, and individual actions. *Journal of Social Issues, 38,* 5–22.

Lorber, J. (2000) *Gender and the social construction of illness,* New York: AltaMira Press.

Lorde, A. 1984. *Sister/outsider: Essays and speeches.* Freedom, CA: The Crossing Press.

Lorentzen, L. A., and J. Turpin. 1996. Introduction: The gendered new world order. In *The gendered new world,* edited by J. Turpin and L. A. Lorentzen. New York: Routledge.

Louie, M. C. Y. 2001. *Sweatshop warriors.* Cambridge, MA: South End Press.

Lovenduski, J. 2008. State feminism and women's movements. *West European Politics, 31,* 169–194.

Lozano, A. 2009. Controversial Afghan law leaves Shiite women's rights in question. *Online News Hour.* http://www.pbs.org/newshour/updates/law/july-dec09/afghanwomen_08-21.html Retrieved on August 28, 2009.

Lyness, K. S., and M. E. Heilman. 2006. When fit is fundamental. Performance evaluations and promotions of upper-level female and male managers. *Journal of Applied Psychology, 91,* 777–785.

Mabee, C. 1995. *Sojourner Truth: Slave, prophet, legend.* New York: New York University Press.

MacKinnon, C. 1979. *The sexual harassment of working women.* New Haven: Yale University Press.

Mak, A., K. Hui, J. Poone, and M. A. King. 1995. Country report on lesbians in Argentina. In *Unspoken rules: Sexual orientation and women's human rights,* edited by R. Rosenbloom. San Francisco: International Gay and Lesbian Human Rights Commission.

Malinowski, M. 2008. Chile Birth-Control Case Spurs 'Apostasy' Planning. *Women's eNews, http://www.womensenews.org/article.cfm?aid=3574.* Retrieved on April 8, 2009.

Maloney, C. 2004. A better future for Afghan women? *Ms.,* Spring, 33.

Mangis, M. W. 1995. Religious beliefs, dogmatism, and attitudes toward women. *Journal of Psychology and Christianity, 14,* 13–25.

Margolis, D. R. 1993. Women's movements around the world: Cross-cultural comparisons. *Gender and Society, 7,* 379–399.

Martinez, A. 1995. Country report on lesbians in Uruguay. In *Unspoken rules: Sexual orientation and women's human rights,* edited by R. Rosenbloom. San Francisco: International Gay and Lesbian Human Rights Commission.

Matynia, E. 1995. Finding a voice: Women in postcommunist Central Europe. In *The challenge of local feminisms: Women's movements in global perspective,* edited by A. Basu. Boulder, CO: Westview Press.

Mayer, A. M. 1995a. Cultural particularism as a bar to women's rights: Reflections on the Middle Eastern experience. In *Women's rights, human rights: International feminist perspectives,* edited by J. Peters and A. Wolper. New York: Routledge.

———. 1995b. *Islam and human rights: Tradition and politics,* 2d ed. Boulder, CO: Westview Press.

Mazur, A. G. 2001. Introduction. *State feminism, women's movements, and job training.* London: Routledge.

Mbachu, D. 2003. Women activists in peaceful takeover of Nigerian oil site. *Associated Press,* 29 July.

Mbon, F. M. 1987. Women in African traditional religions. In *Women in the world's religions, past and present,* edited by U. King. New York: Paragon House.

McBride, D. E. and A. G. Mazur. 2005. *Comparative study of women's movements: Conceptual puzzles and RNGS solutions.* Paper presented at the annual meeting of the American Political Science Association, Marriott Wardman Park, Omni Shoreham, Washington Hilton, Washington, DC. http://www.allacademic.com/meta/p41943_index.html Retrieved on October 2, 2009.

McCabe, M. P., and L. Hardman. 2005. Attitudes and perceptions of workers to sexual harassment. *Journal of Social Psychology, 145,* 719–741.

McCann, D. 2005. *Sexual harassment at work: National and international responses.* Geneva, Switzerland: ILO.

McConnell, T. 2009. Woman willing to risk 40 lashes for her human right to wear trousers; Sudan. *The Times (London),* 31. July 30.

McMinn, M. R., S. D. Brooks, M. A. Triplett, W. E. Hoffman, and P. G. Huizinga. 1993. The effects of God-language on perceived attributes of God. *Journal of Psychology & Theology, 21,* 309–314.

Meacham, D., and L. Shallet. 2002. Morning after pill: Chile grapples with sex. *Women's Health Journal,* Fall, 47–52.

Mead, M. 1935. *Sex and temperament in three primitive societies.* London: Morrow.

Meir, G. 1975. *My life.* New York: Putnam.

Menon, S. A., and S. Kanekar. 1992. Attitudes toward sexual harassment of women in India. *Journal of Applied Social Psychology, 22,* 1940–1952.

Mermel, A., and J. Simons, 1991. *Women and world development: An education and action guide.* Washington, DC: OEF International.

Mernissi, F. 1987. *The veil and the male elite: A feminist interpretation of women's rights in Islam.* Reading, MA: Addison-Wesley.

Merry, S. E. 2009. *Gender violence: A cultural perspective.* Sussex, United Kingdom: Wiley-Blackwell.

Mertus, J. 1995. State discriminatory family law and customary abuses. In *Women's rights, human rights: International feminist perspectives,* edited by J. Peters and A. Wolper. New York: Routledge.

Meyer, I. 2003. Prejudice, social stress, and mental health in lesbian, gay, and bisexual populations: Conceptual issues and research evidence. *Psychological Bulletin, 129,* 674–697.

Millenium Development Goals Report. 2008. www.un.org/**millenniumgoals**/pdf/mdg2007.pdf Retrieved on August 22, 2009.

Minter, S. 1995. Country report on lesbians in the United States. In *Unspoken rules: Sexual orientation and women's human rights,* edited by R. Rosenbloom. San Francisco: International Gay and Lesbian Human Rights Commission.

Mir-Hosseini, Z. 2001. Iran: Emerging women's voices. In *Women's rights: A global view,* edited by L. Walter. Westport, CT: Greenwood Press.

Moaveni, A., and S. Rotella. 2003. Iranian jurist wins Nobel Peace Prize. *Los Angeles Times,* 11 October, A1, A5.

Moghadam, V. M. 1991. Islamist movements and women's responses in the Middle East. *Gender and History, 3,* 268–284.

———1999. Gender and globalization: Female labor and women's mobilization. *Journal of World-Systems Research, 5,* 367–388.

———. 2003. *Modernizing women: Gender and social change in the Middle East,* 2d ed. Boulder: Lynne Rienner Publishers.

———. 2005. *Globalizing women: Transnational feminist networks.* Baltimore, MD: Johns Hopkins University Press.

———. 2007. An introduction and overview. In *From Patriarchy to empowerment,* edited by V. M. Moghadam. Syracuse: Syracuse University Press.

Mohanty, C. 1991. *Third World women and feminism.* Bloomington: Indiana University Press.

———. 2003. *Feminism without borders: Decolonizing theory, practicing solidarity.* Durham, NC: Duke University Press.

Molinelli, N. G. 1994. Argentina: The (no) ceteris paribus case. In *Electoral systems in comparative perspective: Their impact on women and minorities,* edited by W. Rule and J. F. Zimmerman. Westport, CT: Greenwood Press.

Molyneaux, M. 1985. Mobilization with emancipation? Women's interests, the state, and revolution in Nicaragua. *Feminist Studies, 11,* 227–255.

———. 1996. Women's rights and international context in the post-communist states. In *Mapping the women's movement: Feminist politics and social transformation in the North,* edited by M. Threlfall. London: Verso and New Left Review.

Moncrieffe, J. 2005. Beyond categories: Power, recognition and the conditions for equity. Background paper for the *World Development Report 2006: Equity and development.* New York: The World Bank.

Moran, T. H. 2002. *Beyond sweatshops: Foreign direct investment and globalization in developing countries.* Washington, DC: Brookings Institution Press.

Morgan, R., ed. 1996. *Sisterhood is global.* 2d ed. New York: Feminist Press.

Moser, C. 1989. Gender planning in the Third World: Meeting practical and strategical gender needs. *World Development, 17,* 1799–1825.

———. 1995. From Nairobi to Beijing: The transition from women in development to gender and development. In *Seeds 2,* edited by A. Leonard. New York: Feminist Press.

Mosse, J. C. 1993. *Half the world, half a chance: An introduction to gender and development.* Oxford: Oxfam.

Mostaghim, R., and B. Daragahi. 2009. Iranian Nobel Peace Prize winter Shirin Ebadi threatened in her home. *Los Angeles Times,* Jan 3. http://articles.latimes.com/2009/jan/03/world/fg-iran-ebadi3 Retrieved on August 28, 2009.

Mulama, J. 2009. Health Kenya: Contraceptives: Stock-Outs Threaten Family Planning. *IPS News,* http://ipsnews.net/news.asp?idnews=46854 Retrieved on April 9, 2009.

Murrell, A. J. 1996. Sexual harassment and women of color: Issues, challenges, and future directions. In *Sexual harassment in the workplace: Perspectives, frontiers, and response strategies,* edited by M. S. Stockdale. Thousand Oaks, CA: Sage.

Muteshi J., and J. Sass. 2005. *Female Genital Mutilation in Africa: An Analysis of Current Abandonment Approaches.* Nairobi: PATH.

Naples, N. A. 2002. Changing the terms: Community activism, globalization, and the dilemmas of transnational praxis. In *Women's activism and globalization: Linking local struggles transnational politics,* edited by N. A. Naples and M. Desai. New York: Routledge.

Narayanan, V. 1999. Brimming with *Bhakti,* embodiments of *Shakti:* Devotees, deities, performers, reformers, and other women of power in the Hindu tradition. In *Feminism and world religions,* edited by A. Sharma and K. K. Young. Albany, NY: State University Press of New York.

———. 2003. Hinduism. In *Her voice, her faith,* edited by A. Sharma and K. K. Young. Boulder, CO: Westview Press.

———. 2006. Hinduism in North America: Including emerging issues. In *Encyclopedia of women and religion in North America (Vol. 2),* edited by R. S. Keller, R. R. Ruether, and M. Canton. Bloomington: Indiana University Press.

National Association of Women Lawyers. 2008. National Association of Women Lawyers releases third annual survey: Groundbreaking data reveal impact of lateral moves, firm structure on women. http://www.nawl.org/Assets/Documents/2008+Survey+Press+Release.pdf Retrieved on July 10, 2009.

National Labor Committee. 2008. *Women Exploiting Women: Women in the U.S. are purchasing clothing sewn by women who are exploited in Guatemala.* http://www.nlcnet.org/reports.php?id=614 Retrieved on August 15, 2009.

———. 2009. High-tech misery in China. http://www.nlcnet.org/reports.php?id=613 Retrieved on August 15, 2009.

Nauman, A. K., and M. Hutchison. 1997. The integration of women into the Mexican labor force since NAFTA. *American Behavioral Scientist, 40,* 950–956.

Navarro, M. 2001. Argentina: The long road to women's rights. In *Women's rights: A global view,* edited by L. Walter. Westport, CN: Greenwood Press.

Neft, N., and A. D. Levine. 1998. *Where women stand: An international report on the status of women in 140 countries 1997–1998.* New York: Random House.

Nelson, D. L., J. C. Quick, M. A. Hitt, and D. Moesel. 1990. Politics, lack of career progress, and work/home conflict: Stress and strain for working women. *Sex Roles, 23,* 169–184.

Nelson, M. R., and H. Paek. 2005. Cross-cultural differences in sexual advertising content in a transnational women's magazine. *Sex Roles, 53,* 371–383.

New Internationalist. 2007. *Sex trafficking: The facts.* http://www.newint.org/features/2007/09/01/the-facts/ Retrieved on August 21, 2009.

Ng, V. 1996. Looking for lesbians in Chinese history. In *The new lesbian studies: Into the twenty-first century,* edited by B. Zimmerman and T. A. H. McNaron. New York: Feminist Press.

Niarchos, C. N. 1995. Women, war, and rape: Challenges facing the international tribunal for the former Yugoslavia. *Human Rights Quarterly, 17,* 649–690.

Niditch, S. 1991. Portrayals of women in the Hebrew Bible. In *Jewish women in historical perspective,* edited by J. Baskin. Detroit, MI: Wayne State University Press.

Nikolic-Ristanovic, V. 1996. War and violence against women. In *The gendered new world order: Militarism, development and the environment,* edited by J. Turpin and L. A. Lorentzen. New York: Routledge.

Nkomo, S. M., and T. Cox, Jr. 1989. Gender differences in the upward mobility of black managers: Double whammy or double advantage? *Sex Roles, 21,* 825–839.

Nnaemeka, O. 2005. African women, colonial discources, and imperialist interventions: Female circumcision as impetus. In *Circumcision and the politics of knowledge,* edited by O. Nnaemeka. Westport, CT: Praeger.

Nobelprize.org. 2003. *Shirin Ebadi, Nobel Peace Prize 2003.* http://nobelprize.org/nobel_prizes/peace/laureates/2003/ebadi-lecture-e.html Retrieved on August 28, 2009.

Noe, R. A. 1988. Women and mentoring: A review and research agenda. *Academy of Management Review, 13,* 65–78.

Norris, P., and J. Lovenduski, 1995. *Political recruitment, gender, race, and class in the British Parliament.* Cambridge: Cambridge University Press.

Nur, R. 1995. Country report on lesbians in Malaysia. In *Unspoken rules: Sexual orientation and women's human rights,* edited by R. Rosenbloom. San Francisco: International Gay and Lesbian Human Rights Commission.

Nussbaum, M. 1992. Human functioning and social justice: In defense of Aristotelian essentialism. *Political Theory,* 20, 202–246.

Obiora, L.A. 2005. The anti-female circumcision campaign deficit. In O. Nnaemeka (Ed.), *Circumcision and the politics of knowledge.* Westport, CT: Praeger.

Obiora, L. A. 2003. The little foxes that spoil the vine: Revisisting the feminist critique of female circumcision. In *African women and feminism: Reflecting on the politics of sisterhood,* edited by O. Oyewumi. Asmara, Eritrea: Africa World Press.

Oduyoye, M. A. 2001. *Introducing African women's theology.* Sheffield, England: Sheffield Academic Press.

Olson, J. E., and I. H. Frieze. 1987. Income determinants for women in business. In *Women and work: An annual review.* Vol. 2, edited by A. H. Stromberg, L. Larwood, and B. A. Gutek. Newbury Park, CA: Sage.

Onyejekwe, C. J. 2008. Nigeria: The dominance of rape. *Journal of International Women's Studies,* 10, 48–63.

OXFAM. 2007. *Signing away the future.* http://www.oxfam.org.uk/resources/policy/trade/downloads/bp101_ftas.pdf?m=234&url=http://www.oxfam.org.uk/resources/policy/trade/downloads/bp92_afghanistan.pdf Retrieved on July 20, 2009.

Oyewumi, O. 2003. Introduction: Feminism, sisterhood, and other foreign relations. In *African women and feminism: Reflecting on the politics of sisterhood, edited by* O. Oyewumi. Asmara, Eritrea: Africa World Press.

Pablos, E. T. 1992. Women's struggles for empowerment in Mexico: Accomplishments, problems, and challenges. In *Women transforming politics: Worldwide strategies for empowerment,* edited by J. Bystydzienski. Bloomington: Indiana University Press.

Padavic, I., and B. Reskin. 2002. *Women and men at work,* 2d ed. Thousand Oaks, CA: Sage.

Pagels, E. H. 1976. What became of God the Mother? Conflicting images of God in early Christianity. In *Womanspirit rising: A feminist reader in religion,* edited by C. P. Christ and J. Plaskow. San Francisco: Harper and Row.

Parrenas, R. S. 2001. *Servants of globalization: Women, migration, and domestic work.* Stanford, CA: Stanford University Press.

———. 2008. *The force of domesticity: Filipina migrants and globalization.* New York: New York University Press.

Parrot, A., and N. Cummings. 2006. *Forsaken females: The global brutalization of women.* New York: Rowman & Littlefield Publishers, INC.

———. 2008. *Sexual enslavement of girls and women worldwide.* Westport, CT: Praeger.

Pateman, C. 1992. Equality, difference, subordination: The politics of motherhood and women's citizenship. In *Beyond equality and difference,* edited by G. Bock and S. James. London: Routledge.

Patterson, C. J., and R. E. Redding. 1996. Lesbian and gay families with children: Implications of social science research for policy. *Journal of Social Issues, 52,* 29–50.

Patton, L. L. 2007. The cat in the courtyard: The performance of Sanskrit and the religious experience of women. In *Women's Lives: Women's rituals in the hindu tradition,* edited by T. Pintchman. New York: Oxford University Press.

Paxton, P. and M. M. Hughes. 2007. *Women, politics, and power: A global perspective.* Thousand Oaks, CA: Sage Pine Forge Press.

Paxton, P., P. Kunovich, and M. M. Hughes. 2007. Gender in politics. *Annual Review of Sociology, 33,* 263–284.

Peach, L. J. 2001. *Women and world religions.* Upper Saddle River, NJ: Prentice Hall.

Pesantobbee, M. 2005. *Choctaw women in a chaotic world.* Albuquerque: University of New Mexico Press.

Penelope, J. 1990. Introduction. RU12? In *Finding the lesbians: Personal accounts from around the world,* edited by J. Penelope and S. Valentine. Freedom, CA: Crossing Press.

Perez, G. C., and P. Jimenez. 1995. Country report on lesbians in Mexico. In *Unspoken rules: Sexual orientation and women's human rights,* edited by R. Rosenbloom. San Francisco: International Gay and Lesbian Human Rights Commission.

Petchesky, R. P. 1984. Abortion and women's choice. New York: Longman.

———. 1990. Beyond a woman's right to choose: Feminist ideas about reproductive rights. In *Abortion and women's choice: The state, sexuality, and reproductive freedom,* edited by R. P. Petchesky. Hanover, NH: Northeastern University Press.

Peters, J., and A. Wolper. 1995. Introduction. In *Women's rights, human rights: International feminist perspectives,* edited by J. Peters and A. Wolper. New York: Routledge.

Peterson, V. S., and A. S. Runyan. 2010. *Global gender issues,* 2d ed. Boulder, CO: Westview Press.

Pettit, B., and J. Hook. 2005. The structure of women's employment in comparative perspective. *Social Forces, 84,* 779–801.

Pharr, S. 1988. Homophobia: A weapon of sexism. In *Issues in feminism,* 3d ed., edited by S. Ruth. Mountain View, CA: Mayfield.

Plaskow, J. 1979. The coming of Lilith: Toward a feminist theology. In *Womanspirit rising: A feminist reader in religion,* edited by C. P. Christ and J. Plaskow. New York: Harper Collins.

———. 1991. *Standing again at Sinai.* San Francisco: HarperCollins.

———. 2005. The coming of Lilith: Essays on feminism, Judaism, and sexual ethics (1972–2003).

Plata, M. I. 1994. Reproductive rights as human rights: The Colombian case. In *Human rights of women: National and international perspectives,* edited by R. J. Cook. Philadelphia: University of Pennsylvania Press.

Pollit, K. 2002. Introduction. In *Nothing sacred: Women respond to religious fundamentalism and terror,* edited by B. Reed. New York: Thunder's Mouth Press/ Nation Books.

Porter, M. 2007. Transnational feminism in a globalized world: Challenges, analysis, and resistance. *Feminist Studies, 33,* 43–63.

Powell, G. N., and L. A. Mainiero. 1992. Cross-currents in the river of time: Conceptualizing the complexities of women's careers. *Journal of Management, 18,* 215–237.

Prugl, E., and A. Lustgarten. 2006. Mainstreaming gender in international organizations. In *Women and gender equity in development theory and practice: Institutions, resources, and mobilization,* edited by J. S. Jaquette and G. Summerfield. Durham, NC: Duke University Press.

Prusak, B. P. 1974. Woman: Seductive siren and source of sin? In *Religion and sexism: Images of woman in the Jewish and Christian traditions,* edited by R. R. Ruether. New York: Simon and Schuster.

Pryor, J. B., J. L. Giedd, and K. B. Williams. 1995. A social psychological model for predicting sexual harassment. *Journal of Social Issues, 51,* 69–84.

Pui-lan, K. 2007. *Postcolonial imagination and feminist theology.* Louisville, KY: Westminster John Knox Press.

Pyne, H. H. 1995. AIDS and gender violence: The enslavement of Burmese women in the Thai sex industry. In *Women's rights, human rights: International feminist perspectives,* edited by J. Peters and A. Wolper. New York: Routledge.

Rachels, J. 1993. *The elements of moral philosophy,* 2d ed. New York: McGraw-Hill.

Raday, F. 2005. Women of the Wall. *Jewish Women's Archive.* http://jwa.org/encyclopedia/article/ women-of-wall Retrieved on August 29, 2009.

Ragins, B. R. 1999. Gender and mentoring relationships: A review and research agenda for the next decade. In *Handbook of gender and work,* edited by G. N. Powell. Thousand Oaks, CA: Sage.

Ragins, B. R., and E. Sundstrom. 1989. Gender and power in organizations: A longitudinal perspective. *Psychological Bulletin 105,* 51–88.

Ragins, B. R., R. Singh, and J. M. Cornwell. 2007. Making the invisible visible: Fear and disclosure of sexual orientation at work. *Journal of Applied Psychology, 92,* 1103–1118.

RAINN. 2009. *Statistics.* http://rainn.org/statistics Retrieved on January 9, 2009.

Ramshaw, G. 1995. *God beyond gender: Feminist Christian God-language.* Minneapolis, MN: Argsburg Fortress.

Rao, A. 1995. The politics of gender and culture in international human rights discourse. In *Women's rights, human rights: International feminist perspectives,* edited by J. Peters and A. Wolper. New York: Routledge.

Reanda, L. 1992. The commission on the status of women. In *The United Nations and human rights: A critical appraisal,* edited by P. Alston. Oxford, UK: Oxford University Press.

Report of the UN Secretary General, 2006. In-depth study on all forms of violence against women: Report of the Secretary General (Sixty-first session). http://www.stopvaw.org/sites/3f6d15f4-c12d-4515-8544-26b7a3a5a41e/uploads/Sec_Gen_Study_VAW.pdf Retrieved on July 29, 2009.

Rich, A. 1976. *Of woman born: Motherhood as experience and institution.* New York: Norton.

———. 1980. Compulsory heterosexuality and lesbian existence. *Signs, 5,* 631–660.

Ridgeway, C. L. 2001. Social status and group structure. In *Group processes,* edited by M. A. Hogg and S. Tinsdale. Oxford, UK: Blackwell.

Rios Tobar, M. 2008. Seizing a window of opportunity: The election of President Bachelet of Chile. *Politics and Gender, 4,* 509–519.

Roberts, T. 2009. Free God language: fired parish worker's thesis. *National Catholic Reporter.* http://ncronline.org/news/faith-parish/free-god-language-fired-parish-workers-thesis Retrieved on August 26, 2009.

Robinson, S. P. 1985. Hindu paradigms of women: Images and values. In *Women, religion, and social change,* edited by Y. Y. Haddad and E. B. Findly. Albany: State University of New York Press.

Rogers, B. 1980. *The domestication of women: Discrimination in developing societies.* New York: St. Martin's Press.

Roman Catholic Woman Priests. 2009. *Ordinations.* http://www.romancatholicwomenpriests.org/ordained.htm Retrieved on September 2, 2009.

Rondon, E. 1995. Country report on lesbians in Colombia. In *Unspoken rules: Sexual orientation and women's human rights,* edited by R. Rosenbloom. San Francisco: International Gay and Lesbian Human Rights Commission.

Rosaldo, M. Z. 1974. Women, culture, and society: A theoretical overview. In *Women, culture, and society,* edited by M. Z. Rosaldo and L. Lamphere. Stanford, CA: Stanford University Press.

Rose, S. D. 1999. Christian fundamentalism: Patriarchy, sexuality, and human rights. In *Religious fundamentalisms and the human rights of women,* edited by C. W. Howland. New York: St. Martin's Press.

Rosenthal, R., and D. B. Rubin. 1982. Further meta-analytic procedures for assessing cognitive gender differences. *Journal of Educational Psychology, 74,* 706–712.

Ross, S. D. 2008. *Women's human rights: The international and comparative law casebook.* Philadelphia: University of Pennsylvania Press.

Rothschild, C. 2005. *Written out: How sexuality is used to attack women's organizing.* IGLHRC/CWGL http://www.cwgl.rutgers.edu/globalcenter/publications/written2005.pdf Retrieved on June 25, 2009.

Ruan, F. F., and V. Bullough. 1992. Lesbianism in China. *Archives of Sexual Behavior, 21,* 217–228.

Ruether, R. R. 1985. *Womanguides: Readings toward a feminist theology,* Boston: Beacon Press.

———. 1974. *Religion and sexism: Images of woman in the Jewish and Christian traditions.* New York: Simon and Schuster.

———. 1999. Feminism in World Christianity. In *Feminism and world religions,* edited by A. Sharma and K. K. Young. Albany: State University Press of New York.

———. 2002. The war on women. In *Nothing sacred: Women respond to religious fundamentalism and terror,* edited by B. Reed. New York: Thunder's Mouth Press/Nation Books.

———. 2008. *Christianity and social systems: Historical constructions and ethical challenges.* Lanham, MD: Rowman & Littlefield.

Rule, W. 1994. Parliaments of, by, and for the people: Except for women? In *Electoral systems in comparative perspective: Their impact on women and minorities,* edited by W. Rule and J. F. Zimmerman. Westport, CT: Greenwood Press.

Rupp, L. J. 1996. Finding the lesbians in lesbian history: Reflections on female same-sex sexuality in the western world. In *The new lesbian studies: Into the twenty-first century,* edited by B. Zimmerman and T. A. H. McNaron. New York: Feminist Press.

———. 1997. "Imagine my surprise": Women's relationships in historical perspective. *Journal of Lesbian Studies, 1,* 155–176.

Ruth, S. 1995. *Issues in feminism,* 3d ed. Mountain View, CA: Mayfield.

Saint-Germain, M. A. 1993. Women in power in Nicaragua: Myth and reality. In *Women as national leaders,* edited by M. A. Genovese. Newbury Park, CA: Sage.

Saint-Germain, M. A., and C. C. Metoyer. 2008. *Women legislators in Central America: Politics, democracy, and policy.* Austin: University of Texas Press.

Salinas, G. A. 1994. Women and politics: Gender relations in Bolivian political organizations and labor unions. In *Women and politics worldwide,* edited by B. J. Nelson and N. Chowdhury. New Haven, CT: Yale University Press.

Salzinger, L. 2003. *Genders in production: Making workers in Mexico's global factories.* Berkeley: University of California Press.

Sanchez, L. 1993. Women's power and the gendered division of domestic labor in the third world. *Gender and Society,* 7, 434–459.

Sanchez-Hucles, J. V., and D. Davis. 2010. Women and women of color in leadership: Complexity, identity, and intersectionality. *American Psychologist,* 65, 171–181.

Sanday, P. R. 1974. Female status in the public domain. In *Women, culture, and society,* edited by M. Z. Rosaldo and L. Lamphere. Stanford, CA: Stanford University Press.

———. 1981. *Female power and male dominance: On the origins of sexual inequality.* Cambridge: Cambridge University Press.

Sanghari, P., K. Balla, and V. Das. 2009. Fire-related deaths in India in 2001: A retrospective analysis of data. *The Lancet, 373,* 1282–1288.

Santiago, L. Q. 1995. Rebirthing *Babaye:* The women's movement in the Philippines. In *The challenge of local feminisms: Women's movements in global perspective,* edited by A. Basu. Boulder, CO: Westview Press.

Sassen, S. 2002. Global cities and survival circuits. In *Global woman: Nannies, maids, and sex workers in the new economy,* edited by B. Ehrenreich and A. R. Hochschild. New York: Metropolitan Books.

Sawer, M. 1994. Locked out or locked in? Women and politics in Australia. In *Women and politics worldwide,* edited by B. J. Nelson and N. Chowdhury. New Haven, CT: Yale University Press.

Schein, V. E., and R. Mueller. 1992. Sex role stereotyping and requisite management characteristics: A cross-cultural look. *Journal of Organizational Behavior, 13,* 439–447.

Schein, V. E., R. Mueller, and C. Jacobson. 1989. The relationship between sex role stereotypes and requisite management characteristics among college students. *Sex Roles, 20,* 103–111.

Schein, V. E., R. Mueller, T. Lituchy, and J. Liu. 1996. Think manager—think male: A global phenomenon? *Journal of Organizational Behavior, 17,* 33–41.

Schneider, K. T., S. Swann, and L. F. Fitzgerald. 1997. Job-related and psychological effects of sexual harassment in the workplace: Empirical evidence from two organizations. *Journal of Applied Psychology, 82,* 401–415.

Schulman, G. B. 1974. View from the back of the synagogue. In *Sexist religion and women in the church,* edited by A. L. Hageman. New York: Association Press.

Schüssler Fiorenza E. 1992. *But she said: Feminist practices of Biblical interpretation.* Boston, MA: Beacon Press.

———. 1995. *Bread not stone: The challenge of feminist biblical interpretation, 10th anniversary edition.* Boston: Beacon Press.

———. 2007. *The power of the Word: Scripture and the rhetoric of empire.* Minneapolis, MN: Fortress.

Schwindt-Bayer, L. A. 2006. Still supermadres? Gender and the policy priorities of Latin American legislators. *American Journal of Political Science, 50,* 570–585.

Sciolino, E., and S. Mekhennet. 2008. Muslim women and virginity: Two worlds collide. *New York Times,* June 11, 1.

Sczesny, S., J. Bosak, D. Neff, and B. Schyns. 2004. Gender stereotypes and the attribution of leadership Traits: A cross-cultural comparison. *Sex Roles, Vol. 51,* 631–645.

Seager, J. 1993. *Earth follies.* New York: Routledge.

———.1997. *The State of the World Atlas: New Revised Second Edition.* London: Penguin.

———. 2009. *The Penguin Atlas of women in the world,* 4th ed. New York: Penguin.

Segal, L. 1987. *Is the future female? Troubled thoughts on contemporary feminism.* London: Virago.

Sekhon, J., and J. M. Bystydzienski. 2001. Conclusion. In *Democratization and women's grassroots movements,* edited by J. M. Bystydzienski and J. Sekhon. Bloomington: Indiana University Press.

Sen, G., and C. Grown. 1987. *Development crises and alternative visions.* New York: Monthly Review Press.

Sentilles, S. 2008. *A Church of Her Own: What Happens When a Woman Takes the Pulpit.* Orlando: Harcourt Brace.

Sered, S. S. 1994. *Priestess, mother, sacred sister.* Oxford: Oxford University Press.

———. 1999. *Women of the sacred groves: Divine priestesses of Okinawa.* Oxford, UK: Oxford University Press.

Serhan, R. B. 2003. Virginity: Arab states. In *Encyclopedia of Women and Islamic Cultures* (vol. 3), edited by S. Joseph and A. Najmabadi. Boston: Brill.

SEWA. 2009. *Annual report 2007–2008*. http://www .sewabank.com/financialdata.htm Retrieved on July 29, 2009.

Shaaban, B. 1995. The muted voices of women interpreters. In *Faith and freedom: Women's rights in the Muslim world*, edited by M. Afkami. London: I. B. Tauris.

Shalev, C. 1995. Women in Israel: Fighting tradition. In *Women's rights, human rights: International feminist perspectives*, edited by J. Peters and A. Wolper. New York: Routledge.

Shapiro, D. N., Peterson, C., and Stewart, A. 2009. Legal and social contexts and mental health among lesbian and heterosexual mothers. *Journal of Family Psychology, 23*, 255–262.

Sharma, M. 2007. "She has come from the world of the spirits . . .": Life stories of working-class lesbian women in northern India. In *Women's sexualities and masculinities in a globalizing Asia*, edited by S. E. Wieringa, E. Blackwood, and A. Bhaiya. New York: Palgrave Macmillan.

Sherif, B. 2001. Egypt: Multiple Perspectives on Women's Rights. In *Women's rights: A global view*, edited by L. Walter. Westport, CT: Greenwood Press.

Simelela, N. 2006. Women's access to modern methods of fertility regulation. *International Journal of Gynecology and Obstetrics, 94*, 292–300.

Singer, N. 2009. Contraceptive sponge makes a return to pharmacy shelves. *New York Times*, May 23, Section B; Column 0; Business/Financial Desk; 1.

Sjöberg, O. 2004. The role of family policy institutions in explaining gender-role attitudes: A comparative multilevel analysis of thirteen industrialized countries. *Journal of European Social Policy, 14*, 107–123.

Skattebol, J. and Ferfolja, T. 2007. Voices from an enclave: Lesbian mothers' experiences of child care. *Australian Journal of Early Childhood, 32*, 10–19.

Smith, A. 2009. Elisabeth Schüssler Fiorenza and the future of Native American theology. *Journal of Feminist Studies in Religion, 25*, 143–150.

Soares, V., A. A. Alcantara Costa, C. M. Buarque, D. D. Dora, and W. Sant'Anna. 1995. Brazilian feminism and women's movements: A two-way street. In *The challenge of local feminisms: Women's movements in global perspective*, edited by A. Basu. Boulder, CO: Westview Press.

Sommers, C. H. (2000). *The war against boys*. New York: Simon & Schuster.

Sontheimer, S. 1991. *Women and the environment: A reader on crisis and development in the Third World*. New York: Monthly Review Press.

Srinivasan, S. 2005. Daughters or dowries? The changing nature of dowry practices in south India. *World Development, 33*, 593–615.

Srinivasan, S., and A. S. Bedi. 2007. Domestic violence and dowry: Evidence from a South Indian Village. *World Development, 35*, 857–880.

Stamatopoulou, E. 1995. Women's rights and the United Nations. In *Women's rights, human rights: International feminist perspectives*, edited by J. Peters and A. Wolper. New York: Routledge.

Stankiewicz, J. M. and F. Roselli. 2008. Women as sex objects and victims in print advertising. *Sex Roles, 58*, 575–589.

Stark, R. 1995. Reconstructing the rise of Christianity: The role of women. *Sociology of Religion, 56*, 229–244.

Staudt, K. 1995. Planting *Seeds 2* in the classroom. In *Seeds 2*, edited by A. Leonard. New York: Feminist Press.

Steady, F. C. 1995. Women and the environment in developing countries: The challenge of implementing Agenda 21. In *Women and the United Nations*, edited by F. C. Steady and R. Toure. Rochester, VT: Schenkman Books.

Stearns, J. 1998. *Gender and international relations: An introduction*. New Brunswick, NJ: Rutgers University Press.

Stetson, D. M., and A. G. Mazur. 1995. Introduction. In *Comparative state feminism*, edited by D. M. Stetson and A. G. Mazur. Newbury Park, CA: Sage.

Stevens, A. 2007. *Women, power, and politics*. New York: Palgrave Macmillan.

Stevens, G. E. 1984. Women in business: The view of future male and female managers. *Journal of Business Education, 59*, 314–317.

Stevens, P. E., and J. M. Hall. 1991. A critical historical analysis of the medical construction of lesbianism. *International Journal of Health Services, 21*, 291–307.

Stienstra, D. 1994. *Women's movements and international organizations*. New York: St. Martin's Press.

Stone, M. *When God was a woman*. San Diego, CA: Harcourt Brace Jovanovich.

Stop Rape Now. 2009. http://www.stoprapenow.org/ news.html Retrieved on January 9, 2009.

Strange, C. 1990. Mothers on the march: Maternalism in women's protest for peace in North America and Western Europe, 1900–1985. In *Women and social protest,* edited by G. West and R. L. Blumberg. Oxford, UK: Oxford University Press.

Sugirtharajah, S. 1994. Hinduism. In *Women in religion,* edited by J. Holm. New York: St. Martin's Press.

Sullins, P. 2000. The stained glass ceiling: Career attainment for women clergy. *Sociology of Religion, 61,* 243–277.

Sullivan, D. 1995. The public/private distinction in international human rights law. In *Women's rights, human rights: International feminist perspectives,* edited by J. Peters and A. Wolper. New York: Routledge.

Sussman, A. S. 2009. Liberia stresses need for female peacemakers. *Women's e-news.* March 13. http://www.womensenews.org/article.cfm/dyn/aid/3949/context/cover/ Retrieved on September 21, 2009.

Tanaka, K. 1995. Work, education, and the family. In *Japanese women: New feminist perspectives on the past, present and future,* edited by K. Fujimura-Fanselow and A. Kameda. New York: Feminist Press.

Tangri, S. S., Burt, M. R., and L. B. Johnson. 1982 Sexual harassment at work: Three explanatory models. *Journal of Social Issues, 28,* 33–54.

Taylor, D. 2002. Women in search of peace. *The Guardian,* 22 January, 8.

Taylor, V., and L. J. Rupp. 1993. Women's culture and lesbian feminist activism: A reconsideration of cultural feminism. *Signs,* Autumn, 32–61.

The Carter Center. 2009. *Liberia.* http://www .cartercenter.org/countries/liberia.html. Retrieved on September 21, 2009.

Threlfall, M. 1996. Feminist politics and social change in Spain. In *Mapping the women's movement: Feminist politics and social transformation in the North,* edited by M. Threlfall. London: Verso and New Left Review.

Tinker, I. 1990. A context for the field and for the book. In *Persistent inequalities: Women and world development,* edited by I. Tinker. Oxford: Oxford University Press.

———. 1994. Women and community forestry in Nepal: Expectations and realities. *Society and Natural Resources, 7,* 367–381.

———. 1995. The human economy of microentrepreneurs. In *Women in micro- and small-scale enterprise development,* edited by L. Divard and J. Havet. Boulder, CO: Westview Press.

Todosijevic, J. 1995. Country report on lesbians in Serbia. In *Unspoken rules: Sexual orientation and women's human rights,* edited by R. Rosenbloom.

San Francisco: International Gay and Lesbian Human Rights Commission.

Tomasevski, K. 1993. *Women and human rights.* London: Zed. Toro, M. S. 1995. Popularizing women's human rights at the local level: A grassroots methodology for setting the international agenda. In *Women's rights, human rights: International feminist perspectives,* edited by J. Peters and A. Wolper. New York: Routledge.

Tomlinson, J. 2008. Causes and consequences of the divergent working-time patterns of employed mothers in the UK and the US: Developing a comparative analysis. *Gender Issues, 25,* 246–266.

Tong, R. 2009. *Feminist thought: A more comprehensive introduction,* 3rd ed. Boulder, CO: Westview.

Townes, E. M. 2006. Womanist theology. In *Encyclopedia of women and religion in North America (vol. 3),* edited by R. S. Keller, R. R. Ruether, and M. Canton. Bloomington: Indiana University Press.

Trible, P. 1973. Eve and Adam: Genesis 2–3 reread. In *Womanspirit rising: A feminist reader in religion,* edited by C. P. Christ and J. Plaskow. New York: Harper and Row.

Tripp, A. M. 2006a. The evolution of transnational feminisms: Consensus, conflict, and new dynamics. In *Global feminism,* edited by M. M. Ferree and A. M. Tripp. New York: New York University Press.

———. 2006b. Challenges in transnational feminist mobilization. In *Global feminism,* edited by M. M. Ferree and A. M. Tripp. New York: New York University Press.

Tripp, A. M., and A. Kang. 2008. The global impact of quotas: On the fast track to increased female legislative representation. *Comparative Political Studies, 41,* 338–361.

Tripp, A. M., I. Casimiro, J. Kwesiga, and A. Mungwa. 2009. *African women's movements: Changing political landscapes.* New York: Cambridge University Press.

Trujillo, C. 1991. Chicana lesbians: Fear and loathing in the Chicano community. In *Women images and realities: A multicultural anthology,* edited by A. Kesselman, L. D. McNair, and N. Schniedewind. Mountain View, CA: Mayfield.

Tucker, P. 2008. The daughter also rises: how son preference is impacting Asia. *The Futurist, 42,* 3.

Uchino, K. 1987. The status elevation process of Soto sect nuns in modern Japan. In *Speaking of faith: Global perspectives on women, religion, and social change,* edited by D. L. Eck and D. Jain. Philadelphia: New Society Publishers.

Umanksy, E. M. 1999. Feminism in Judaism. In *Feminism and world religions,* edited by A. Sharma and K. K. Young. Albany: State University Press of New York.

UN (United Nations). 1994. Equal pay, urban women problems discussed by commission. *UN Chronicle,* August, 60–61.

———. 1999. *World survey on the role of women in development: Globalization, gender and work.* New York: Author.

———. 2008. *Millennium development goals report 2008.* New York: Author.

UNAIDS. 2008. *2008 report on the global AIDS epidemic.* Geneva, Switzerland: UNAIDS.

UN DESA (United Nations Department of Economic and Social Affairs). 2009. Division of unpaid and paid work: A source of inequality. *DESA News, 13.* http://www.un.org/esa/desa/desaNews/v13n03/feature.html

UNDP (United Nations Development Programme). 1995. *Human development report.* Oxford, UK: Oxford University Press.

———. 2003. *Human development report 2003.* Oxford, UK: Oxford University Press.

———. 2007. *Asian son preference will have severe social consequences, new studies warn.* United Nations Population Fund. http://www.unfpa.org/public/News/pid/301 Retrieved on January 9, 2009.

———. 2008a. *Statistics of the human development report.* http://hdr.undp.org/en/statistics/ Retrieved on August 1, 2009.

———. 2008b. *The gender equality strategy 2008–2011.* New York, New York: Author.

———. 2008c. *Human development report 2007–2008: Fighting climate change.* http://hdr.undp.org/en/media/HDR_20072008_EN_Complete.pdf Retrieved on August 6, 2009.

———. 2009a. *Gender and poverty.* http://www.undp.org/poverty/focus_gender_and_poverty.shtml Retrieved on August 1, 2009.

———. 2009b. *Resource guide on gender and climate change.* http://www.un.org/womenwatch/downloads/Resource_Guide_English_FINAL.pdf Retrieved on August 20, 2009.

———. 2009c. *Climate change affects all the MDGs.* http://www.undp.org/climatechange/climateMDGs.htm Retrieved on August 6, 2009.

———. 2009. United Nations Development Program Asia Pacific Regional Center (2006). Gender facts. *Inside, 1, 1.*

UN End Poverty Millennium Campaign. 2009. *Goal #3: Gender Equity.* http://endpoverty2015.org/goals/gender-equity Retrieved on August 1, 2009.

UNFPA (United Nations Population Fund). 2006. *State of the world population 2006: A Passage to hope—women and international migration.* http://www.unfpa.org/swp/2006/ Retrieved on August 17, 2009.

———. 2009a. *Ending widespread violence against women.* United Nations Population Fund. http://www.unfpa.org/gender/violence/htm Retrieved on January 9, 2009.

———. 2009b. *Improving reproductive health.* http://www.unfpa.org/rh/index.htm Retrieved on March 9, 2009.

———. 2009c. *Stepping up efforts to save women's lives.* http://www.unfpa.org/mothers/index.htm Retrieved on March 9, 2009.

———. 2009d. *Facts about safe motherhood.* http://www.unfpa.org/mothers/facts.htm Retrieved on March 9, 2009.

———. 2009e. *Maternal mortality figures show limited progress in making motherhood safer.* http://www.unfpa.org/mothers/statistics.htm Retrieved on March 9, 2009.

———. 2009f. *Calling for an end to female genital cutting.* http://www.unfpa.org/gender/practices1.htm Retrieved on February 9, 2009.

———. 2008a. *State of the world population 2008. Reaching common ground: Culture, gender, and human rights.* United Nations Population Fund. http://www.unfpa.org/swp/2008/en/index.html Retrieved on February 10, 2009.

———. 2008b. *Contraceptives save lives.* http://www.unfpa.org/rh/planning/mediakit/docs/new_docs/sheet2-english.pdf Retrieved on March 9, 2009.

———. 2005a. *State of the world population.* United Nations Population Fund. www.unfpa.org/swp/**2005**/english/ch1/index.htm Retrieved on April 9, 2009.

———. 2005b. *International Conference on Population and Development - ICPD Programme of Action.* http://www.unfpa.org/webdav/site/global/shared/documents/publications/2004/icpd_eng.pdf

UNFPA Campaign to End Fistula. 2009. http://www.endfistula.org/ Retrieved on March 16, 2009.

UN High Commissioner for Human Rights. 2009. *Fact Sheet No.23, Harmful traditional practices affecting the health of women and children.* http://www.unhchr .ch/html/menu6/2/fs23.htm

UNICEF (United Nations Children's Fund). 2006. *The state of the world's children 2007: Women and Children.* New York: United Nations Children's Fund.

———. 2009. *Child trafficking.* http://www.unicef.org/ protection/index_exploitation.html Retrieved on August 21, 2009.

UNIFEM (United Nations Development Fund for Women). 2003. Women's human rights: Addressing the gender dimensions of HIV/AIDS. http://www.unifem.org

———. 2005. *Progress of the world's women 2005.* http://www.ilo.org/dyn/infoecon/docs/903/ F1194308449/PoWW2005_eng.pdf

———. 2009a. *Progress of the world's women 2008/2009. Who answers to women? Gender and accountability.* http://www.unifem.org/progress/2008

———. 2009b. *Facts and figures on VAW: Sexual violence.* http://www.unifem.org/gender_issues/violence_ against_women/facts_figures.php?page=3

UN Integrated Regional Information Networks. 2003. *Zimbabwe: Focus on rape as a political weapon.* 8 April.

United States Department of State. 2009. *Trafficking in persons report.* http://www.state.gov/g/tip/rls/ tiprpt/2009/ Retrieved on August 21, 2009.

UNODC (United Nations Office of Drugs and Crime). 2009. *Global report on trafficking in persons.* United Nations Office of Drugs and Crime. http://www.unodc.org/documents/human_ trafficking Retrieved on April 15, 2009.

UN Secretary General. 2006. *In-depth study on all forms of violence against women: Report of the Secretary General,* 2006. A/61/122/Add.1. 6 July 2006.

———. 2009. UN Secretary General's Database on Violence Against Women. http://webapps01 .un.org/vawdatabase/advancedSearch.action;jse ssionid=0F20808E99272B142AF9361467A867B1 Retrieved on February 9, 2009.

UN Statistics Division. 2007a. *Under five mortality rate.* UN Data: Gender Info 2007. http://data .un.org/Browse.aspx?d=GenderStat Retrieved on February 9, 2009.

———. 2007b. *Prevalence of underweight children.* UN Data: Gender Info 2007. http://data.un.org/ Browse .aspx?d=GenderStat Retrieved on February 9, 2009.

———. 2007c. *Female/male ratio of population.* UN Data: Gender Info 2007. http://data.un.org/Browse .aspx?d=GenderStat Retrieved on February 9, 2009.

———. 2007d. Labour force participation rate. *Gender Info 2007.* http://data.un.org/Data.aspx? d=GenderStat&f=inID%3a106#GenderStat Retrieved on July 14, 2009.

UN Treaty Collection. 2009. *Protocol to Prevent, Suppress and Punish Trafficking in Persons, Especially Women and Children, supplementing the United Nations Convention against Transnational Organized Crime.* http://treaties.un.org/Pages/ViewDetails .aspx?src=TREATY&mtdsg_no=XVIII-12-a& chapter=18&lang=en Retrieved on August 21, 2009.

University of Bath. 2008. Marriage dowry as major cause of poverty in Bangladesh. *Science Daily.* 31 October.

Valenti, J. 2009. How 'virginity' is a dangerous idea. *The Toronto Star,* April 25, IN04.

Valiente, C. 2005. The women's movement, gender equality agencies, and central-state debates on political representation in Spain. In *State feminism and political representation,* edited by J. Lovenduski. New York: Cambridge University Press.

Van Vianen, A. E. M., and T. M. Willemsen. 1992. The employment interview: The role of sex stereotypes in the evaluation of male and female job appli- cants in the Netherlands. *Journal of Applied Social Psychology, 22,* 471–491.

Vasudev, S., A. K. Menon, R. Vinayak, S. David, and K. Muralideharan. 2003. Groom showroom. *India Today,* 9 June, 64.

Violence Policy Center. 2008. *When men murder women: An analysis of 2006 homicide data.* http://www.vpc .org/studies/wmmw2008.pdf

Vitema, J., and K. M. Fallon. 2008. Democratization, women's movements, and gender-equitable States: A framework for comparison. *American Sociological Review, 73,* 668–688.

VOA News. 2009. *Trafficking in women and girls.* August 8. http://www.voanews.com/uspolicy/2009-08- 10-voa1.cfm Retrieved on August 21, 2009.

Wadud, A. 1999. *Qu'ran and women: Rereading the sacred text from a woman's perspective.* New York: Oxford USA.

———. 2006. *Inside the gender jihad: Women's reform in Islam.* Oxford, UK: Oneworld.

Walter, L. 2001. Introduction. In *Women's rights as human rights: A global view,* edited by L. Walter. Westport, CT: Greenwood Press.

Ward, K. B., and J. L. Pyle. 1995. Gender, industrialization, transnational corporations, and development: An overview of trends and patterns. In *Women in the Latin American development process,* edited by C. E. Bose and E. Acosta-Belen. Philadelphia: Temple University Press.

Ward, O. 2009. Women to get UN advocate. *Toronto Star.* October 2. A15.

Waring, M. 1988. *If women counted: A new feminist economics.* New York: Harper and Row.

Waters, E., and A. Posadskaya. 1995. Democracy without women is no democracy: Women's struggles in postcommunist Russia. In *The challenge of local feminisms: Women's movements in global perspective,* edited by A. Basu. Boulder, CO: Westview Press.

Watson, N. K. 2003. *Feminist theology: A reader.* Grand Rapids, MI: Eerdmans Publishing.

Waylen, G. 2008. Enhancing the substantive representation of women: Lessons from transitions to democracy. *Parliamentary Affairs, 61,* 518–534.

WEDO. 2007. *Challenging Nike to deliver on worker rights.* http://www.wedo.org/tag/corporate-campaigns Retrieved on August 17, 2009.

———. 2009. *Corporate accountability.* http://www.wedo.org/category/learn/campaigns/corporateaccountability/policy-advocacy Retrieved on August 17, 2009.

———. 2009. UN reform: The GEAR campaign. http://www.wedo.org/category/learn/campaigns/governance/unreform Retrieved on October 24, 2009.

Weeks, J. 1999. Sexuality and history revisited. In *State, private life and political change,* edited by L. Jamieson and Helen Corr. New York: St. Martin's Press.

Weissinger, C. 1993. Introduction: Going beyond and retaining charisma: *Women's leadership in marginal religions: Explorations outside the mainstream.* Chicago: University of Illinois Press.

Wekker, G. 1993. Mati-ism and black lesbianism: Two ideal typical expressions of female homosexuality in Black communities of the Diaspora. *Journal of Homosexuality, 24,* 11–24.

Werner, M., and J. Blair. 2009. After sweatshops? Apparel politics in the circum-Caribbean (UPDATE). *NACLA Report on the Americas, 42,* 6–12.

West, G., and R. L. Blumberg. 1990. Reconstructing social protest from a feminist perspective. In *Women and social protest,* edited by G. West and R. L. Blumberg. New York: Oxford University Press.

West, L. 1999. The United Nations women's conferences and feminist politics. In *Gender politics in global governance,* edited by M. K. Meyer and E. Prugl. Lanham, MD: Rowman & Littlefield.

WHO (World Health Organization). 2009. 10 facts about women's health. http://www.who.int/features/factfiles/women/en/index.html

———. 2007. *What is a gender-based approach to public health?* http://www.who.int/features/qa/56/en/index.html Retrieved on May 28, 2009.

———. 2008. *Violence against women.* World Health Organization. http://www.who.int/mediacentre/factsheets/fs239/en Retrieved on March 18, 2009.

———. 2005. *WHO multi-country study on women's health and domestic violence against women. Initial results on prevalence, health outcomes and women's responses.* Geneva: World Health Organization.

Wiliarity, S. E. 2008. Chancellor Angela Merkel: A sign of hope or the exception that proves the rule? *Politics and Gender, 4,* 485–496.

Wilkinson, T. 1998. She seeks women's rights—quietly. *Los Angeles Times,* 7 October, A1, A6.

———. 2007. Taking the honor out of killing women. *Los Angeles Times,* 9 January.

Williams, D. S. 1994. Womanist theology: Black women's voices. In *Feminist theology from the Third World,* edited by U. King. Maryknoll, NY: Orbis.

Williams, H. 1995. Violeta Barrios de Chamorro. In *Women in world politics: An introduction,* edited by F. D'Amico and P. R. Beckman. Westport, CT: Bergin and Garvey.

Willness, C. R., Steel, P., and K. Lee. 2007. A meta-analysis of the antecedents and consequences of workplace sexual harassment. *Personnel Psychology, 60,* 127–162.

WIN. 1992. Sexual harassment at work. *Women's International Network News, 18,* 46–47.

———. 2003. UNIFEM: Women's political participation a most positive change. *Women's International Network News, 29,* 3.

Wise, C. 2008. *Hidden circles in the web: Feminist wicca, occult knowledge, and process thought.* Lanham, MD: Altamira Press.

Wolbrecht, C., and D. E. Campbell. 2007. Leading by Example: Female Members of Parliament as Political Role Models. *American Journal of Political Science, 51,* 921–939.

Wolfe, L. R., and J. Tucker. 1995. Feminism lives: Building a multicultural women's movement. In *The united rights,* edited by R. Rosenbloom. San Francisco, CA: International Gay and Lesbian Human Rights Commission.

Women Living Under Muslim Laws (WLUML). 2009. *About WLUML.* http://www.wluml.org/node/5408 Retrieved on October 30, 2009.

WomenWarPeace.org. 2009. *Peace negotiations.* http://www.womenwarpeace.org/node/11 Retrieved on September 26, 2009.

World Bank. 2001. *Engendering development: Through gender equality in rights, resources, and voice.* Oxford: Oxford University Press and the World Bank.

———. 2009. Women in 33 countries highly vulnerable to financial crisis effects—World Bank estimates increase in infant mortality, less girl education and reduced earnings', press release 6 March. http://web.worldbank.org/WBSITE/EXTERNAL/NEWS/0,contentMDK:22092604~pagePK:34370~piPK:34424~theSitePK:4607,00.html Retrieved on August 14, 2009.

———. 2009. *Gender in agriculture sourcebook.* Washington, DC: Author.

World Commission on Environment and Development. 1987. *Our common future.* Oxford, UK: Oxford University Press.

World Resources Institute. 1994–95. *World resources: A guide to the global environment.* Oxford, UK: Oxford University Press.

———. 2009. *Earth trends: Climate protection in a disparate world.* http://earthtrends.wri.org/features/view_feature.php?theme=3&fid=31 Retrieved on August 5, 2009.

Xu, F. 2009. Chinese feminisms encounter international feminisms: Identity, power, and knowledge production. *International Journal of Politics, 11,* 196–215.

Yogyakarta Principles. 2007. http://www.yogyakartaprinciples.org/index.php?item=1 Retrieved on June 25, 2009.

Young, K. K. 1987. Hinduism. In *Women in world religions,* edited by A. Sharma. Albany: State University of New York Press.

———. 1994. Women in Hinduism. In *Today's woman in world religions,* edited by A. Sharma. Albany: State University of New York Press.

Youseff, N. H. 1995. Women's access to productive resources: The need for legal instruments to protect women's development rights. In *Women's rights, human rights: International feminist perspectives,* edited by J. Peters and A. Wolper. New York: Routledge.

Yuan, L. 2005. *Reconceiving women's equality in China: A critical examination of models of sex equality.* Oxford, UK: Lexington.

Zhang, N., and W. Xu. 1995. Discovering the positive within the negative: The women's movement in a changing China. In *The challenge of local feminisms: Women's movements in global perspective,* edited by A. Basu. Boulder, CO: Westview Press.

Index

Key terms and the pages on which they are defined are boldfaced.